Map pages south

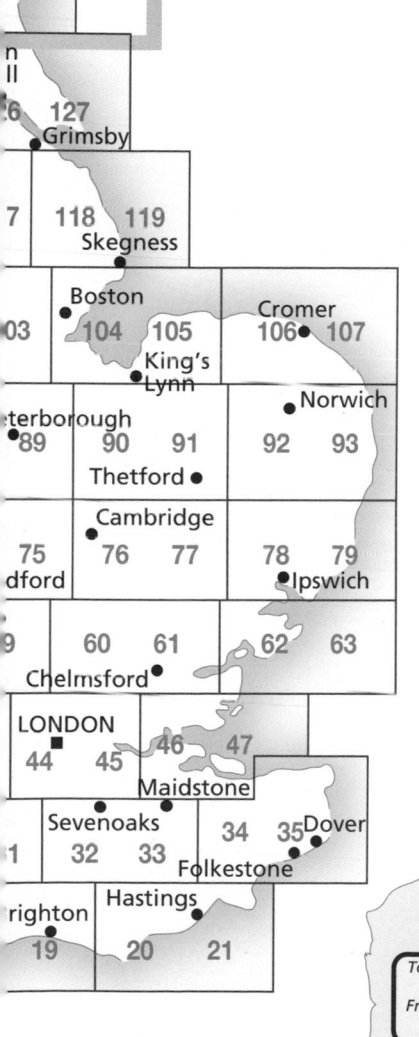

35

n
ll

6 127
   Grimsby

7   118   119
      Skegness

     Boston
03   104   105   Cromer
                    106   107
           King's
           Lynn
                         Norwich
terborough
  89   90   91   92   93
      Thetford

      Cambridge
75   76   77   78   79
dford   Ipswich

9   60   61   62   63
   Chelmsford

LONDON   46   47
44   45
      Maidstone
   Sevenoaks   34   35 Dover
1   32   33   Folkestone

righton   Hastings
   19   20   21

To help you navigate safely
and easily, see the AA's
France and Europe atlases...
theAA.com/shop

Available on Android & iOS
RoadPilot mobile
by ROAD ANGEL
Your personal driving companion
Road Pilot Mobile is an invaluable driving aid, alerting to fixed and mobile speed cameras, recording your trips and providing real-time driver behaviour stats to help improve your safety.
✓ Journey recording & view trip history
✓ Real-time driver behaviour score
✓ Eco driving gauge to help reduce fuel consumption
✓ Industry-leading database
✓ Fixed and mobile camera alerts
✓ Background alerts - continues to run in the background
For more information on Road Pilot Mobile visit www.roadpilot.com or to download visit the Apple or Google Play app store
RoadPilot mobile
RoadPilot Ltd Clark House | Silverstone Technology Park
Silverstone Circuit | Northants | NN12 8GX
Available on the App Store
GET IT ON Google play

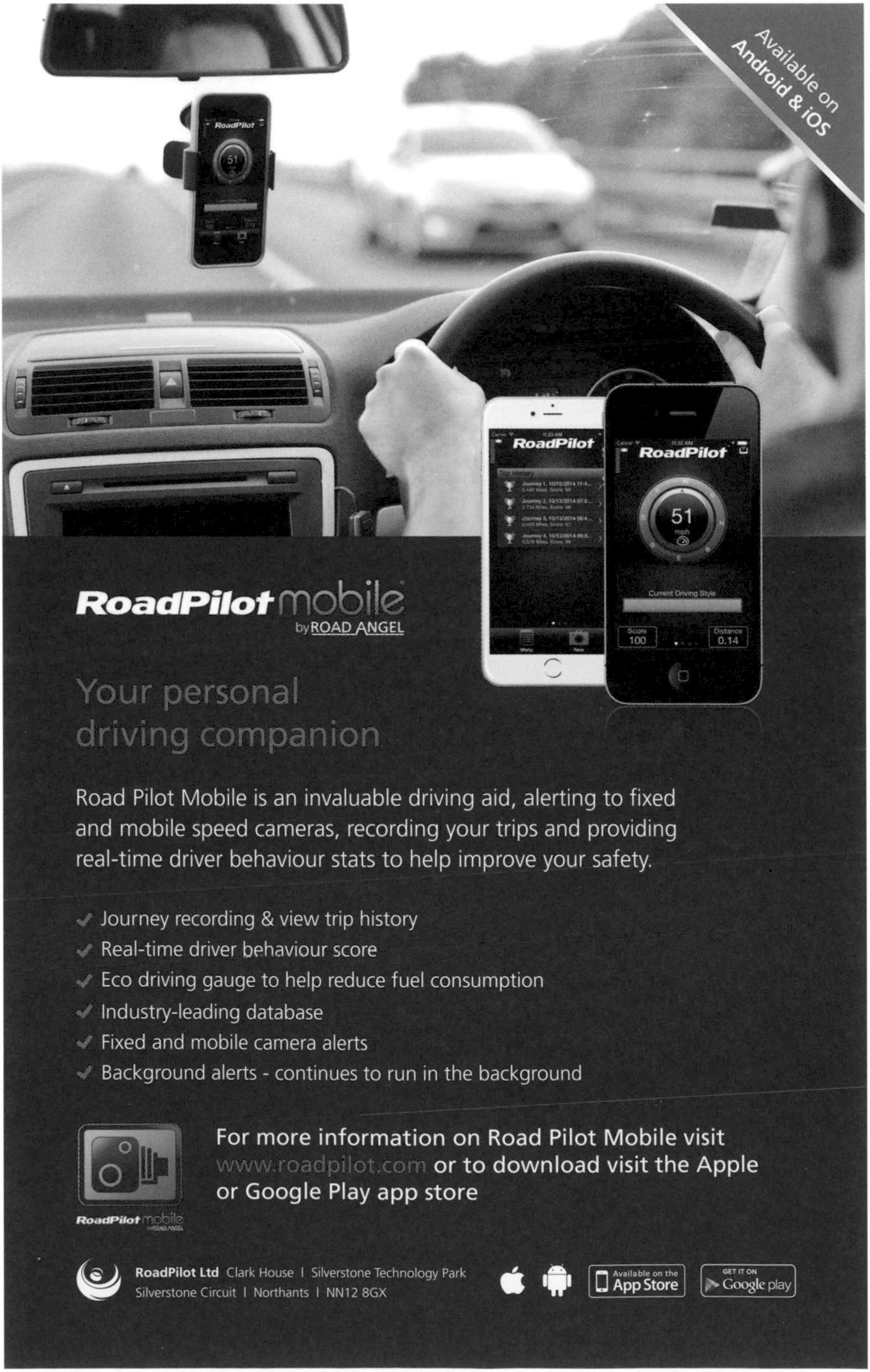

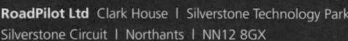

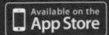

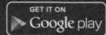

Atlas contents

Scale 1:250,000 or 3.95 miles to 1 inch

Map pages south	inside front cover
Route planner	II–VII
Mileage chart	VIII
Atlas Symbols	1
Road maps 1:250,000 scale	2–237

Western Isles 1:700,000 scale — 232–233
Orkney Islands 1:636,000 scale — 234
Shetland Islands 1:636,000 scale — 235
Channel Islands 1:150,000 scale — 236
Isle of Man 1:317,000 scale — 237

Restricted junctions	238–239
Index to place names	240–320

County, administrative area map — 240–241
Place name index — 242–320

Ireland	endpaper
Map pages north	inside back cover

14th edition June 2015

© AA Media Limited 2015

Cartography:

All cartography in this atlas edited, designed and produced by the Mapping Services Department of AA Publishing (A05306).

This atlas contains Ordnance Survey data © Crown copyright and database right 2015.

This atlas is based upon Crown Copyright and is reproduced with the permission of Land & Property Services under delegated authority from the Controller of Her Majesty's Stationery Office, © Crown copyright and database right 2015, PMLPA No. 100497

Ireland's National Mapping Agency

© Ordnance Survey Ireland/ Government of Ireland. Copyright Permit No. MP000115

Publisher's notes:

Published by AA Publishing (a trading name of AA Media Limited, whose registered office is Fanum House, Basing View, Basingstoke, Hampshire RG21 4EA, UK. Registered number 06112600).

All rights reserved. No part of this publication may be reproduced, stored in a retrieval system, or transmitted in any form or by any means – electronic, mechanical, photocopying, recording or otherwise – unless the permission of the publisher has been given beforehand.

ISBN: 978 0 7495 7683 7 (flexibound)

A CIP catalogue record for this book is available from The British Library.

Disclaimer:

The contents of this atlas are believed to be correct at the time of the latest revision, it will not contain any subsequent amended, new or temporary information including diversions and traffic control or enforcement systems. The publishers cannot be held responsible or liable for any loss or damage occasioned to any person acting or refraining from action as a result of any use or reliance on material in this atlas, nor for any errors, omissions or changes in such material. This does not affect your statutory rights.

The publishers would welcome information to correct any errors or omissions and to keep this atlas up to date. Please write to the Atlas Editor, AA Publishing, Fanum House, Basing View, Basingstoke, Hampshire RG21 4EA, UK. E-mail: roadatlasfeedback@theaa.com

Acknowledgements:

AA Publishing would like to thank the following for their assistance in producing this atlas:

RoadPilot mobile by ROAD ANGEL

Information on fixed speed camera locations provided by and © 2015 RoadPilot Ltd. Crematoria database provided by Cremation Society of Great Britain. Cadw, English Heritage, Forestry Commission, Historic Scotland, Johnsons, National Trust and National Trust for Scotland, RSPB, The Wildlife Trust, Scottish Natural Heritage, Natural England, The Countryside Council for Wales.

Printer:

1010 Printing International Ltd.

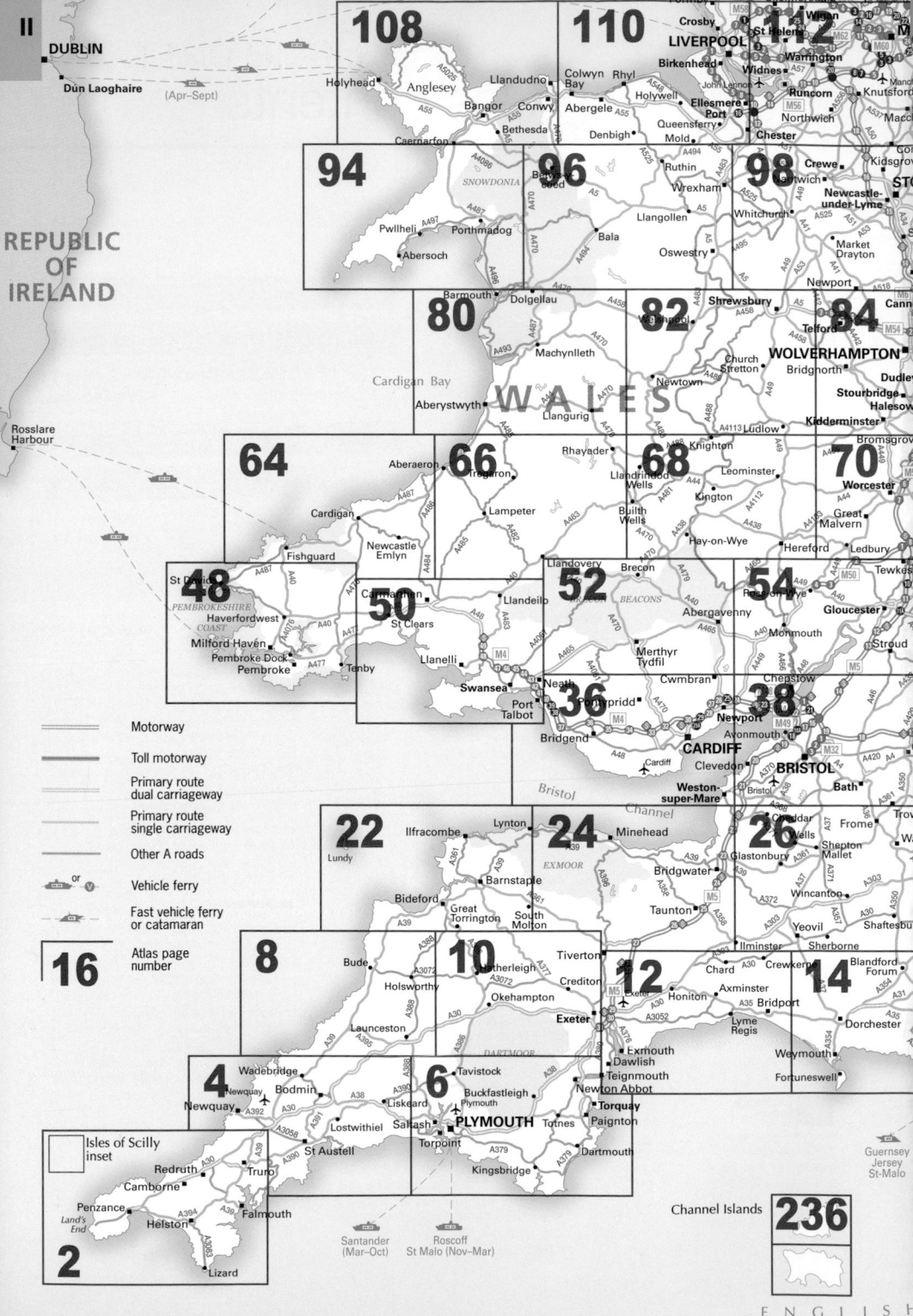

ENGLAND

114 MANCHESTER, Glossop, Stockport, SHEFFIELD, Chesterfield, Buxton, Bakewell, PEAK DISTRICT, Barnsley, Rotherham, Worksop

116 Doncaster, Bawtry, Robin Hood Doncaster Sheffield, Gainsborough, Retford, Lincoln, Mansfield, Market Rasen

118 Grimsby, Cleethorpes, Humberside, Louth, Mablethorpe, Skegness, Horncastle, Brigg

100 STOKE-ON-TRENT, Ashbourne, Ilkeston, DERBY, Burton upon Trent, Stafford, Rugeley, Lichfield, Tamworth, Uttoxeter, Long Eaton, Loughborough, East Midlands, Alfreton

102 NOTTINGHAM, Newark-on-Trent, Sleaford, Grantham, Melton Mowbray, Oakham, Bourne, Spalding

104 Boston, The Wash, King's Lynn, Hunstanton

106 Sheringham, Cromer, North Walsham, Aylsham, Dereham, Fakenham, Swaffham

86 Walsall, Nuneaton, BIRMINGHAM, COVENTRY, LEICESTER, Hinckley, Wigston, Market Harborough, Rugby

88 Stamford, Peterborough, Corby, Kettering, A1(M)

90 Wisbech, March, Downham Market, Chatteris, Ely, Huntingdon

92 Norwich, Attleborough, Bungay, Diss, Beccles, Great Yarmouth, Lowestoft, Southwold, Caister-on-Sea, THE BROADS

72 Redditch, Stratford-upon-Avon, Warwick, Royal Leamington Spa, Daventry, Evesham, Banbury

74 Northampton, Bedford, St Neots, Milton Keynes, Brackley, Towcester, Iowcester

76 Cambridge, Newmarket, Royston, Haverhill, St Edmunds, Bury St Edmunds, Thetford

78 Stowmarket, Sudbury, Woodbridge, Ipswich, Aldeburgh, Felixstowe

56 Swindon, Cheltenham, Cirencester, Chipping Norton, Witney, Burford, Bicester

58 Leighton Buzzard, Dunstable, Aylesbury, Thame, Oxford, Luton, St Albans, Hatfield

60 Stevenage, Hertford, Harlow, Bishop's Stortford, Chelmsford, Stansted, Braintree, Witham, Maldon

62 Colchester, Clacton-on-Sea, Harwich, Hoek van Holland, Esbjerg

40 Swindon, Marlborough, Devizes, Newbury, Reading, Wantage, Abingdon-on-Thames, Faringdon

42 Maidenhead, Slough, Windsor, Bracknell, Staines-upon-Thames, High Wycombe, Beaconsfield, Woking

44 LONDON, Richmond, Heathrow, Croydon, Watford, Brentwood, City, Dartford

46 Southend-on-Sea, Basildon, Canvey Island, Sheerness, Tilbury, Gravesend, Chatham, Rochester

28 Basingstoke, Andover, Amesbury, Salisbury, Winchester, Romsey, Alton, Farnham

30 Guildford, Dorking, Leatherhead, Reigate, Gatwick, Crawley, Horsham, Billingshurst

32 Redhill, East Grinstead, Tonbridge, Royal Tunbridge Wells, Crowborough, Sevenoaks

34 Maidstone, Ashford, Tenterden, Canterbury, New Romney, Hythe, Folkestone, Dover, CHANNEL TUNNEL TERMINAL

Margate, Ramsgate, Sandwich, Deal, Kent International

16 SOUTHAMPTON, Eastleigh, Portsmouth, Gosport, Lymington, Cowes, Ryde, Newport, Sandown, Shanklin, Isle of Wight, Bournemouth, Christchurch, Swanage, NEW FOREST

18 Chichester, Bognor Regis, Arundel, Worthing, Shoreham-by-Sea, Midhurst, Petersfield

20 Brighton, Newhaven, Lewes, Uckfield, Heathfield, Hastings, Bexhill, Eastbourne, Rye

Calais, Dunkerque, CALAIS / COQUELLES TERMINAL, Strait of Dover, CHANNEL TUNNEL

FRANCE

CHANNEL

Cherbourg (Jan–Oct), Santander, Gijón

Guernsey, Jersey, St-Malo, Caen (Ouistreham), Le Havre (Mar–Oct), Bilbao (Mar–Oct), Santander

Cherbourg (May–Sept), Le Havre (May–Sept)

Dieppe

Rotterdam (Europoort), Zeebrugge

To help you navigate safely and easily, see the AA's France and Europe atlases... theAA.com/shop

0 10 20 30 miles
0 10 20 30 40 kilometres

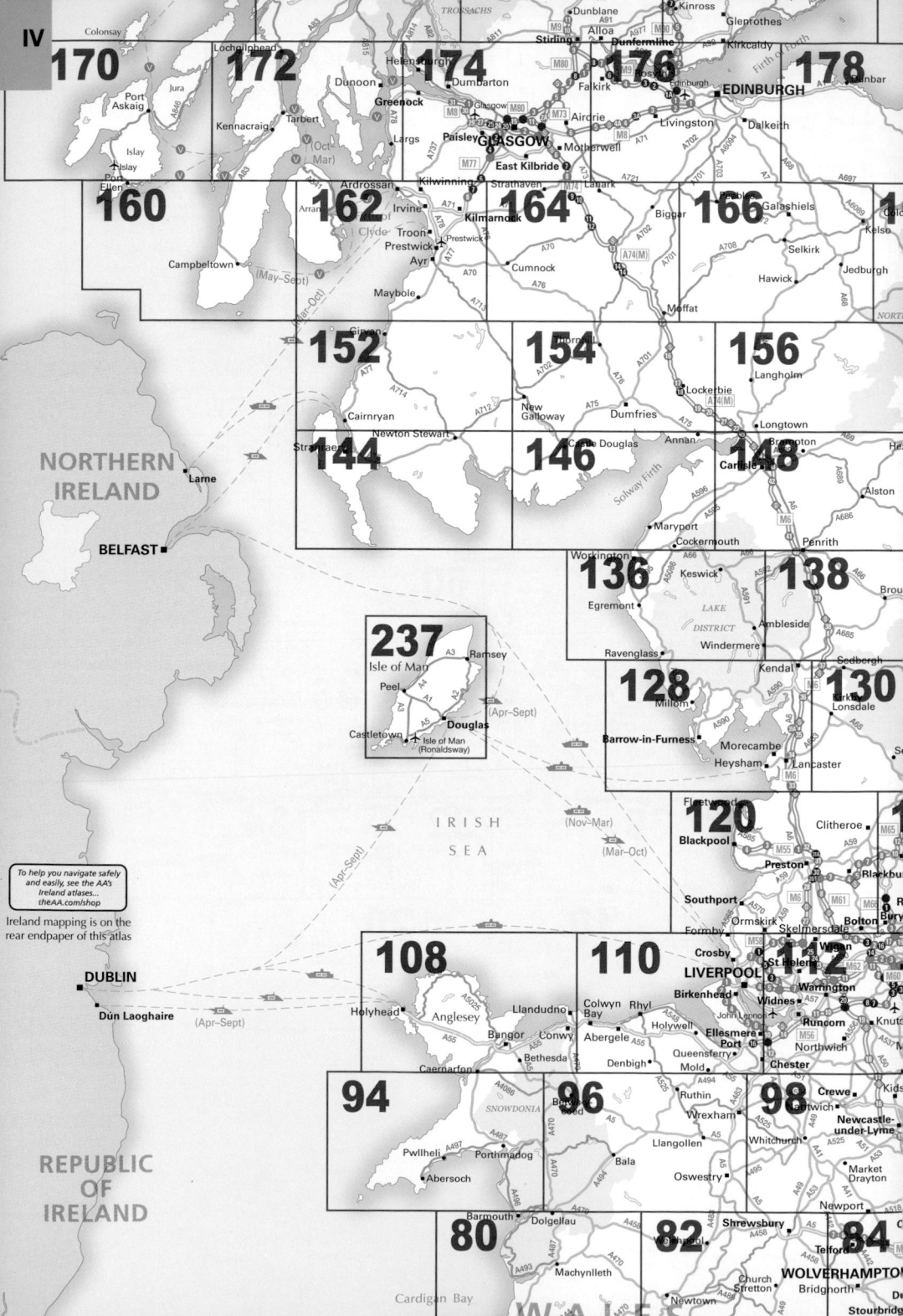

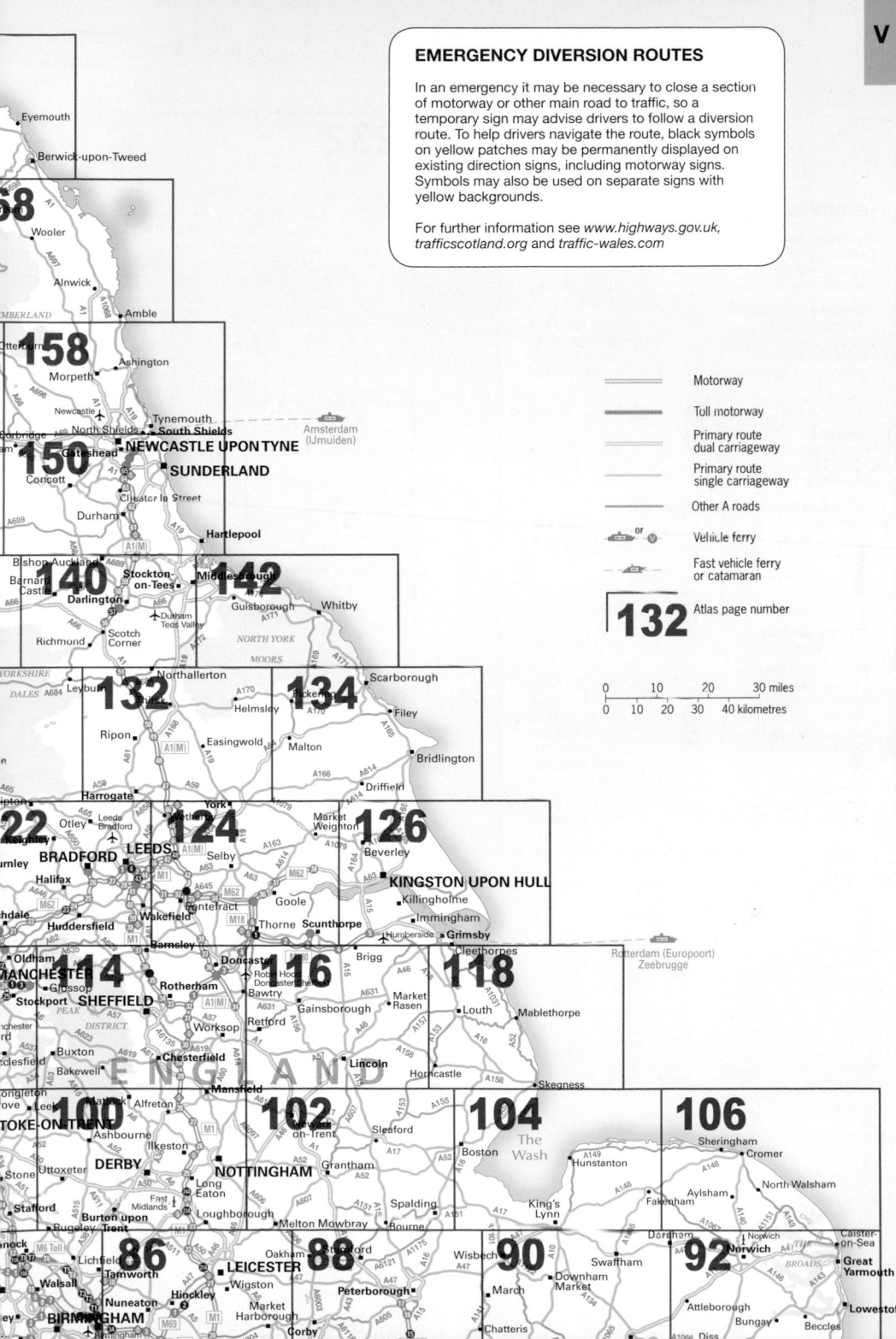

EMERGENCY DIVERSION ROUTES

In an emergency it may be necessary to close a section of motorway or other main road to traffic, so a temporary sign may advise drivers to follow a diversion route. To help drivers navigate the route, black symbols on yellow patches may be permanently displayed on existing direction signs, including motorway signs. Symbols may also be used on separate signs with yellow backgrounds.

For further information see *www.highways.gov.uk*, *trafficscotland.org* and *traffic-wales.com*

Legend:
- ──────── Motorway
- ──────── Toll motorway
- ──────── Primary route dual carriageway
- ──────── Primary route single carriageway
- ──────── Other A roads
- Vehicle ferry
- Fast vehicle ferry or catamaran
- **132** Atlas page number

0   10   20   30 miles
0 10 20 30 40 kilometres

FERRY INFORMATION

Hebrides and west coast Scotland
calmac.co.uk | 0800 066 5000
skyeferry.co.uk |
western-ferries.co.uk | 01369 704 452

Orkney and Shetland
northlinkferries.co.uk | 0845 6000 449
pentlandferries.co.uk | 0800 688 8998
orkneyferries.co.uk | 01856 872 044
shetland.gov.uk/ferries | 01595 743 970

Isle of Man
steam-packet.com | 08722 992 992

Ireland
irishferries.com | 08717 300 400
poferries.com | 08716 642 020
stenaline.co.uk | 08447 70 70 70

North Sea (Scandinavia and Benelux)
dfdsseaways.co.uk | 08715 229 955
poferries.com | 08716 642 020
stenaline.co.uk | 08447 70 70 70

Isle of Wight
wightlink.co.uk | 0333 999 7333
redfunnel.co.uk | 0844 844 9988

Channel Islands
condorferries.co.uk | 0845 609 1024

France and Belgium
brittany-ferries.co.uk | 0871 244 0744
condorferries.co.uk | 0845 609 1024
eurotunnel.com | 08443 35 35 35
dfdsseaways.co.uk | 08715 229 955
poferries.com | 08716 642 020
myferrylink.com | 0844 2482 100

Northern Spain
brittany-ferries.co.uk | 0871 244 0744
ldlines.co.uk | 0844 576 8836

Motorway
Toll motorway
Primary route dual carriageway
Primary route single carriageway
Other A roads
Vehicle ferry
Fast vehicle ferry or catamaran

192 Atlas page number

0 10 20 30 miles
0 10 20 30 40 kilometres

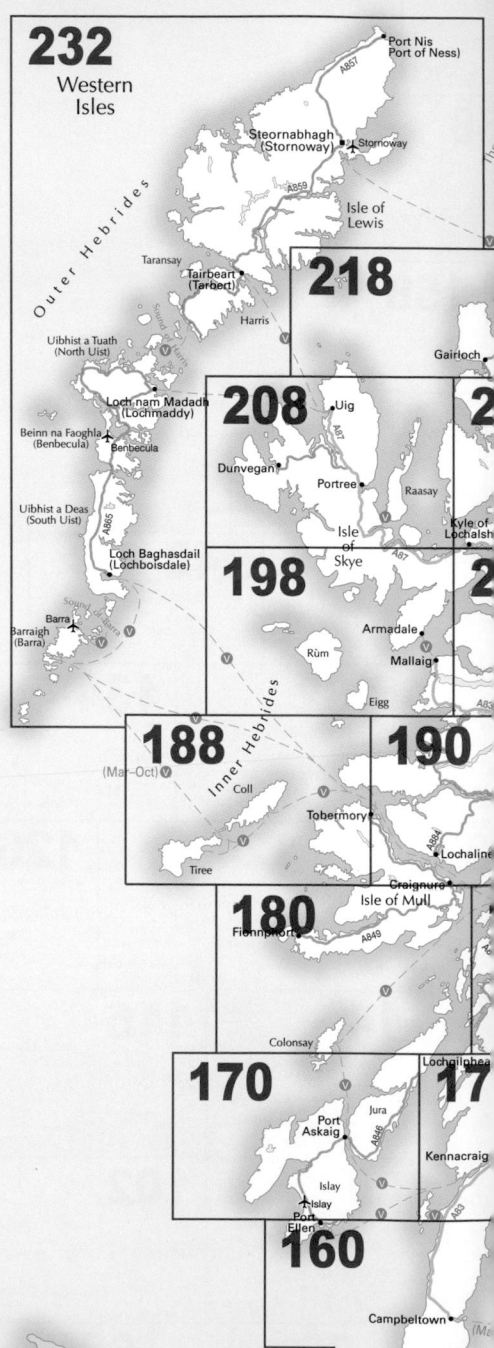

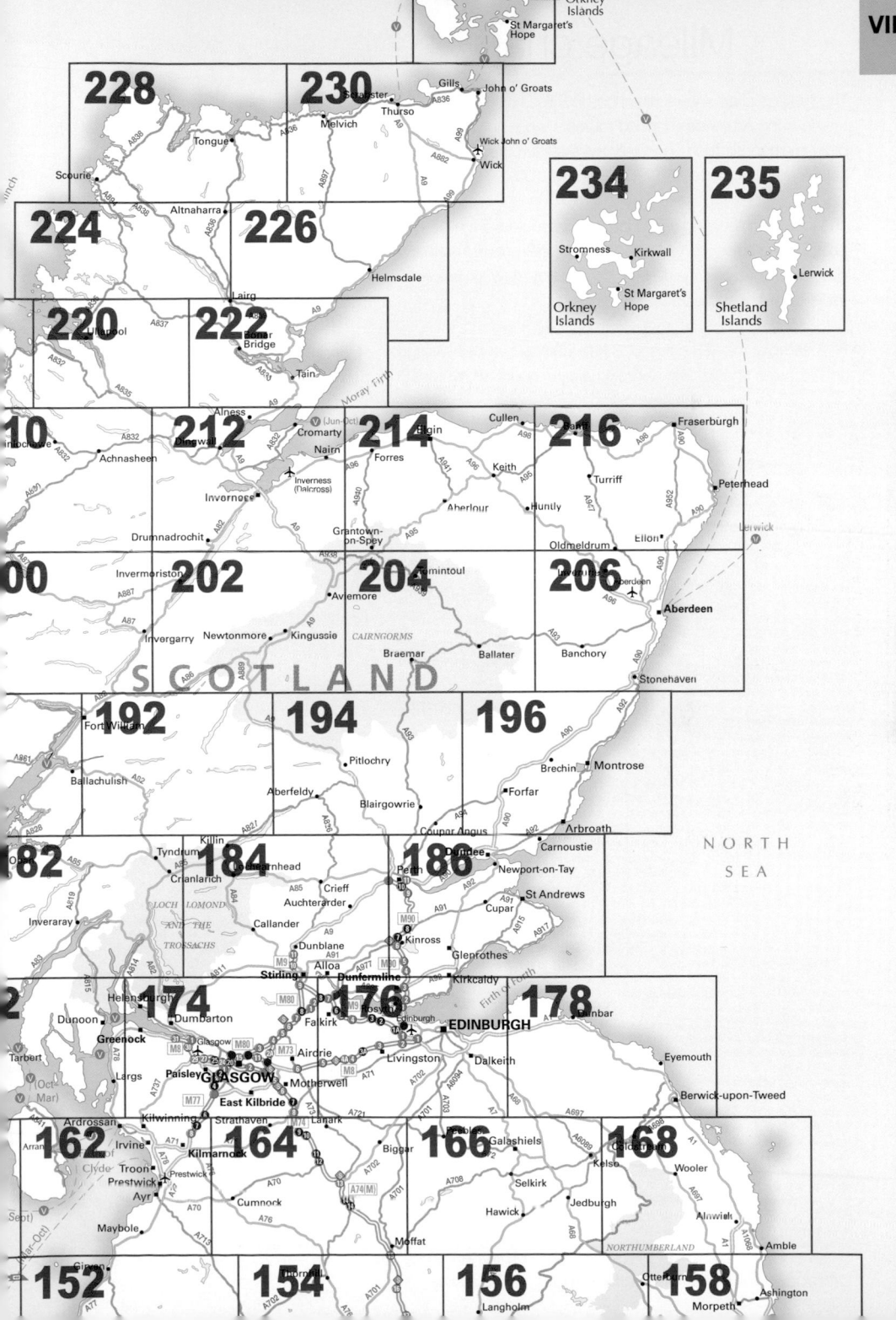

Mileage chart

The mileage chart shows distances in miles between two towns along AA-recommended routes. Using motorways and other main roads this is normally the fastest route, though not necessarily the shortest.

The journey times, shown in hours and minutes, are average off-peak driving times along AA-recommended routes. These times should be used as a guide only and do not allow for unforeseen traffic delays, rest breaks or fuel stops.

For example, the 378 miles (608 km) journey between Glasgow and Norwich should take approximately 7 hours 28 minutes.

Journey times

The mileage chart below shows distances in miles between two towns, with city reference labels along the diagonal: Aberdeen, Aberystwyth, Barnstaple, Birmingham, Brighton, Bristol, Cambridge, Cardiff, Carlisle, Carmarthen, Dorchester, Dover, Edinburgh, Exeter, Fort William, Glasgow, Gloucester, Guildford, Hereford, Holyhead, Hull, Inverness, Kendal, Leeds, Lincoln, Liverpool, Maidstone, Manchester, Middlesbrough, Newcastle, Northampton, Norwich, Nottingham, Oxford, Penzance, Perth, Peterborough, Plymouth, Portsmouth, Preston, Salisbury, Sheffield, Shrewsbury, Southampton, Stoke-on-Trent, Stranraer, Taunton, Wick, York, LONDON.

Distances in miles (one mile equals 1.6093 km)

Atlas symbols

M4	Motorway with number
Toll / T4	Toll motorway with toll station
3	Restricted motorway junctions
S Fleet	Motorway service area
	Motorway and junction under construction
A3	Primary route single/dual carriageway
1	Primary route junction with and without number
3	Restricted primary route junctions
S	Primary route service area
BATH	Primary route destination
A1123	Other A road single/dual carriageway
B2070	B road single/dual carriageway

	Minor road, more than 4 metres wide, less than 4 metres wide
	Roundabout
	Interchange/junction
	Narrow primary/other A/B road with passing places (Scotland)
	Road under construction/ approved
	Road tunnel
Toll	Road toll, steep gradient (arrows point downhill)
5	Distance in miles between symbols
	Railway line, in tunnel
	Railway station and level crossing
	Tourist railway
628 / 637 Lecht Summit	Height in metres, mountain pass

30	Safety camera site (fixed location) with speed limit in mph
40	Section of road with two or more fixed safety cameras, with speed limit in mph
50 — 50	Average speed (SPECS™) camera system with speed limit in mph
V	Fixed safety camera site with variable speed limit
or V	Vehicle ferry
	Fast vehicle ferry or catamaran
⊕ H F	Airport, heliport, international freight terminal
H	24-hour Accident & Emergency hospital
C	Crematorium
P•R	Park and Ride (at least 6 days per week)
	City, town, village or other built-up area
	National boundary, county or administrative boundary

	Scenic route
	Tourist Information Centre (all year/seasonal)
	Visitor or heritage centre
	Picnic site
	Caravan site (AA inspected)
	Camping site (AA inspected)
	Caravan & camping site (AA inspected)
	Abbey, cathedral or priory
	Ruined abbey, cathedral or priory
	Castle
	Historic house or building
	Museum or art gallery
	Industrial interest

	Aqueduct or viaduct
	Garden, arboretum
	Vineyard
	Country park
	Agricultural showground
	Theme park
	Farm or animal centre
	Zoological or wildlife collection
	Bird collection, aquarium
	RSPB site
	National Nature Reserve (England, Scotland, Wales)
	Local nature reserve
	Wildlife Trust reserve

	Forest drive
	National trail
	Viewpoint
	Hill-fort
	Prehistoric monument, Roman antiquity
1066	Battle site with year
	Steam railway centre
	Cave
	Windmill, monument
	Golf course (AA listed)
	County cricket ground
	Rugby Union national stadium
	International athletics stadium

	Horse racing, show jumping
	Air show venue, motor-racing circuit
	Ski slope (natural, artificial)
	National Trust property (England & Wales, Scotland)
	English Heritage site
	Historic Scotland site
	Cadw (Welsh heritage) site
	Major shopping centre, other place of interest
	Attraction within urban area
	World Heritage Site (UNESCO)
	National Park and National Scenic Area (Scotland)
	Forest Park
	Heritage coast

2

Isles of Scilly

White Island
ST MARTIN'S
St Martin's Head
King Charles's
Old Grimsby
BRYHER
Cromwell's
Old Blockhouse
Higher Town
New Lizard Point
Grimsby
Great Ganilly
Isles of Scilly Heritage Coast
Tresco Abbey
TRESCO
Innisidgen Tomb
Great Arthur
Samson
Bant's Carn Burial
Harry's Walls
A3111
ST MARY'S
St Mary's Quay
Longstone
Deep Point
Hugh Town
Porth Hellick Downs Tombs
Isles of Scilly (St Mary's)
Garrison Walls
Old Town
Peninnis Head
Annet
St Mary's Sound
Middle Town
Gugh
ST AGNES
Horse Point
Western Rocks
Smith Sound
North West Channel
Broad Sound
Crow Sound
Crow Bar

0 1 2 3 miles
0 1 2 3 4 5 kilometres

Godrevy
Carn Naun Point
The Island or St Ives Head
St Ives Bay
St Ives
Zennor Head
Carbis Bay
Gurnards Head
Halsetown
Lelant
Zennor
Towednack
B3306
South West Coast Path
Canonstown
A30
Pendeen Watch
Lighthouse
Carn Galver Mine
Men-An-Tol
Mulfra Quoit
Chysauster Ancient Village
St Erth
Morvah
Penwith Heritage Coast
New Mill
Crowlas
Geevor Tin Mine
Lanyon Quoit
Ludgvan
Relubbus
Levant Mine and Beam Engine
Pendeen
B3318
Trengwainton Garden
Gulval
Longrock
St Hilary
Botallack
St Just Mining District
Madron
Heamoor
Chyandour
Marazion
Cape Cornwall
St Just
A3071
Newbridge
Chyandour
Goldsithney
Ballowall Barrow
A30
Penzance
St Michael's Mount
Perranuthnoe
Kelynack
Carn Euny Ancient Village
Sancreed
Newlyn
Cudden Point
Whitesand Bay
Land's End
Drift
Kerris
B3306
A30
Crows-an-Wra
Paul
Sennen Cove
Mousehole
MOUNT'S BAY
LAND'S END
Sennen
St Buryan
Trevescan
B3315
The Merry Maidens
Lamorna
Porthcurno
Trethewey
B3315
Lamorna Cove
Treen
Merthen Point
Porthgwarra
Telegraph
St Levan
Minack Cribba Head Open Air Theatre
Gwennap Head

0 1 2 3 4 miles
0 1 2 3 4 5 kilometres

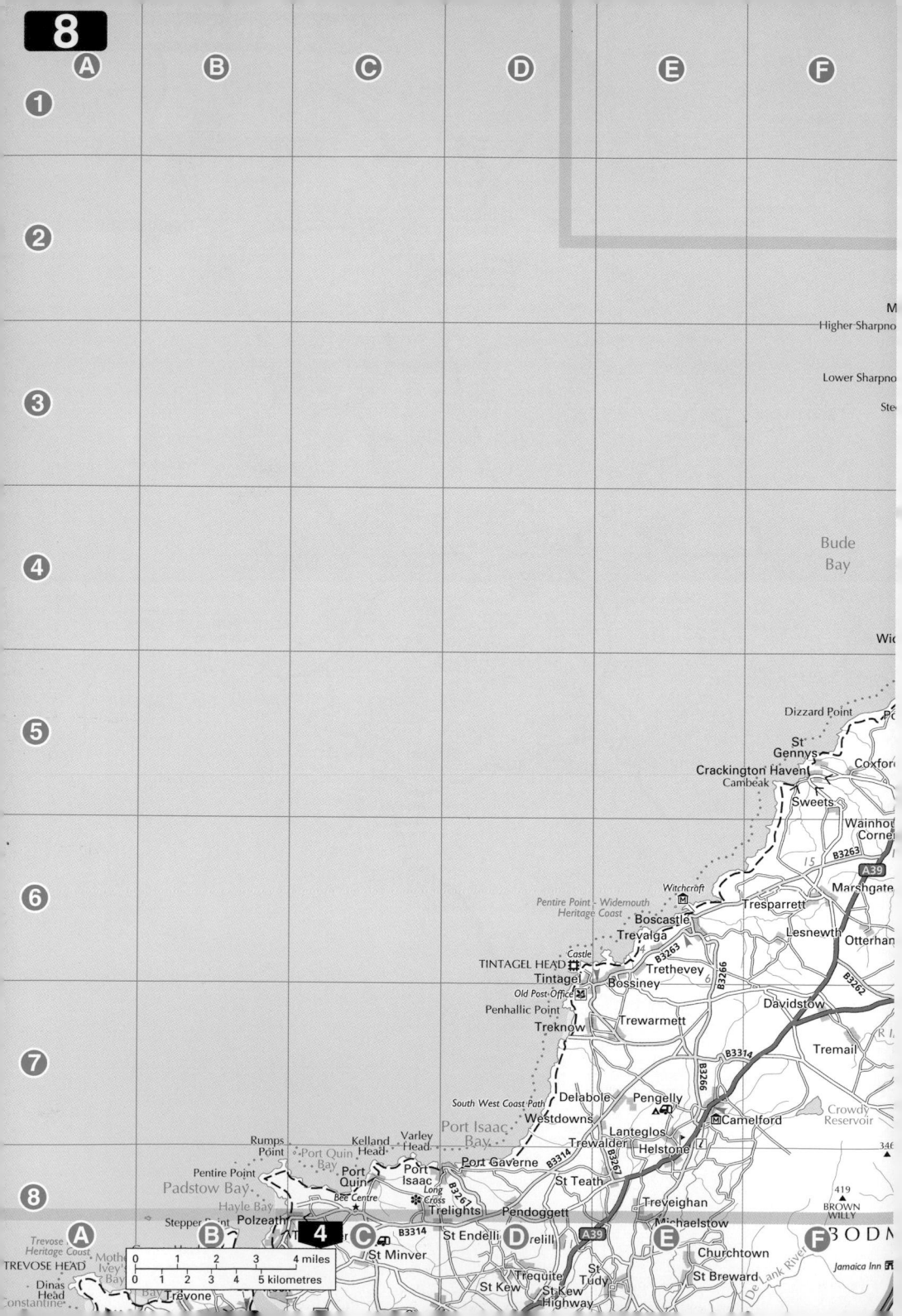

A B C D E F

1

2

3

4

5

6

7

8

M

Higher Sharpno

Lower Sharpno

Ste

Bude
Bay

Wid

Dizzard Point

PC

St
Gennys

Crackington Haven
Cambeak

Coxfor

Sweets

Wainho
Corne

Witchcroft

A39

Pentire Point - Widemouth
Heritage Coast

Boscastle

Marshgate

Trevalga

B3263

Tresparrett

Lesnewth

Otterhan

Castle

TINTAGEL HEAD

Tintagel

Trethevey

B3266

Bossiney

Old Post Office

Trewarmett

Penhallic Point

Treknow

Davidstow

B3262

Tremail

R

South West Coast Path

Delabole

Pengelly

B3314

B3266

Crowdy
Reservoir

Westdowns

Lanteglos

Camelford

Port Isaac
Bay

Trewarden

Helstone

Rumps
Point

Kelland
Head

Varley
Head

Port Gaverne

B3314

St Teath

346

Port Quin
Bay

Port
Quin

Port
Isaac

Long
Cross

Pentire Point

Pendoggett

Treveighan

419
BROWN
WILLY

Padstow Bay

Hayle Bay

Bee Centre

Trelights

Michaelstow

BODM

Trevose
Heritage Coast

Stepper Point

Polzeath

A B **4** C

B3314

St Endelli

D relill

A39

E

Churchtown

F

TREVOSE HEAD

St Minver

St Breward

Jamaica Inn

Dinas
Head

Constantine

Trevone

St Kew

Trequite

St Kew
Highway

St
Tudy

De Lank River

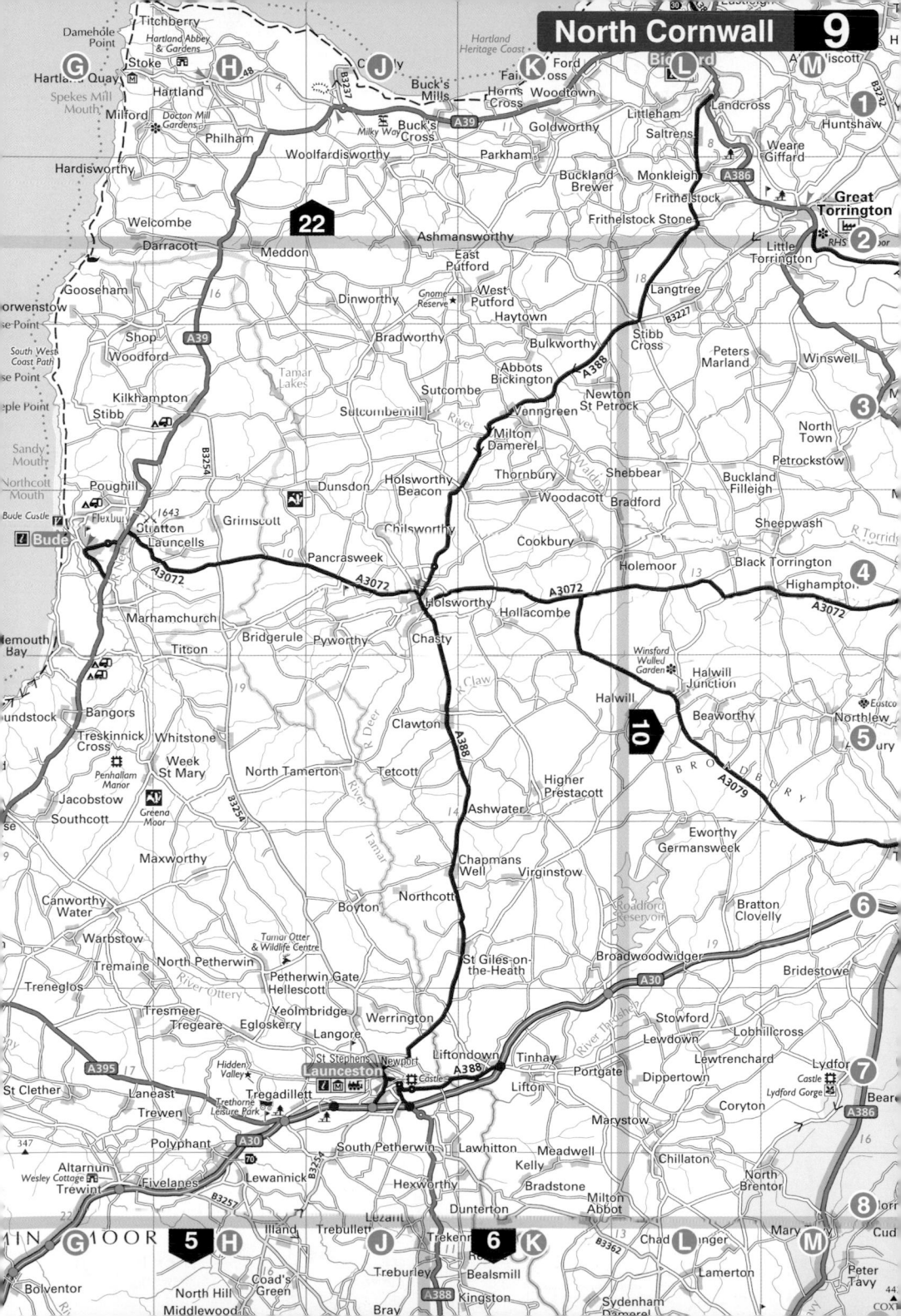

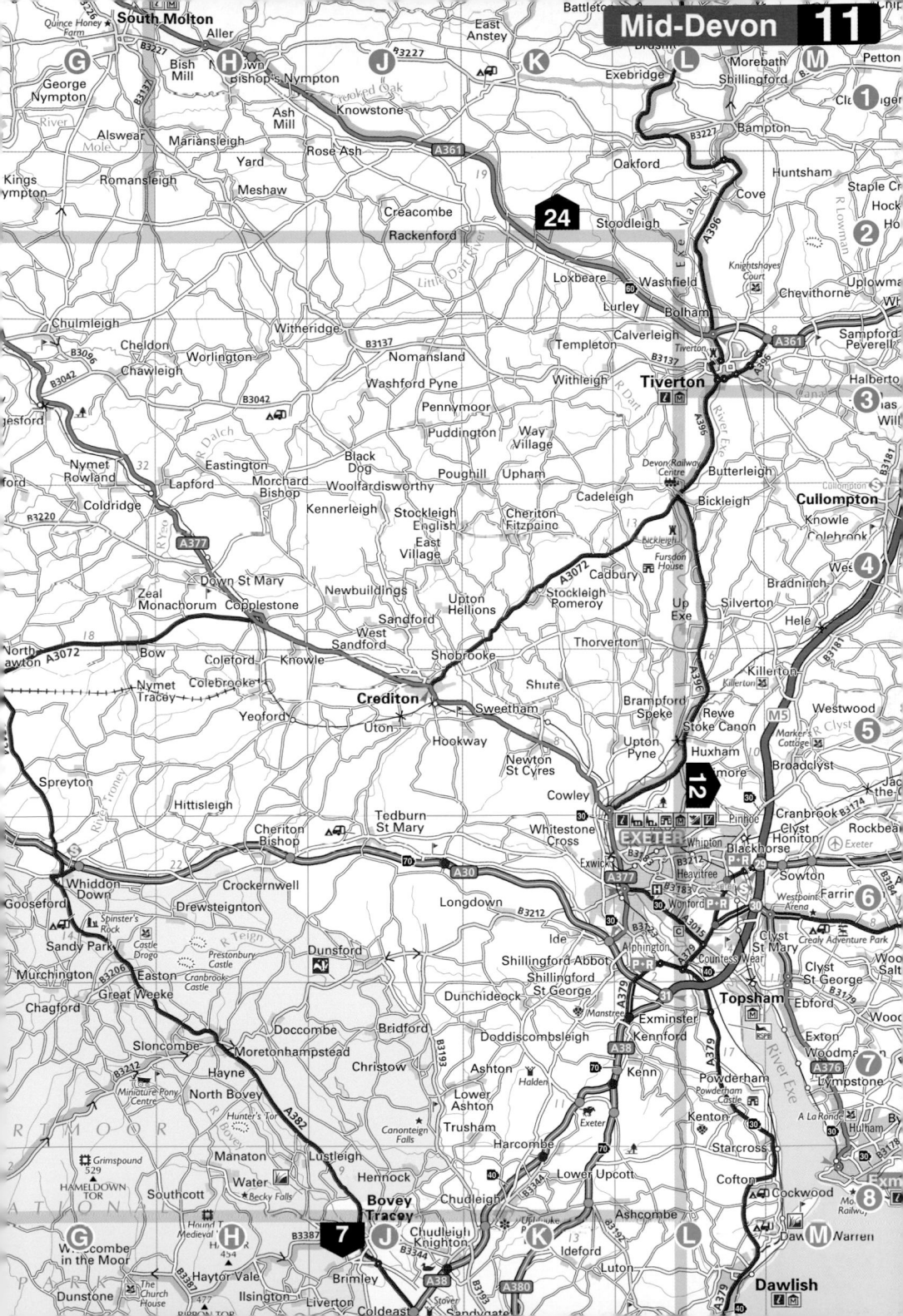

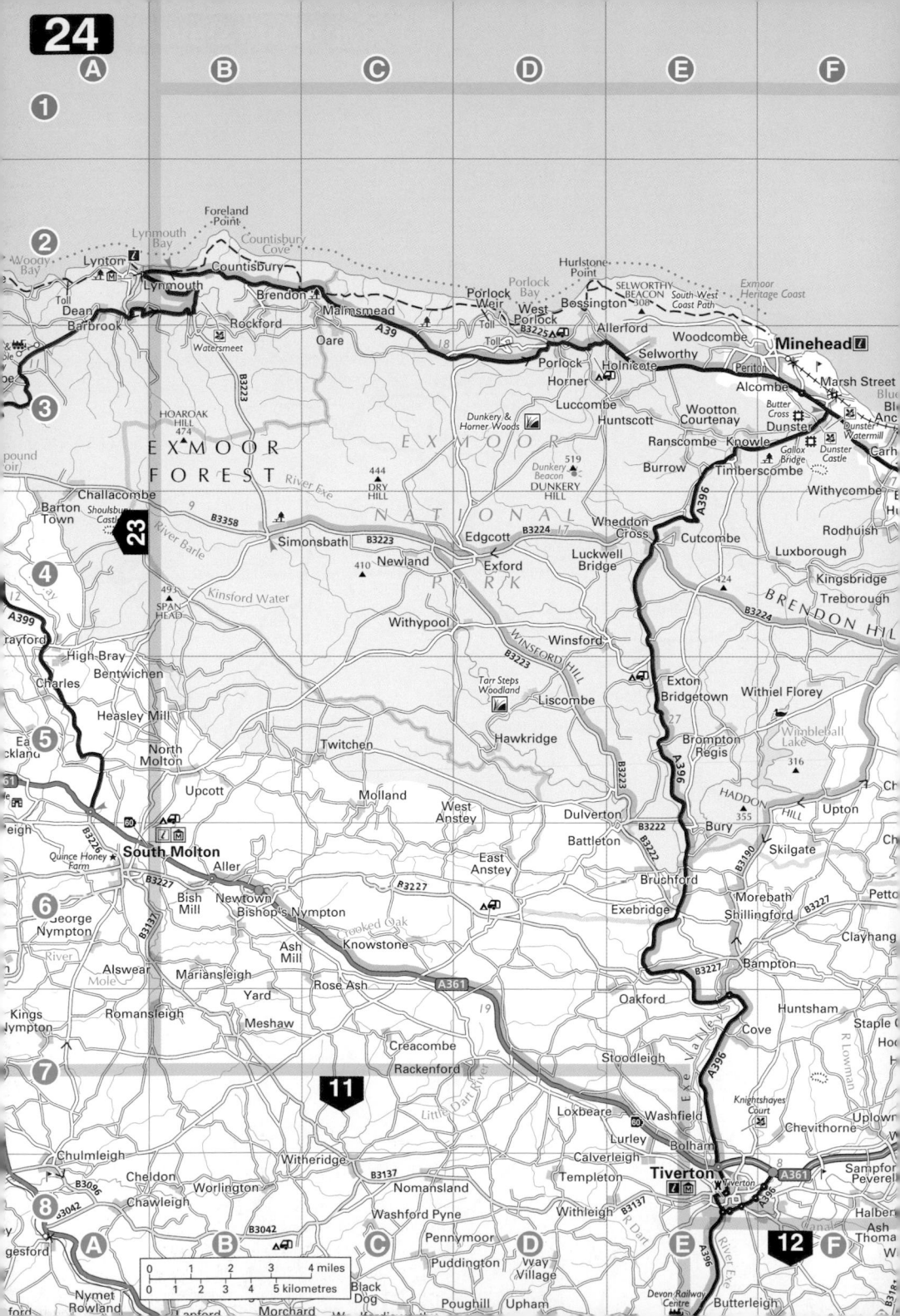

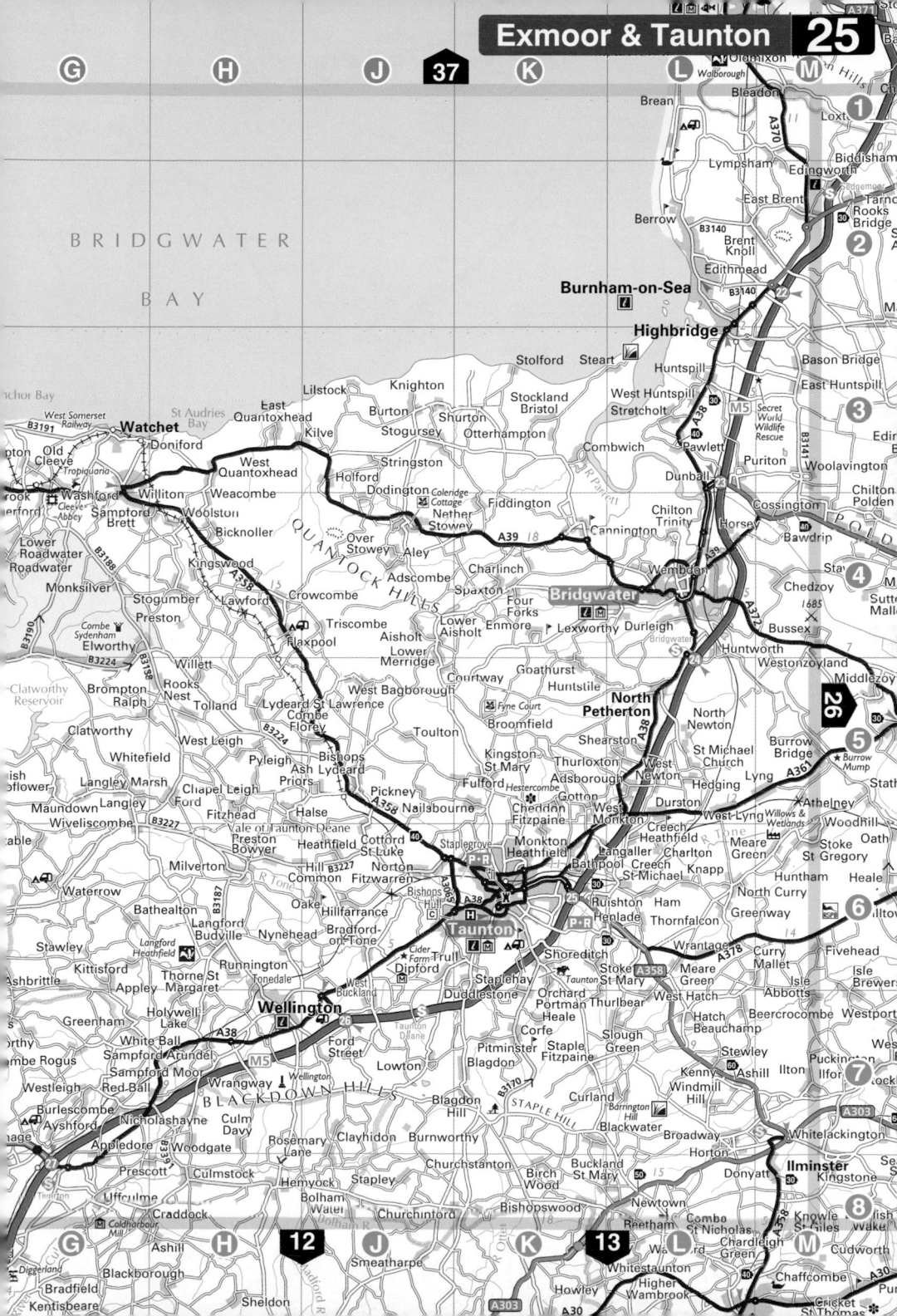

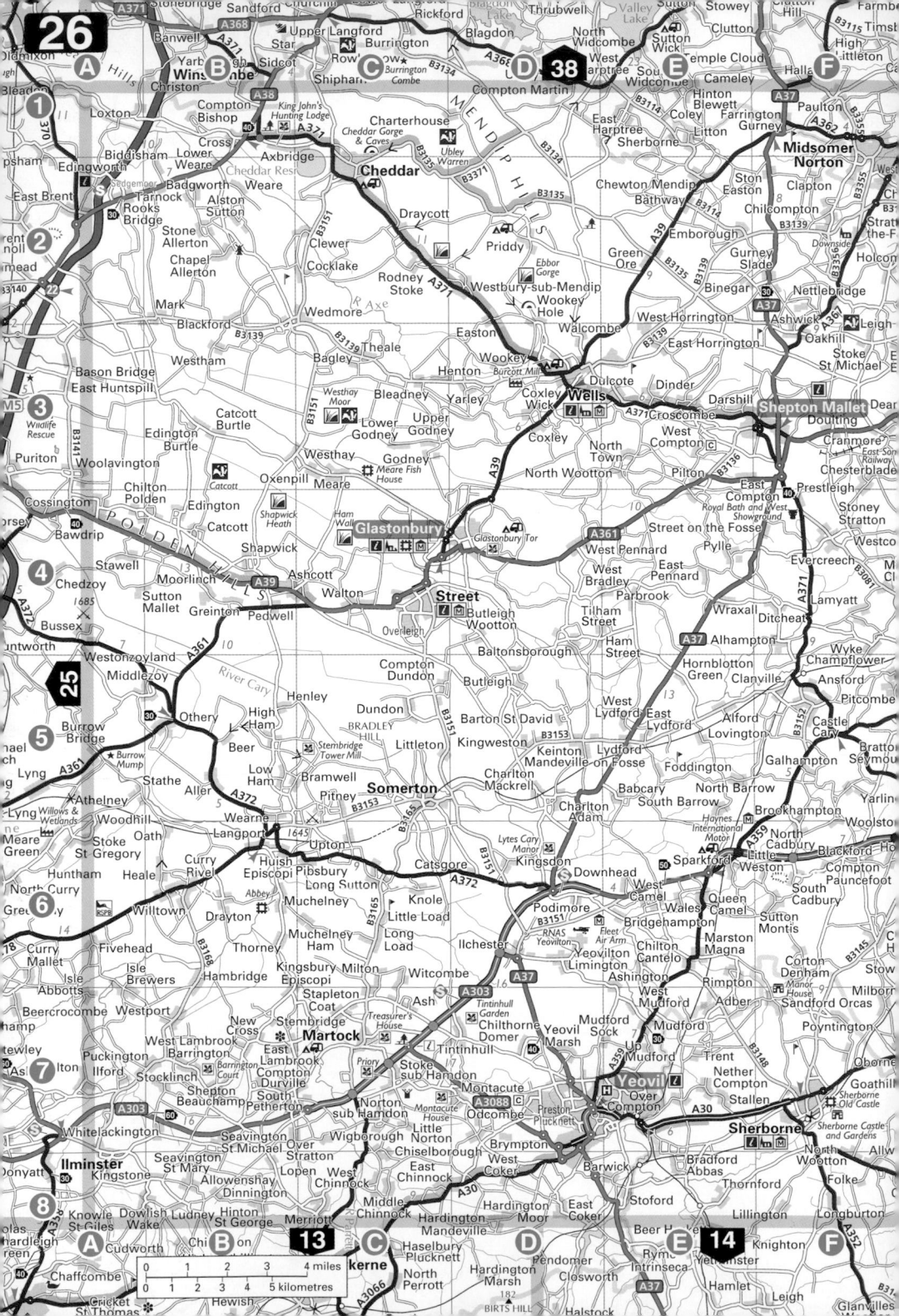

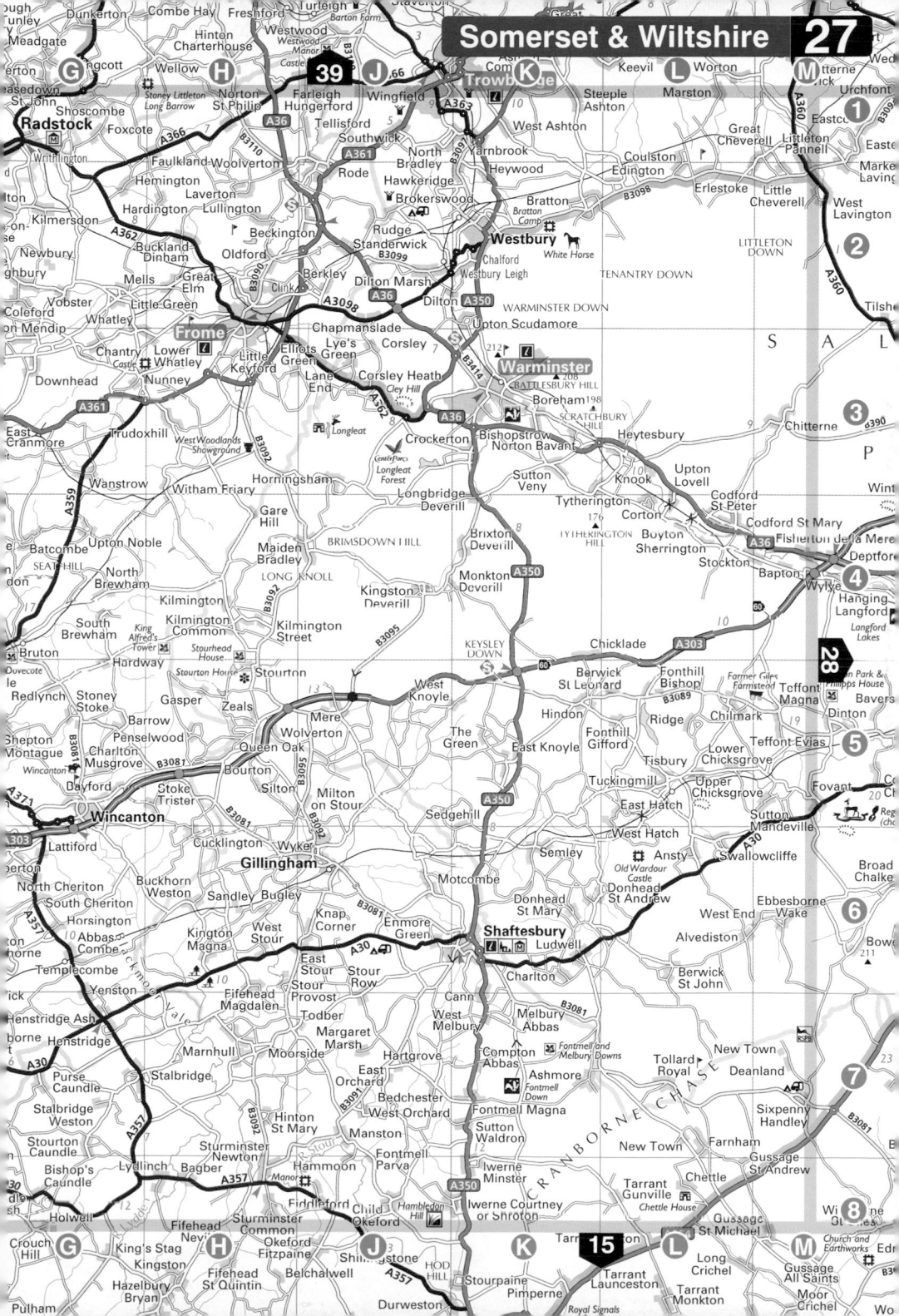

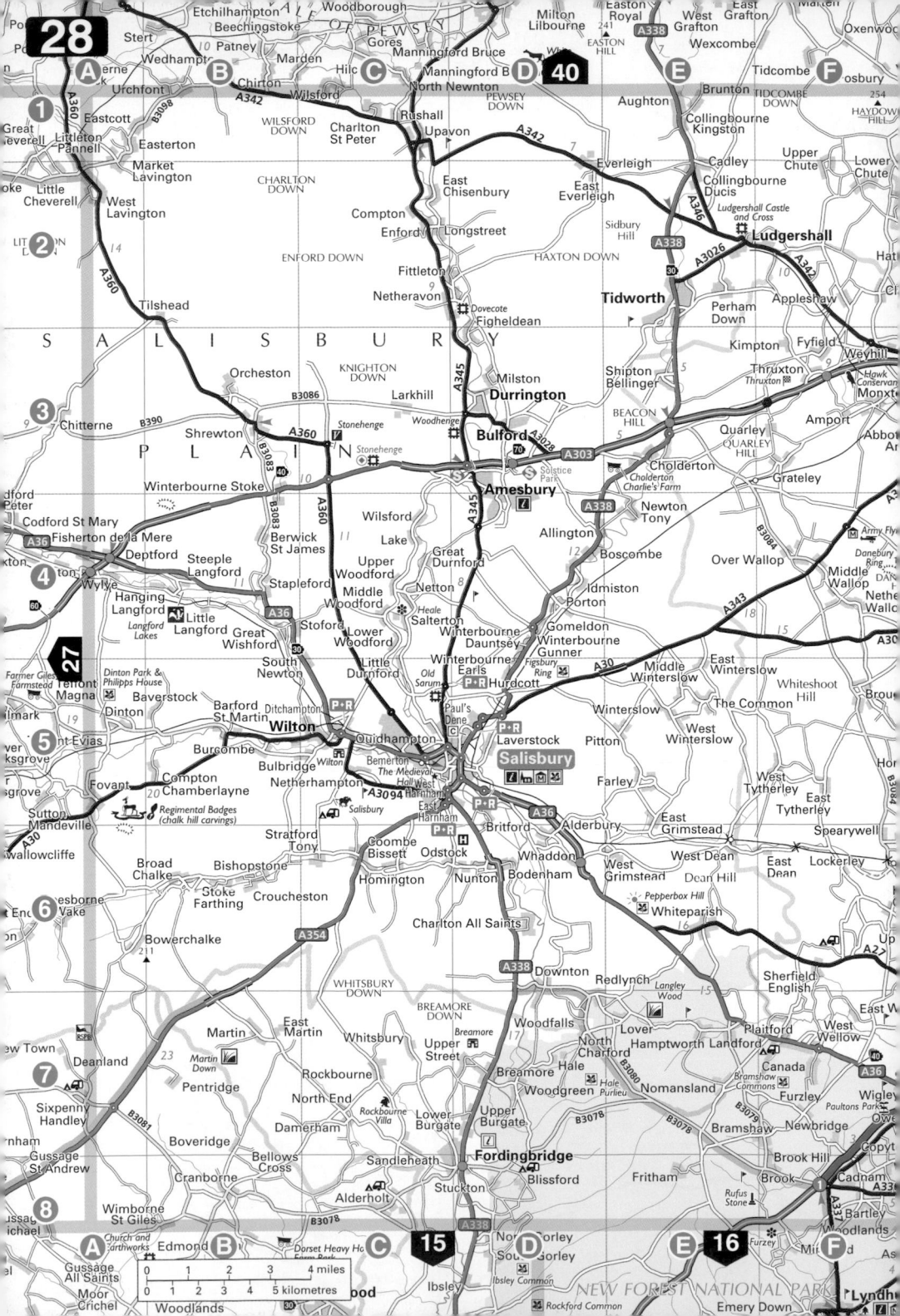

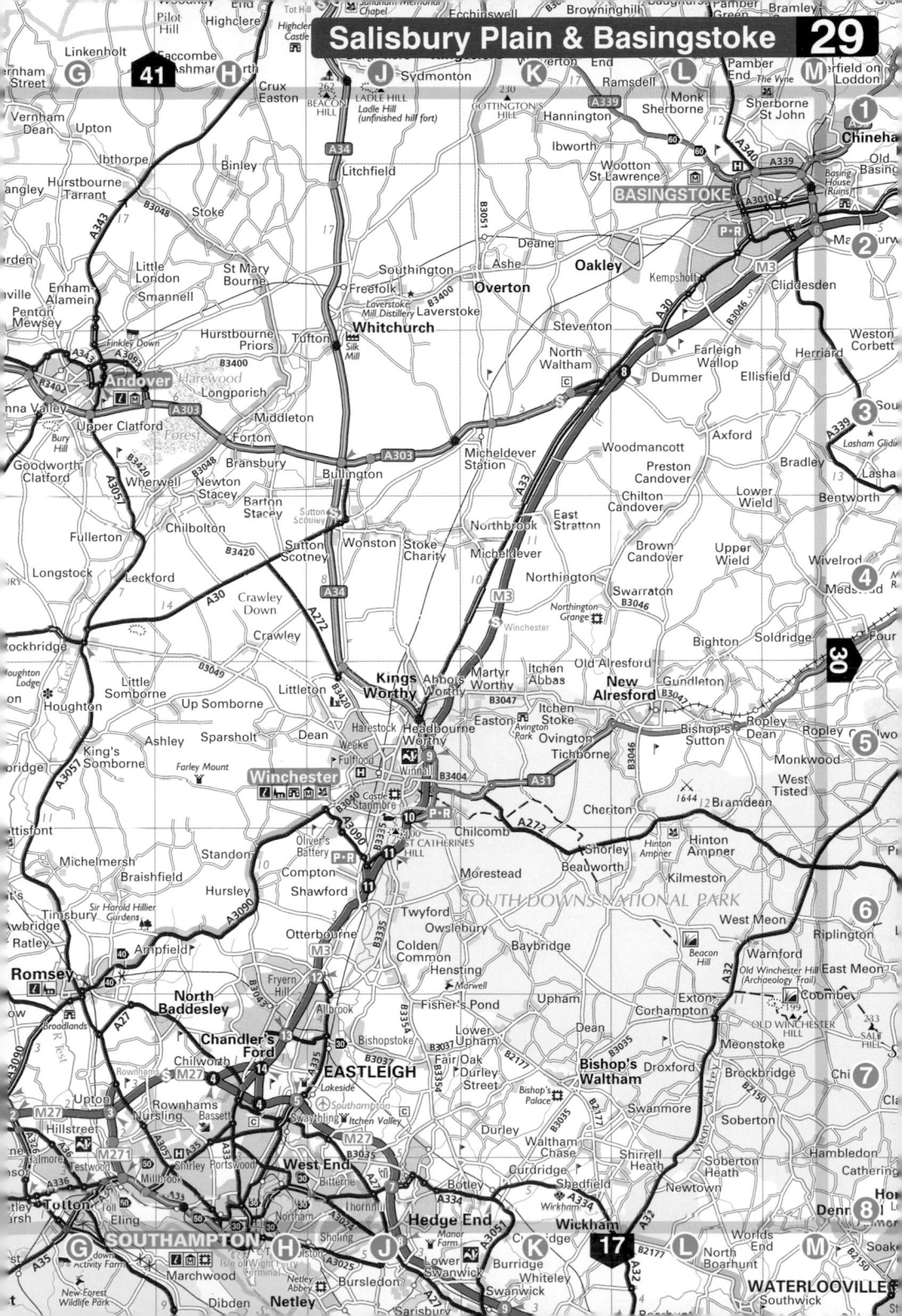

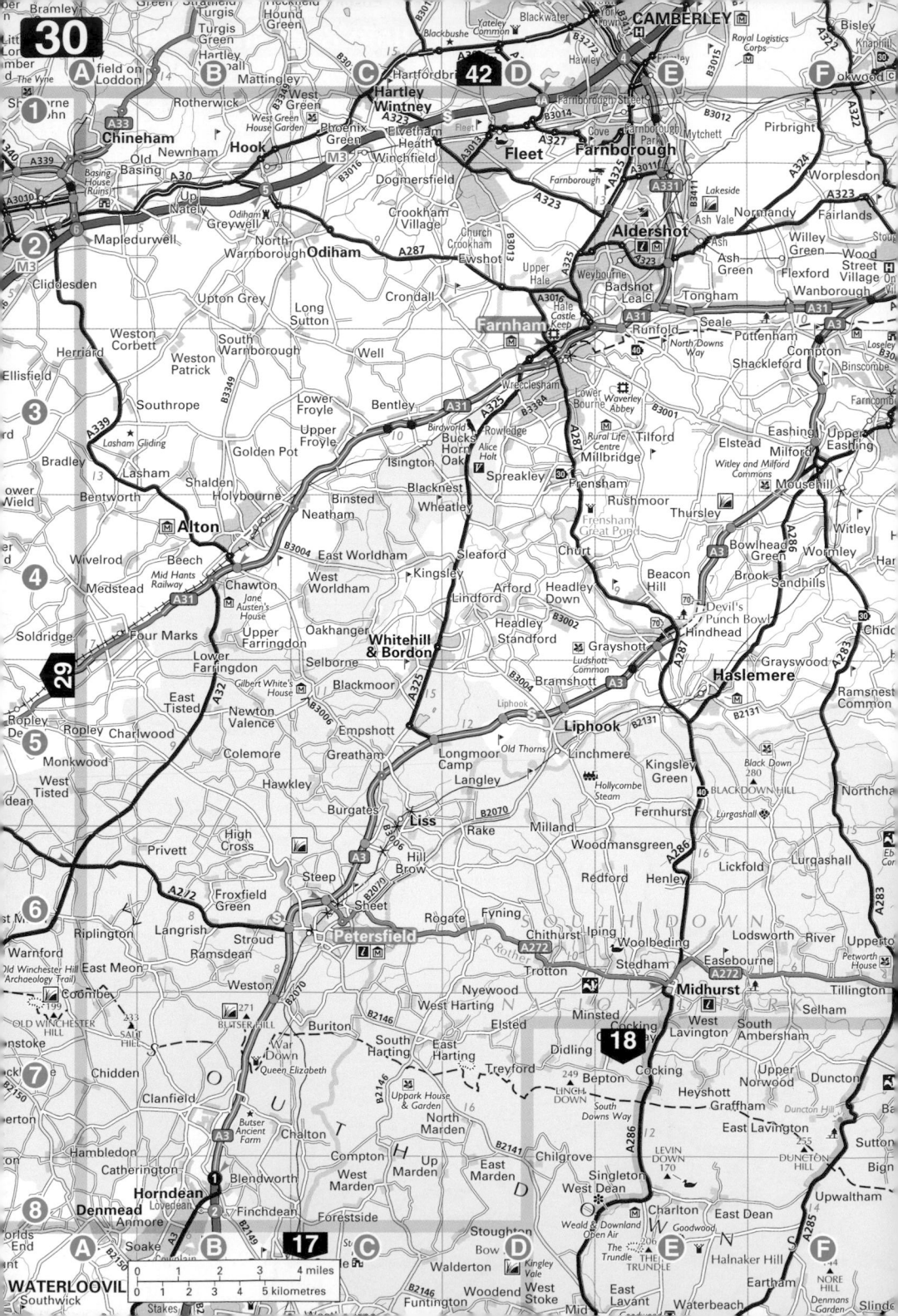

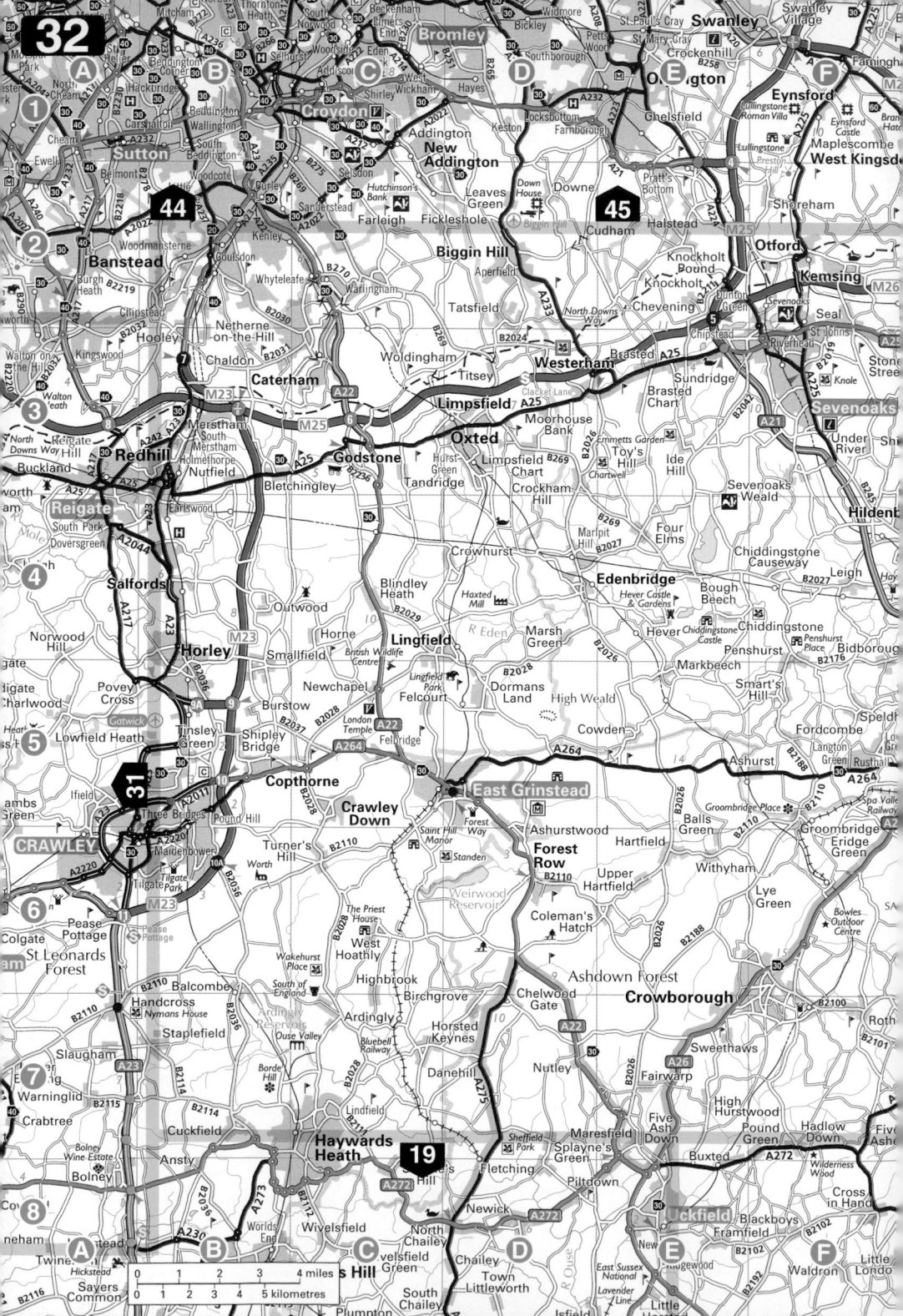

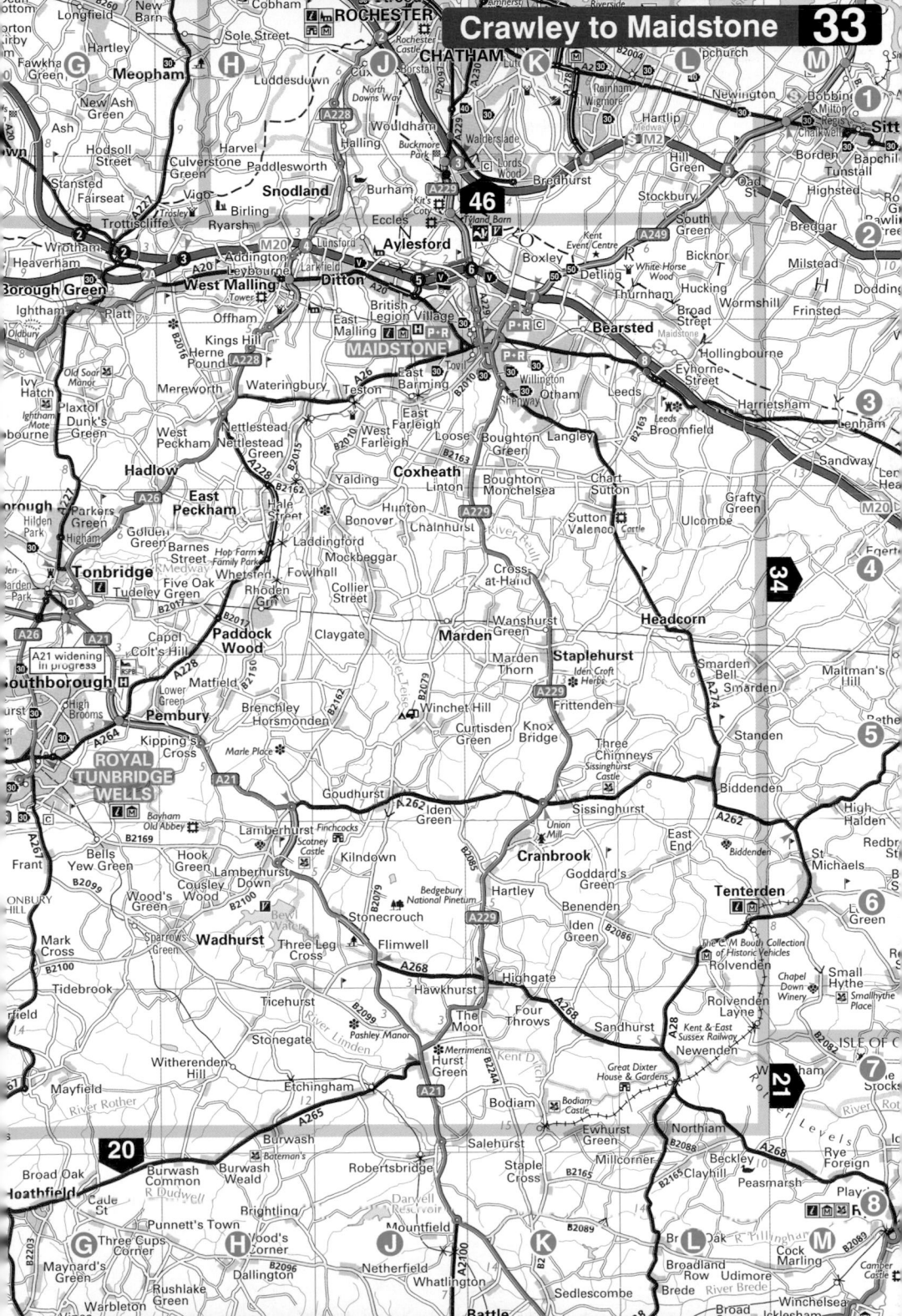

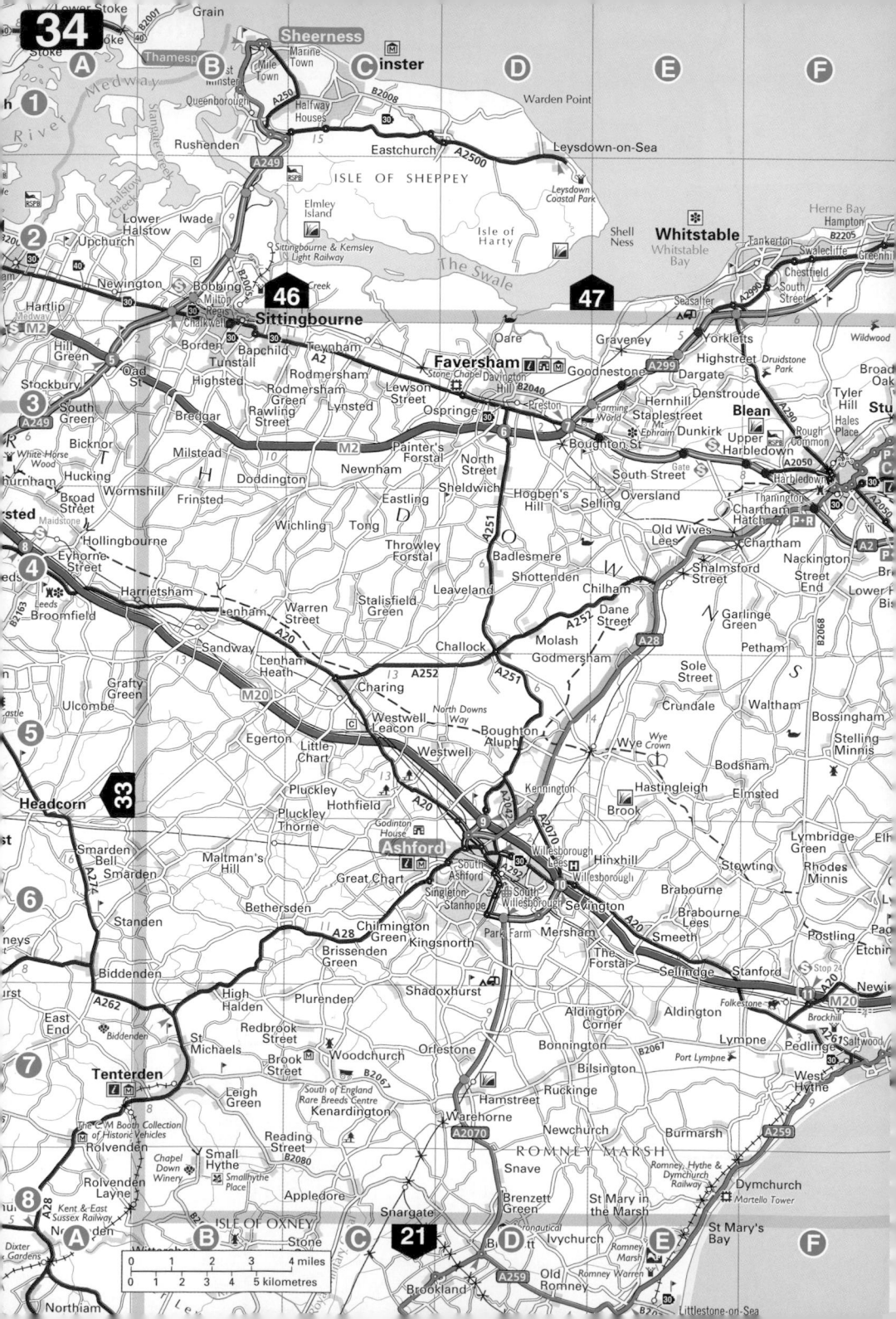

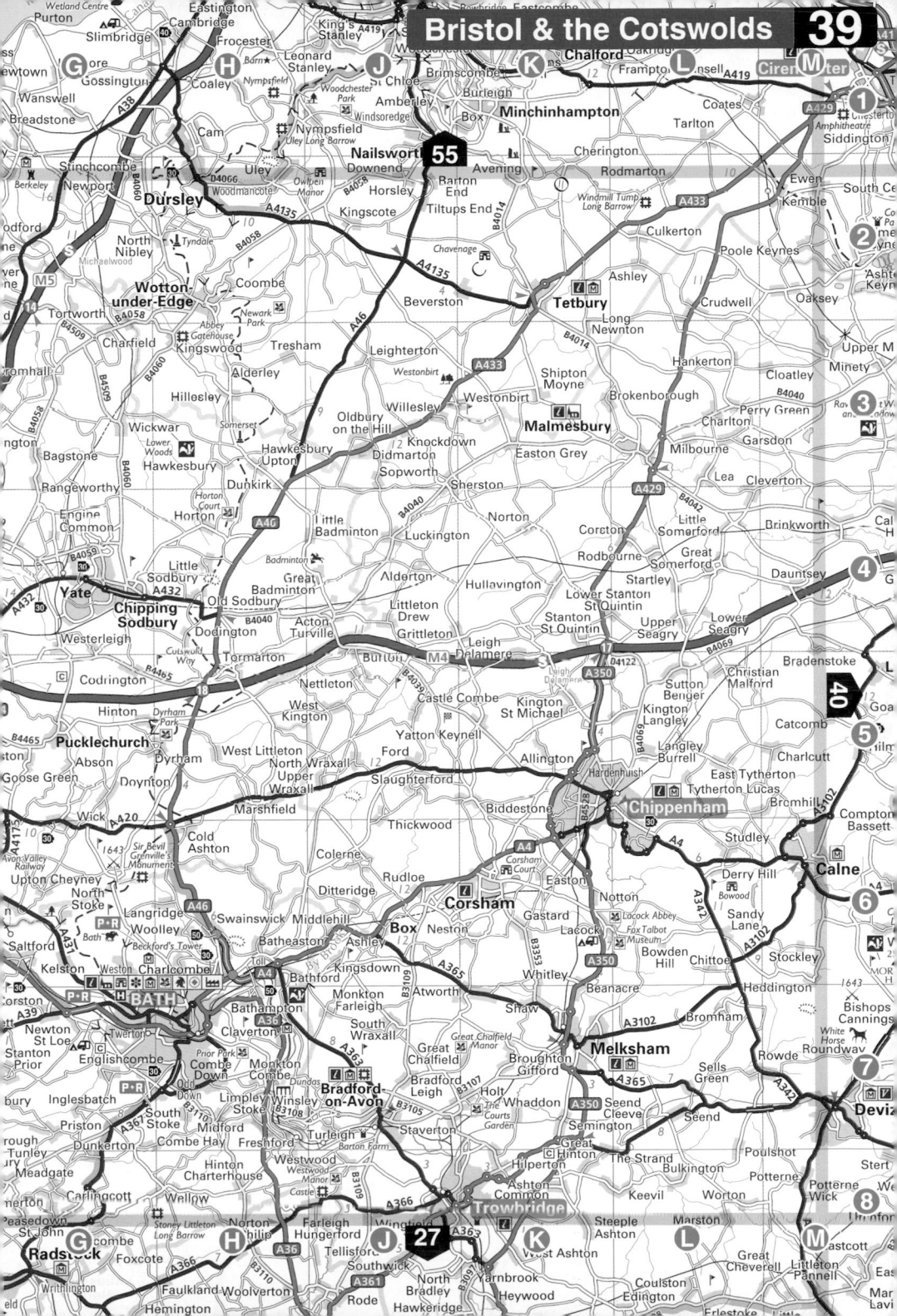

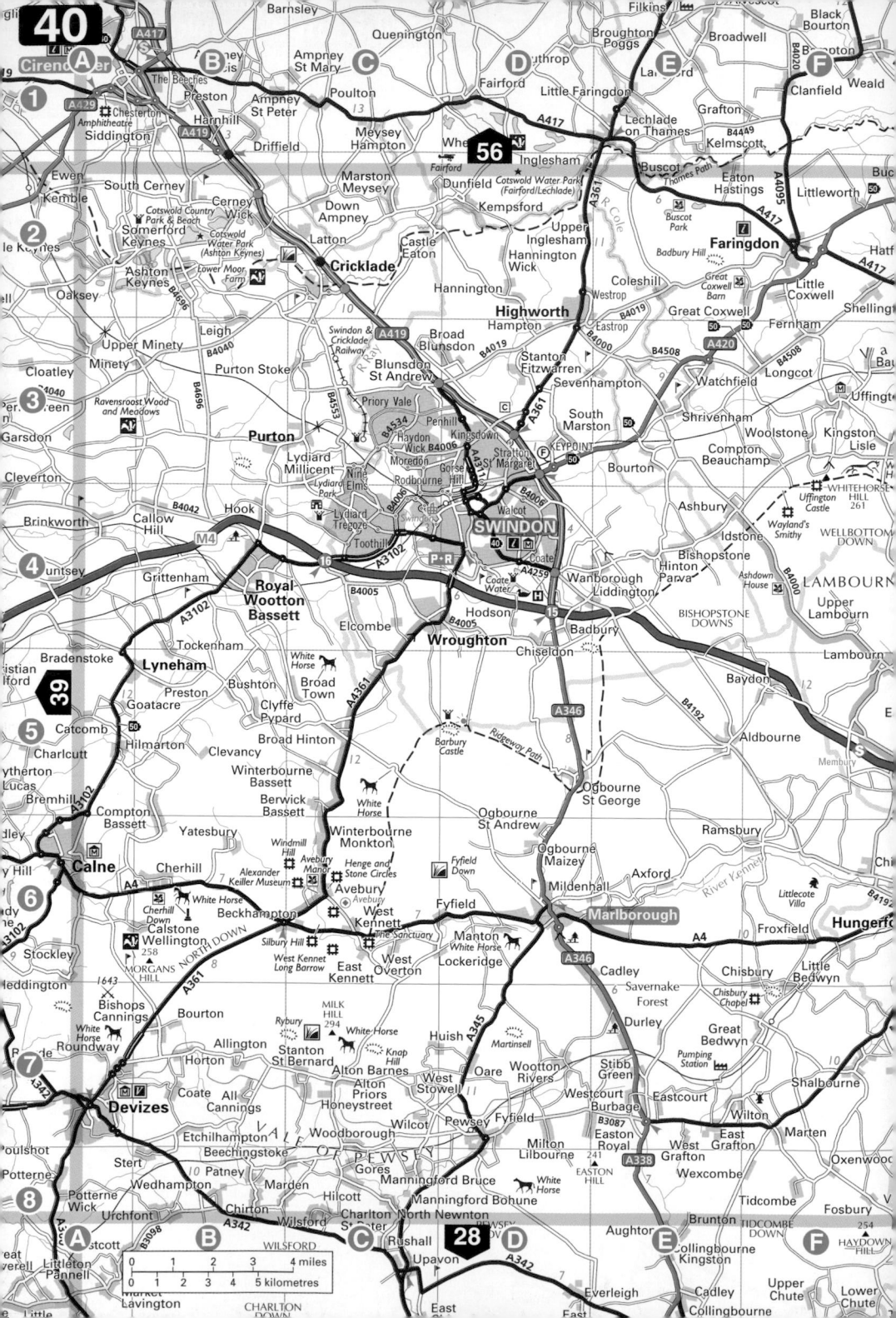

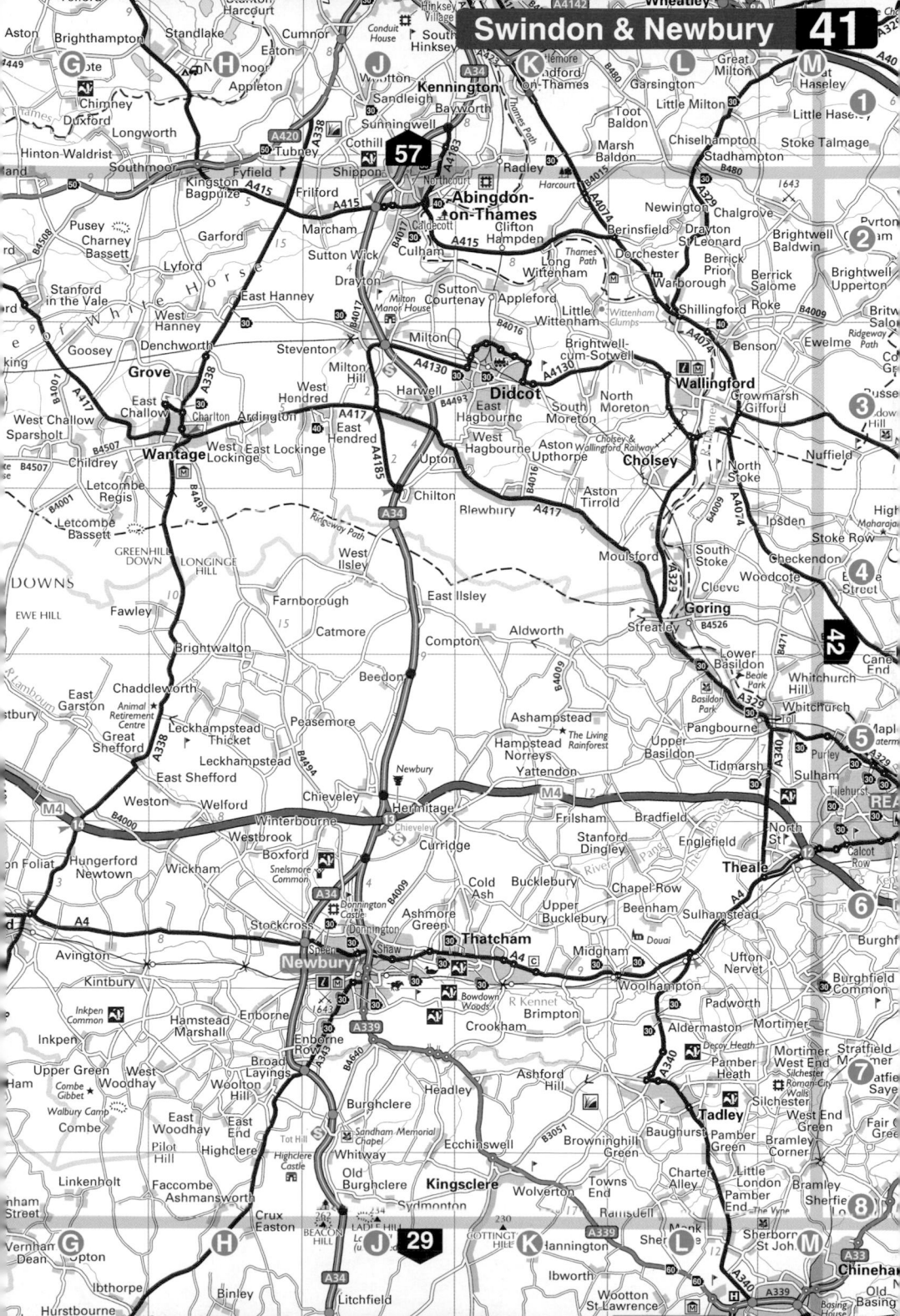

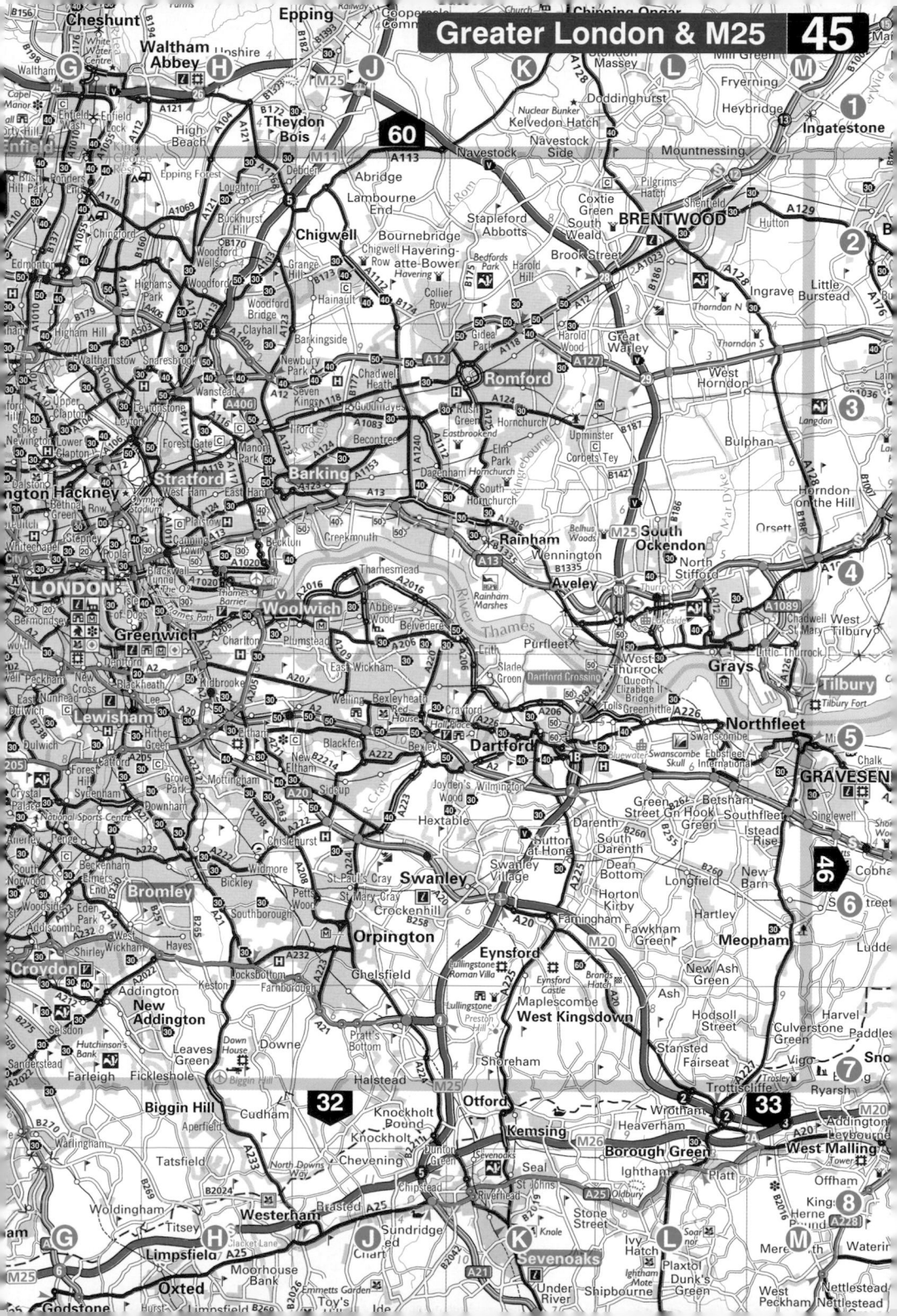

G H J K L M

1

2

3

4

5

6

7

8

62

Dengie
eldham **G**
minster
on-Crouch
Holliwell Point
Foulness Point
Courtsend
Churchend
FOULNESS ISLAND

Warden Point
Leysdown-on-Sea
ch **A2500**
SHEPPEY
Isle of Harty
Leysdown Coastal Park
Shell Ness
The Swale

35
MA
Westgate on Sea
Minnis Bay
Birchington
Acol
Monkton
Durlock
ISLE OF NET
B2190
A299
6
A253
17
A28

Whitstable
Whitstable Bay
Tankerton
Swalecliffe
Chestfield
South Street
Seasalter
Yorkletts
Highstreet
Druidstone Park
Dargate
Denstroude
Hernhill
Staplestreet
Dunkirk
Mt Ephraim
Upper Harbledown
Blean
Rough Common

Herne Bay
Herne Bay Hampton
Beltinge
Bishopstone
Reculver Towers & Roman Fort
Reculver
Broomfield
Greenhill
Herne
Hoath
Upstreet
A299
St Nicholas at Wade
Boyden Gate
Sarre
Chislet
West Stourmouth
East Stourmouth
Westmarsh
Minster
R Stour

34
Faversham
Stone Chapel Davington Hill
Oare
Preston
B2040
Ospringe
Farming World
Boughton St
South Street
North Street
Sheldwich
Hogben's Hill
Selling
Oversland
Overland
Gate
Harbledown
Chartham Hatch
Chartham
Old Wives Lees

35
Wildwood
Broad Oak
Tyler Hill
Sturry
Stodmarsh
Hersden
Westbere
Fordwich
Town Hall
Wickhambreaux
Ickham
Littlebourne
Preston
Elmstone
Hoaden
Cop Street
Stourmouth
Durlock
Wingham
Marshborough
Ash
A257
Woodnesborough
Staple
Statenborough
Eastry
7
8

Canterbury
P·R
Thanington
A2
Bramling
Bekesbourne
Patrixbourne
Adisham
Goodnestone
Nonington
Chillenden
Betteshanger

G H **J** **K** **L** **M**
Badlesmere
Leaveland
Shottenden
Chilham
Dane Street
Shalmsford Street End
Garlinge Green
Lower Hardres
Bishopsbourne
Bridge
Aylesham
North Downs Way
2068
Rackington Street End
Great Mong
Stone Cross
Richbor

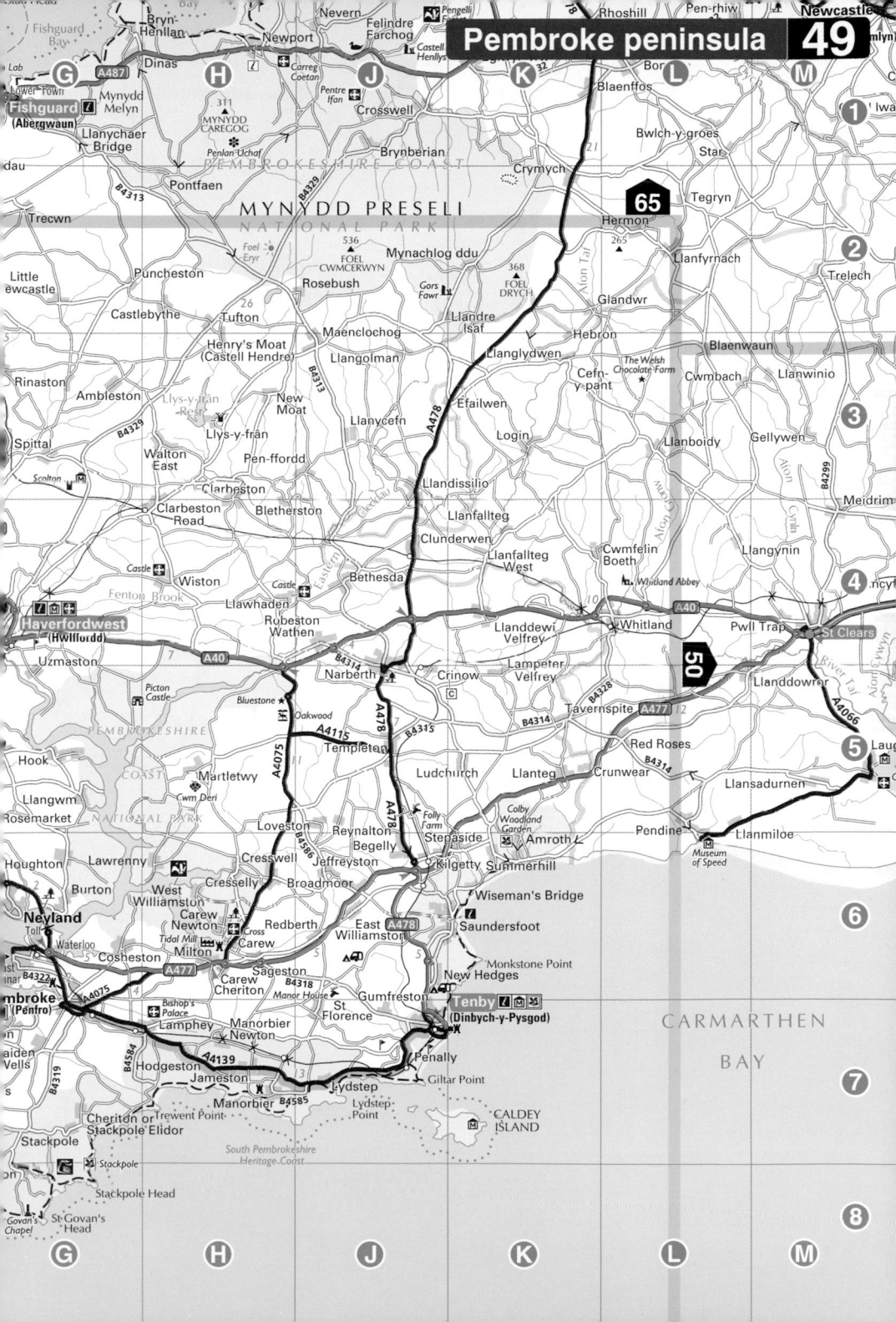

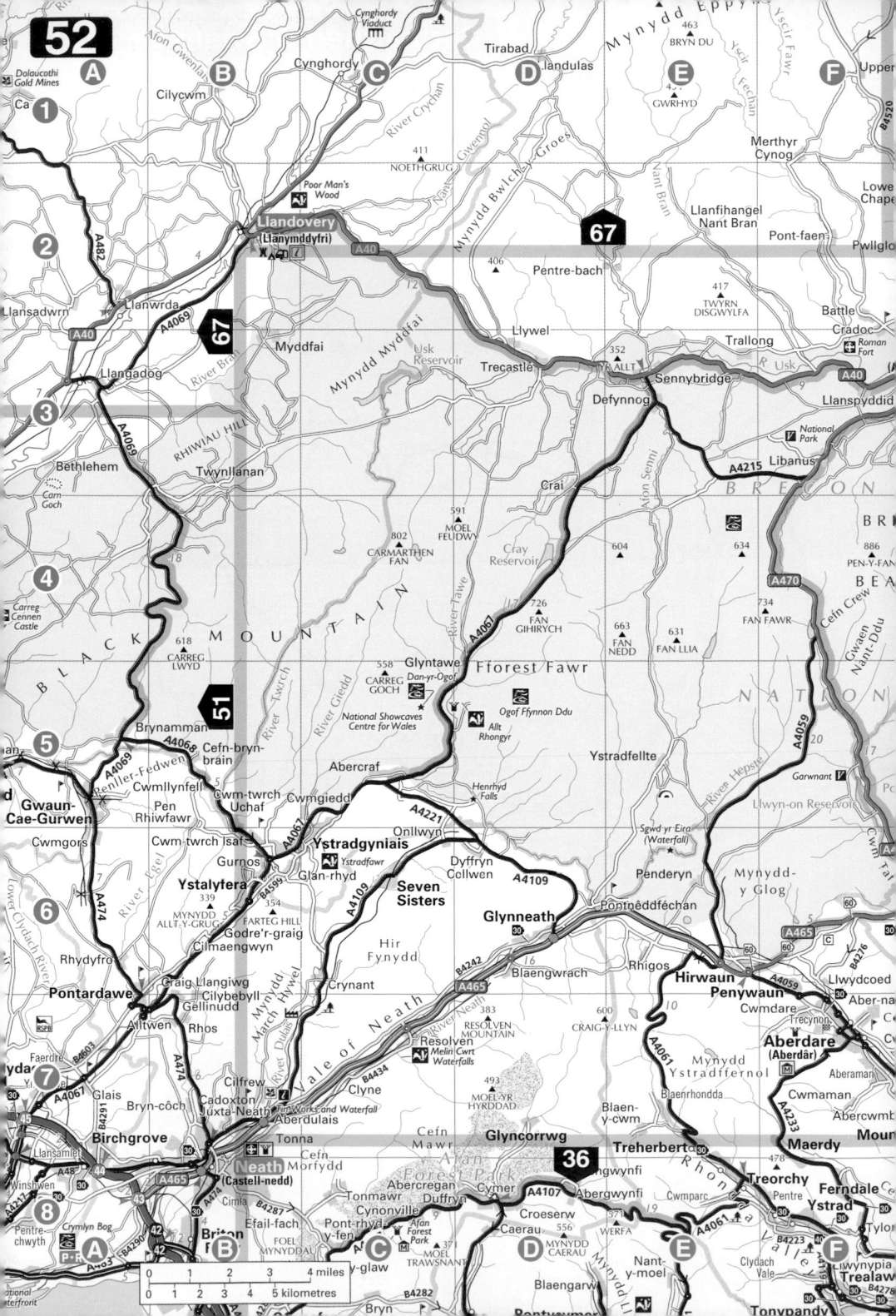

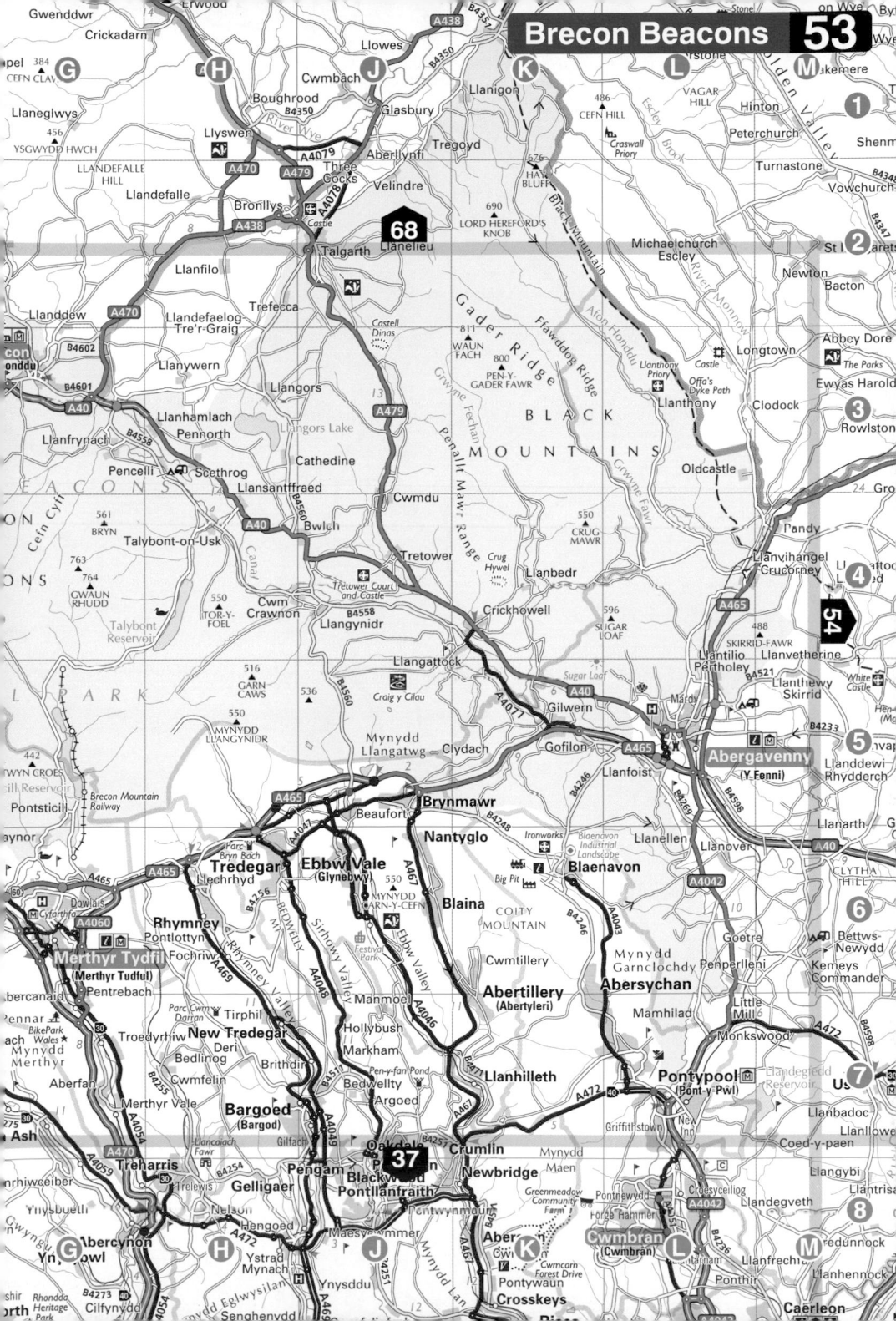

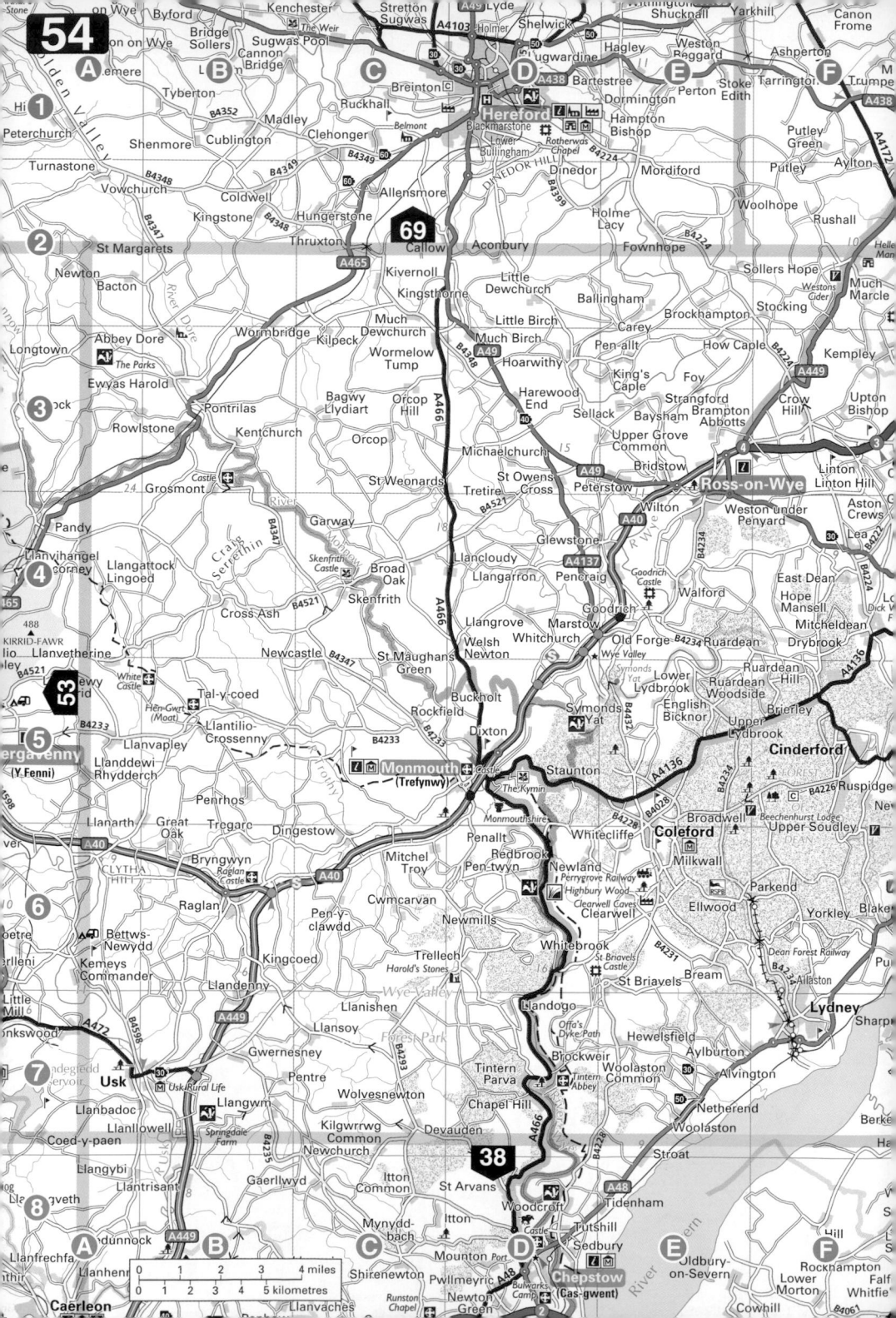

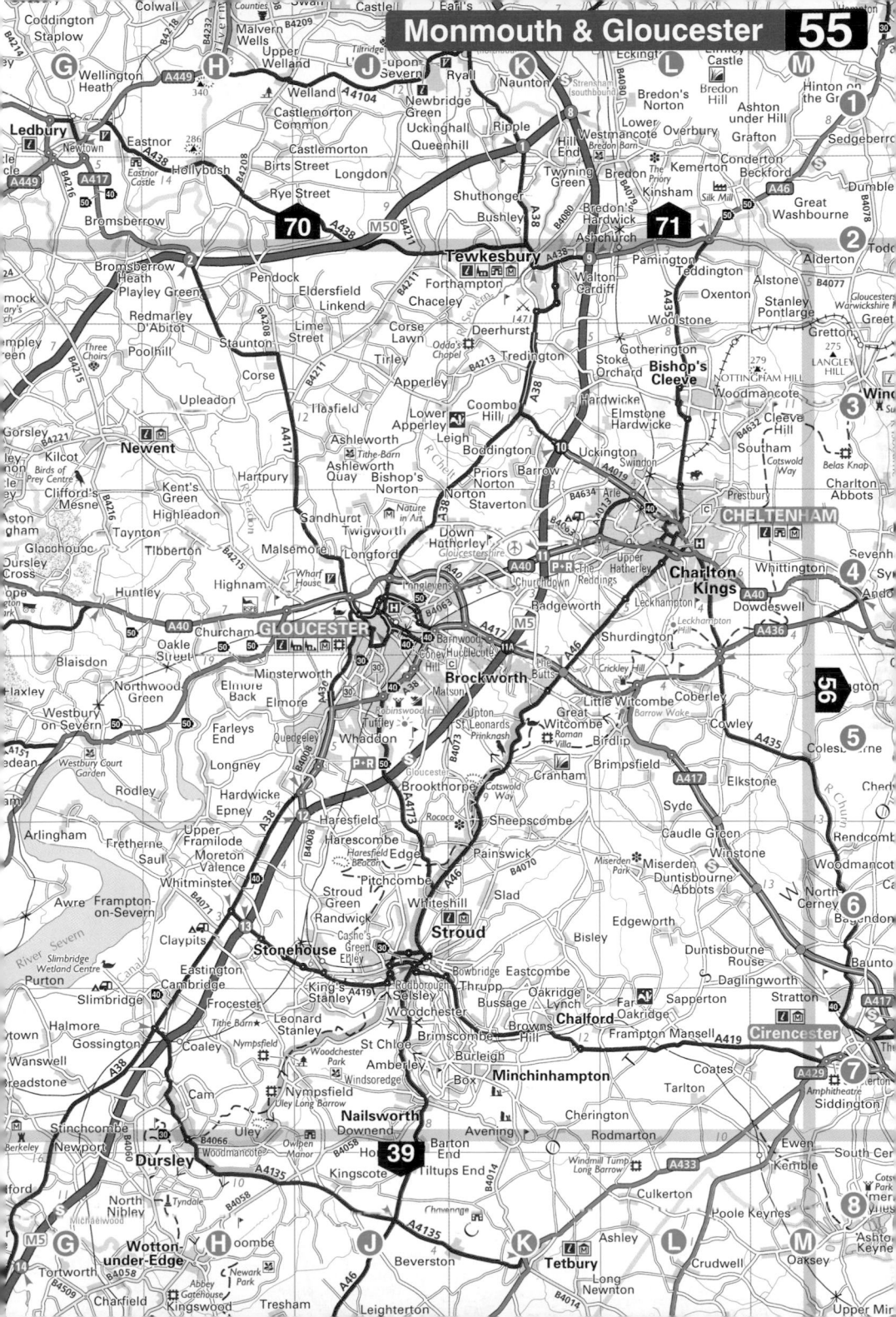

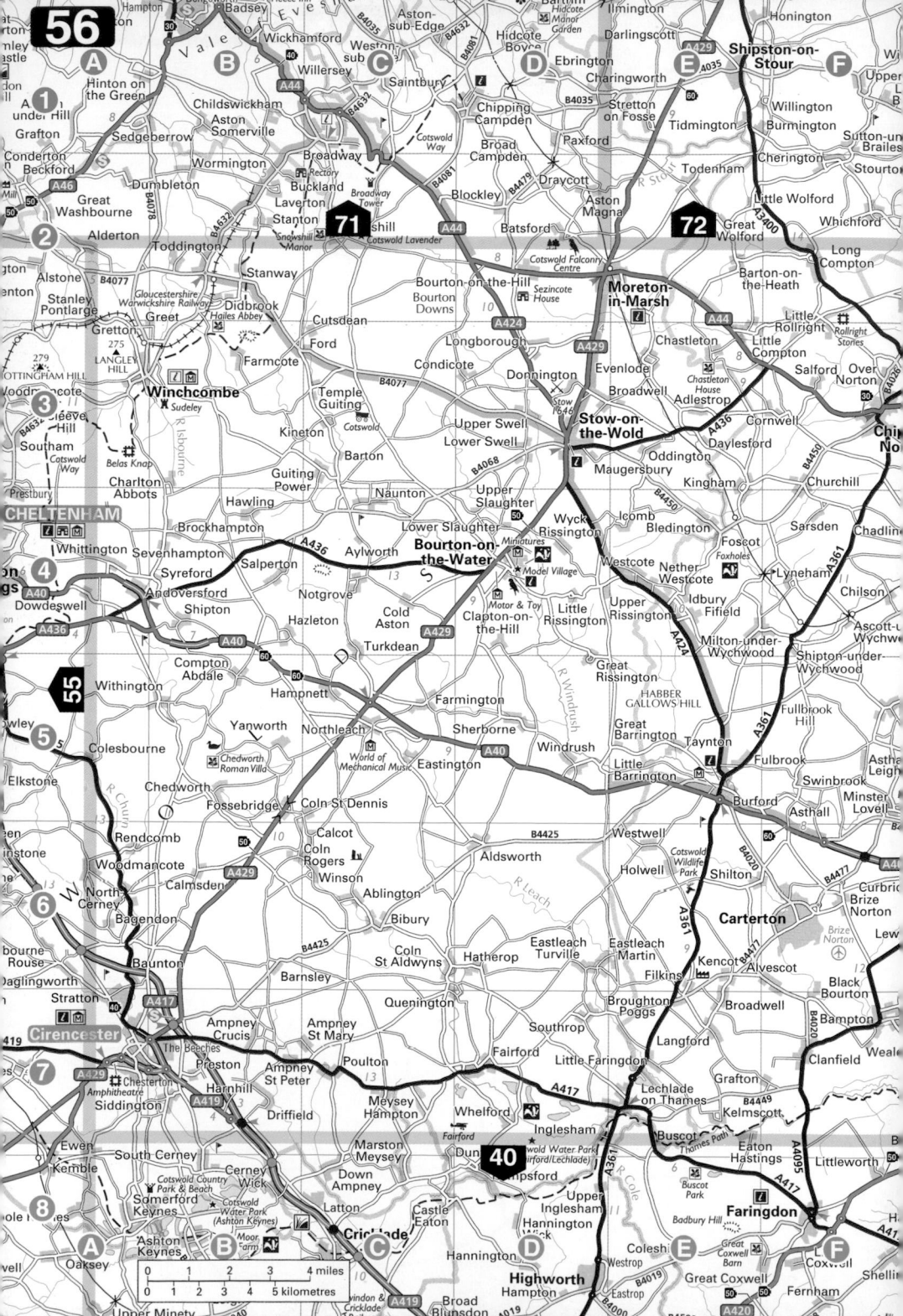

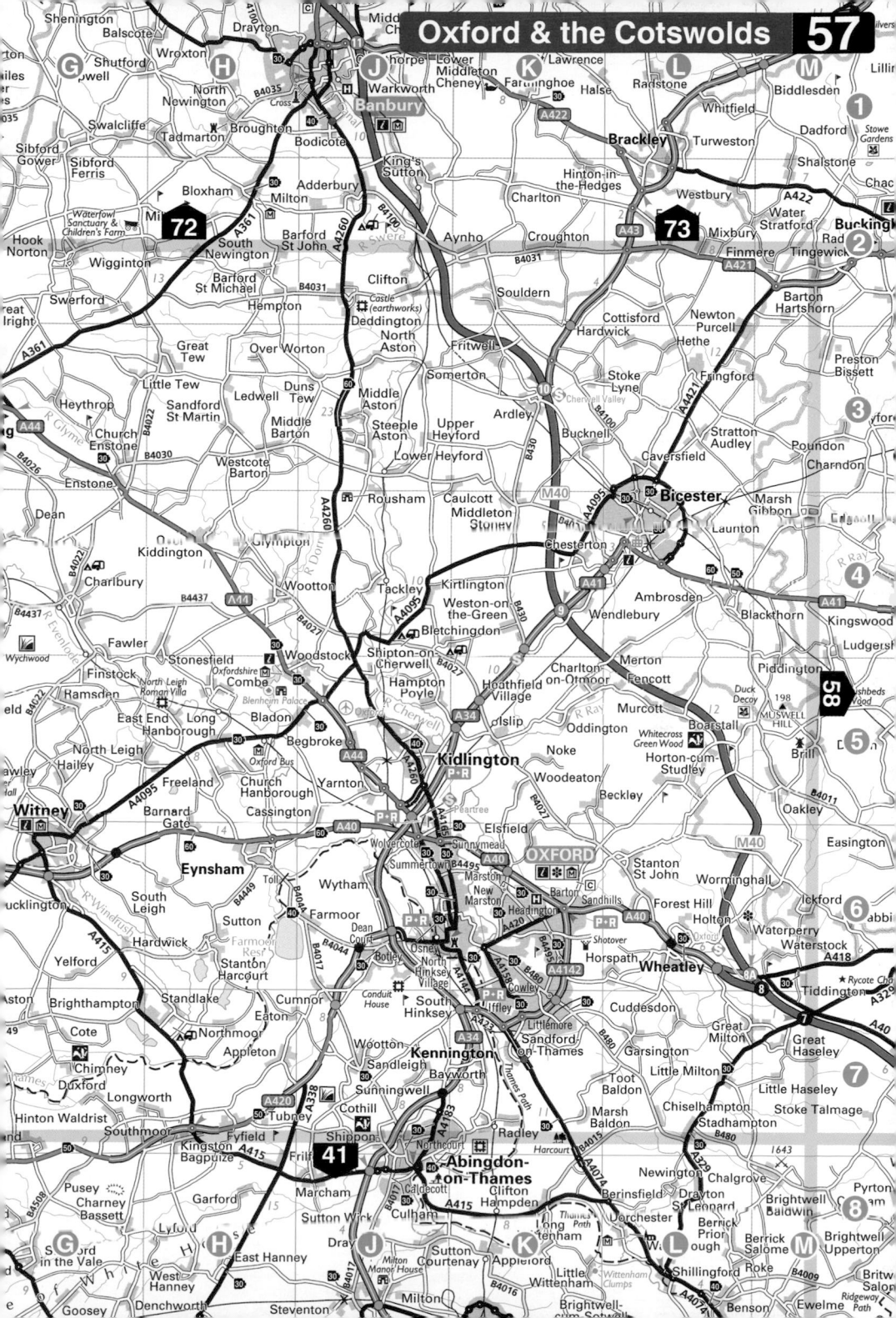

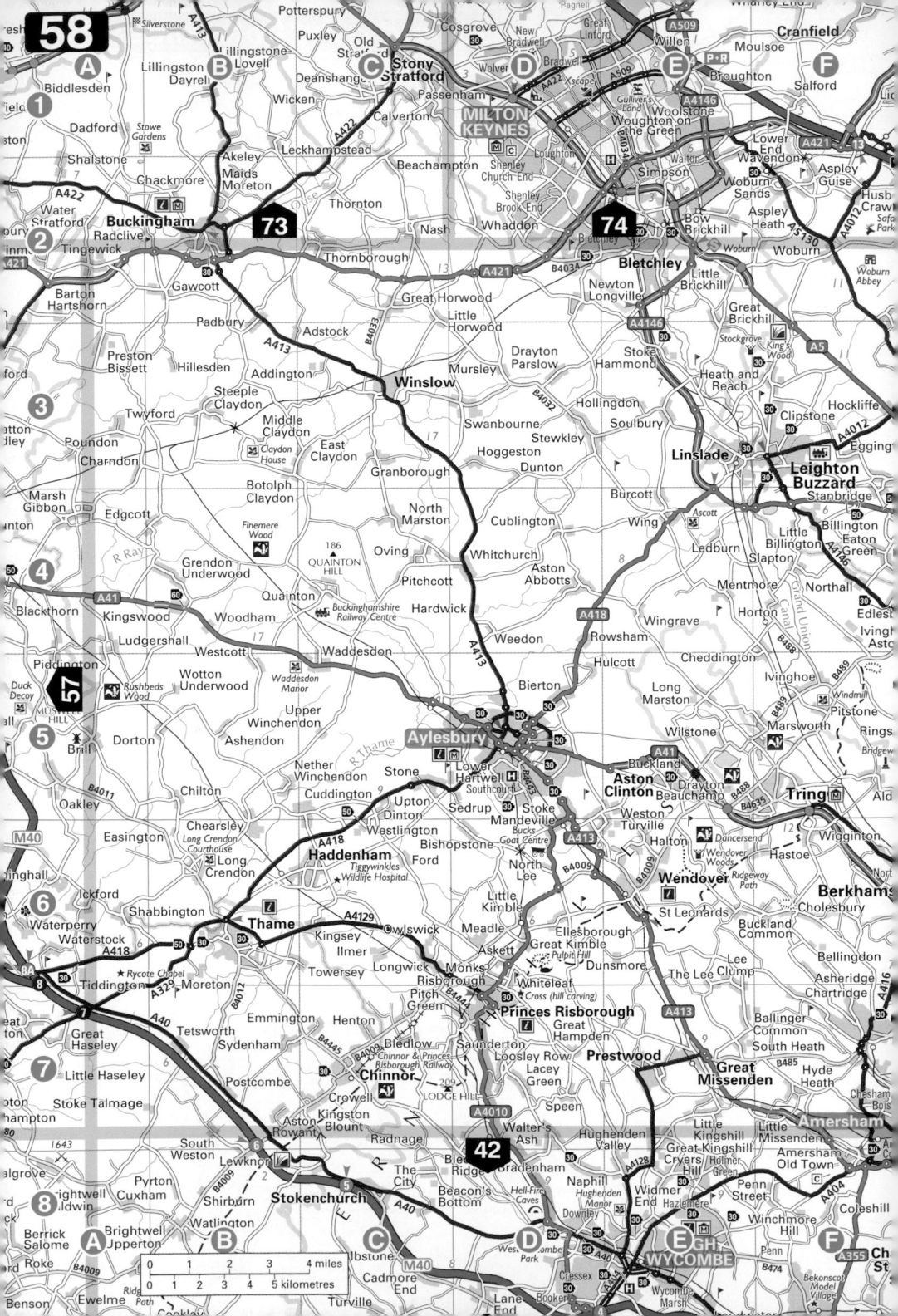

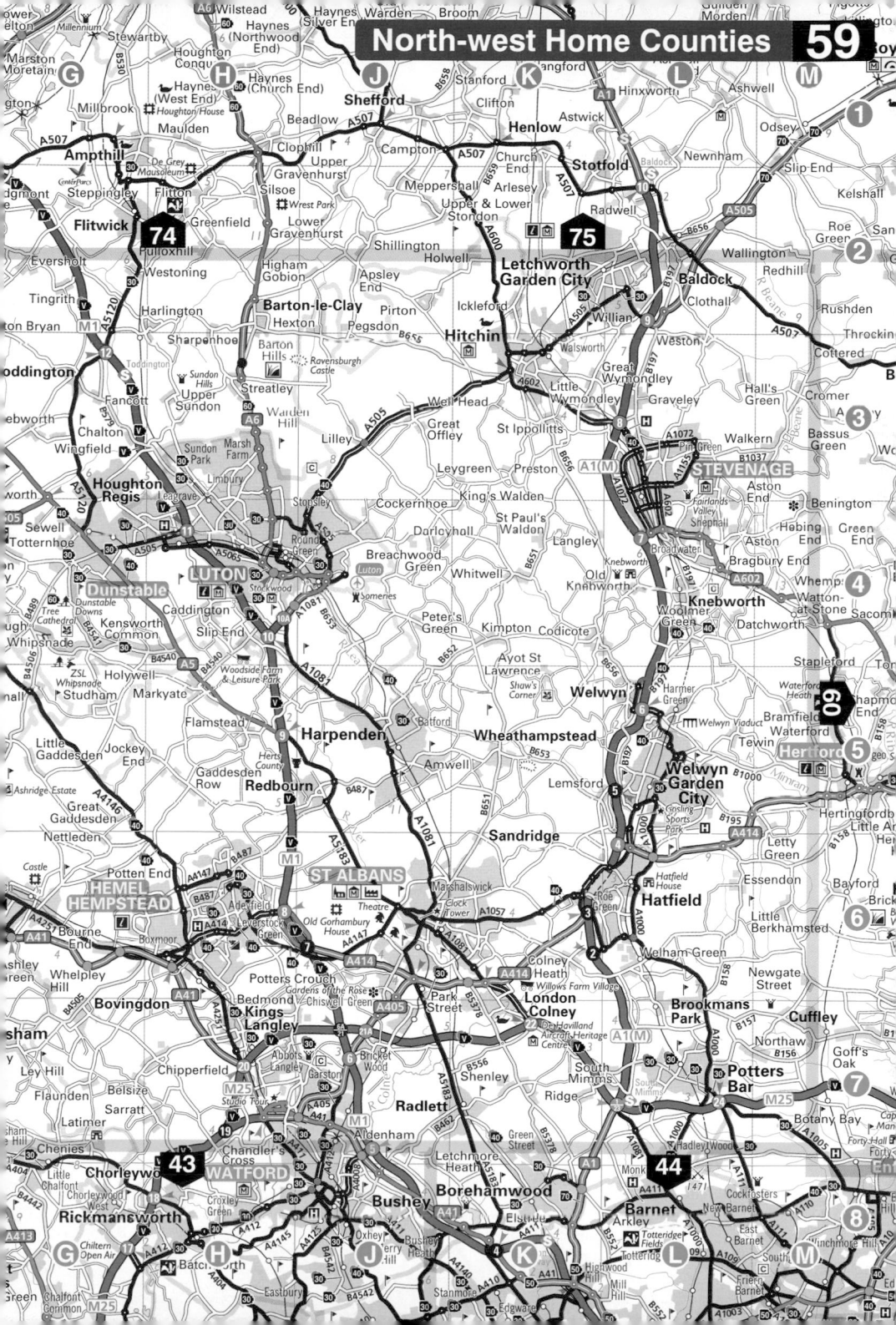

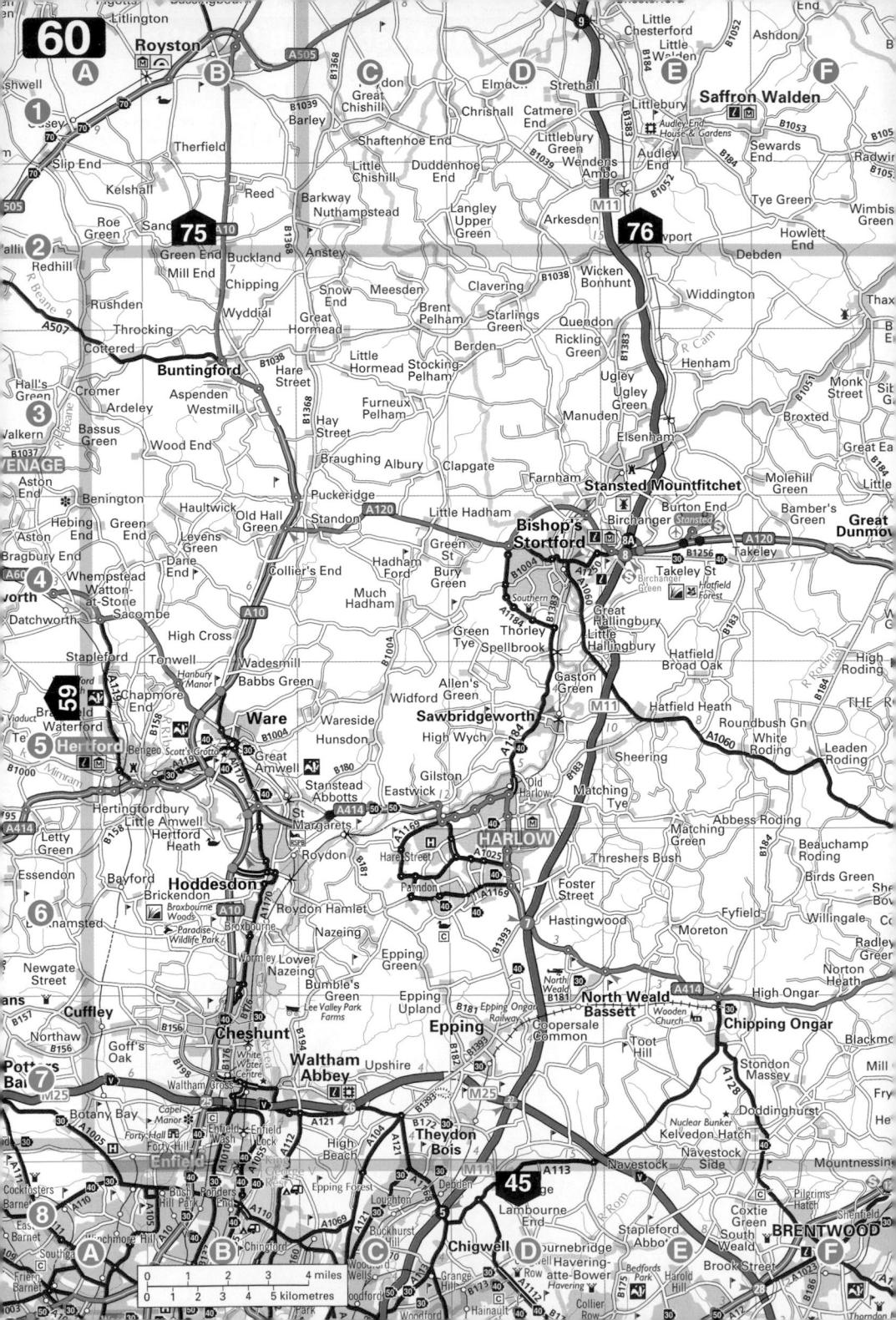

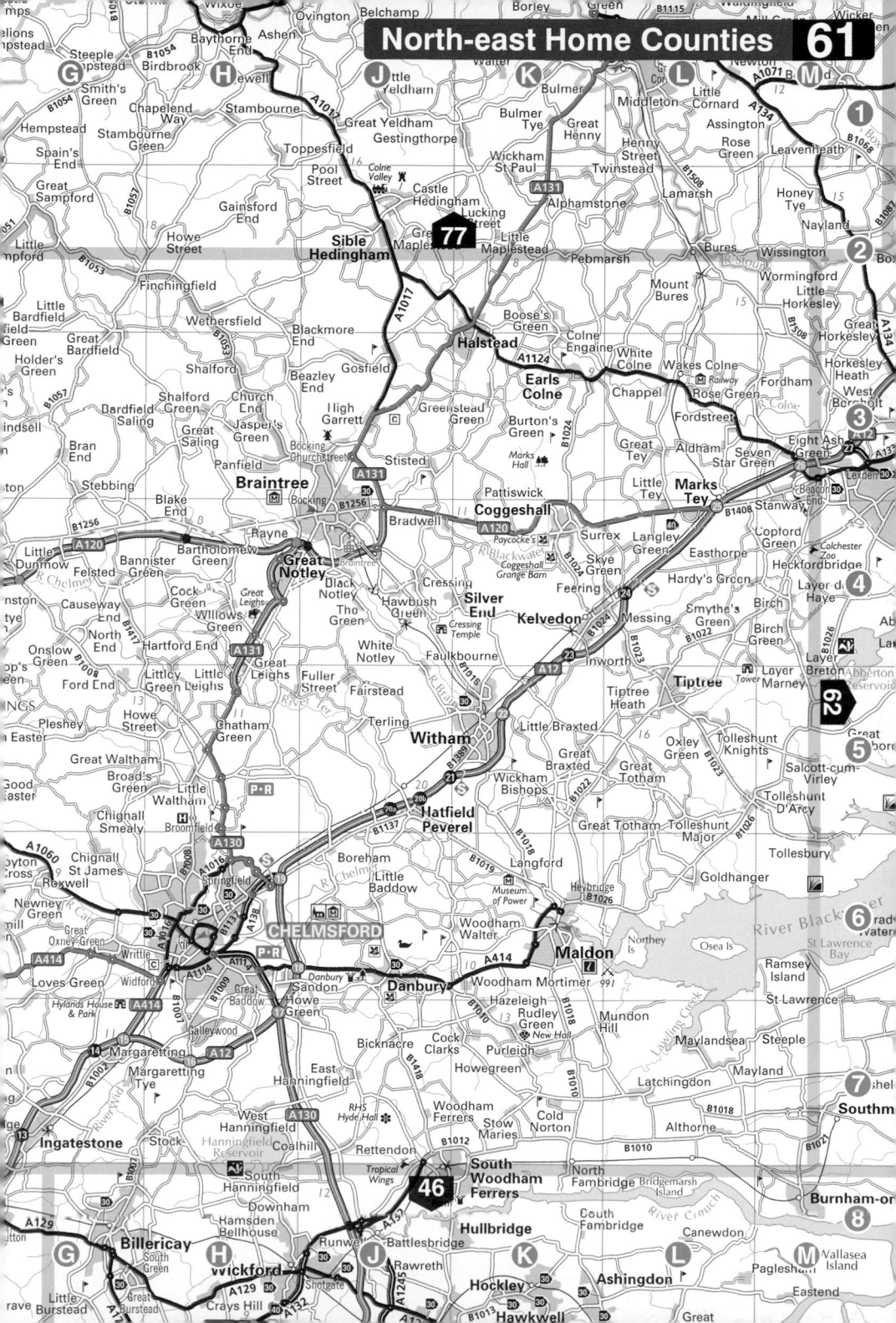

ewbourne
Hemley

Alderton

Bawdsey

Hollesley
Bay

Kirton
Falkenham

Trimley
St Mary

Old
Felixstowe

Walton

61

Felixstowe

79

Landguard Fort

Landguard
Point

Hoek van Holland
Esbjerg

Naze

on
aze

Sea

G   H   J   K   L   M

1
2
3
4
5
6
7
8

G   H   J   K   L   M

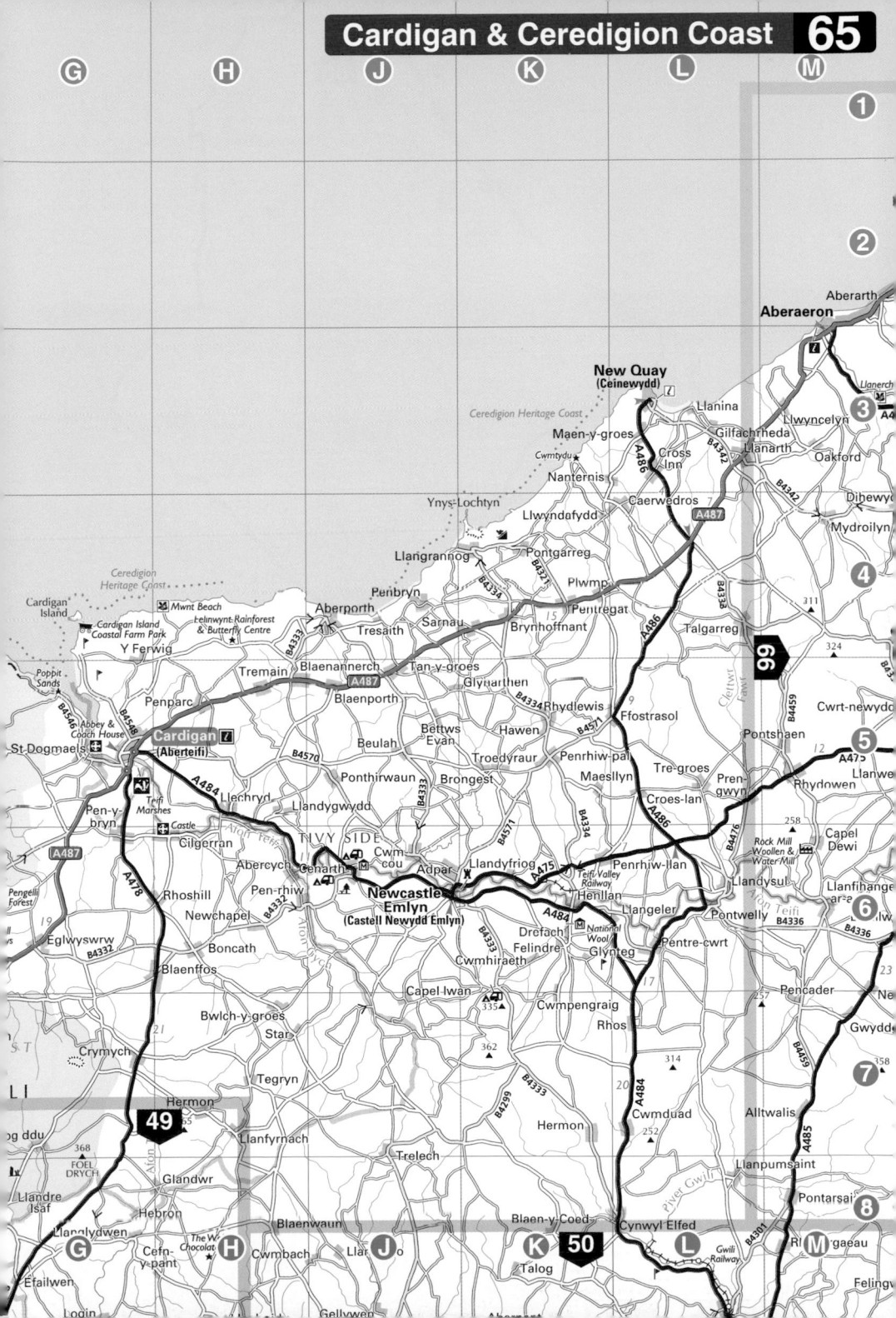

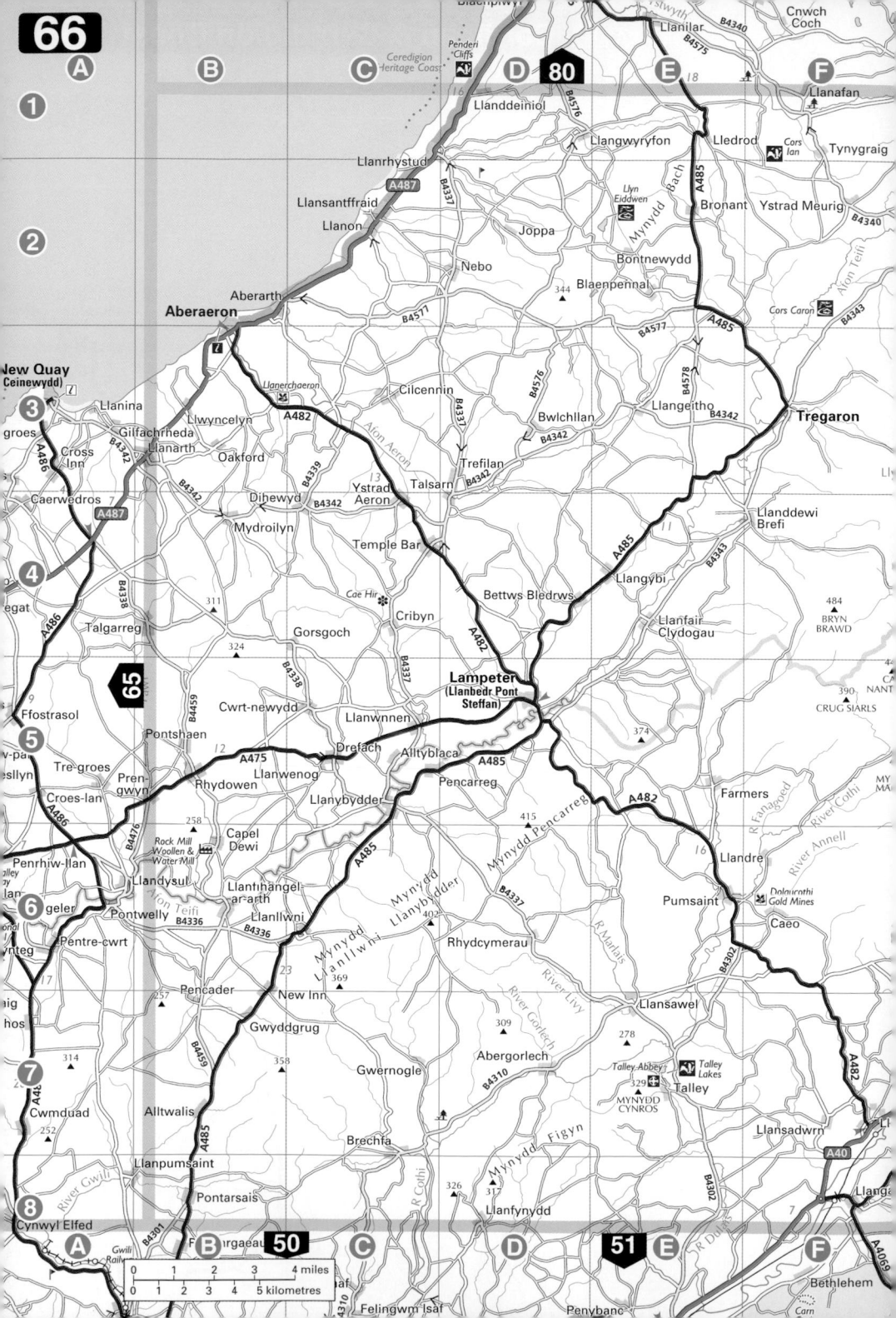

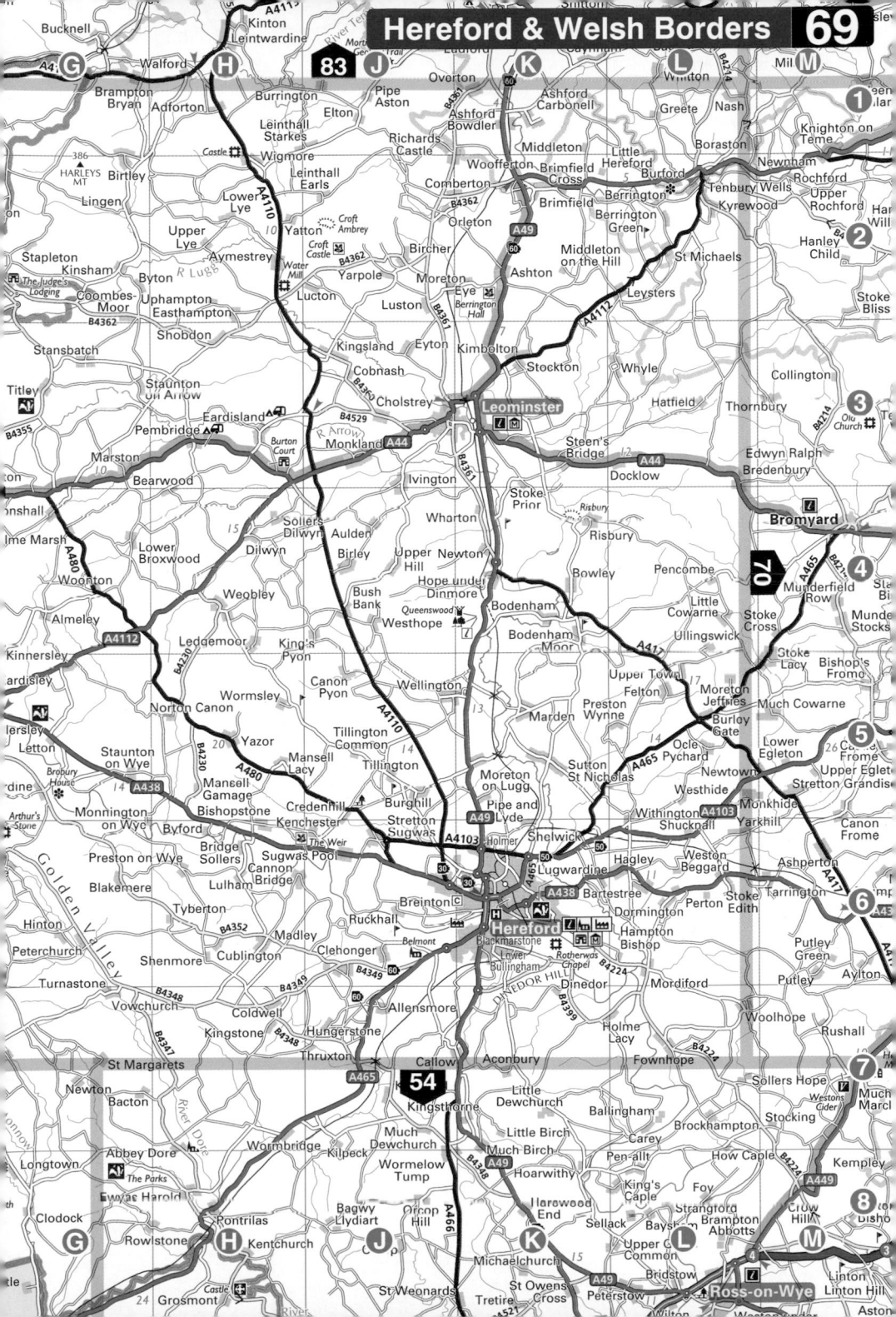

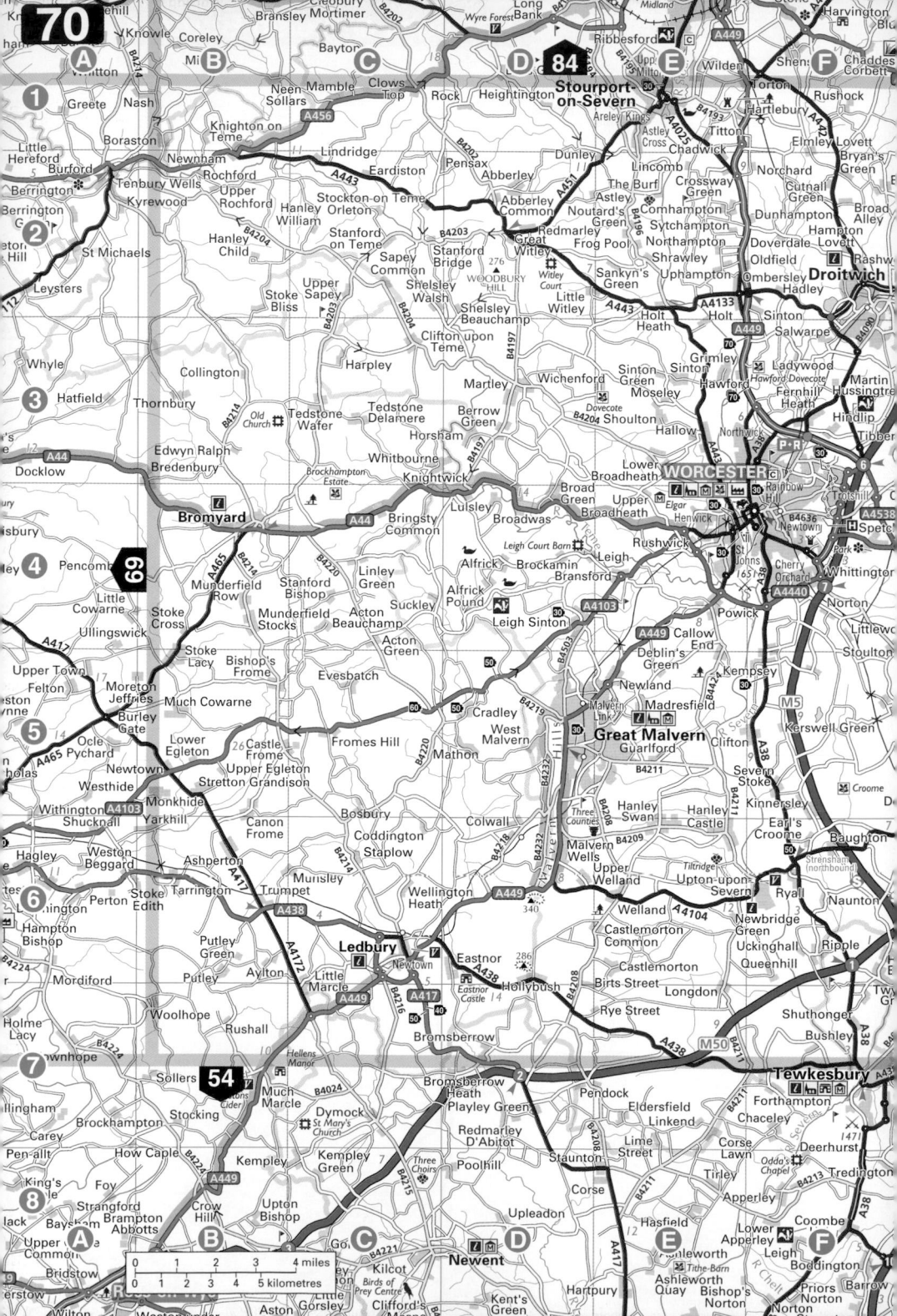

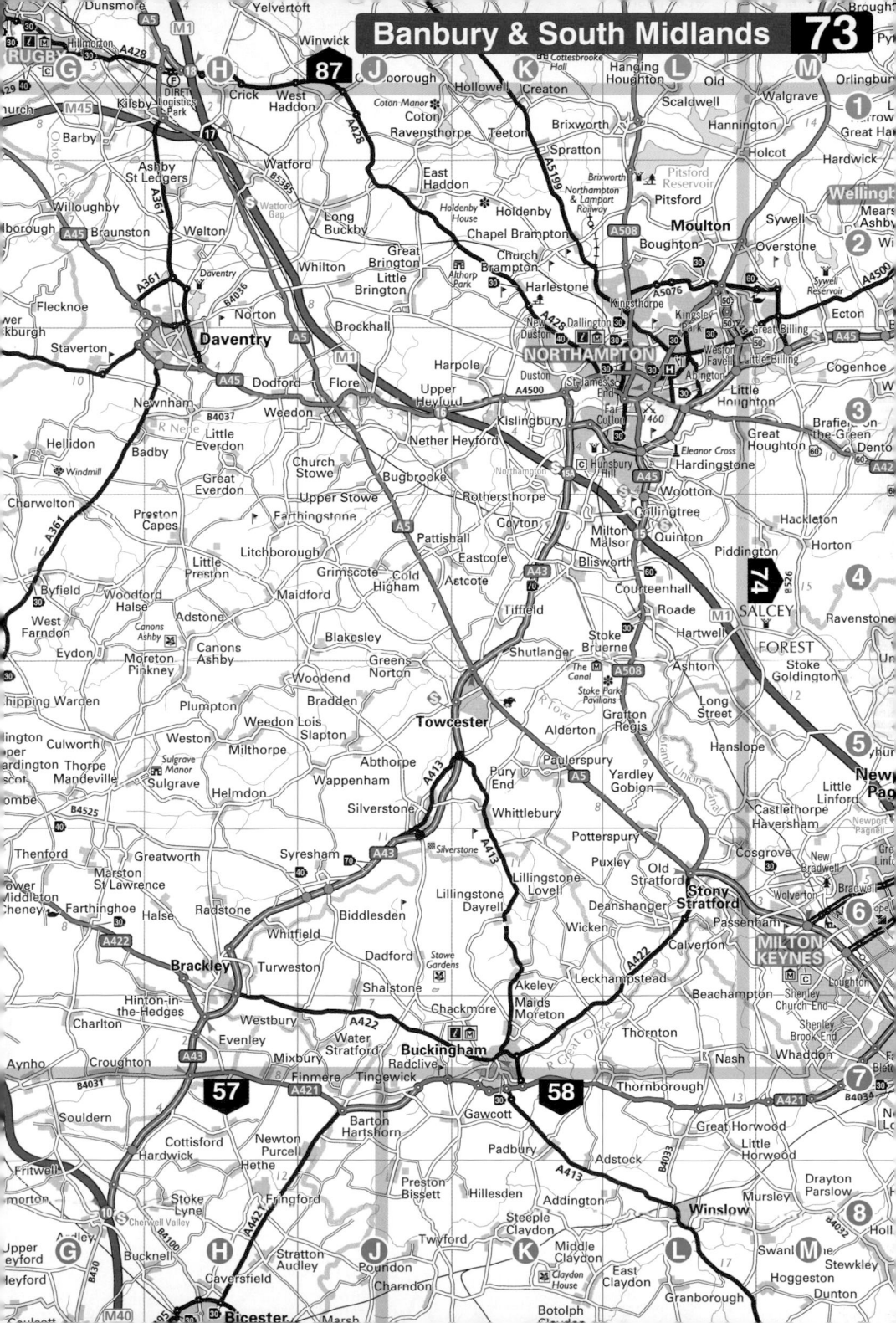

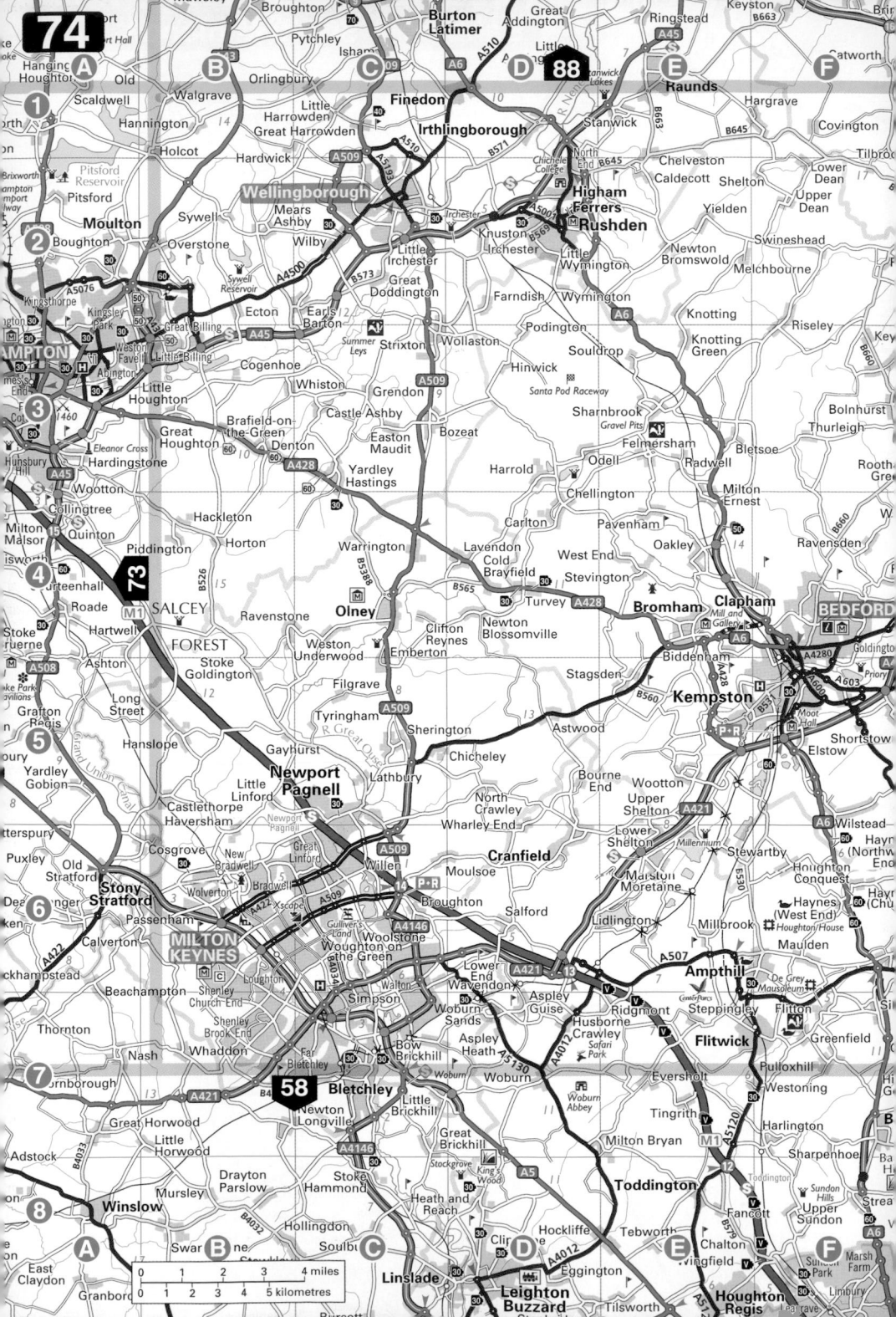

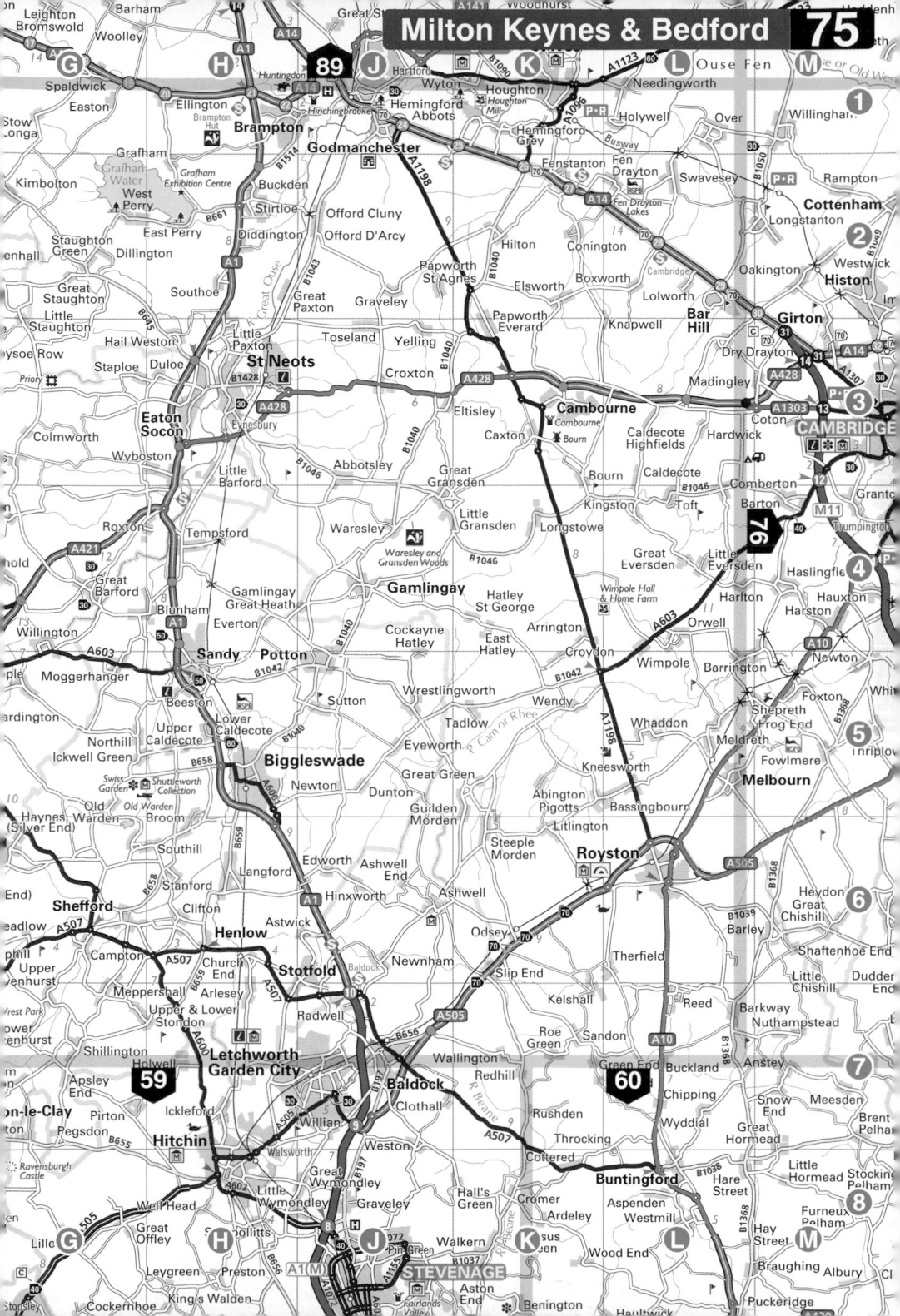

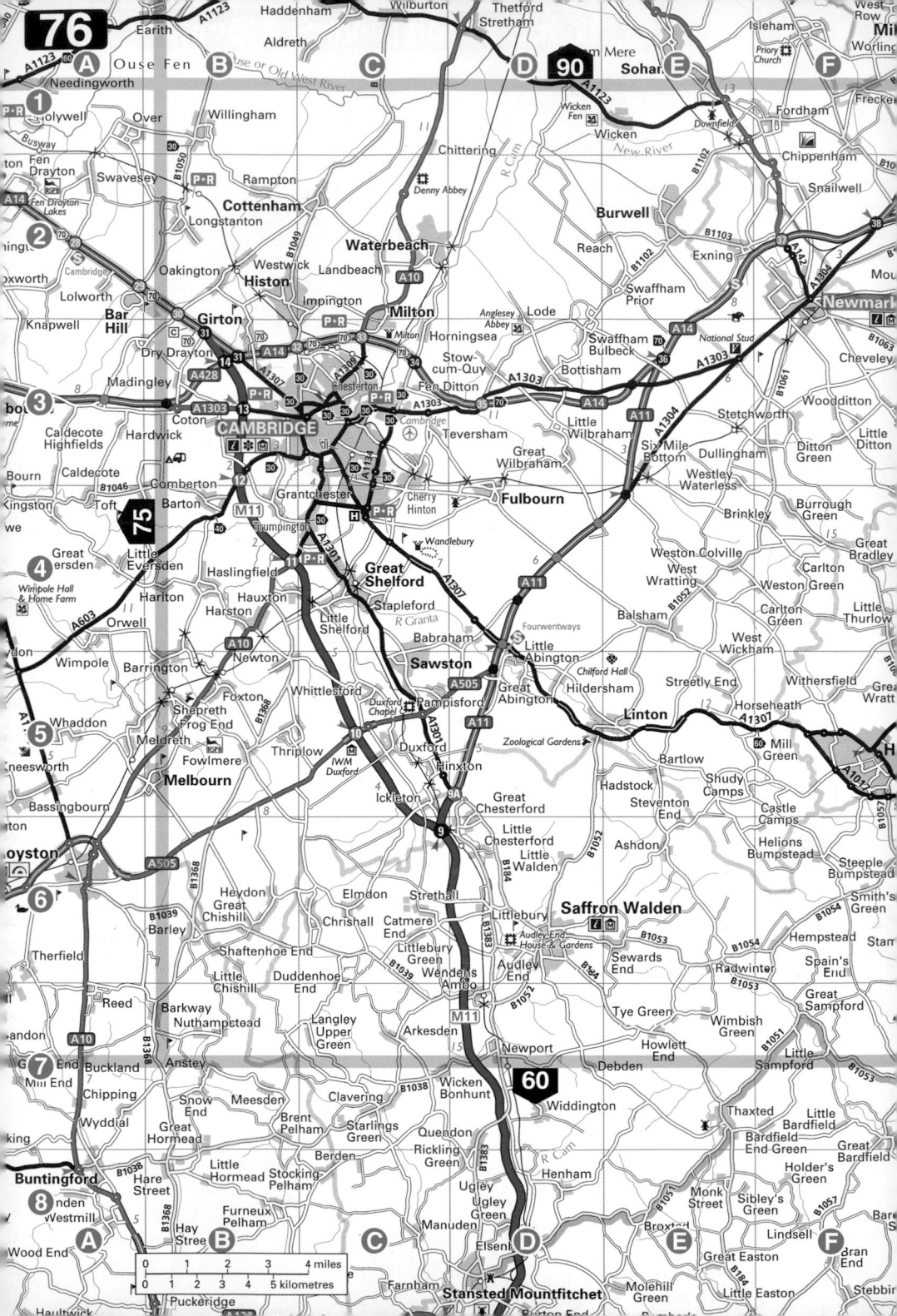

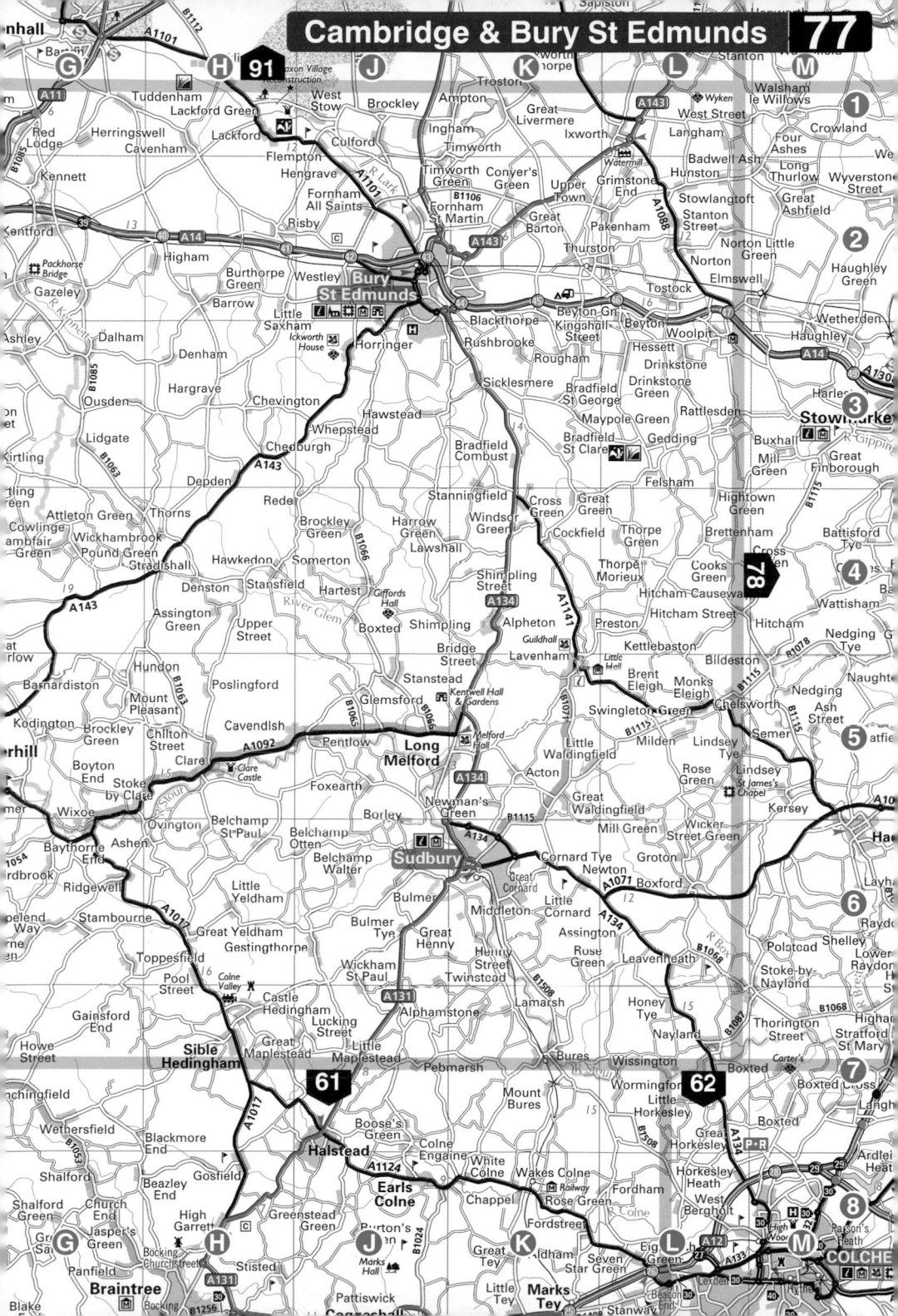

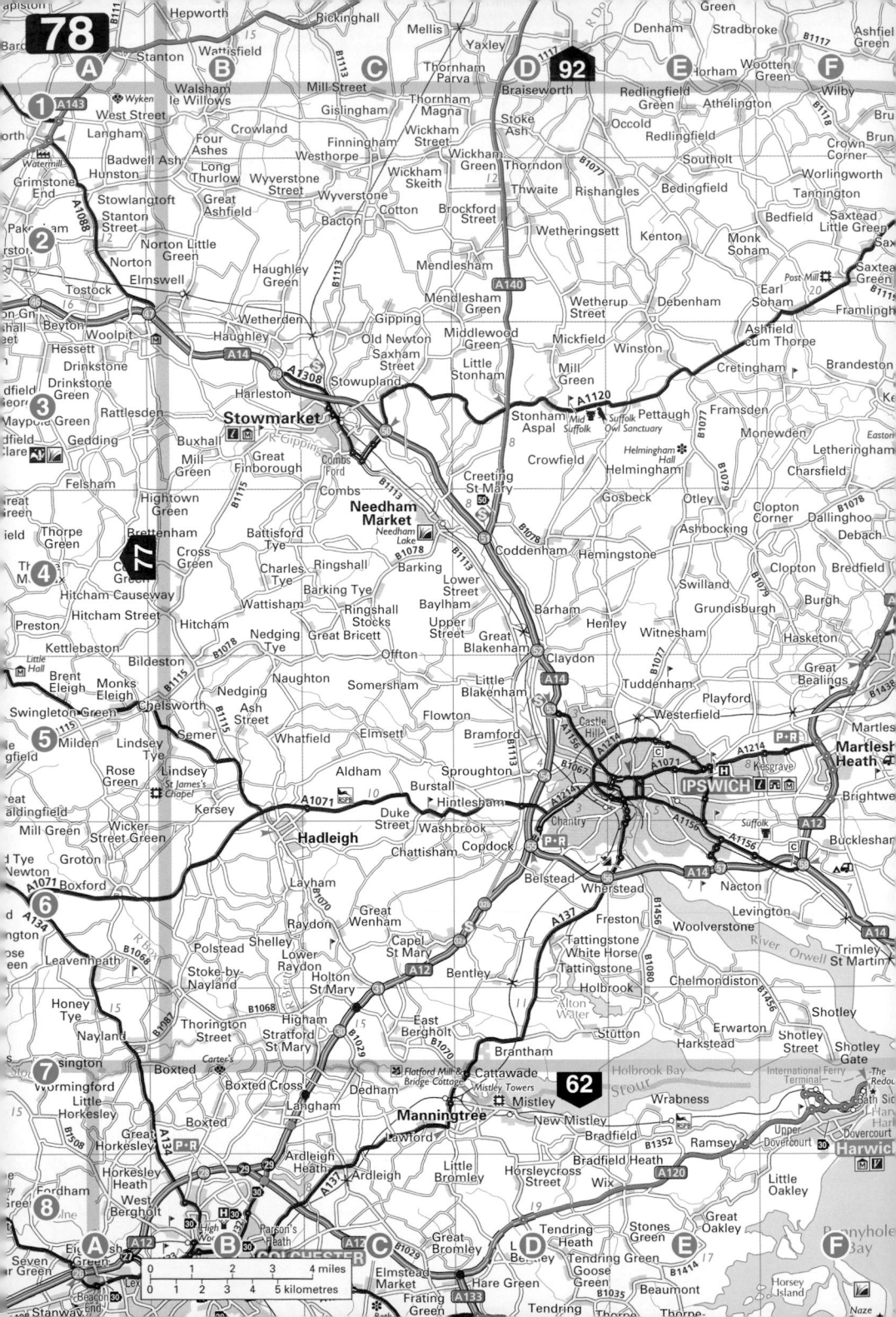

A B C **95** D E F

1

2

3

4

5

6

7

8

A B C **66** D E F

Llanelltyd
Toll
Penmaenpool

Barmouth
Barmouth Bridge ★
Barmouth Bay
A496
A493
Fairbourne
Steam Railway
Fairbourne

SNOWDONIA

621
NATIONAL

CADER I
892

Llwyngwril
PARK
Tal-y-llyn

Castell y Bere
Afon Dysynni

Llangelynin
Kin
Abergynolwyn
667

Rhoslefain
A493
Llanegryn
Tal-y-llyn Railway
633
Bryncrug B4405
Dolgoch
Falls
TAREN
HENDRE

Aber
Dysynni

Tywyn
Pennal

Dovey

CARDIGAN

Aberdovey
Aberdyfi A493
Glandy

Ynys-hir
Gland

BAY

Afon Dyfi (River Dovey)
A487
Dyfi
Furnace
PEN

Cwm
Clettwr

B4353
Tre Taliesin

Borth
Tal-y-bont

B4353

Ceredigion
Heritage Coast
Llandre
Bont-goch
or Elerch
Rhyd-y pennau
Salem
Bow
Street
Pen-bont
Rhydybeddau

Clarach
Bay
Garth
Penrhyncoch

Cliff Railway
Capel
Dewi
A4159
Capel
Bangor
Goginan

Aberystwyth
Waunfawr
Llanbadarn
Fawr
P·R

Rheidol
power station

Capel
Coed Seion
Penglanowen
12
A4120

Llanfarian

Llanfihangel-
y-Creuddyn

Blaenplwyf
A485
Afon Ystwyth
Cnwch
Coch

Llanilar
B4340

B4575

Ceredigion
Heritage Coast
Penderi
Cliffs
18
Llanafan

Llanddeiniol
B4576
Llangwyryfon
Lledrod
Cors
Ian
Tynygrai

Llanrhystud
85

0 1 2 3 4 miles
0 1 2 3 4 5 kilometres

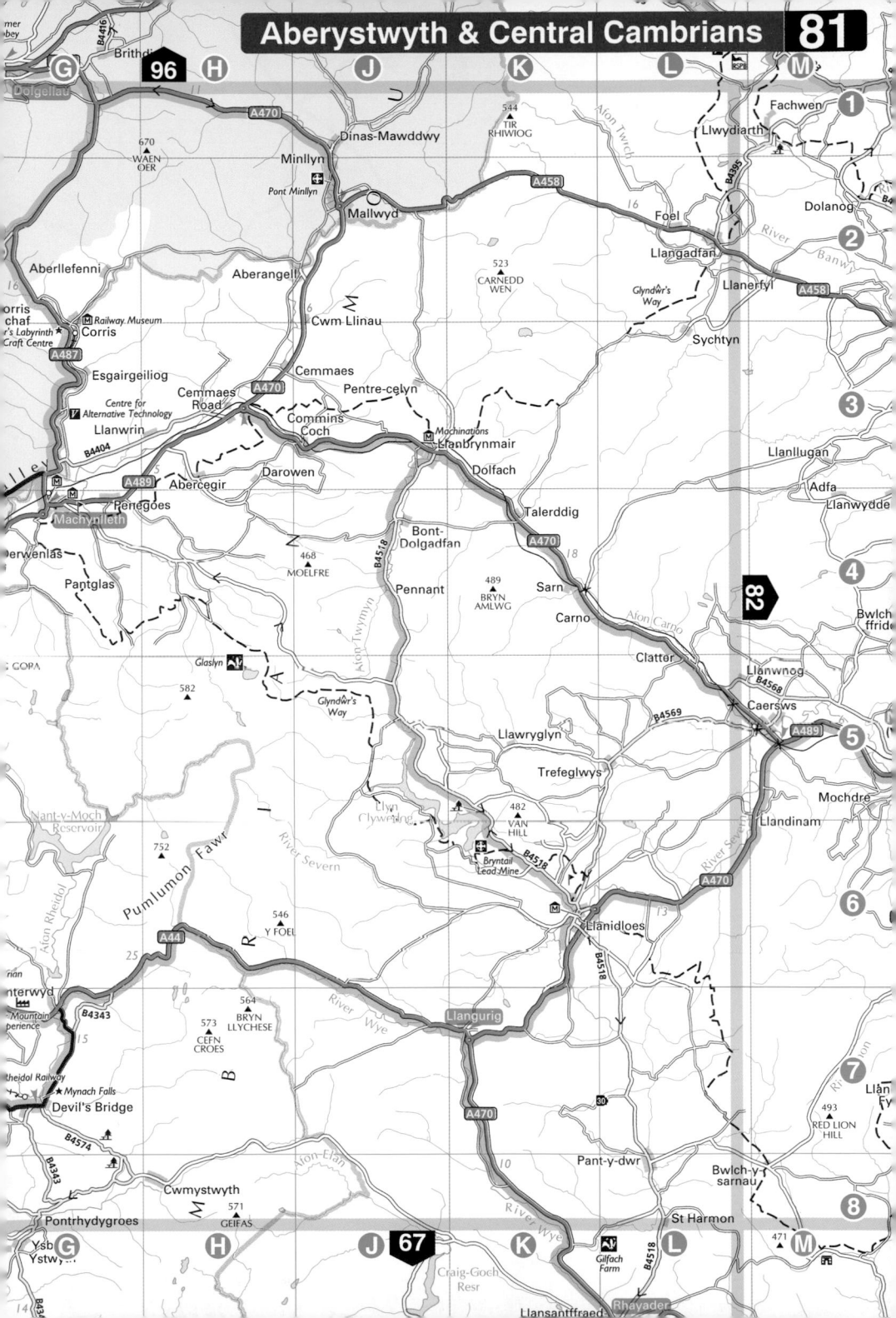

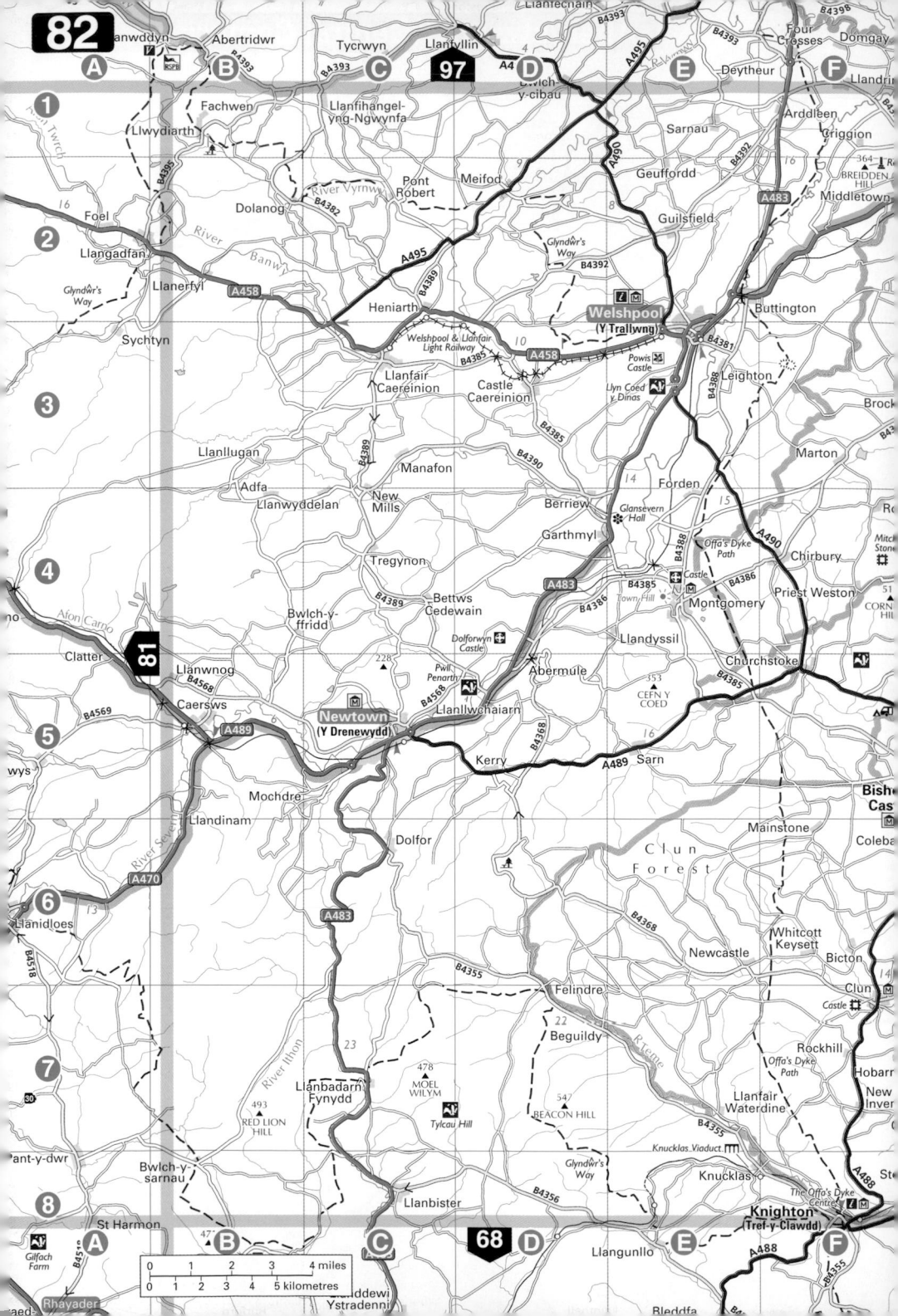

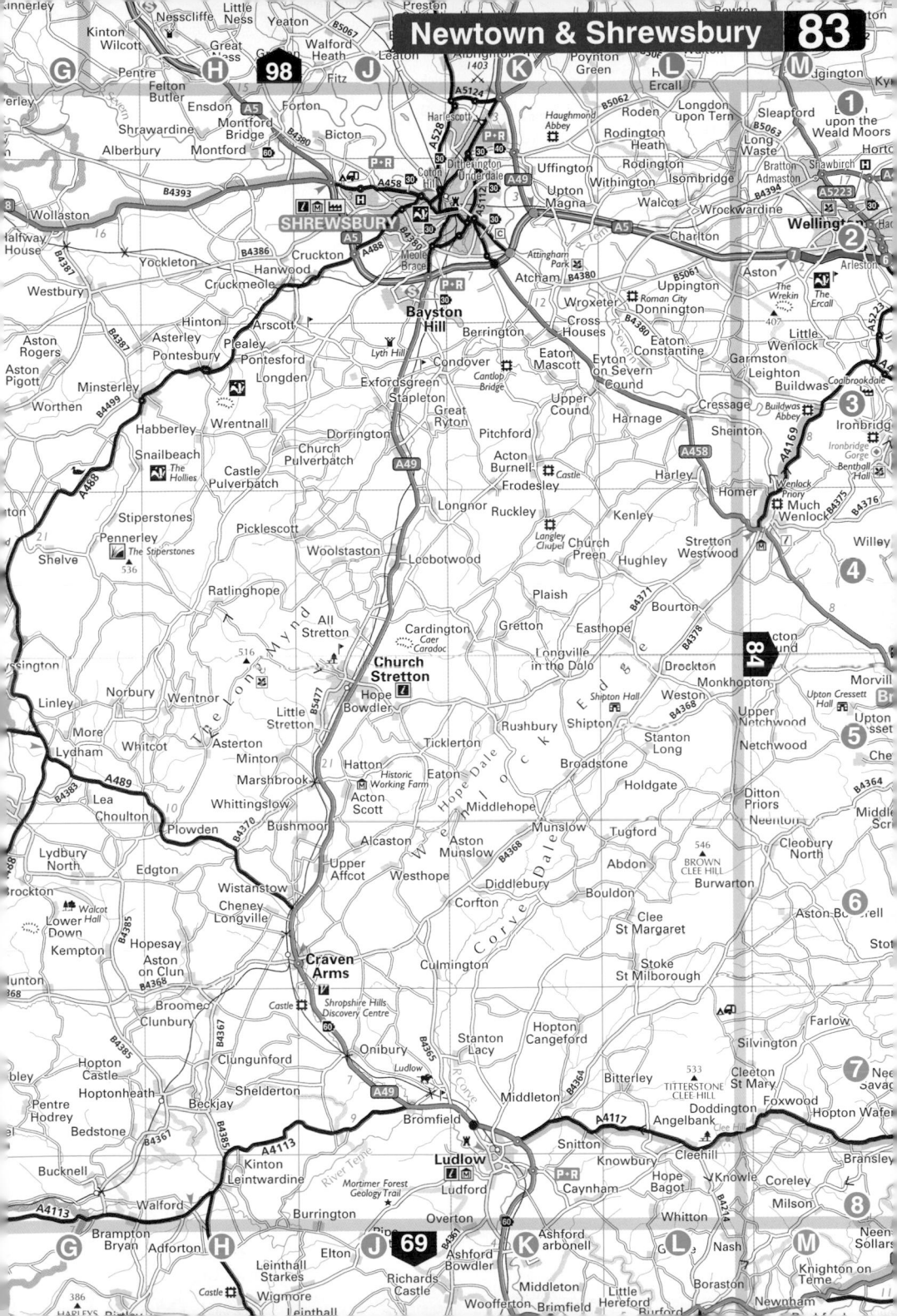

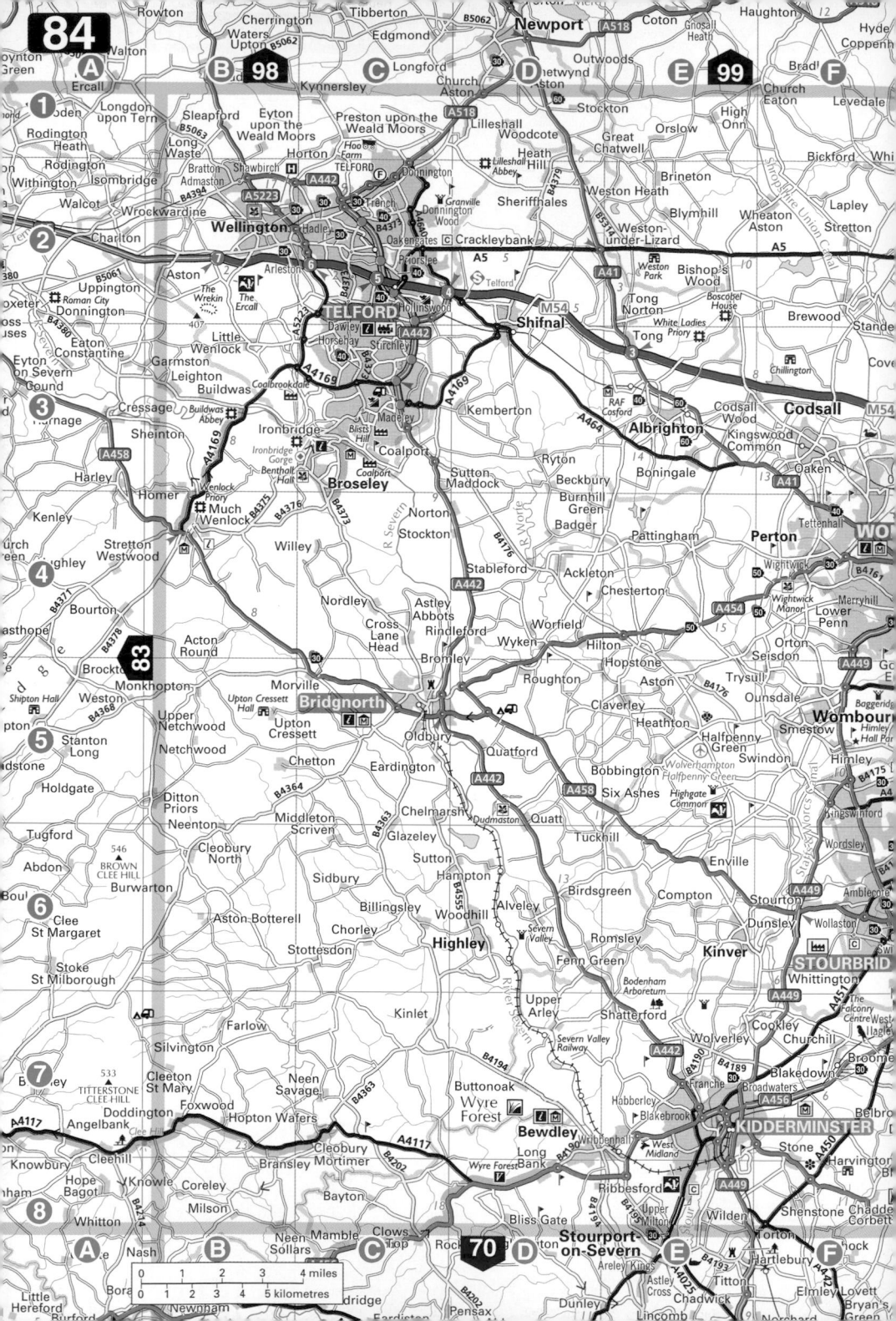

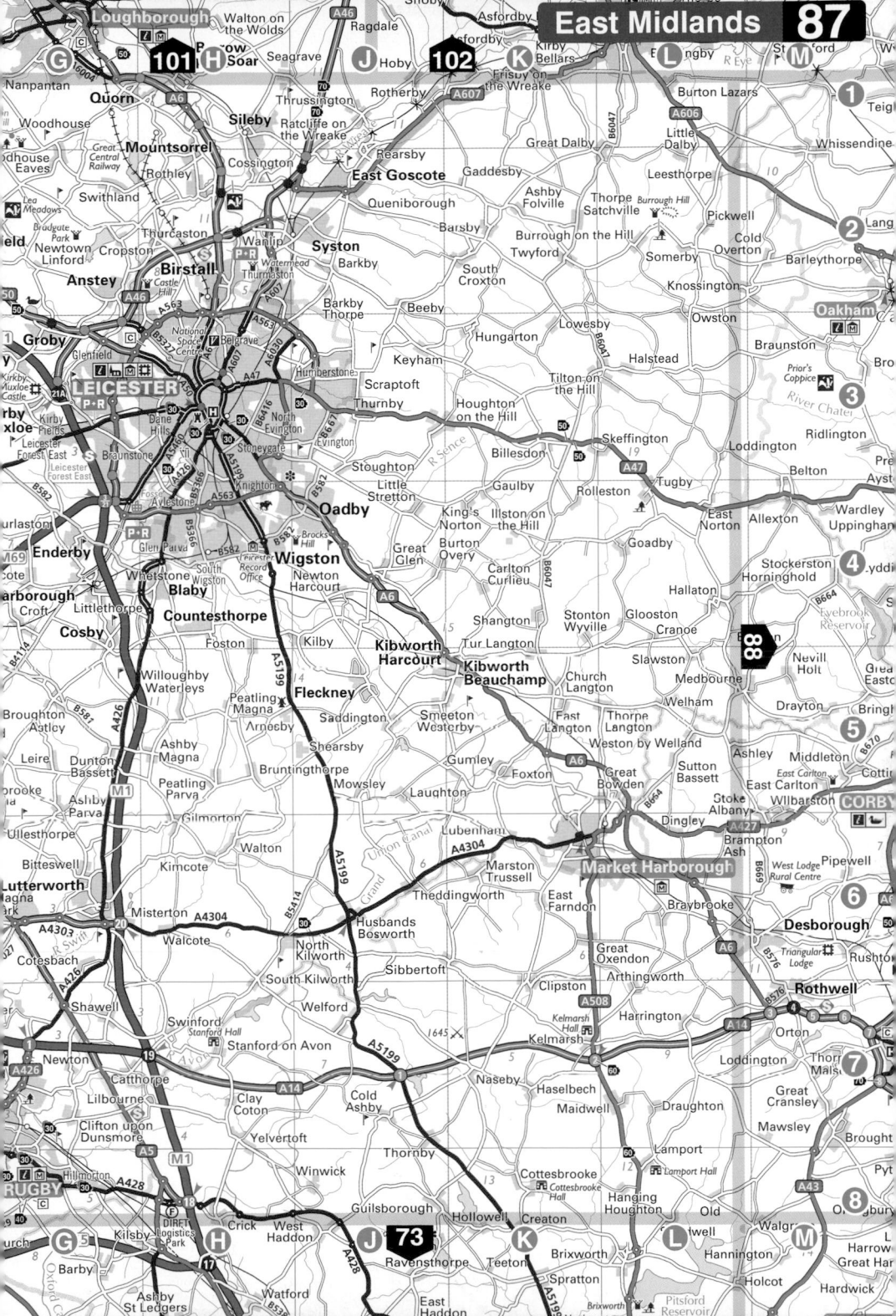

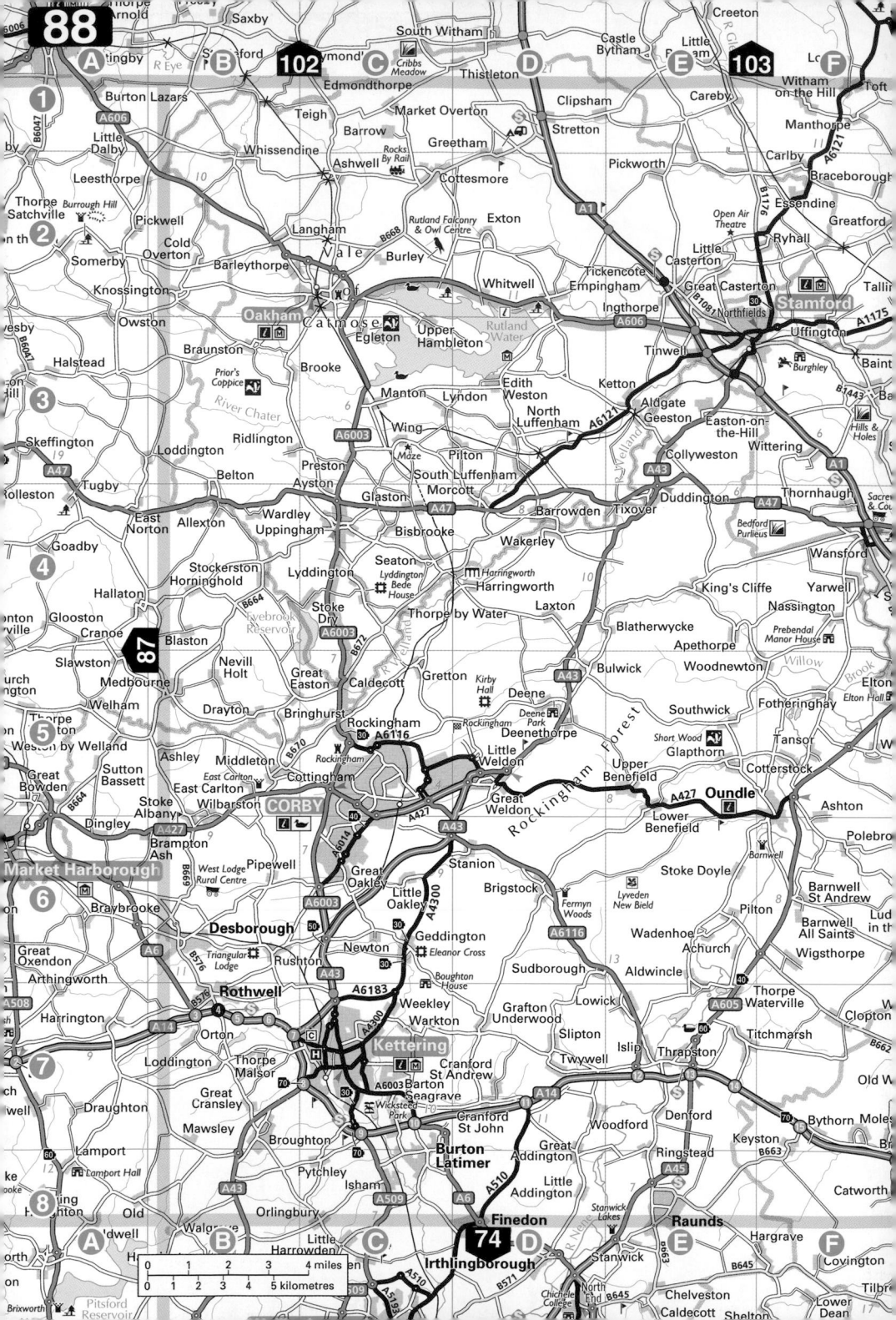

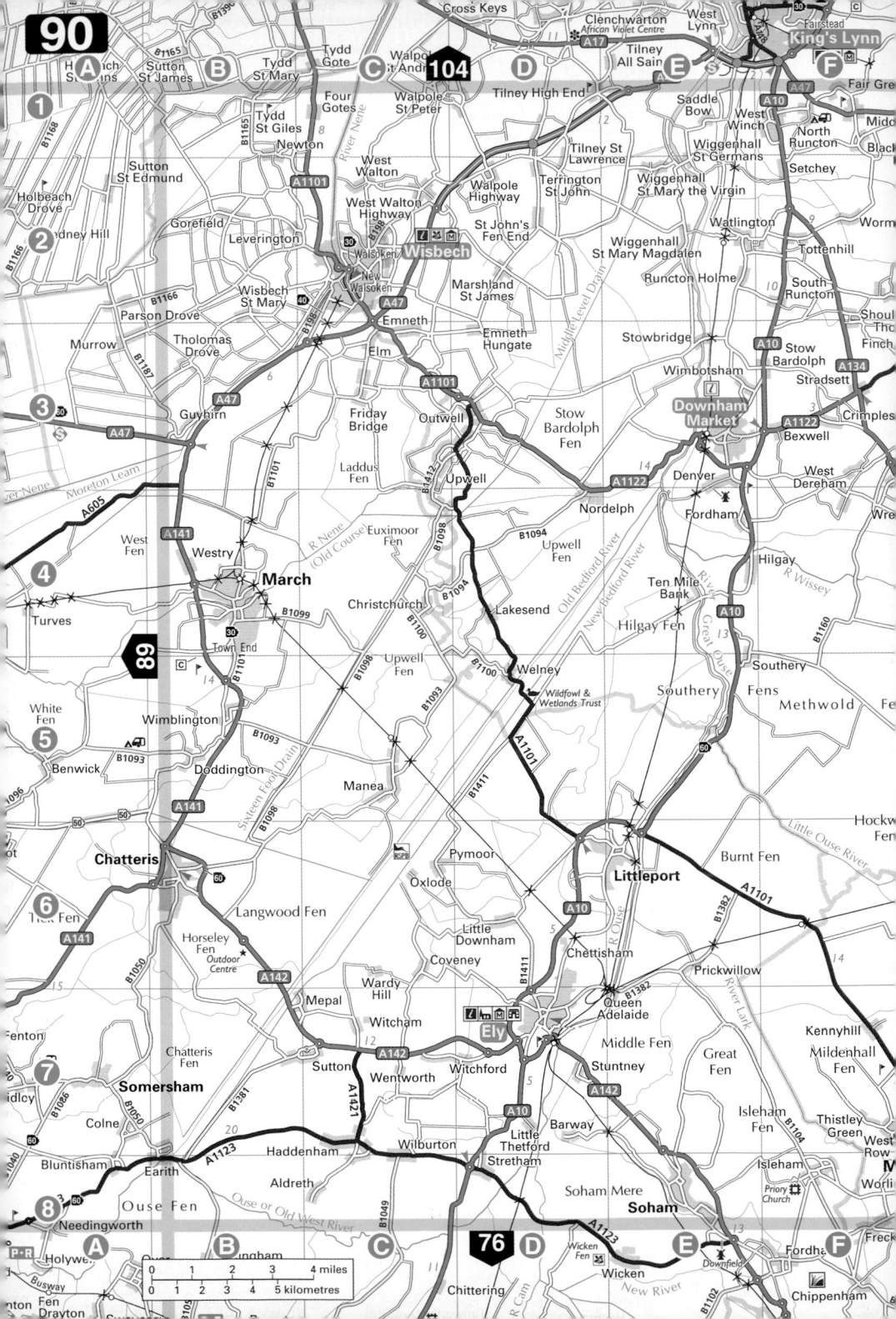

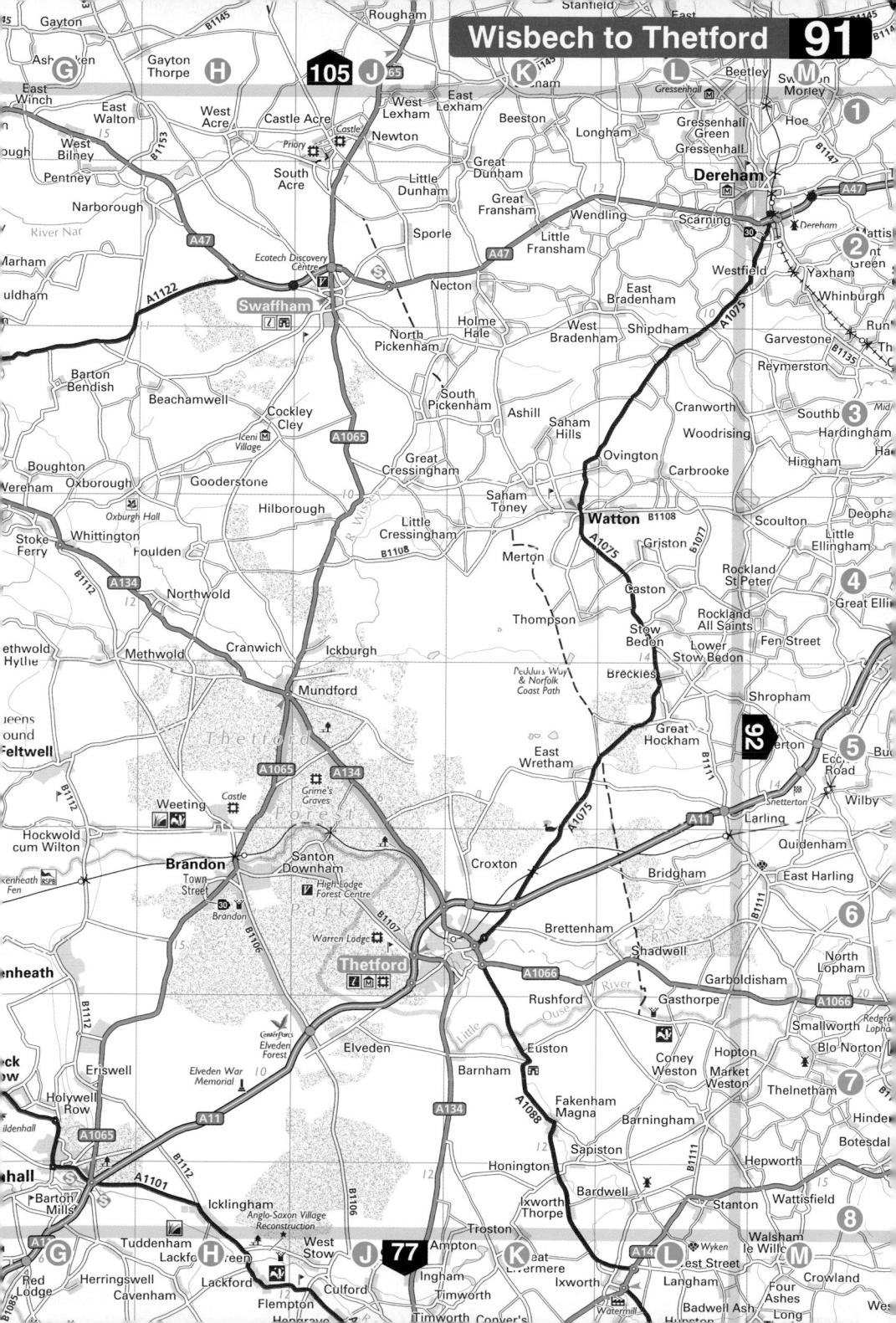

Wisbech to Thetford 91

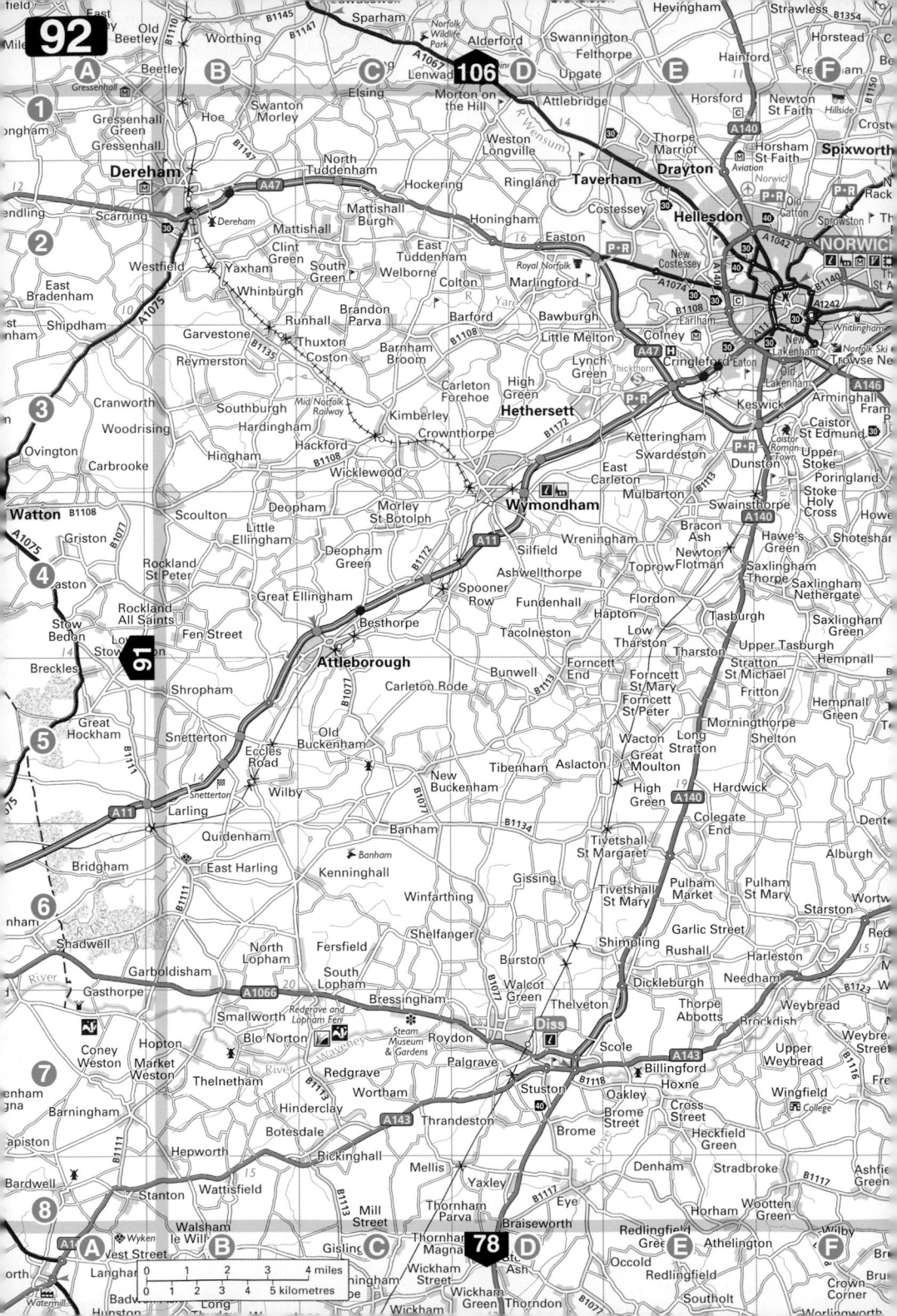

A B C D E F

1 2 3 4 5 6 7 8

Aberffraw Bay
Heritage Coast
Malltraeth

Llanddwyn

C A E R N A R F O N

B A Y

Lleyn Heritage
Coast

Trefo

564
YR EIFL
Trwyn y
Grolech

Llithfa

20

Carreg Ddu

Porth
Nefyn

Morfa
Nefyn

Pistyll

B434

Nefyn

B4417

Edern

Bodfuan

Llann

Porth Ysgaden

Tudweiliog

Dinas

LLEYN

A497

7

Efailnev

Porth
Colman

Carn
Fadrun
371

B4415

Rhyd-y-clafdy

Pen-y-graig

Bryn-
mawr

Llaniestyn

A499

B4417

14

Meyllteyrn

Penrhos

Llangwnnadl

Sarn

Botwnnog

Llanbedrog

7

Porthoer

Bryncroes

B4413

B4413

Trwyn Llanbedr

Rhoshirwaun

Plas yn
Rhiw

Llangian

St Tudwal's
Road

B4413

Y Rhiw

Llanengan

Abersoch

Aberdaron

Llanfaelrhys

Porth Neigwl
or
Hell's Mouth

Bwlchtocyn

Marchros

St Tudwal's
Island East

Aberdaron
Bay

Porth
Ysgo

St Tudwal's
Island West

Bardsey Sound

Porth
Geiriad

Lleyn Heritage
Coast

St Mary's

Ynys Enlli

BARDSEY ISLAND

A B C D E F

0 1 2 3 4 miles
0 1 2 3 4 5 kilometres

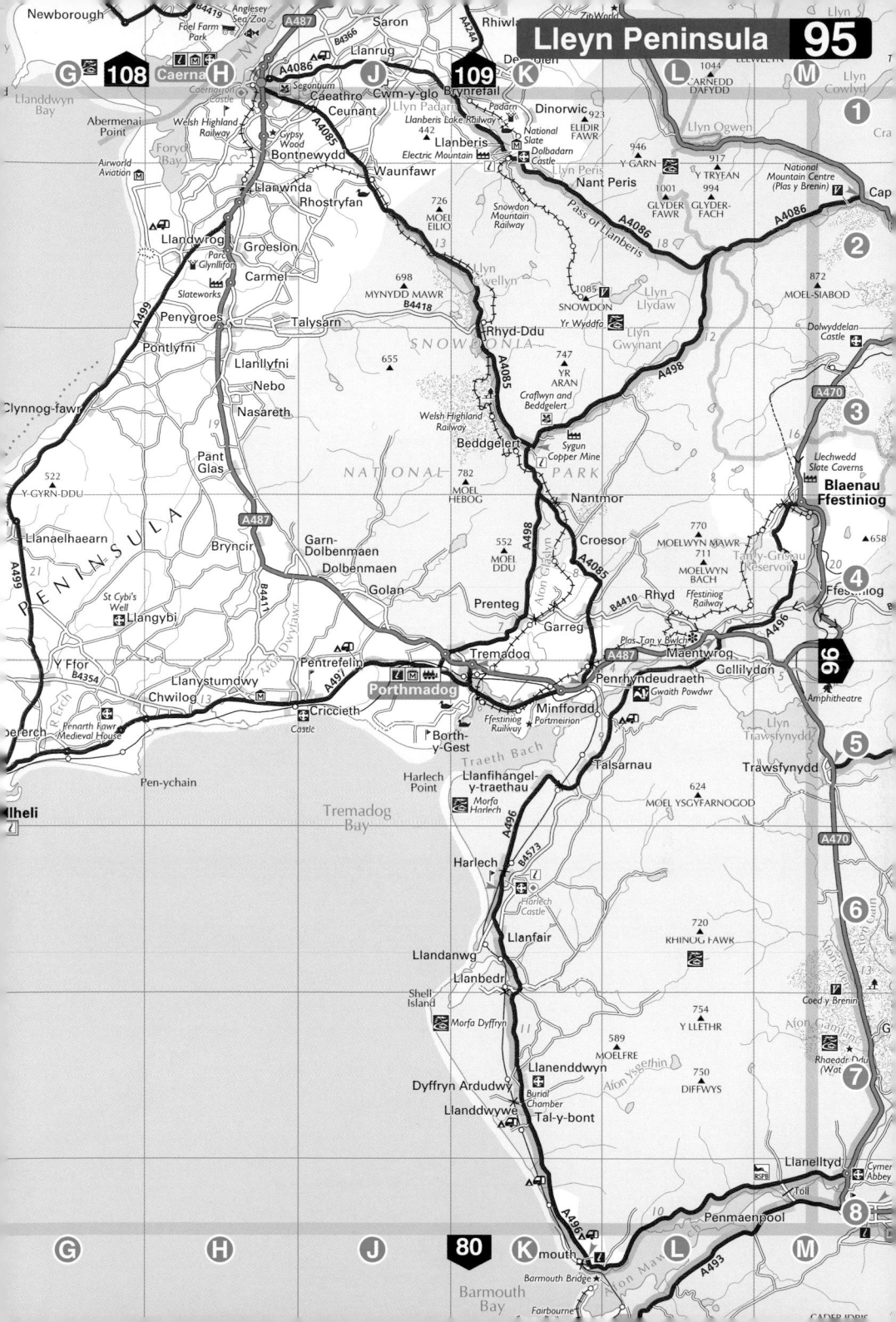

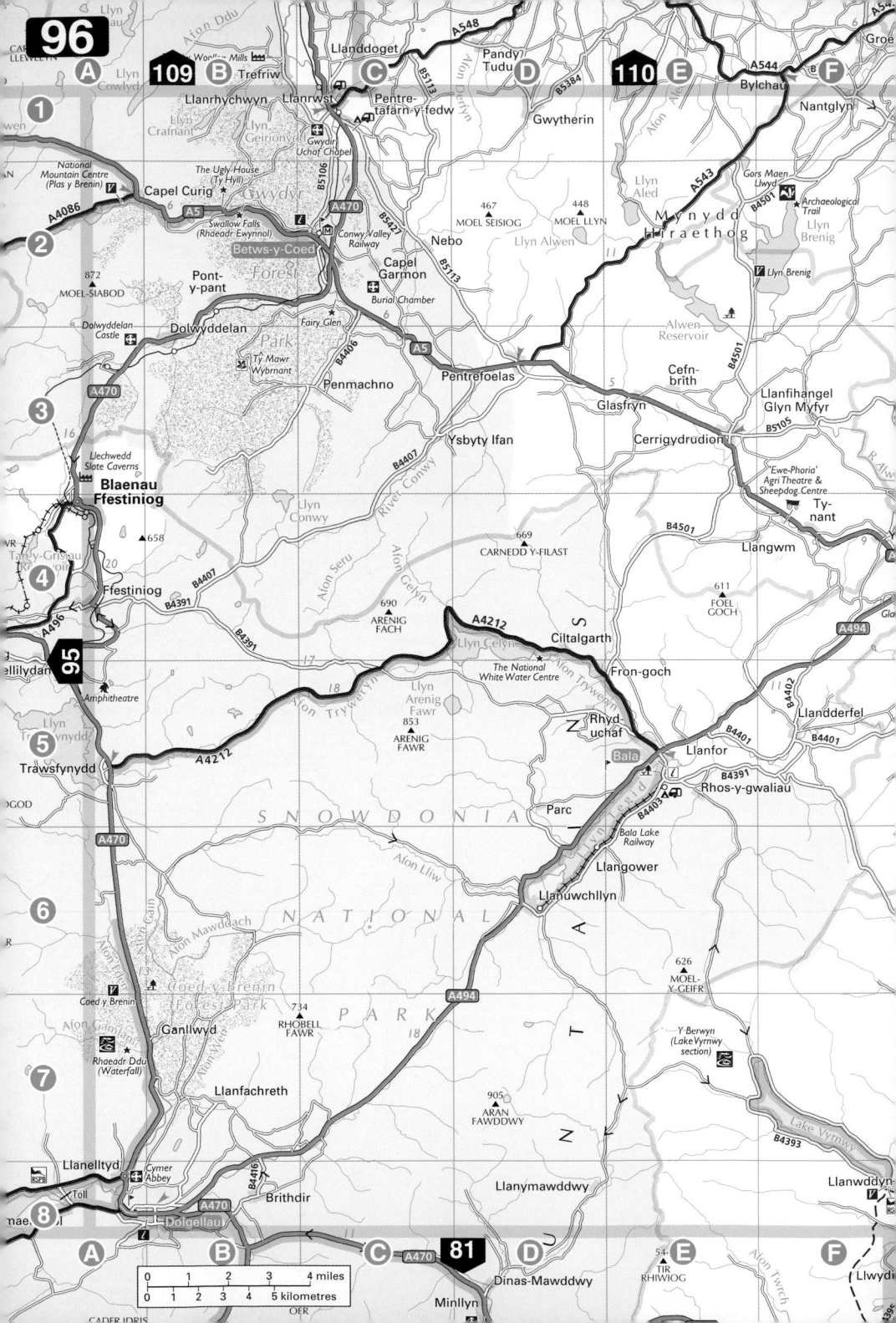

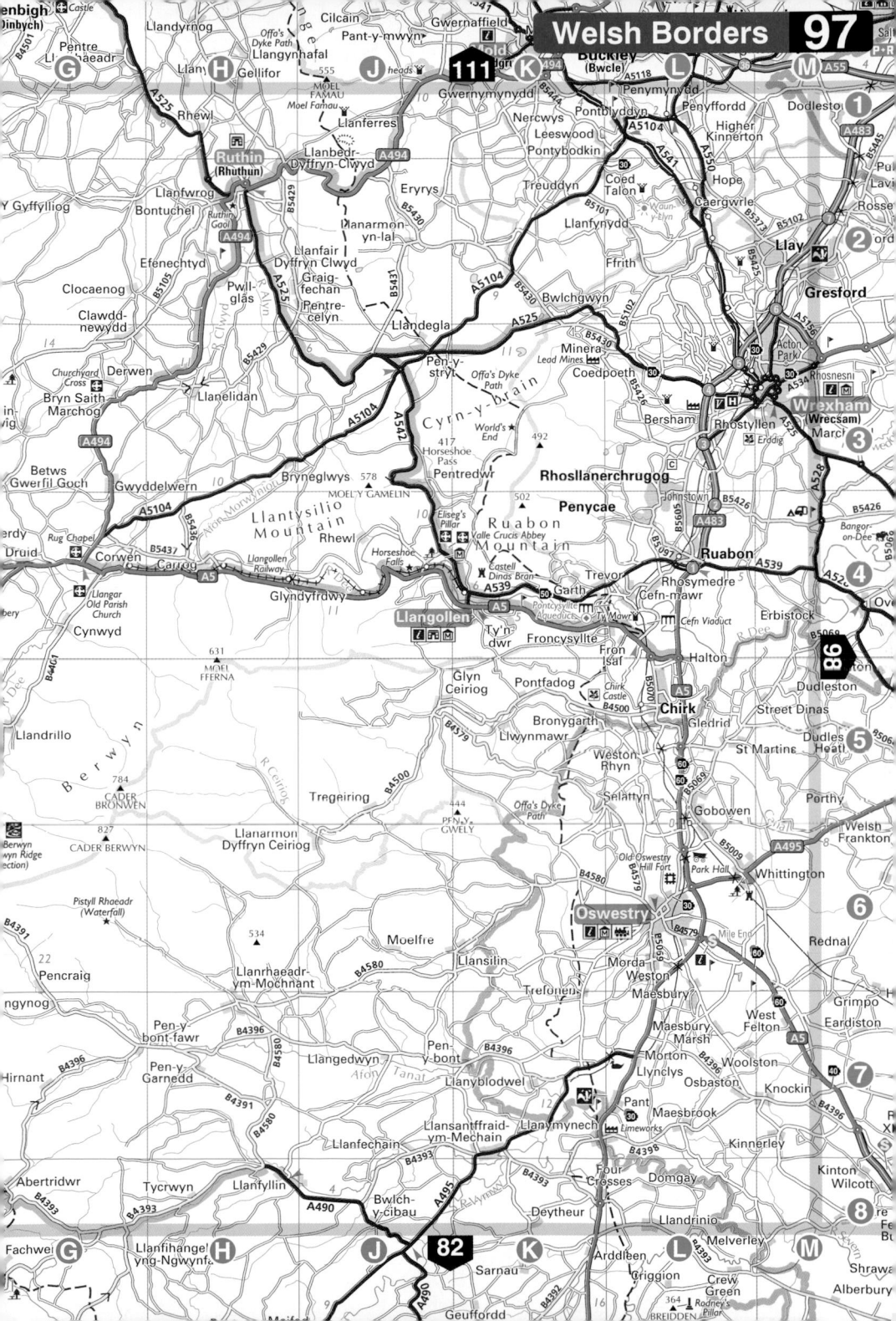

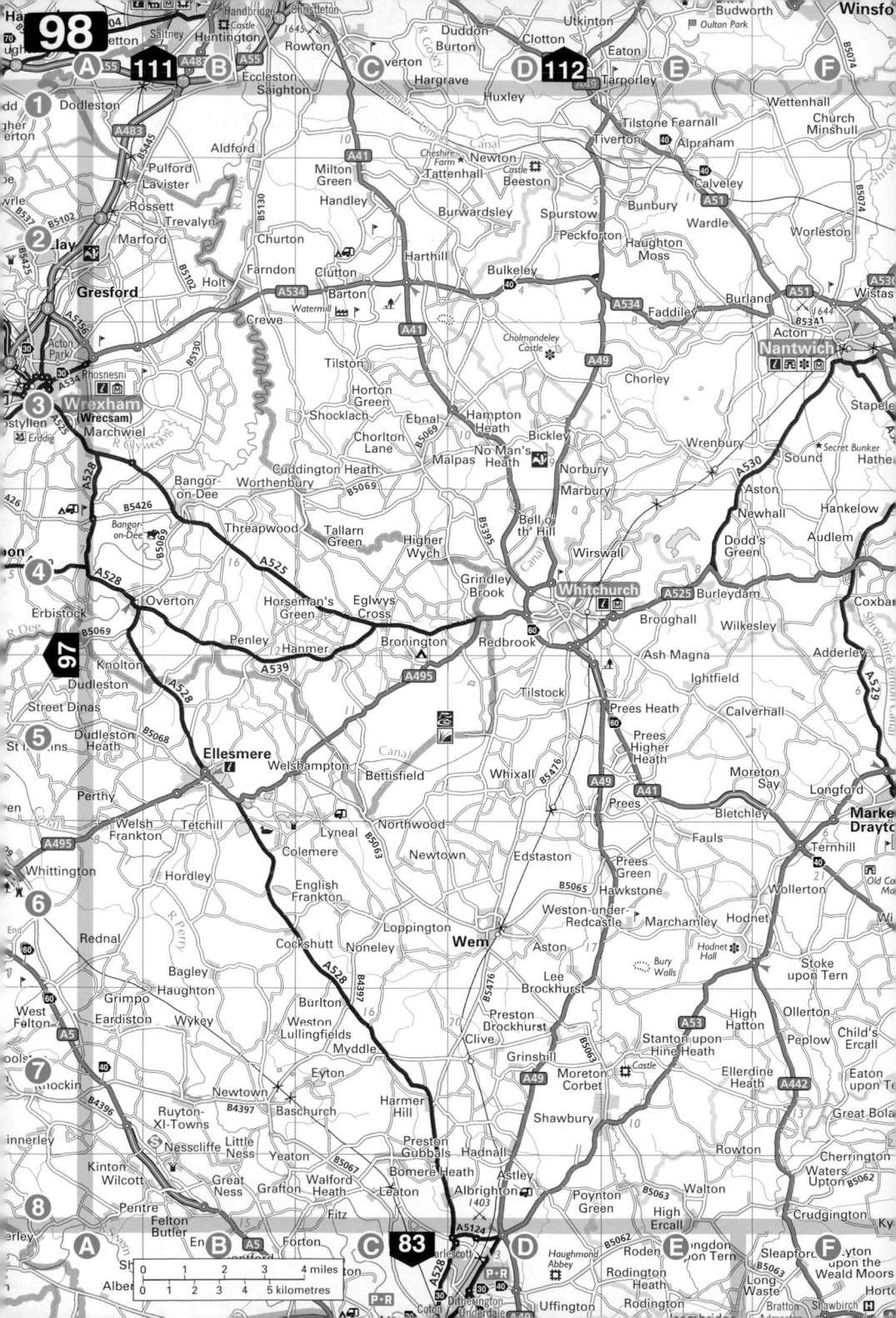

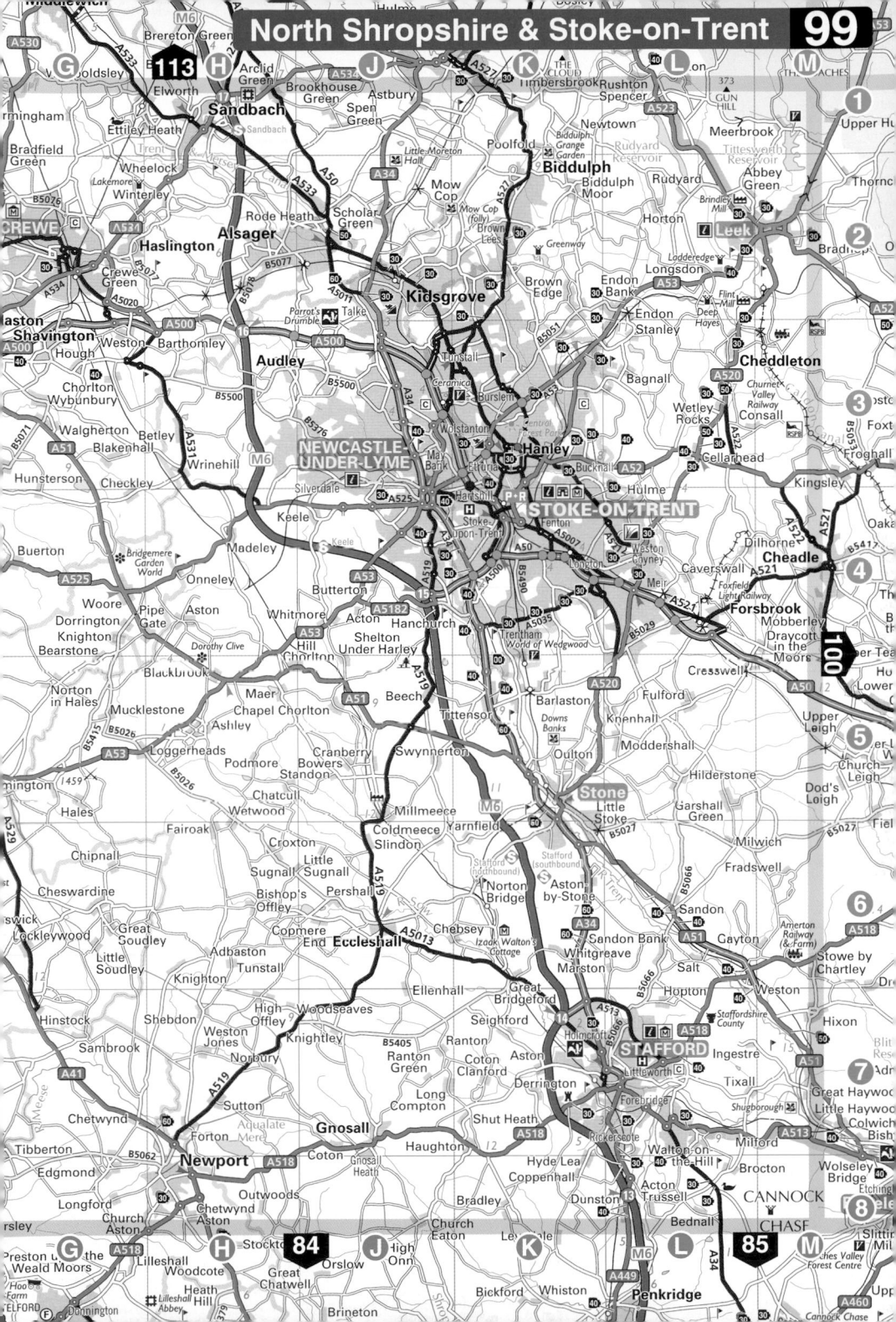

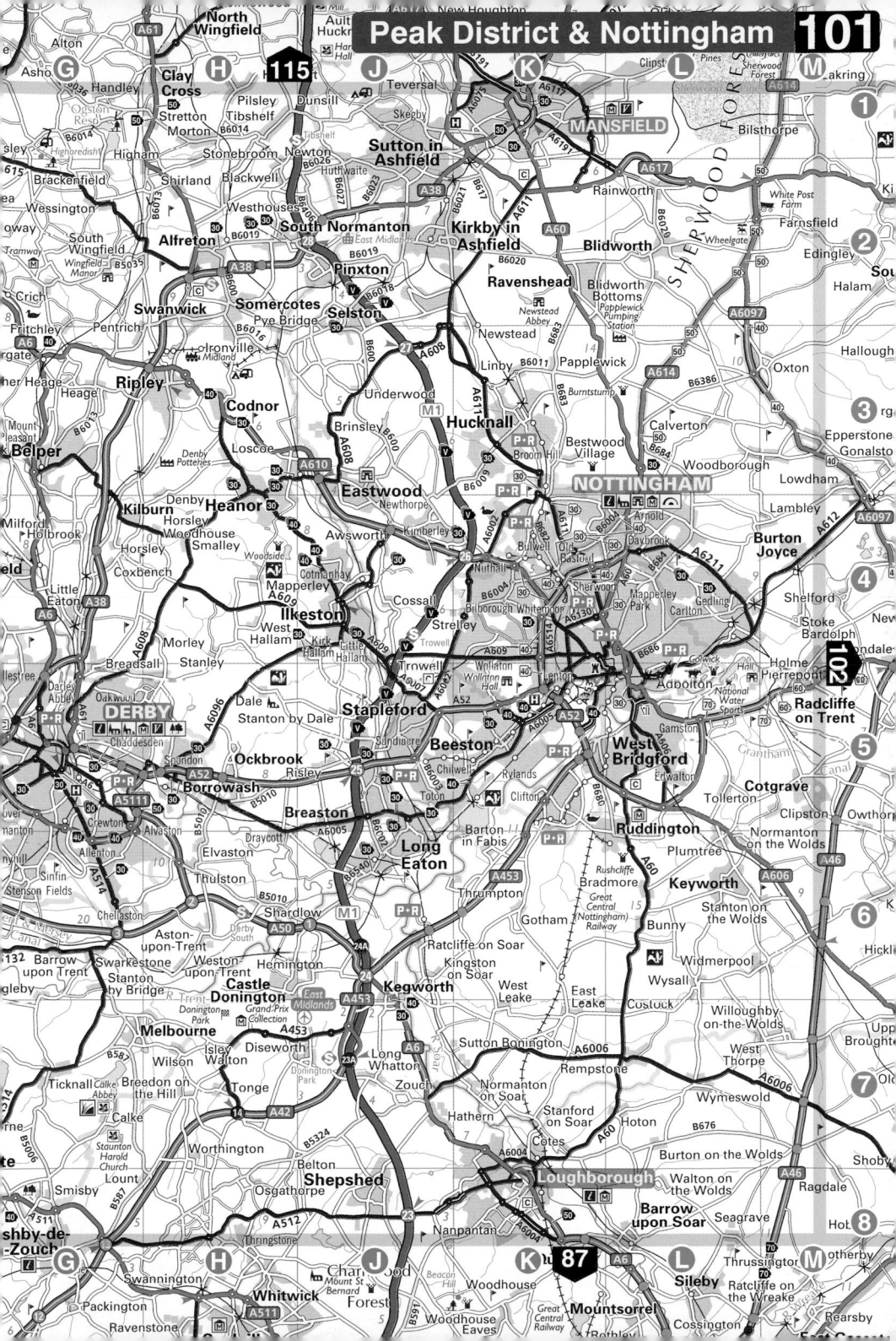

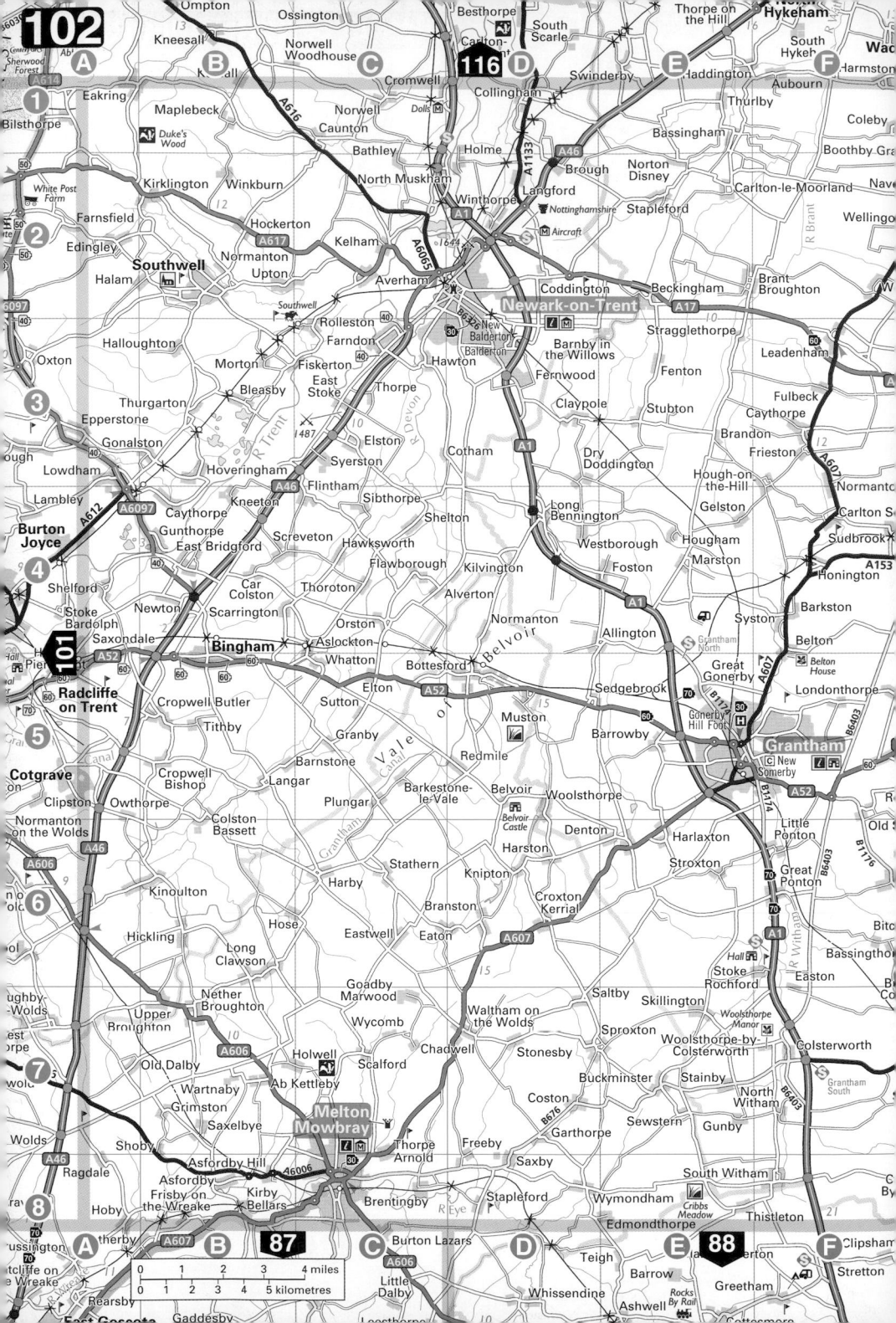

Map grid references: G, H, J, K, L, M (top and bottom) and 1, 2, 3, 4, 5, 6, 7, 8 (right side)

Trimingham

ham

Mundesley
Stow Mill
Knapton Paston B1159
Bacton
Edingthorpe
Walcott

Edingthorpe
Green Witton Ridlington Happisburgh

Meeting Whimpwell Green
House Hill
Happisburgh Hempstead
Honing Common
Lessingham
Briggate East Ingham Sea Palling
Ruston Corner
Worstead Ingham Waxham
Stalham Calthorpe
Dilham Street
Smallburgh Hickling
Sutton Hickling Green Horsey
Barton Horsey Windpump
Turf Wood
Tunstead Street Hickling
Barton Broad
Neatishead Broad Catfield
Wroxham Irstead
Barns Potter
Heigham Winterton-on-Sea
Hoveton BeWILDerwood Ludham
Martham Hemsby Hemsby
Upper A1062 Bastwick Hole
Street Thurne
Horning er Street Repps esby Orr y Scratby
Woodbastwick Bure Broadland Thurne St Margaret
Marshes Conservation Centre Burgh St California
ckheath Salhouse Ranworth Pilson Margaret Ormesby
Green Clippesby St Michael
Fairhaven Cargate Billockby Caister-on-

A149, A1151, B1150, B1140, A1062, B1152, A47, 93

Hemsby

G H J K L M

① ② ③ ④

110

⑤ ⑥ ⑦ ⑧

nt Lynas

Dulas
Bay

Seawatch Centre

Moelfre
Llanallgo

Benllech

Red Wharf Bay

nbedrgoch

Red Wharf
Bay

Llanddona

Pentraeth

ddyfnan

Talwrn

B5109

B5420

enmynydd

Llanfairpwllgwyngyll

Beaumaris

Llansadwrn

Llandegfan

Menai
Bridge
(Porthaethwy)

Bangor

Bryn
Celli Ddu

Britannia
Bridge

Plas
Newydd

Penrhyn

Llandygai

A55

Tal-y-
bont

Glasinfryn

Y Felinheli

GreenWood
Forest Park

Pentir

Rhye y-
groes

Tregarth

Bethesda

Seion

Bethel

Llanddeiniolen

Saron

Llanrug

Rhiwlas

Deiniolen

ZipWorld

A5

Puffin Island

Penmon Priory

Black Point

Llangoed

Gaol

Beaumaris
Castle

Courthouse

Llanfairfechan

Abergwyngregyn

Coedydd
Aber

Aber Falls

MOEL
WNION

Llanllechid

Rachub

B4409

Penmaenmawr

Dwygyfylchi

Capelulo

Conwy

Conwy
Castle

Henryd

SNOWDONIA

610
TAL-Y-FAN

Rowen

Ty'n-y-Groes

Llanbedr-y-Cennin

Y DROSGL

757

FOEL FRAS

942

Tal-y-Bont

Dolgarrog

Afon Dulyn

Llyn
Eigiau

Afon Ddu

Great Orme
Heritage Coast

GREAT ORMES HEAD

Great Orme
Tramway

Toll

Conwy
Bay

Conwy Bay

Llandudno

Deganwy

Little Orme

Penr
ay

Llandrillo-
yn-Rhos

Llandudno
Junction

Llansanffraid
Glan Conwy

A470

Bodnant

Graig

Tal-y-Cafn

Eglwysbach

Llanddoget

Vale of Conwy

NATIONAL

PARK

Trefriw Woollen Mills

Trefriw

Geirionydd

CARNEDD
LLEWELYN

1062

CARNEDD
DAFYDD

1044

Llyn
Cowlyd

Llyn
Crafnant

Pentre-
tafarn-y-fe

Llanrwst

Gwydir
Uchaf Chapel

The Ugly House
(Ty Hyll)

G H **95** J K L **96** M

Caeathro

Cwm-y-glo

Brynrefail

wic

Llanberis Lake Rd

Electric Mountain

Llanberis

Waunfawr

National
Slate

Dolbadarn
Castle

ELIDIR
FAWR

Y GARN

Llyn
Peris

Nant Peris

Llyn Ogwen

Y TRYFAN

National
Mountain Centre

Segontium

Gypsy
Wood
ntnewydd

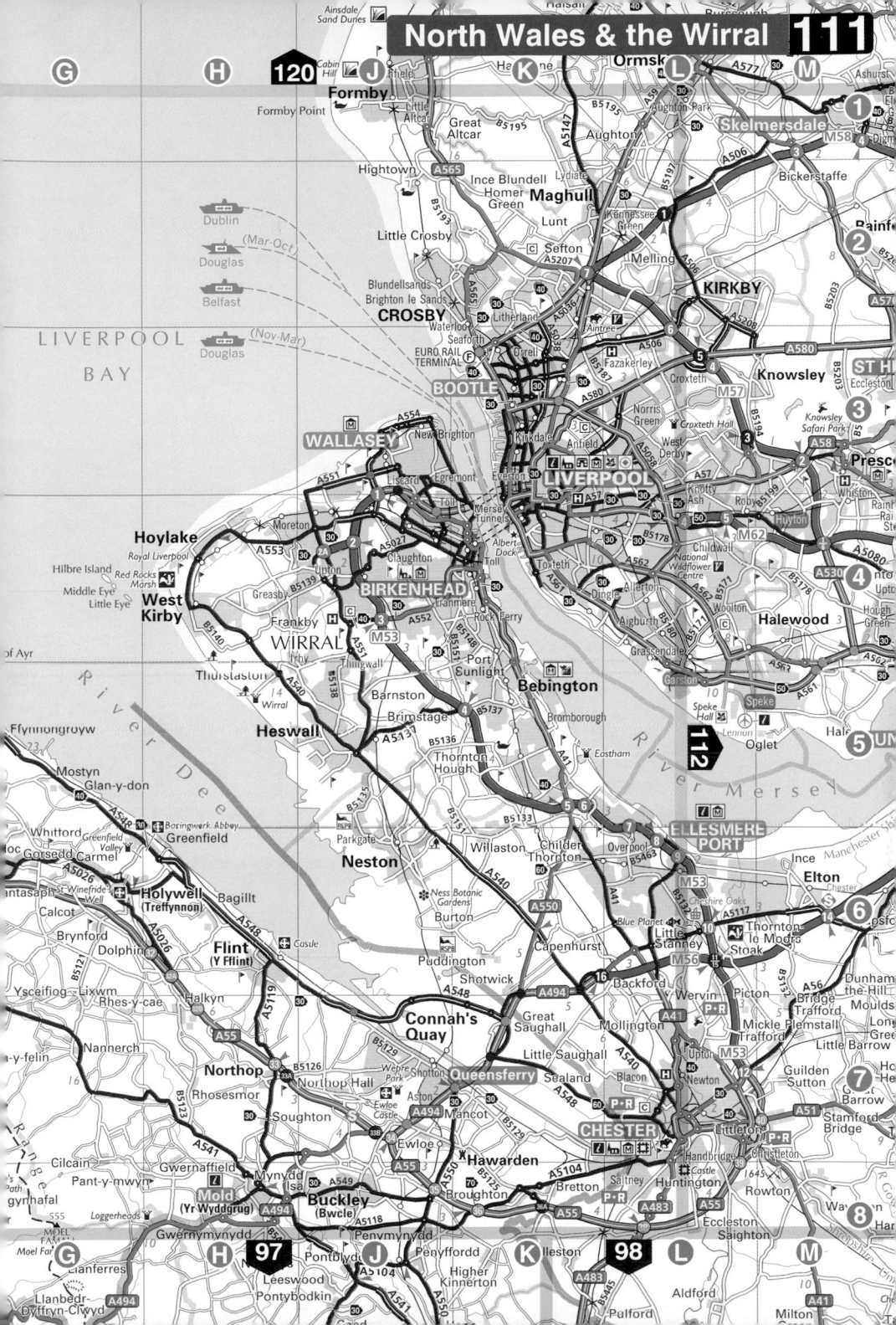

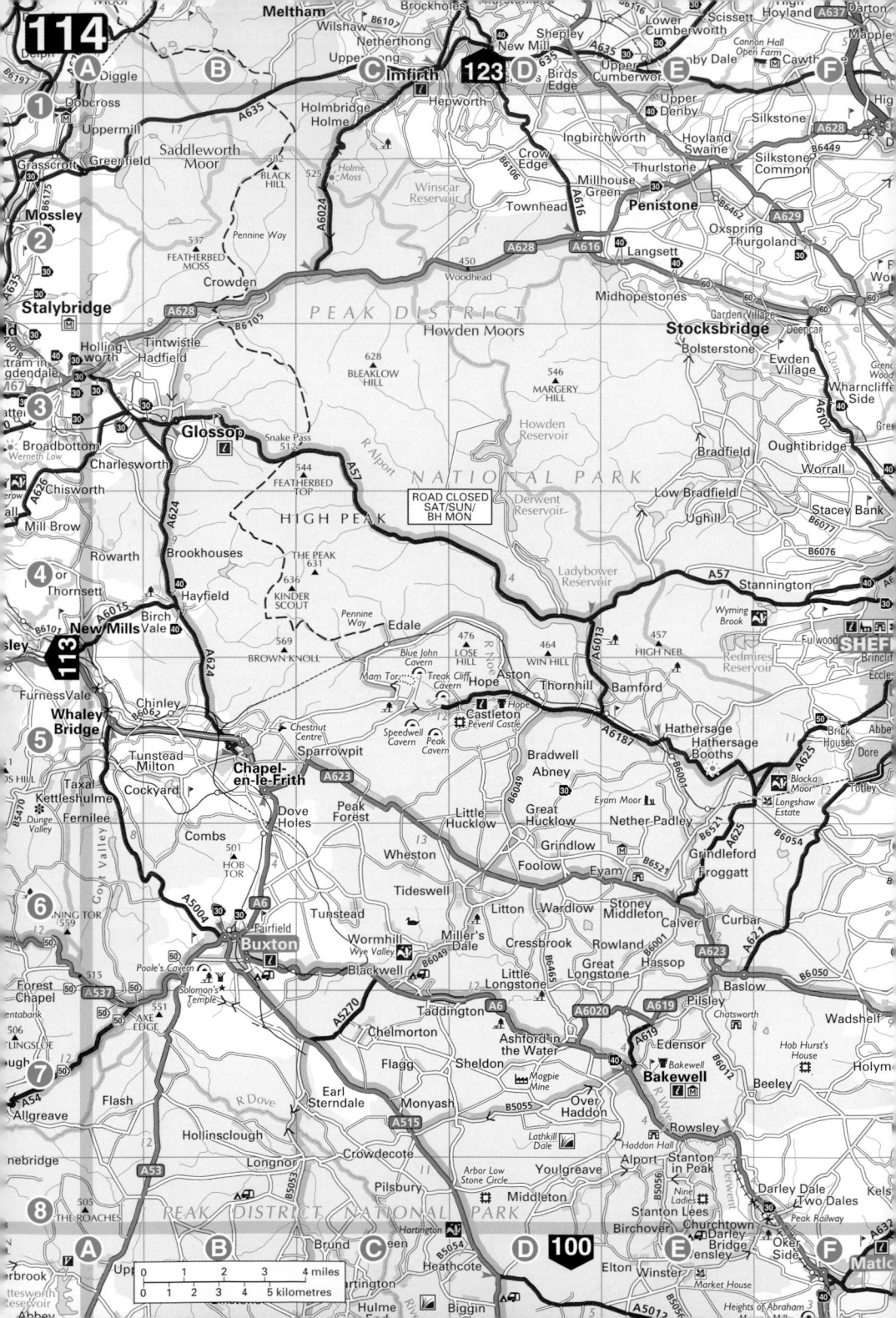

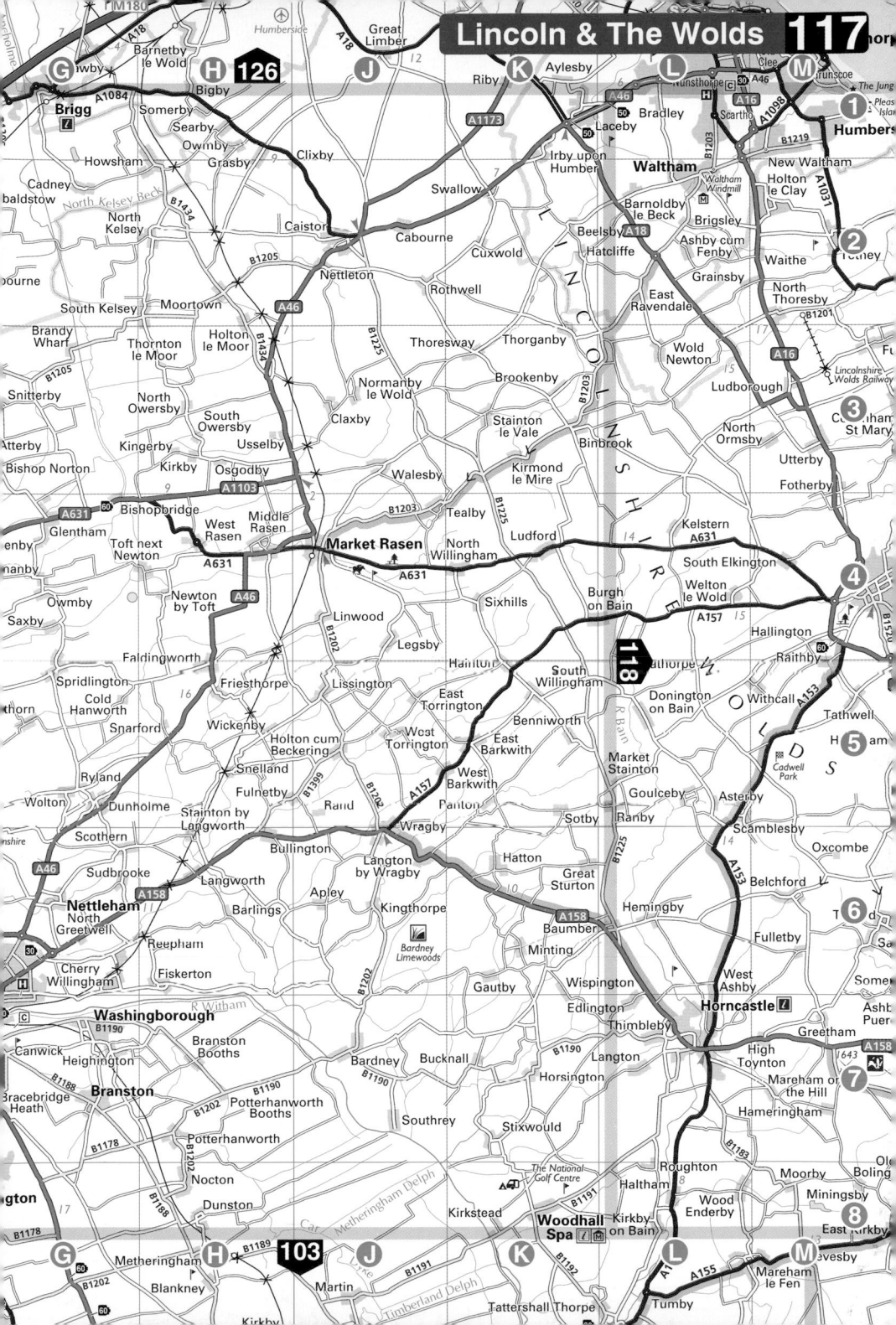

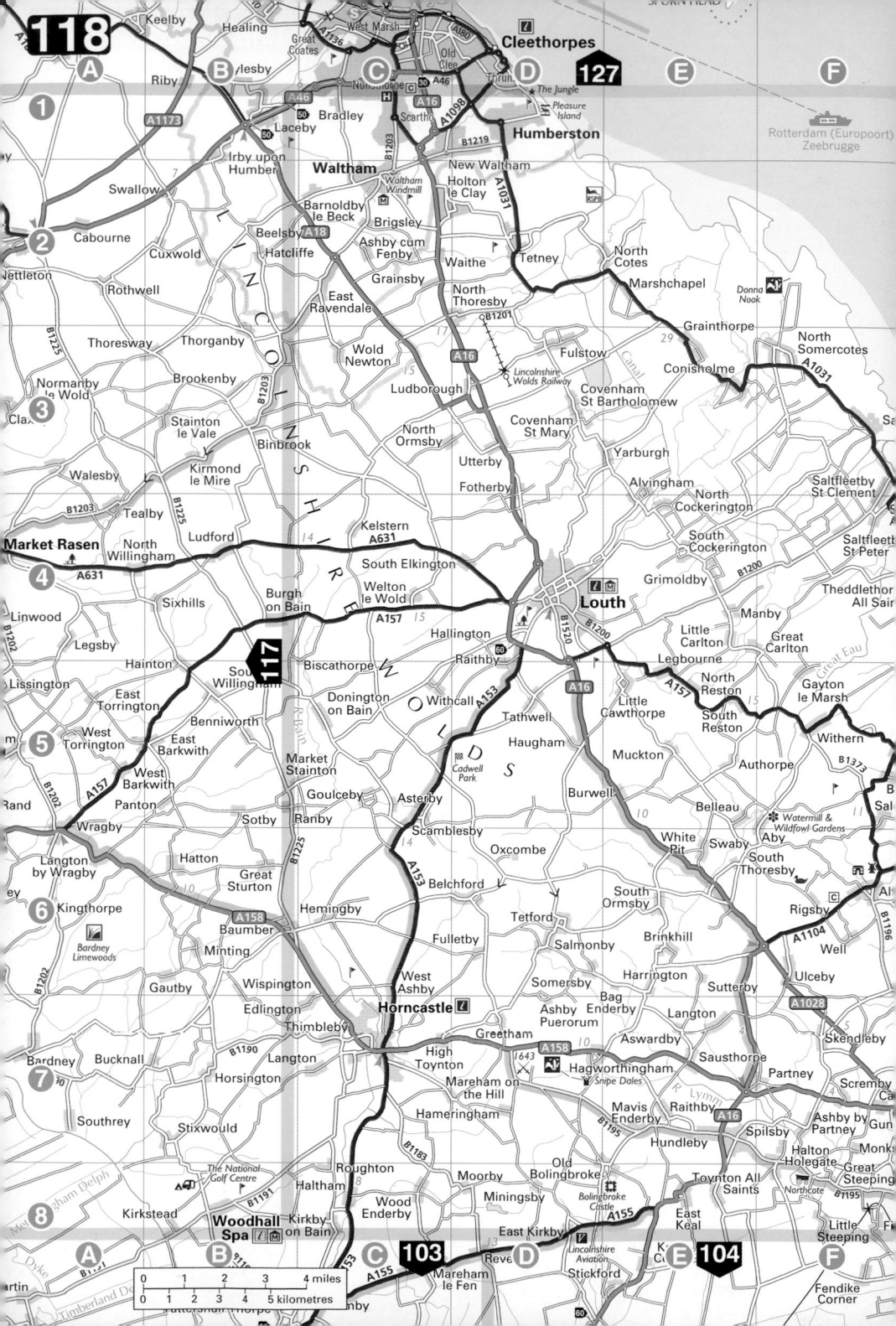

G   H   J   K   L   M

1

2

3

4

etby
nts
Theddlethorpe
St Helen
A1031

Mablethorpe
ℹ️

A1104
Trusthorpe
A52
Sutton on Sea
altby
Marsh
A1111
Sandilands

5

A52
Markby

Huttoft
Bilsby
Thurlby
B1449
Anderby Creek
Anderby
Farlesthorpe
Mumby
mberworth
Chapel Point

6

Willoughby
Hogsthorpe
**Chapel
St Leonards**

Sloothby
Habertoft
Addlethorpe
🎡 Fantasy Island
Ingoldmells
Welton
e Marsh
by
Ingoldmells
Point

7

Orby
Hall
pe
Burgh le Marsh
A158
Bratoft
rby in the Marsh
ℹ️ 🏛️ 🔊
Skegness

8

G   **104** H   J   K   L   M

Croft
Thorpe St Peter
Wainfleet
Haven
Wainfleet

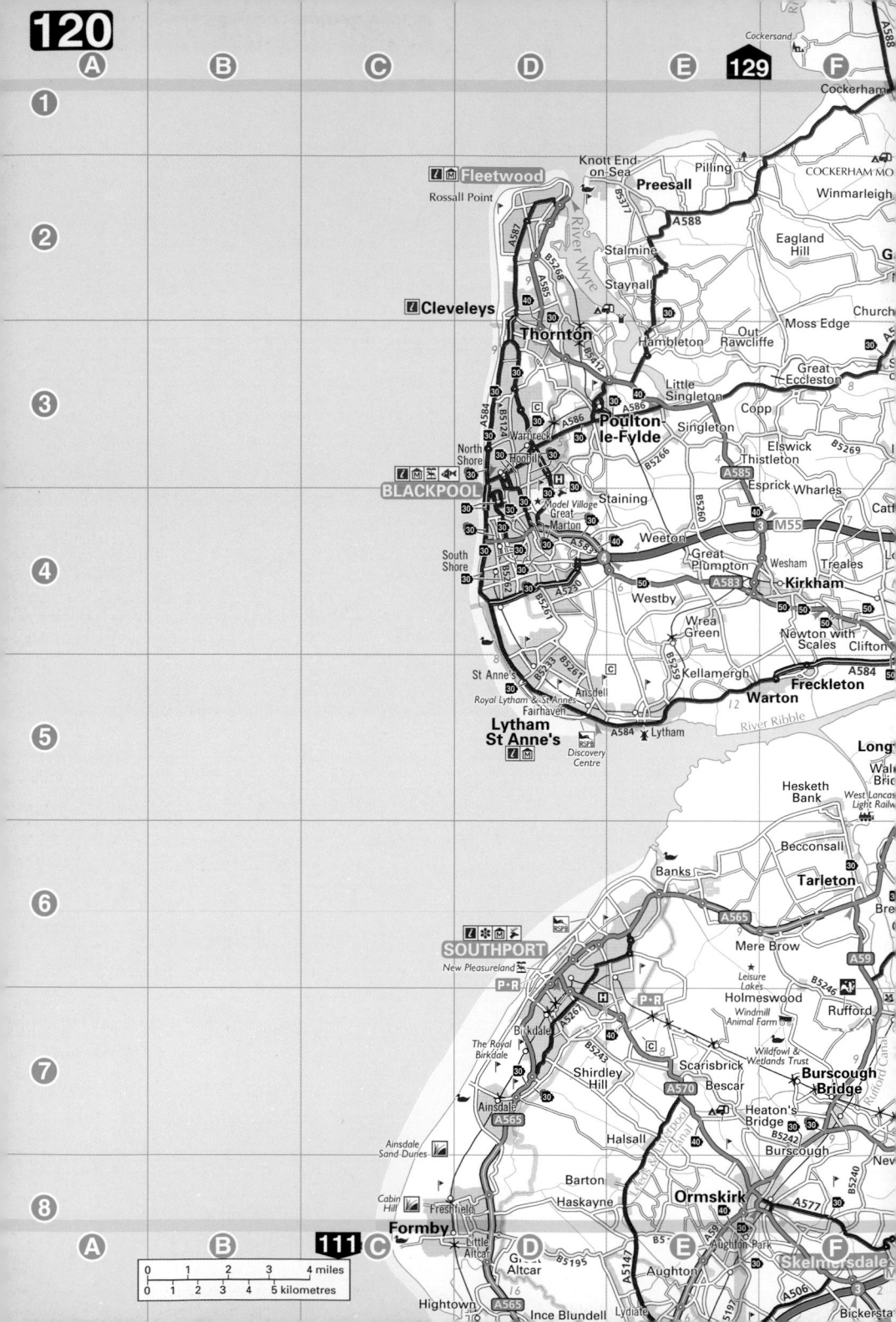

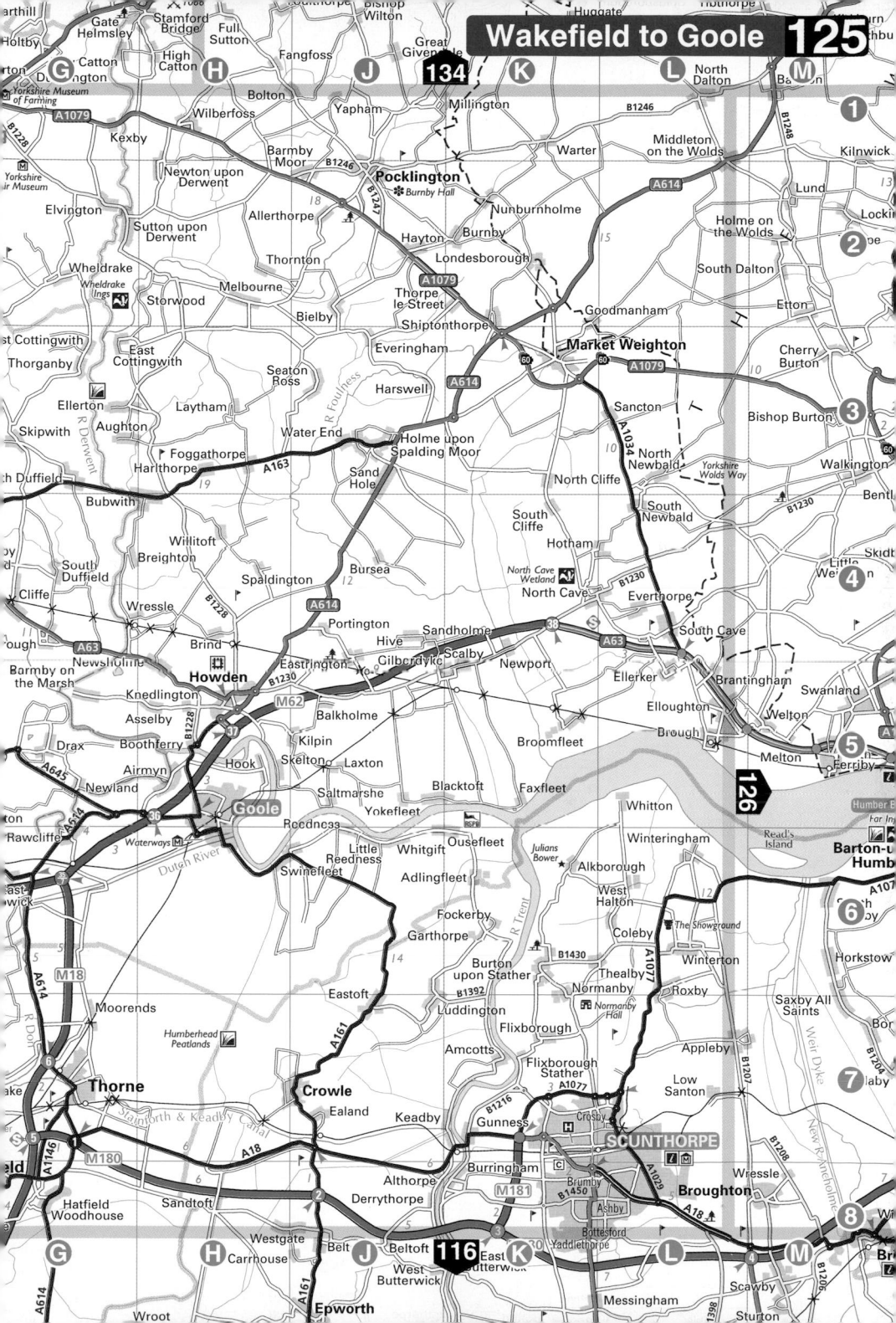

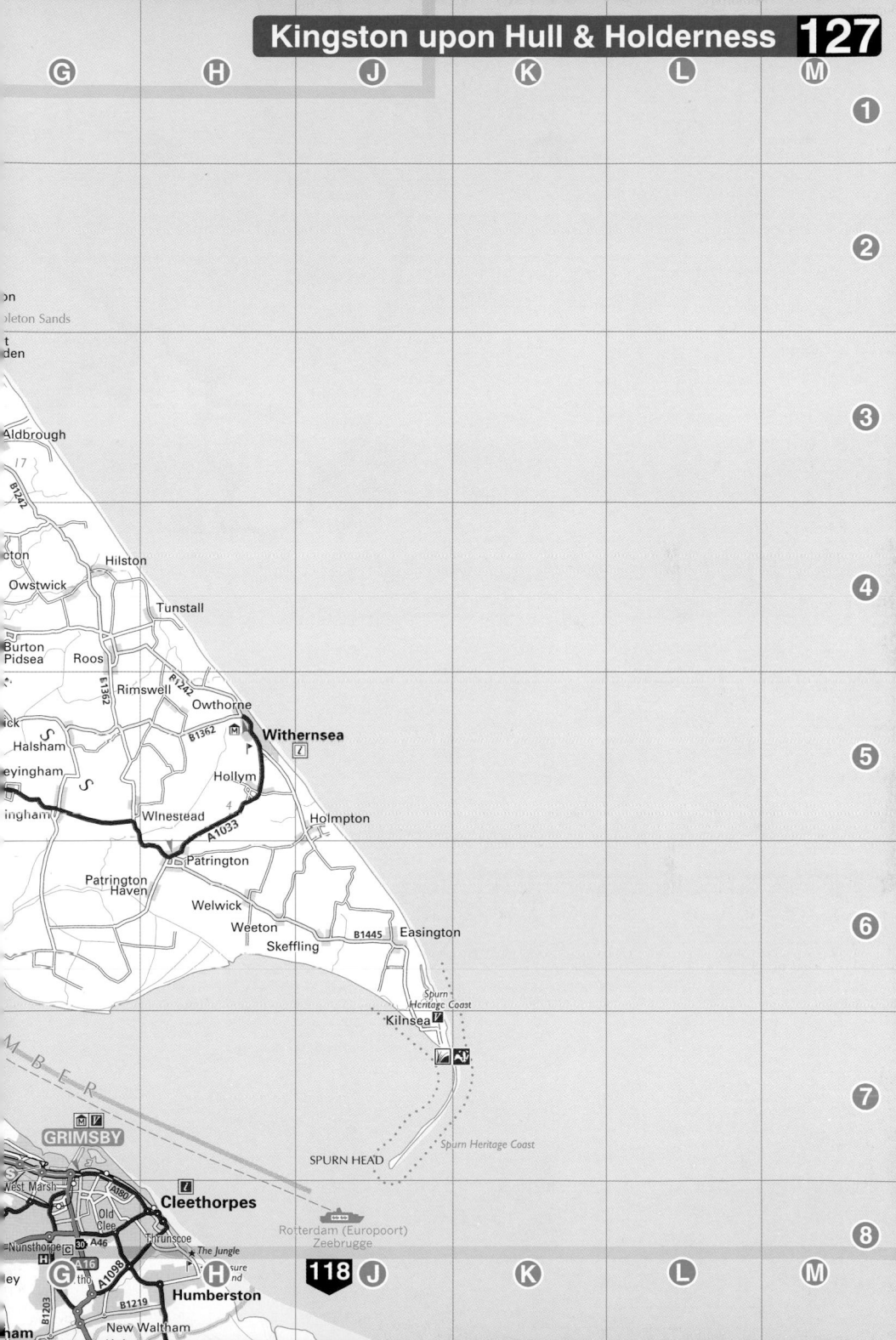

G   H   J   K   L   M

1
2
3
4
5
6
7
8

oleton Sands
t
den
ham

Aldbrough

B1242
17

cton
Owstwick

Hilston

Tunstall

Burton
Pidsea   Roos
B1362

ick
Halsham

eyingham

ingham

Rimswell
B1242
Owthorne
B1362
Withernsea

Hollym

Winestead
A1033
Holmpton

Patrington

Patrington
Haven

Welwick

Weeton
Skeffling   B1445   Easington

Spurn
Heritage Coast
Kilnsea

GRIMSBY
West Marsh
A180
Cleethorpes
Old
Clee
Nunsthorpe   A46   Thrunscoe
G   A16   thc   ★ The Jungle
A1098   sure
ley   nd
Humberston
B1203   B1219
ham   New Waltham

Spurn
Heritage Coast

SPURN HEAD

Rotterdam (Europoort)
Zeebrugge

A   B   C   D   E   F

1

Seascale
Hallsenna Moor
Drigg   Holmrook
Muncaster
Mill
13
Ravenglass
and Eskdale
Railway
ESKDALE
652
HARTER
FELL
Fu
eathwaite
Tarn

Ravenglass
Roman
Bath
House
Muncaster
Muncaster
A595
Devoke
Water
Hall
Dunnerdale
Seathwaite

136   **137**

2

Waberthwaite
573
WHITFELL
Ulpha
LAKE   DISTRICT
NATIONAL
Broughton
Mills
A593

Hycemoor
Selker Bay
PARK
Bootle
Swinside
Stone Circle
Broughton-in-Furn

3

600
BLACK
COMBE
Whitbeck
The Green
A595
Lady
Hall
Foxfield
Grizebe
Gutterby Spa
Whicham
The Hill
A5093
Kirkby-in-Fu
Beck Sid
Silecroft
8
Soutergate
A595

4

Kirksanton
Millom
12
U
Haverigg
Ireleth
Penn
Haverigg
Point
Askam
in Furness
Lindal
in Furness
South Lakes
Animal Park
Little
Urswic

Sandscale Haws

5

North Walney
BARROW-
IN-FURNESS
Dalton-
in-Furness
H
Newton
Stain
with Ad
Furness
Abbey
Bow
Bridge
Dendron

6

Vickerstown
Barrow
Island
30
A5087
Leec
A590
Rampsi

ISLE OF
WALNEY
Sheep
Island
Piel
Castle
Foul
Piel Island

Hilpsford Point
South
Walney
Piel Bar

7

8

A   B   C   D   E   F

0   1   2   3   4 miles
0 1 2 3 4 5 kilometres

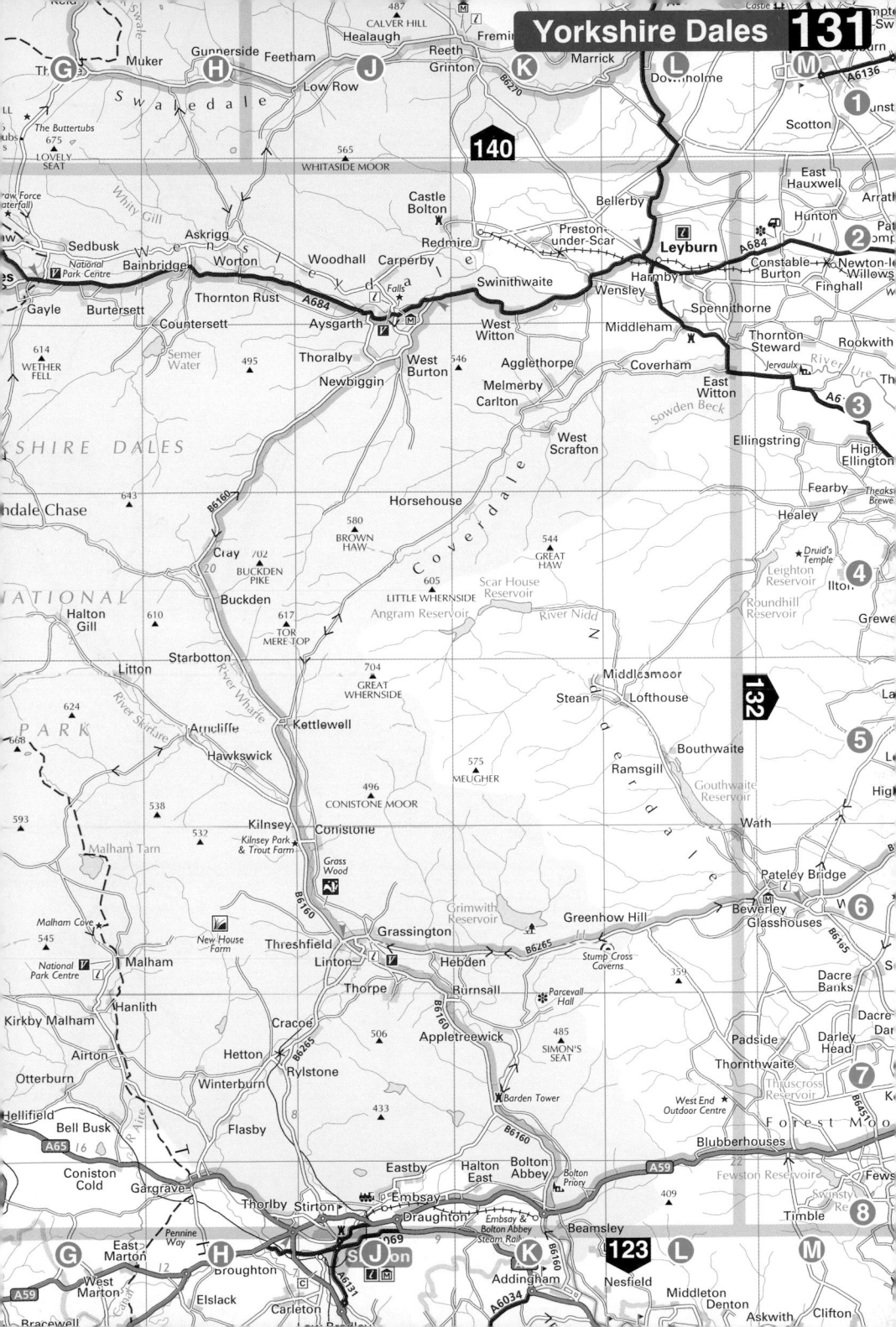

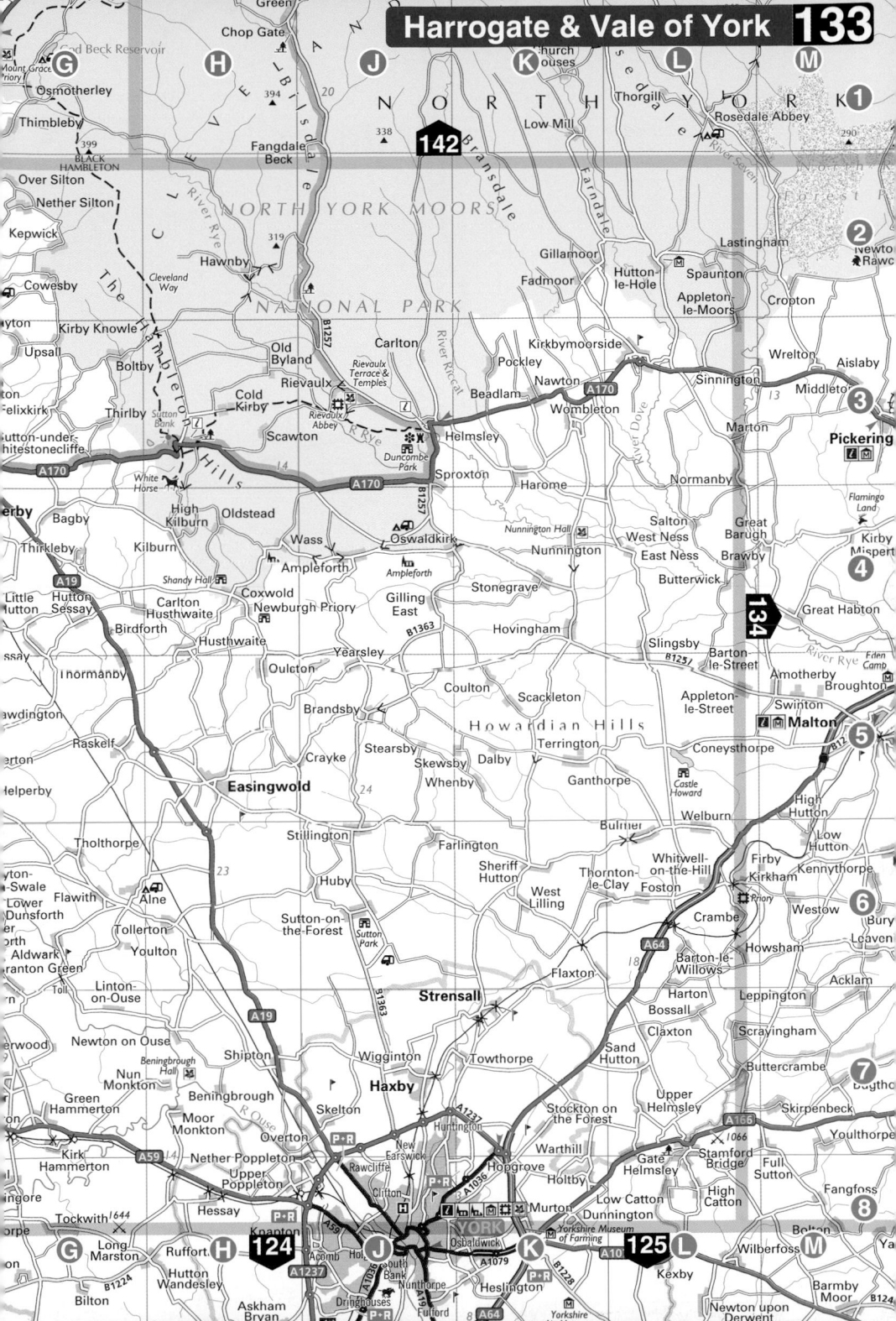

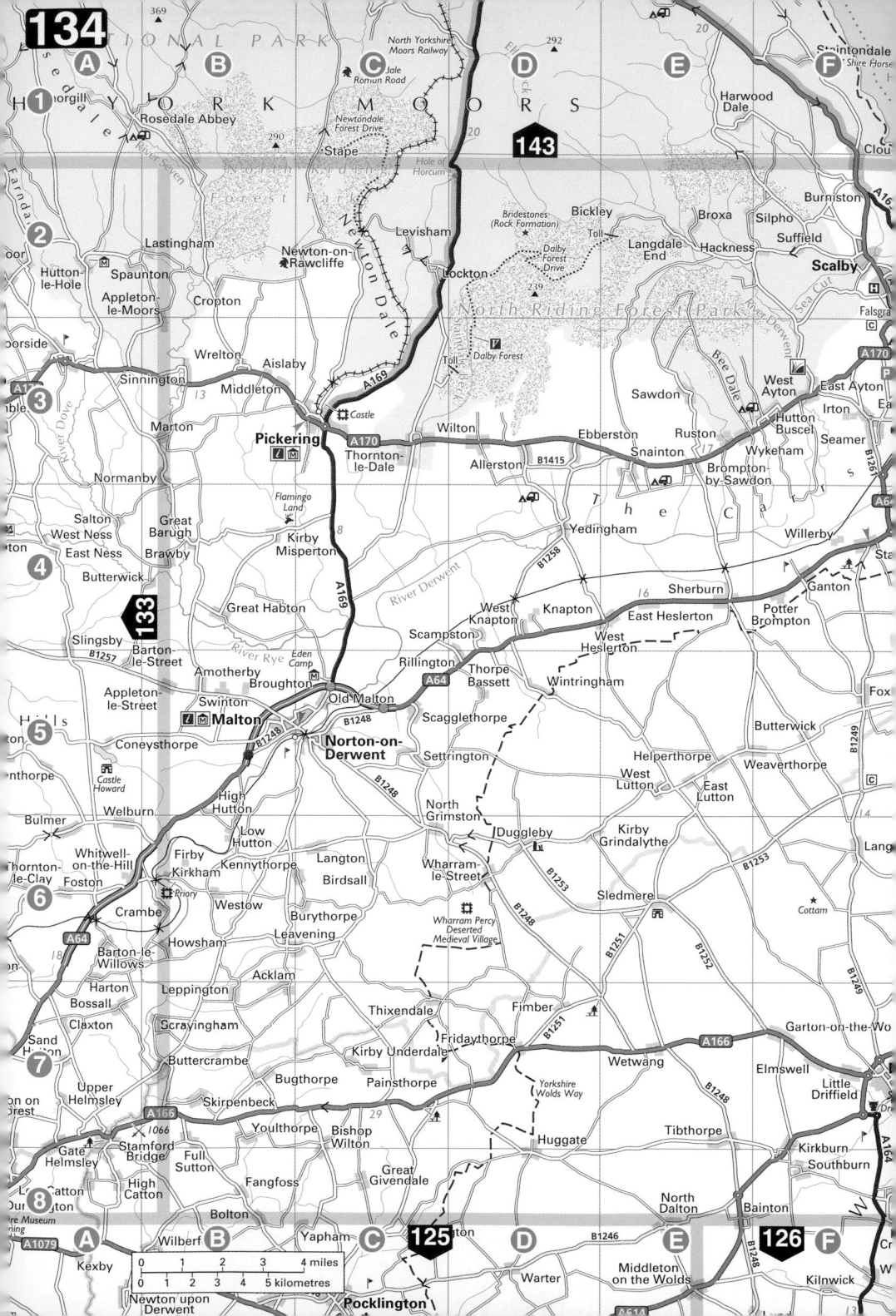

G H J K L M

1

2

3

4

5

6

7

8

Cloughton
Wyke

Cromer Point

Cleveland Way

Scarborough
Castle

Oliver's Mount

A165
P·R Osgodby
Cayton
Bay
The
Wyke
B1261
sgates
Cayton
Lebberston
Gristhorpe
A1039
Filey Brigg
Folkton
Muston
A1039
Filey
R. Hertford

Flixton

Hunmanby

Fordon
Reighton
Filey Bay

Wold
Newton
B1229
Speeton
Bempton
Cliffs
RSPB
Flamborough Head
Heritage Coast
Thornwick
Bay

Burton
Fleming
Buckton
Bempton
North Landing
Selwicks
Bay
B1259
**FLAMBOROUGH
HEAD**
Lighthouse

Grindale
A165
B1229

Thwing
B1255
Flamborough

Sewerby
Bondville
Miniature Village

B1253
Boynton

Rudston
Monolith
Bessingby
Bridlington
**BRIDLINGTON
BAY**

Carnaby
Hilderthorpe

Haisthorpe
Thornholme

Kilham
Burton Agnes
Norman
Manor House
A165

Ruston Parva
Harpham
Fraisthorpe

Lowthorpe
A614
Nafferton
Gransmoor

field
Great Kelk
Lissett
Barmston

R. Hull
Wansford
Gembling
Ulrome

Skerne
B1249
Foston on
the Wolds
Skipsea
Castle
Skipsea

Brigham
Beeford

North
Frodingham
126
Dunnington

Yorkshire
Wolds Way

wick
Atwick

Bewholme

Honeysuckle
B1242

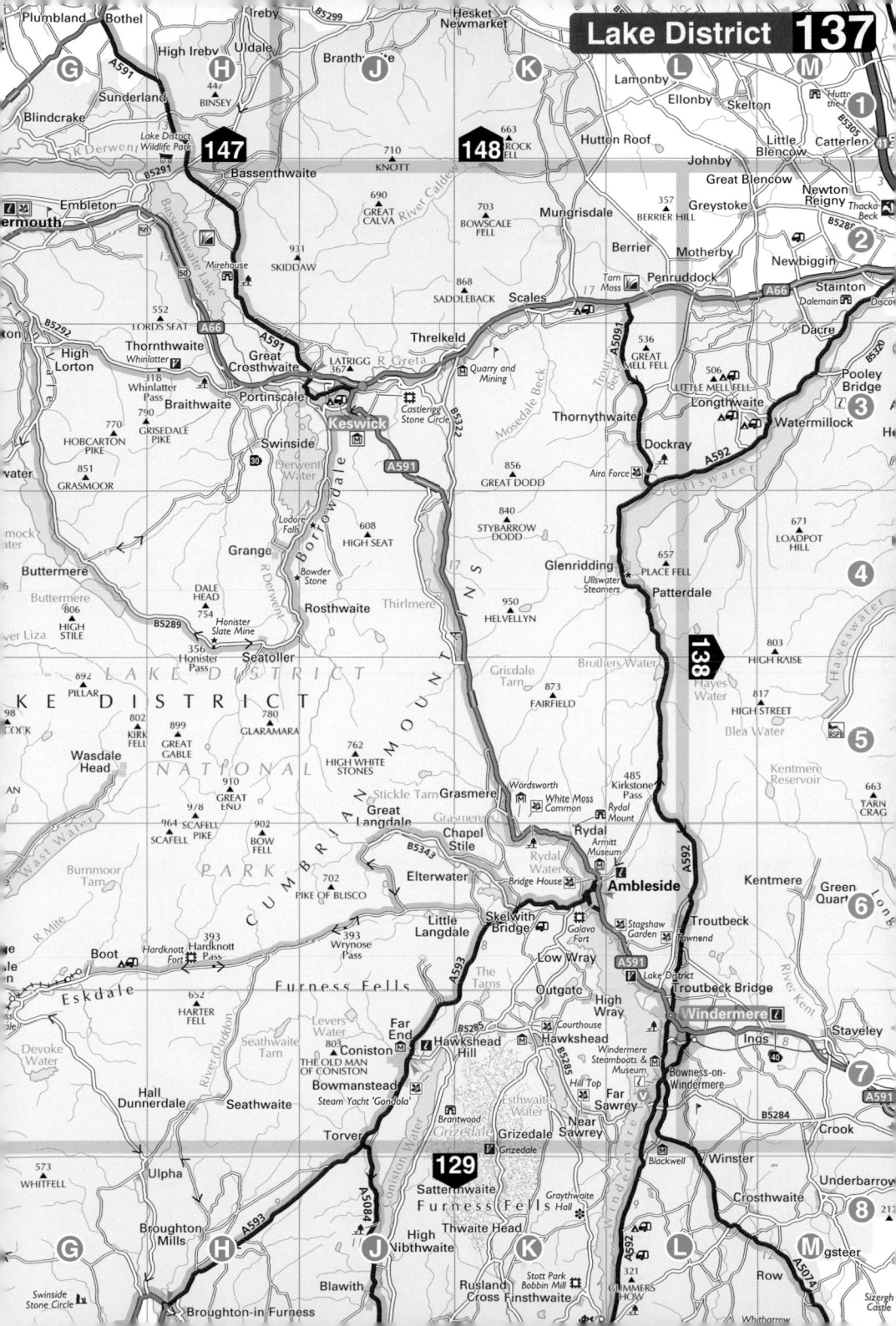

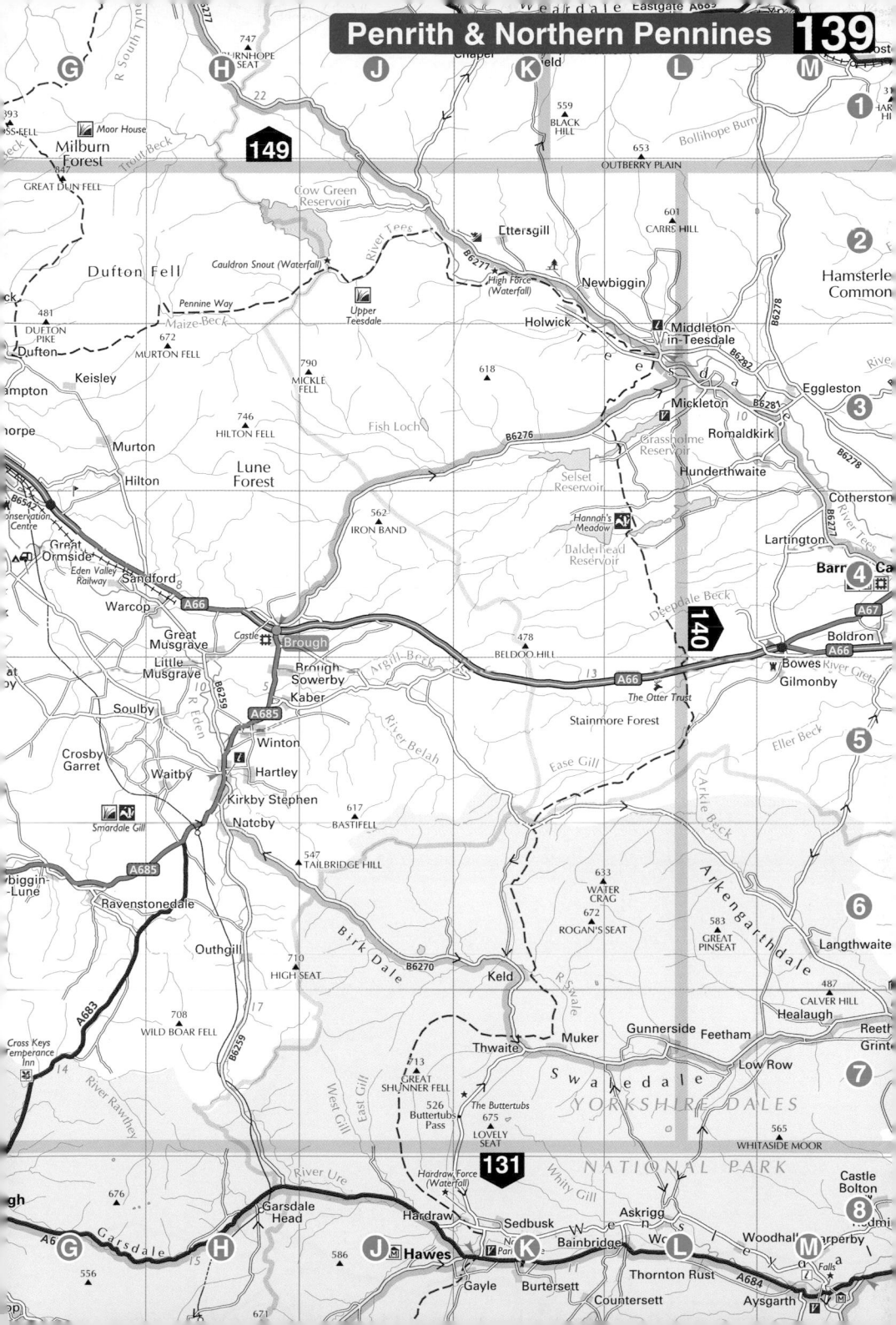

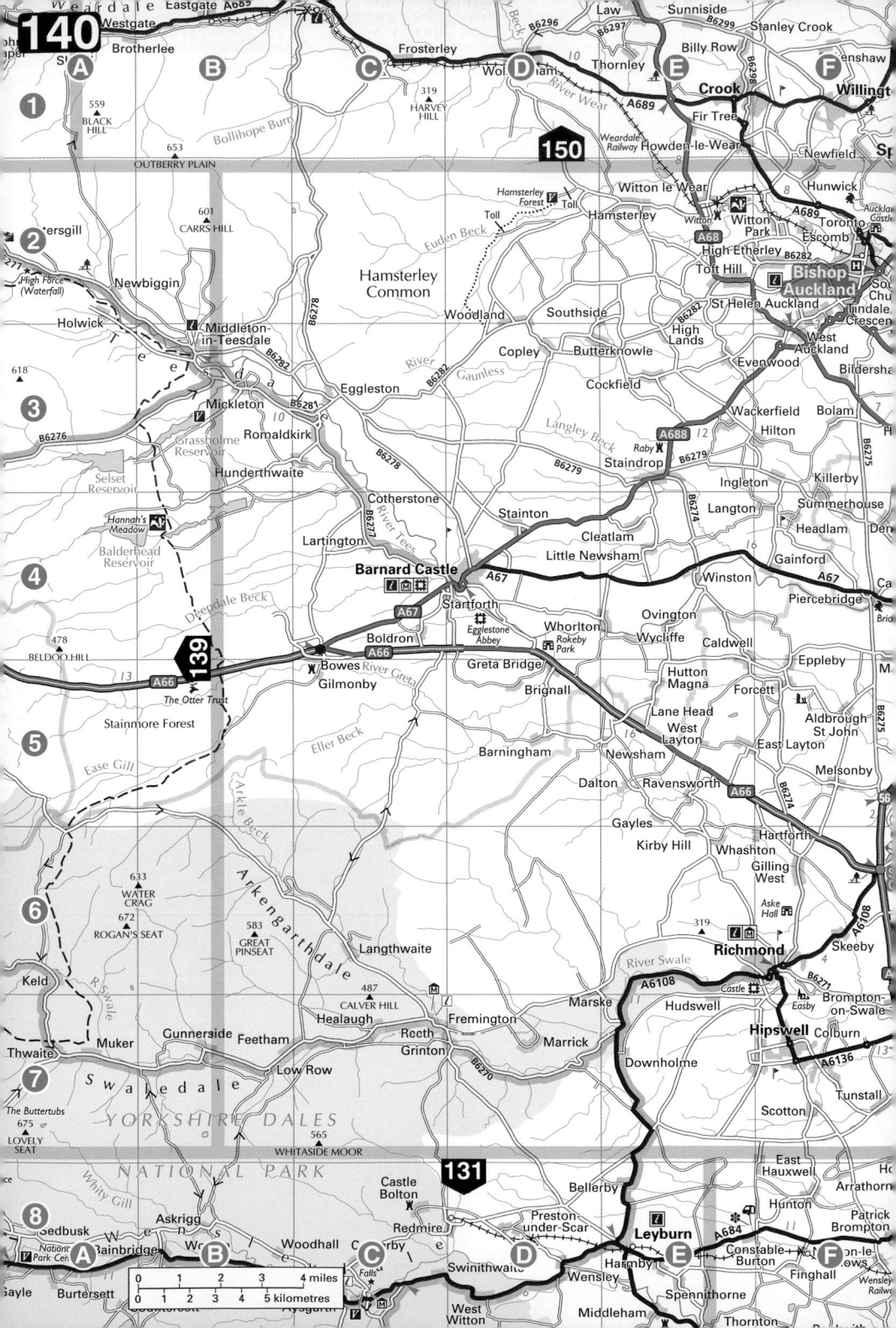

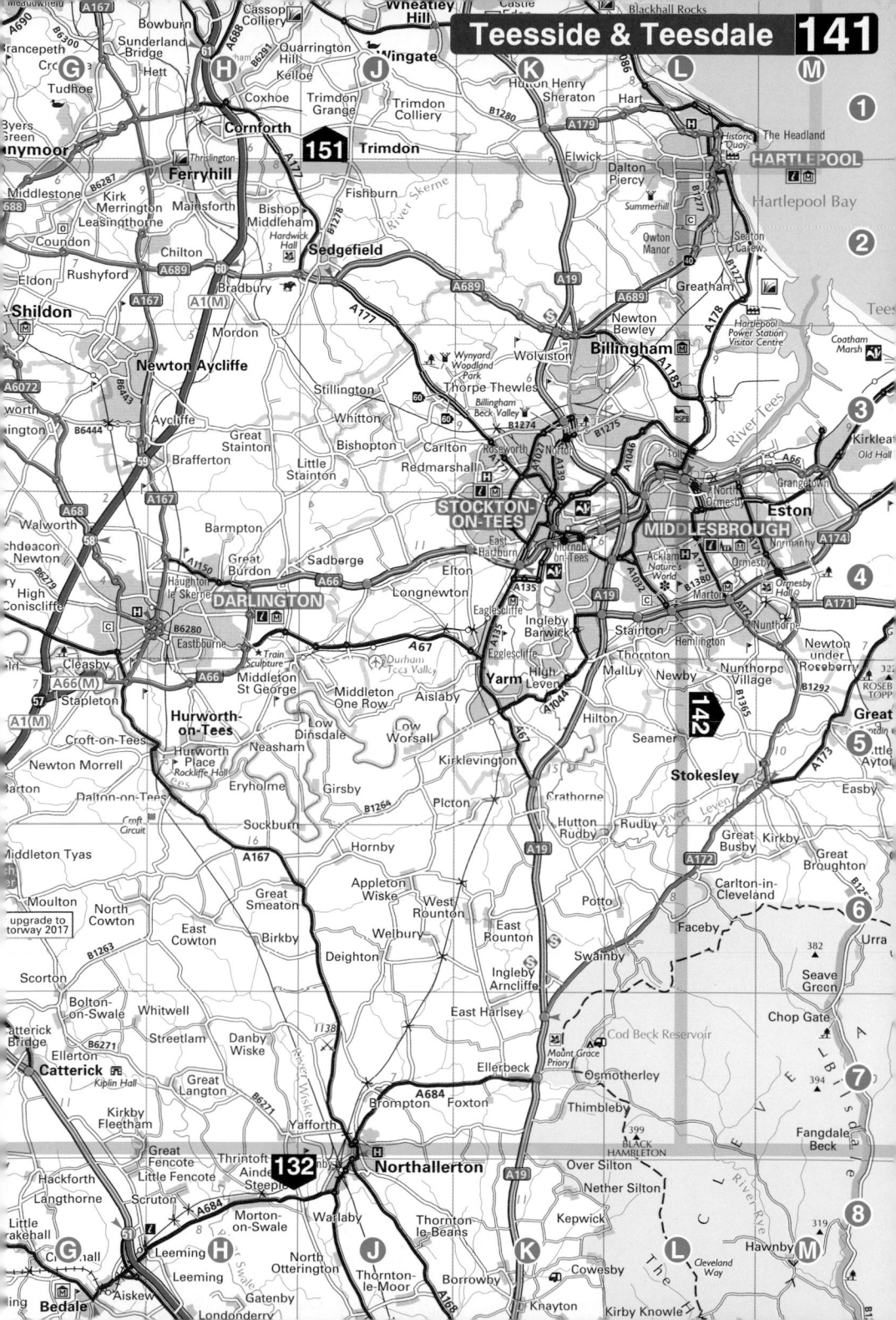

Staithes
Heritage Centre
derwell
Runswick Bay
Runswick
North Yorkshire and Cleveland Heritage Coast
Goldsborough
Overdale Wyke
Ellerby
B1266
Lythe
A174
Mickleby
Sandsend
Sandsend Wyke
West Barnby
East Barnby
Dunsley
Whitby
Saltwick Bay
Ugthorpe
Newholm
Abbey
Ruswarp
A171
Briggswath
Stainsacre
The Green
Aislaby
Sneaton
High Hawsker
Egton
Sleights
Ugglebarnby
B1447
on Bridge
Iburndale
Grosmont
A169
Ness Point or North Cheek
Robin Hood's Bay
OORS
B1416
Fylingthorpe
Robin Hood's Bay
Old Peak or South Cheek
ILL
A171
Ravenscar
Goathland
North Yorkshire Moors Railway
292
20
Staintondale
Shire Horse Centre
Hayburn Wyke
ARK
Wheeldale Roman Road
Eller Beck
Harwood Dale
MOORS
Newtondale Forest Drive
290
20
Cloughton Wyke
Stape
Hole of Horcum
Cloughton
t Park
134
Cromer Point
A165
Burniston
Cleveland Way
Bridestones (Rock Formation)
Bickley
Broxa
Silpho
Levisham
Toll
Suffield
Newton Raw
Dalby Forest Drive
Langdale End
Hackness
Scalby
Scarborough
Lock
239
Sea Cut
Falsgrave
North Riding Forest Park

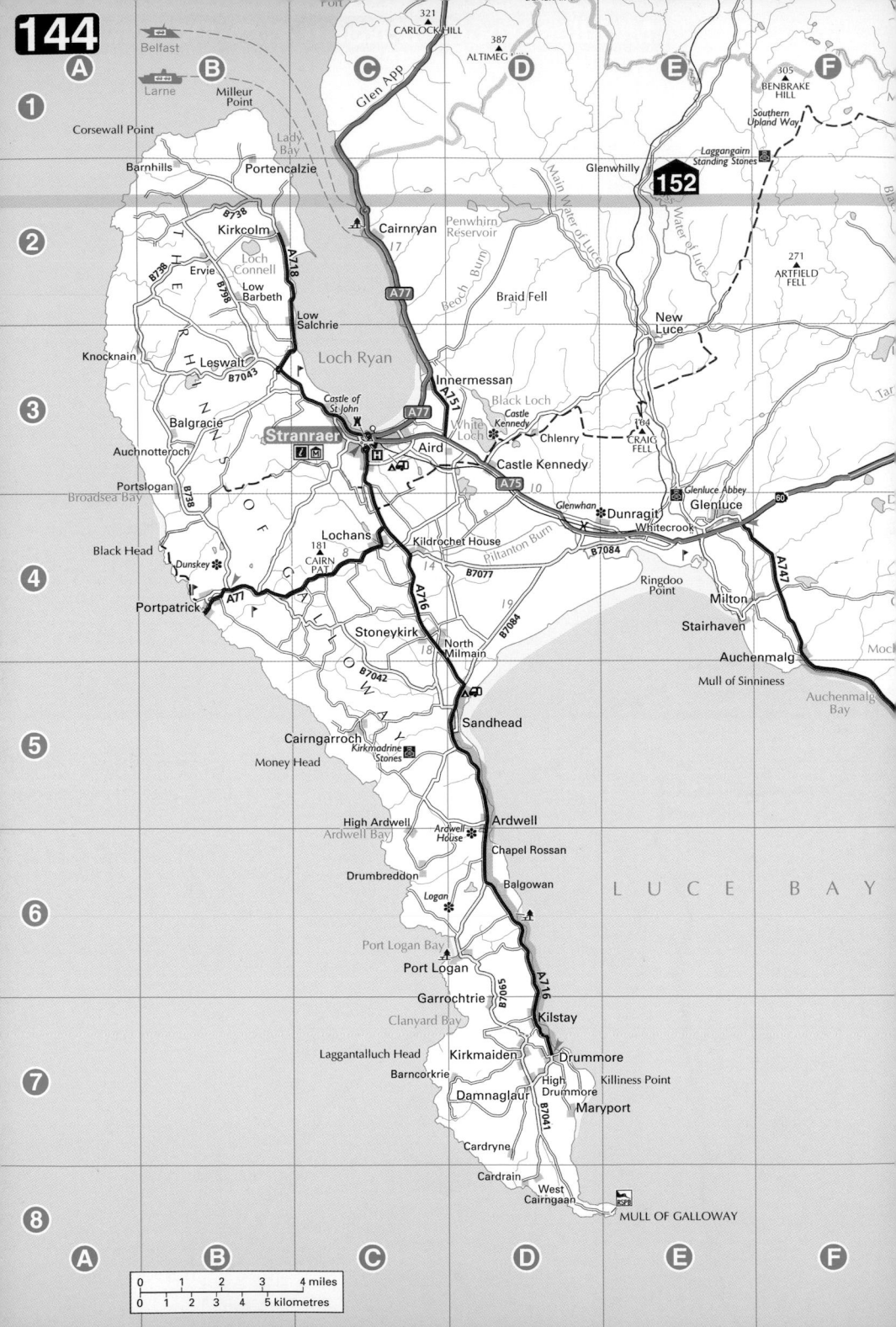

A   B   C   D   E   F

1 Belfast
Larne
Milleur Point
Corsewall Point
321
CARLOCK HILL
387
ALTIMEG HILL
305
BENBRAKE HILL
Southern Upland Way
Lady Bay
Glen App
Laggangairn Standing Stones
Barnhills   Portencalzie
Glenwhilly
152

2 B738
Kirkcolm
A718
Cairnryan
17
Penwhirn Reservoir
Main Water of Luce
New Luce
271
ARTFIELD FELL
Water of Luce
B798   Ervie
Loch Connell
Low Barbeth
Beoch Burn
Braid Fell
Knocknain
Leswalt
B7043
Low Salchrie
Loch Ryan
Innermessan
Black Loch
Castle Kennedy
Chlenry
CRAIG FELL

3 Balgracie
Castle of St John
A751
White Loch
Castle Kennedy
Stranraer
Aird
Castle Kennedy
Auchnotteroch
H
A75   10
Glenluce Abbey
Glenluce
60
Portslogan
Broadsea Bay
B738
Glenwhan
Dunragit
Whitecrook

4 Black Head
Lochans
181 CAIRN PAT
8
Kildrochet House
14
B7077
B7084
Ringdoo Point
Milton
Dunskey
A716
19
Stairhaven
Portpatrick
A71
B7084
Auchenmalg
Stoneykirk
18   North Milmain
Mull of Sinniness
Auchenmalg Bay
B7042

5 Cairngarroch
Kirkmadrine Stones
Sandhead
Money Head
L U C E   B A Y

6 High Ardwell
Ardwell Bay
Ardwell House
Ardwell
Chapel Rossan
Drumbreddon
Logan
Balgowan
Port Logan Bay
B716

7 Port Logan
Garrochtrie
B7065
Kilstay
Clanyard Bay
Laggantalluch Head
Kirkmaiden
Drummore
Barncorkrie
High Drummore
Killiness Point
Damnaglaur
Maryport
B7041
Cardryne
Cardrain
West Cairngaan
RSPB

8 MULL OF GALLOWAY

A   B   C   D   E   F

0   1   2   3   4 miles
0   1   2   3   4   5 kilometres

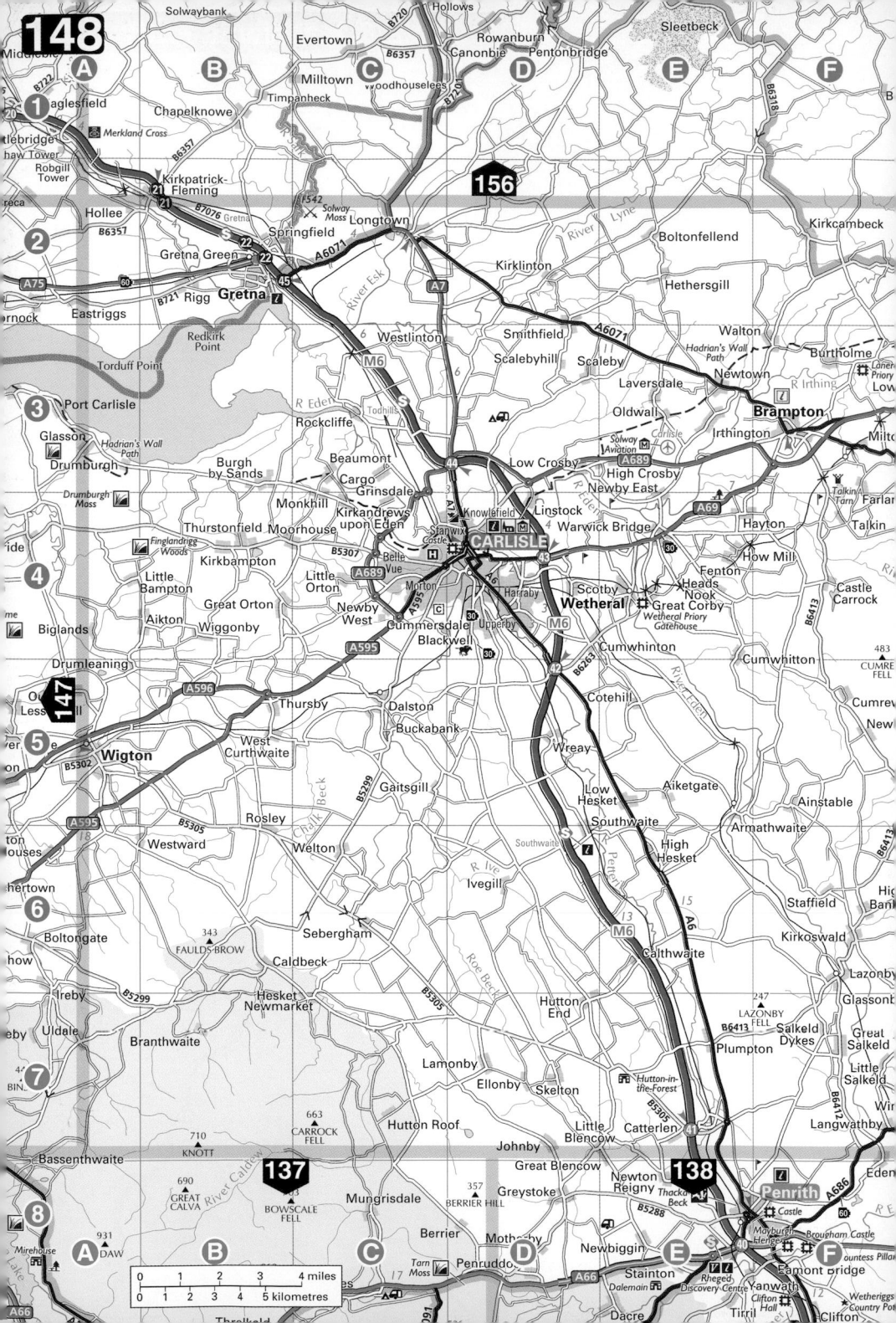

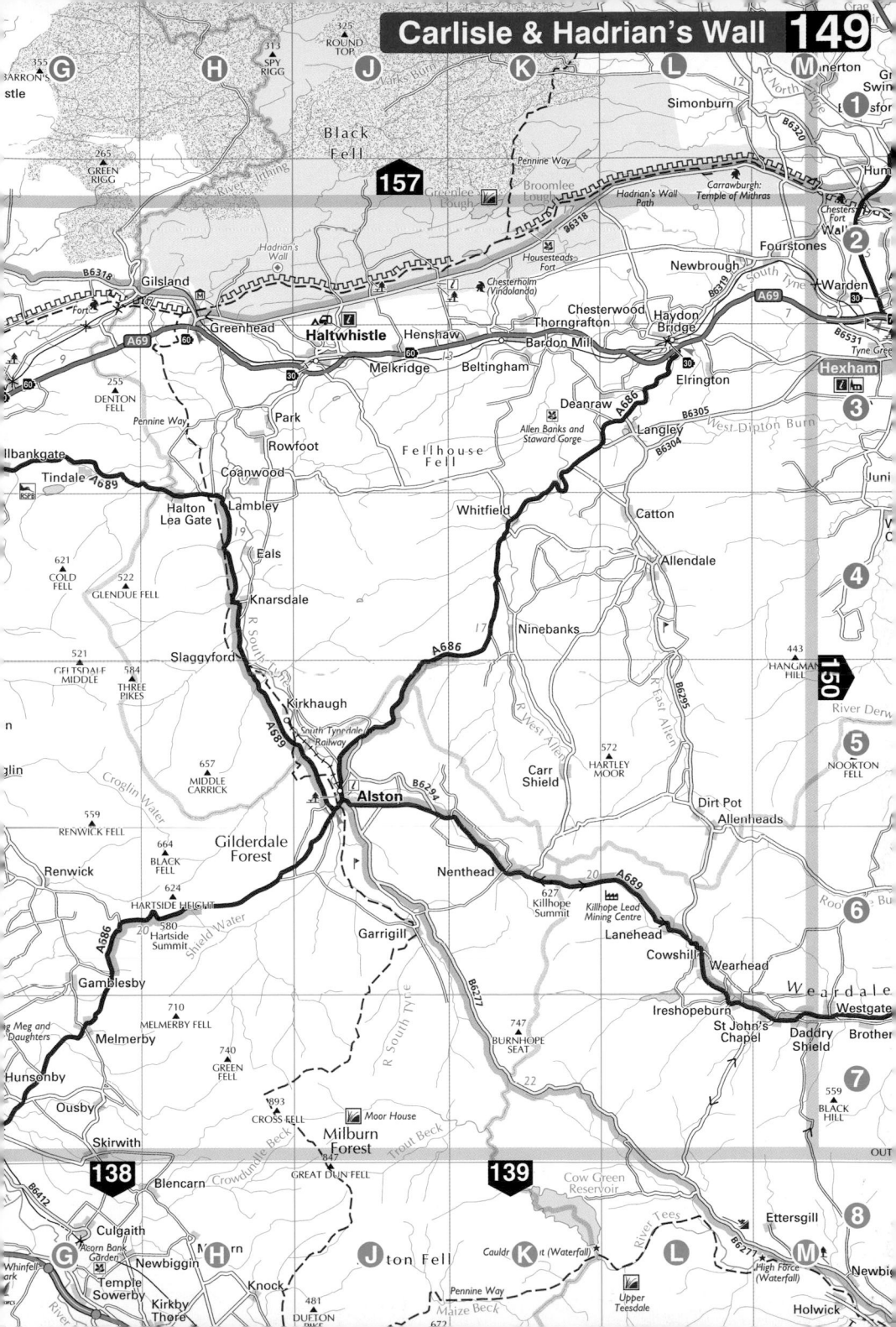

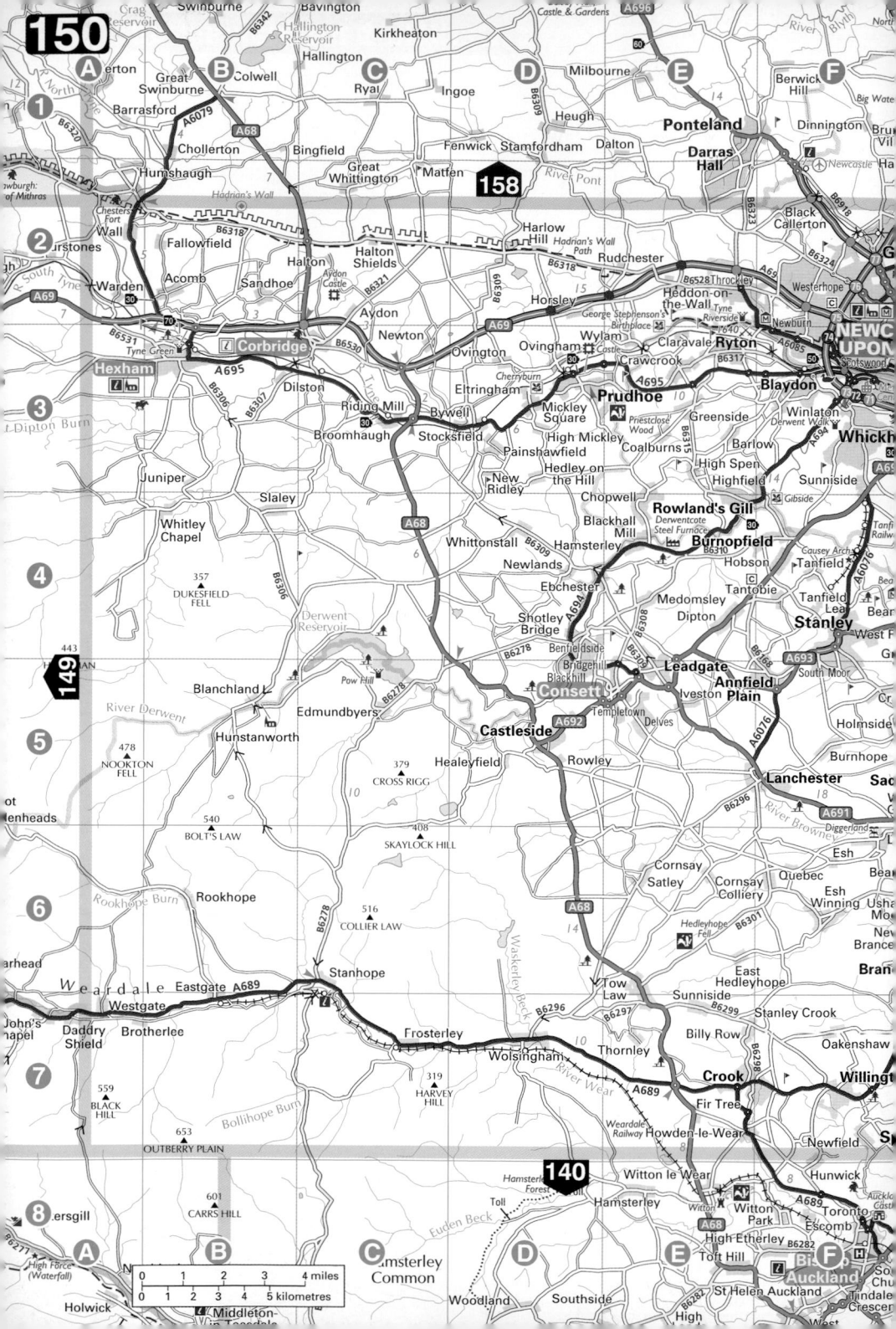

A B C D E F

162

1

2

3

4

5

6

7

8

Cro (Elect Kno

Culzean Bay
Culzean C & Country Park

Penny

Maidenhead Bay

Maidens

A719

22

Kirkoswal
Souter Johnnie Cottage

12

Turnberry

Turnberry
Turnberry Bay

A77

60

Ro

Dipple

Wallaceto

Kilgrammie

A741

B741

Water of Girvan

B7035

Old Dailly

60

Girvan

Dounepark

B7035

Penkill

B734

340 Ailsa Craig
RSPB

Woodland

60

Pinminnoch

C

A

8

60

297
GREY HILL

Pinmore

Balligmorrie

13

Lendalfoot

A77

A714

Muck Water

Bennane Head

Colmonell

B734

Pinwherry

River Stinchar

B734

Duisk River

Heronsford

Water of Tig

Ballantrae

Barrhill

Feoc

Belfast

Currarie Port

437
BENERAIRD

Loch

Larne

321
CARLOCK HILL

387
ALTIMEG HILL

305
BENBRAKE HILL

Milleur Point

Glen App

Lady Bay

Southern Upland Way

Corsewall Point

Glenwhilly

Laggangairn Standing Stones

Barnhills

Portencalzie

Main Water of Luce

Cross Water of Luce

B738

Kirkcolm

A718

New

271
ARTFIELD FELL

B738

Ervie

Loch Connell

Low Barbeth

B738

Braid Fell

A77

Low Salchrie

E

F

A B C D

Knockna

0   1   2   3   4 miles
0 1 2 3 4 5 kilometres

h Ryan

Innermessan

A751

Castle of St John

Black Loch

144

Cairnryan

A77

Beoch Burn

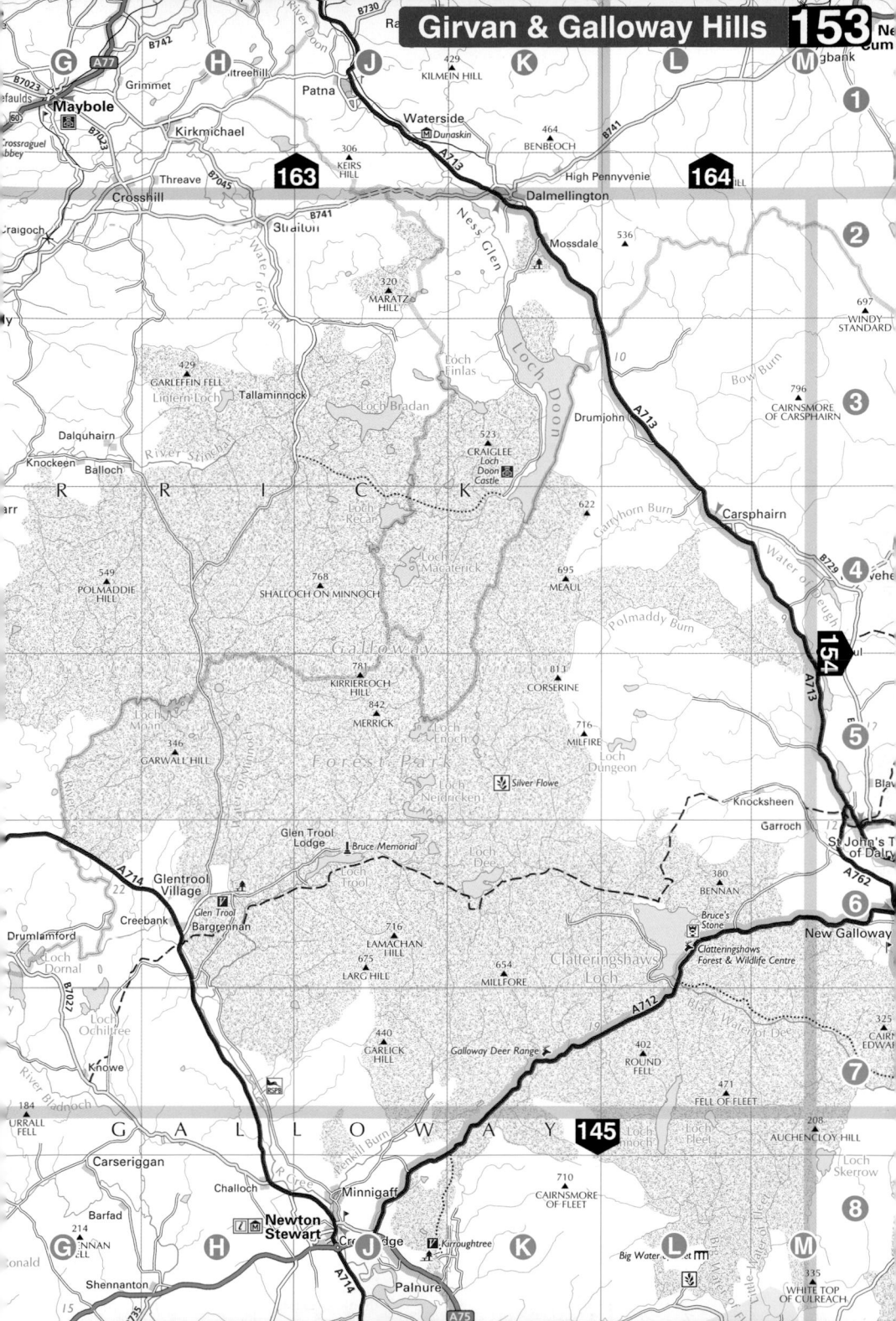

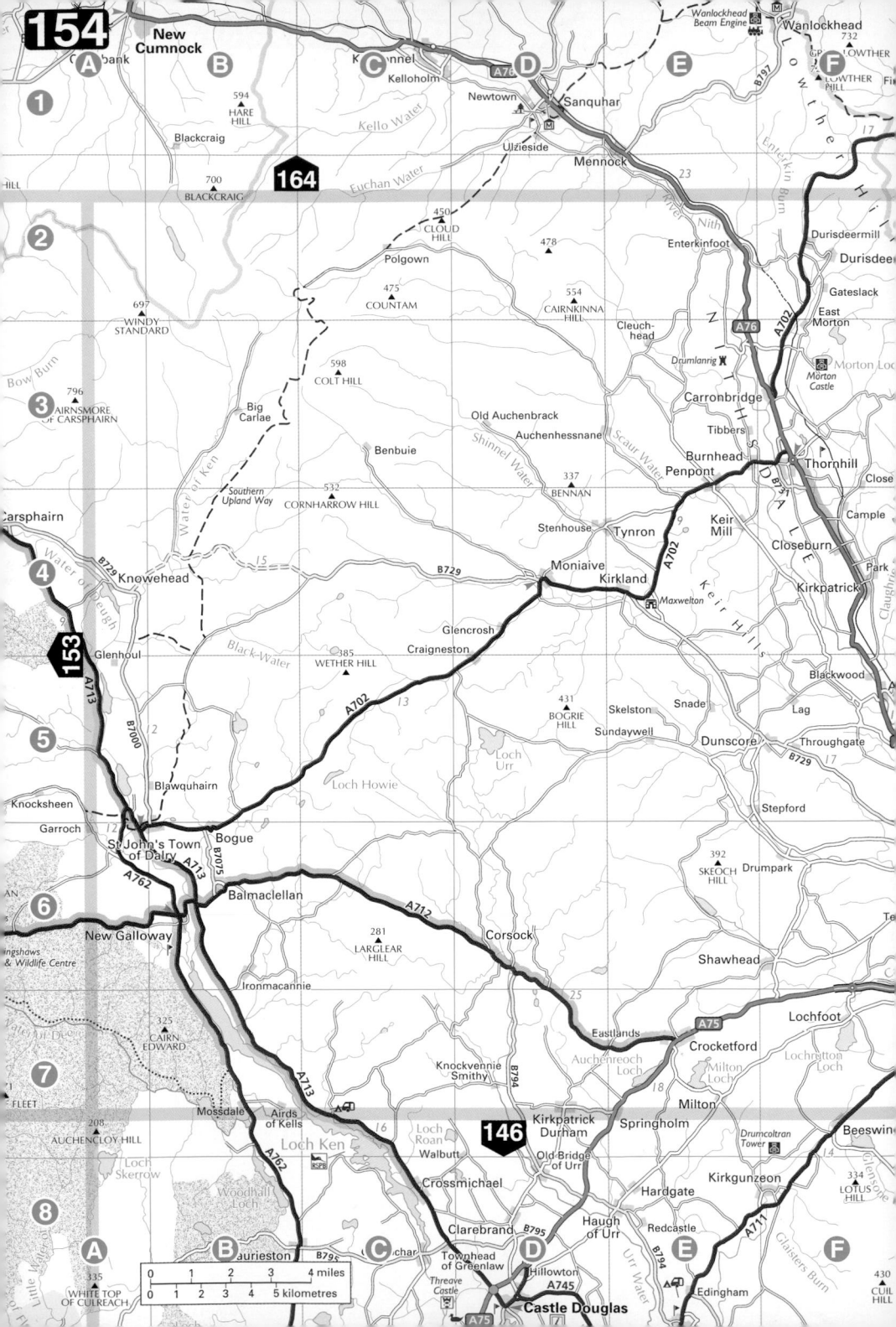

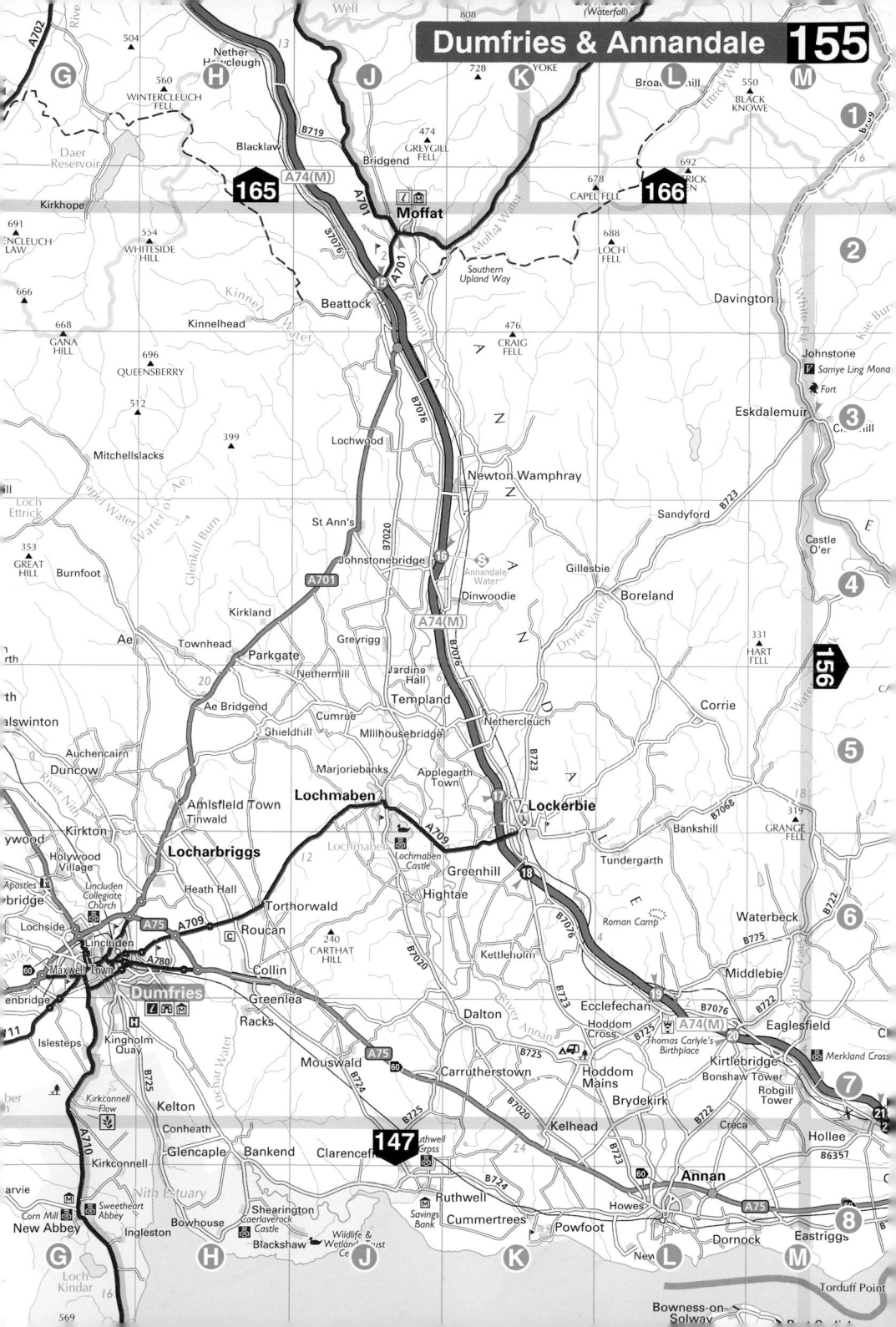

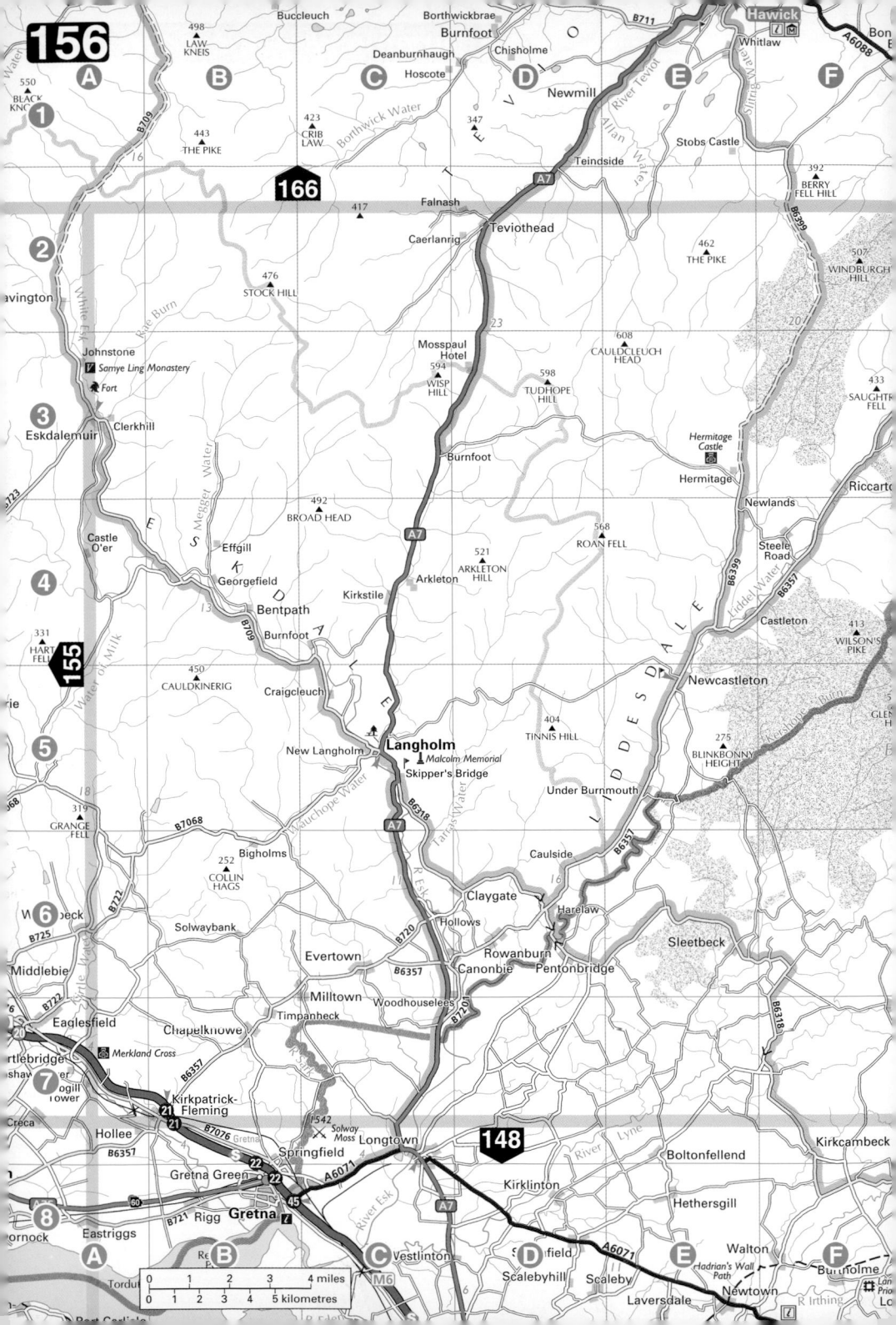

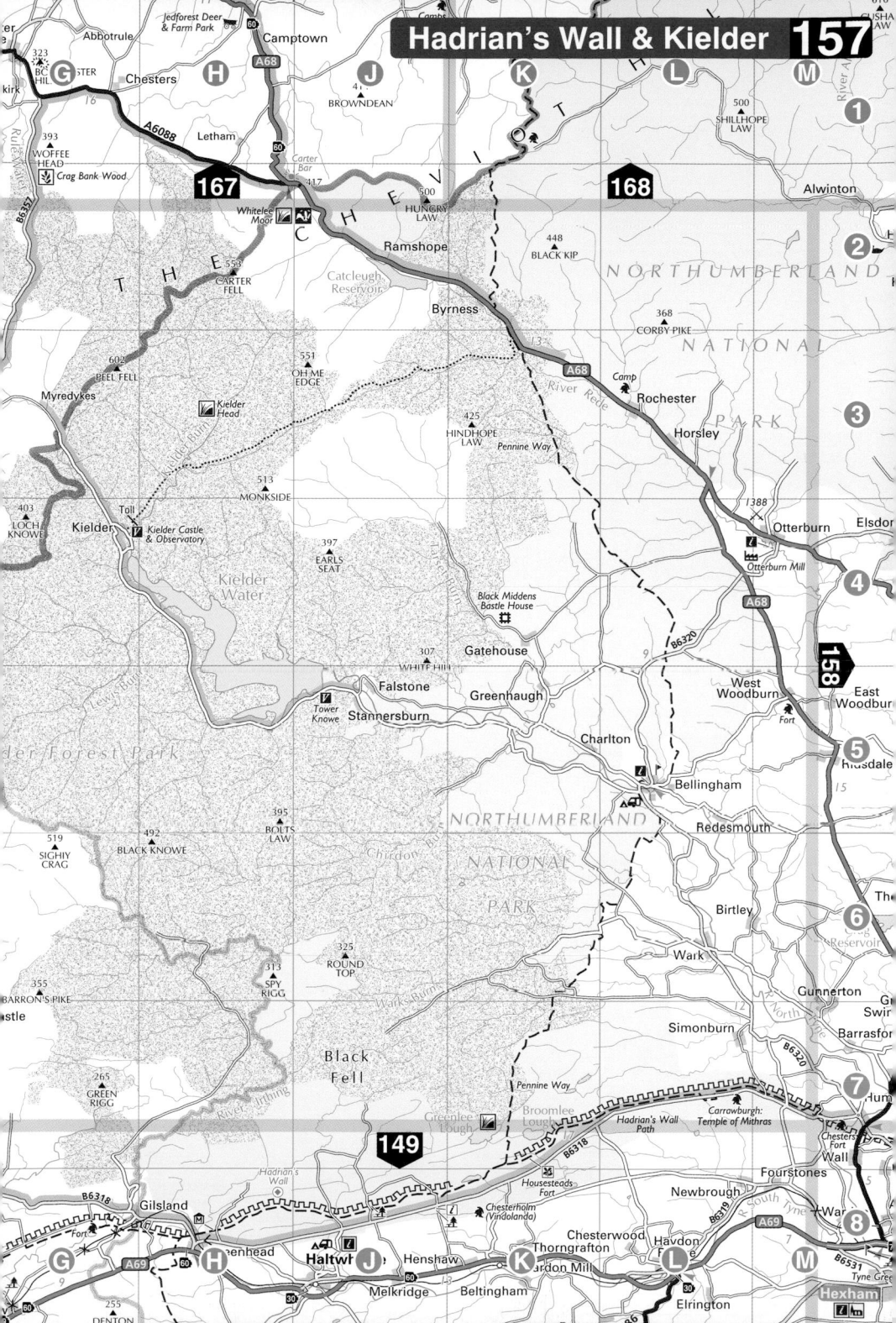

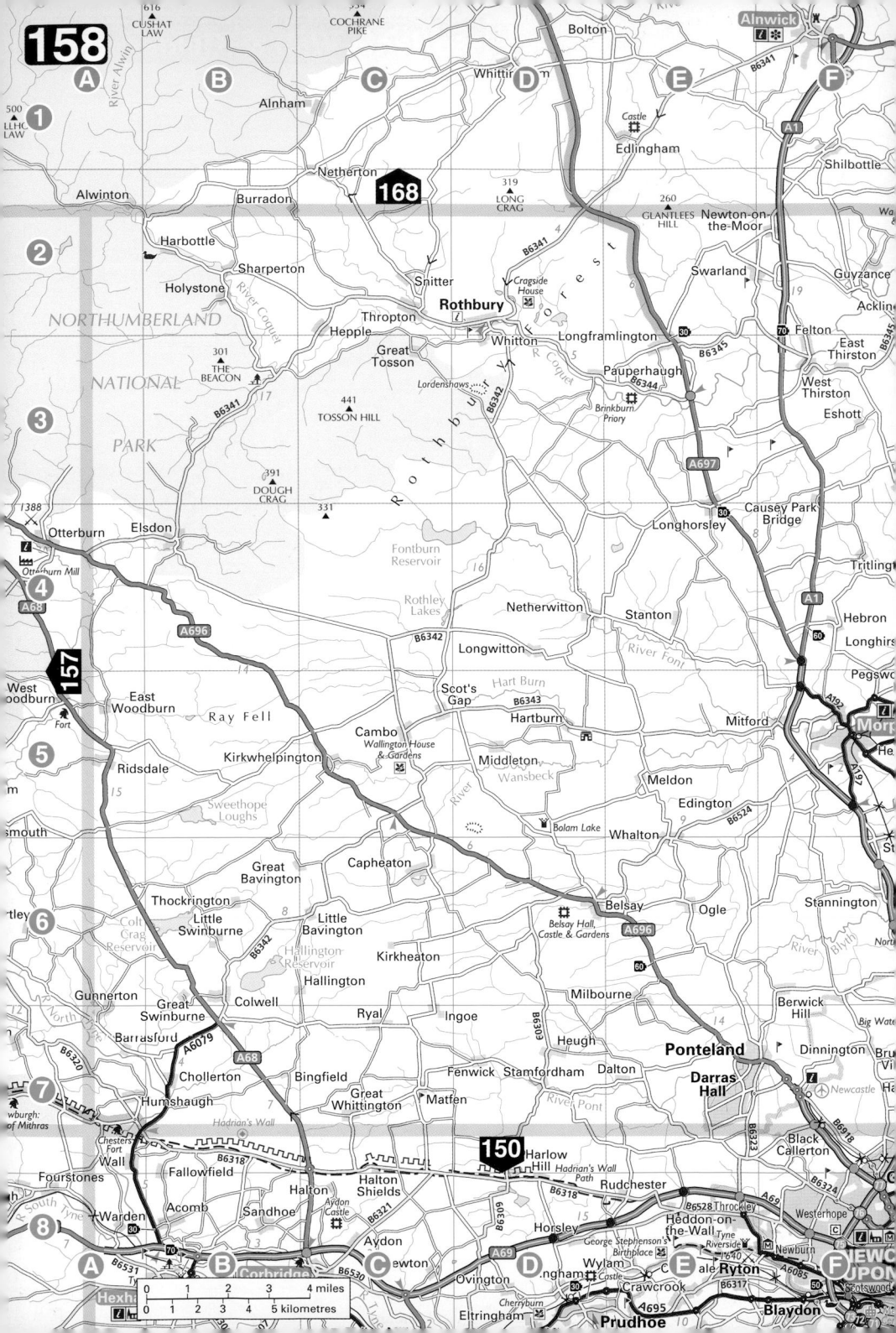

A B C D E F

616
CUSHAT
LAW

1
500
LLHO
LAW

River Alwin

COCHRANE
PIKE

Bolton

B6341

Alnwick

Alnham

Whitti

Netherton

168

Castle
Edlingham

2
Alwinton

Burradon

319
LONG
CRAG

B6341

260
GLANTLEES
HILL

Newton-on-
the-Moor

A1

Shilbottle

Harbottle

Sharperton

Snitter

Cragside
House

Rothbury

Swarland

Guyzance

NORTHUMBERLAND

Holystone

River Coquet

Hepple

Thro, ton

Whitton

Longframlington

Acklin

Felton

B6345

East
Thirston

3
NATIONAL

301
THE
BEACON

B6341

Great
Tosson

441
TOSSON HILL

Lordenshaws

Pauperhaugh

B6344

Brinkburn
Priory

West
Thirston

Eshott

PARK

391
DOUGH
CRAG

331

Fontburn
Reservoir

R Coquet

A697

Causey Park
Bridge

A1

Tritling

4
1388

Otterburn

Elsdon

Rothley
Lakes

Netherwitton

Longhorsley

Hebron

Longhirs

A68

Ottriburn Mill

A696

B6342

Longwitton

Stanton

River Font

Pegswo

Fort

5
West
oodburn

East
Woodburn

Ray Fell

Kirkwhelpington

Scot's
Gap

Hart Burn

B6343

Hartburn

Middleton

Wansbeck

Meldon

Mitford

Edington

B6524

Mor

He

157

Ridsdale

Sweethope
Loughs

Cambo
Wallington House
& Gardens

River

Whalton

St

6
Thockrington

Great
Bavington

Capheaton

Bolam Lake

Belsay
Belsay Hall,
Castle & Gardens

Ogle

Stannington

Berwick
Hill

Big Wate

tley

Gunnerton

Colt
Crag
Reservoir

Little
Swinburne

B6342

Little
Bavington

Hallington
Reservoir

Kirkheaton

Hallington

A696

Milbourne

River Blyth

Dinnington

Bru
Vi

7
wburgh:
of Mithras

Great
Swinburne

Colwell

Ryal

Ingoe

B6309

Heugh

Ponteland

Darras
Hall

Newcastle

B6320

Barrasford

A6079

A68

Chollerton

Bingfield

Great
Whittington

Fenwick

Stamfordham

Dalton

River Pont

Black
Callerton

B9918

B6324

Westerhope

Humshaugh

Hadrian's Wall

Chesters
Fort

150

Harlow
Hill
Hadrian's Wall
Path

Rudchester

B6528 Throckley

A69

Newburn

C

8
Fourstones

Wall

Fallowfield

B6318

Halton

Aydon
Castle

Halton
Shields

B6321

B6318

Horsley

B6309

A69

Heddon-on-
the-Wall
Tyne
Riverside

George Stephenson's
Birthplace

Wylam

Ryton

B6317

Spotswo

R South Tyne

Warden

Acomb

Sandhoe

Aydon

ewton

gham

Castle

ale

Blaydon

NEWC
UPON

A B C D E F

Hexha

Corbridge

B6530

Ovington

Crawcrook

Prudhoe

Eltringham

Cherryburn

A695

0 1 2 3 4 miles
0 1 2 3 4 5 kilometres

Lesbury
Seaton Point
G
H
J
K
L
M
1

A1068
8

169

Alnmouth
Alnmouth
Bay
Castle
Heritage
Warkworth

Gloster Hill
Amble
Coquet Island
2

High
Hauxley

Togston

B1339
30
Broomhill
South
Coombhill
Druridge Bay
3
Red Row
Druridge
Bay
swood
Widdrington
8
North Northumberland
Heritage Coast

Widdrington
Station
Cresswell
A1068
Ulgham
Ellington
4
Lynemouth
A189
Beacon Point
A1068
Woodhorn
Ashington
A197
Kirst
H
A197
30
Newbiggin-by-the-Sea
Bothal
Wansbeck
Riverside
A196
Guide Post
B1334
Stakeford
5
ppington
30
30
7
Bedlington
B1331
B1331
A193
C
Blyth
gton A1068
Cowpen
B1505
Newsham
A189
30
A192
A1061
A193
6
Cramlington
A192
New
Hartley
A190
30
Seaton
Sluice
S
50
B1326
**Seaton
Delaval**
A192
St. Mary's Lighthouse
C
A19
B1325
Dudley
A192
B1322
Earsdon
A1148
**Whitley
Bay**
7
Wide
Open
A186
Killingworth
B1317
Monkseaton
Cullercoats
Forest
Hall
A191
Shiremoor
H
A193
Tynemouth
B1318
Rising
Sun
C
A189 1058
South
Gosforth
C
North
Shields
Tynemouth Priory
& Castle
151
Amsterdam
(IJmuiden)
orth
Jesmond
50
Willington
Quay
A187
8
Wallsend
A187
Heaton
A1058
Jarrow
Int. Ferry
Terminal
Westoe
A183
**SOUTH
SHIELDS**
Marsden
Bay
TLE
NE
Walker
B1313
Tyne Tunnel
Souter Lighthouse
G
Byker
Hepburn
H
J
K
L
M
swick
A184
Monkton
Marsden
Souter Point
ston
40
West
Boldon
B1298
Cleadon
A183
Whitburn

BEINN SHOLUM

Eilean
a' Chuirn

Rudha Mòr

Port Ellen · Kennacraig

Rudha na
Gainmhich

165
MAOL BUIDHE

Port
Ellen

A846

Ardbeg

Lagavulin

THE OA

Laphroaig
Distillery

3
Laphroaig

ISLAY

Texa

Lower
Killeyan

Risabus

Kinnabus

Loch
Kinnabus

American
Monument

MULL
OF OA

Rudha nan Leacan

Earadale

MULL
OF
KINTY

0   1   2   3   4 miles
0 1 2 3 4 5 kilometres

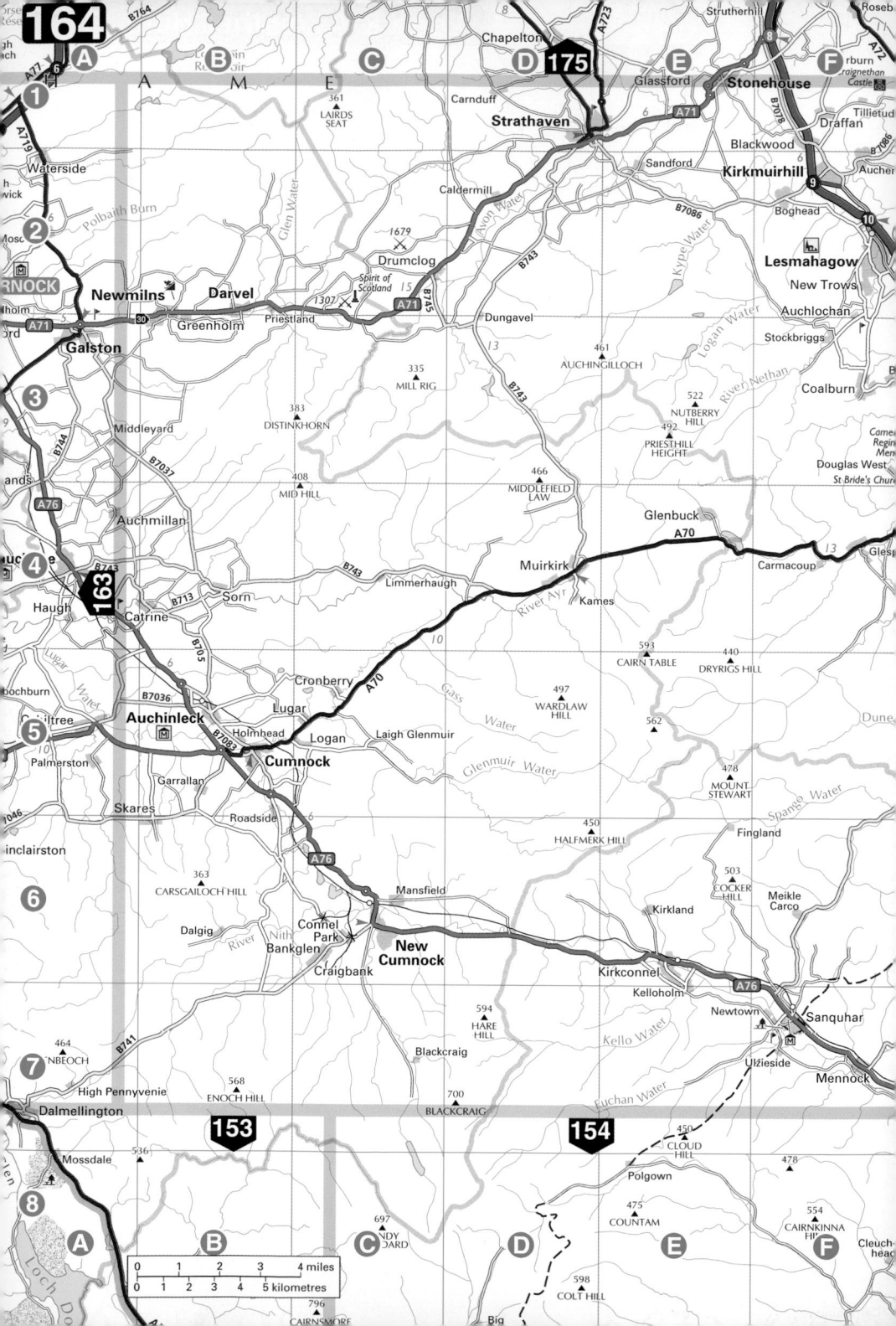

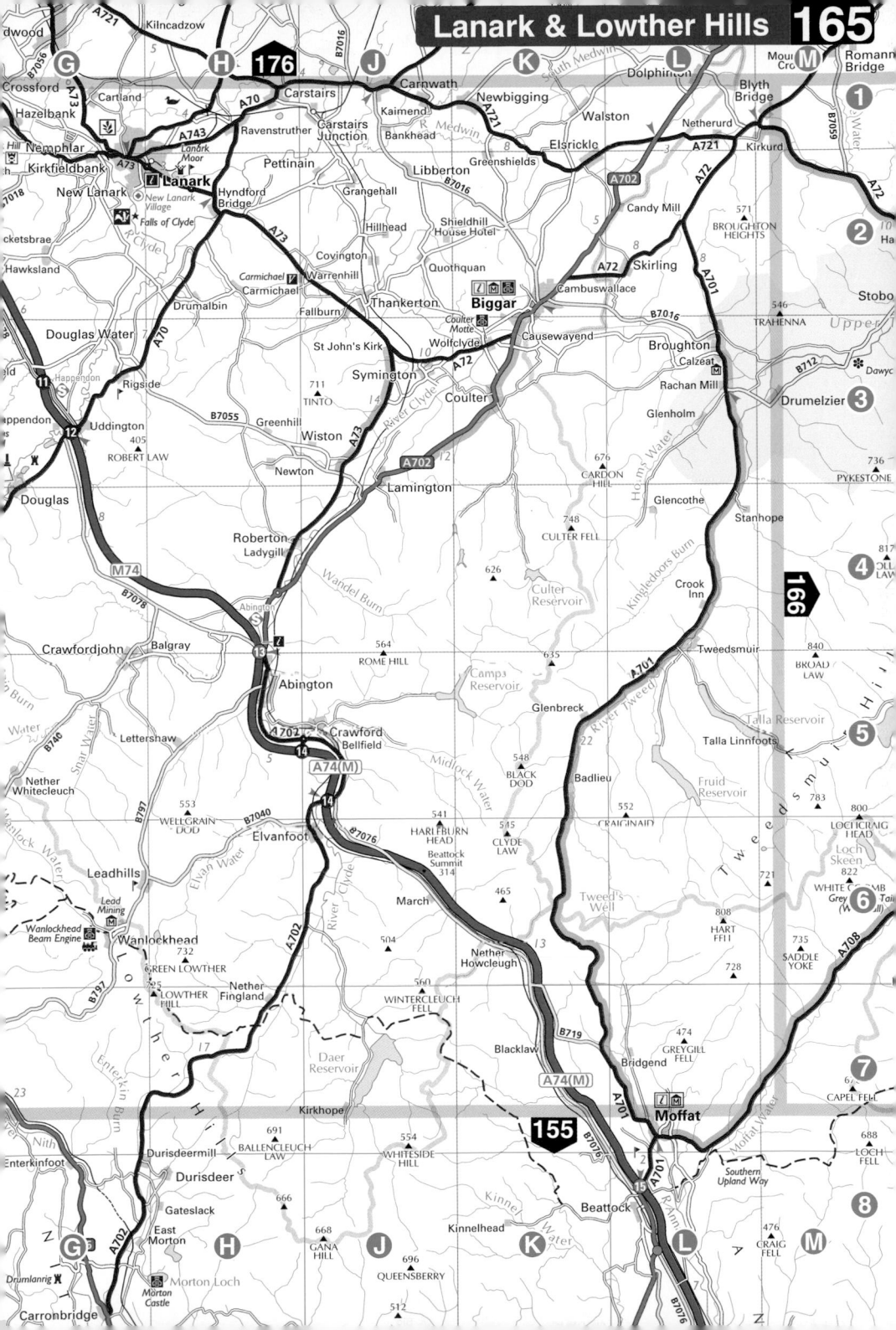

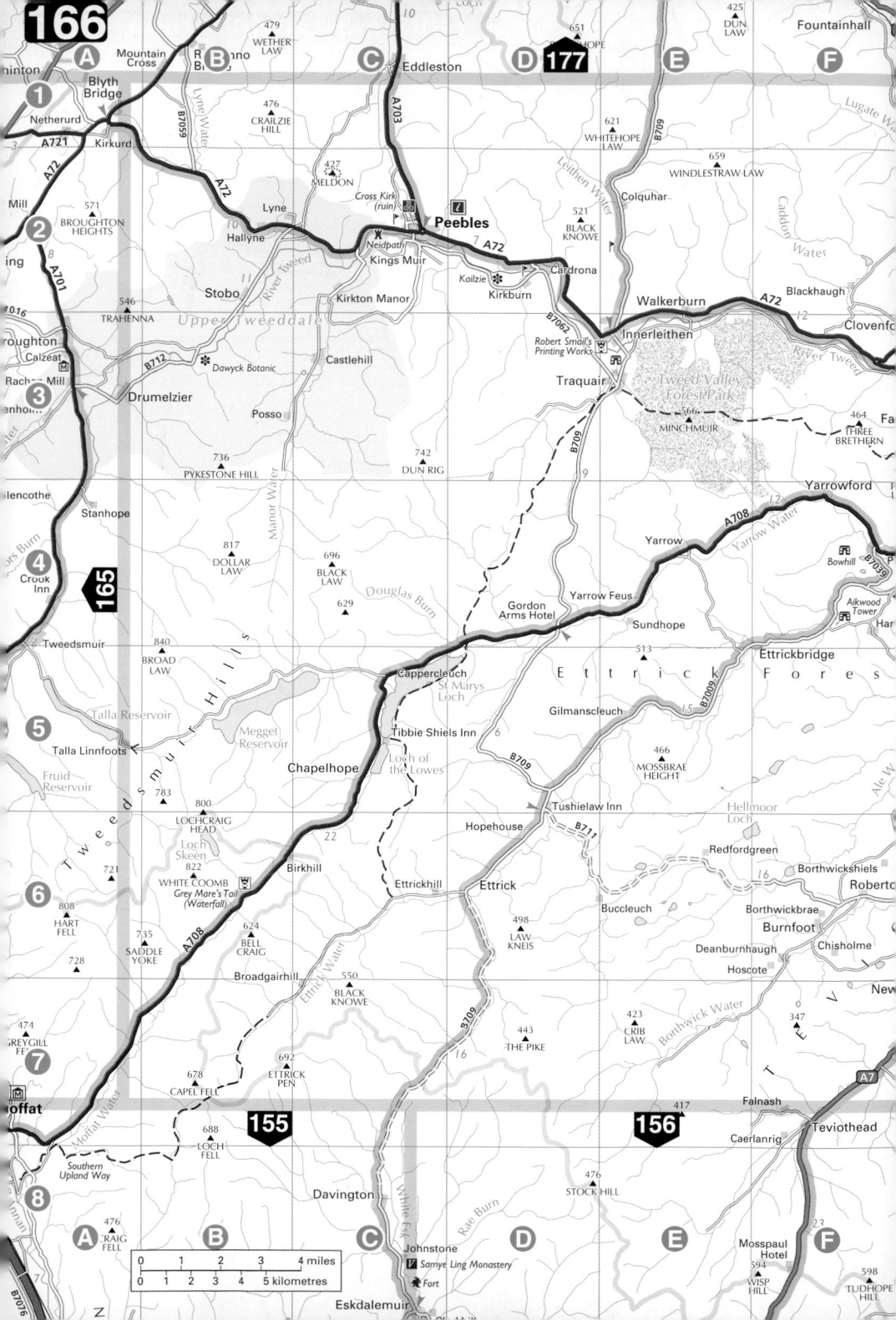

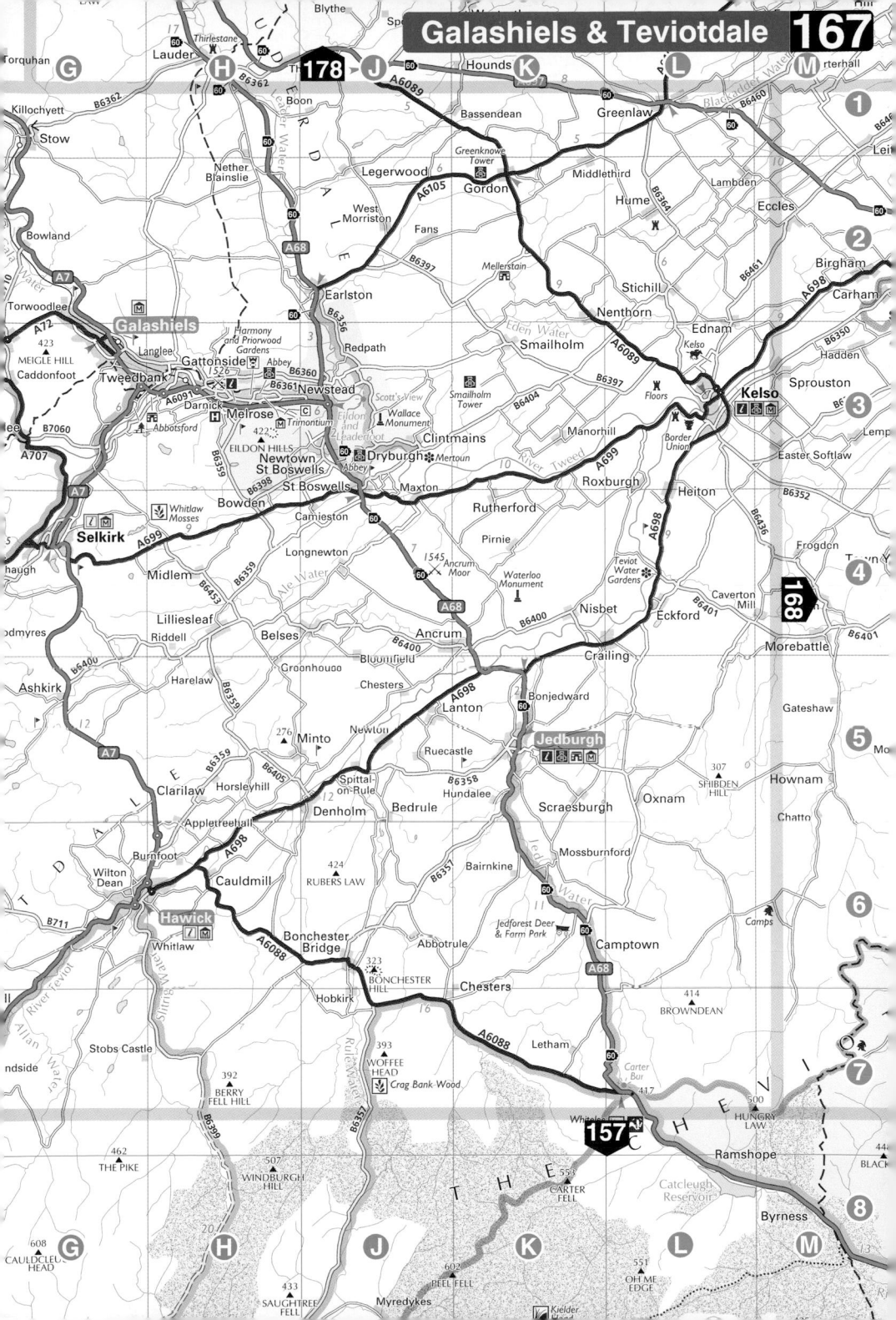

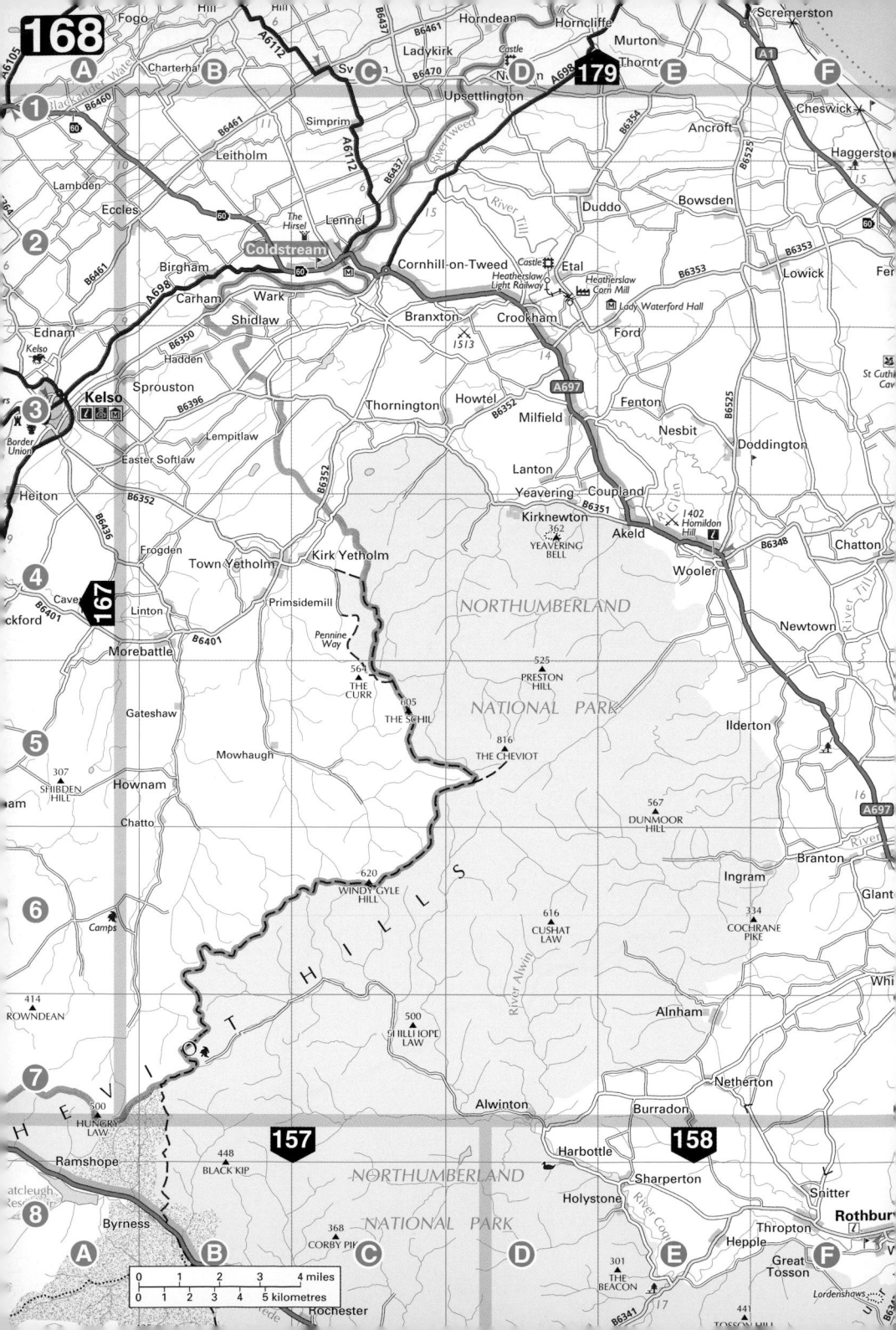

CAUSEWAY FLOODED AT HIGH TIDE

HOLY ISLAND

Holy Island

Lindisfarne Priory
Lindisfarne Castle
Castle Point
Guile Point

Beal

Longstone Lighthouse

FARNE ISLANDS

Staple Sound

Inner Sound

North Northumberland Heritage Coast

Budle Bay

Bamburgh
B1342
Bamburgh
B1340

Belford

B6349

Seahouses

North Sunderland

Lucker
B1341
60

Warenford

A1

Beadnell

Swinhoe

Chathill
Tughall
B1340

Newstead
Ellingham
Preston

Wild Cattle Park

Ros Castle

267
CATERAN HILL

Preston Pele Tower

Christon Bank

Embleton & Newton Links

Embleton

Newton-by-the-Sea

Beadnell Bay

Old Bewick

B6346

North Charlton

South Charlton
Falloden
B6347

Rock

60

Embleton Bay

Dunstanburgh Castle

Dunstan

Craster

Eglingham

B6341

B6341

Rennington

Stamford

Howick Hall

Howick

Cullernose Point

Beanley

Bolton

B6346

River Aln

Denwick

Longhoughton

Boulmer

Alnwick

Seaton Point

burn

Lesbury

Alnmouth

Castle
Edlingham

B6341

A1

Shilbottle

A1068

Alnmouth Bay

260
GLANTLEES HILL

Newton-on-the-Moor

Warkworth Castle & Hermitage

Warkworth

159

Amble
Coquet Island

B6341

Swarland

19

Guyzance

Gloster Hill

High Hauxley

gside ouse

Acklington

Togston

amlington
80
B63

Felton
70

Pauperhaugh

B6344

Brinkburn

East Thirston

West Thirston

South Broomhill

Red Row

Broomhill
30

Drudge Bay

1

2

3

Dubh Eilean

ISLAY

Nave Island

Ardnave
Point

Gortantac
Point

4

Ton Mhòr

Kilnave

Eilean Mòr

Sanaigmore

Loch
Gruinart

Rudha Lamanais

Loch
Gòrr

Lecht Gruinart

B8017

B8018

Saligo Bay

B8017

Gruinart

Gleann Mòr

5

Loch
Gorm

Coul Point

Sunderland

B8018

Machir
Bay

Kilchoman

A847

Bruichladdich

Loch
Indaal

6

Kilchiaran Bay

15

Bowmore

Port
Charlotte

River Lag

231
BEINN TART A'MHILL

RHINNS

OF

ISLAY

Duich R.

A846

Lossit Bay

Nereabolls

7

Rudha na
Faing

A847

A847

Portnahaven

Port Wemyss

Islay

Orsay

RHINNS
POINT

Laggan
Bay

8

Rudha Mòr

Kintra

165
MAOL BU

THE O

0 1 2 3 4 miles

0 1 2 3 4 5 kilometres

Lower
Killeyan

Risabus

Scalasaig
B8086
Machrins
Colon
G
Garvard
Oronsay
Rudha
Bàn
ORONSAY
Eilean
Ghurdmail

H
Colonsay-Port Askaig

J

181

Coipach Bay
K

Glen Grundale
Lussa River
L
466
BEINN
BHREAC

M
Lea
1

Ardlussa
Lussa Point
Lussagiven
2

SHIAN Bay
453
RAINBERG MÒR

J U R A

Loch
Righ Mòr
A846

3
Keills Ch
Loch Cille
Da
Isla

Rudh' ant-Sàilein

Loch Tarbert

St Cormac's
Chapel
Kilmory Kna
Chapel
Kilmory Ba

Rudha
Bholsa
Rudha' a' Mhàil
363
SGARBH
BREAC
506
SCRINADLE
398
BEINN
TARSUINN

24
Knockrome
Ardfernal
4
Point Knap

Bunnahabhain
316
GUIR-
BHEINN
Loch a'
Chnuic Bhric
Jura Forest
784
BEINN
AN OIR
734
Paps of Jura
J u r a

5
Kilb
Sculp
Sta
Kilberry He
Keppoch Po

Port Askaig
Kiells
Finlaggan
Loch
Finlaggan
Feolin Ferry
560
GLASS BHEINN
529
DUBHA
BHEINN
Keils
Craighouse
Small
Isles
A846

172

Ballygrant
Loch
Ballygrant
Loch
Lossit
266
BEINNE
DUBH
342
BRAT
BHEINN
Cabrach
Rudha na Gaillich

A846
ridgend
Gartachossan
Kilennan Burn
429
SGORR NAM
FAOILEANN
471
Am-Fraoch
Eilean
Brosdale
Island
Rudha na Tràille

McArthur's
Head

6

490
BEINN BHEIGEIR
Port Askaig - Kennacraig

454
BEINN URARAIDH
Loch Uraraidh
Rudha Liath
Ardtalla
Claggain
Bay

Kinerar
7
Tarbert
GIGHA

edale
Kintour
Kildalton
Cross
346
BEINN SHOLUM
Ardmore
Point
Eilean
a' Chuirn

Port Ellen - Kennacraig

Ardminish
Achamore
Rhunahaorin
Point

G
Port
en
A846
Lagavulin
Laphroaig
Distillery
Laphroaig
Texa
Ar
H
Rudha na
Gainn

160

J

K

L

Tayinloan
8

M

Cara

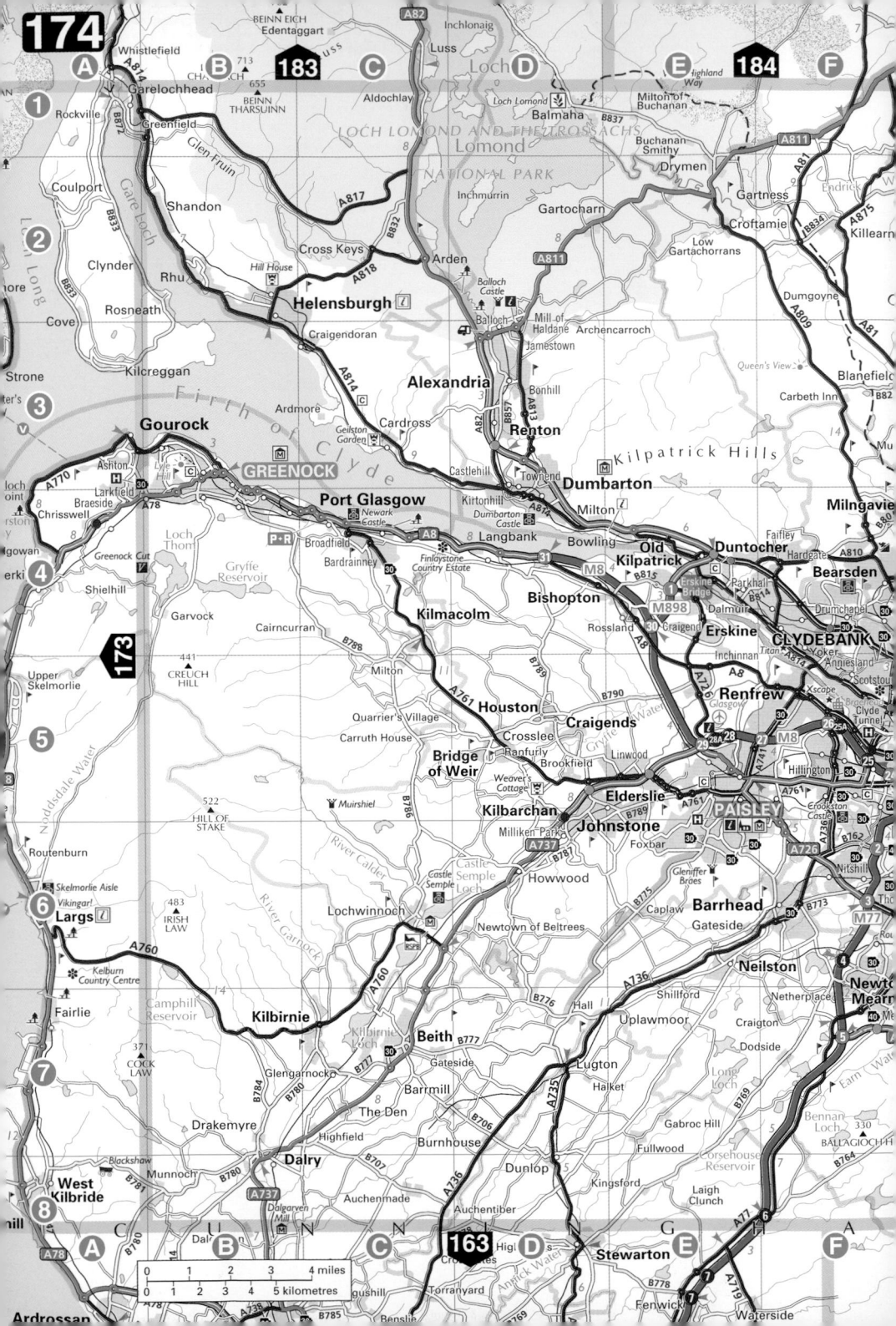

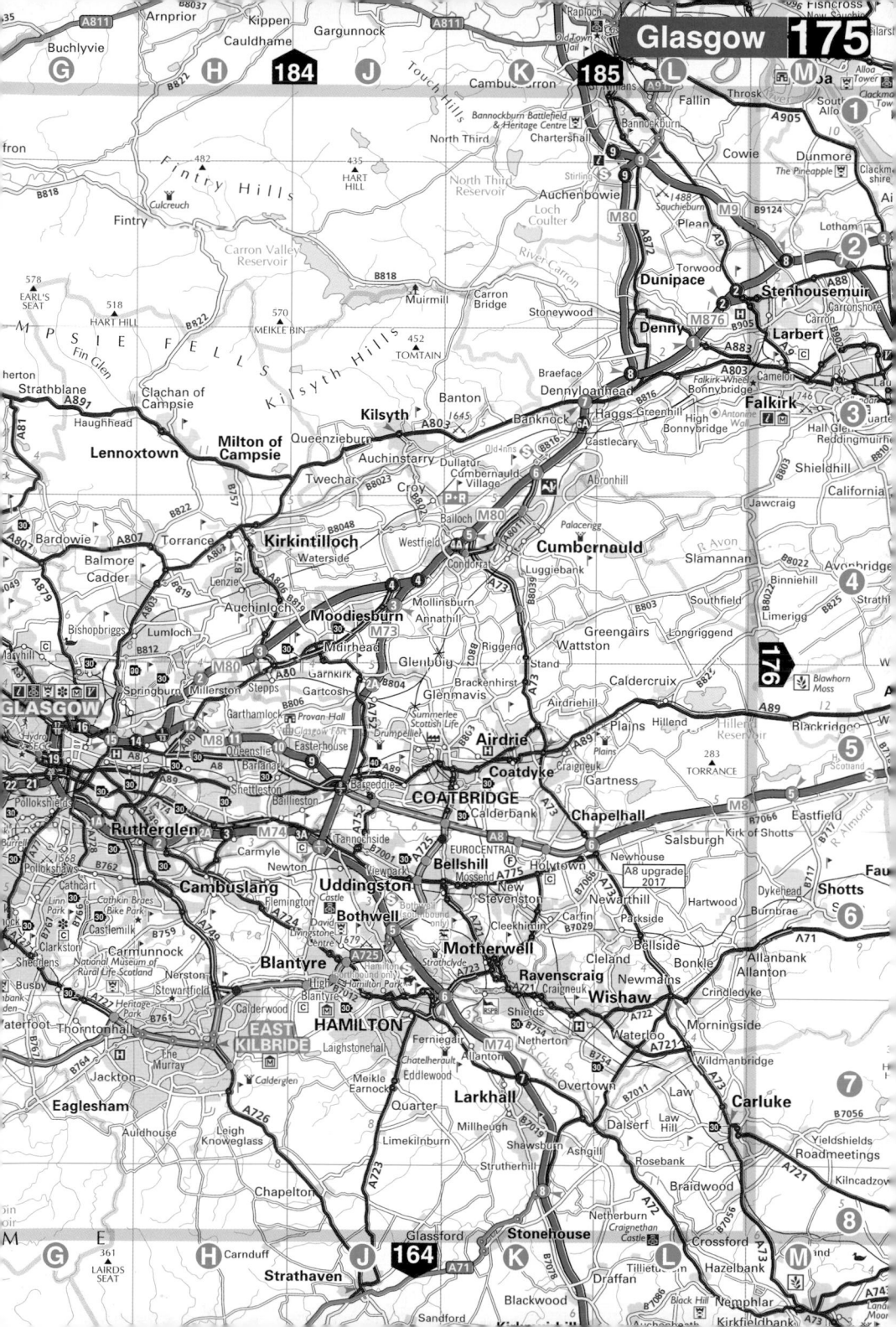

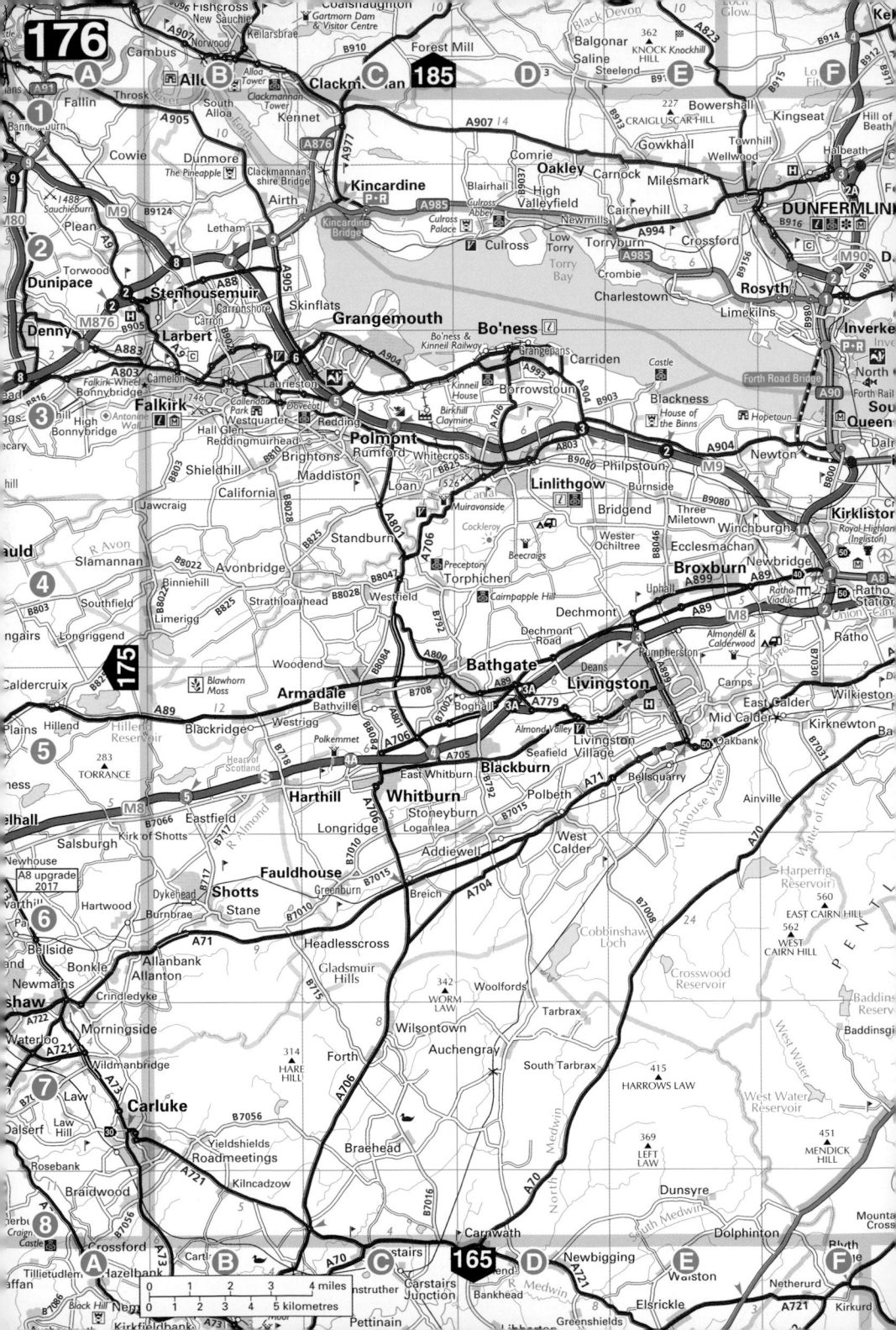

G   H   J   K   L   M

① ② ③ ④ ⑤ ⑥ ⑦ ⑧

loch

Reed Point
Cove Pease Bay
Siccar Point
Fast Castle Head
rnspath
A1107
Pease Dean
196
ST ABB'S HEAD
BROWN RIG
Coldingham Loch
St Abbs
Grantshouse
Coldingham
Coldingham Bay
Southern Upland Way
Butterdean
B6438
A1107 22
Fye Water
21
Houndwood
Heugh Head
Cairncross
Eyemouth
uixwood
262
HORSELEY HILL
A1
Ayton
B6355
Burnmouth
din's
l Broch
14
B6438
Reston
Auchencrow
URN
Marygold
Lamberton
Lintlaw
A6112
70
Marshall Meadows Bay
North Northumberland Heritage Coast
ehill
Preston
Cumledge
Edrom Church
B6355
Chirnside
B6437
B6355
Foulden
1333
B6365
Edrom
Chirnsidebridge
Foulden Tithe Barn
A6105
Berwick-upon-Tweed
Manderston
Broadhaugh
Edington
Whiteadder Water
Castle
Barracks
M
A6105
Allanton
Hutton
Town Ramparts
Duns
Blackadder
B6437
Paxton
70
Tweedmouth
B6460
Paxton
B6461
Whitsome
B6460
Hilton
Spittal
Nisbet Hill
Sinclair's Hill
13
Horndean
Horncliffe
Huds Head
A6112
Ladykirk
Murton
Scremerston
A1
charterhall
Swinton
B6461
Castle
Norham
Thornton
B6470
A698
Cheswick
CAUSEWAY FLOODED AT HIGH TIDE

G   H   J   K   L   M

B6461
Simprim
A6112
Upsettlington
168
B6354
Ancroft
Leitholm
River Tweed
B437
Haggerston
B6525

1

ULVA

Bac Mòr or Dutchmans Cap

⬧eag

Staffa

Fingal's Cave

Little Colonsay

Loch na Keal
Isle of Mull

Inch Kenneth
Inchkenneth Chapel
(ruin)

2

491
CREACH BHEINN

Fossil Tree

Burg

3

Loch

Rudha nan Cearc

IONA

Iona Abbey
& Nunnery

Baile Mòr

Kintra

MacLean's Cross

Sound of Iona

Loch na Lathaich

Fionnphort

(Mar–
Oct)

A849

Aridhglas

376
CRUACH
MIN

St Columba
Exhibition
Centre

Bunessan

Loch Assapol

ROSS OF MULL

4

Soa Island

Erraid

Ardchiavaig

Uisken

Rudha
Braithe

Rudha
Ardalanish

5

Torran Rocks

6

7

Eilean
Dubh

Kiloran Bay

Balnahard

Rudh' a'

COLONSAY

Kiloran

Kilchattan

B8087

Scalasaig

B8086

Machrins

Colonsay

B8085

8

Ⓐ   Ⓑ   Ⓒ   Ⓓ   **171**   Gar   Ⓔ   Ⓕ

Oronsay

Rudha
Bàn

Dubh Eilean

0 1 2 3 4 miles
0 1 2 3 4 5 kilometres

Eorsa

Macquarie Mausoleum

BEINN NAN LUS

ISLE

G   H   190   J   K   L   M

5   BEINN A'... AIG

B8035 17

ahard

966
BEN
MORE

704
CRUACHAN
DEARG

OF

BEINN
MHEADHO

766
DUN DA
GHAOITHE

Craignure

Seallastle Bay

Rudha an
Ridire   Kilch

1

Duart
Bay   Duart
Point
Torosay   Duart

MULL

A849   17

Lochdonhead
Lochdon

Gorten

Grass Point

Strathcoil

247
CARN
BAN

KERRE

2

Tiroran

Aird of
Kinloch

A849

Loch-Fuaran

717
BEN
BUIE

698
BEN CREACH

Loch Don

Croggan

Rudha Seanach

3

Pennycross

Pennyghael

503
BEINN NA
CROISE

Lochbuie

Loch
Uisg

337
MAOL
BAN

Leidle Water

14

376
BEINN
CHREAGACH

Carsaig

Rudha
Dubh

Loch Buie

377
DRUIM
FADA

Malcolm's
Point

Insh
Island

Clachan

Clachan Seil

B844

SEIL

Ellenabeich

Easdale

Balvicar

Easdale

B8003

Cuan

4

182

Garbh Eileach

Eilean
Dubh Mòr

GARVELLACHS
Monastery & Beehive Cells

Eileach
an Naoimh

LUNGA

Scarba, Lunga

and the

Garvellachs

Cullipool

Torsa

LUING

Toberonochy

SHUNA

Shuna
Point

Degnish

Loch Melf

Arduai

Craobh
Haven

Craigd

5

6

Ardfe   K

SCARBA

448
CRUACH SCARBA

Gulf of Corryvreckan

Aird

Craignish Point

Island
Macaskin

B8002

En M

En

Clackav
Wood
Circles

Ri Cruir
Poltal

7

Glengarrisdale
Bay

295
CRUACH NA
SEILCHEIG

Glendebadel Bay

JURA

364
BEN
GARRISDALE

Lussa River

Lealt Burn

Loch Crinan

Crinan

Kilmahumaig

Bellanoch

B8025
Cri

8

Corpach Bay

G   H   171   466
BEINI
BHREAC   J   len Grundale   K   L   172   M   Barnluasgan

Carsaig Bay

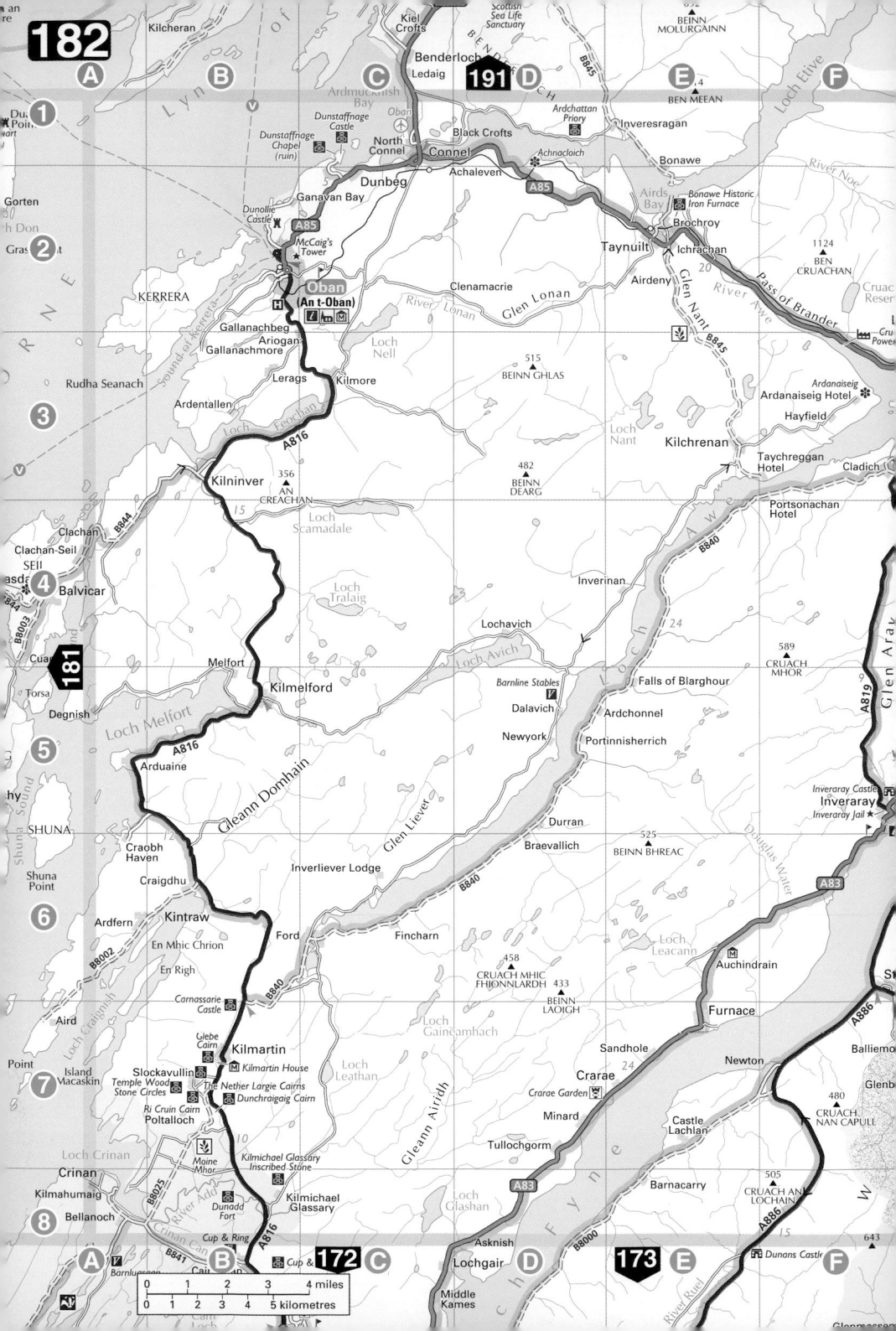

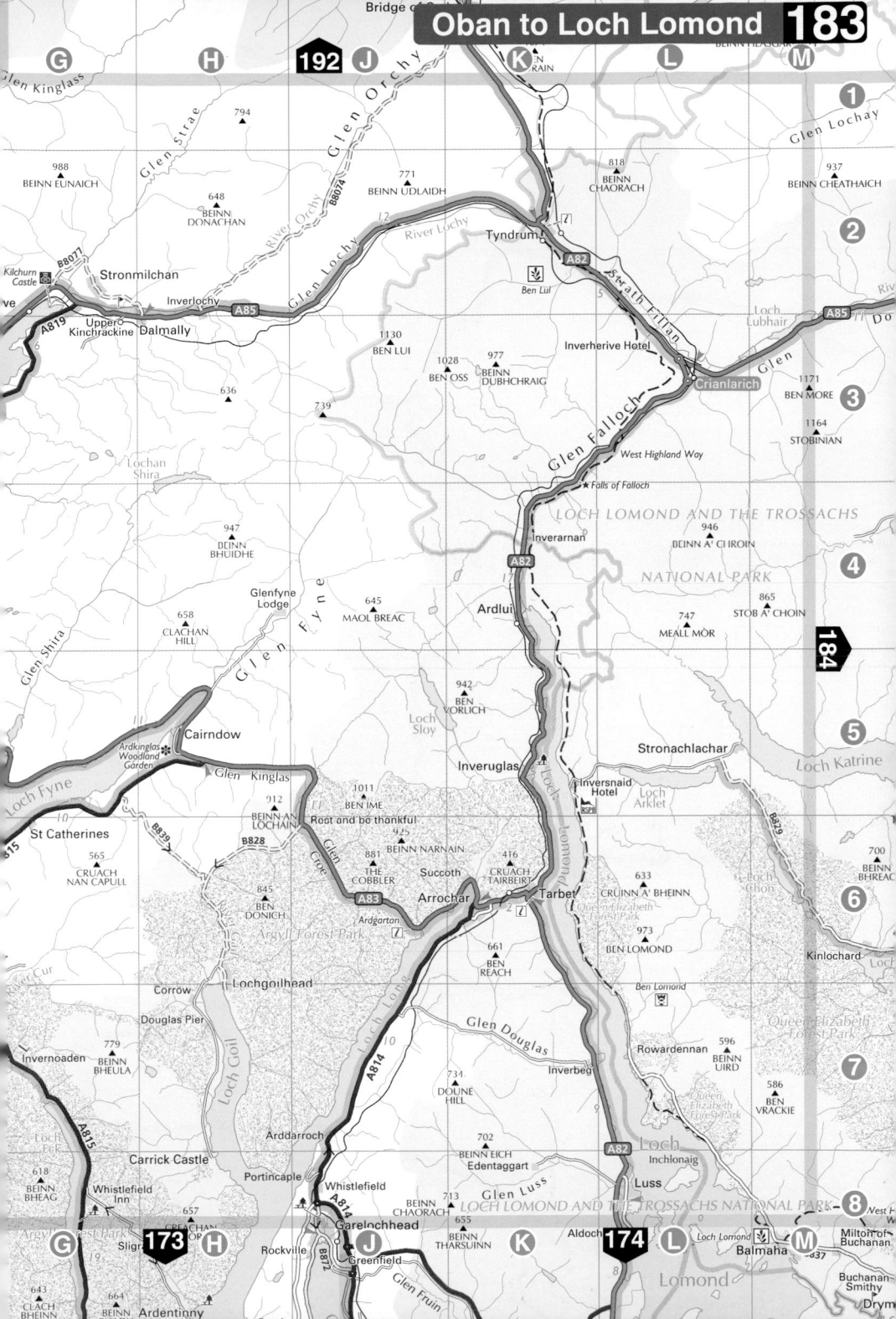

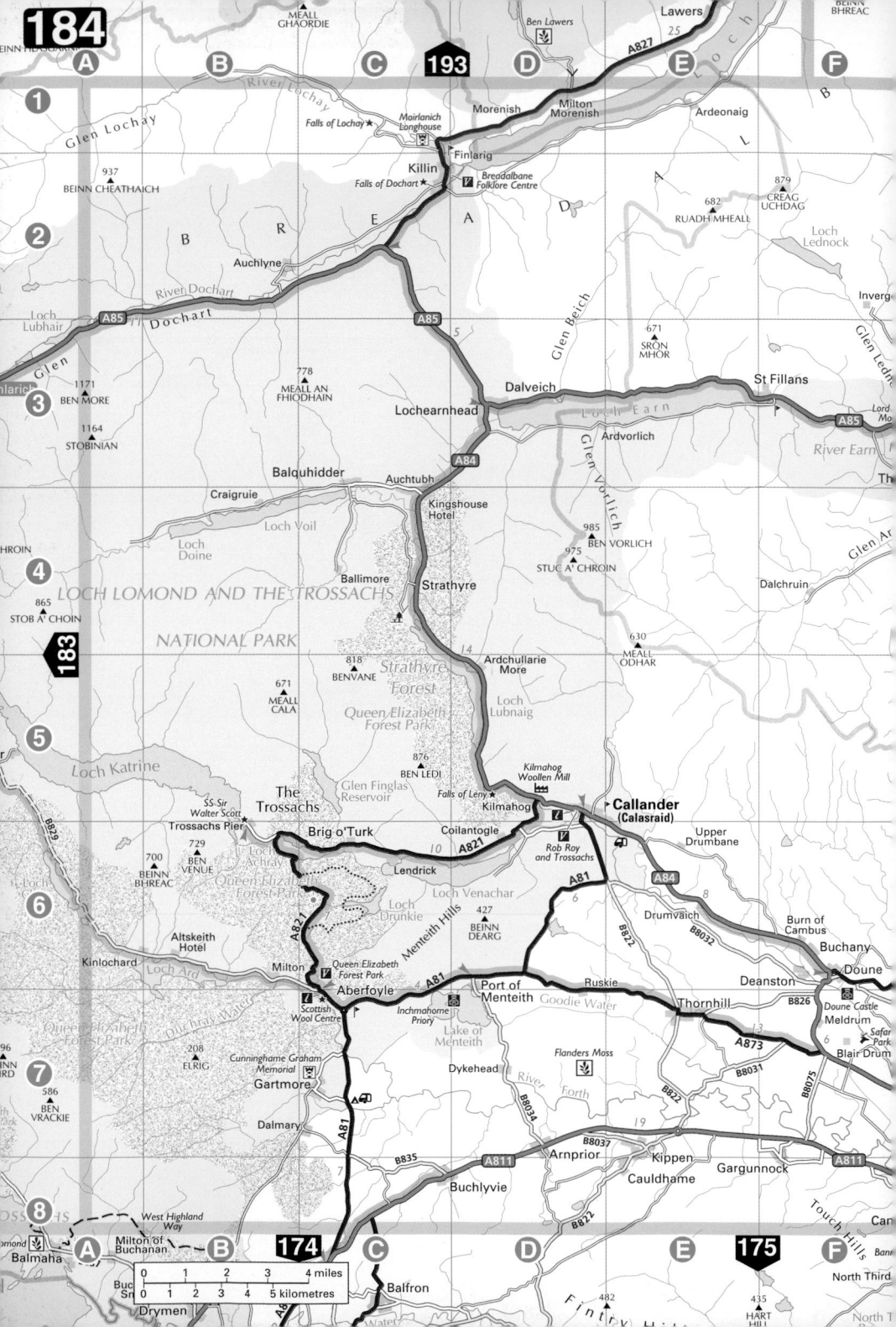

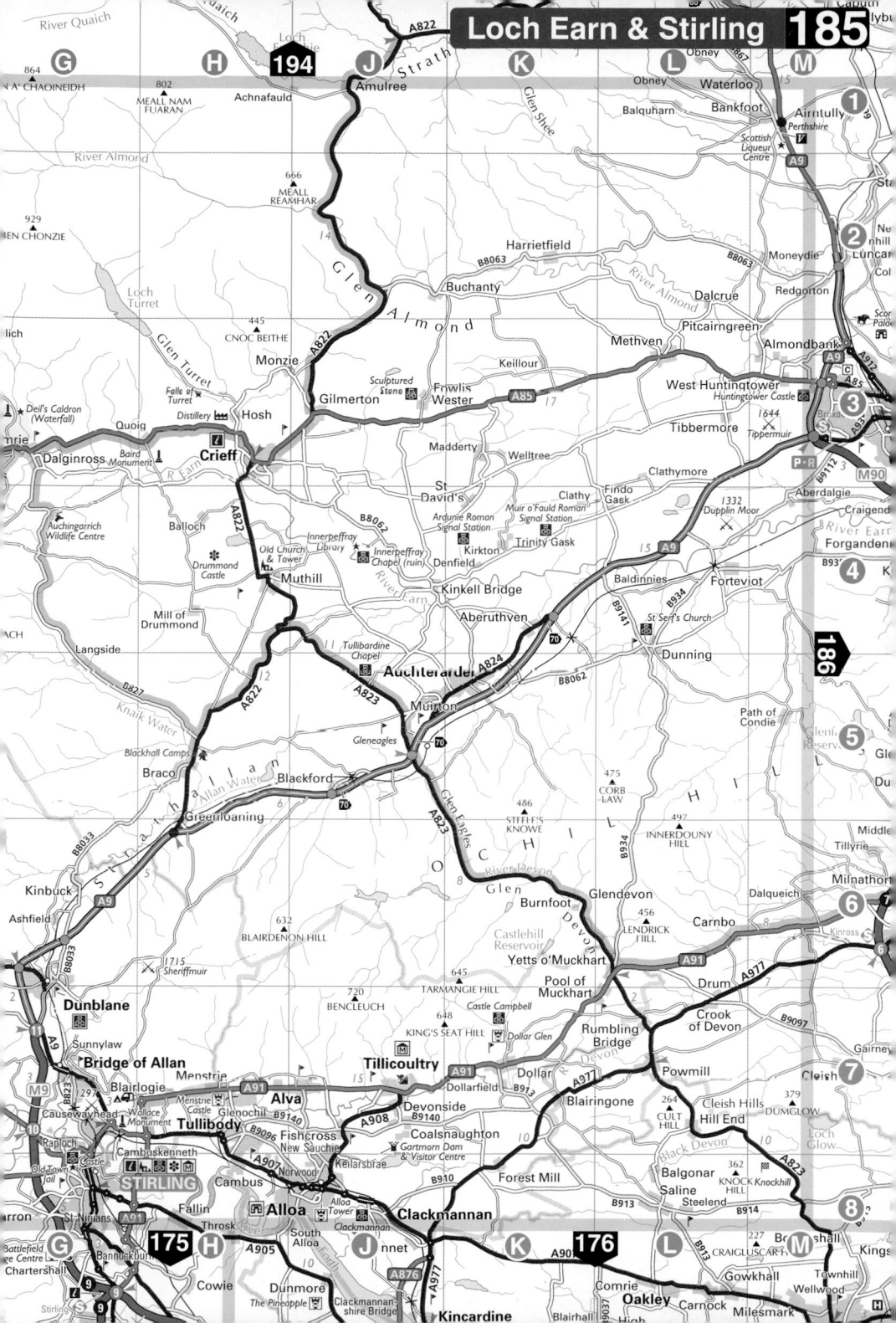

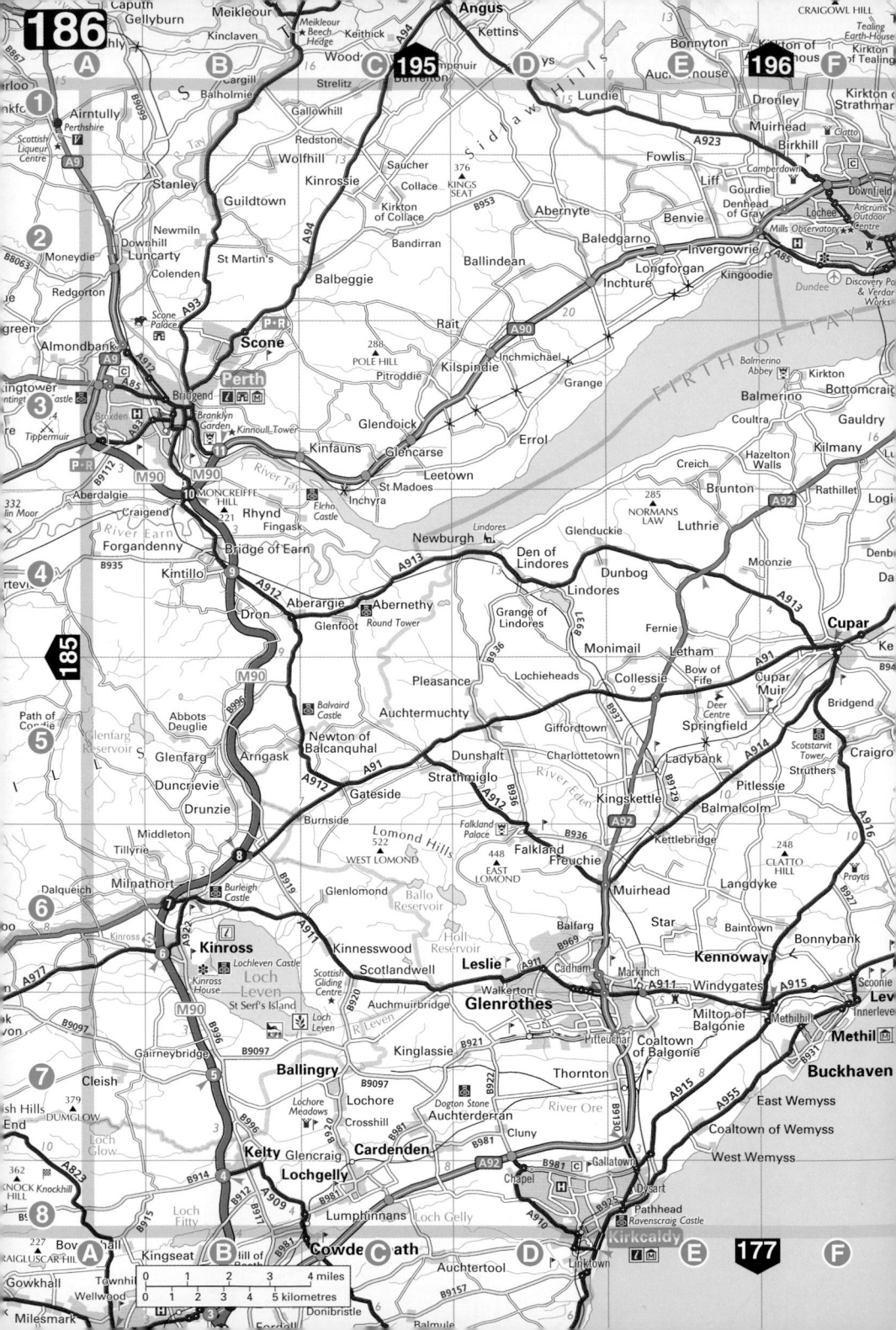

A B C D E F

1

2

3

4

Arnabos
Grishipoll
Clabhach   Loch
                  Cliac
              Ballyhaugh   Ar
Hogh Bay

Bagh a Chaisteil   Totronald
(Castlebay)   *Coll*
                                        Acha
5   Feall   Arileod
                               Bay   Uig

                    (Mar.Oct)   RSPB
                                                  Rudha
                    Calgary Point   Crossapol   Fàsachd
                                    Bay
              Gunna

6   Loch Bheachacha
                          Caoles
        Rudha Port   Clachan   Rudha Dubh
        Bhiosd   Mor   Balephetrish
                            Bay   B8069
                                    Ruaig
        Haugh   Loch   B8068
        Bay   Bhasapoll
        Ballevullin Cornoigmore   Kenovay   Gott
                                                   Bay
        Kilkenneth   *Tiree*
                            B8068
        Middleton   Moss   Heylipoll   B8065   Scarinish
7   Barrapoll   B8065   TIREE
                    B8067   Balemartine
              Loch a   Mannel
              Phuill
        Rinn
        Thorbhais   Hynish
              Balephuil
              Bay

8

A B C D E F

0   1   2   3   4 miles
0 1 2 3 4 5 kilometres

G   H   **198** J   K   L   M

1

2

393

Kildonnan

Eilean
nan Each

MUCK

Port Mor

of Eigg

C   L   tail

Ockle
Point

Sanna Point

Sanna
Bay

Sanna Bay

Achnaha

Kilmory

Ockle

Ru
D

3

Portuairk

Ardnamurchan
Point

Achosnich

MEALL NAN CON

436

Branault

ARDNAM

Bagh a Chaisteil
(Castlebay)
Loch Baghasdail
(Lochboisdale)

B8007

Loch
Mùdle

Eilean Mòr

Rudha
Mòr

Rudha
Sgor-innis

Sorisdale

Bousd

B8072

Kilchoan

Ormsaigmore

BEINN
NA SEILG

342

Mingary

527
BEN
HIANT

4

Ardslignish

Coll   Oban

Ardmore Point

Auliston
Point

Ord

COLL

Eilean
Ornsay

Sorne
Point

Quinish Point

Glengorm Castle

Tobermory

190

V

Calve
Island

Drim

5

Caliach Point

'S AIRDE
BEINN

292

Dervaig

Achnadrish House

A848

Sou

Calgary

B8073

5

6

SPEINNE MÒR

444

6

Calgary Bay

Treshnish Point

Ensay

CÀRN MÒR

342

ISLE

Loch Frisa

10

Rudh' a' Chaoil

Burg

OF

MULL

Glen Aros

Aro

Fladda

Fanmore

CNOC AN DÀ CHINN

390

Glenaros House

7

Lunga

Ballygown

Eas Fors (Waterfall)

BEINN
NAN CÀRN

333

Killiechronan

B8035

2

TRESHNISH
ISLES

Gometra

ULVA

Oskamull

B8073

Gruline

Macquarie
Mausoleum

Loch

Tuath

Loch na

Keal

Bac Mòr or Dutchmans Cap

Bac Beag

Little Colonsay

Eorsa

Loch na Keal,
Isle of Mull

BEINN A' GH

591

8

G   H   **180** J   K   L   M

Staffa

Fingal's Cave

Inch   neth

Inchkenneth Chapel
(ruin)

Balnahard

966

704

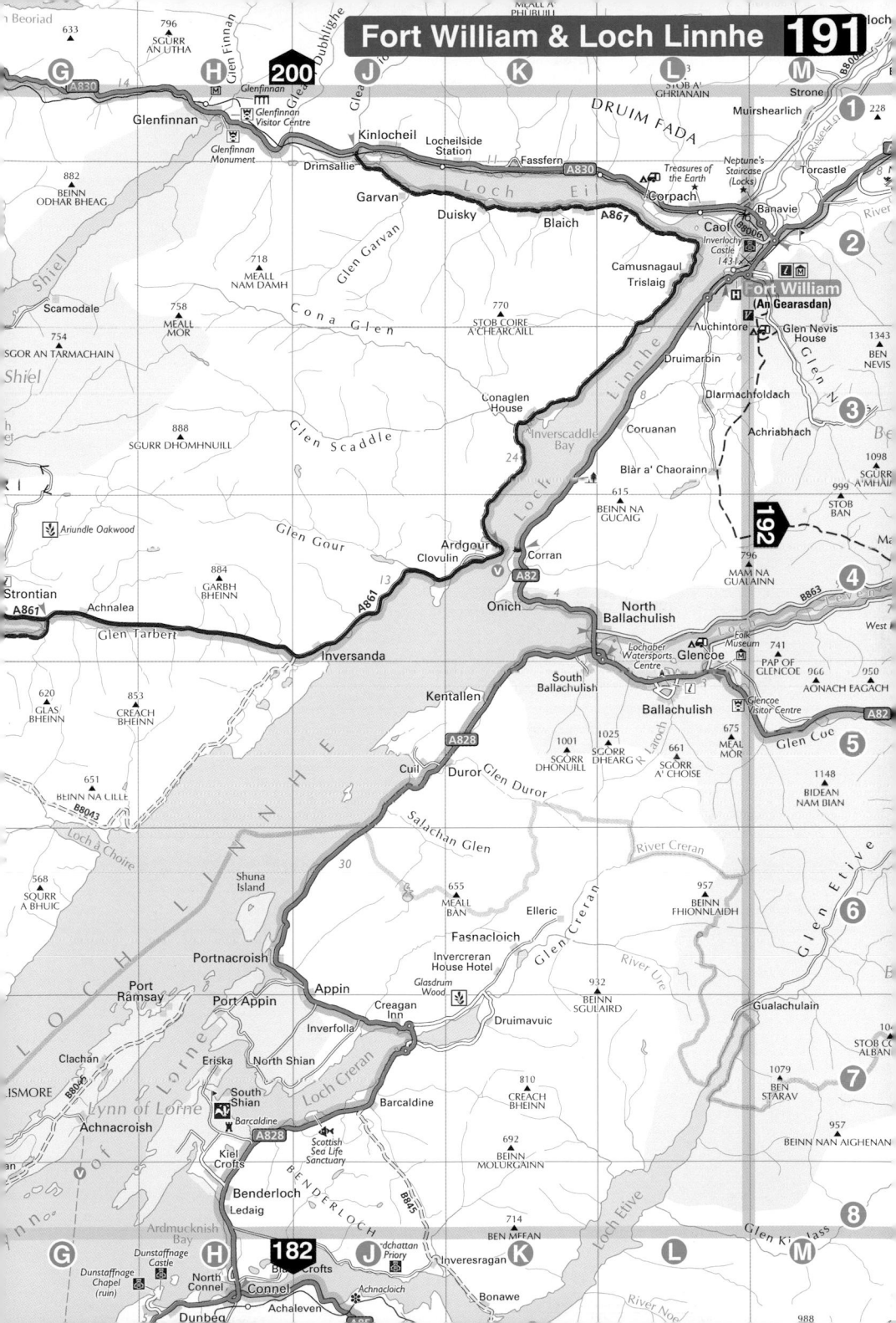

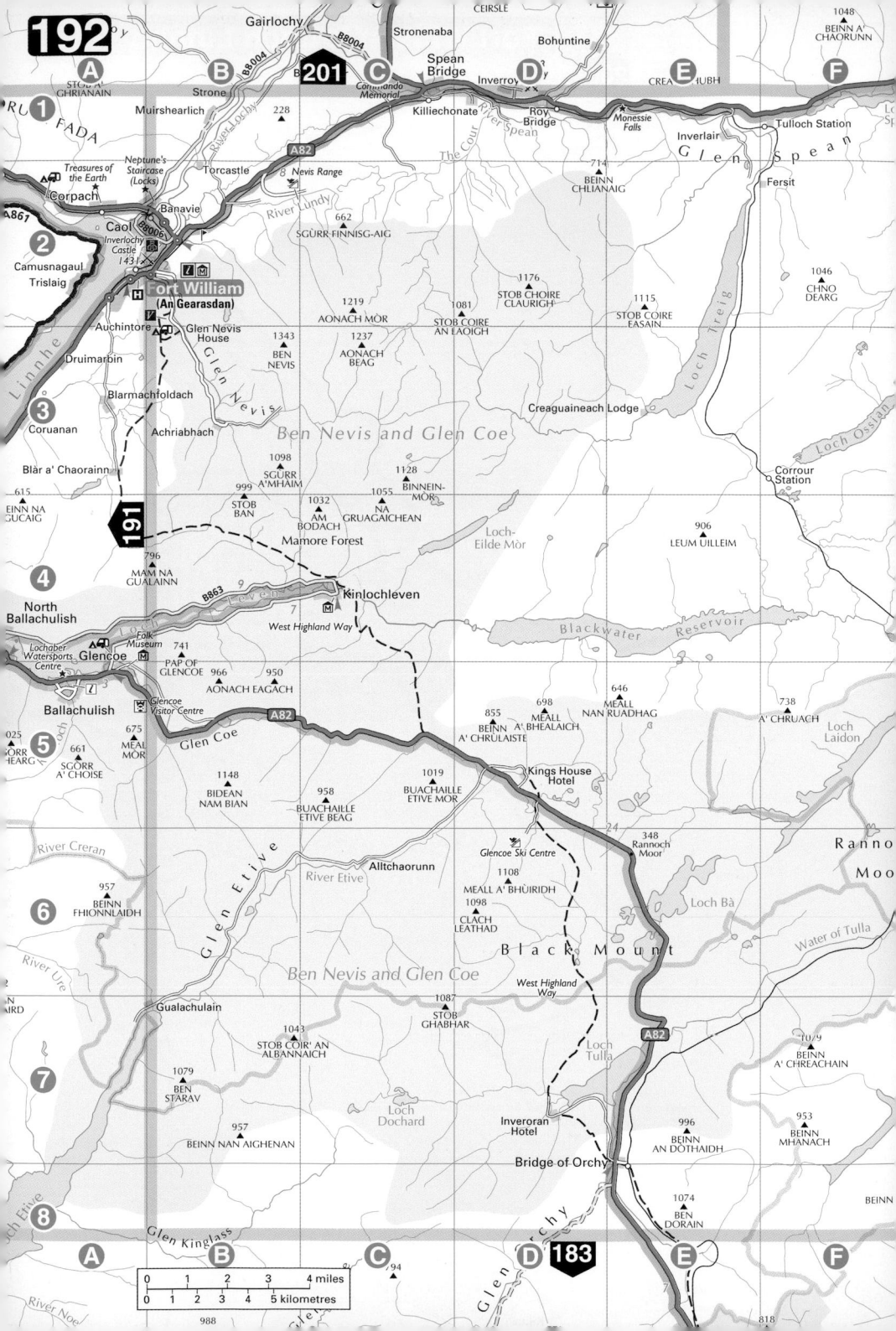

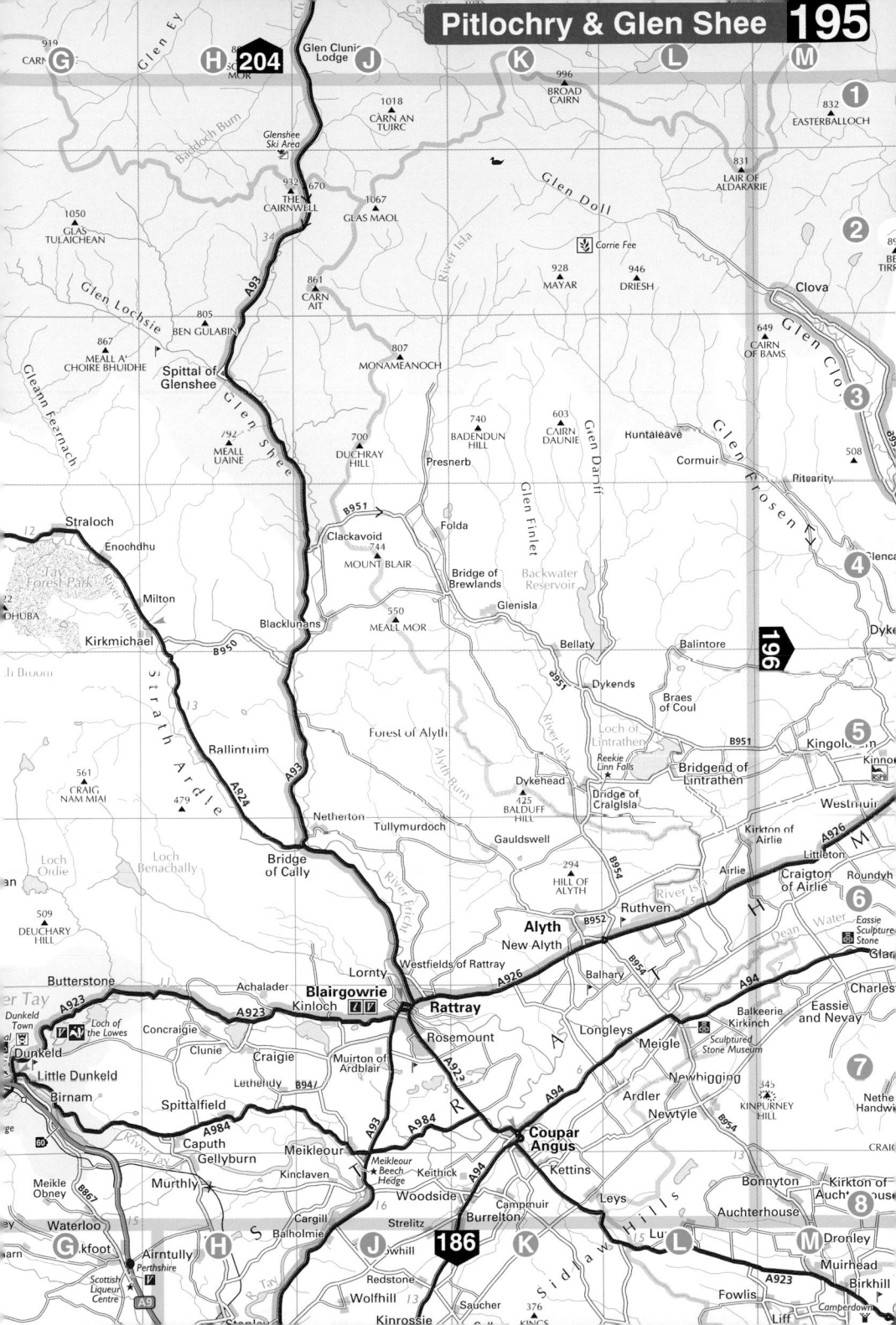

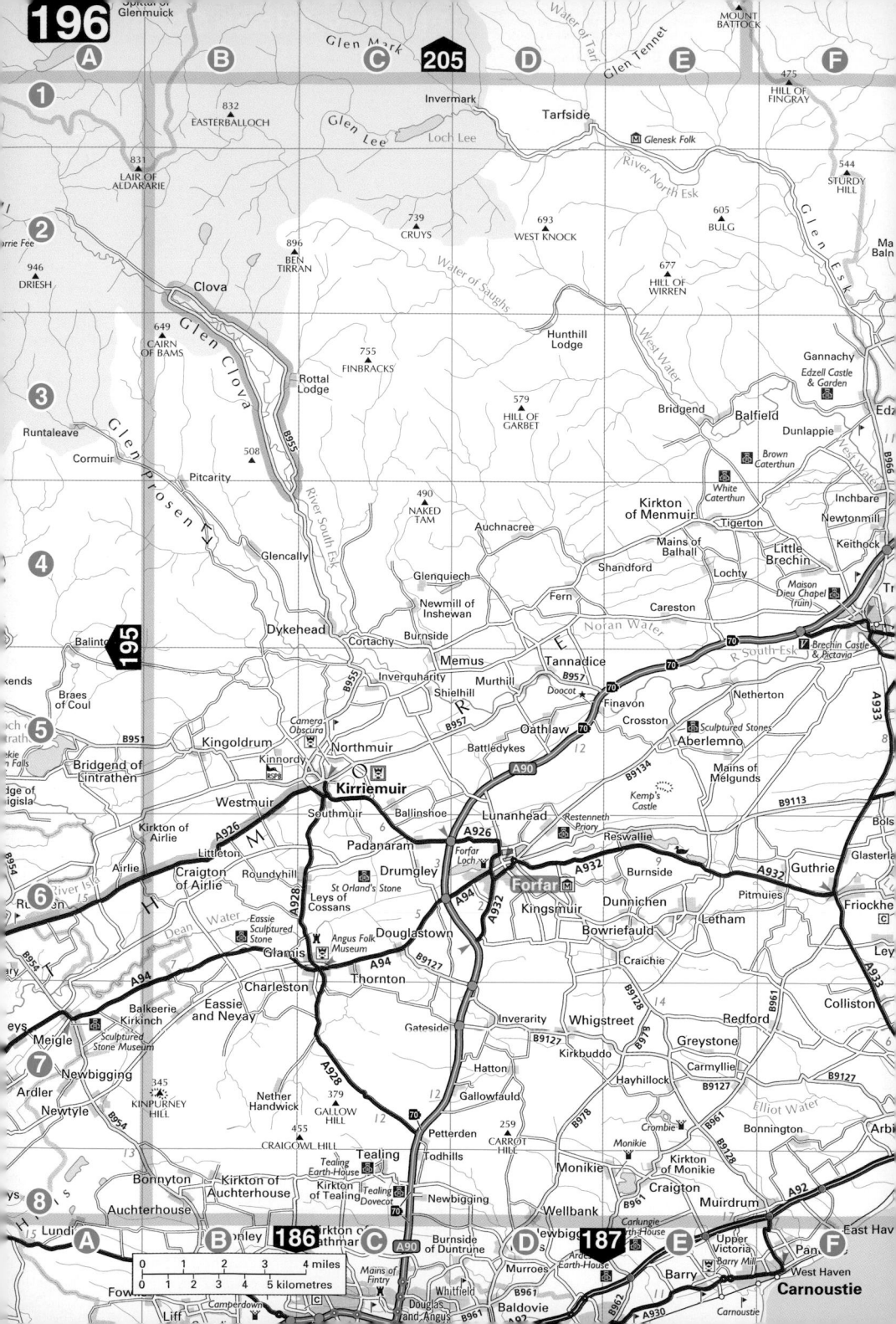

G H 206 J K L M

1

er of Dye
Goosecruives
465
GOYLE
HILL
Drumlithie
v Mill
Tar
Crawton
Fowlsheugh
Trelong
Bay
Glenbervie
Temple
of Fiddes
RSPB
454
Cairn
O'Mount
Mondynes
Catterline
414
FINELLA
HILL
Auchenblae
Kinneff
Todhead Point

2

B966
Fordoun
Redmyre
Arbuthnott
Pittarrow
Mains of
Haulkerton
25
Inverbervie
ettercairn
Laurencekirk
Bervie
Bay
B9120
Bogmuir
B974
Sauchieburn
B9120
Gourdon
Edzell
Woods
50
Redford
Luthermuir
Dykelands
Benholm

3

A90
B974
Johnshaven
River North Esk
Marykirk
Logie Pert
Craigo
Lochside
Bush
Milton Ness
Logie
Morphie
St Cyrus

4

Hillside
A937
A92
chin
House of
Dun
Dun
A935
Montrose Air Station
9
Montrose
Caledonian
Railway
Montrose
Basin
Haughs of
Kinnaird
Barnhead
Scurdie Ness
Maryton
Ferryden

5

A934
Craig
Usan
nell
Westerton
of Rossie
11
132
WUDDY
LAW
Braehead
Boddin Point
ell
Lunan
Boysack
Lunan Bay

6

Inverkeilor
13
Red Head
Chapelton
Cauldcots
Letham
Grange
A92
Marywell

7

St Vigeans
Auchmithie
Carlingheugh
Bay
The Deil's
Head
Arbroath

8

G H J K L M

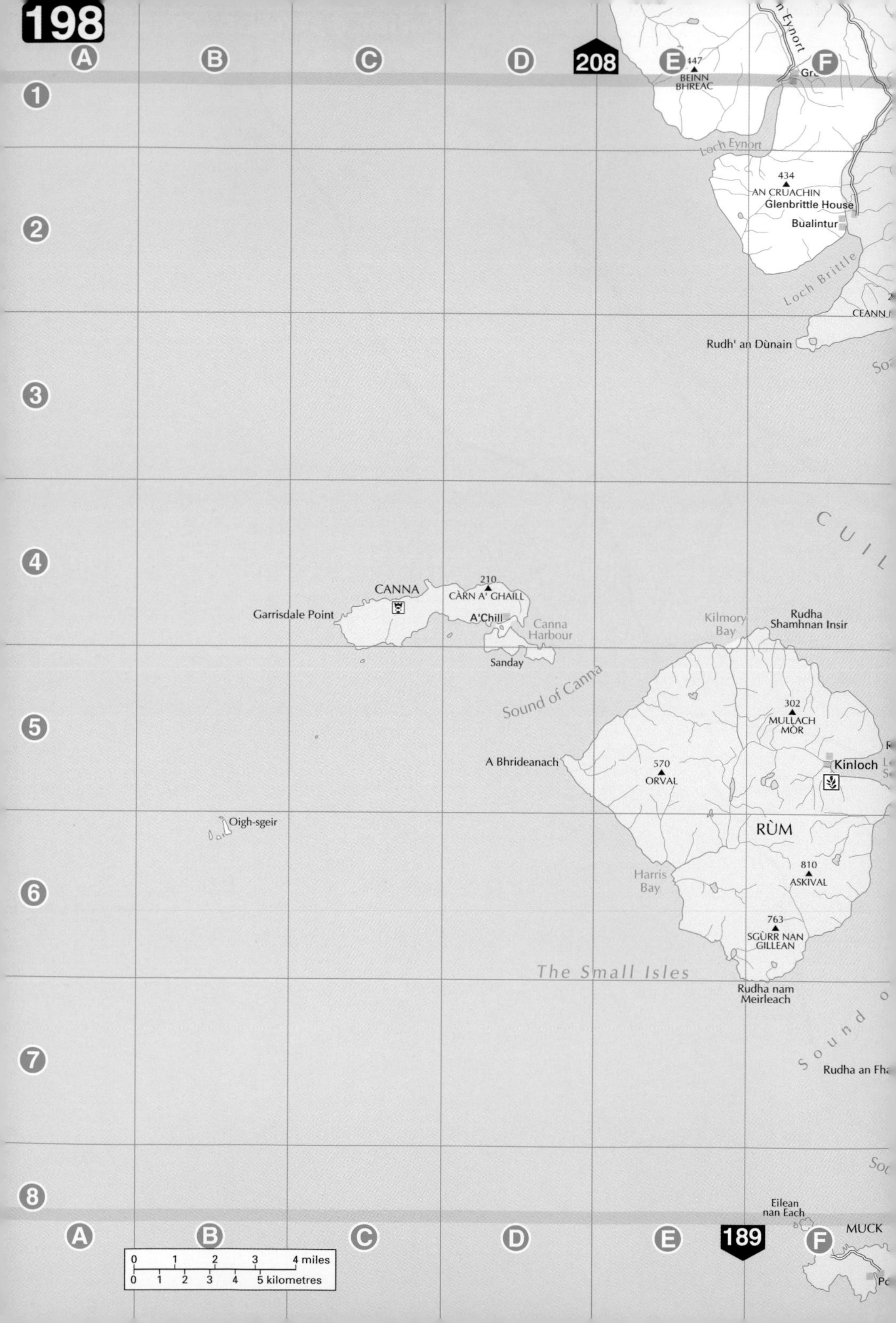

A B C D **208** E F

1

2

3

4

5

6

7

8

A B C D E **189** F

BEINN BHREAC 447

Loch Eynort

AN CRUACHIN 434
Glenbrittle House
Bualintur

Loch Brittle

CEANN

Rudh' an Dùnain

So

CUIL

CANNA
Garrisdale Point
CÀRN A' GHAILL 210
A'Chill
Canna Harbour
Sanday

Kilmory Bay
Rudha Shamhnan Insir

MULLACH MÒR 302

Kinloch

A Bhrideanach
ORVAL 570

RÙM

Oigh-sgeir

Harris Bay

ASKIVAL 810

SGÙRR NAN GILLEAN 763

The Small Isles

Rudha nam Meirleach

Sound o

Rudha an Fha

So

Eilean nan Each

MUCK

Po

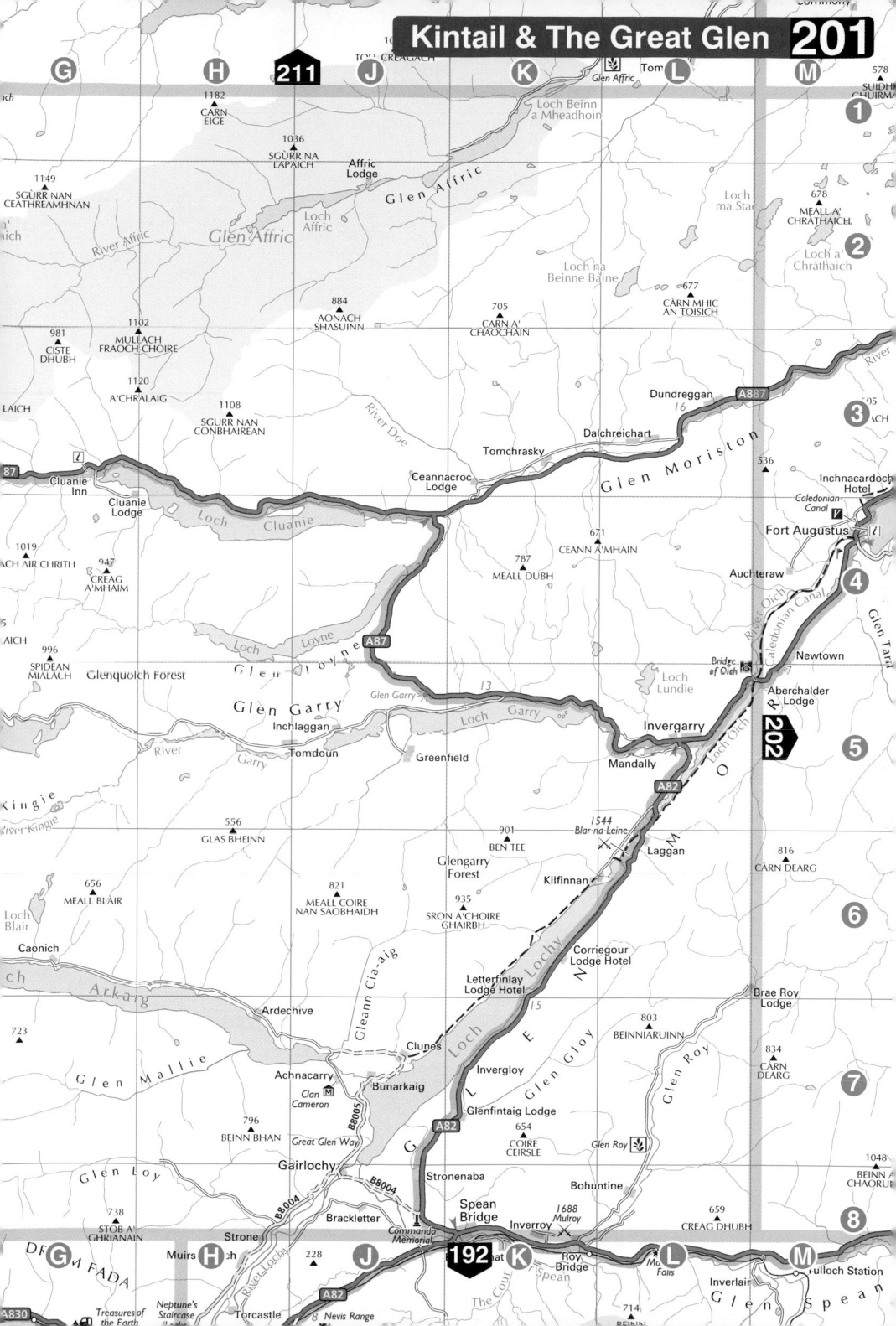

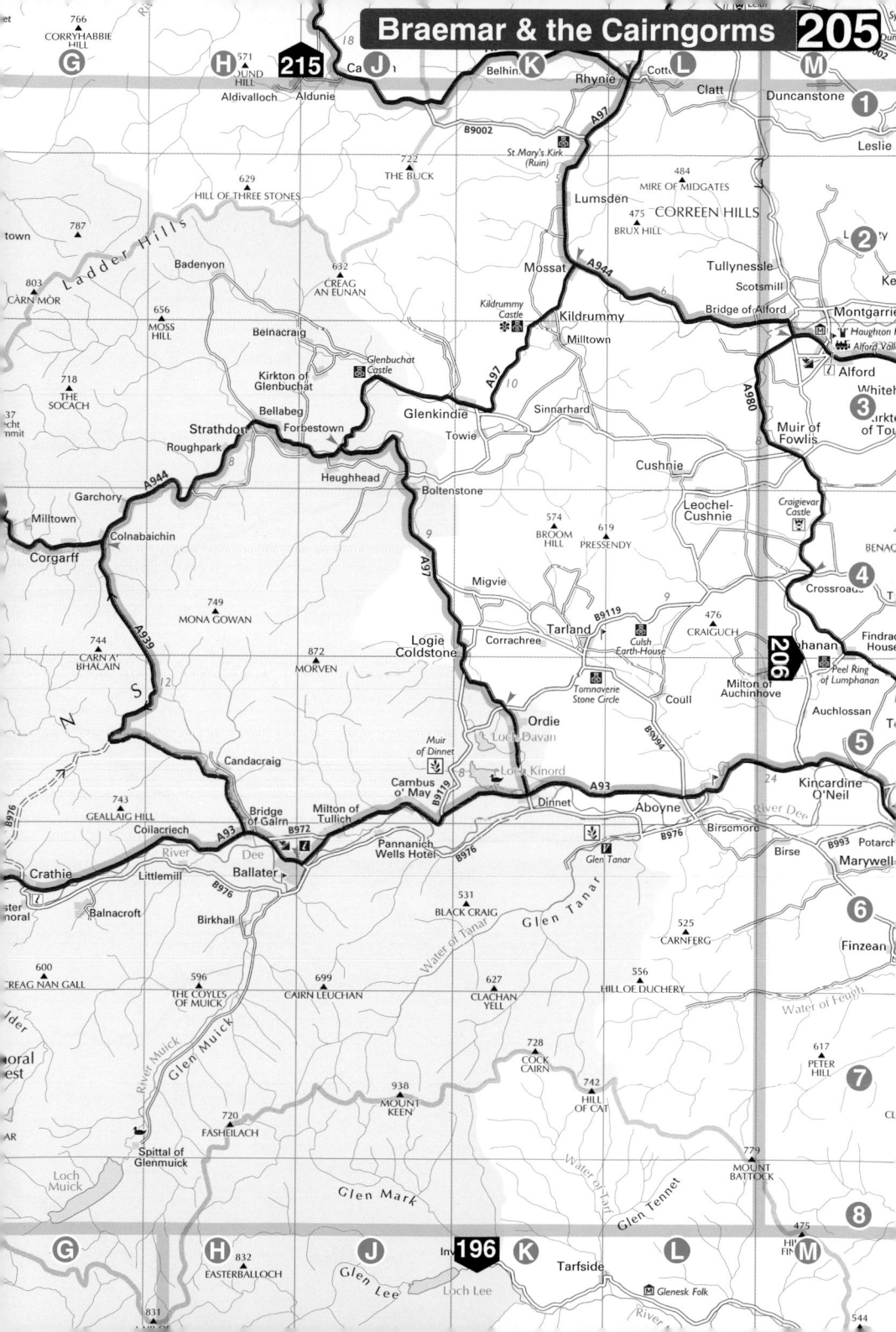

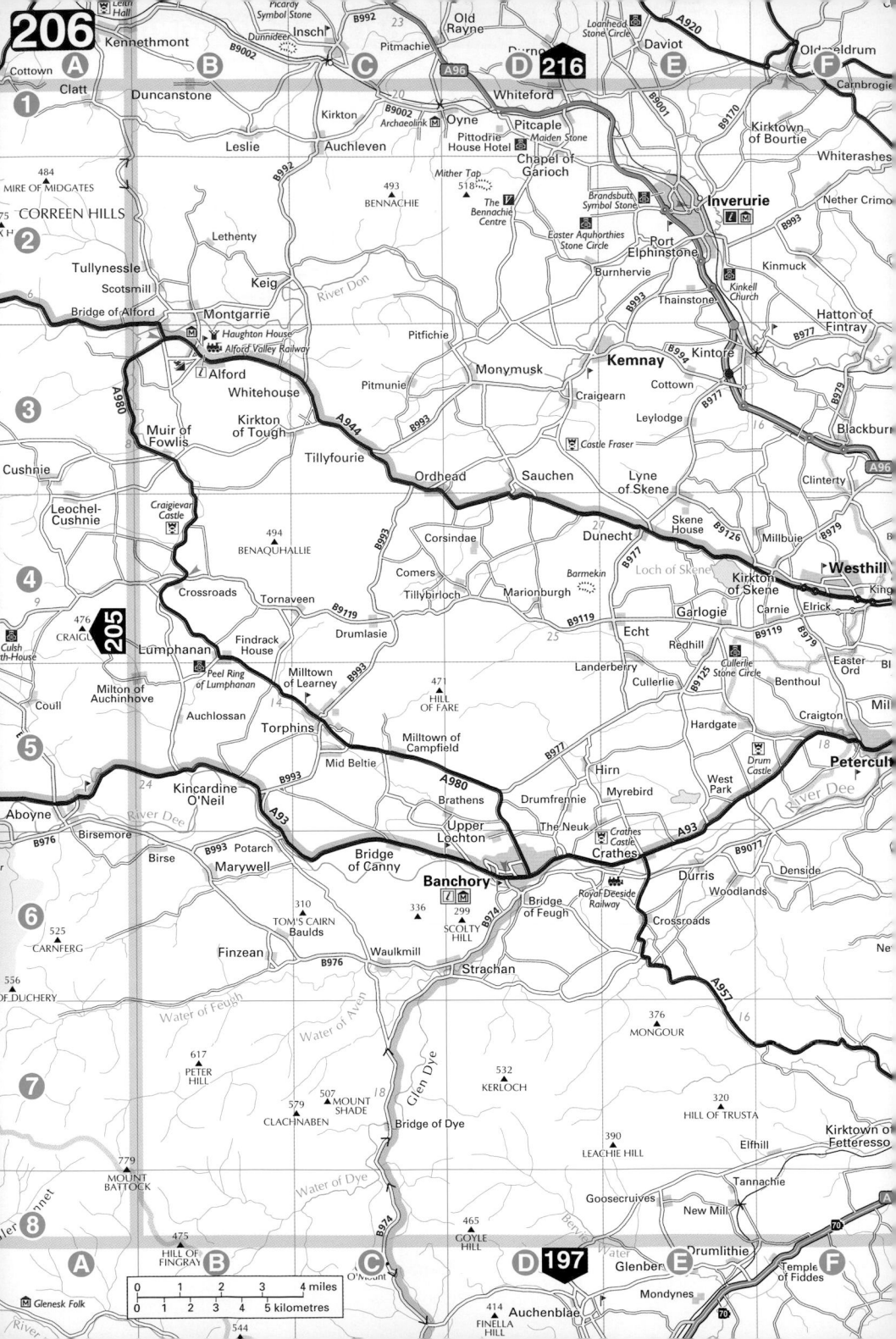

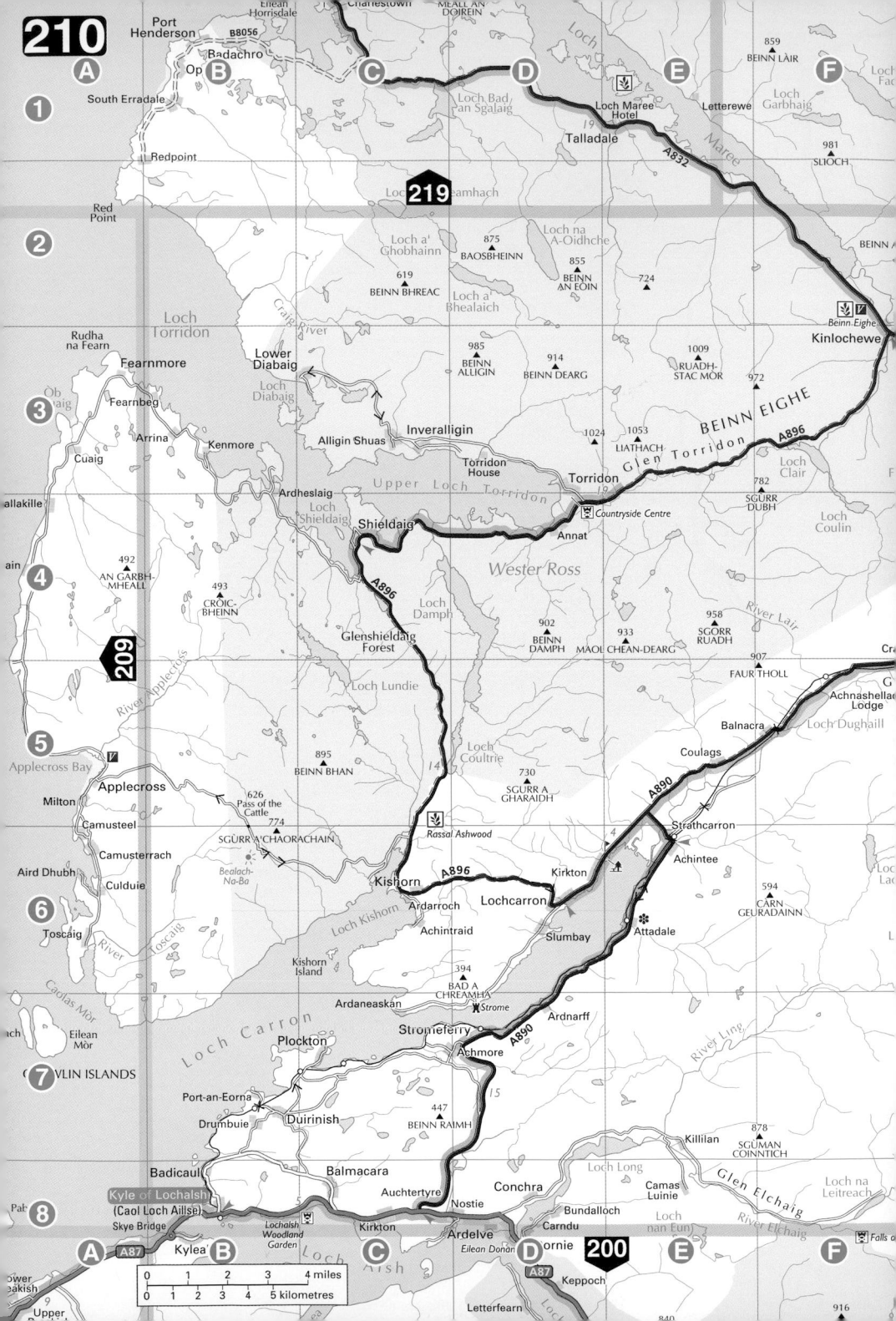

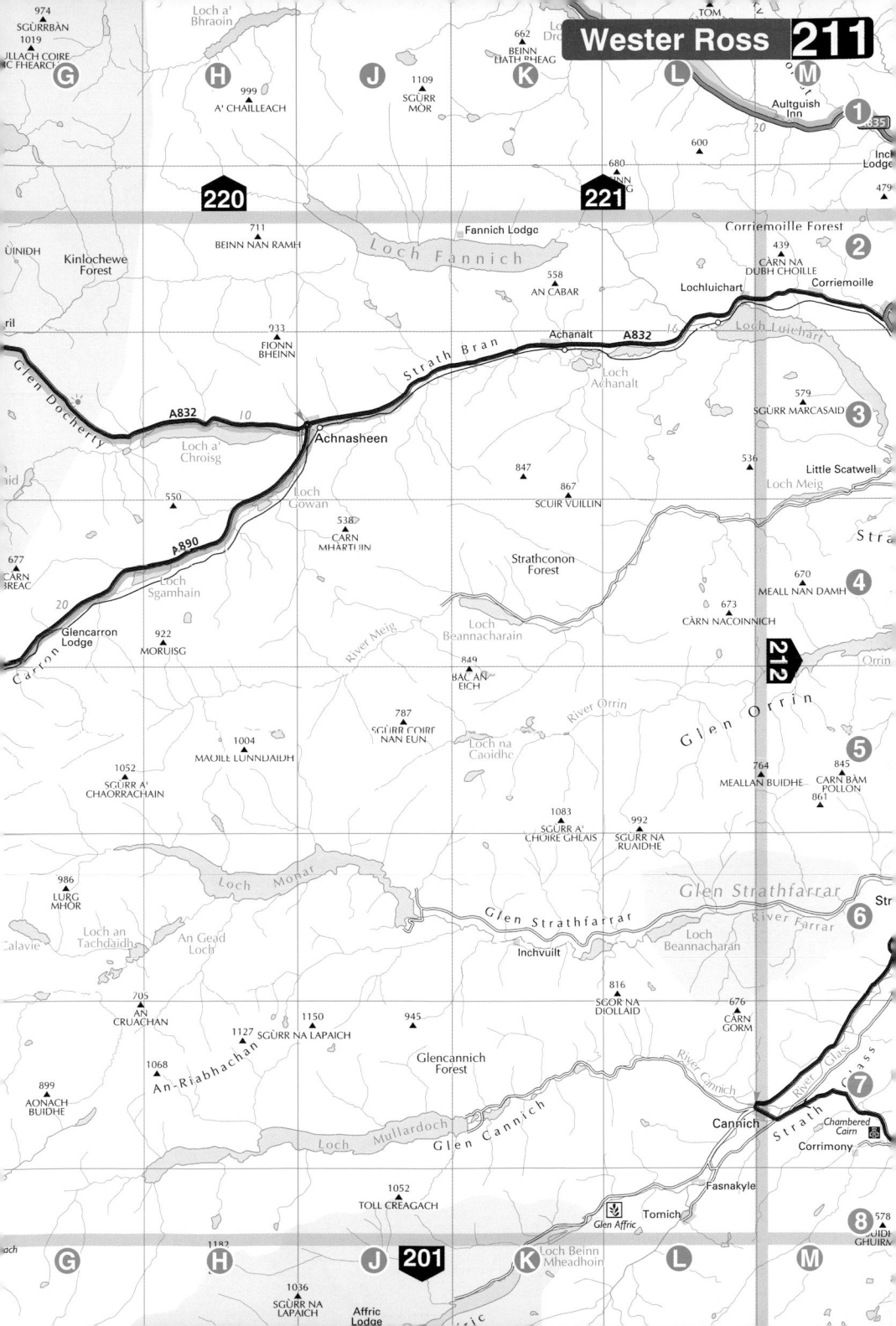

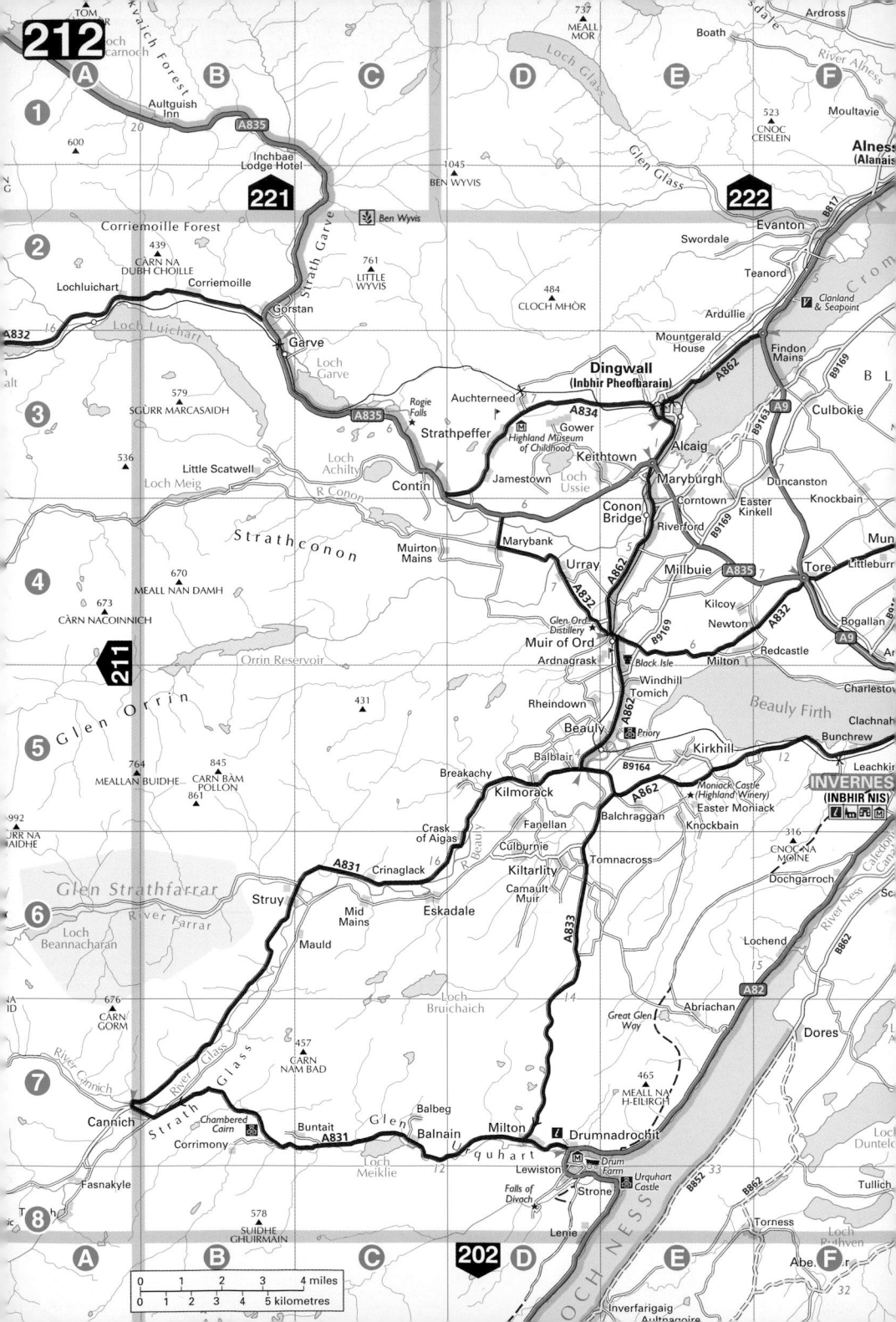

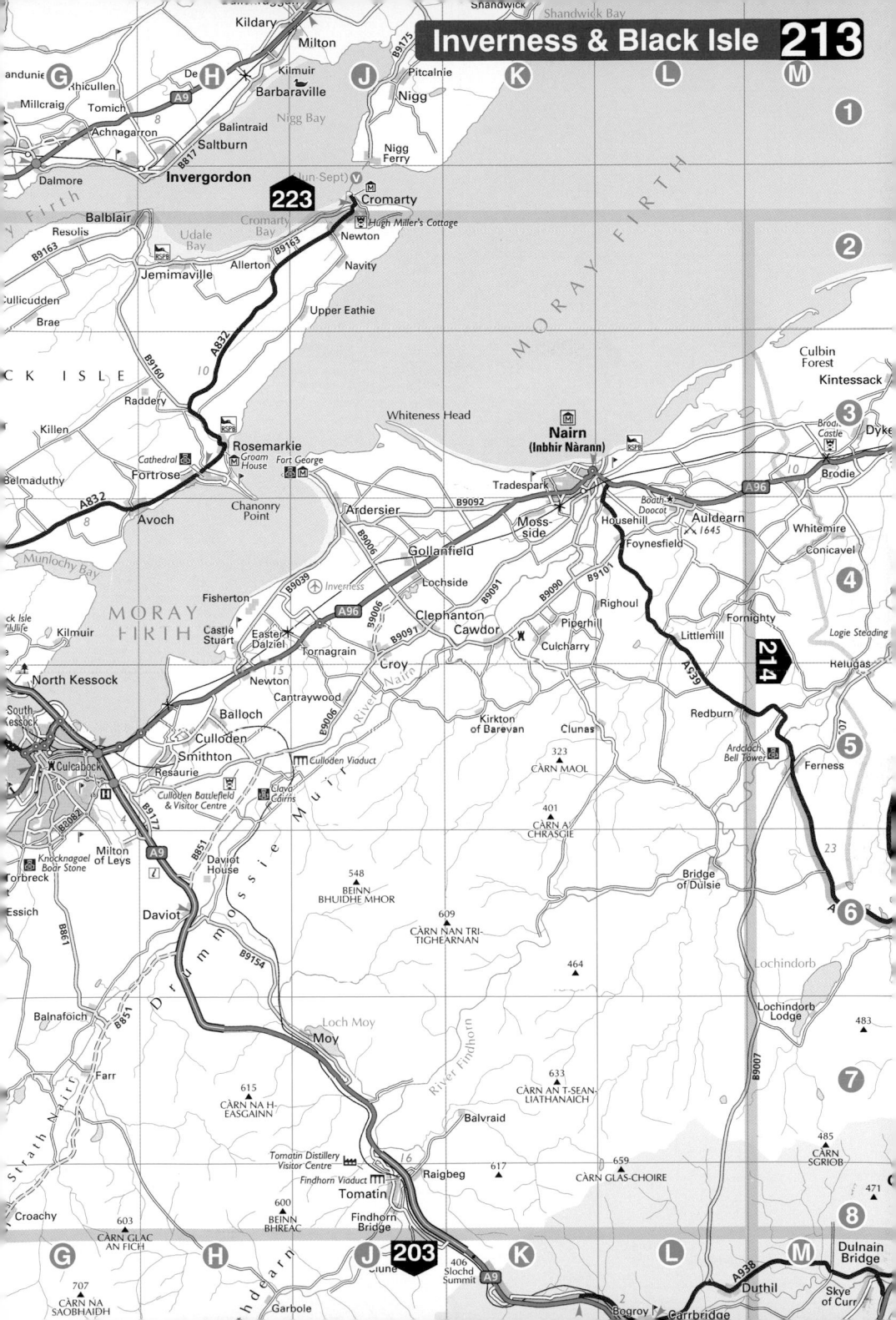

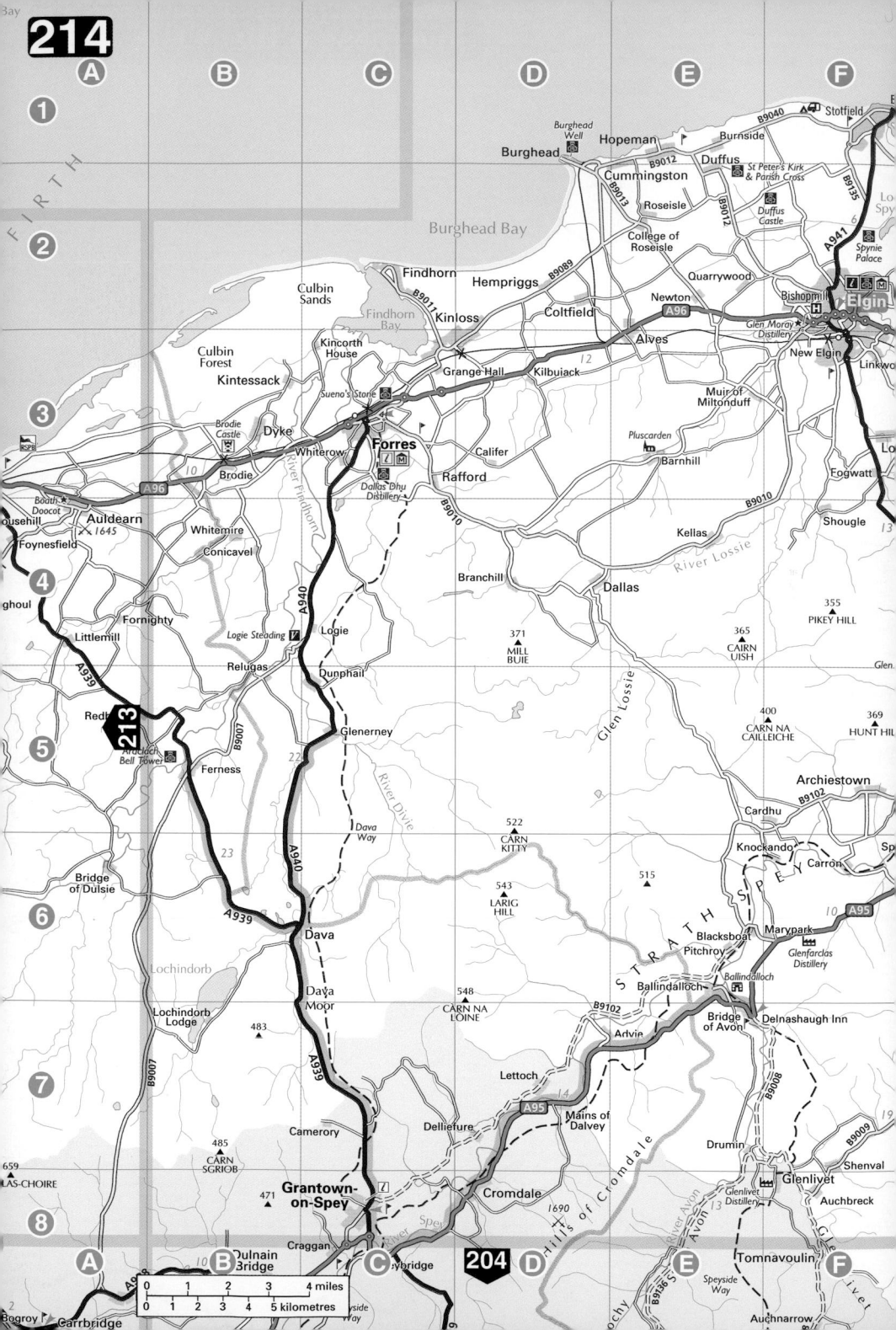

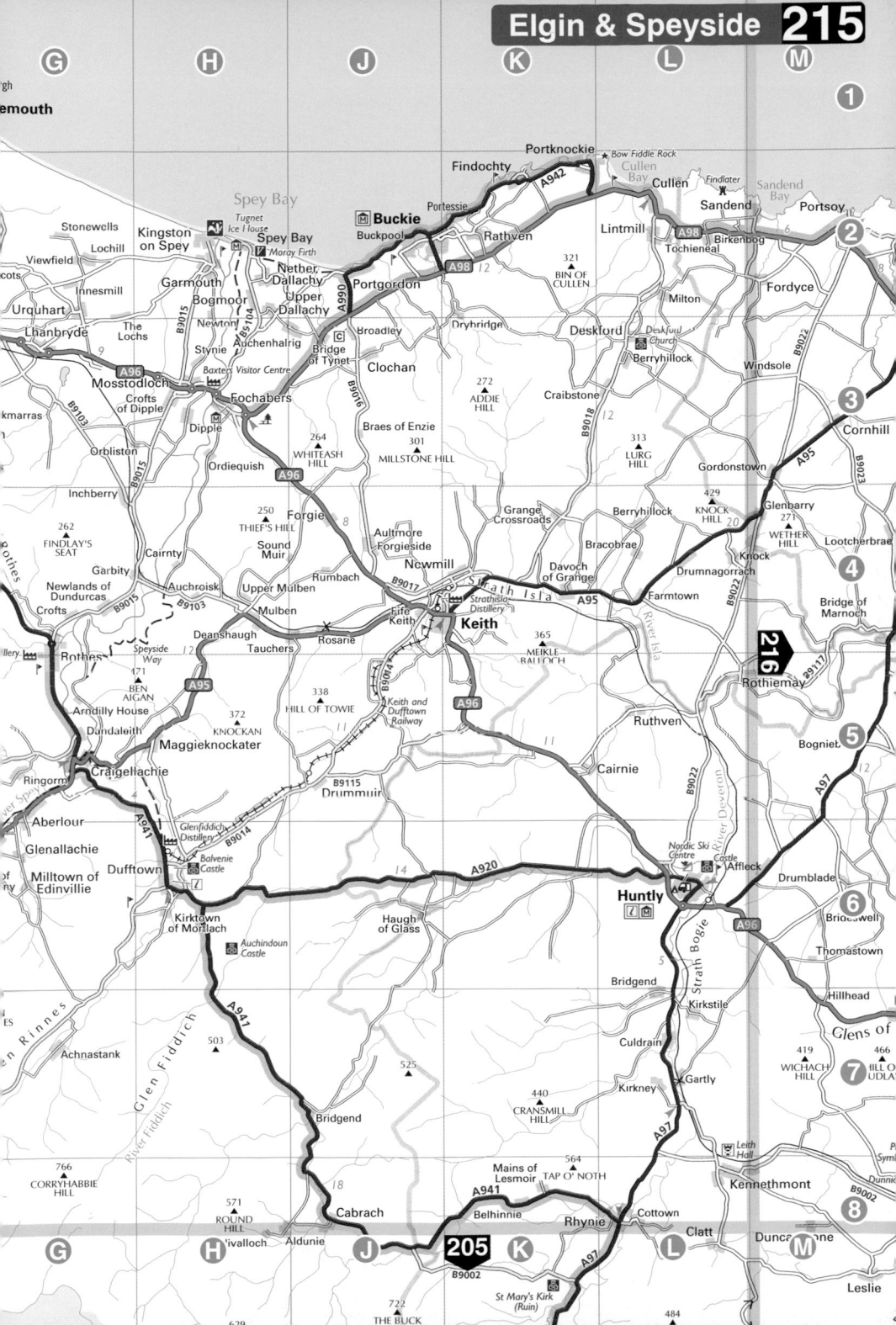

G   H   J   K   L   M

1

Portknockie
Findochty ★ Bow Fiddle Rock
A942   Cullen
Portessie   Bay   Cullen
🏰 Buckie   Findlater
Buckpool   Rathven   Lintmill   Sandend
Spey Bay   A98   Tochieneal   Birkenbog   Sandend Bay
Stonewells   Kingston   Tugnet   Moray Firth   Portsoy   2
Lochill   on Spey   Ice House   Portgordon   BIN OF   Milton   Fordyce
Viewfield   Spey Bay   A990   CULLEN   321
Innesmill   Garmouth   Nether   A98   12   Deskford   Windsole
Urquhart   Bogmoor   Dallachy   DryhDeskford
Lhanbryde   The   Newton   Upper   Broadley   Church   3
Lochs   Stynie   Dallachy   Clochan   Berryhillock   Cornhill
Mosstodloch   Auchenhalrig   Bridge   272   Craibstone   A95
Crofts   Baxters Visitor Centre   of Tynet   ADDIE   313
of Dipple   Fochabers   HILL   LURG   Gordonstown
Orbliston   Dipple   Braes of Enzie   HILL   429   Glenbarry   4
Inchberry   Ordiequish   264   301   Grange   KNOCK   271   Lootcherbrae
WHITEASH   MILLSTONE HILL   Crossroads   Berryhillock   HILL   WETHER
262   HILL   Forgie   8   Bracobrae   20   Knock   HILL
FINDLAY'S   250   Aultmore   Drumnagorrach   Bridge of
SEAT   THIEF'S HILL   Forgieside   Newmill   Davoch   Marnoch
Garbity   Sound   of Grange   5
Cairnty   Muir   Rumbach   Strathisla   Farmtown   216
Auchroisk   Upper Mulben   Fife   Distillery   Rothiemay
Newlands of   Keith   A95   Bogniet   5
Dundurcas   Mulben   Rosarie   365
Crofts   Deanshaugh   MEIKLE   6
Rothes   Tauchers   338   BALLOCH   Ruthven
171   Speyside   HILL OF TOWIE   Keith and   Cairnie
BEN   Way   A95   Dufftown   11
AIGAN   372   Railway   A96
Arndilly House   KNOCKAN   11
Dandaleith   Maggieknockater   Nordic Ski
Ringorm   B9115   Centre   Affleck   Drumblade
Craigellachie   Drummuir   Bridgewell   6
Aberlour   Glenfiddich   Castle   Thomastown
Glenallachie   Distillery   B9014   Huntly   A96   Hillhead
Milltown of   Balvenie   A920   Glens of
Edinvillie   Dufftown   Castle   Kirkstile   7
Kirktown   Haugh   Bridgend   WICHACH
of Mortlach   of Glass   419   HILL   466
Auchindoun   Culdrain   Gartly   HILL O
Castle   Kirkney   UDLA
A941   503   Bridgend   CRANSMILL   440   Kennethmont   8
Achnastank   525   HILL   Kirkney
766   Mains of   564   Leith
CORRYHABBIE   571   Lesmoir   TAP O' NOTH   Hall
HILL   ROUND   Belhinnie   Cottown
Glen Fiddich   HILL   Cabrach   A941   Rhynie   Clatt   Duncanstone
Aldunie   205   A97   Leslie
G   H   J   B9002   K   L   M
722
THE BUCK   St Mary's Kirk   484
629   (Ruin)

Rosehearty
Pittulie
Craigiefold
Peathill
Sandhaven
Castle Lighthouse & Museum
Kinnaird Head
Fraserburgh
Kirktown
Fraserburgh Bay
Maggie's Hoosie
Cairnbulg
Inverallochy
Whitelinks Bay
Percyhorner
Coburby
B9031
Pitblae
New berdour
Boyndlie
Mid Ardlaw
B9032
Memsie
St Combs
B9033
Aberdour Bay
A98
A90
Memsie Cairn
Rathen
Newburgh
Lonmay
Crofts of Savoch
Rattray Head
234
WAUGHTON HILL
A952
Crimond
Blackhill
Loch of Strathbeg
New Pitsligo
B9093
Strichen
New Leeds
18
B9093
Leys
Backfolds
Kirktown
St Fergus
Bonnykelly
A981
A950
Denhead
Rora
A90
Fetterangus
4
Deer Abbey
Dunshillock
Maud
Aden
Mintlaw
Longside
Inverugie
Buchanhaven
Peterhead
New Deer
B9029
B9029
Old Deer
Stuartfield
Inverquhomery
A950
Peterhead
Peterhead Bay
Blackhill of Clackriach
Bulwark
Drymuir
Nethermuir
Millbreck
Nether Kinmundy
Hillhead of Cocklaw
Burnhaven
Knaven
B9030
Kinnadie
Clola
Blackhill
Stirling
Buchan Ness
Boddam
Auchnagatt
12
Coldwells
Kinknockie
Lendrum Terrace
Cairnorrie
Brownhill
Inkhorn
A952
Ardallie
A90
Longhaven
ethlick
Arthrath
Muirtack
Hatton
Auchiries
Bullers of Buchan
North Haven
Slains
Cruden Bay
Bogbrae
Chapel Hill
A975
Bay of Cruden
Whinnyfold
The Skares
Ythanbank
B9005
Auchedly
Artrochie
Birness
derlairs
Altar Tomb of William Forbes
Kinharrachie
Ythsie
Ellon
P+R
Esslemont
Kirkton of Logie Buchan
Kirkton of Slains
quhon castle
B999
A920
B9005
Collieston
Pitmedden Garden
Pitmedden
Logierieve
Forvie
Ud Gre.
Housieside
B90
Udny Station
207
Newburgh
B9000
A90
Ud oodland
Pettymuk
Cultercullen
Foveran

A
B
C
D
E
F

1

2

Loch
ollum

SOUND OF SHIANT

SHIANT
ISLANDS

3

4

5 Fladda-chùain

Eilean Troday

Rudha Hunish

North
Duntulm Kilmaluag
6 Duntulm A855
Tairbeart Lùb Score Skye Museum
(Tarbert) of Island Life Flodigarry
Borneskitaig Eilean Flodigarry
Kilmuir Heribusta
Kilvaxter 542 Staffin
Balgown MEAL NA Digg Bay Staffin Island
SUIREAMACH
Brogaig
Linicro Stenscholl Staffin
Totscore 464 Kilt Rock Waterfall
Loch nam Madadh 208 BIODA Trotternish Ellishader 209
(Lochmaddy) BUIDHE
Maligar Valtos
Idrigill Marishader Rudha nam Brathairean
Culnaknock
611 Garros
8 BEINN Le
Loch S ort EDRA Tote
A Uig Bay B C D E F
Uig
(Uige) A855 RONA
Ear

0   1   2   3   4 miles
0 1 2 3 4 5 kilometres

608
CREAG A' LAIN

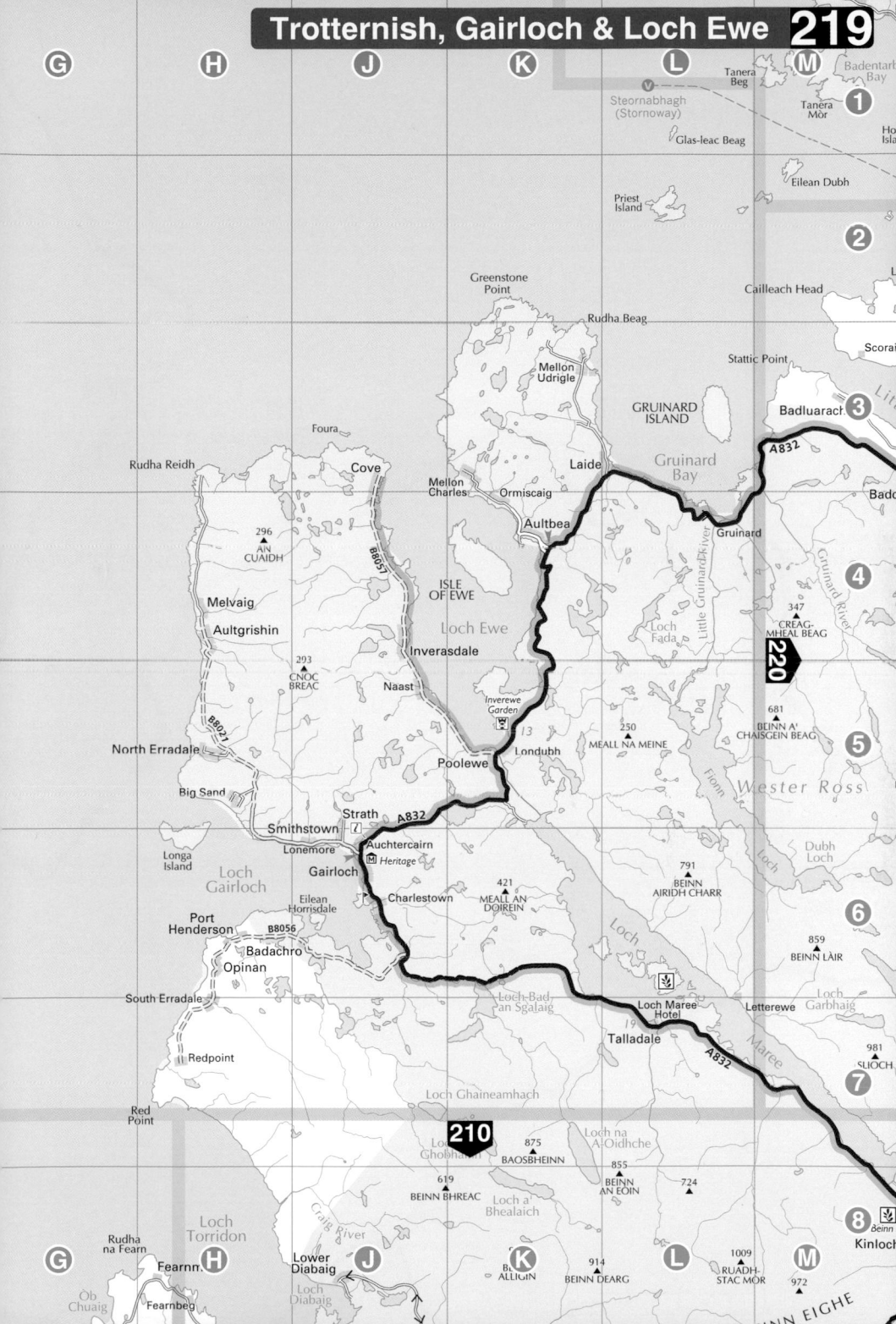

G   H   J   K   L   M

Tolb

Badentarb
Bay

1

Steornabhagh
(Stornoway)

Tanera Beg

Tanera Mòr

Ho
Isla

Glas-leac Beag

Eilean Dubh

2

Cailleach Head

Scorai

Priest
Island

Greenstone
Point

Rudha Beag

Stattic Point

Badluarach

3

A832

GRUINARD
ISLAND

Gruinard
Bay

Bad

Mellon
Udrigle

Laide

Gruinard

Foura

Cove

Mellon
Charles

Ormiscaig

Aultbea

4

347
CREAG-
MHEAL BEAG

Rudha Reidh

296
AN
CUAIDH

B8057

ISLE
OF EWE

Loch
Fada

220

681
BEINN A'
CHAISGEIN BEAG

5

Melvaig

Aultgrishin

293
CNOC
BREAC

Loch Ewe

Inverasdale

Naast

250
MEALL NA MEINE

Wester Ross

B8021

North Erradale

Inverewe
Garden

13

Londubh

Dubh
Loch

Poolewe

Big Sand

Longa
Island

Loch
Gairloch

Smithstown

Lonemore

Strath

Gairloch

Auchtercairn

Heritage

A832

421
MEALL AN
DOIREIN

791
BEINN
AIRIDH CHARR

Loch

6

Eilean
Horrisdale

Charlestown

859
BEINN LÀIR

Port
Henderson

Badachro

Opinan

B8056

Loch-Bad
an Sgalaig

Loch Maree
Hotel

Letterewe

Loch
Garbhaig

South Erradale

Talladale

19

A832

981
SLIOCH

7

Redpoint

Red
Point

Loch Ghaineamhach

875
BAOSBHEINN

Loch na
A-Oidhche

210

619
BEINN BHREAC

Loch a'
Bhealaich

855
BEINN
AN EOIN

724

8

Rudha
na Fearn

Fearn

Loch
Torridon

Lower
Diabaig

Loch
Diabaig

BEINN
ALLIGIN

914
BEINN DEARG

1009
RUADH-
STAC MÒR

Kinloch

972

Òb
Chuaig

Fearnbeg

Craig River

BEINN EIGHE

G   H   J   K   L   M

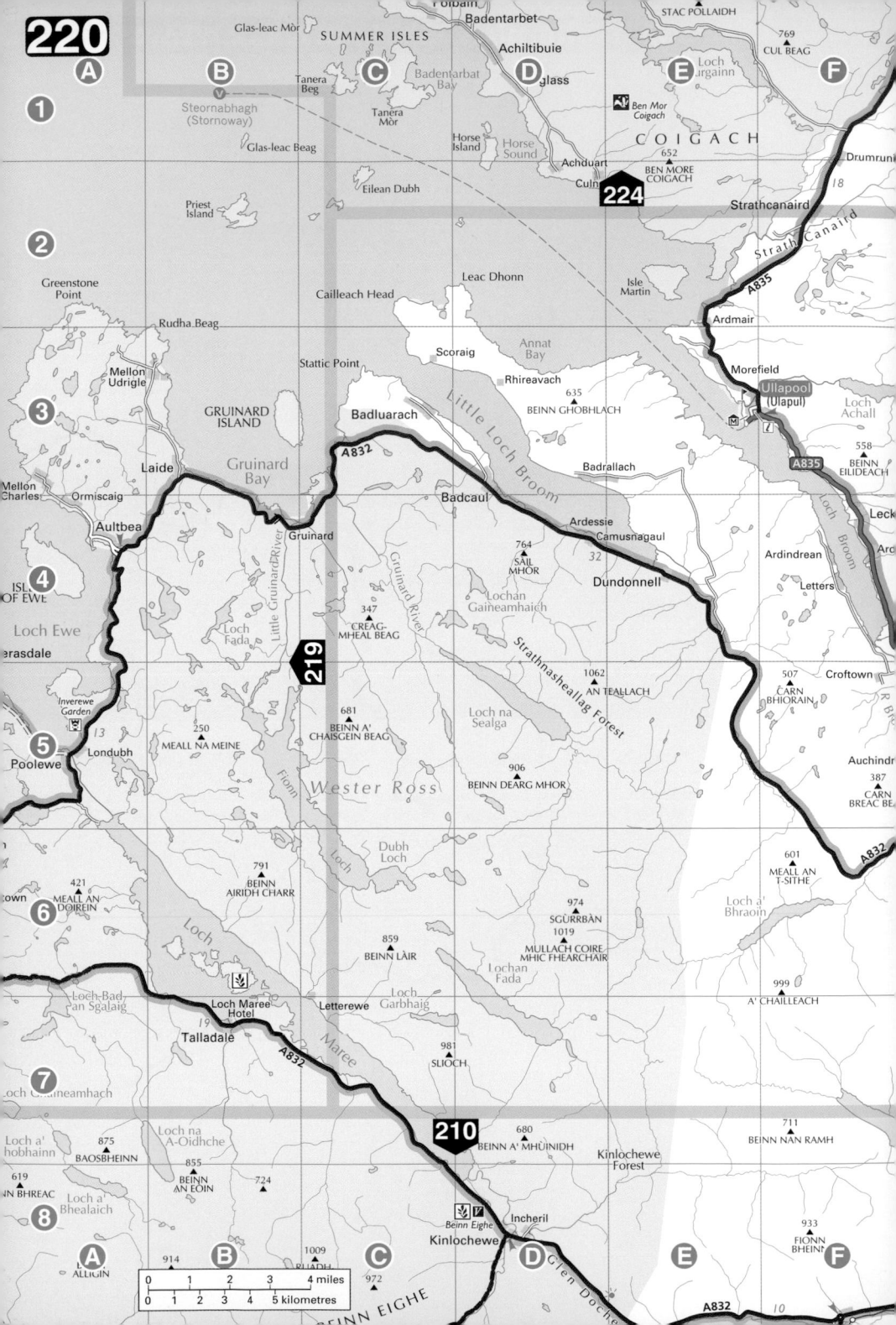

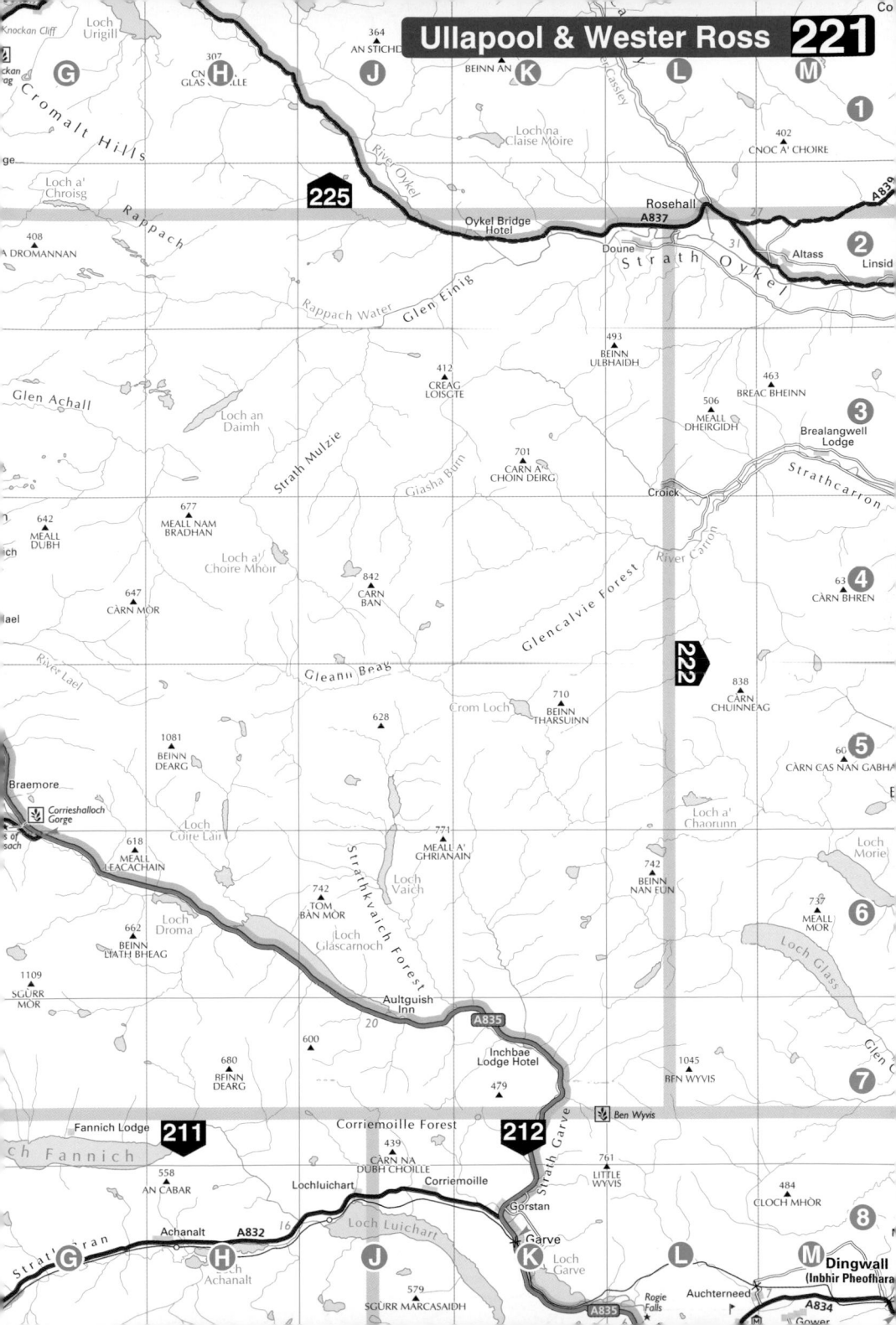

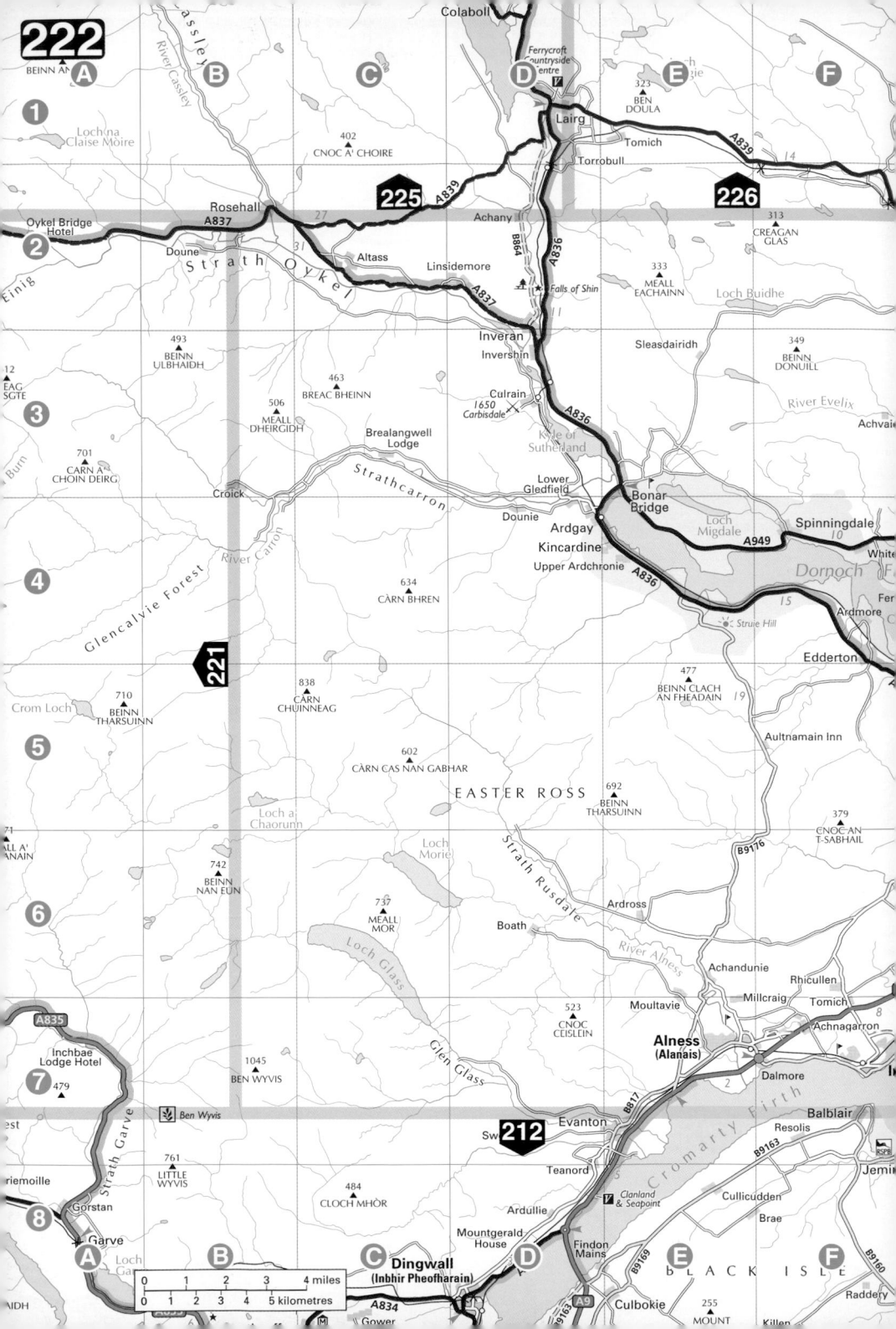

G **H** **J** **K** **L** **M**

1 **2** **3** **4** **5** **6** **7** **8**

Stra[...]
River Brora
BHEINN

Dalreavoch Lodge

Loch Horn
520 BEN HORN

Dalchalm

Brora
227

Golspie Burn
378 CAGAR FEOSAIG
Doll
Backies
Carn Liath
A9

446 BEN LUNDIE
383 BEN BHRAGGIE
Rhives
Dunrobin Castle

Torboll
Golspie

Cambusavie Platform
Loch Fleet

Badninish
Skelbo 7
Skelbo Street
Fourpenny

Birichin
B9168
Embo

Astle
Embo Street
Pitgrudy

Evelix
A949
Royal Dornoch

Clashmore
A9
Camore
Dornoch

6
Historylinks

Cuthill

uscurrie
Ferry Point

Dornoch Firth

Innis Mhor
Tarbat Ness
Brucefield
Wilkhaven

Glenmorangie Distillery
Portmahomack

Morangie
Inver
Rockfield
B9165

284
Tain
(Baile Dhubhthaich)
Arboll
Toulvaddie
Lochslin
Loch Eye
Rhynio
Hill of Fearn
Balmuchy
Hilton of Cadboll Chapel (ruin)

Newfield
B9165
Fearn
Tullich
Hilton
Balintore

Ballchraggan
Arabella
Shandwick
Shandwick Bay

Kildary
Ankerville
B9175

Milton
Pitcalnie

Iny
Kilmuir
Nigg
Barbaraville

Balintraid
Nigg Bay

Saltburn
Nigg Ferry

rgordon
(Jun–Sept) **V**
Cromarty

Cromarty Bay
B9163
Hugh Miller's Cottage
Newton
213

ale
Allerton
Navity
214

ille
A832
Upper Eathie

MORAY FIRTH
Burghe[...]

Findhorn
B9011

Culbin Sands

Culbin Forest
Findhorn Bay
Findhorn House
Kincorth House

Whiteness Head
Kintessack
Sueno's Stone

10
Grange

G **H** **J** **K** **L** **M**

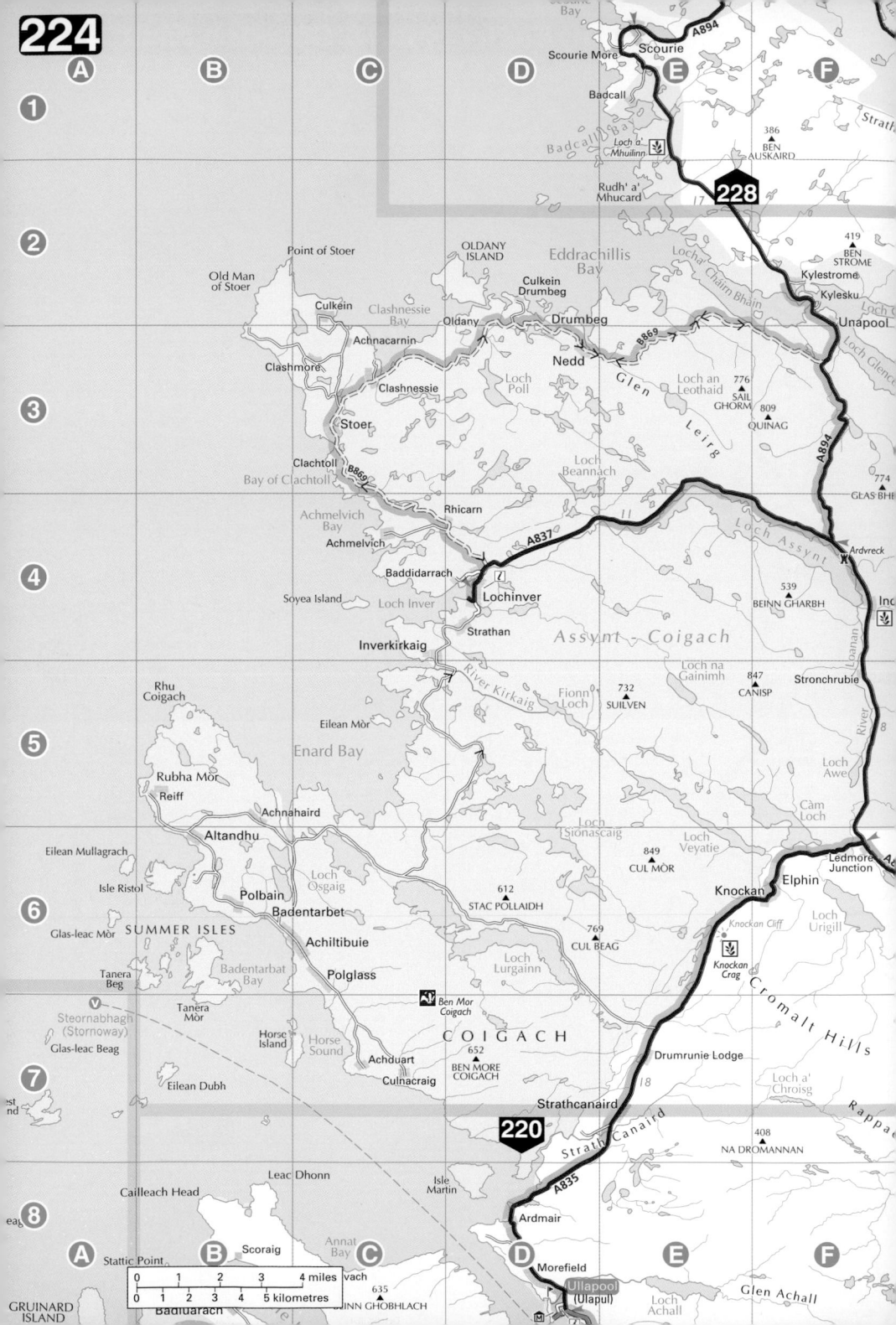

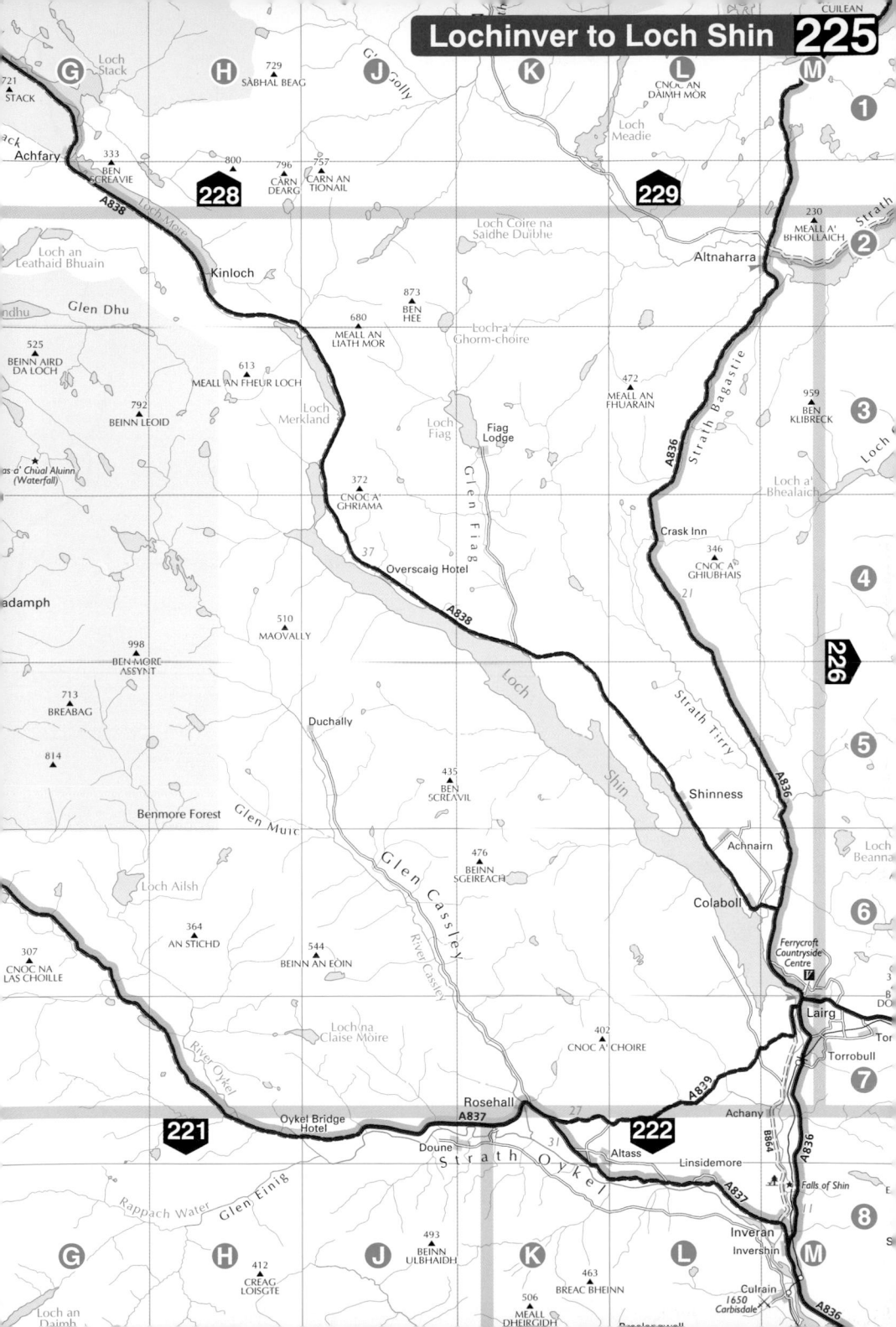

CUILEAN

G Loch Stack
721 STACK

H 729 SÀBHAL BEAG

G'olly

J

K

L CNOC AN DÀIMH MÒR

Loch Meadie

M

1

A838
Achfary

333 BEN SCREAVIE

800

228

796 CARN DEARG

757 CARN AN TIONAIL

Loch Coire na Saidhe Duibhe

229

Altnaharra

230 MEALL A' BHROLLAICH

Strath

2

Loch Mòre

Kinloch

Loch an Leathaid Bhuain

Glen Dhu

525 BEINN AIRD DA LOCH

680 MEALL AN LIATH MOR

873 BEN HEE

Loch-a'-Ghorm-choire

472 MEALL AN FHUARAIN

Strath Bagastie

A836

959 BEN KLIBRECK

Loch

3

dhu

613 MEALL AN FHEUR LOCH

792 BEINN LEOID

Loch Merkland

Loch Fiag

Fiag Lodge

Loch a' Bhealaich

as a' Chual Aluinn (Waterfall)

372 CNOC A' GHRIAMA

Glen Fiag

Crask Inn

346 CNOC A' GHIUBHAIS

4

37

Overscaig Hotel

21

226

adamph

998 BEN MORE ASSYNT

510 MAOVALLY

A838

Loch

5

713 BREABAG

814

Duchally

Shin

Strath Tirry

Shinness

Loch Beanna

Benmore Forest

Glen Muic

435 BEN SCREAVIL

476 BEINN SGEIREACH

Achnairn

6

Loch Ailsh

364 AN STICHD

Glen Cassley

Colaboll

Ferrycroft Countryside Centre

307 CNOC NA LAS CHOILLE

544 BEINN AN EOIN

River Cassley

Loch na Claise Mòire

402 CNOC A' CHOIRE

Lairg

Torrobull

Tor

DO

7

River Oykel

221

Oykel Bridge Hotel

Rosehall

A837

27

222

A839

Achany

B864

A836

Doune

31

Altass

Linsidemore

Falls of Shin

8

Glen Einig

Strath Oykel

A837

Inveran

Invershin

M

Rappach Water

G

H 412 CREAG LOISGTE

493 BEINN ULBHAIDH

J

K 463 BREAC BHEINN

L

Culrain 1650 Carbisdale

A836

Loch an Daimh

506 MEALL DHEIRGIDH

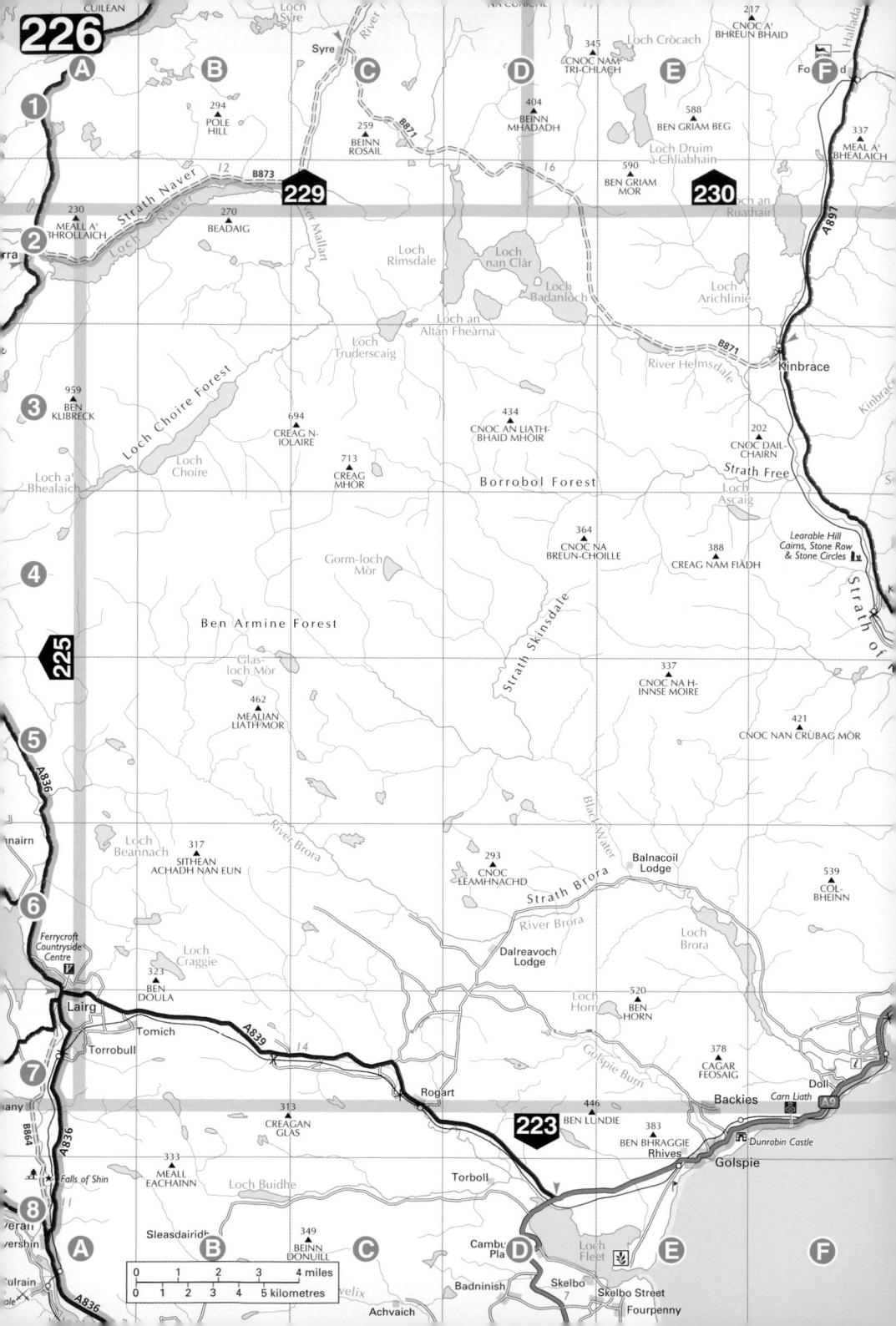

G CNOC NAN GALL

H

J Strathmore

K Achavanich

L Loch Stemster

M

1

Rumsdale Water

Dalnawillan Lodge

226 COIRE NA BEINN

248 STEMSTER HILL

Gre of

Glutt Water

348 ▲ BEN ALISKY

230

287 ▲ BEN-A-CHIELT

231

Upper Lybster

2

Glutt Lodge

264 ▲ CNOCAN CONACHREAG

Houstry

Landhallow

Swiney

Invershore

Lybster

440 ▲

Smerral

Forse

Lybster Bay

KNOCKFIN HEIGHTS

432 ▲

313 ▲ CNOC LOCH MHADADH

Dunbeath Water

Latheronwheel

Latheron

Janetstown

437 ▲ CNOC COIRE NA FEARNA

Berriedale Water

484 ▲ MAIDEN PAP

Braemore

Knockally

Laidhay Croft

Dunbeath

3

518 ▲ CNOC AN EIREANNAICH

Gill Burn

705 ▲ MORVEN

626 ▲ SCARABEN

Ramscraigs

554 ▲ CREAG SCALABSDALE

Langwell Forest

Borgue

20

Newport

4

onan Lodge

401 ▲ CNOC NA MAOILE

Langwell House

Berriedale

Gildonan 416 ▲ BEINN DUBHAIN

A897

404 ▲ CREAG THORARAIDH

A9

Badbea Historic Village

onan

River Helmsdale

Torrish

Ord of Caithness

5

674 ▲ BEINN DHORAIN

591 ▲ BEINN NA MEILICH

West Helmsdale

Timespan

Navidale House Hotel

East Helmsdale

Gartymore

Helmsdale

Glen Loth

Portgower

6

Lothmore

Lothbeg

21

Dalchalm

7

rora

8

G **H** **J** **K** **L** **M**

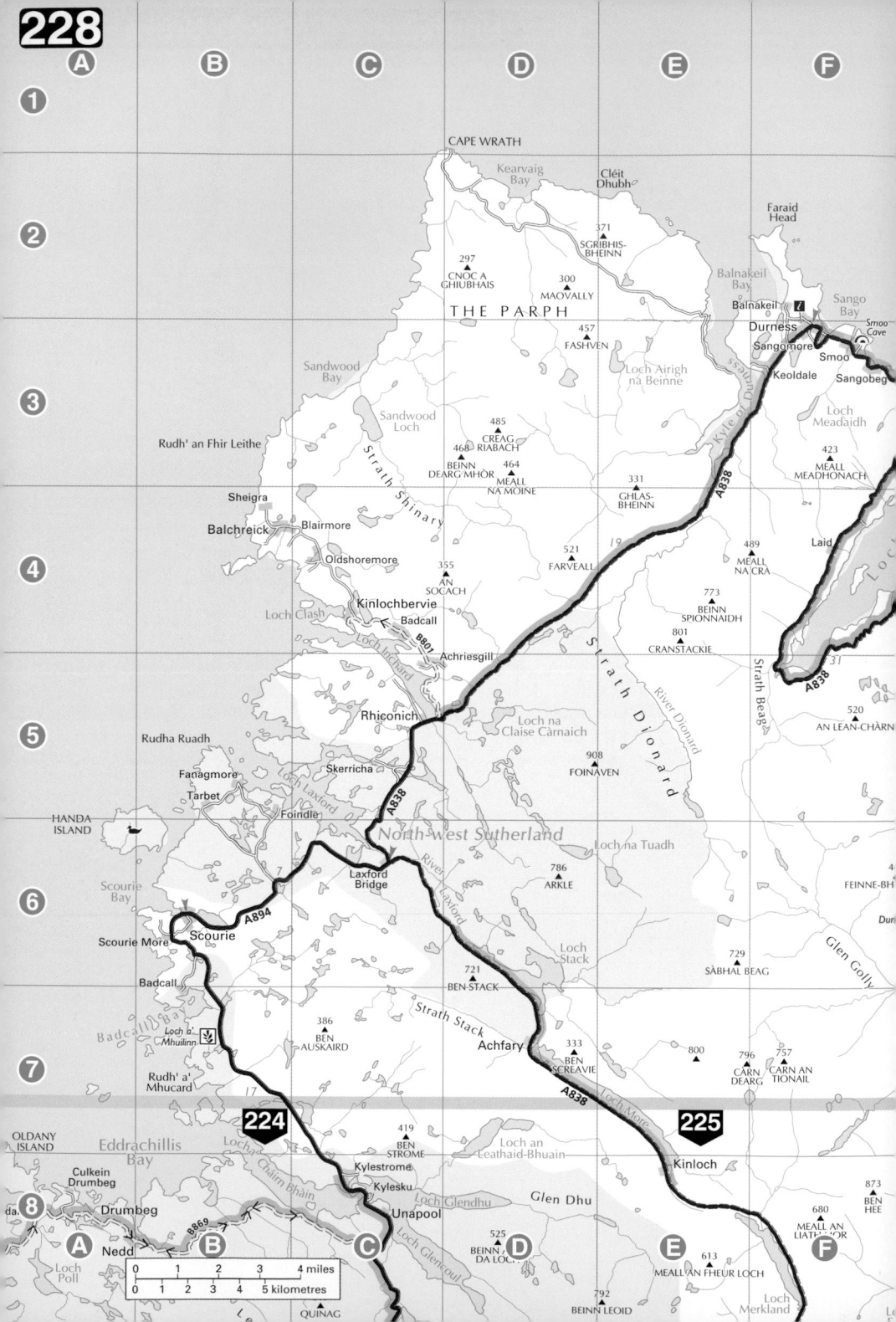

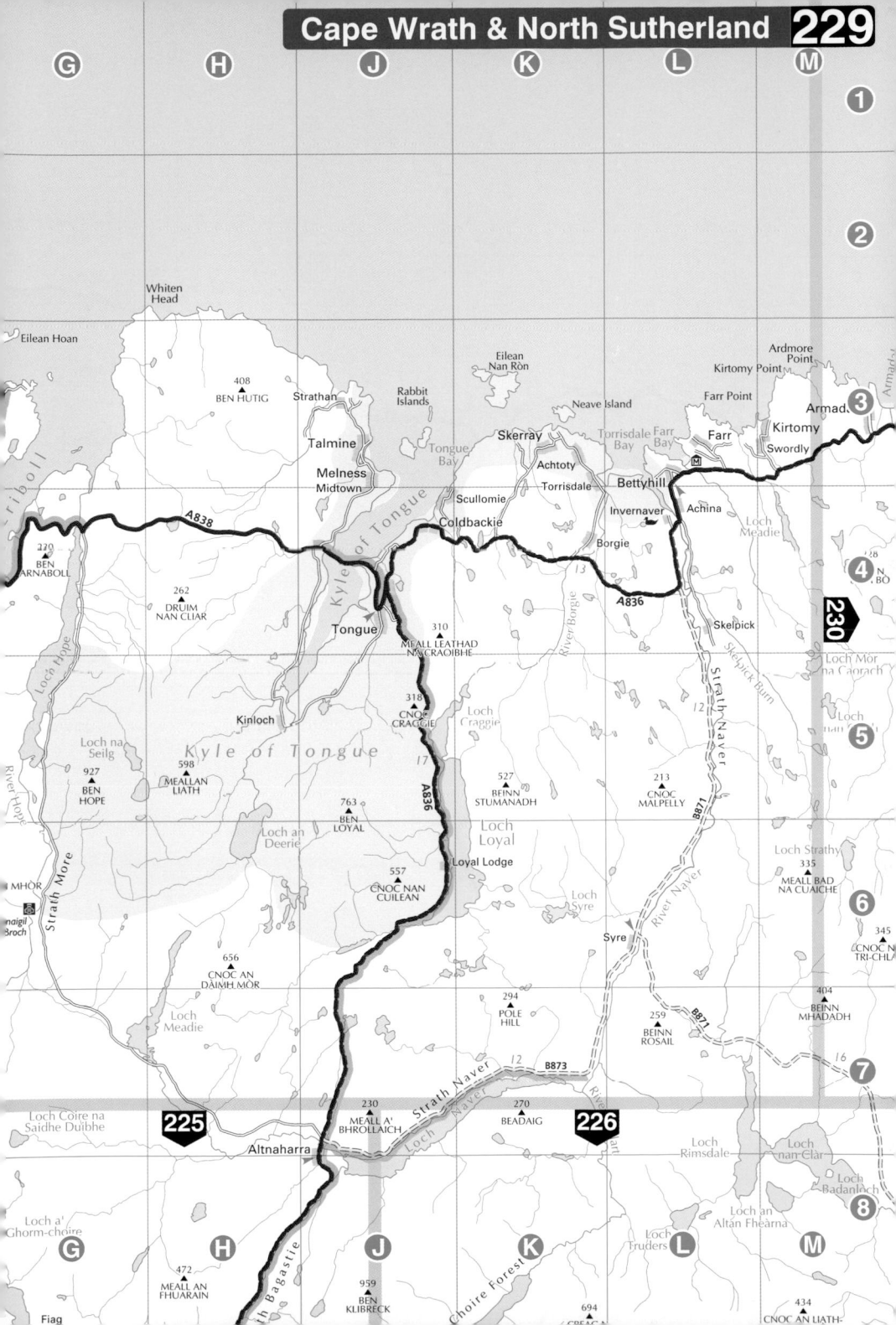

G   H   J   K   L   M

1

2

Whiten
Head

Eilean Hoan

3

Ardmore
Point

Kirtomy Point

Farr Point

Armad

408
BEN HUTIG

Strathan

Rabbit
Islands

Eilean
Nan Ròn

Neave Island

Talmine

Skerray

Torrisdale
Bay

Farr
Bay

Farr

Kirtomy

Swordly

Tongue
Bay

Achtoty

Melness

Midtown

Scullomie

Torrisdale

Bettyhill

Achina

A838

Coldbackie

Invernaver

220
BEN
ARNABOLL

Kyle of Tongue

Borgie

A836

Skelpick

230

262
DRUIM
NAN CLIAR

Tongue

310
MEALL LEATHAD
NA CRAOIBHE

13

Loch Mòr
na Caorach

Strath Naver

318
CNOC
CRAGGIE

Loch
Craggie

Loch
nan

Kinloch

Kyle of Tongue

17

527
BEINN
STUMANADH

213
CNOC
MALPELLY

Loch

5

598
MEALLAN
LIATH

A836

B871

927
BEN
HOPE

763
BEN
LOYAL

Loch
Loyal

Loch Strathy

335
MEALL BAD
NA CUAICHE

6

Loch an
Deerie

Loyal Lodge

River Naver

345
CNOC N
TRI-CHL

MHÒR

557
CNOC NAN
CUILEAN

Loch
Syre

Syre

Strath More

656
CNOC AN
DÀIMH MÒR

294
POLE
HILL

259
BEINN
ROSAIL

B871

404
BEINN
MHADADH

7

Loch
Meadie

B873

16

225

230
MEALL A'
BHROLLAICH

Strath Naver

12

270
BEADAIG

226

Loch
Rimsdale

8

Loch Coire na
Saidhe Duibhe

Altnaharra

Loch an
Altàn Fhearna

Loch a'
Ghorm-choire

G   H   J   K   L   M

472
MEALL AN
FHUARAIN

959
BEN KLIBRECK

694

434
CNOC AN LIATH

Fiag

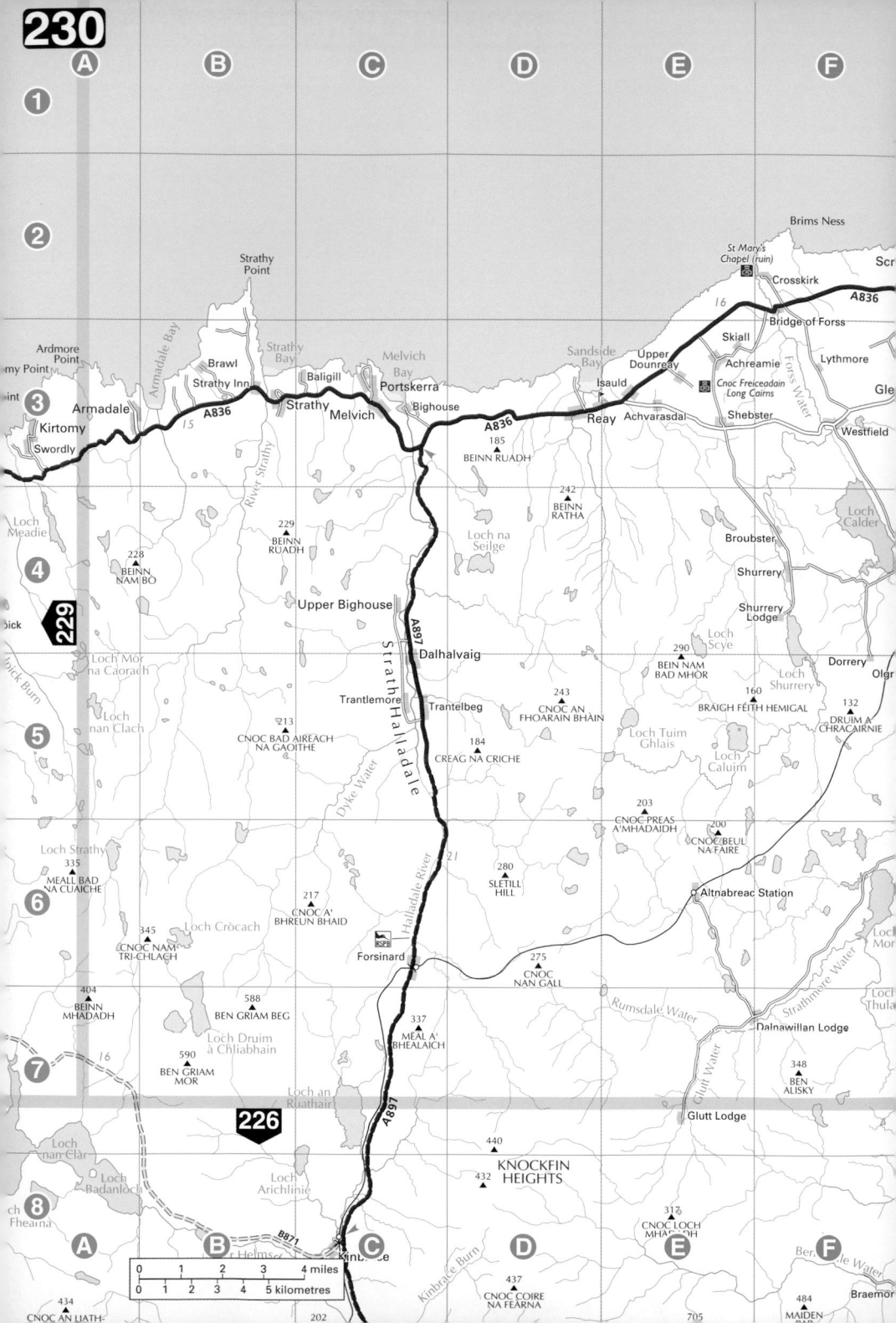

Western Isles

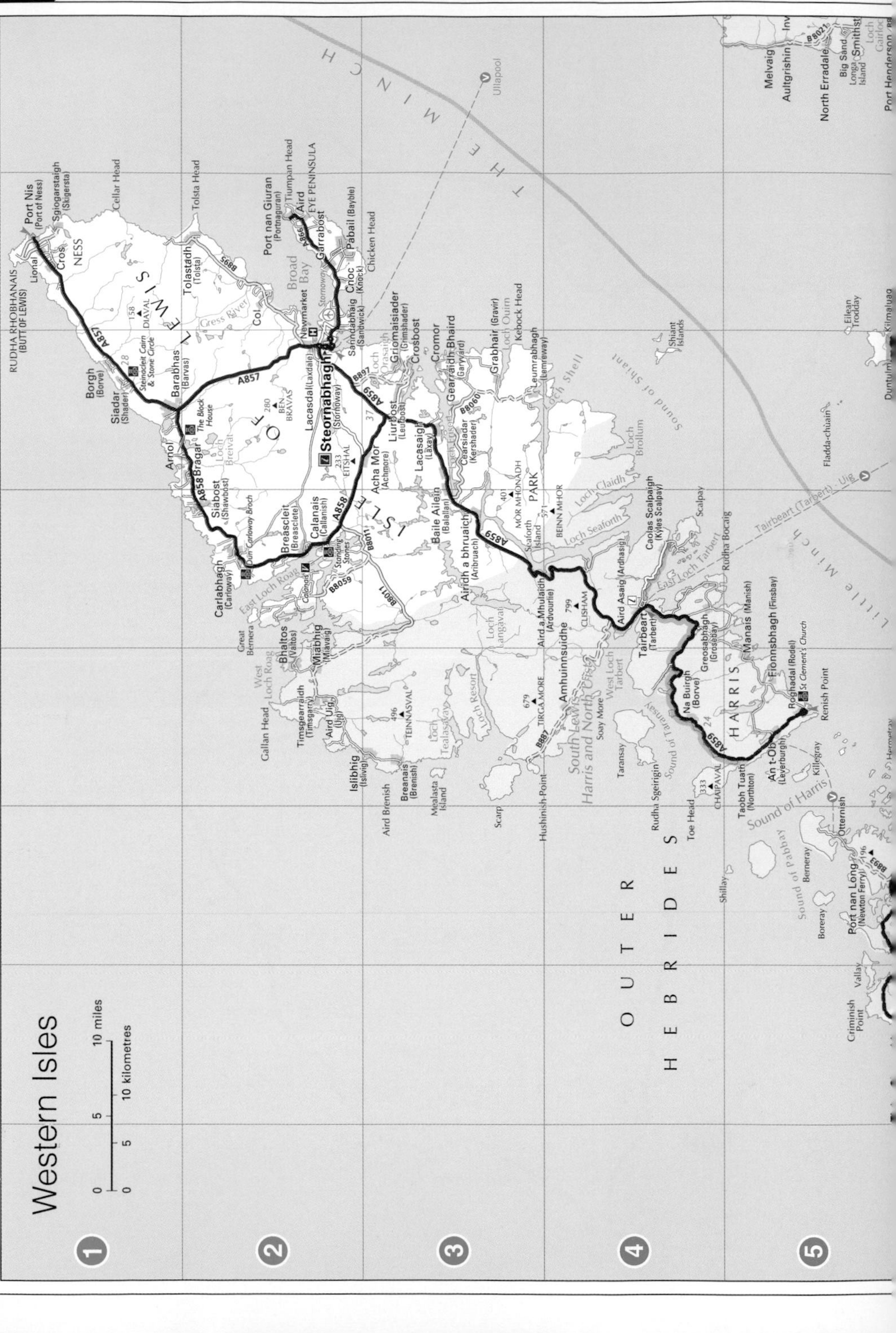

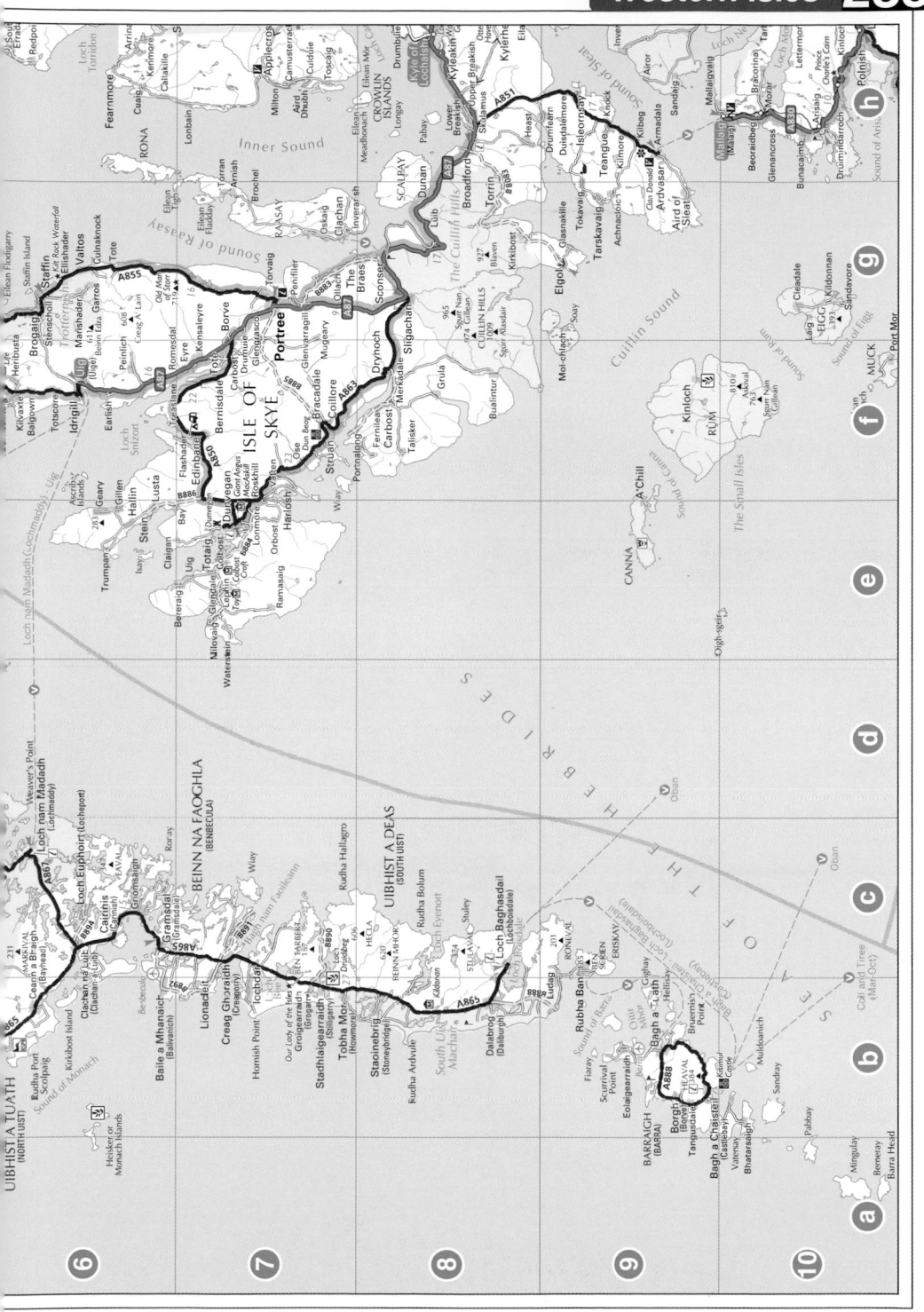

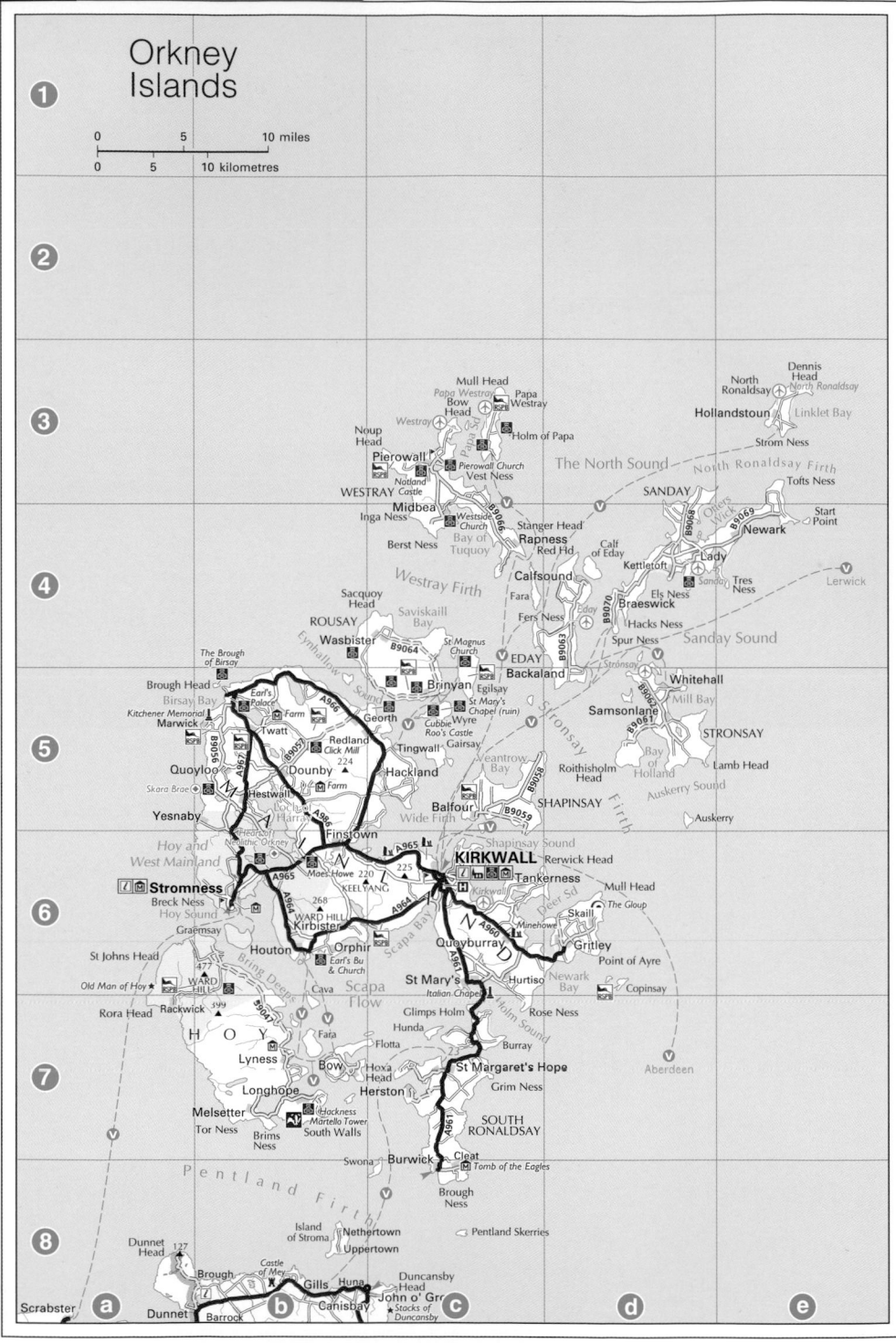

Orkney
Islands

0   5   10 miles
0   5   10 kilometres

Mull Head
Papa Westray
Bow
Head
Papa
Westray
Noup
Head
Holm of Papa
North
Ronaldsay
Dennis
Head
North Ronaldsay
Hollandstoun
Linklet Bay
Pierowall
Westray
Pierowall Church
Vest Ness
Strom Ness
Tofts Ness
The North Sound
North Ronaldsay Firth
Notland
Castle
SANDAY
Start
Point
WESTRAY
Midbea
Westside
Church
Stanger Head
Red Hd
Kettletoft
Lady
Sanday
Newark
Inga Ness
Berst Ness
Bay of
Tuquoy
Rapness
Calf
of Eday
Els Ness
Tres
Ness
Westray Firth
Calfsound
Fara
Fers Ness
Eday
Sanday
Sound
Lerwick
Sacquoy
Head
Saviskaill
Bay
St Magnus
Church
EDAY
Braeswick
Hacks Ness
ROUSAY
Wasbister
B9064
Backaland
Spur Ness
Sanday Sound
The Brough
of Birsay
Egilsay
Whitehall
Mill Bay
Brough Head
Earl's
Palace
A966
Farm
St Mary's
Chapel (ruin)
Wyre
Samsonlane
Birsay Bay
Kitchener Memorial
Marwick
B9056
Twatt
Redland
Click Mill
Georth
Cubbie
Roo's Castle
Gairsay
STRONSAY
Bay
of
Holland
Lamb Head
Quoyloo
224
Dounby
Farm
Hackland
Veantrow
Bay
Auskerry Sound
Yesnaby
Skara Brae
Hestwall
Loch of
Harray
Finstown
Balfour
B9059
SHAPINSAY
Auskerry
Hoy and
West Mainland
Ring of
Neolithic Orkney
Wide Firth
Stromness
A965
Maes Howe 220
225
KIRKWALL
Rerwick Head
Breck Ness
Hoy Sound
268
KEELYANG
A960
Tankerness
Mull Head
Graemsay
Houton
WARD HILL
Kirbister
Orphir
Earl's Bu
& Church
Quoyburray
Minehowe
Skaill
The Gloup
St Johns Head
Old Man of Hoy
WARD
HILL
479
St Mary's
Italian Chapel
Hurtiso
Newark
Bay
Gritley
Point of Ayre
Copinsay
Rora Head
Rackwick
B9047
Cava
Scapa
Flow
Glimps Holm
Hunda
Rose Ness
HOY
Lyness
Fara
Flotta
Burray
Aberdeen
Longhope
Bow
Hoxa
Head
St Margaret's Hope
Grim Ness
Melsetter
Hackness
Martello Tower
South Walls
Herston
SOUTH
RONALDSAY
Tor Ness
Brims
Ness
Swona
Burwick
Cleat
Tomb of the Eagles
Pentland Firth
Brough
Ness
Dunnet
Head
127
Island
of Stroma
Nethertown
Uppertown
Pentland Skerries
Brough
Castle
of Mey
Gills
Huna
Duncansby
Head
John o' Grc
Stacks of
Duncansby
Scrabster
Dunnet
Barrock
Canisbay

a   b   c   d   e

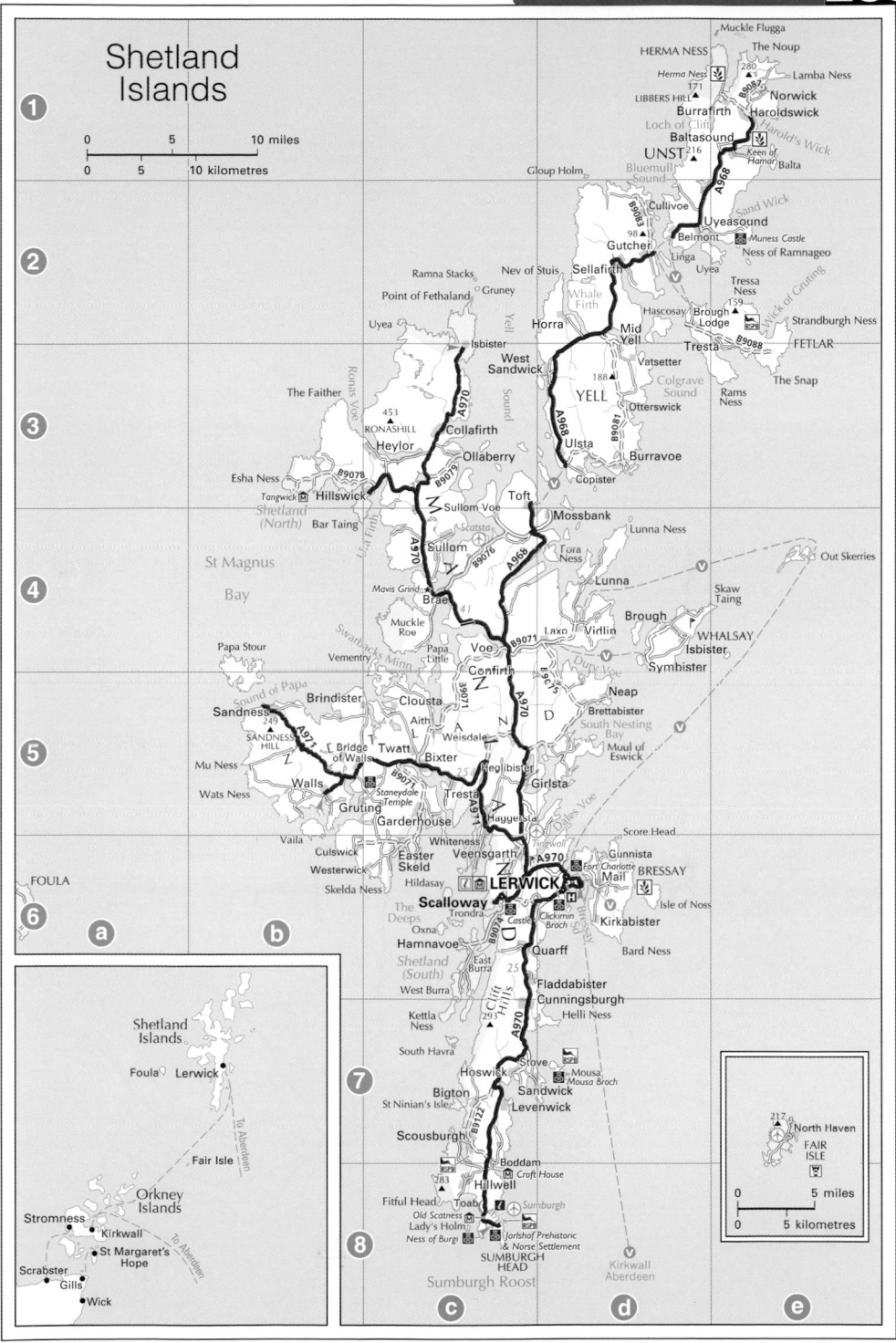

Shetland Islands

0 5 10 miles
0 5 10 kilometres

Muckle Flugga
The Noup
HERMA NESS
Herma Ness
280
Lamba Ness
LIBBERS HILL
171
Burrafirth
Norwick
Baltasound
Haroldswick
UNST
216
Balta
Harold's Wick
Gloup Holm
Sand Wick
Bluemull
Cullivoe
Sound
Belmont
Uyeasound
Gutcher
Muness Castle
98
Linga
Ness of Ramnageo
Uyea
Ramna Stacks
Nev of Stuis
Sellafirth
Tressa
Point of Fethaland
Gruney
Ness
159
Uyea
Whale
Horra
Mid
Hascosay
Brough
Strandburgh Ness
Firth
Yell
Lodge
FETLAR
Isbister
West
Tresta
B9088
The Faither
Sandwick
Vatsetter
The Snap
Ronas Voe
188
YELL
Colgrave
RONASHILL
Collafirth
A970
Sound
453
Otterswick
Rams
Heylor
Ollaberry
A968
Ness
Esha Ness
Ulsta
Burravoe
B9078
Toft
Copister
Tangwick
Hillswick
Sullom Voe
Mossbank
Bar Taing
Lunna Ness
Shetland
(North)
Sullom
Fora
Lunna
St Magnus
A970
Ness
Virdlin
Out Skerries
Mavis Grind
Brough
Skaw
Bay
Brae
Taing
Laxo
WHALSAY
Muckle
Voe
Roe
B9071
Isbister
Papa
Confirth
Symbister
Vementry
Little
Papa Stour
Neap
Brindister
Clousta
Brettabister
Sandness
Aith
South Nesting
Twatt
Weisdale
Bay
SANDNESS
Bixter
Muul of
HILL
Bridge
Eswick
Mu Ness
of Walls
Reglibister
Girlsta
Wats Ness
Walls
B9071
Gunnista
Gruting
Tresta
Haggrsta
Score Head
Staneydale
Temple
Vaila
Garderhouse
Whiteness
Fort
Culswick
Easter
Veensgarth
Charlotte
BRESSAY
Skeld
A970
Gunnista
Westerwick
Hildasay
Mail
Skelda Ness
LERWICK
Isle of Noss
Scalloway
Castle
Clickimin
Foula
The
Trondra
Broch
Kirkabister
Deeps
Oxna
Quarff
Bard Ness
Hamnavoe
East
Burra
Fladdabister
Cunningsburgh
West Burra
Helli Ness
Kettla
Cliff
Ness
Hills
South Havra
297
Hoswick
Stove
Mousa
Mousa Broch
Bigton
Sandwick
St Ninian's Isle
Levenwick
Scousburgh
Boddam
283
Croft House
Fitful Head
Hillwell
Toab
Old Scatness
Sumburgh
Lady's Holm
Jarlshof Prehistoric
Ness of Burgi
& Norse Settlement
SUMBURGH
HEAD
Sumburgh Roost

Inset (bottom left)
Shetland
Islands
Foula   Lerwick
To Aberdeen
Fair Isle
Orkney
Islands
Stromness
Kirkwall
St Margaret's
Hope
Scrabster
Gills
Wick

Inset (bottom right)
217
North Haven
FAIR
ISLE
0 5 miles
0 5 kilometres

a b c d e
1 2 3 4 5 6 7 8

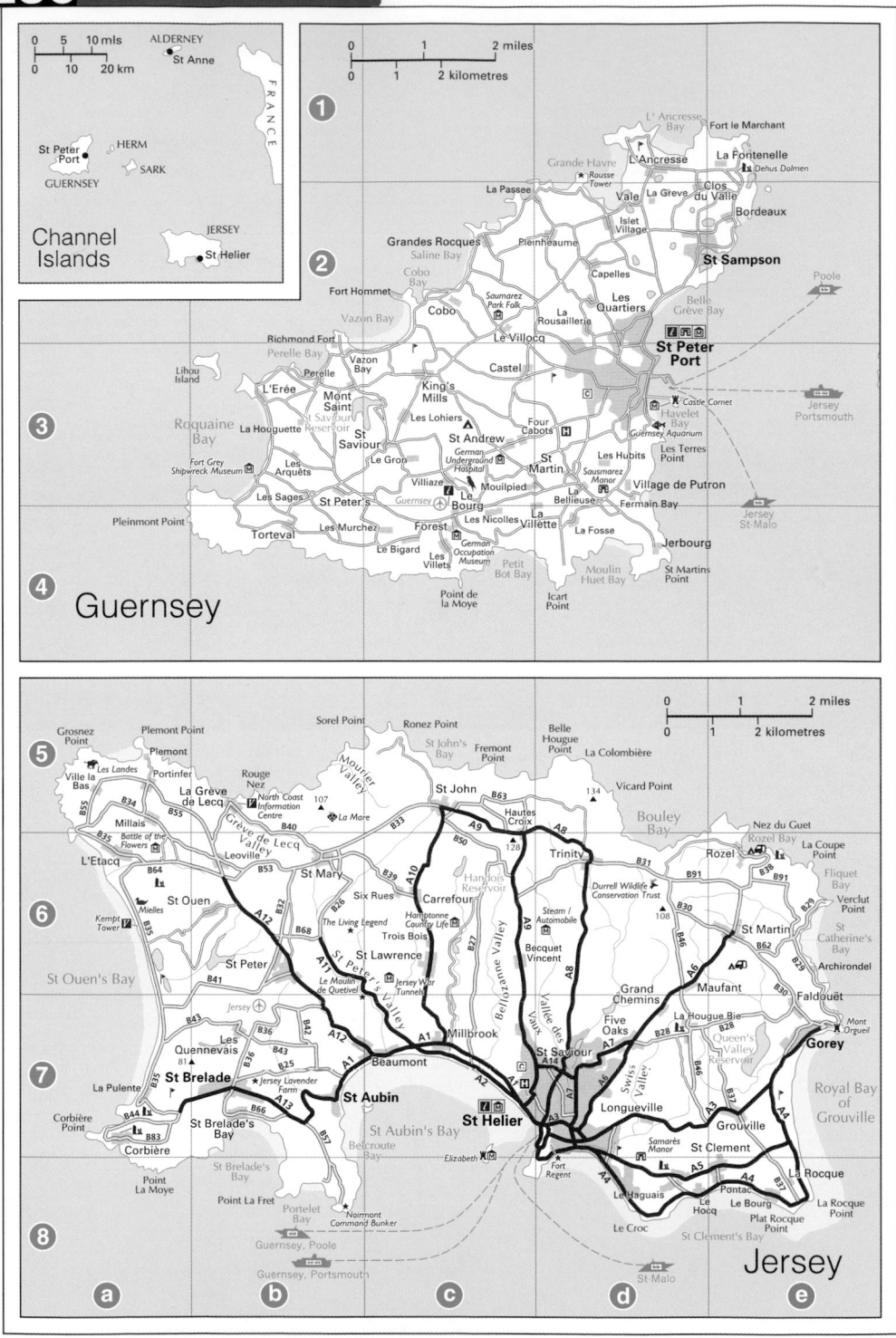

Channel Islands

ALDERNEY
• St Anne

0 5 10 mls
0 10 20 km

FRANCE

St Peter
Port •   HERM
GUERNSEY   SARK

JERSEY
• St Helier

0   1   2 miles
0   1   2 kilometres

Guernsey

L'Ancresse Bay
Fort le Marchant
La Fontenelle
Dehus Dolmen
Grande Havre
Rousse Tower
L'Ancresse
Clos du Valle
Bordeaux
La Passee
Vale
La Greve
St Sampson
Grandes Rocques
Pleinheaume
Saline Bay
Capelles
Poole
Cobo Bay
Islet Village
Les Quartiers
Soumarez Park Folk
Fort Hommet
Cobo
La Rousaillerie
Belle Greve Bay
Vazon Bay
Le Villocq
St Peter Port
Richmond Fort
Perelle Bay
Vazon Bay
Castel
Castle Cornet
Jersey Portsmouth
Lihou Island
L'Erée
Perelle
King's Mills
Guernsey Aquarium
Mont Saint
Havelet Bay
Roquaine Bay
La Houguette
St Saviour Reservoir
Les Lohiers
Four Cabots
St Andrew
Les Hubits
Les Terres Point
Fort Grey Shipwreck Museum
Les Arquêts
Le Gron
German Underground Hospital
St Martin
Sausmarez Manor
Village de Putron
Les Sages
St Peter's
Villiaze
Le Bourg
Moulpied
La Bellieuse
Fermain Bay
Pleinmont Point
Les Murchez
Forest
Les Nicolles
La Villette
La Fosse
Jerbourg
Torteval
Le Bigard
German Occupation Museum
Les Villets
St Martins Point
Petit Bot Bay
Moulin Huet Bay
Point de la Moye
Icart Point

Jersey

Grosnez Point
Plemont Point
Sorel Point
Ronez Point
Belle Hougue Point
La Colombière
Les Landes
Plemont
St John's Bay
Fremont Point
Ville la Bas
Portinfer
Rouge Nez
Mourier Valley
Vicard Point
North Coast Information Centre
St John
Bouley Bay
Nez du Guet
Battle of the Flowers
107
La Mare
Hautes Croix
134
Rozel Bay
La Coupe Point
L'Etacq
B64
Leoville
B33
A9
A8
Rozel
Fliquet Bay
Millais
Mielles
St Mary
A10
Trinity
Durrell Wildlife Conservation Trust
B91
Verclut Point
Kempt Tower
Six Rues
Carrefour
Handois Reservoir
Steam / Automobile
108
St Martin
St Catherine's Bay
St Ouen
The Living Legend
Hamptonne Country Life
Trois Bois
Becquet Vincent
Archirondel
St Ouen's Bay
St Peter
St Lawrence
Maufant
Faldouët
Le Moulin de Quetivel
Jersey War Tunnels
Grand Chemins
La Hougue Bie
Mont Orgueil
Les Quennevais
81
Millbrook
Five Oaks
Queen's Valley Reservoir
Gorey
La Pulente
Beaumont
St Saviour
Royal Bay of Grouville
Corbière Point
St Brelade
St Aubin
St Aubin's Bay
St Helier
Longueville
Grouville
Corbière
St Brelade's Bay
Belcroute Bay
Elizabeth
Fort Regent
Samarès Manor
St Clement
La Rocque
Point La Moye
St Brelade's Bay
Le Haguais
Le Bourg
La Rocque Point
Portelet Bay
Normont Command Bunker
Le Hocq
Plat Rocque Point
Guernsey, Poole
Le Croc
Pontac
St Clement's Bay
Guernsey, Portsmouth
St-Malo

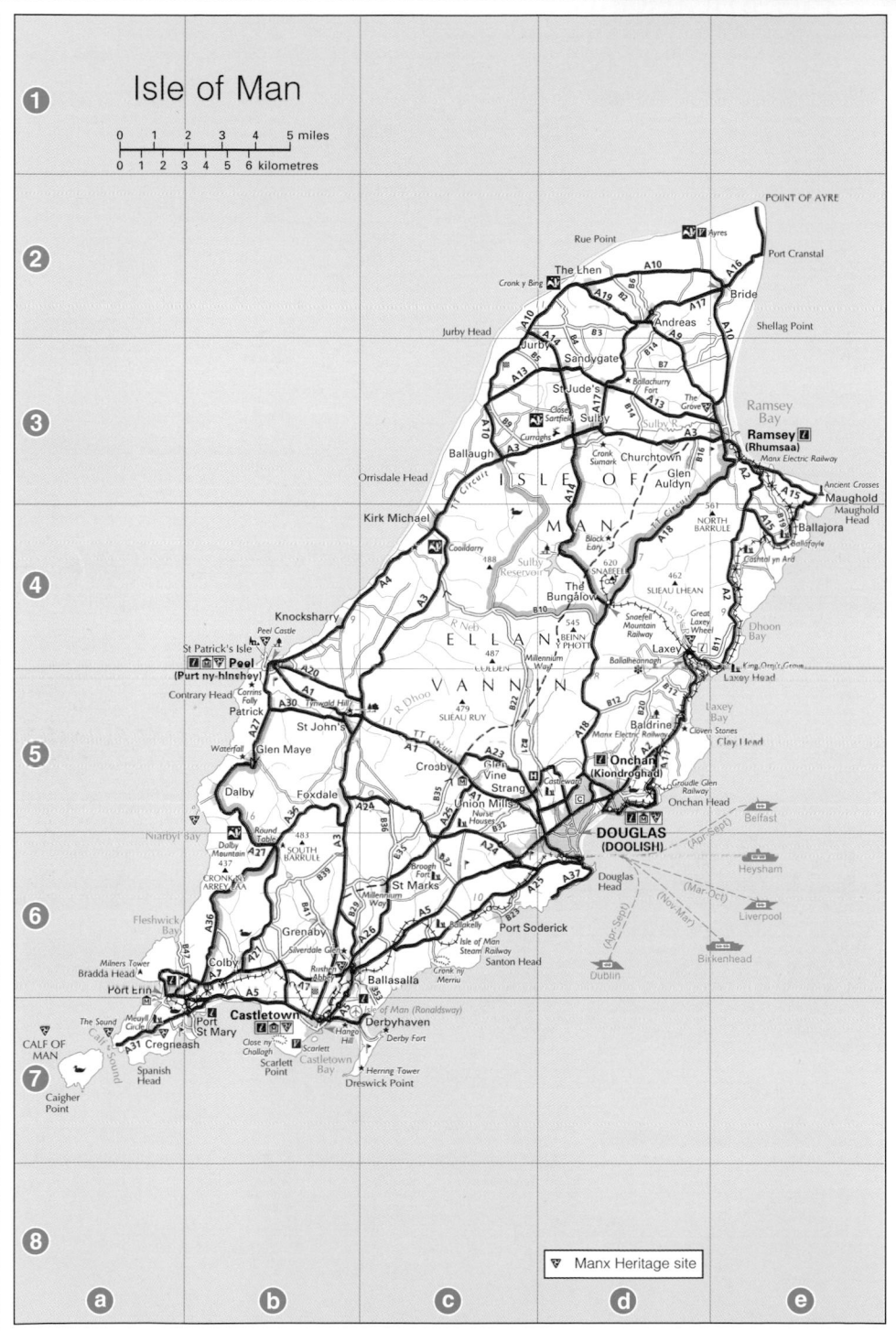

Isle of Man

0 1 2 3 4 5 miles
0 1 2 3 4 5 6 kilometres

POINT OF AYRE

Rue Point
Ayres
The Lhen
Cronk y Bing
Port Cranstal
A10
Bride
A16
Jurby Head
Jurby
A19
Andreas
A9
Shellag Point
A10
A14
B3
A10
B14
Sandygate
A13
St Jude's
Ballachurry
Fort
The
Grove
Sulby
Curraghs
Sulby R.
B14
A13
Ramsey
Bay
Ballaugh
A3
A14
Churchtown
Crank
Sumark
Glen
Auldyn
Ramsey
(Rhumsaa)
Orrisdale Head
I S L E   O F
A2
Ancient Crosses
Maughold
Maughold
Head
Kirk Michael
M A N
Block ★
Eary
NORTH
BARRULE
561
A18
Ballajora
Ballafayle
Coaildarry
188
Sulby
Reservoir
620
SNAEFELL
462
SLIEAU LHEAN
A2
Cashtal yn Ard
Knocksharry
Peel Castle
R. Neb
The
Bungalow
B10
545
BEINN-Y-
PHOTT
Snaefell
Mountain
Railway
Great
Laxey
Wheel
Dhoon
Bay
St Patrick's Isle
Peel
(Purt ny-hInshey)
E L L A N
487
Millennium
Way
Laxey
B11
Contrary Head
Corrins
Folly
A20
V A N N I N
R. Dhoo
479
SLIEAU RUY
Manx Electric Railway
B11
King Orry's Grave
Laxey Head
Patrick
A1
A30
Tynwald Hill
St John's
TT Circuit
128
B12
B20
Laxey
Bay
Waterfall
Glen Maye
A1
A3
A23
A18
Baldrine
Cloven Stones
Clay Head
Dalby
Foxdale
A24
Crosby
Glen
Vine
Strang
Groudle Glen
Railway
Belfast
Round
Table
483
SOUTH
BARRULE
Union Mills
Nurse
Houses
Onchan
(Kiondroghad)
Onchan Head
Niarbyl Bay
Dolby
Mountain
437
A27
A36
B35
B32
Castletown
DOUGLAS
(DOOLISH)
Heysham
CRONK NY
ARREY LAA
A3
Broogh
Fort
St Marks
10
A25
A37
Douglas
Head
Liverpool
Fleshwick
Bay
A36
Grenaby
Silverdale Glen
Millennium
Way
B41
Rushen
Abbey
Isle of Man
Steam Railway
Port Soderick
Santon Head
Birkenhead
Colby
A31
A7
A5
B26
Isle of Man (Ronaldsway)
Cronk ny
Merriu
Dublin
Bradda Head
Milners Tower
Port Erin
Ballasalla
Derbyhaven
Derby Fort
CALF OF
MAN
The Sound
Meayll
Circle
Port
St Mary
Castletown
A31
Cregneash
Close ny
Chollagh
Hango
Hill
Castletown
Bay
Scarlett
Point
Herring Tower
Spanish
Head
Scarlett
Dreswick Point
Caigher
Point

▽ Manx Heritage site

Restricted junctions

Motorway and Primary Route junctions which have access or exit restrictions are shown on the map pages thus:

M1 London - Leeds

Junction	Northbound	Southbound
2	Access only from A1 (northbound)	Exit only to A1 (southbound)
4	Access only from A41 (northbound)	Exit only to A41 (southbound)
6A	Access only from M25 (no link from A405)	Exit only to M25 (no link from A405)
7	Access only from A414	Exit only to A414
17	Exit only to M45	Access only from M45
19	Exit only to M6 (northbound)	Access only from M6
21A	Exit only, no access	Access only, no exit
23A	Access only from A42	No restriction
24A	Exit only, no access	Exit only, no access
35A	Exit only, no access	Access only, no exit
43	Exit only to M621	Access only from M621
48	Exit only to A1(M) (northbound)	Access only from A1(M) (southbound)

M2 Rochester - Faversham

Junction	Westbound	Eastbound
1	No exit to A2 (eastbound)	No access from A2 (westbound)

M3 Sunbury - Southampton

Junction	Northeastbound	Southwestbound
8	Access only from A303, no exit	Exit only to A303, no access
10	Exit only, no access	Access only, no exit
14	Access from M27 only, no exit	No access to M27 (westbound)

M4 London - South Wales

Junction	Westbound	Eastbound
1	Access only from A4 (westbound)	Exit only to A4 (eastbound)
21	Exit only to M48	Access only from M48
23	Access only from M48	Exit only to M48
25	Exit only, no access	Access only, no exit
25A	Exit only, no access	Access only, no exit
29	Exit only to A48(M)	Access only from A48(M)
38	Exit only, no access	No restriction
39	Access only, no exit	No access or exit

M5 Birmingham - Exeter

Junction	Northeastbound	Southwestbound
10	Access only, no exit	Exit only, no access
11A	Access only from A417 (westbound)	Exit only to A417 (eastbound)
18A	Exit only to M49	Access only from M49
18	Exit only, no access	Access only, no exit

M6 Toll Motorway

Junction	Northwestbound	Southeastbound
T1	Access only, no exit	No access or exit
T2	No access or exit	Exit only, no access
T3	Staggered junction; follow signs - access only from A38 (northbound)	Staggered junction; follow signs - access only from A38 (southbound)
T5	Access only, no exit	Exit only to A5148 (northbound), no access
T7	Exit only, no access	Access only, no exit
T8	Exit only, no access	Access only, no exit

M6 Rugby - Carlisle

Junction	Northbound	Southbound
3A	Exit only to M6 Toll	Access only from M6 Toll
4A	Access only from M42 (southbound)	Exit only to M42
5	Exit only, no access	Access only, no exit
10A	Exit only to M54	Access only from M54

11A	Access only from M6 Toll	Exit only to M6 Toll
with M56 (jct 20A)	No restriction	Access only from M56 (eastbound)
20	Access only, no exit	No restriction
24	Access only, no exit	Exit only, no access
25	Exit only, no access	Access only, no exit
29	No direct access, use adjacent slip road to jct 29A	No direct exit, use adjacent slip road from jct 29A
29A	Access only, no exit	Exit only, no access
30	Access only from M61	Exit only to M61
31A	Exit only, no access	Access only, no exit
45	Exit only, no access	Access only, no exit

M8 Edinburgh - Bishopton

Junction	Westbound	Eastbound
8	No access from M73 (southbound) or from A8 (eastbound) & A89	No exit to M73 (northbound) or to A8 (westbound) & A89
9	Access only, no exit	Exit only, no access
13	Access only from M80 (southbound)	Exit only to M80 (northbound)
14	Access only, no exit	Exit only, no access
16	Exit only to A804	Access only from A879
17	Exit only to A82	No restriction
18	Access only from A82 (eastbound)	Exit only to A814
19	No access from A814 (westbound)	Exit only to A814 (westbound)
20	Exit only, no access	Access only, no exit
21	Access only, no exit	Exit only to A8
22	Exit only to M77 (southbound)	Access only from M77 (northbound)
23	Exit only to B768	Access only from B768
25	No access or exit from or to A8	No access or exit from or to A8
25A	Exit only, no access	Access only, no exit
28	Access only, no exit	Exit only, no access
28A	Exit only to A737	Access only from A737

M9 Edinburgh - Dunblane

Junction	Northwestbound	Southeastbound
2	Access only, no exit	Exit only, no access
3	Exit only, no access	Access only, no exit
6	Access only, no exit	Exit only to A905
8	Exit only to M876 (southwestbound)	Access only from M876 (northeastbound)

M11 London - Cambridge

Junction	Northbound	Southbound
4	Access only from A406 (eastbound)	Exit only to A406
5	Exit only, no access	Access only, no exit
9	Exit only to A11	Access only from A11
13	Access only, no exit	Exit only, no access
14	Exit only, no access	Access only, no exit

M20 Swanley - Folkestone

Junction	Northwestbound	Southeastbound
2	Staggered junction; follow signs - access only	Staggered junction; follow signs - exit only
3	Exit only to M26 (westbound)	Access only from M26 (eastbound)
5	Access only from A20	For access follow signs - exit only to A20
6	No restriction	For exit follow signs
11A	Access only, no exit	Exit only, no access

M23 Hooley - Crawley

Junction	Northbound	Southbound
7	Exit only to A23 (northbound)	Access only from A23 (southbound)
10A	Access only, no exit	Exit only, no access

M25 London Orbital Motorway

Junction	Clockwise	Anticlockwise
1B	No direct access, use slip road to Jct 2. Exit only	Access only, no exit
5	No exit to M26 (eastbound)	No access from M26
19	Exit only, no access	Access only, no exit
21	Access only from M1 (southbound). Exit only to M1 (northbound)	Access only from M1 (southbound). Exit only to M1 (northbound)
31	No exit (use slip road via jct 30), access only	No access (use slip road via jct 30), exit only

M26 Sevenoaks - Wrotham

Junction	Westbound	Eastbound
with M25 (jct 5)	Exit only to clockwise M25 (westbound)	Access only from anticlockwise M25
with M20 (jct 3)	Access only from M20 (northwestbound)	Exit only to M20 (southeastbound)

M27 Cadnam - Portsmouth

Junction	Westbound	Eastbound
4	Staggered junction; follow signs - access only from M3 (southbound). Exit only to M3 (northbound)	Staggered junction; follow signs - access only from M3 (southbound). Exit only to M3 (northbound)
10	Exit only, no access	Access only, no exit
12	Staggered junction; follow signs - exit only to M275 (southbound)	Staggered junction; follow signs - access only from M275 (northbound)

M40 London - Birmingham

Junction	Northwestbound	Southeastbound
3	Exit only, no access	Access only, no exit
7	Exit only, no access	Access only, no exit
8	Exit only to M40/A40	Access only from M40/A40
13	Exit only, no access	Access only, no exit
14	Access only, no exit	Exit only, no access
16	Access only, no exit	Exit only, no access

M42 Bromsgrove - Measham

Junction	Northeastbound	Southwestbound
1	Access only, no exit	Access only, no exit
7	Exit only to M6 (northwestbound)	Access only from M6 (northwestbound)
7A	Exit only to M6 (southwestbound)	No access or exit
8	Access only from M6 (southeastbound)	Exit only to M6 (northwestbound)

M45 Coventry - M1

Junction	Westbound	Eastbound
Dunchurch (unnumbered)	Access only from A45	Exit only, no access
with M1 (jct 17)	Access only from M1 (northbound)	Exit only to M1 (southbound)

M53 Mersey Tunnel - Chester

Junction	Northbound	Southbound
11	Access only from M56 (westbound). Exit only to M56 (eastbound)	Access only from M56 (westbound). Exit only to M56 (eastbound)

M54 Telford

Junction	Westbound	Eastbound
with M6 (jct 10A)	Access only from M6 (northbound)	Exit only to M6 (southbound)

M56 North Cheshire

Junction	Westbound	Eastbound
1	Access only from M60 (westbound)	Exit only to M60 (eastbound) & A34 (northbound)
2	Exit only, no access	Access only, no exit
3	Access only, no exit	Exit only, no access
4	Exit only, no access	Access only, no exit
7	Exit only, no access	No restriction
8	Access only, no exit	No access or exit
15	Exit only to M53	Access only from M53
16	No access or exit	No restrictions

M57 Liverpool Outer Ring Road

Junction	Northwestbound	Southeastbound
3	Access only, no exit	Exit only, no access
5	Access only from A580 (westbound)	Exit only, no access

M58 Liverpool - Wigan

Junction	Westbound	Eastbound
1	Exit only, no access	Access only, no exit

M60 Manchester Orbital

Junction	Clockwise	Anticlockwise
2	Access only, no exit	Exit only, no access
3	No access from M56	Access only from A34 (northbound)
4	Access only from A34 (northbound). Exit only to M56	Access only from M56 (eastbound). Exit only to A34 (southbound)
5	Access and exit only from and to A5103 (northbound)	Access and exit only from and to A5103 (southbound)
7	No direct access, use slip road to jct 8. Exit only to A56	Access only from A56. No exit - use jct 8
14	Access from A580 (eastbound)	Exit only to A580 (westbound)
16	Access only, no exit	Exit only, no access
20	No access, no exit	Access only, no exit
22	No restriction	Exit only, no access
25	Exit only, no access	No restriction
26	No restriction	Exit only, no access
27	Access only, no exit	Exit only, no access

M61 Manchester - Preston

Junction	Northwestbound	Southeastbound
3	No access or exit	Exit only, no access
with M6 (jct 30)	Exit only to M6 (northbound)	Access only from M6 (southbound)

M62 Liverpool - Kingston upon Hull

Junction	Westbound	Eastbound
23	Access only, no exit	Exit only, no access
32A	No access to A1(M) (southbound)	No restriction

M65 Preston - Colne

Junction	Northeastbound	Southwestbound
9	Exit only, no access	Access only, no exit
11	Access only, no exit	Exit only, no access

M66 Bury

Junction	Northbound	Southbound
with A56	Exit only to A56 (northbound)	Access only from A56 (southbound)
1	Exit only, no access	Access only, no exit

M67 Hyde Bypass

Junction	Westbound	Eastbound
1	Access only, no exit	Exit only, no access
2	Access only, no exit	Access only, no exit
3	Exit only, no access	No restriction

M69 Coventry - Leicester

Junction	Northbound	Southbound
2	Access only, no exit	Exit only, no access

M73 East of Glasgow

Junction	Northbound	Southbound
2	No access from or exit to A89. No access from M8 (eastbound).	No access from or exit to A89. No exit to M8 (westbound)

M74 and A74(M) Glasgow - Gretna

Junction	Northbound	Southbound
3	Access only, no access	Access only, no exit
3A	Access only, no exit	Exit only, no access
7	Access only, no exit	Exit only, no access
9	No access or exit	Exit only, no access
10	No restrictions	Access only, no exit
11	Access only, no exit	Exit only, no access
12	Exit only, no access	Access only, no exit
18	Access only, no exit	Access only, no exit

M77 South of Glasgow

Junction	Northbound	Southbound
with M8 (jct 22)	No exit to M8 (westbound)	No access from M8 (eastbound)
4	Access only, no exit	Exit only, no access
6	Access only, no exit	Exit only, no access
7	Access only, no exit	No restriction

M80 Glasgow - Stirling

Junction	Northbound	Southbound
4A	Exit only, no access	Access only, no exit
6A	Access only, no exit	Exit only, no access
8	Exit only to M876 (northeastbound)	Access only from M876 (southwestbound)

M90 Forth Road Bridge - Perth

Junction	Northbound	Southbound
2A	Exit only to A92 (eastbound)	Access only from A92 (westbound)
7	Access only, no exit	Exit only, no access
8	Exit only, no access	Access only, no exit
10	No access from A912. No exit to A912 (southbound)	No access from A912 (northbound). No exit to A912

M180 Doncaster - Grimsby

Junction	Westbound	Eastbound
1	Access only, no exit	Exit only, no access

M606 Bradford Spur

Junction	Northbound	Southbound
2	Exit only, no access	No restriction

M621 Leeds - M1

Junction	Clockwise	Anticlockwise
2A	Access only, no exit	Exit only, no access
4	No exit or access	No restriction
5	Access only, no exit	Exit only, no access
6	Exit only, no access	Access only, no exit
with M1 (jct 43)	Exit only to M1 (southbound)	Access only from M1 (northbound)

M876 Bonnybridge - Kincardine Bridge

Junction	Northeastbound	Southwestbound
with M80 (jct 5)	Access only from M80 (northbound)	Exit only to M80 (southbound)
with M9 (jct 8)	Exit only to M9 (eastbound)	Access only from M9 (westbound)

A1(M) South Mimms - Baldock

Junction	Northbound	Southbound
2	Exit only, no access	Access only, no exit
3	No restriction	Exit only, no access
5	Access only, no exit	No access or exit

A1(M) Pontefract - Bedale

Junction	Northbound	Southbound
41	No access to M62 (eastbound)	No restriction
43	Access only from M1 (northbound)	Exit only to M1 (southbound)

A1(M) Scotch Corner - Newcastle upon Tyne

Junction	Northbound	Southbound
57	Exit only to A66(M) (eastbound)	Access only from A66(M) (westbound)
65	No access Exit only to A194(M) & A1 (northbound)	No exit Access only from A194(M) & A1 (southbound)

A3(M) Horndean - Havant

Junction	Northbound	Southbound
1	Access only from A3	Exit only to A3
4	Exit only, no access	Access only, no exit

A48(M) Cardiff Spur

Junction	Westbound	Eastbound
29	Access only from M4 (westbound)	Exit only to M4 (eastbound)
29A	Exit only to A48 (westbound)	Access only from A48 (eastbound)

A66(M) Darlington Spur

Junction	Westbound	Eastbound
with A1(M) (jct 57)	Exit only to A1(M) (southbound)	Access only from A1(M) (northbound)

A194(M) Newcastle upon Tyne

Junction	Northbound	Southbound
with A1(M) (jct 65)	Access only from A1(M) (northbound)	Exit only to A1(M) (southbound)

A12 M25 - Ipswich

Junction	Northeastbound	Southwestbound
13	Access only, no exit	No restriction
14	Exit only, no access	Access only, no exit
20A	Exit only, no access	Access only, no exit
20B	Access only, no exit	Exit only, no access
21	No restriction	Access only, no exit
23	Exit only, no access	Access only, no exit
24	Access only, no exit	Exit only, no access
27	Exit only, no access	Access only, no exit
Dedham & Stratford St Mary (unnumbered)	Exit only	Access only

A14 M1 - Felixstowe

Junction	Westbound	Eastbound
with M1/M6 (jct 19)	Exit only to M6 and M1 (northbound)	Access only from M6 and M1 (southbound)
4	Exit only, no access	Access only, no exit
31	Access only, no exit	Exit only to A1307
34	Access only, no exit	Exit only, no access
36	Exit only to A11, access only from A1303	Access only from A11
38	Access only from A11	Exit only to A11
39	Exit only, no access	Access only, no exit
61	Access only, no exit	Exit only, no access

A55 Holyhead - Chester

Junction	Westbound	Eastbound
8A	Access only, no exit	Access only, no exit
23A	Access only, no exit	Exit only, no access
24A	Exit only, no access	No access or exit
33A	Exit only, no access	No access or exit
33B	Exit only, no access	Access only, no exit
37	Exit only to A5104	Access only from A5104

Index to place names

This index lists places appearing in the main-map section of the atlas in alphabetical order. The reference following each name gives the atlas page number and grid reference of the square in which the place appears. The map shows counties and administrative areas, together with a list of the abbreviated name forms used in the index. The top 100 places of tourist interest are indexed in **red**, World Heritage sites in **green**, motorway service areas in **blue**, airports in blue *italic* and National Parks in green *italic*.

Scotland

Abers	**Aberdeenshire**
Ag & B	**Argyll and Bute**
Angus	**Angus**
Border	**Scottish Borders**
C Aber	**City of Aberdeen**
C Dund	**City of Dundee**
C Edin	**City of Edinburgh**
C Glas	**City of Glasgow**
Clacks	**Clackmannanshire (1)**
D & G	**Dumfries & Galloway**
E Ayrs	**East Ayrshire**
E Duns	**East Dunbartonshire (2)**
E Loth	**East Lothian**
E Rens	**East Renfrewshire (3)**
Falk	**Falkirk**
Fife	**Fife**
Highld	**Highland**
Inver	**Inverclyde (4)**
Mdloth	**Midlothian (5)**
Moray	**Moray**
N Ayrs	**North Ayrshire**
N Lans	**North Lanarkshire (6)**
Ork	**Orkney Islands**
P & K	**Perth & Kinross**
Rens	**Renfrewshire (7)**
S Ayrs	**South Ayrshire**
Shet	**Shetland Islands**
S Lans	**South Lanarkshire**
Stirlg	**Stirling**
W Duns	**West Dunbartonshire (8)**
W Isls	**Western Isles**
	(Na h-Eileanan an Iar)
W Loth	**West Lothian**

Wales

Blae G	**Blaenau Gwent (9)**
Brdgnd	**Bridgend (10)**
Caerph	**Caerphilly (11)**
Cardif	**Cardiff**
Carmth	**Carmarthenshire**
Cerdgn	**Ceredigion**
Conwy	**Conwy**
Denbgs	**Denbighshire**
Flints	**Flintshire**
Gwynd	**Gwynedd**
IoA	**Isle of Anglesey**
Mons	**Monmouthshire**
Myr Td	**Merthyr Tydfil (12)**
Neath	**Neath Port Talbot (13)**
Newpt	**Newport (14)**
Pembks	**Pembrokeshire**
Powys	**Powys**
Rhondd	**Rhondda Cynon Taff (15)**
Swans	**Swansea**
Torfn	**Torfaen (16)**
V Glam	**Vale of Glamorgan (17)**
Wrexhm	**Wrexham**

Channel Islands & Isle of Man

Guern	**Guernsey**
Jersey	**Jersey**
IoM	**Isle of Man**

England

BaNES	**Bath & N E Somerset (18)**
Barns	**Barnsley (19)**
Bed	**Bedford**
Birm	**Birmingham**
Bl w D	**Blackburn with Darwen (20)**
Bmouth	**Bournemouth**
Bolton	**Bolton (21)**
Bpool	**Blackpool**
Br & H	**Brighton & Hove (22)**
Br For	**Bracknell Forest (23)**
Bristl	**City of Bristol**
Bucks	**Buckinghamshire**
Bury	**Bury (24)**
C Beds	**Central Bedfordshire**
C Brad	**City of Bradford**
C Derb	**City of Derby**
C KuH	**City of Kingston upon Hull**
C Leic	**City of Leicester**
C Nott	**City of Nottingham**
C Pete	**City of Peterborough**
C Plym	**City of Plymouth**
C Port	**City of Portsmouth**
C Sotn	**City of Southampton**
C Stke	**City of Stoke-on-Trent**
C York	**City of York**
Calder	**Calderdale (25)**
Cambs	**Cambridgeshire**
Ches E	**Cheshire East**
Ches W	**Cheshire West and Chester**
Cnwll	**Cornwall**
Covtry	**Coventry**
Cumb	**Cumbria Darltn**
Derbys	**Derbyshire**
Devon	**Devon**
Donc	**Doncaster (27)**
Dorset	**Dorset**
Dudley	**Dudley (28)**
Dur	**Durham**
E R Yk	**East Riding of Yorkshire**
E Susx	**East Sussex**
Essex	**Essex**
Gatesd	**Gateshead (29)**
Gloucs	**Gloucestershire**
Gt Lon	**Greater London**
Halton	**Halton (30)**
Hants	**Hampshire**
Hartpl	**Hartlepool (31)**
Herefs	**Herefordshire**
Herts	**Hertfordshire**
IoS	**Isles of Scilly**
IoW	**Isle of Wight**
Kent	**Kent**
Kirk	**Kirklees (32)**
Knows	**Knowsley (33)**
Lancs	**Lancashire**
Leeds	**Leeds**
Leics	**Leicestershire**
Lincs	**Lincolnshire**
Lpool	**Liverpool**
Luton	**Luton**
M Keyn	**Milton Keynes**
Manch	**Manchester**
Medway	**Medway**

Middsb	**Middlesbrough**
NE Lin	**North East Lincolnshire**
N Linc	**North Lincolnshire**
N Som	**North Somerset (34)**
N Tyne	**North Tyneside (35)**
N u Ty	**Newcastle upon Tyne**
N York	**North Yorkshire**
Nhants	**Northamptonshire**
Norfk	**Norfolk**
Notts	**Nottinghamshire**
Nthumb	**Northumberland**
Oldham	**Oldham (36)**
Oxon	**Oxfordshire**
Poole	**Poole**
R & Cl	**Redcar & Cleveland**
Readg	**Reading**
Rochdl	**Rochdale (37)**
Rothm	**Rotherham (38)**
Rutlnd	**Rutland**
S Glos	**South Gloucestershire (39)**
S on T	**Stockton-on-Tees (40)**
S Tyne	**South Tyneside (41)**
Salfd	**Salford (42)**
Sandw	**Sandwell (43)**
Sefton	**Sefton (44)**
Sheff	**Sheffield**
Shrops	**Shropshire**
Slough	**Slough (45)**
Solhll	**Solihull (46)**
Somset	**Somerset**
St Hel	**St Helens (47)**
Staffs	**Staffordshire**
Sthend	**Southend-on-Sea**
Stockp	**Stockport (48)**
Suffk	**Suffolk**
Sundld	**Sunderland**
Surrey	**Surrey**
Swindn	**Swindon**
Tamesd	**Tameside (49)**
Thurr	**Thurrock (50)**
Torbay	**Torbay**
Traffd	**Trafford (51)**
W & M	**Windsor and Maidenhead (52)**
W Berk	**West Berkshire**
W Susx	**West Sussex**
Wakefd	**Wakefield (53)**
Warrtn	**Warrington (54)**
Warwks	**Warwickshire**
Wigan	**Wigan (55)**
Wilts	**Wiltshire**
Wirral	**Wirral (56)**
Wokham	**Wokingham (57)**
Wolves	**Wolverhampton (58)**
Worcs	**Worcestershire**
Wrekin	**Telford & Wrekin (59)**
Wsall	**Walsall (60)**

ORKNEY
ISLANDS

SHETLAND
ISLANDS

WESTERN ISLES (NA H-EILEANAN AN IAR)

HIGHLAND

MORAY

S C O T L A N D

• Aberdeen

ABERDEENSHIRE

ANGUS

PERTH &
KINROSS

• Dundee

ARGYLL
& BUTE

STIRLING

FIFE

1

FALK

8   2
4 • Glasgow
7
3

W
LOTH

6

Edinburgh

E LOTH

5

NORTH
AYRSHIRE

S LANS

SCOTTISH
BORDERS

E AYRS

S AYRS

DUMFRIES &
GALLOWAY

NORTHUMBERLAND

Newcastle
upon Tyne

35
41

29   Sunderland

IoM

CUMBRIA

DURHAM

31

R & CL.

26 40   Middlesbrough

NORTH YORKSHIRE

Blackpool

LANCASHIRE

Bradford

York

EAST RIDING
OF YORKSHIRE

Kingston
upon Hull

20

Leeds

25

53

N LINC

N E
LIN

IoA

44
56
33
30

21 24 37
55   36
42   49
54 51
40

32

19

27

Liverpool

Manchester

38

Sheffield

CONWY

FLINTS

CHES
W

CHES
E

DERBYS

NOTTS

LINCOLNSHIRE

DENBGS

WREXHAM

Stoke-on-
Trent

Derby

Nottingham

GWYNEDD

59

STAFFS

LEICS

RUTLAND

Peterborough

NORFOLK

SHROPSHIRE

58 60
28 43

Birmingham

Coventry

Leicester

N'HANTS

Milton
Keynes

CAMBS

SUFFOLK

46

BED

PEMBKS

CERDGN

POWYS

WORCS

WARWKS

W A L E S

HEREFS

E N G L A N D

BEDS   Luton

HERTS

ESSEX

Southend-
on-Sea

CARMTH

13

MONS

12 9
15 16
11
14

GLOUCS

OXON

Swindon

BUCKS

52 45

GREATER
LONDON

50

MEDWAY

Swansea

10

Cardiff

Bristol

39

Reading

W BERK

57 23

KENT

17

34

18

WILTSHIRE

SURREY

HAMPSHIRE

W SUSX

E SUSX

22

SOMERSET

DEVON

DORSET

Southampton

Bournemouth
Poole

Portsmouth

IoW

CORNWALL

Plymouth

Torbay

CHANNEL
ISLANDS

Guernsey

Jersey

IoS

A

Abbas Combe Somset....27 G6
Abberley Worcs..............70 D2
Abberley Common
  Worcs.............................70 D2
Abberton Essex..............62 B4
Abberton Worcs..............71 H4
Abbess Roding Essex....60 F5
Abbeydale Sheff............114 F5
Abbey Dore Herefs.........54 B3
Abbey Green Staffs.........99 L2
Abbey St Bathans
  Border.........................178 F6
Abbeystead Lancs........130 B8
Abbey Town Cumb........147 L5
Abbey Village Lancs......121 J6
Abbey Wood Gt Lon......45 J4
Abbotrule Border...........167 J6
Abbots Bickington
  Devon.............................9 K3
Abbots Bromley Staffs..100 B7
Abbotsbury Dorset.........14 B5
Abbots Deuglie P & K...186 B5
Abbotsham Devon..........22 F6
Abbotskerswell
  Devon.............................7 K3
Abbots Langley Herts....59 H7
Abbots Leigh N Som......38 D5
Abbotsley Cambs...........75 J3
Abbots Morton Worcs....71 H4
Abbots Ripton Cambs....89 J7
Abbot's Salford
  Warwks.........................71 J4
Abbots Worthy Hants....29 J5
Abbotts Ann Hants.........29 G3
Abbott Street Dorset....15 J3
Abdon Shrops.................83 L6
Aberaeron Cerdgn.........66 B3
Aberaman Rhondd.........52 F7
Aberangell Gwynd.........81 J2
Aberarder Highld.........202 F1
Aberargie P & K............186 B4
Aberarth Cerdgn...........66 B2
Aberavon Neath.............51 L7
Abercanaid Myr Td........53 G7
Abercarn Caerph............37 K2
Abercastle Pembks........64 B7
Abercegir Powys............81 H3
Aberchalder Lodge
  Highld.........................202 B5
Aberchirder Abers........216 C4
Abercraf Powys..............52 C5
Abercregan Neath.........36 D2
Abercwmboi Rhondd....52 F7
Abercych Pembks...........65 H6
Abercynon Rhondd........37 G2
Aberdalgie P & K..........185 M4
Aberdare Rhondd...........52 F7
Aberdaron Gwynd..........94 C7
Aberdeen C Aber..........207 H4
Aberdeen Airport
  C Aber........................207 G3
Aberdeen
  Crematorium
  C Aber........................207 G4
Aberdour Fife................177 G2
Aberdulais Neath...........52 B7
Aberdyfi Gwynd.............80 E4
Aberedw Powys..............68 C5
Abereiddy Pembks.........48 D2
Abererch Gwynd.............95 G5
Aberfan Myr Td..............53 G7
Aberfeldy P & K............194 D6
Aberffraw IoA...............108 D7
Aberford Leeds..............124 C3
Aberfoyle Stirlg............184 C7
Abergavenny Mons........53 L5
Abergele Conwy............110 C6
Abergorlech Carmth......66 D7
Abergwesyn Powys........67 J4
Abergwili Carmth............50 F2
Abergwynfi Neath..........36 D2
Abergwyngregyn
  Gwynd.........................109 J6

Abergynolwyn
  Gwynd...........................80 F3
Aberkenfig Brdgnd........36 D4
Aberlady E Loth...........178 B3
Aberlemno Angus........196 E5
Aberllefenni Gwynd.......81 G2
Aberllynfi Powys............68 D6
Aberlour Moray.............215 G5
Abermule Powys............82 D5
Abernant Carmth............50 D2
Abernethy P & K...........186 C4
Abernyte P & K.............186 D2
Aberporth Cerdgn..........65 J4
Abersoch Gwynd............94 E6
Abersychan Torfn.........53 K7
Aberthin V Glam............36 F5
Abertillery Blae G.........53 K7
Abertridwr Caerph.........37 H3
Abertridwr Powys..........97 G8
Aberuthven P & K.........185 K4
Aberystwyth Cerdgn......80 D6
Aberystwyth
  Crematorium
  Cerdgn...........................80 E6
Abingdon-on-
  Thames Oxon...............41 J2
Abinger Common
  Surrey...........................31 J3
Abinger Hammer
  Surrey...........................31 H2
Abington Nhants...........73 L3
Abington S Lans...........165 H5
Abington Pigotts
  Cambs...........................75 K5
Abington Services
  S Lans.........................165 H4
Abingworth W Susx.......18 F3
Ab Kettleby Leics........102 B7
Ablington Gloucs...........56 C6
Abney Derbys...............114 D5
Aboyne Abers...............205 L5
Abram Wigan................112 E2
Abriachan Highld.........212 E7
Abridge Essex................45 J2
Abronhill N Lans..........175 K3
Abson S Glos.................39 G5
Abthorpe Nhants...........73 J5
Aby Lincs.....................118 F5
Acaster Malbis C York..124 E2
Acaster Selby N York...124 E3
Accrington Lancs.........121 L5
Accrington
  Crematorium
  Lancs...........................121 L5
Acha Ag & B................188 F5
Achahoish Ag & B........172 D3
Achalader P & K..........195 H7
Achaleven Ag & B........182 D1
Acha Mor W Isls..........232 f3
Achanalt Highld...........211 K3
Achandunie Highld.......222 E6
Achany Highld..............222 D2
Acharacle Highld.........190 D3
Acharn Highld..............190 E6
Acharn P & K................194 B7
Achavanich Highld.......231 H6
Achduart Highld...........224 C7
Achfary Highld.............228 D7
A'Chill Highld...............198 D4
Achiltibuie Highld.........224 C6
Achina Highld...............229 L4
Achinhoan Ag & B........161 J6
Achintee Highld............210 E6
Achintraid Highld.........210 C6
Achlyness Highld.........228 C4
Achmelvich Highld.......224 C4
Achmore Highld...........210 D7
Achmore W Isls............232 f3
Achnacarnin Highld......224 C3
Achnacarry Highld........201 J7
Achnacloich Highld......199 J4
Achnaconeran Highld ..202 C2
Achnacroish Ag & B....191 G7
Achnadrish House
  Ag & B.........................189 L6
Achnafauld P & K........185 J1

Achnagarron Highld......222 F7
Achnaha Highld............189 L3
Achnahaird Highld........224 B5
Achnairn Highld............225 L6
Achnalea Highld...........191 G4
Achnamara Ag & B.......172 D2
Achnasheen Highld......211 J3
Achnashellach Lodge
  Highld.........................210 F5
Achnastank Moray........215 G7
Achosnich Highld.........189 K3
Achranich Highld..........190 E6
Achreamie Highld.........230 E3
Achriabhach Highld......192 B3
Achriesgill Highld.........228 C5
Achtoty Highld.............229 K3
Achurch Nhants.............88 E6
Achvaich Highld...........222 F3
Achvarasdal Highld......230 E3
Ackergill Highld...........231 L5
Acklam Middsb............141 L4
Acklam N York.............134 B7
Ackleton Shrops............84 D4
Acklington Nthumb......159 G2
Ackton Wakefd............124 C6
Ackworth Moor Top
  Wakefd.......................124 C7
Acle Norfk.....................93 J2
Acock's Green Birm......85 K6
Acol Kent.......................35 J2
Acomb C York..............124 E1
Acomb Nthumb............150 B2
Aconbury Herefs...........54 D2
Acton Ches E.................98 F2
Acton Gt Lon.................44 D4
Acton Staffs...................99 J4
Acton Suffk....................77 K5
Acton Beauchamp
  Herefs...........................70 C4
Acton Bridge Ches W..112 E6
Acton Burnell Shrops....83 K3
Acton Green Herefs......70 C4
Acton Park Wrexhm......97 M3
Acton Round Shrops......84 B4
Acton Scott Shrops.......83 J5
Acton Trussell Staffs....99 L8
Acton Turville S Glos....39 J4
Adbaston Staffs.............99 H6
Adber Dorset..................26 E7
Adbolton Notts............101 L5
Adderbury Oxon............72 F7
Adderley Shrops............98 F4
Addiewell W Loth........176 D5
Addingham C Brad......123 G1
Addington Bucks...........58 C3
Addington Gt Lon..........45 G7
Addington Kent.............33 H2
Addiscombe Gt Lon......45 G6
Addlestone Surrey........43 H7
Addlethorpe Lincs........119 H7
Adeyfield Herts.............59 H6
Adfa Powys....................82 B4
Adforton Herefs............69 H1
Adisham Kent................35 G4
Adlestrop Gloucs..........56 E3
Adlingfleet E R Yk.......125 K6
Adlington Lancs...........121 J7
Admaston Staffs..........100 B7
Admaston Wrekin..........84 B2
Adpar Cerdgn................65 J6
Adsborough Somset......25 L5
Adscombe Somset.........25 J4
Adstock Bucks...............58 C3
Adstone Nhants.............73 H4
Adversane W Susx........31 H6
Advie Highld................214 D7
Adwick Le Street
  Donc............................115 J2
Adwick upon Dearne
  Donc............................115 J2
Ae D & G.....................155 H4
Ae Bridgend D & G......155 H5
Afan Forest Park
  Neath............................36 D2
Affleck Abers...............216 B6
Affpuddle Dorset..........14 F4

Affric Lodge Highld......201 J2
Afon-wen Flints...........110 F6
Afton IoW.......................16 D5
Agecroft
  Crematorium
  Salfd...........................113 J2
Agglethorpe N York.....131 K3
Aigburth Lpool.............111 L4
Aike E R Yk.................126 C2
Aiketgate Cumb...........148 E5
Aikton Cumb................148 B4
Ailsworth C Pete...........89 G4
Ainderby Quernhow
  N York.........................132 E4
Ainderby Steeple
  N York.........................132 D2
Aingers Green Essex....62 D4
Ainsdale Sefton...........120 D7
Ainstable Cumb...........148 F5
Ainsworth Bury............121 L8
Ainthorpe N York.........142 E5
Ainville W Loth............176 F5
Aird Ag & B..................181 M7
Aird D & G...................144 D3
Aird W Isls...................232 g2
Aird a Mhulaidh
  W Isls.........................232 e3
Aird Asaig W Isls.........232 e4
Aird Dhubh Highld.......209 L6
Airdeny Ag & B............182 E2
Aird of Kinloch
  Ag & B.........................181 H2
Aird of Sleat Highld.....199 J5
Airdrie N Lans.............175 K5
Airdriehill N Lans........175 K5
Airds of Kells D & G....154 B7
Aird Uig W Isls............232 d2
Airidh a bhruaich
  W Isls.........................232 e3
Airieland D & G...........146 D4
Airlie Angus................195 L6
Airmyn E R Yk.............125 H5
Airntully P & K............186 A1
Airor Highld.................199 L4
Airth Falk....................176 B2
Airton N York...............131 G7
Aisby Lincs..................103 G5
Aisby Lincs..................116 E3
Aish Devon.....................7 G4
Aish Devon.....................7 J4
Aisholt Somset..............25 J4
Aiskew N York.............132 D2
Aislaby N York.............134 B3
Aislaby N York.............143 H5
Aislaby S on T.............141 J5
Aisthorpe Lincs...........116 F5
Aith Shet.....................235 c5
Akeld Nthumb..............168 E4
Akeley Bucks.................73 K6
Albaston Cnwll................6 B2
Alberbury Shrops..........83 G1
Albourne W Susx..........19 H3
Albrighton Shrops.........84 E3
Albrighton Shrops.........98 C8
Alburgh Norfk................92 F6
Albury Herts..................60 C3
Albury Surrey................31 H2
Albury Heath Surrey.....31 H3
Alcaig Highld...............212 F3
Alcaston Shrops............83 J6
Alcester Warwks...........71 K3
Alciston E Susx.............20 B5
Alcombe Somset...........24 F3
Alconbury Cambs..........89 H7
Alconbury Weston
  Cambs...........................89 H7
Aldborough N York.......132 F6
Aldborough Norfk........106 E5
Aldbourne Wilts............40 E5
Aldbrough E R Yk........127 G3
Aldbrough St John
  N York.........................140 F5
Aldbury Herts................58 F5
Aldcliffe Lancs............129 K7
Aldclune P & K............194 E4
Aldeburgh Suffk............79 K3

Aldeby Norfk..................93 J5
Aldenham Herts...............43 J2
Alderbury Wilts...............28 D6
Alderford Norfk.............106 D8
Alderholt Dorset..............28 C8
Alderley Gloucs..............39 H3
Alderley Edge Ches E....113 J3
Aldermans Green
    Covtry.....................86 D6
Aldermaston W Berk 41 L7
Alderminster Warwks ...72 B5
Aldershot Hants.............30 E2
Alderton Gloucs.............55 M2
Alderton Nhants.............73 K5
Alderton Suffk................79 M6
Alderton Wilts................39 J4
Aldfield N York..............132 D5
Aldford Ches W..............98 B2
Aldgate Rutlnd..............88 E3
Aldham Essex................61 L3
Aldham Suffk..................78 C5
Aldingbourne W Susx....18 C5
Aldingham Cumb..........129 G5
Aldington Kent...............34 E7
Aldington Worcs............71 J5
Aldington Corner
    Kent.......................34 E7
Aldivalloch Moray 205 H1
Aldochlay Ag & B..........174 C1
Aldreth Cambs...............90 C8
Aldridge Wsall................85 J4
Aldringham Suffk............79 J3
Aldsworth Gloucs...........56 D6
Aldunie Moray...............215 H8
Aldwark Derbys.............100 E2
Aldwark N York.............133 G6
Aldwick W Susx..............18 C6
Aldwincle Nhants...........88 E6
Aldworth W Berk............41 K4
Alexandria W Duns.......174 D3
Aley Somset....................25 J4
Alfington Devon.............12 E3
Alfold Surrey..................31 H5
Alfold Crossways
    Surrey......................31 H4
Alford Abers.................206 B3
Alford Lincs..................118 F6
Alford Somset.................26 E5
Alford Crematorium
    Lincs......................118 F6
Alfreton Derbys.............101 H2
Alfrick Worcs..................70 D4
Alfrick Pound Worcs.......70 D4
Alfriston E Susx..............20 B5
Algarkirk Lincs..............103 M5
Alhampton Somset.........26 F4
Alkborough N Linc.........125 K6
Alkham Kent...................35 H6
Alkmonton Derbys........100 D5
Allaleigh Devon................7 J5
Allanaquoich Abers 204 D6
Allanbank N Lans..........175 L6
Allanton Border............179 H7
Allanton N Lans............175 L6
Allanton S Lans.............175 K7
Allaston Gloucs...............54 F6
Allbrook Hants................29 J7
All Cannings Wilts...........40 B7
Allendale Nthumb.........149 L4
Allenheads Nthumb......149 L6
Allen's Green Herts.........60 D5
Allensmore Herefs.........69 J7
Allenton C Derb............101 G6
Aller Devon.....................24 B6
Aller Somset...................26 B5
Allerby Cumb................147 J6
Allercombe Devon..........12 D4
Allerford Somset.............24 D3
Allerston N York...........134 D3
Allerthorpe E R Yk........125 J2
Allerton C Brad.............123 G4
Allerton Highld.............213 H2
Allerton Lpool...............111 L4
Allerton Bywater
    Leeds....................124 C5

Allerton Mauleverer
    N York..................132 F7
Allesley Covtry................86 C7
Allestree C Derb............101 G5
Allexton Leics..................88 B4
Allgreave Ches E...........113 L7
Allhallows Medway..........46 D4
Alligin Shuas Highld.....210 C3
Allington Dorset.............13 L4
Allington Lincs..............102 E4
Allington Wilts................28 D4
Allington Wilts................39 K5
Allington Wilts................40 B7
Allithwaite Cumb..........129 J4
Alloa Clacks..................185 J8
Allonby Cumb................147 J6
Alloway S Ayrs..............163 J5
Allowenshay Somset......26 B8
All Stretton Shrops.........83 J4
Alltchaorunn Highld.....192 C6
Alltwalis Carmth.............66 B7
Alltwen Neath.................51 K5
Alltyblaca Cerdgn...........66 C5
Allweston Dorset.............26 F8
Almeley Herefs................69 G4
Almington Staffs.............99 G5
Almondbank P & K........185 M3
Almondbury Kirk...........123 H7
Almondsbury S Glos......38 E4
Alne N York...................133 G6
Alness Highld...............222 E7
Alnham Nthumb............168 E7
Alnmouth Nthumb........169 J7
Alnwick Nthumb...........169 J6
Alperton Gt Lon..............44 D4
Alphamstone Essex........77 K7
Alpheton Suffk................77 K4
Alphington Devon...........11 L6
Alport Derbys................114 E8
Alpraham Ches E............98 E1
Alresford Essex...............62 C4
Alrewas Staffs.................85 L1
Alsager Ches E................99 H2
Alsop en le Dale
    Derbys...................100 D2
Alston Cumb.................149 J5
Alston Devon..................13 H2
Alstone Gloucs................55 M2
Alstonefield Staffs........100 C2
Alston Sutton Somset....26 B2
Alswear Devon................23 L6
Altandhu Highld...........224 B6
Altarnun Cnwll.................9 G8
Altass Highld................222 C4
Altcreich Ag & B...........190 D8
Altgaltraig Ag & B.........173 H4
Althorne Essex................61 L7
Althorpe N Linc............125 K8
Altnabreac Station
    Highld...................230 E6
Altnaharra Highld.........225 M2
Alton Derbys.................115 G8
Alton Hants.....................30 B4
Alton Staffs..................100 B4
Alton Barnes Wilts..........40 C7
Alton Pancras Dorset.....14 D3
Alton Priors Wilts...........40 C7
Alton Towers Staffs......100 B4
Altrincham Traffd.........113 H4
Altrincham
    Crematorium
    Traffd....................113 G4
Aitskelth Hotel Stirlg ...184 B6
Alva Clacks...................185 J7
Alvanley Ches W...........112 D6
Alvaston C Derb............101 H5
Alvechurch Worcs...........85 J8
Alvecote Warwks...........86 B3
Alvediston Wilts..............27 L6
Alveley Shrops................84 D6
Alverdiscott Devon..........23 H6
Alverstoke Hants.............17 H3
Alverstone IoW................17 H5
Alverthorpe Wakefd.....123 L6
Alverton Notts...............102 C4
Alves Moray.................214 E3

Alvescot Oxon................56 F6
Alveston S Glos..............38 F3
Alveston Warwks............72 B3
Alvingham Lincs............118 E4
Alvington Gloucs.............54 E7
Alwalton C Pete..............89 G4
Alwinton Nthumb.........168 D7
Alwoodley Leeds...........123 K3
Alyth P & K...................195 K6
Ambergate Derbys........101 G3
Amberley Gloucs.............55 J7
Amberley W Susx............18 D3
Amble Nthumb..............159 G2
Amblecote Dudley...........84 F6
Ambler Thorn C Brad....123 G5
Ambleside Cumb...........137 K6
Ambleston Pembks.........49 G3
Ambrosden Oxon............57 L4
Amcotts N Linc.............125 K7
Amersham Bucks............42 F2
Amersham Common
    Bucks.....................42 F2
Amersham Old Town
    Bucks.....................42 F2
Amersham on the
    Hill Bucks..............58 F7
Amerton Railway &
    Farm Staffs...........99 M6
Amesbury Wilts...............28 D3
Amhuinnsuidhe W Isls..232 d4
Amington Staffs..............86 B3
Amisfield Town D & G...155 H5
Amlwch IoA..................108 F3
Ammanford Carmth........51 J3
Amotherby N York........134 B5
Ampfield Hants................29 H6
Ampleforth N York........133 J4
Ampney Crucis
    Gloucs.....................56 B7
Ampney St Mary
    Gloucs.....................56 C7
Ampney St Peter
    Gloucs.....................56 B7
Amport Hants..................28 F3
Ampthill C Beds...............74 F6
Ampton Suffk..................77 J1
Amroth Pembks...............49 K6
Amulree P & K...............185 J1
Amwell Herts...................59 K5
Anaheilt Highld.............191 G4
Ancaster Lincs...............103 G4
Ancroft Nthumb............168 E1
Ancrum Border..............167 K4
Anderby Lincs................119 G6
Andover Hants................29 G3
Andoversford Gloucs......56 A4
Andreas IoM..................237 d2
Anerley Gt Lon................45 G6
Anfield Lpool.................111 K3
Anfield Crematorium
    Lpool......................111 K3
Angarrack Cnwll................3 G4
Angelbank Shrops...........83 L7
Angle Pembks..................48 E6
Anglesey IoA.................108 E5
Anglesey Abbey
    Cambs......................76 D3
Angmering W Susx..........18 E5
Angram N York..............124 D2
Ankerville Highld...........223 H6
Anlaby E R Yk...............126 C5
Anmer Norfk.................105 H6
Anmore Hants..................17 J1
Annan D & G.................147 L2
Annandale Water
    Services D & G.......155 J4
Annat Highld................210 D4
Annathill N Lans............175 J4
Anna Valley Hants..........29 G3
Annbank S Ayrs.............163 K5
Anne Hathaway's
    Cottage Warwks.....71 L4
Annfield Plain Dur........150 F5
Anniesland C Glas........174 F5
Ansdell Lancs................120 D5
Ansford Somset...............26 F5

Ansley Warwks................86 C5
Anslow Staffs................100 E7
Anslow Gate Staffs......100 D7
Anstey Herts...................60 C2
Anstey Leics...................87 G2
Anstruther Fife.............187 J6
Ansty W Susx..................19 J2
Ansty Warwks.................86 E6
Ansty Wilts.....................27 L6
Anthorn Cumb..............147 L4
Antingham Norfk..........106 F5
An t-Ob W Isls..............232 d5
Antonine Wall Falk.......175 L3
Anton's Gowt Lincs.......103 M3
Antony Cnwll....................6 B5
Antrobus Ches W...........112 F5
Anwick Lincs..................103 J3
Anwoth D & G...............145 M4
Aperfield Gt Lon.............32 D2
Apethorpe Nhants..........88 E4
Apley Lincs...................117 J6
Apperknowle Derbys.....115 G5
Apperley Gloucs..............55 K3
Appin Ag & B................191 J6
Appleby N Linc.............126 B7
Appleby-in-
    Westmorland
    Cumb....................139 G3
Appleby Magna Leics....86 C2
Appleby Parva Leics......86 C2
Applecross Highld........209 L5
Appledore Devon............23 G5
Appledore Devon............25 G8
Appledore Kent...............34 C8
Appleford Oxon...............41 K2
Applegarth Town
    D & G....................155 J5
Appleshaw Hants.............28 F2
Appleton Halton............112 D4
Appleton Oxon.................57 H7
Appleton Warrtn...........112 F5
Appleton-le-Moors
    N York...................155 L3
Appleton-le-Street
    N York...................134 B5
Appleton Roebuck
    N York...................124 E3
Appleton Thorn
    Warrtn..................112 F5
Appleton Wiske
    N York...................141 J6
Appletreehall Border....167 H6
Appletreewick
    N York...................131 K7
Appley Somset................25 G6
Appley Bridge Lancs....121 G8
Apse Heath IoW..............17 G5
Apsley End C Beds..........59 J2
Apuldram W Susx............18 A5
Arabella Highld.............223 H6
Arbirlot Angus...............196 F7
Arboll Highld................223 J5
Arborfield Wokham........42 C6
Arborfield Cross
    Wokham..................42 C6
Arbroath Angus.............197 G7
Arbuthnott Abers..........197 K2
Archdeacon Newton
    Darltn....................141 G4
Archencarroch
    W Duns..................174 D3
Archiestown Moray 214 F5
Archirondel Jersey........236 e6
Arclid Green Ches E.......99 H1
Ardallie Abers...............217 J6
Ardanaiseig Hotel
    Ag & B...................182 F3
Ardaneaskan Highld.....210 C7
Ardarroch Highld.........210 C6
Ardbeg Ag & B..............160 D1
Ardbeg Ag & B..............173 J5
Ardbeg Ag & B..............173 K2
Ardcharnich Highld......220 F4
Ardchiavaig Ag & B......180 E4
Ardchonnel Ag & B......182 D5

Ardchullarie More
Stirlg 184 D5
Arddarroch Ag & B.........183 J7
Arddleen Powys...........82 F1
Ardechive Highld.........201 H7
Ardeer N Ayrs.............163 H2
Ardeley Herts..............60 A3
Ardelve Highld............210 D8
Arden Ag & B...............174 C2
Ardens Grafton
Warwks.......................71 K4
Ardentallen Ag & B......182 B3
Ardentinny Ag & B........173 L2
Ardentraive Ag & B......173 H4
Ardeonaig Stirlg..........184 E1
Ardersier Highld..........213 J4
Ardessie Highld...........220 D4
Ardfern Ag & B............182 A6
Ardfernal Ag & B..........171 K4
Ardgay Highld.............222 D4
Ardgour Highld............191 K4
Ardgowan Inver...........173 L4
Ardhallow Ag & B.........173 K4
Ardhasig W Isls...........232 e4
Ardheslaig Highld........210 B3
Ardindrean Highld........220 F4
Ardingly W Susx............32 C7
Ardington Oxon............41 H3
Ardlamont Ag & B.........173 G5
Ardleigh Essex.............62 C3
Ardleigh Heath Essex....62 C2
Ardler P & K................195 L7
Ardley Oxon.................57 K3
Ardlui Ag & B...............183 K4
Ardlussa Ag & B...........172 B2
Ardmair Highld............220 E2
Ardmaleish Ag & B........173 J5
Ardmolich Highld.........190 E3
Ardmore Ag & B...........174 C3
Ardmore Highld...........222 F4
Ardnadam Ag & B.........173 K3
Ardnagrask Highld........212 E4
Ardnarff Highld...........210 D7
Ardnastang Highld........190 F4
Ardpatrick Ag & B........172 C6
Ardrishaig Ag & B.........172 E2
Ardross Highld.............222 E6
Ardrossan N Ayrs.........163 G2
Ardsley East Leeds.......123 K5
Ardslignish Highld........190 B4
Ardtalla Ag & B.............171 J7
Ardtoe Highld..............190 C3
Arduaine Ag & B...........182 A5
Ardullie Highld............212 E2
Ardvasar Highld...........199 K5
Ardvorlich P & K...........183 D3
Ardvourlie W Isls..........232 e3
Ardwell D & G..............144 D5
Ardwick Manch............113 J3
Areley Kings Worcs........70 E1
Arevegaig Highld..........190 D3
Arford Hants.................30 D4
Argoed Caerph.............53 J7
Argyll Forest Park
Ag & B.......................183 J6
Aribruach W Isls...........232 e3
Aridhglas Ag & B..........180 D3
Arileod Ag & B..............188 F5
Arinagour Ag & B..........189 G5
Ariogan Ag & B.............182 C3
Arisaig Highld..............199 K7
Arisaig House Highld....199 L7
Arkendale N York..........132 F7
Arkesden Essex.............76 C7
Arkholme Lancs...........130 B5
Arkleton D & G.............156 C4
Arkley Gt Lon................44 E2
Arksey Donc.................115 L1
Arkwright Town
Derbys......................115 H7
Arle Gloucs...................55 L4
Arlecdon Cumb............136 E4
Arlesey C Beds..............75 H7
Arleston Wrekin............84 B2
Arley Ches E................112 F5

Arley Warwks................86 C5
Arlingham Gloucs..........55 G6
Arlington Devon.............23 K4
Arlington E Susx............20 B4
Armadale Highld..........199 K5
Armadale Highld..........230 A3
Armadale W Loth..........176 C5
Armathwaite Cumb.......148 E5
Arminghall Norfk...........92 F3
Armitage Staffs............85 J1
Armley Leeds...............123 K4
Armscote Warwks.........72 B5
Armthorpe Donc..........115 L1
Arnabost Ag & B..........188 F4
Arncliffe N York............131 H5
Arncroach Fife.............187 H6
Arndilly House Moray...215 G5
Arne Dorset...................15 H5
Arnesby Leics...............87 H5
Arngask P & K..............186 B5
Arnisdale Highld...........200 C3
Arnish Highld...............209 J5
Arnol W Isls..................232 f1
Arnold E R Yk...............126 E3
Arnold Notts................101 L4
Arnprior Stirlg.............184 D7
Arnside Cumb..............129 K4
Aros Ag & B..................190 B7
Arrad Foot Cumb..........129 G4
Arram E R Yk...............126 C2
Arran N Ayrs................162 B3
Arrathorne N York........132 C2
Arreton IoW..................17 G5
Arrina Highld...............210 B3
Arrington Cambs...........75 K4
Arrochar Ag & B...........183 K6
Arrow Warwks...............71 J3
Arscott Shrops..............83 J2
Artafallie Highld...........212 F4
Arthington Leeds.........123 K2
Arthingworth Nhants......87 L7
Arthrath Abers.............217 H6
Artrochie Abers............217 J7
Arundel W Susx.............18 D4
Asby Cumb..................136 E3
Ascog Ag & B................173 J5
Ascot W & M.................42 F6
Ascott-under-
Wychwood Oxon......56 F4
Asenby N York.............132 F4
Asfordby Leics............102 B8
Asfordby Hill Leics.......102 B8
Asgarby Lincs..............103 J4
Ash Kent.......................35 H3
Ash Kent.......................45 L6
Ash Somset...................26 C7
Ash Surrey....................30 E2
Ashampstead W Berk.....41 K5
Ashbocking Suffk..........78 E4
Ashbourne Derbys........100 D3
Ashbrittle Somset.........25 G6
Ashburton Devon.............7 H2
Ashbury Devon.............10 D5
Ashbury Oxon...............40 E4
Ashby N Linc...............125 L8
Ashby by Partney
Lincs.......................118 F7
Ashby cum Fenby
NE Lin......................118 C2
Ashby de la Launde
Lincs.......................103 H2
Ashby-de-la-Zouch
Leics..........................86 D1
Ashby Folville Leics.......87 K2
Ashby Magna Leics........87 H5
Ashby Parva Leics.........87 G5
Ashby Puerorum
Lincs.......................118 D7
Ashby St Ledgers
Nhants........................73 H2
Ashby St Mary Norfk......93 G3
Ashchurch Gloucs.........55 L2
Ashcombe Devon...........11 L8
Ashcombe N Som...........37 M7
Ashcott Somset.............26 C4

Ashdon Essex................76 E6
Ashe Hants....................29 K2
Asheldham Essex...........62 A7
Ashen Essex..................77 H6
Ashendon Bucks............58 B5
Asheridge Bucks............58 F6
Ashfield Stirlg..............185 G6
Ashfield cum Thorpe
Suffk..........................78 E3
Ashfield Green Suffk......92 F8
Ashford Devon.................7 G6
Ashford Devon...............11 G5
Ashford Kent.................34 D6
Ashford Surrey..............43 H6
Ashford Bowdler
Shrops.......................69 K1
Ashford Carbonell
Shrops.......................69 K1
Ashford Hill Hants.........41 K7
Ashford in the Water
Derbys......................114 D7
Ashgill S Lans..............175 K7
Ash Green Surrey...........30 E2
Ash Green Warwks.........86 D6
Ashill Devon...................12 E1
Ashill Norfk...................91 K3
Ashill Somset................25 L7
Ashingdon Essex...........46 E2
Ashington Nthumb........159 G5
Ashington Somset..........26 E6
Ashington W Susx..........18 F3
Ashkirk Border..............167 G5
Ashleworth Gloucs.........55 J3
Ashleworth Quay
Gloucs........................55 J3
Ashley Cambs................77 G3
Ashley Ches E...............113 H5
Ashley Devon.................10 F3
Ashley Gloucs................39 L2
Ashley Hants.................16 B4
Ashley Hants.................29 G5
Ashley Kent...................35 J5
Ashley Nhants................87 L5
Ashley Staffs.................99 H5
Ashley Wilts...................39 J6
Ashley Green Bucks........58 F6
Ash Magna Shrops.........98 E4
Ashmansworth Hants......41 H8
Ashmansworthy
Devon........................22 E7
Ash Mill Devon...............24 C6
Ashmore Dorset.............27 K7
Ashmore Green
W Berk........................41 J6
Ashorne Warwks............72 C3
Ashover Derbys............115 G8
Ashow Warwks...............72 C1
Ashperton Herefs..........70 B6
Ashprington Devon..........7 J4
Ash Priors Somset..........25 J5
Ashreigney Devon..........10 F3
Ash Street Suffk............78 B5
Ashtead Surrey..............44 D8
Ash Thomas Devon.........12 C1
Ashton Ches W..............112 D7
Ashton Cnwll...................3 G5
Ashton Devon.................11 K7
Ashton Herefs...............69 K2
Ashton Inver................173 L3
Ashton Nhants...............73 L5
Ashton Nhants...............88 E7
Ashton Common
Wilts..........................39 K8
Ashton-in-Makerfield
Wigan.......................112 E2
Ashton Keynes Wilts.......40 B2
Ashton under Hill
Worcs.........................71 H6
Ashton-under-Lyne
Tamesd......................113 L2
Ashurst Hants................16 D1
Ashurst Kent.................32 F5
Ashurst Lancs..............121 G8
Ashurst W Susx.............19 G3
Ashurstwood W Susx......32 D5
Ash Vale Surrey.............30 E2

Ashwater Devon..............9 K5
Ashwell Herts................75 J4
Ashwell Rutlnd...............88 C2
Ashwell End Herts.........75 J4
Ashwellthorpe Norfk......92 D4
Ashwick Somset.............26 F2
Ashwicken Norfk..........105 H8
Askam in Furness
Cumb........................128 F4
Askern Donc................124 E7
Askerswell Dorset..........14 A4
Askett Bucks.................58 D6
Askham Cumb...............138 D3
Askham Notts...............116 C6
Askham Bryan C York....124 E2
Askham Richard
C York.......................124 E2
Asknish Ag & B.............172 F1
Askrigg N York..............131 H2
Askwith N York.............123 H2
Aslackby Lincs.............103 H6
Aslacton Norfk...............92 D5
Aslockton Notts............102 C4
Aspatria Cumb.............147 K6
Aspenden Herts.............60 B3
Aspley Guise C Beds.......74 D7
Aspley Heath C Beds.......74 D7
Aspull Wigan................121 J8
Asselby E R Yk.............125 H5
Assington Suffk.............77 L6
Assington Green
Suffk..........................77 H4
Astbury Ches E.............99 J1
Astcote Nhants..............73 J4
Asterby Lincs...............118 C5
Asterley Shrops.............83 H3
Asterton Shrops............83 H5
Asthall Oxon..................56 F5
Asthall Leigh Oxon.........56 F5
Astle Highld..................223 G3
Astley Shrops................98 D8
Astley Warwks................86 C5
Astley Wigan................113 G2
Astley Worcs..................70 D2
Astley Abbots Shrops.....84 C4
Astley Bridge Bolton....121 K7
Astley Cross Worcs........70 E1
Aston Ches E.................98 E3
Aston Ches W...............112 E5
Aston Derbys................114 D5
Aston Flints.................111 J7
Aston Herts...................59 L4
Aston Oxon....................57 G7
Aston Rothm................115 J4
Aston Shrops.................84 E5
Aston Shrops.................98 D6
Aston Staffs...................99 H4
Aston Staffs...................99 K7
Aston Wokham...............42 C4
Aston Wrekin.................84 B2
Aston Abbotts
Bucks.........................58 D4
Aston Botterell
Shrops.......................84 B6
Aston-by-Stone
Staffs..........................99 K6
Aston Cantlow
Warwks.......................71 K3
Aston Clinton Bucks.......58 E5
Aston Crews Herefs.......54 F4
Aston End Herts............59 L3
Aston Fields Worcs........71 G1
Aston Flamville Leics......86 F6
Aston Ingham Herefs......55 G4
Aston le Walls Nhants.....72 F4
Aston Magna Gloucs......71 L7
Aston Munslow
Shrops.......................83 K6
Aston on Clun Shrops.....83 H6
Aston Pigott Shrops.......83 G3
Aston Rogers Shrops......83 G3
Aston Rowant Oxon.......58 B7
Aston Somerville
Worcs.........................71 J6
Aston-sub-Edge
Gloucs.......................71 K6

Aston Tirrold - Balmedie

245

Aston Tirrold Oxon 41 K3
Aston-upon-Trent Derbys 101 H6
Aston Upthorpe Oxon 41 K3
Astwick C Beds 75 J6
Astwood M Keyn 74 D5
Astwood Worcs 71 G2
Astwood Bank Worcs 71 J3
Aswarby Lincs 103 H4
Aswardby Lincs 118 E7
Atcham Shrops 83 K2
Athelhampton Dorset 14 E4
Athelington Suffk 78 E1
Athelney Somset 25 M5
Athelstaneford E Loth 178 C3
Atherington Devon 23 J6
Atherstone Warwks 86 C4
Atherstone on Stour Warwks 72 B4
Atherton Wigan 113 G2
Atlow Derbys 100 E3
Attadale Highld 210 E6
Atterby Lincs 117 G3
Attercliffe Sheff 115 G4
Atterton Leics 86 D4
Attingham Park Shrops 83 K2
Attleborough Norfk 92 C4
Attleborough Warwks 86 D5
Attlebridge Norfk 92 D1
Attleton Green Suffk 77 G4
Atwick E R Yk 126 F1
Atworth Wilts 39 J7
Aubourn Lincs 116 F8
Auchbreck Moray 214 F8
Auchedly Abers 217 G7
Auchenblae Abers 197 H1
Auchenbowie Stirlg 175 L2
Auchencairn D & G 146 D5
Auchencairn D & G 155 G5
Auchencairn N Ayrs 162 D4
Auchencrow Border 179 H6
Auchendinny Mdloth 177 H6
Auchengray S Lans 176 D7
Auchenhalrig Moray 215 J3
Auchenheath S Lans 164 F2
Auchenhessnane D & G 154 E3
Auchenlochan Ag & B 173 G4
Auchenmade N Ayrs 174 C8
Auchenmalg D & G 144 F4
Auchentiber N Ayrs 174 C8
Auchindrain Ag & B 182 E6
Auchindrean Highld 221 G5
Auchininna Abers 216 C5
Auchinleck E Ayrs 164 B5
Auchinloch N Lans 175 H4
Auchinstarry N Lans 175 J3
Auchintore Highld 191 L2
Auchiries Abers 217 K6
Auchlean Highld 203 K5
Auchlee Abers 207 G6
Auchleven Abers 206 C1
Auchlochan S Lans 164 F3
Auchlossan Abers 206 B5
Auchlyne Stirlg 184 B2
Auchmillan E Ayrs 164 A4
Auchmithie Angus 197 G7
Auchmuirbridge Fife 186 C6
Auchnacree Angus 196 D4
Auchnagatt Abers 217 H6
Auchnarrow Moray 204 F2
Auchnotteroch D & G 144 B3
Auchroisk Moray 215 H4
Auchterarder P & K 185 K5
Auchteraw Highld 202 B4
Auchterblair Highld 203 L2
Auchtercairn Highld 219 J6
Auchterderran Fife 186 C7
Auchterhouse Angus 196 B8
Auchterless Abers 216 D6
Auchtermuchty Fife 186 D5
Auchterneed Highld 212 D3
Auchtertool Fife 177 H1
Auchtertyre Highld 210 C8
Auchtubh Stirlg 184 C4
Auckengill Highld 231 L3
Auckley Donc 115 M2
Audenshaw Tamesd 113 K3
Audlem Ches E 98 F4
Audley Staffs 99 J3
Audley End Essex 76 D6
Audley End House & Gardens Essex 76 D6
Aughton E R Yk 125 G3
Aughton Lancs 111 L1
Aughton Lancs 129 L6
Aughton Rothm 115 J4
Aughton Wilts 28 E1
Aughton Park Lancs 112 B1
Auldearn Highld 213 L4
Aulden Herefs 69 J4
Auldgirth D & G 154 F5
Auldhouse S Lans 175 H7
Ault a' chruinn Highld 200 E2
Aultbea Highld 219 K4
Aultgrishin Highld 219 H4
Aultguish Inn Highld 221 J7
Ault Hucknall Derbys 115 J7
Aultmore Moray 215 J4
Aultnagoire Highld 202 E2
Aultnamain Inn Highld 222 F5
Aunsby Lincs 103 H5
Aust S Glos 38 E3
Austerfield Donc 116 A3
Austrey Warwks 86 C3
Austwick N York 130 E5
Authorpe Lincs 118 E5
Avebury Wilts 40 C6
Avebury Wilts 40 C6
Aveley Thurr 45 L4
Avening Gloucs 39 K2
Averham Notts 102 C2
Aveton Gifford Devon 7 G6
Aviemore Highld 203 L3
Avington W Berk 41 G6
Avoch Highld 213 G4
Avon Hants 15 L3
Avonbridge Falk 176 B4
Avon Dassett Warwks 72 E4
Avonmouth Bristl 38 D5
Avonwick Devon 7 G4
Awbridge Hants 28 F6
Awliscombe Devon 12 E3
Awre Gloucs 55 G6
Awsworth Notts 101 J4
Axbridge Somset 26 B1
Axford Hants 29 L3
Axford Wilts 40 E6
Axminster Devon 13 H3
Axmouth Devon 13 G4
Aycliffe Dur 141 G3
Aydon Nthumb 150 C2
Aylburton Gloucs 54 E7
Aylesbeare Devon 12 D4
Aylesbury Bucks 58 D5
Aylesby NE Lin 126 F8
Aylesford Kent 33 J2
Aylesham Kent 35 H4
Aylestone C Leic 87 H4
Aylmerton Norfk 106 E5
Aylsham Norfk 106 E6
Aylton Herefs 70 B6
Aylworth Gloucs 56 C4
Aymestrey Herefs 69 H2
Aynho Nhants 57 K2
Ayot St Lawrence Herts 59 K5
Ayr S Ayrs 163 J5
Aysgarth N York 131 J2
Ayshford Devon 25 G7
Ayside Cumb 129 J3
Ayston RutInd 88 C4
Ayton Border 179 J6
Azerley N York 132 C5

B

Babbacombe Torbay 7 L3
Babbs Green Herts 60 C5
Babcary Somset 26 E5
Babraham Cambs 76 D4
Babworth Notts 116 B5
Backaland Ork 234 d4
Backfolds Abers 217 J4
Backford Ches W 111 L6
Backies Highld 223 H2
Back of Keppoch Highld 199 K7
Backwell N Som 38 C6
Baconsthorpe Norfk 106 D5
Bacton Herefs 54 A2
Bacton Norfk 107 H5
Bacton Suffk 78 C2
Bacup Lancs 122 C6
Badachro Highld 219 J6
Badbury Swindn 40 D4
Badby Nhants 73 H3
Badcall Highld 228 B7
Badcall Highld 228 C4
Badcaul Highld 220 D3
Baddesley Clinton Warwks 86 B8
Baddesley Ensor Warwks 86 C4
Baddidarrach Highld 224 D4
Baddinsgill Border 176 F7
Badenscoth Abers 216 D6
Badentarbet Highld 224 B6
Badenyon Abers 205 H2
Badger Shrops 84 D4
Badgeworth Gloucs 55 K4
Badgworth Somset 26 B2
Badicaul Highld 210 B8
Badingham Suffk 79 G2
Badlesmere Kent 34 D4
Badlieu Border 165 K5
Badlipster Highld 231 J5
Badluarach Highld 220 C3
Badninish Highld 223 G3
Badrallach Highld 220 D3
Badsey Worcs 71 J5
Badshot Lea Surrey 30 E2
Badsworth Wakefd 124 C7
Badwell Ash Suffk 78 B2
Bagber Dorset 27 H8
Bagby N York 133 G4
Bag Enderby Lincs 118 E6
Bagendon Gloucs 56 A6
Bagh a Chaisteil W Isls 233 b9
Bagh a Tuath W Isls 233 b9
Bagillt Flints 111 H6
Baginton Warwks 86 D8
Baglan Neath 51 L6
Bagley Shrops 98 B6
Bagley Somset 26 C3
Bagnall Staffs 99 L3
Bagshot Surrey 42 E7
Bagstone S Glos 39 G3
Bagworth Leics 86 F2
Bagwy Llydiart Herefs 54 C3
Baildon C Brad 123 H3
Baildon Green C Brad 123 H3
Baile Ailein W Isls 232 f3
Baile a Mhanaich W Isls 233 b6
Baile Mor Ag & B 180 D3
Baillieston C Glas 175 J5
Bainbridge N York 131 H2
Bainshole Abers 216 B7
Bainton C Pete 89 G3
Bainton E R Yk 126 B1
Baintown Fife 186 F6
Bairnkine Border 167 K6
Bakewell Derbys 114 E7
Bala Gwynd 96 E5
Balallan W Isls 232 f3
Balbeg Highld 212 C7
Balbeggie P & K 186 C2
Balblair Highld 212 D5
Balblair Highld 213 G2
Balby Donc 115 K2
Balcary D & G 146 E5
Balchraggan Highld 212 E5
Balchreick Highld 228 B4
Balcombe W Susx 32 B6
Balcomie Links Fife 187 K5
Baldersby N York 132 E4
Baldersby St James N York 132 E4
Balderstone Lancs 121 J4
Balderton Notts 102 D3
Baldinnie Fife 187 G5
Baldinnies P & K 185 L4
Baldock Herts 75 J7
Baldock Services Herts 75 J6
Baldovie C Dund 187 G2
Baldrine IoM 237 d5
Baldslow E Susx 20 F3
Bale Norfk 106 B5
Baledgarno P & K 186 D2
Balemartine Ag & B 188 C7
Balerno C Edin 177 G5
Balfarg Fife 186 D6
Balfield Angus 196 E3
Balfour Ork 234 c5
Balfron Stirlg 174 F1
Balgaveny Abers 216 C6
Balgonar Fife 185 L8
Balgowan D & G 144 D6
Balgowan Highld 202 F6
Balgown Highld 218 B7
Balgracie D & G 144 D3
Balgray S Lans 165 H5
Balham Gt Lon 44 F5
Balhary P & K 195 L6
Balholmie P & K 186 B1
Baligill Highld 230 C3
Balintore Angus 195 L5
Balintore Highld 223 J6
Balintraid Highld 223 G7
Balivanich W Isls 233 b6
Balkeerie Angus 196 B7
Balkholme E R Yk 125 J5
Ballachulish Highld 191 L5
Ballajora IoM 237 e4
Ballanlay Ag & B 173 H6
Ballantrae S Ayrs 152 C5
Ballasalla IoM 237 b6
Ballater Abers 205 J6
Ballaugh IoM 237 c3
Ballchraggan Highld 223 G6
Ballencrieff E Loth 178 B3
Ballevullin Ag & B 188 B6
Ballidon Derbys 100 D2
Balliekine N Ayrs 161 L2
Balliemore Ag & B 182 F7
Balligmorrie S Ayrs 152 F4
Ballimore Stirlg 184 C4
Ballindalloch Moray 214 E6
Ballindean P & K 186 D2
Ballinger Common Bucks 58 E7
Ballingham Herefs 54 E2
Ballingry Fife 186 C7
Ballinluig P & K 194 F6
Ballinshoe Angus 196 C5
Ballintuim P & K 195 H5
Balloch Highld 213 H5
Balloch N Lans 175 K4
Balloch P & K 185 H4
Balloch S Ayrs 153 G3
Balloch W Duns 174 D3
Balls Cross W Susx 31 G6
Balls Green E Susx 32 E6
Ballygown Ag & B 189 K7
Ballygrant Ag & B 171 G5
Ballyhaugh Ag & B 188 F5
Balmaclellan D & G 154 B6
Balmae D & G 146 C6
Balmaha Stirlg 174 D1
Balmalcolm Fife 186 E5
Balmangan D & G 146 B5
Balmedie Abers 207 H2

Balmerino Fife......186 F3
Balmichael N Ayrs......162 B3
Balmore E Duns......175 G4
Balmuchy Highld......223 J5
Balmule Fife......177 G2
Balmullo Fife......187 G4
Balnacoil Lodge
  Highld......226 E6
Balnacra Highld......210 F5
Balnacroft Abers......205 G6
Balnafoich Highld......213 G7
Balnaguard P & K......194 E6
Balnahard Ag & B......180 F1
Balnahard Ag & B......180 F7
Balnain Highld......212 C7
Balnakeil Highld......228 F2
Balne N York......124 F6
Balquharn P & K......185 L1
Balquhidder Stirlg......184 C3
Balsall Common Solhll......86 B7
Balsall Heath Birm......85 J6
Balscote Oxon......72 E6
Balsham Cambs......76 E4
Baltasound Shet......235 e1
Baltersan D & G......145 J3
Baltonsborough
  Somset......26 D4
Balvicar Ag & B......181 M4
Balvraid Highld......200 C3
Balvraid Highld......213 K7
Bamber Bridge Lancs...121 H5
Bamber's Green
  Essex......60 F4
Bamburgh Nthumb...169 H3
Bamburgh Castle
  Nthumb......169 H3
Bamford Derbys......114 E5
Bampton Cumb......138 D4
Bampton Devon......24 E6
Bampton Oxon......56 F7
Bampton Grange
  Cumb......138 D4
Banavie Highld......191 L2
Banbury Oxon......72 F6
Banbury
  Crematorium
  Oxon......72 F6
Bancffosfelen
  Carmth......50 F3
Banchory Abers......206 D6
Banchory-Devenick
  Abers......207 G5
Bancycapel Carmth......50 E3
Bancyfelin Carmth......50 D2
Bandirran P & K......186 C2
Banff Abers......216 D2
Bangor Gwynd......109 H6
Bangor Crematorium
  Gwynd......109 H6
Bangor-on-Dee
  Wrexhm......98 B4
Bangors Cnwll......9 G5
Banham Norfk......92 C6
Bank Hants......16 C2
Bankend D & G......147 H2
Bankfoot P & K......185 M1
Bankglen E Ayrs......164 C6
Bankhead C Aber......207 G4
Bankhead S Lans......165 J1
Banknock Falk......175 K3
Banks Lancs......120 E6
Bankshill D & G......155 L5
Banningham Norfk......106 F6
Bannister Green
  Essex......61 H4
Bannockburn Stirlg...175 L1
Banstead Surrey......44 E7
Bantham Devon......6 F6
Banton N Lans......175 K3
Banwell N Som......38 B4
Bapchild Kent......34 C3
Bapton Wilts......27 M4
Barabhas W Isls......232 f1
Barassie S Ayrs......163 J3
Barbaraville Highld......223 G6
Barbieston S Ayrs......163 K5

Barbon Cumb......130 C3
Barbrook Devon......23 L2
Barby Nhants......73 G1
Barcaldine Ag & B......191 J7
Barcombe E Susx......19 L3
Barcombe Cross
  E Susx......19 L3
Barden Park Kent......33 G4
Bardfield End Green
  Essex......61 G2
Bardfield Saling Essex...61 G3
Bardney Lincs......117 J7
Bardon Leics......86 F2
Bardon Mill Nthumb...149 K3
Bardowie E Duns......175 G4
Bardrainney Inver......174 C4
Bardsea Cumb......129 G5
Bardsey Leeds......124 B2
Bardsey Island Gwynd...94 B7
Bardwell Suffk......91 L8
Bare Lancs......129 K6
Barfad D & G......145 G2
Barford Norfk......92 D3
Barford Warwks......72 C3
Barford St John Oxon...57 H2
Barford St Martin
  Wilts......28 B5
Barford St Michael
  Oxon......57 H2
Barfrestone Kent......35 H5
Bargeddie N Lans......175 J5
Bargoed Caerph......53 J7
Bargrennan D & G......153 H6
Barham Cambs......89 G7
Barham Kent......35 G5
Barham Suffk......78 D4
Barham
  Crematorium
  Kent......35 G5
Bar Hill Cambs......75 L2
Barholm Lincs......88 F2
Barkby Leics......87 J2
Barkby Thorpe Leics...87 J2
Barkestone-le-Vale
  Leics......102 C5
Barkham Wokham......42 C6
Barking Gt Lon......45 H3
Barking Suffk......78 C4
Barkingside Gt Lon......45 H3
Barking Tye Suffk......78 C4
Barkisland Calder......122 F6
Barkla Shop Cnwll......3 J2
Barkston Lincs......102 F4
Barkston Ash N York...124 D4
Barkway Herts......75 L7
Barlanark C Glas......175 H5
Barlaston Staffs......99 K5
Barlavington W Susx...18 C3
Barlborough Derbys...115 J6
Barlby N York......124 F4
Barlestone Leics......86 E3
Barley Herts......76 B6
Barley Lancs......122 B3
Barleythorpe Rutlnd...88 B2
Barling Essex......46 F3
Barlings Lincs......117 H6
Barlochan D & G......146 E4
Barlow Derbys......115 G6
Barlow Gatesd......150 E3
Barlow N York......124 F5
Barmby Moor E R Yk...125 J2
Barmby on the
  Marsh E R Yk......125 G5
Barmollack Ag & B......161 K1
Barmouth Gwynd......80 E1
Barmpton Darltn......141 H4
Barmston E R Yk......135 J7
Barnacarry Ag & B......182 E8
Barnack C Pete......88 F3
Barnard Castle Dur...140 D4
Barnard Gate Oxon...57 H6
Barnardiston Suffk......77 G5
Barnbarroch D & G...146 E4
Barnburgh Donc......115 J2
Barnby Suffk......93 K5
Barnby Dun Donc......124 F8

Barnby in the
  Willows Notts......102 E3
Barnby Moor Notts...116 A5
Barncorkrie D & G......144 B7
Barnes Gt Lon......44 E5
Barnes Street Kent......33 H4
Barnet Gt Lon......44 E2
Barnetby le Wold
  N Linc......126 C8
Barney Norfk......106 B6
Barnham Suffk......91 K7
Barnham W Susx......18 C5
Barnham Broom
  Norfk......92 C3
Barnhead Angus......197 G5
Barnhill C Dund......187 H2
Barnhill Moray......214 E3
Barnhills D & G......152 B7
Barningham Dur......140 D5
Barningham Suffk......91 L7
Barnoldby le Beck
  NE Lin......118 C2
Barnoldswick Lancs...122 C2
Barns Green W Susx...31 J6
Barnsley Barns......115 G1
Barnsley Gloucs......56 B6
Barnsley
  Crematorium
  Barns......115 G1
Barnstaple Devon......23 J5
Barnston Essex......61 G4
Barnston Wirral......111 J5
Barnstone Notts......102 B5
Barnt Green Worcs......85 H8
Barnton C Edin......177 G4
Barnton Ches W......112 F6
Barnwell All Saints
  Nhants......88 F6
Barnwell St Andrew
  Nhants......88 F6
Barnwood Gloucs......55 K4
Barr S Ayrs......153 G4
Barra W Isls......233 b9
Barra Airport W Isls...233 b9
Barrachan D & G......145 H5
Barraigh W Isls......233 b9
Barrapoll Ag & B......188 B7
Barrasford Nthumb...158 A4
Barrhead E Rens......174 F6
Barrhill S Ayrs......152 F5
Barrington Cambs......76 B5
Barrington Somset......26 B7
Barripper Cnwll......3 H4
Barrmill N Ayrs......174 C7
Barrock Highld......231 J2
Barrow Gloucs......55 K3
Barrow Lancs......121 L3
Barrow Rutlnd......88 C1
Barrow Somset......27 G5
Barrow Suffk......77 H2
Barrowby Lincs......102 E5
Barrowden Rutlnd......88 D4
Barrowford Lancs......122 C3
Barrow Gurney
  N Som......38 D6
Barrow Haven N Linc...126 D6
Barrow-in-Furness
  Cumb......128 E5
Barrow Island Cumb...128 E5
Barrow-upon-
  Humber N Linc......126 D6
Barrow upon Soar
  Leics......101 L8
Barrow upon Trent
  Derbys......101 G6
Barry Angus......187 J1
Barry V Glam......37 H6
Barry Island V Glam...37 H6
Barsby Leics......87 K2
Barsham Suffk......93 H5
Barston Solhll......86 B7
Bartestree Herefs......69 L6
Barthol Chapel Abers...216 F7
Bartholomew Green
  Essex......61 H4
Barthomley Ches E...99 H3

Bartley Hants......28 F8
Bartley Green Birm......85 H6
Bartlow Cambs......76 E5
Barton Cambs......76 B4
Barton Ches W......98 C2
Barton Gloucs......56 C3
Barton Lancs......120 E8
Barton Lancs......121 G3
Barton N York......141 G5
Barton Oxon......57 K6
Barton Torbay......7 K3
Barton Bendish Norfk...91 G3
Barton End Gloucs......39 J2
Barton Hartshorn
  Bucks......57 M2
Barton in Fabis Notts...101 K6
Barton in the Beans
  Leics......86 E3
Barton-le-Clay C Beds...59 H2
Barton-le-Street
  N York......133 L5
Barton-le-Willows
  N York......133 L6
Barton Mills Suffk......91 G8
Barton-on-Sea Hants...16 B4
Barton-on-the-Heath
  Warwks......56 E2
Barton St David
  Somset......26 D5
Barton Seagrave
  Nhants......88 C7
Barton Stacey Hants...29 H3
Barton Town Devon...23 L4
Barton Turf Norfk......107 H7
Barton-under-
  Needwood Staffs...100 D8
Barton-upon-
  Humber N Linc......126 C6
Barton Waterside
  N Linc......126 C6
Barvas W Isls......232 f1
Barway Cambs......90 D7
Barwell Leics......86 F4
Barwick Devon......10 E4
Barwick Somset......26 E8
Barwick in Elmet
  Leeds......124 B3
Baschurch Shrops......98 B7
Bascote Warwks......72 E2
Bashall Eaves Lancs...121 K2
Basildon Essex......46 B3
Basildon & District
  Crematorium
  Essex......46 C3
Basingstoke Hants...29 M2
Basingstoke
  Crematorium
  Hants......29 K3
Baslow Derbys......114 E6
Bason Bridge Somset...25 M3
Bassaleg Newpt......37 L3
Bassendean Border...167 K1
Bassenthwaite Cumb...137 H2
Bassett C Sotn......29 H7
Bassingbourn Cambs...75 K5
Bassingham Lincs......102 E1
Bassingthorpe Lincs...102 F6
Bassus Green Herts......60 A3
Baston Lincs......89 G2
Bastwick Norfk......107 J8
Batchworth Herts......43 H2
Batcombe Dorset......14 C2
Batcombe Somset......27 G4
Batford Herts......59 J5
Bath BaNES......39 H7
Bathampton BaNES......39 H7
Bath, City of BaNES......39 H7
Bathealton Somset......25 G6
Batheaston BaNES......39 H6
Bathford BaNES......39 H6
Bathgate W Loth......176 D5
Bathley Notts......102 C2
Bathpool Cnwll......5 L2
Bathpool Somset......25 K6
Bath Side Essex......62 F2
Bathville W Loth......176 C5

Bathway Somset............26 E2
Batley Kirk............123 J5
Batsford Gloucs............71 L7
Battersby N York............142 D5
Battersea Gt Lon............44 F5
Battisford Tye Suffk............78 B4
Battle E Susx............20 F3
Battle Powys............52 F2
Battledykes Angus............196 D5
Battlesbridge Essex............46 C2
Battleton Somset............24 E6
Baughton Worcs............70 F6
Baughurst Hants............41 L7
Baulds Abers............206 B6
Baulking Oxon............40 F3
Baumber Lincs............117 L6
Baunton Gloucs............56 A6
Baverstock Wilts............28 B5
Bawburgh Norfk............92 D2
Bawdeswell Norfk............106 C7
Bawdrip Somset............25 M4
Bawdsey Suffk............79 H6
Bawtry Donc............115 M3
Baxenden Lancs............122 B5
Baxterley Warwks............86 C4
Bay Highld............208 D4
Bayble W Isls............232 g2
Baybridge Hants............29 K6
Baycliff Cumb............129 G5
Baydon Wilts............40 F5
Bayford Herts............60 A6
Bayford Somset............27 G5
Bayhead W Isls............233 b6
Baylham Suffk............78 D4
Baysham Herefs............54 E3
Bayston Hill Shrops............83 J2
Baythorne End Essex............77 H4
Bayton Worcs............84 C8
Bayworth Oxon............57 J7
Beachampton Bucks............73 L6
Beachamwell Norfk............91 H3
Beachy Head E Susx............20 C6
Beacon Devon............12 F2
Beacon End Essex............62 A3
Beacon Hill Surrey............30 E4
Beacon's Bottom
    Bucks............42 C2
Beaconsfield Bucks............42 F3
Beaconsfield
    Services Bucks............42 F3
Beadlam N York............133 K3
Beadlow C Beds............75 G6
Beadnell Nthumb............169 J4
Beaford Devon............10 E2
Beal N York............124 E5
Beal Nthumb............169 G2
Bealsmill Cnwll............6 A1
Beaminster Dorset............13 L3
Beamish Dur............150 F4
Beamish Museum
    Dur............150 F4
Beamsley N York............131 K8
Beanacre Wilts............39 K7
Beanley Nthumb............169 G5
Beardon Devon............10 D7
Beare Green Surrey............31 K3
Bearley Warwks............71 L3
Bearpark Dur............151 G6
Bearsden E Duns............174 F4
Bearsted Kent............33 K3
Bearstone Shrops............99 G5
Bearwood Birm............85 H6
Bearwood Herefs............69 H4
Bearwood Poole............15 K3
Beattock D & G............155 J2
Beauchamp Roding
    Essex............60 F6
Beaufort Blae G............53 J5
Beaulieu Hants............16 E3
Beauly Highld............212 E5
Beaumaris IoA............109 H6
Beaumaris Castle IoA............109 J6
Beaumont Cumb............148 C3
Beaumont Essex............62 E3
Beaumont Jersey............236 c7
Beausale Warwks............72 B1

Beauworth Hants............29 L6
Beaworthy Devon............10 C5
Beazley End Essex............61 H3
Bebington Wirral............111 K5
Beccles Suffk............93 J5
Becconsall Lancs............120 F6
Beckbury Shrops............84 D3
Beckenham Gt Lon............45 G6
Beckenham
    Crematorium
    Gt Lon............45 G6
Beckermet Cumb............136 E6
Beckfoot Cumb............147 J5
Beckford Worcs............71 H7
Beckhampton Wilts............40 C6
Beckingham Lincs............102 E2
Beckingham Notts............116 C4
Beckington Somset............27 J2
Beckjay Shrops............83 H7
Beckley E Susx............21 G2
Beckley Oxon............57 K5
Beck Row Suffk............91 G7
Beck Side Cumb............128 F3
Beckton Gt Lon............45 H4
Beckwithshaw N York............132 D8
Becontree Gt Lon............45 J3
Becquet Vincent
    Jersey............236 c6
Bedale N York............132 D2
Bedchester Dorset............27 J7
Beddau Rhondd............37 G4
Beddgelert Gwynd............95 K3
Beddingham E Susx............19 L4
Beddington Gt Lon............44 F6
Beddington Corner
    Gt Lon............44 F6
Bedfield Suffk............78 F2
Bedford Bed............74 F5
Bedford
    Crematorium Bed............75 G4
Bedhampton Hants............17 K2
Bedingfield Suffk............78 E2
Bedlam N York............132 D7
Bedlington Nthumb............159 G5
Bedlinog Myr Td............53 H7
Bedminster Bristl............38 E6
Bedminster Down
    Bristl............38 E6
Bedmond Herts............59 J7
Bednall Staffs............99 L8
Bedrule Border............167 J5
Bedstone Shrops............83 G7
Bedwas Caerph............37 J3
Bedwellty Caerph............53 J7
Bedworth Warwks............86 D6
Beeby Leics............87 J2
Beech Hants............30 B4
Beech Staffs............99 J5
Beech Hill W Berk............42 B7
Beechingstoke Wilts............40 C8
Beedon W Berk............41 J5
Beeford E R Yk............135 H8
Beeley Derbys............114 E7
Beelsby NE Lin............117 K2
Beenham W Berk............41 L6
Beer Devon............13 G5
Beer Somset............26 B5
Beercrocombe
    Somset............25 L7
Beer Hackett Dorset............14 B1
Beesands Devon............7 J7
Beesby Lincs............118 F5
Beeson Devon............7 J7
Beeston C Beds............75 H5
Beeston Ches W............98 D2
Beeston Leeds............123 K4
Beeston Norfk............91 K1
Beeston Notts............101 K5
Beeston Regis Norfk............106 E4
Beeswing D & G............146 F2
Beetham Cumb............129 K4
Beetham Somset............25 L8
Beetley Norfk............106 A8
Begbroke Oxon............57 J5
Begelly Pembks............49 J6
Beguildy Powys............82 D7

Beighton Norfk............93 H2
Beighton Sheff............115 H5
Beinn Na Faoghla
    W Isls............233 c7
Beith N Ayrs............174 C7
Bekesbourne Kent............35 G4
Belaugh Norfk............107 G8
Belbroughton Worcs............85 G7
Belchalwell Dorset............14 E1
Belchamp Otten
    Essex............77 J6
Belchamp St Paul
    Essex............77 H6
Belchamp Walter
    Essex............77 J6
Belchford Lincs............118 D6
Belford Nthumb............169 G3
Belgrave C Leic............87 H3
Belhaven E Loth............178 E3
Belhelvie Abers............207 H2
Belhinnie Abers............215 K8
Bellabeg Abers............205 H3
Bellanoch Ag & B............182 A8
Bellaty Angus............195 K4
Bell Busk N York............131 G7
Belleau Lincs............118 E5
Bell End Worcs............85 G7
Bellerby N York............131 L2
Belle Vue Cumb............148 C4
Belle Vue Wakefd............123 L6
Bellfield S Lans............164 F3
Bellfield S Lans............165 J5
Bellingdon Bucks............58 F6
Bellingham Nthumb............157 L5
Belloch Ag & B............161 H2
Bellochantuy Ag & B............161 H3
Bell o' th' Hill Ches W............98 D4
Bellshill N Lans............175 J6
Bellside N Lans............175 L6
Bellsquarry W Loth............176 E5
Bells Yew Green
    E Susx............33 G6
Belluton BaNES............38 F7
Belmaduthy Highld............213 G3
Belmont Bl w D............121 K7
Belmont Gt Lon............44 E7
Belmont S Ayrs............163 J5
Belmont Shet............235 d2
Belnacraig Abers............205 J3
Belper Derbys............101 G3
Belsay Nthumb............158 D6
Belses Border............167 J4
Belsford Devon............7 H4
Belsize Herts............59 G7
Belstead Suffk............78 D6
Belstone Devon............10 F6
Belthorn Lancs............121 L5
Beltinge Kent............47 K6
Beltingham Nthumb............149 K3
Beltoft N Linc............116 D1
Belton Leics............101 H7
Belton Lincs............102 F4
Belton N Linc............116 C1
Belton Norfk............93 K3
Belton Rutlnd............88 B3
Belton House Lincs............102 F5
Belvedere Gt Lon............45 J4
Belvoir Leics............102 D5
Bembridge IoW............17 J5
Bemerton Wilts............28 C5
Bempton E R Yk............135 J5
Benacre Suffk............93 K6
Benbecula W Isls............233 c7
Benbecula Airport
    W Isls............233 c6
Benbuie D & G............154 C3
Benderloch Ag & B............191 H8
Benenden Kent............33 K6
Benfieldside Dur............150 D4
Bengeo Herts............60 A5
Bengeworth Worcs............71 J5
Benhall Green Suffk............79 H3
Benhall Street Suffk............79 H3
Benholm Abers............197 K3
Beningbrough N York............133 H7
Benington Herts............59 M4

Benington Lincs............104 C3
Benllech IoA............109 G5
Benmore Ag & B............173 K2
Bennan N Ayrs............162 C5
Ben Nevis Highld............192 B3
Benniworth Lincs............117 K5
Benover Kent............33 J4
Ben Rhydding C Brad............123 H2
Benslie N Ayrs............163 J2
Benson Oxon............41 L3
Benthoul C Aber............206 F5
Bentley Donc............115 K1
Bentley E R Yk............126 C4
Bentley Hants............30 C3
Bentley Suffk............78 D6
Bentley Warwks............86 C4
Bentley
    Crematorium
    Essex............45 L2
Bentpath D & G............156 B4
Bentwichen Devon............24 B5
Bentworth Hants............30 A4
Benvie Angus............186 E2
Benville Dorset............14 A2
Benwick Cambs............89 L5
Beoley Worcs............71 J1
Beoraidbeg Highld............199 L6
Bepton W Susx............18 B3
Berden Essex............60 D3
Berea Pembks............48 D2
Bere Alston Devon............6 C3
Bere Ferrers Devon............6 C3
Bere Regis Dorset............14 F4
Bergh Apton Norfk............93 G4
Berinsfield Oxon............41 L2
Berkeley Gloucs............55 G7
Berkhamsted Herts............59 G6
Berkley Somset............27 J2
Berkswell Solhll............86 B7
Bermondsey Gt Lon............45 G4
Bernera Highld............200 C2
Bernisdale Highld............208 F4
Berrick Prior Oxon............41 L2
Berrick Salome Oxon............41 L2
Berriedale Highld............227 K4
Berrier Cumb............137 L2
Berriew Powys............82 D4
Berrington Shrops............83 K3
Berrington Worcs............69 L2
Berrington Green
    Worcs............69 L2
Berrow Somset............25 L2
Berrow Green Worcs............70 D3
Berryhillock Moray............215 L3
Berryhillock Moray............215 L4
Berrynarbor Devon............23 J3
Berry Pomeroy
    Devon............7 J4
Bersham Wrexhm............97 L3
Berwick E Susx............20 B5
Berwick Bassett Wilts............40 C5
Berwick Hill Nthumb............158 F6
Berwick St James
    Wilts............28 B4
Berwick St John Wilts............27 L6
Berwick St Leonard
    Wilts............27 L5
Berwick-upon-
    Tweed Nthumb............179 K7
Bescar Lancs............120 E7
Besford Worcs............71 G5
Bessacarr Donc............115 L2
Bessingby E R Yk............135 J6
Bessingham Norfk............106 E5
Besthorpe Norfk............92 C4
Besthorpe Notts............116 D8
Bestwood Village
    Notts............101 K3
Beswick E R Yk............126 C2
Betchworth Surrey............31 K2
Bethel Gwynd............109 G7
Bethel IoA............108 E7
Bethersden Kent............34 C6
Bethesda Gwynd............109 J7
Bethesda Pembks............49 J4
Bethlehem Carmth............51 K1

Bethnal Green Gt Lon 45 G4
Betley Staffs 99 H3
Betsham Kent 45 L5
Betteshanger Kent 35 J4
Bettiscombe Dorset 13 K3
Bettisfield Wrexhm 98 C5
Bettws Newpt 37 L3
Bettws Bledrws
    Cerdgn 66 D4
Bettws Cedewain
    Powys 82 C4
Bettws Evan Cerdgn 65 J5
Bettws-Newydd
    Mons 54 A6
Bettyhill Highld 229 L3
Betws Brdgnd 36 D3
Betws Gwerfil Goch
    Denbgs 97 G3
Betws-y-Coed Conwy 96 C2
Betws-yn-Rhos
    Conwy 110 C6
Beulah Cerdgn 65 J5
Beulah Powys 67 K4
Bevercotes Notts 116 B6
Beverley E R Yk 126 C3
Beverston Gloucs 39 K2
Bewcastle Cumb 156 F7
Bewdley Worcs 84 D7
Bewerley N York 132 B6
Bewholme E R Yk 126 E1
Bexhill E Susx 20 E4
Bexley Gt Lon 45 J5
Bexleyheath Gt Lon 45 J5
Bexwell Norfk 90 F3
Beyton Suffk 77 L2
Beyton Green Suffk 77 L2
Bhaltos W Isls 232 d2
Bhatarsaigh W Isls 233b10
Bibury Gloucs 56 C6
Bicester Oxon 57 L4
Bickenhill Solhll 85 L6
Bicker Lincs 103 L5
Bickerstaffe Lancs 112 C2
Bickerton N York 124 C1
Bickford Staffs 84 F2
Bickington Devon 7 J2
Bickington Devon 23 H5
Bickleigh Devon 6 D4
Bickleigh Devon 12 B2
Bickley Ches W 98 D3
Bickley Gt Lon 45 H6
Bickley N York 134 E2
Bicknacre Essex 61 J7
Bicknoller Somset 25 H4
Bicknor Kent 33 L2
Bicton Shrops 82 F6
Bicton Shrops 83 J1
Bidborough Kent 32 F5
Biddenden Kent 33 L5
Biddenham Bed 74 E4
Biddestone Wilts 39 K5
Biddisham Somset 26 B2
Biddlesden Bucks 73 J6
Biddulph Staffs 99 K2
Biddulph Moor Staffs 99 K2
Bideford Devon 23 G6
Bidford-on-Avon
    Warwks 71 K4
Bielby E R Yk 125 J2
Bieldside C Aber 207 G5
Bierley IoW 17 G6
Bierton Bucks 58 D5
Big Balcraig D & G 145 H6
Bigbury Devon 6 F6
Bigbury-on-Sea
    Devon 6 F6
Bigby Lincs 117 H1
Big Carlae D & G 154 B3
Biggar S Lans 165 K2
Biggin Derbys 100 D2
Biggin Hill Gt Lon 32 D2
Biggin Hill Airport
    Gt Lon 45 H7
Biggleswade C Beds 75 H5
Bigholms D & G 156 B6
Bighouse Highld 230 C3

Bighton Hants 29 L4
Biglands Cumb 148 A4
Bignor W Susx 18 D3
Bigrigg Cumb 136 D5
Big Sand Highld 219 H5
Bigton Shet 235 c7
Bilborough C Nott 101 K4
Bilbrook Somset 25 G3
Bilbrough N York 124 E2
Bilbster Highld 231 K5
Bildershaw Dur 140 F3
Bildeston Suffk 78 B5
Billericay Essex 46 B2
Billesdon Leics 87 K3
Billesley Warwks 71 K3
Billingborough Lincs 103 J5
Billinge St Hel 112 D2
Billingford Norfk 92 E7
Billingford Norfk 106 B7
Billingham S on T 141 K3
Billinghay Lincs 103 J2
Billingley Barns 115 H1
Billingshurst W Susx 31 H6
Billingsley Shrops 84 C6
Billington C Beds 58 F4
Billington Lancs 121 L4
Billockby Norfk 93 J2
Billy Row Dur 150 E7
Bilsborrow Lancs 121 G3
Bilsby Lincs 119 G6
Bilsham W Susx 18 D5
Bilsington Kent 34 D7
Bilsthorpe Notts 101 M1
Bilston Mdloth 177 H5
Bilston Wolves 85 G4
Bilstone Leics 86 D3
Bilton E R Yk 126 E4
Bilton N York 124 D1
Bilton N York 132 D7
Bilton Warwks 86 F8
Binbrook Lincs 117 K3
Bincombe Dorset 14 D5
Binegar Somset 26 E2
Binfield Br For 42 D6
Binfield Heath Oxon 42 C5
Bingfield Nthumb 158 B7
Bingham Notts 102 B4
Bingley C Brad 123 G3
Binham Norfk 106 B5
Binley Covtry 86 E7
Binley Hants 29 H2
Binley Woods Warwks 86 E7
Binnegar Dorset 15 G5
Binniehill Falk 176 B4
Binscombe Surrey 30 F3
Binstead IoW 17 H4
Binsted Hants 30 C3
Binsted W Susx 18 D4
Binton Warwks 71 K4
Bintree Norfk 106 B7
Birch Essex 61 M4
Bircham Newton
    Norfk 105 J5
Bircham Tofts Norfk 105 J6
Birchanger Green
    Services Essex 60 E4
Birch Cross Staffs 100 C6
Bircher Herefs 69 J2
Birch Green Essex 61 M4
Birchgrove Cardif 37 J4
Birchgrove Swans 51 K5
Birchgrove W Susx 32 D7
Birchington Kent 35 J2
Birchley Heath
    Warwks 86 C5
Birchover Derbys 100 E1
Birch Services Rochdl .. 122 C8
Birch Vale Derbys 114 A4
Birchwood Lincs 116 F7
Birch Wood Somset 25 K8
Birchwood Warrtn 112 F4
Bircotes Notts 115 M3
Birdbrook Essex 77 G6
Birdforth N York 133 G4
Birdham W Susx 17 M3

Birdingbury Warwks 72 E2
Birdlip Gloucs 55 L5
Birdsall N York 134 C6
Birds Edge Kirk 123 J8
Birds Green Essex 60 F6
Birdsgreen Shrops 84 D6
Birdsmoorgate
    Dorset 13 K3
Birdwell Barns 115 G2
Birgham Border 168 B2
Birichin Highld 223 G3
Birkby N York 141 H6
Birkdale Sefton 120 D7
Birkenbog Abers 215 L2
Birkenhead Wirral 111 K4
Birkenhills Abers 216 E5
Birkenshaw Kirk 123 J5
Birkhall Abers 205 H6
Birkhill Angus 186 F1
Birkhill D & G 166 B6
Birkin N York 124 E5
Birley Herefs 69 J4
Birley Carr Sheff 115 G3
Birling Kent 46 B7
Birlingham Worcs 71 G5
Birmingham Birm 85 J6
Birmingham Airport
    Solhll 85 L6
Birnam P & K 195 G7
Birness Abers 217 J7
Birse Abers 206 B6
Birsemore Abers 205 L5
Birstall Kirk 123 J5
Birstall Leics 87 H2
Birstwith N York 132 C7
Birtley Gatesd 151 G4
Birtley Herefs 69 G2
Birtley Nthumb 157 L6
Birtley Crematorium
    Gatesd 151 G4
Birts Street Worcs 70 D7
Bisbrooke Rutlnd 88 C4
Biscathorpe Lincs 118 C5
Bisham W & M 42 D4
Bishampton Worcs 71 H4
Bish Mill Devon 24 B6
Bishop Auckland Dur ... 140 F2
Bishopbridge Lincs 117 G4
Bishopbriggs E Duns 175 G4
Bishop Burton E R Yk ... 126 B3
Bishop Middleham
    Dur 141 H2
Bishopmill Moray 214 F2
Bishop Monkton
    N York 132 E6
Bishop Norton Lincs 117 G3
Bishopsbourne Kent 35 G4
Bishops Cannings
    Wilts 40 B7
Bishop's Castle
    Shrops 83 G5
Bishop's Caundle
    Dorset 27 G8
Bishop's Cleeve
    Gloucs 55 L3
Bishop's Frome
    Herefs 70 B5
Bishop's Green Essex 61 G4
Bishops Hull Somset 25 J6
Bishop's Itchington
    Warwks 72 E3
Bishops Lydeard
    Somset 25 J5
Bishop's Norton
    Gloucs 55 J3
Bishop's Nympton
    Devon 24 B6
Bishop's Offley Staffs 99 H6
Bishop's Stortford
    Herts 60 D4
Bishop's Sutton
    Hants 29 L5
Bishop's Tachbrook
    Warwks 72 C3
Bishop's Tawton
    Devon 23 J5

Bishopsteignton
    Devon 7 K2
Bishopstoke Hants 29 J7
Bishopston Swans 51 H7
Bishopstone Bucks 58 D6
Bishopstone E Susx 19 M5
Bishopstone Herefs 69 H5
Bishopstone Kent 47 K6
Bishopstone Swindn 40 E4
Bishopstone Wilts 28 B6
Bishopstrow Wilts 27 K3
Bishop Sutton BaNES 38 E7
Bishop's Waltham
    Hants 29 K7
Bishopswood Somset 25 K8
Bishop's Wood Staffs 84 E2
Bishopsworth Bristl 38 E6
Bishop Thornton
    N York 132 D6
Bishopthorpe
    C York 124 F2
Bishopton Darltn 141 J3
Bishopton Rens 174 E4
Bishop Wilton
    E R Yk 134 C7
Bishton Newpt 38 B3
Bishton Staffs 100 A7
Bisley Gloucs 55 K6
Bisley Surrey 42 F8
Bissoe Cnwll 3 K3
Bisterne Hants 15 L3
Bitchfield Lincs 103 G6
Bittadon Devon 23 J3
Bittaford Devon 6 F4
Bitterley Shrops 83 L7
Bitterne C Sotn 29 J8
Bitteswell Leics 87 G6
Bitton S Glos 39 G6
Bix Oxon 42 B4
Bixter Shet 235 c5
Blaby Leics 87 H4
Blackadder Border 179 H7
Blackawton Devon 7 J5
Blackborough Devon 12 E1
Blackborough End
    Norfk 90 F1
Black Bourton Oxon 56 F6
Blackboys E Susx 20 B2
Blackbrook Derbys 101 G3
Blackbrook St Hel 112 D3
Blackbrook Staffs 99 H5
Blackburn Abers 206 F3
Blackburn Bl w D 121 K5
Blackburn W Loth 176 D5
Blackburn with
    Darwen Services
    Bl w D 121 K5
Black Callerton N u Ty .. 150 F2
Blackcraig E Ayrs 164 C7
Black Crofts Ag & B 182 D1
Blackdog Abers 207 H3
Black Dog Devon 11 J3
Blackdown Dorset 13 K2
Blacker Hill Barns 115 G2
Blackfen Gt Lon 45 J5
Blackfield Hants 16 E3
Blackford P & K 185 J5
Blackford Somset 26 B2
Blackford Somset 26 F6
Blackfordby Leics 101 G8
Blackhall C Edin 177 G4
Blackhall Colliery Dur .. 151 K6
Blackhall Mill Gatesd ... 150 E4
Blackhaugh Border 166 F2
Blackheath Gt Lon 45 G5
Blackheath Sandw 85 H6
Blackheath Suffk 93 J8
Blackheath Surrey 31 G3
Blackhill Abers 217 K3
Blackhill Abers 217 K5
Blackhill Dur 150 D5
Blackhill of
    Clackriach Abers 217 H5
Blackhorse Devon 12 C4
Blacklaw D & G 165 K7
Blackley Manch 113 J2

Blackley
  Crematorium
    Manch 113 J2
Blacklunans P & K 195 J4
Blackmarstone
  Herefs 69 K6
Blackmill Brdgnd........36 E3
Blackmoor Hants........30 C5
Blackmoor N Som.......38 C7
Blackmoorfoot Kirk....123 G7
Blackmore Essex........60 F7
Blackmore End Essex..61 H2
Blackness Falk..........176 E3
Blacknest Hants........30 D3
Black Notley Essex......61 J4
Blacko Lancs.............122 C3
Black Pill Swans........51 J7
Blackpool Bpool........120 D4
Blackpool Devon..........7 K6
Blackridge W Loth......176 B5
Blackrod Bolton........121 J7
Blacksboat Moray......214 E6
Blackshaw D & G.......147 J2
Blackshaw Head
  Calder....................122 E5
Blackstone W Susx......19 H3
Black Street Suffk......93 K6
Blackthorn Oxon........57 L4
Blackthorpe Suffk......77 K2
Blacktoft E R Yk........125 J5
Blacktop C Aber........207 G4
Black Torrington
  Devon......................10 C4
Blackwall Derbys......100 E3
Blackwater Cnwll.........3 J3
Blackwater Hants........42 D7
Blackwater IoW..........17 G5
Blackwater Somset.....25 K7
Blackwaterfoot
  N Ayrs....................162 A4
Blackwell Cumb........148 D4
Blackwell Derbys......101 H2
Blackwell Derbys......114 C6
Blackwell Warwks......72 B5
Blackwell Worcs........71 H1
Blackwood Caerph......37 J2
Blackwood D & G......154 F5
Blackwood S Lans.....164 F1
Blacon Ches W.........111 L7
Bladnoch D & G.......145 J4
Bladon Oxon.............57 J5
Blaenannerch Cerdgn..65 H5
Blaenau Ffestiniog
  Gwynd......................96 A4
Blaenavon Torfn........53 K6
Blaenavon Industrial
  Landscape Torfn......53 K6
Blaenffos Pembks......65 H6
Blaengarw Brdgnd......36 D2
Blaengwrach Neath.....52 D6
Blaengwynfi Neath......36 D2
Blaenpennal Cerdgn....66 E2
Blaenplwyf Cerdgn......80 D7
Blaenporth Cerdgn......65 J5
Blaenrhondda
  Rhondd...................52 E7
Blaenwaun Carmth....50 B1
Blaen-y-Coed Carmth..50 D1
Blaen-y-cwm Rhondd..52 E7
Blagdon N Som.........38 D8
Blagdon Somset........25 K4
Blagdon Torbay..........7 K4
Blagdon Hill Somset...25 K4
Blaich Highld...........191 K2
Blain Highld............190 D3
Blaina Blae G...........53 J6
Blair Atholl P & K.....194 D4
Blair Drummond
  Stirlg....................184 F7
Blairgowrie P & K......195 J7
Blairhall Fife...........176 D2
Blairingone P & K......185 K7
Blairlogie Stirlg........185 H7
Blairmore Ag & B......173 L2
Blairmore Highld......228 C4
Blair's Ferry Ag & B...173 G4

Blaisdon Gloucs........55 G5
Blakebrook Worcs......84 E7
Blakedown Worcs.......84 F7
Blake End Essex........61 H4
Blakemere Ches W....112 D7
Blakemere Herefs......69 G6
Blakenall Heath Wsall.85 H3
Blakeney Gloucs........54 F6
Blakeney Norfk........106 B4
Blakenhall Ches E......99 G3
Blakenhall Wolves......85 G4
Blakesley Nhants.......73 J4
Blanchland Nthumb..150 B5
Blandford Forum
  Dorset....................15 G2
Blandford St Mary
  Dorset....................15 G2
Blanefield Stirlg.......174 F3
Blankney Lincs.........103 H1
Blantyre S Lans........175 J6
Blar a' Chaorainn
  Highld...................191 L3
Blargie Highld.........202 F6
Blarmachfoldach
  Highld...................191 L3
Blaston Leics............88 B4
Blatherwycke Nhants..88 D4
Blawith Cumb..........129 G2
Blawquhairn D & G...154 B5
Blaxhall Suffk...........79 H3
Blaxton Donc..........116 A2
Blaydon Gatesd.......150 F3
Bleadney Somset.......26 C3
Bleadon N Som.........25 M1
Blean Kent..............34 F3
Bleasby Notts..........102 B3
Blebocraigs Fife......187 G4
Bleddfa Powys..........68 E2
Bledington Gloucs......56 E4
Bledlow Bucks..........58 C7
Bledlow Ridge Bucks..42 D2
Blegbie E Loth.........178 B6
Blencarn Cumb........138 F2
Blencogo Cumb........147 L5
Blendworth Hants......30 B8
Blenheim Palace
  Oxon......................57 H5
Blennerhasset Cumb..147 L6
Bletchingdon Oxon....57 J4
Bletchingley Surrey...32 B3
Bletchley M Keyn......58 E2
Bletchley Shrops.......98 F5
Bletherston Pembks...49 H4
Bletsoe Bed.............74 E3
Blewbury Oxon.........41 K4
Blickling Norfk........106 E6
Blidworth Notts.......101 L2
Blidworth Bottoms
  Notts....................101 L2
Blindcrake Cumb......147 K7
Blindley Heath
  Surrey....................32 C4
Blisland Cnwll............5 H2
Blissford Hants.........28 D8
Bliss Gate Worcs.......84 D8
Blisworth Nhants......73 K4
Blithbury Staffs.......100 B8
Blockley Gloucs........71 L7
Blofield Norfk..........93 G2
Blofield Heath Norfk..93 G2
Blo Norton Norfk......92 B7
Bloomfield Border....167 J4
Blore Staffs............100 C3
Bloxham Oxon..........72 E7
Bloxholm Lincs........103 H2
Bloxwich Wsall.........85 H3
Bloxworth Dorset......15 G4
Blubberhouses
  N York...................132 B7
Blue Anchor Somset...24 F3
Blue Bell Hill Kent.....46 C7
Blue John Cavern
  Derbys..................114 C5
Blundellsands Sefton.111 J2
Blundeston Suffk......93 L4
Blunham C Beds.......75 H4

Blunsdon St Andrew
  Swindn....................40 C3
Bluntington Worcs.....84 F8
Bluntisham Cambs.....89 L8
Blyborough Lincs.....116 F3
Blyford Suffk............93 J7
Blymhill Staffs..........84 E2
Blyth Notts............115 L4
Blyth Nthumb.........159 H5
Blyth Bridge Border.165 M1
Blythburgh Suffk......93 J7
Blyth Crematorium
  Nthumb.................159 H5
Blythe Border.........178 D7
Blyton Lincs...........116 D3
Boarhills Fife..........187 J5
Boarhunt Hants........17 H2
Boarstall Bucks........57 L5
Boath Highld..........222 D6
Boat of Garten Highld.203 L2
Bobbing Kent..........46 E6
Bobbington Staffs......84 E5
Bocking Essex..........61 J4
Bocking
  Churchstreet
    Essex................61 J3
Boddam Abers.........217 L6
Boddam Shet..........235 C7
Boddington Gloucs....55 K3
Bodedern IoA.........108 D5
Bodelwyddan
  Denbgs..................110 D6
Bodenham Herefs......69 K4
Bodenham Wilts........28 D6
Bodenham Moor
  Herefs....................69 K4
Bodewryd IoA.........108 E4
Bodfari Denbgs.......110 F7
Bodffordd IoA.........108 F6
Bodfuan Gwynd........94 F5
Bodham Norfk.........106 D4
Bodiam E Susx.........33 K7
Bodicote Oxon..........72 F6
Bodinnick Cnwll.........5 H5
Bodle Street Green
  E Susx....................20 D3
Bodmin Cnwll...........5 G3
Bodmin Moor Cnwll....5 J1
Bodsham Kent..........34 E5
Bodwen Cnwll...........5 G4
Bogallan Highld.......212 F4
Bogbrae Abers.........217 J7
Bogend S Ayrs.........163 K3
Boggs Holdings
  E Loth...................177 L4
Boghall Mdloth........177 H5
Boghall W Loth........176 D5
Boghead S Lans.......164 F2
Bogmoor Moray........215 H2
Bogmuir Abers.........197 G3
Bogniebrae Abers.....216 B5
Bognor Regis W Susx.18 C6
Bogroy Highld.........203 L2
Bogue D & G..........154 B6
Bohortha Cnwll..........3 L5
Bohuntine Highld.....201 L8
Bolam Dur.............140 F3
Bolberry Devon..........7 G7
Boldmere Birm.........85 K5
Boldre Hants...........16 C3
Boldron Dur...........140 C4
Bole Notts.............116 C4
Bolehill Derbys........100 F2
Bolham Devon..........24 E7
Bolham Water Devon..25 J8
Bolingey Cnwll...........3 K1
Bollington Ches E.....113 L6
Bolney W Susx.........31 L6
Bolnhurst Bed..........74 F3
Bolshan Angus........197 G6
Bolsover Derbys......115 J7
Bolsterstone Sheff....114 F3
Boltby N York.........133 G3
Bolton Bolton.........121 L8
Bolton Cumb..........138 F3

Bolton E Loth.........178 B4
Bolton E R Yk.........125 J1
Bolton Nthumb........169 G6
Bolton Abbey N York.131 K8
Bolton-by-Bowland
  Lancs....................122 B1
Boltonfellend Cumb..148 E2
Boltongate Cumb.....147 M6
Bolton le Sands Lancs.129 K6
Bolton Low Houses
  Cumb....................147 M6
Bolton-on-Swale
  N York...................141 G7
Bolton Percy N York.124 E3
Bolton Upon Dearne
  Barns....................115 J2
Bolventor Cnwll..........5 J1
Bomere Heath Shrops.98 C8
Bonar Bridge Highld.222 E3
Bonawe Ag & B.......182 E2
Bonby N Linc.........126 C7
Boncath Pembks......65 H6
Bonchester Bridge
  Border...................167 J6
Bondleigh Devon......10 F4
Bonds Lancs...........121 G2
Bo'ness Falk...........176 D3
Boney Hay Staffs......85 J2
Bonhill W Duns.......174 D3
Boningale Shrops......84 E3
Bonjedward Border..167 K5
Bonkle N Lans........175 L6
Bonnington Angus...196 F7
Bonnington Kent......34 E7
Bonnybank Fife.......186 F6
Bonnybridge Falk.....175 L3
Bonnykelly Abers.....217 G4
Bonnyrigg Mdloth....177 J5
Bonnyton Angus......196 B8
Bonsall Derbys........100 F2
Bonshaw Tower
  D & G...................155 M7
Bont-Dolgadfan
  Powys.....................81 J4
Bont-goch or Elerch
  Cerdgn....................80 F6
Bontnewydd Cerdgn..66 E2
Bontnewydd Gwynd..95 H1
Bontuchel Denbgs....97 G2
Bonvilston V Glam....37 G5
Boode Devon...........23 H4
Booker Bucks..........42 D3
Boon Border..........167 J1
Boosbeck R & Cl....142 E4
Boose's Green Essex..61 K2
Boot Cumb............137 G6
Booth Calder.........122 F5
Boothby Graffoe
  Lincs....................103 G2
Boothby Pagnell
  Lincs....................102 F6
Boothferry E R Yk...125 H5
Boothstown Salfd....113 G2
Bootle Cumb..........128 D2
Bootle Sefton.........111 K3
Boraston Shrops......70 B1
Bordeaux Guern.....236 e2
Borden Kent...........34 B3
Border Forest Park..157 G5
Borders
  Crematorium
    Border.............167 H3
Boreham Essex........61 J6
Boreham Wilts.........27 K3
Boreham Street
  E Susx....................20 D4
Borehamwood Herts.44 D2
Boreland D & G.....155 L4
Boreraig Highld......208 C4
Borgh W Isls..........232 f1
Borgh W Isls..........233 b9
Borgie Highld.........229 K4
Borgue D & G........146 B5
Borgue Highld........227 K4
Borley Essex...........77 J6
Borneskitaig Highld.218 B7

Borness D & G ... 146 A5
Boroughbridge N York ... 132 F6
Borough Green Kent ... 33 G2
Borrowash Derbys ... 101 H5
Borrowby N York ... 132 F2
Borrowstoun Falk ... 176 D3
Borstal Medway ... 46 B6
Borth Cerdgn ... 80 E5
Borthwickbrae Border ... 166 F6
Borthwickshiels Border ... 166 F6
Borth-y-Gest Gwynd ... 95 K5
Borve Highld ... 209 G5
Borve W Isls ... 232 d4
Borve W Isls ... 232 f1
Borve W Isls ... 233 b9
Borwick Lancs ... 129 L5
Bosbury Herefs ... 70 C5
Boscastle Cnwll ... 8 E6
Boscombe Bmouth ... 15 L4
Boscombe Wilts ... 28 D4
Bosham W Susx ... 17 L2
Bosherston Pembks ... 49 G8
Bosley Ches E ... 113 K7
Bossall N York ... 133 L7
Bossiney Cnwll ... 8 E6
Bossingham Kent ... 34 F5
Bossington Somset ... 24 D2
Bostock Green Ches W ... 112 F7
Boston Lincs ... 104 B4
Boston Crematorium Lincs ... 104 A4
Boston Spa Leeds ... 124 C2
Boswinger Cnwll ... 4 F7
Botallack Cnwll ... 2 C5
Botany Bay Gt Lon ... 59 M7
Botesdale Suffk ... 92 C7
Bothal Nthumb ... 159 G5
Bothamsall Notts ... 116 A6
Bothel Cumb ... 147 L6
Bothenhampton Dorset ... 13 L4
Bothwell S Lans ... 175 J6
Bothwell Services S Lans ... 175 J6
Botley Bucks ... 59 G7
Botley Hants ... 29 K8
Botley Oxon ... 57 J6
Botolph Claydon Bucks ... 58 B3
Botolphs W Susx ... 19 G4
Bottesford Leics ... 102 D5
Bottesford N Linc ... 116 E1
Bottisham Cambs ... 76 D3
Bottomcraig Fife ... 186 F3
Bottoms Calder ... 122 D6
Botusfleming Cnwll ... 6 B4
Botwnnog Gwynd ... 94 E6
Bough Beech Kent ... 32 E4
Boughrood Powys ... 68 C6
Boughton Nhants ... 73 L2
Boughton Norfk ... 91 G3
Boughton Notts ... 116 B7
Boughton Aluph Kent ... 34 D5
Boughton Green Kent ... 33 K3
Boughton Monchelsea Kent ... 33 K3
Boughton Street Kent ... 34 E3
Bouldon Shrops ... 83 K6
Boulmer Nthumb ... 169 K6
Boultham Lincs ... 116 F7
Bourn Cambs ... 75 K3
Bourne Lincs ... 103 H7
Bournebridge Essex ... 45 J2
Bournebrook Birm ... 85 J6
Bourne End Bucks ... 42 E3
Bourne End C Beds ... 74 D5
Bourne End Herts ... 59 G6
Bournemouth Bmouth ... 15 K4

Bournemouth Airport Dorset ... 15 L3
Bournemouth Crematorium Bmouth ... 15 L4
Bournes Green Sthend ... 46 E3
Bournheath Worcs ... 85 G8
Bournmoor Dur ... 151 H5
Bournville Birm ... 85 J7
Bourton Dorset ... 27 H5
Bourton Oxon ... 40 E3
Bourton Shrops ... 83 L4
Bourton Wilts ... 40 B7
Bourton on Dunsmore Warwks ... 72 E1
Bourton-on-the-Hill Gloucs ... 56 D2
Bourton-on-the-Water Gloucs ... 56 D4
Bousd Ag & B ... 189 G4
Bouth Cumb ... 129 H3
Bouthwaite N York ... 131 L5
Boveridge Dorset ... 28 B7
Bovey Tracey Devon ... 7 J1
Bovingdon Herts ... 59 G7
Bow Devon ... 11 G4
Bow Gt Lon ... 45 G4
Bow Ork ... 234 b7
Bow Brickhill M Keyn ... 74 C7
Bowbridge Gloucs ... 55 J6
Bowburn Dur ... 151 H7
Bowcombe IoW ... 16 F5
Bowd Devon ... 12 E4
Bowden Border ... 167 H4
Bowden Hill Wilts ... 39 L6
Bowdon Traffd ... 113 H4
Bower Highld ... 231 J3
Bowerchalke Wilts ... 28 A6
Bowermadden Highld ... 231 J3
Bowers Staffs ... 99 J5
Bowers Gifford Essex ... 46 C3
Bowershall Fife ... 176 F1
Bower's Row Leeds ... 124 B5
Bowes Dur ... 140 C4
Bowgreave Lancs ... 121 G2
Bowhouse D & G ... 147 H2
Bowland Border ... 167 G2
Bowley Herefs ... 69 K4
Bowlhead Green Surrey ... 30 E4
Bowling C Brad ... 123 H4
Bowling W Duns ... 174 E4
Bowmanstead Cumb ... 137 J7
Bowmore Ag & B ... 170 F6
Bowness-on-Solway Cumb ... 147 L3
Bowness-on-Windermere Cumb ... 137 L7
Bow of Fife Fife ... 186 E5
Bowriefauld Angus ... 196 E6
Bowsden Nthumb ... 168 E2
Bow Street Cerdgn ... 80 E6
Box Gloucs ... 55 K7
Box Wilts ... 39 J6
Boxford Suffk ... 77 L6
Boxford W Berk ... 41 H6
Boxgrove W Susx ... 18 B4
Boxley Kent ... 33 K2
Boxmoor Herts ... 59 H6
Boxted Essex ... 62 B2
Boxted Essex ... 62 B2
Boxted Suffk ... 77 J4
Boxted Cross Essex ... 62 B2
Boxworth Cambs ... 75 L2
Boyden Gate Kent ... 47 L6
Boylestone Derbys ... 100 D5
Boyndie Abers ... 216 D2
Boyndlie Abers ... 217 G2
Boynton E R Yk ... 135 H6
Boysack Angus ... 197 G6
Boyton Cnwll ... 9 J6
Boyton Suffk ... 79 H5
Boyton Wilts ... 27 L4
Boyton Cross Essex ... 61 G6

Boyton End Suffk ... 77 G5
Bozeat Nhants ... 74 C3
Brabourne Kent ... 34 E6
Brabourne Lees Kent ... 34 E6
Brabstermire Highld ... 231 K2
Bracadale Highld ... 208 E6
Braceborough Lincs ... 88 F2
Bracebridge Heath Lincs ... 117 G7
Bracebridge Low Fields Lincs ... 116 F7
Braceby Lincs ... 103 G5
Bracewell Lancs ... 122 C2
Brackenfield Derbys ... 101 G2
Brackenhirst N Lans ... 175 K5
Bracklesham W Susx ... 17 L3
Brackletter Highld ... 201 J8
Brackley Nhants ... 73 H6
Bracknell Br For ... 42 E6
Braco P & K ... 185 H5
Bracobrae Moray ... 215 L4
Bracon Ash Norfk ... 92 E4
Bracora Highld ... 199 L6
Bracorina Highld ... 199 L6
Bradbourne Derbys ... 100 D3
Bradbury Dur ... 141 H2
Bradden Nhants ... 73 J5
Bradenham Bucks ... 42 D2
Bradenstoke Wilts ... 39 M4
Bradfield Devon ... 12 D1
Bradfield Essex ... 62 D2
Bradfield Norfk ... 106 F5
Bradfield Sheff ... 114 F3
Bradfield W Berk ... 41 L6
Bradfield Combust Suffk ... 77 K3
Bradfield Green Ches E ... 99 G2
Bradfield Heath Essex ... 62 D3
Bradfield St Clare Suffk ... 77 K3
Bradfield St George Suffk ... 77 K3
Bradford C Brad ... 123 H4
Bradford Devon ... 9 L4
Bradford Abbas Dorset ... 26 E8
Bradford Leigh Wilts ... 39 J7
Bradford-on-Avon Wilts ... 39 J7
Bradford-on-Tone Somset ... 25 J6
Bradford Peverell Dorset ... 14 C4
Bradiford Devon ... 23 J5
Brading IoW ... 17 H5
Bradley Derbys ... 100 E4
Bradley Hants ... 29 M3
Bradley NE Lin ... 118 C1
Bradley Staffs ... 99 K8
Bradley Wolves ... 85 G4
Bradley Worcs ... 71 H3
Bradley Green Worcs ... 71 H3
Bradley in the Moors Staffs ... 100 B4
Bradley Stoke S Glos ... 38 E4
Bradmore Notts ... 101 L6
Bradninch Devon ... 12 C2
Bradnop Staffs ... 100 A2
Bradpole Dorset ... 13 L4
Bradshaw Calder ... 123 G4
Bradstone Devon ... 9 K8
Bradwall Green Ches E ... 113 H8
Bradwell Derbys ... 114 D5
Bradwell Essex ... 61 J4
Bradwell M Keyn ... 74 B6
Bradwell Norfk ... 93 K3
Bradwell Crematorium Staffs ... 99 J3
Bradwell-on-Sea Essex ... 62 B6
Bradwell Waterside Essex ... 62 B6
Bradworthy Devon ... 9 J3

Brae Highld ... 213 G2
Brae Shet ... 235 c4
Braeface Falk ... 175 K3
Braehead Angus ... 197 H5
Braehead D & G ... 145 J4
Braehead S Lans ... 176 C7
Braemar Abers ... 204 E6
Braemore Highld ... 221 G5
Braemore Highld ... 227 J3
Brae Roy Lodge Highld ... 201 L6
Braeside Inver ... 173 L4
Braes of Coul Angus ... 195 L5
Braes of Enzie Moray ... 215 J3
Braeswick Ork ... 234 d4
Braevallich Ag & B ... 182 D6
Brafferton Darltn ... 141 H3
Brafferton N York ... 132 F5
Brafield-on-the-Green Nhants ... 74 B3
Bragar W Isls ... 232 f2
Bragbury End Herts ... 59 L4
Braidwood S Lans ... 175 L8
Brailsford Derbys ... 100 E4
Braintree Essex ... 61 J4
Braiseworth Suffk ... 78 D1
Braishfield Hants ... 29 G6
Braithwaite Cumb ... 137 H3
Braithwell Donc ... 115 K3
Bramber W Susx ... 19 G4
Bramcote Warwks ... 86 E5
Bramcote Crematorium Notts ... 101 J5
Bramdean Hants ... 29 L5
Bramerton Norfk ... 93 G3
Bramfield Herts ... 59 M5
Bramfield Suffk ... 93 H8
Bramford Suffk ... 78 D5
Bramhall Stockp ... 113 K5
Bramham Leeds ... 124 C2
Bramhope Leeds ... 123 K2
Bramley Hants ... 41 M8
Bramley Leeds ... 123 K4
Bramley Rothm ... 115 J3
Bramley Surrey ... 31 G3
Bramley Corner Hants ... 41 M8
Bramling Kent ... 35 G4
Brampford Speke Devon ... 11 L5
Brampton Cambs ... 75 J1
Brampton Cambs ... 138 F3
Brampton Cumb ... 148 F3
Brampton Lincs ... 116 D5
Brampton Norfk ... 106 F7
Brampton Rothm ... 115 H2
Brampton Suffk ... 93 J6
Brampton Abbotts Herefs ... 54 E3
Brampton Ash Nhants ... 87 L6
Brampton Bryan Herefs ... 83 G8
Brampton-en-le-Morthen Rothm ... 115 J4
Bramshall Staffs ... 100 B6
Bramshaw Hants ... 28 F7
Bramshott Hants ... 30 D5
Bramwell Somset ... 26 B5
Branault Highld ... 190 B3
Brancaster Norfk ... 105 J4
Brancaster Staithe Norfk ... 105 J4
Brancepeth Dur ... 150 F7
Branchill Moray ... 214 D4
Branderburgh Moray ... 214 F1
Brandesburton E R Yk ... 126 E2
Brandeston Suffk ... 78 F3
Brandiston Norfk ... 106 D7
Brandon Dur ... 151 G6
Brandon Lincs ... 102 E3
Brandon Suffk ... 91 H6
Brandon Warwks ... 86 E7
Brandon Parva Norfk ... 92 C2
Brandsby N York ... 133 J5

Brandy Wharf Lincs 117 G3
Bran End Essex 61 G3
Branksome Poole 15 K4
Branksome Park
  Poole 15 K4
Bransbury Hants 29 H3
Bransby Lincs 116 E5
Branscombe Devon 12 F5
Bransford Worcs 70 E4
Bransgore Hants 16 A3
Bransholme C KuH 126 D4
Bransley Shrops 84 B7
Branston Leics 102 D6
Branston Lincs 117 G7
Branston Staffs 100 E7
Branston Booths
  Lincs 117 H7
Branstone IoW 17 G5
Brant Broughton
  Lincs 102 E2
Brantham Suffk 78 D7
Branthwaite Cumb 136 E3
Branthwaite Cumb 148 B7
Brantingham E R Yk 125 L5
Branton Donc 115 M2
Branton Nthumb 168 F6
Branton Green N York . 132 F6
Branxton Nthumb 168 D2
Brassington Derbys 100 E2
Brasted Kent 32 E3
Brasted Chart Kent 32 E3
Brathens Abers 206 D5
Bratoft Lincs 119 G8
Brattleby Lincs 116 F5
Bratton Wilts 27 K2
Bratton Wrekin 84 B2
Bratton Clovelly
  Devon 10 C6
Bratton Fleming
  Devon 23 K4
Bratton Seymour
  Somset 26 F5
Braughing Herts 60 C5
Braunston Nhants 73 G2
Braunston Rutlnd 88 B3
Braunstone Leics 87 G3
Braunton Devon 23 H4
Brawby N York 134 D4
Brawl Highld 230 B3
Bray W & M 42 E4
Braybrooke Nhants 87 L6
Brayford Devon 23 L4
Bray Shop Cnwll 5 M2
Brayton N York 124 F4
Braywick W & M 42 E4
Breachwood Green
  Herts 59 J4
Breadsall Derbys 101 G5
Breadstone Gloucs 55 G7
Breage Cnwll 3 G5
Breakachy Highld 212 D5
Breakspear
  Crematorium
  Gt Lon 43 H3
Brealangwell Lodge
  Highld 222 C3
Bream Gloucs 54 E6
Breamore Hants 28 D7
Brean Somset 25 L1
Breanais W Isls 232 d3
Brearton N York 132 E7
Breascleit W Isls 232 e2
Breasclete W Isls 232 e2
Breaston Derbys 101 J5
Brechfa Carmth 66 C7
Brechin Angus 196 F4
Breckles Norfk 91 L5
Brecon Powys 53 G3
Brecon Beacons
  National Park 52 F3
Bredbury Stockp 113 L3
Brede E Susx 21 G3
Bredenbury Herefs 69 L3
Bredfield Suffk 78 F4
Bredgar Kent 34 B3
Bredhurst Kent 46 D7

Bredon Worcs 71 G6
Bredon's Hardwick
  Worcs 71 G7
Bredon's Norton
  Worcs 71 G6
Bredwardine Herefs 69 G5
Breedon on the Hill
  Leics 101 H7
Breich W Loth 176 C6
Breightmet Bolton 121 L8
Breighton E R Yk 125 G4
Breinton Herefs 69 J6
Bremhill Wilts 39 L5
Brenchley Kent 33 H5
Brendon Devon 24 B2
Brenfield Ag & B 172 E2
Brenish W Isls 232 d3
Brent Cross Gt Lon 44 E3
Brent Eleigh Suffk 77 L5
Brentford Gt Lon 44 D5
Brentingby Leics 102 C8
Brent Knoll Somset 25 M2
Brent Mill Devon 7 G4
Brent Pelham Herts 60 C2
Brentwood Essex 45 L2
Brenzett Kent 21 K1
Brenzett Green Kent ... 34 D8
Brereton Staffs 85 J1
Brereton Green
  Ches E 113 H8
Bressay Shet 235 d6
Bressingham Norfk 92 C7
Bretby Derbys 100 F7
Bretby Crematorium
  Derbys 100 F7
Bretford Warwks 86 E7
Bretforton Worcs 71 K5
Bretherton Lancs 121 G6
Brettabister Shet 235 d5
Brettenham Norfk 91 L6
Brettenham Suffk 77 L4
Bretton Flints 111 K8
Brewood Staffs 84 F2
Briantspuddle Dorset.. 14 F4
Brickendon Herts 60 A6
Bricket Wood Herts 59 J7
Brick Houses Sheff 114 F5
Bricklehampton
  Worcs 71 H6
Bride IoM 237 e2
Bridekirk Cumb 147 K7
Bridestowe Devon 10 D6
Brideswell Abers 216 B6
Bridford Devon 11 J7
Bridge Kent 35 G4
Bridgehampton
  Somset 26 E6
Bridge Hewick
  N York 132 E5
Bridgehill Dur 150 D5
Bridgemary Hants 17 H2
Bridgend Abers 215 L7
Bridgend Ag & B 161 K2
Bridgend Ag & B 171 G6
Bridgend Angus 196 E3
Bridgend Brdgnd 36 E4
Bridgend D & G 165 L7
Bridgend Devon 6 E6
Bridgend Fife 186 F5
Bridgend Moray 215 J7
Bridgend P & K 186 B3
Bridgend W Loth 176 E3
Bridgend of
  Lintrathen Angus.... 195 L5
Bridge of Alford
  Abers 206 B2
Bridge of Allan Stirlg ... 185 G7
Bridge of Avon Moray . 204 E2
Bridge of Avon Moray . 214 E7
Bridge of Balgie
  P & K 193 J6
Bridge of Brewlands
  Angus 195 J4
Bridge of Brown
  Highld 204 D2
Bridge of Cally P & K .. 195 J6

Bridge of Canny
  Abers 206 C6
Bridge of Craigisla
  Angus 195 K5
Bridge of Dee D & G ... 146 C3
Bridge of Don C Aber .. 207 H4
Bridge of Dulsie
  Highld 213 L6
Bridge of Dye Abers 206 C7
Bridge of Earn P & K ... 186 B4
Bridge of Ericht P & K . 193 H5
Bridge of Feugh
  Abers 206 D6
Bridge of Forss
  Highld 230 F2
Bridge of Gairn Abers . 205 H6
Bridge of Gaur P & K .. 193 H5
Bridge of Marnoch
  Abers 216 D4
Bridge of Orchy
  Ag & B 192 E7
Bridge of Tilt P & K 194 D4
Bridge of Tynet
  Moray 215 J3
Bridge of Walls Shet ... 235 D5
Bridge of Weir Rens ... 174 D5
Bridgerule Devon 9 H4
Bridge Sollers Herefs . 69 H6
Bridge Street Suffk 77 K5
Bridgetown Somset 24 E5
Bridge Trafford
  Ches W 112 C7
Bridgham Norfk 91 L6
Bridgnorth Shrops 84 C5
Bridgwater Somset 25 L4
Bridgwater Services
  Somset 25 L4
Bridlington E R Yk 135 J6
Bridport Dorset 13 L4
Bridstow Herefs 54 E3
Brierfield Lancs 122 C3
Brierley Barns 124 C7
Brierley Gloucs 54 F5
Brierley Hill Dudley 85 G6
Brigg N Linc 117 G1
Briggate Norfk 107 G6
Briggswath N York 143 H5
Brigham Cumb 136 F2
Brigham E R Yk 135 G8
Brighouse Calder 123 H6
Brighstone IoW 16 E5
Brighthampton Oxon ... 57 G7
Brightley Devon 10 E5
Brightling E Susx 20 D2
Brightlingsea Essex ... 62 C5
Brighton Br & M 19 J5
Brighton le Sands
  Sefton 111 J2
Brightons Falk 176 C3
Brightwalton W Berk ... 41 H5
Brightwell Suffk 78 F5
Brightwell Baldwin
  Oxon 41 M2
Brightwell-cum-
  Sotwell Oxon 41 L3
Brightwell Upperton
  Oxon 42 A2
Brignall Dur 140 D5
Brig o'Turk Stirlg 184 C6
Brigsley NE Lin 118 C2
Brigsteer Cumb 129 K2
Brigstock Nhants 88 D6
Brill Bucks 58 A5
Brill Cnwll 3 J5
Brilley Herefs 68 F5
Brimfield Herefs 69 K2
Brimfield Cross
  Herefs 69 K2
Brimington Derbys 115 H6
Brimley Devon 7 J1
Brimpsfield Gloucs 55 L5
Brimpton W Berk 41 K7
Brimscombe Gloucs 55 K7
Brimstage Wirral 111 J5
Brincliffe Sheff 115 F4
Brind E R Yk 125 H4

Brindister Shet 235 c5
Brindle Lancs 121 J5
Brineton Staffs 84 E2
Bringhurst Leics 88 B5
Bringsty Common
  Herefs 70 C4
Brington Cambs 88 F7
Briningham Norfk 106 C5
Brinkhill Lincs 118 E6
Brinkley Cambs 76 F4
Brinklow Warwks 86 E7
Brinkworth Wilts 40 A4
Brinscall Lancs 121 J6
Brinsley Notts 101 J3
Brinsworth Rothm 115 H4
Brinton Norfk 106 C5
Brinyan Ork 234 c5
Brisley Norfk 105 M7
Drislington Dristl 30 r6
Brissenden Green
  Kent 34 C6
Bristol Bristl 38 E5
Bristol Airport N Som . 38 D7
Bristol Zoo Gardens
  Bristl 38 E5
Briston Norfk 106 C6
Britford Wilts 28 D5
Brithdir Caerph 53 J7
Brithdir Gwynd 96 B8
British Legion Village
  Kent 33 J2
Briton Ferry Neath 51 L6
Britwell Salome Oxon . 42 A2
Brixham Torbay 7 L5
Brixton Devon 6 E5
Brixton Gt Lon 44 F5
Brixton Deverill Wilts . 27 K4
Brixworth Nhants 73 L1
Brize Norton Oxon 56 F6
Brize Norton Airport
  Oxon 56 F6
Broad Alley Worcs 70 F2
Broad Blunsdon
  Swindn 40 D3
Broadbottom Tamesd . 113 M3
Broadbridge W Susx ... 17 M2
Broadbridge Heath
  W Susx 31 J5
Broad Campden
  Gloucs 71 L6
Broad Carr Calder 123 G6
Broad Chalke Wilts 28 B6
Broadclyst Devon 12 C3
Broadfield Inver 174 C4
Broadford Highld 199 K2
Broadford Bridge
  W Susx 31 H6
Broadgairhill Border ... 166 C7
Broad Green Worcs 70 D4
Broadhaugh Border 179 H7
Broad Haven Pembks .. 48 E5
Broadheath Traffd 113 H4
Broadhembury
  Devon 12 E2
Broadhempston
  Devon 7 J3
Broad Hinton Wilts 40 C5
Broadland Row
  E Susx 21 G2
Broad Layings Hants .. 41 H7
Broadley Moray 215 J3
Broad Marston Worcs . 71 K5
Broadmayne Dorset 14 D5
Broadmoor Pembks 49 J6
Broadoak Dorset 13 K3
Broad Oak E Susx 20 C2
Broad Oak E Susx 21 G2
Broad Oak Herefs 54 C4
Broad Oak Kent 35 G3
Broad Oak St Hel 112 D3
Broad's Green Essex ... 61 H5
Broadstairs Kent 35 K2
Broadstone Poole 15 J4
Broadstone Shrops 83 K5
Broad Street E Susx ... 21 H3
Broad Street Kent 33 L2

Broad Town Wilts..........40 C5
Broadwas Worcs 70 D4
Broadwater Herts..........59 L4
Broadwater W Susx.......18 F5
Broadwaters Worcs........84 E7
Broadway Pembks..........48 E5
Broadway Somset 25 L7
Broadway Worcs............71 K6
Broadwell Gloucs..........54 E5
Broadwell Gloucs..........56 D3
Broadwell Oxon.............56 E6
Broadwell Warwks 72 F2
Broadwindsor Dorset.....13 K2
Broadwood Kelly
  Devon........................10 F4
Broadwoodwidger
  Devon...........................9 K6
Brochel Highld.............209 J5
Brochroy Ag & B.........182 E2
Brockamin Worcs...........70 D4
Brockbridge Hants........29 L7
Brockdish Norfk............92 E7
Brockenhurst Hants.......16 C3
Brocketsbrae S Lans ...164 F2
Brockford Street
  Suffk..........................78 D2
Brockhall Nhants..........73 J2
Brockham Surrey 31 K2
Brockhampton
  Gloucs........................56 B4
Brockhampton
  Hants..........................17 K2
Brockhampton
  Herefs........................54 E2
Brockholes Kirk 123 H7
Brocklesby Lincs 126 E7
Brockley N Som............38 C6
Brockley Suffk..............77 J1
Brockley Green
  Suffk..........................77 G5
Brockley Green
  Suffk..........................77 J4
Brockton Shrops...........83 G3
Brockton Shrops...........83 G6
Brockton Shrops...........83 L5
Brockweir Gloucs..........54 D7
Brockworth Gloucs........55 K5
Brocton Staffs..............99 L8
Brodick N Ayrs............162 C3
Brodie Moray..............214 B3
Brodsworth Donc........115 J1
Brogaig Highld............218 C7
Brokenborough Wilts....39 K3
Broken Cross Ches E....113 K6
Brokerswood Wilts........27 J2
Bromborough Wirral ...111 K5
Brome Suffk..................92 D7
Brome Street Suffk........92 D7
Bromeswell Suffk..........79 G4
Bromfield Cumb 147 L5
Bromfield Shrops..........83 J7
Bromham Bed...............74 E4
Bromham Wilts.............39 L7
Bromley Gt Lon............45 H6
Bromley Shrops............84 D4
Bromley Cross Bolton ..121 L7
Brompton Medway 46 C6
Brompton N York.........141 J7
Brompton-by-
  Sawdon N York........134 E3
Brompton-on-Swale
  N York......................140 F7
Brompton Ralph
  Somset.......................25 G5
Brompton Regis
  Somset.......................24 E5
Bromsberrow Gloucs....70 D7
Bromsberrow Heath
  Gloucs........................55 G2
Bromsgrove Worcs.......71 G1
Bromyard Herefs...........70 B4
Bronant Cerdgn............66 E2
Brongest Cerdgn...........65 K5
Bronington Wrexhm.......98 C4
Bronllys Powys.............68 D7
Bronwydd Carmth.........50 E2

Bronygarth Shrops.......97 K5
Bron-y-Nant
  Crematorium
  Conwy.......................110 A5
Brook Hants..................28 F8
Brook IoW....................16 E5
Brook Kent....................34 E6
Brook Surrey.................30 F4
Brooke Norfk.................93 G4
Brooke Rutlnd...............88 B3
Brookenby Lincs..........117 K3
Brookfield Rens...........174 D5
Brookhampton
  Somset.......................26 F5
Brook Hill Hants............28 F8
Brookhouse Lancs.......129 L6
Brookhouse Rothm......115 K4
Brookhouse Green
  Ches E.........................99 J1
Brookhouses Derbys ...114 B4
Brookland Kent.............21 K1
Brooklands Traffd........113 H4
Brookmans Park
  Herts..........................59 L7
Brook Street Essex......45 L2
Brook Street Kent..........34 C7
Brookthorpe Gloucs......55 J5
Brookwood Surrey 42 F8
Broom C Beds................75 H6
Broom Rothm...............115 H3
Broom Warwks..............71 K4
Broome Norfk................93 H5
Broome Shrops.............83 H7
Broome Worcs...............84 F7
Broomedge Warrtn.......113 G4
Broomfield Essex..........61 H5
Broomfield Kent............33 L3
Broomfield Kent............47 K6
Broomfield Somset........25 K6
Broomfleet E R Yk........125 K5
Broomhaugh
  Nthumb.....................150 C3
Broom Hill Barns.........115 H2
Broom Hill Notts..........101 K3
Broomhill Nthumb........159 G3
Broompark Dur...........151 G6
Brora Highld................226 F7
Broseley Shrops............84 C3
Brotherlee Dur.............150 A7
Brotherton N York.......124 D5
Brotton R & Cl.............142 E4
Broubster Highld.........230 F4
Brough Cumb..............139 H4
Brough E R Yk............125 L5
Brough Highld..............231 J2
Brough Notts...............102 D2
Brough Shet.................235 d4
Brough Lodge Shet......235 d2
Brough Sowerby
  Cumb........................139 H5
Broughall Shrops..........98 E4
Brough Sowerby
  Cumb........................139 H5
Broughton Border........165 L3
Broughton Cambs.........89 K7
Broughton Flints..........111 K8
Broughton Hants...........28 F5
Broughton Lancs..........121 G4
Broughton M Keyn.........74 C6
Broughton N Linc........126 B8
Broughton N York........122 D1
Broughton N York........134 B5
Broughton Nhants.........88 B7
Broughton Oxon............72 E6
Broughton Salfd...........113 J2
Broughton V Glam.........36 E6
Broughton Astley
  Leics...........................87 G5
Broughton Gifford
  Wilts...........................39 K7
Broughton Green
  Worcs.........................71 G3
Broughton Hackett
  Worcs.........................71 G4
Broughton-in-
  Furness Cumb..........128 F3
Broughton Mains
  D & G........................145 J6

Broughton Mills
  Cumb........................128 F2
Broughton Moor
  Cumb........................147 J7
Broughton Poggs
  Oxon...........................56 E7
Broughty Ferry
  C Dund......................187 H2
Brown Candover
  Hants..........................29 L4
Brown Edge Staffs........99 K2
Brownhill Abers...........217 G6
Brownhills Fife.............187 H4
Brownhills Wsall...........85 J3
Browninghill Green
  Hants..........................41 L7
Brown Lees Staffs........99 K2
Brownsea Island
  Dorset.........................15 J5
Browns Hill Gloucs......55 K7
Brownston Devon............7 G5
Broxa N York...............134 E2
Broxbourne Herts..........60 B6
Broxburn E Loth..........178 E3
Broxburn W Loth.........176 E4
Broxted Essex...............60 F3
Bruan Highld................231 K7
Bruar P & K.................194 C3
Brucefield Highld.........223 K4
Bruchag Ag & B..........173 J6
Bruichladdich Ag & B ..170 E6
Bruisyard Suffk.............79 G2
Bruisyard Street
  Suffk...........................79 G2
Brumby N Linc............125 K8
Brund Staffs................100 C1
Brundall Norfk..............93 G2
Brundish Suffk..............78 F1
Brundish Street Suffk....78 F1
Brunery Highld............190 E3
Brunswick Village
  N u Ty.......................159 G7
Brunthwaite C Brad....122 F2
Bruntingthorpe Leics....87 H5
Brunton Fife................186 E3
Brunton Wilts...............28 E1
Brushford Devon...........11 G4
Brushford Somset.........24 E6
Bruton Somset..............27 G4
Bryan's Green Worcs....70 F2
Bryanston Dorset..........15 G2
Brydekirk D & G..........155 L7
Bryher IoS......................2 a1
Brympton Somset.........26 D7
Bryn Carmth.................51 G5
Bryn Neath....................36 C3
Brynamman Carmth......51 K3
Brynberian Pembks......64 F7
Bryncir Gwynd..............95 H4
Bryn-coch Neath..........51 L5
Bryncroes Gwynd.........94 D6
Bryncrug Gwynd...........80 E3
Bryneglwys Denbgs......97 H3
Brynford Flints............111 G6
Bryn Gates Wigan......112 E2
Bryngwran IoA............108 D6
Bryngwyn Mons............54 B6
Bryngwyn Powys...........68 D5
Bryn-Henllan Pembks....64 E6
Brynhoffnant Cerdgn....65 K4
Brynmawr Blae G..........53 J5
Bryn-mawr Gwynd.........94 D5
Brynmenyn Brdgnd........36 D4
Brynmill Swans.............51 J6
Brynna Rhondd.............36 F4
Brynrefail Gwynd.........109 H8
Brynsadler Rhondd........37 G4
Bryn Saith Marchog
  Denbgs.......................97 G3
Brynsiencyn IoA..........108 F7
Brynteg IoA.................109 G5
Bryn-y-Maen Conwy.....110 B6
Bualintur Highld..........198 F2
Bubbenhall Warwks......86 D8
Bubwith E R Yk...........125 H4
Buccleuch Border........166 E6

Buchanan Smithy
  Stirlg.........................174 E1
Buchanhaven Abers....217 L5
Buchanty P & K..........185 J2
Buchany Stirlg............184 F6
Buchlyvie Stirlg...........184 C8
Buckabank Cumb.........148 C5
Buckden Cambs............75 H2
Buckden N York..........131 H4
Buckenham Norfk..........93 H3
Buckerell Devon............12 E3
Buckfast Devon...............7 H3
Buckfastleigh Devon.......7 H3
Buckhaven Fife............186 F7
Buckholt Mons.............54 D5
Buckhorn Weston
  Dorset.........................27 H6
Buckhurst Hill Essex....45 H2
Buckie Moray..............215 J2
Buckingham Bucks.......73 K7
Buckland Bucks............58 E5
Buckland Devon.............7 G6
Buckland Gloucs...........71 J7
Buckland Herts.............75 L7
Buckland Kent..............35 J6
Buckland Oxon.............41 G2
Buckland Surrey...........31 K2
Buckland Brewer
  Devon........................22 F7
Buckland Common
  Bucks.........................58 F6
Buckland Dinham
  Somset.......................27 H2
Buckland Filleigh
  Devon........................10 C3
Buckland in the
  Moor Devon................7 G2
Buckland
  Monachorum
  Devon..........................6 D3
Buckland Newton
  Dorset.........................14 D2
Buckland Ripers
  Dorset.........................14 C6
Buckland St Mary
  Somset.......................25 L8
Buckland-Tout-
  Saints Devon...............7 H6
Bucklebury W Berk 41 K6
Bucklers Hard Hants.....16 E3
Bucklesham Suffk.........78 F6
Buckley Flints.............111 J8
Bucklow Hill Ches E....113 G5
Buckminster Leics.......102 E7
Bucknall C Stke.............99 K3
Bucknall Lincs.............117 K7
Bucknell Oxon...............57 K3
Bucknell Shrops...........83 G8
Buckpool Moray..........215 J2
Bucksburn C Aber.......207 G4
Buck's Cross Devon......22 E6
Bucks Green W Susx 31 H5
Buckshaw Village
  Lancs........................121 H6
Bucks Horn Oak
  Hants..........................30 D3
Buck's Mills Devon......22 E6
Buckton E R Yk...........135 J3
Buckton Nthumb.........169 G2
Buckworth Cambs.........89 G7
Budby Notts................115 L7
Bude Cnwll.....................9 G4
Budge's Shop Cnwll.......5 M4
Budleigh Salterton
  Devon........................12 D3
Budock Water Cnwll.......3 K5
Buerton Ches E.............99 G4
Bugbrooke Nhants.......73 J3
Bugle Cnwll....................4 F4
Bugley Dorset...............27 H6
Bugthorpe E R Yk.......134 B7
Buildwas Shrops...........84 B3
Builth Wells Powys.......68 B4
Bulbridge Wilts.............28 C5
Bulford Wilts................28 D3
Bulkeley Ches E............98 D2

Bulkington Warwks.........86 E6
Bulkington Wilts...........39 L8
Bulkworthy Devon 9 K3
Bullbrook Br For...........42 E6
Bullington Hants 29 J3
Bullington Lincs..........117 H6
Bulmer Essex 77 J6
Bulmer N York.............133 L6
Bulmer Tye Essex 77 J6
Bulphan Thurr 45 M3
Bulwark Abers.............217 H5
Bulwell C Nott............101 K4
Bulwick Nhants 88 D5
Bumble's Green Essex 60 C6
Bunacaimb Highld 199 K7
Bunarkaig Highld 201 J7
Bunbury Ches E............98 E2
Bunchrew Highld 212 F5
Bundalloch Highld 210 D8
Bunessan Ag & B.........180 E3
Bungay Suffk 93 G5
Bunnahabhain
   Ag & B...................171 H4
Bunny Notts...............101 L6
Buntait Highld 212 C7
Buntingford Herts 60 B3
Bunwell Norfk 92 D5
Burbage Leics 86 F5
Burbage Wilts 40 E7
Burchett's Green
   W & M....................42 D4
Burcombe Wilts 28 B5
Burcott Bucks 58 E4
Bures Essex 77 K7
Burford Oxon..............56 E5
Burford Shrops 69 L2
Burg Ag & B...............188 J7
Burgates Hants 30 C5
Burgess Hill W Susx 19 J2
Burgh Suffk 78 F4
Burgh by Sands
   Cumb....................148 D3
Burgh Castle Norfk 93 K5
Burghclere Hants 41 J7
Burghead Moray 214 D1
Burghfield W Berk........42 A6
Burghfield Common
   W Berk...................42 A6
Burgh Heath Surrey.......44 E7
Burgh Island Devon 6 F6
Burgh le Marsh Lincs....119 G7
Burgh next Aylsham
   Norfk....................106 F7
Burgh on Bain Lincs....117 L4
Burgh St Margaret
   Norfk.....................93 J2
Burgh St Peter Norfk 93 K5
Burghwallis Donc.........124 E7
Burham Kent 46 B7
Buriton Hants 30 C7
Burland Ches E 98 E2
Burlawn Cnwll 4 F2
Burleigh Gloucs 55 K7
Burlescombe Devon 25 G7
Burleston Dorset..........14 E4
Burley Hants 16 B2
Burley Rutlnd.............88 C2
Burleydam Ches E.........98 E4
Burley Gate Herefs.......69 L5
Burley in Wharfedale
   C Brad..................123 H2
Burley Street Hants 16 B2
Burley Wood Head
   C Brad..................123 H2
Burlton Shrops 98 C7
Burmarsh Kent 34 E7
Burmington Warwks 72 C6
Burn N York 124 F5
Burnage Manch...........113 K3
Burnaston Derbys 100 F6
Burnbrae N Lans.........176 B6
Burnby E R Yk............125 K2
Burneside Cumb 138 D7
Burneston N York 132 D3
Burnett BaNES.............38 F7

Burnfoot Border 166 F6
Burnfoot Border 167 H6
Burnfoot D & G...........155 G4
Burnfoot D & G...........156 C3
Burnfoot D & G...........156 C4
Burnfoot P & K...........185 K6
Burnham Bucks 42 F4
Burnham Deepdale
   Norfk....................105 J4
Burnham Market
   Norfk....................105 K4
Burnham Norton
   Norfk....................105 K4
Burnham-on-Crouch
   Essex.....................46 F2
Burnham-on-Sea
   Somset....................25 L2
Burnham Overy
   Norfk....................105 K4
Burnham Overy
   Staithe Norfk 105 K4
Burnham Thorpe
   Norfk....................105 K4
Burnhaven Abers.........217 L5
Burnhead D & G...........154 E3
Burnhervie Abers.........206 D2
Burnhill Green Staffs.....84 E4
Burnhope Dur.............150 F5
Burnhouse N Ayrs........174 D7
Burniston N York.........134 F2
Burnley Lancs 122 C4
Burnley
   Crematorium
   Lancs...................122 B4
Burnmouth Border 179 K6
Burn of Cambus Stirlg..184 F6
Burnopfield Dur.........150 F4
Burnsall N York 131 J7
Burnside Angus 196 C4
Burnside Angus 196 E6
Burnside Fife 186 B5
Burnside Moray 214 E1
Burnside W Loth.........176 E3
Burnside of
   Duntrune Angus 187 G1
Burntisland Fife 177 H2
Burntwood Staffs 85 J2
Burntwood Green
   Staffs.....................85 J2
Burnt Yates N York 132 C7
Burnworthy Somset.......25 J7
Burpham Surrey...........31 G2
Burpham W Susx 18 E4
Burradon Nthumb 168 E7
Burrafirth Shet...........235 e1
Burravoe Shet 235 d3
Burrells Cumb............138 F4
Burrelton P & K..........195 K8
Burridge Devon 13 H2
Burridge Hants 17 G1
Burrill N York 132 C3
Burringham N Linc.......125 K8
Burrington Devon.........10 F2
Burrington Herefs........69 J1
Burrington N Som........38 C8
Burrough Green
   Cambs.....................76 F4
Burrough on the Hill
   Leics......................87 L2
Burrow Lancs 130 C4
Burrow Somset...........24 E3
Burrow Bridge
   Somset....................26 A5
Burrowhill Surrey.........42 F7
Burry Green Swans 50 F7
Burry Port Carmth.......50 F5
Burscough Lancs.........120 F7
Burscough Bridge
   Lancs...................120 F7
Bursea E R Yk...........125 J4
Bursledon Hants..........16 F1
Burslem C Stke 99 K3
Burstall Suffk 78 D5
Burstock Dorset..........13 K2
Burston Norfk.............92 D6
Burstow Surrey...........32 B5

Burstwick E R Yk.........126 F5
Burtersett N York........131 G2
Burtholme Cumb..........148 F3
Burthorpe Green
   Suffk.....................77 H2
Burtoft Lincs............103 L5
Burton Ches W...........111 K6
Burton Ches W...........112 D8
Burton Dorset 15 M4
Burton Lincs.............116 F6
Burton Pembks............49 G6
Burton Somset 25 J3
Burton Wilts 39 J4
Burton Agnes E R Yk....135 H6
Burton Bradstock
   Dorset....................13 L4
Burton Coggles Lincs ...103 G7
Burton End Essex.........60 E4
Burton Fleming
   E R Yk...................135 G5
Burton Hastings
   Warwks....................86 E5
Burton-in-Kendal
   Cumb....................129 L4
Burton-in-Kendal
   Services Cumb 129 L4
Burton in Lonsdale
   N York...................130 C5
Burton Joyce Notts.....101 M4
Burton Latimer
   Nhants....................88 C8
Burton Lazars Leics 87 L1
Burton Leonard
   N York...................132 E6
Burton on the Wolds
   Leics.....................101 L7
Burton Overy Leics 87 J4
Burton Pedwardine
   Lincs.....................103 J4
Burton Pidsea E R Yk...127 G4
Burton Salmon
   N York...................124 D5
Burton's Green Essex 61 K3
Burton upon Stather
   N Linc...................125 K6
Burton upon Trent
   Staffs...................100 E7
Burton Waters Lincs....116 F6
Burtonwood Warrtn.....112 E3
Burtonwood
   Services Warrtn......112 E4
Burwardsley Ches W 98 D2
Burwarton Shrops........84 B6
Burwash E Susx...........33 H7
Burwash Common
   E Susx....................20 D2
Burwash Weald
   E Susx....................20 D2
Burwell Cambs 76 E2
Burwell Lincs............118 E5
Burwen IoA 108 E3
Burwick Ork 234 c8
Bury Bury 122 B7
Bury Cambs 89 K6
Bury Somset 24 E6
Bury W Susx 18 D3
Bury Green Herts 60 D4
Bury St Edmunds
   Suffk.....................77 J2
Burythorpe N York......134 C6
Busby E Rens 175 G6
Buscot Oxon..............40 E2
Bush Abers...............197 J4
Bush Bank Herefs.........69 J4
Bushbury Wolves..........85 G3
Bushbury
   Crematorium
   Wolves....................85 G3
Bushey Herts 43 J2
Bushey Heath Herts 43 J2
Bush Hill Park Gt Lon...45 G2
Bushley Worcs............70 F7
Bushmoor Shrops 83 J6
Bushton Wilts 40 B5
Bussage Gloucs...........55 K7
Bussex Somset 26 A4

Butcombe N Som..........38 D7
Bute Ag & B 173 H4
Butleigh Somset..........26 D5
Butleigh Wootton
   Somset....................26 D4
Butlers Marston
   Warwks....................72 D4
Butley Suffk 79 H4
Buttercrambe N York....133 L7
Butterdean Border 179 G5
Butterknowle Dur 140 E3
Butterleigh Devon 12 C2
Buttermere Cumb 137 G4
Buttershaw C Brad......123 H5
Butterstone P & K.......195 G7
Butterton Staffs 99 J4
Butterton Staffs 100 B2
Butterwick Lincs 104 C4
Butterwick N York 133 L4
Butterwick N York 134 F5
Buttington Powys.........82 E2
Buttonoak Shrops........84 D7
Buxhall Suffk.............78 B3
Buxted E Susx 20 A2
Buxton Derbys...........114 B6
Buxton Norfk............106 F7
Buxton Heath Norfk....106 E7
Bwlch Powys 53 J4
Bwlchgwyn Wrexhm......97 K2
Bwlchllan Cerdgn........66 D3
Bwlchtocyn Gwynd........94 E7
Bwlch-y-cibau Powys....97 J8
Bwlch-y-ffridd Powys....82 B4
Bwlch-y-groes
   Pembks...................65 H7
Bwlch-y-sarnau
   Powys.....................82 B8
Byers Green Dur.........150 F7
Byfield Nhants 73 G4
Byfleet Surrey............43 H7
Byford Herefs.............69 H6
Byker N u Ty.............151 G3
Bylchau Conwy...........110 D0
Byley Ches W............113 G7
Byrness Nthumb 157 K2
Bystock Devon 12 D5
Bythorn Cambs 88 F7
Byton Herefs..............69 G2
Bywell Nthumb 150 D3
Byworth W Susx 31 G7

C

Cabourne Lincs..........117 J2
Cabrach Ag & B..........171 J5
Cabrach Moray 215 J8
Cabus Lancs.............121 G2
Cadbury Devon...........11 L4
Cadbury World Birm......85 J7
Cadder E Duns 175 G4
Caddington C Beds.......59 H4
Caddonfoot Border 167 G3
Cadeby Donc 115 K2
Cadeby Leics 86 E3
Cadeleigh Devon 11 L4
Cade Street E Susx 20 C2
Cadgwith Cnwll 3 J7
Cadham Fife 186 D6
Cadishead Salfd.........113 G3
Cadle Swans 51 J6
Cadley Lancs 121 G4
Cadley Wilts 28 E2
Cadley Wilts 40 E6
Cadmore End Bucks......42 C3
Cadnam Hants 28 F8
Cadney N Linc...........117 G2
Cadoxton V Glam.........37 H6
Cadoxton Juxta-
   Neath Neath 51 L5
Caeathro Gwynd..........95 J1
Caenby Lincs............117 G4
Caeo Carmth..............66 F6
Caerau Brdgnd 36 D2
Caerau Cardif 37 H5

Caer Farchell Pembks..... 48 D3
Caergeiliog IoA.............. 108 D5
Caergwrle Flints............... 97 L2
Caerlanrig Border 156 D2
Caerleon Newpt 37 M3
Caernarfon Gwynd....... 108 F8
Caernarfon Castle
  Gwynd....................... 108 F8
Caerphilly Caerph........... 37 J3
Caersws Powys................ 82 B5
Caerwedros Cerdgn 65 L4
Caerwent Mons.............. 38 C3
Caerwys Flints 110 F6
Cairinis W Isls 233 c6
Cairnbaan Ag & B......... 172 E1
Cairnbulg Abers............ 217 J2
Cairncross Border 179 J5
Cairncurran Inver........ 174 C4
Cairndow Ag & B.......... 183 H5
Cairneyhill Fife 176 E2
Cairngarroch D & G..... 144 C5
Cairngorms National
  Park 204 C5
Cairnie Abers................ 215 K5
Cairnorrie Abers............ 217 G6
Cairnryan D & G............ 144 C2
Cairnty Moray............... 215 H4
Caister-on-Sea Norfk...... 93 L2
Caistor Lincs................ 117 J2
Caistor St Edmund
  Norfk 92 F3
Calanais W Isls 232 e2
Calbourne IoW................ 16 E5
Calcot Flints 111 G6
Calcot Gloucs 56 C6
Calcot Row W Berk 42 A6
Calcots Moray............... 215 G2
Caldbeck Cumb............. 148 B6
Caldecote Cambs 75 L3
Caldecote Cambs 89 G5
Caldecote Highfields
  Cambs 75 L3
Caldecott Nhants 74 E2
Caldecott Oxon 41 J2
Caldecott Rutlnd............ 88 C5
Calderbank N Lans 175 K5
Calder Bridge Cumb... 136 E6
Caldercruix N Lans 175 L5
Calder Grove Wakefd... 123 L6
Caldermill S Lans 164 D2
Calder Vale Lancs 121 G2
Calderwood S Lans 175 H7
Caldey Island Pembks... 49 K7
Caldicot Mons................ 38 C3
Caldmore Wsall............. 85 H4
Caldwell N York 140 E5
Calf of Man IoM.............. 237 a7
Calfsound Ork............... 234 d4
Calgary Ag & B.............. 189 J6
Califer Moray................ 214 D3
California Falk................ 176 B3
California Norfk............. 93 K1
Calke Derbys 101 G7
Calke Abbey Derbys.... 101 G7
Callakille Highld............ 209 L4
Callander Stirlg............ 184 D5
Callanish W Isls 232 e2
Callestick Cnwll............... 3 K2
Calligarry Highld........... 199 K5
Callington Cnwll.............. 6 A3
Callow Herefs................. 69 J7
Callow End Worcs.......... 70 E4
Callow Hill Wilts 40 B4
Calmore Hants 29 G7
Calmsden Gloucs 56 B6
Calne Wilts 39 M6
Calshot Hants................ 16 F3
Calstock Cnwll 6 C3
Calstone Wellington
  Wilts 40 B6
Calthorpe Norfk 106 E6
Calthorpe Street
  Norfk 107 J7
Calthwaite Cumb........ 148 E6
Calton Staffs................ 100 C3
Calveley Ches E 98 E2

Calver Derbys................ 114 E6
Calverhall Shrops 98 E5
Calverleigh Devon.......... 11 L3
Calverton M Keyn............ 73 L6
Calverton Notts............ 101 L3
Calvine P & K................ 194 C3
Calzeat Border.............. 165 L3
Cam Gloucs 55 H7
Camasachoirce
  Highld 190 F4
Camasine Highld 190 F4
Camas Luinie Highld ... 210 E8
Camastianavaig
  Highld 209 H6
Camault Muir Highld... 212 D6
Camber E Susx 21 J2
Camberley Surrey 42 E7
Camberwell Gt Lon 44 F5
Camblesforth N York ... 124 F5
Cambo Nthumb............. 158 C5
Camborne Cnwll.............. 3 H4
Camborne and
  Redruth Mining
  District Cnwll 3 H4
Cambourne Cambs....... 75 K3
Cambridge Cambs 76 C3
Cambridge Gloucs........ 55 H7
Cambridge Airport
  Cambs 76 C3
Cambridge City
  Crematorium
  Cambs 76 B3
Cambrose Cnwll 3 H3
Cambus Clacks 185 H8
Cambusavie
  Platform Highld 223 G3
Cambusbarron Stirlg... 185 G8
Cambuskenneth
  Stirlg 185 G8
Cambuslang S Lans 175 H6
Cambus o' May Abers... 205 J5
Cambuswallace
  S Lans 165 K2
Camden Town Gt Lon... 44 F4
Cameley BaNES............. 38 E8
Camelford Cnwll............. 8 E7
Camelon Falk................ 176 B3
Camerory Highld.......... 214 C7
Camerton BaNES........... 39 G8
Camerton Cumb 136 E2
Camghouran P & K 193 J5
Camieston Border........ 167 J4
Cammachmore Abers... 207 G6
Cammeringham Lincs... 116 F5
Camore Highld.............. 223 G4
Campbeltown Ag & B... 161 J5
Campbeltown Airport
  Ag & B 161 H5
Cample D & G................ 154 F4
Campmuir P & K 195 K8
Camps W Loth............... 176 F5
Campsall Donc.............. 124 E7
Campsea Ash Suffk........ 79 G4
Campton C Beds............ 75 G6
Camptown Border........ 167 K6
Camrose Pembks............ 48 F4
Camserney P & K.......... 194 C6
Camusnagaul Highld ... 191 L2
Camusnagaul Highld ... 220 D4
Camusteel Highld......... 209 L6
Camusterrach Highld... 209 L6
Canada Hants................ 28 F7
Candacraig Abers......... 205 H5
Candlesby Lincs............ 118 F7
Candy Mill Border......... 165 L2
Cane End Oxon 42 B4
Canewdon Essex 46 E2
Canford Cliffs Poole 15 K5
Canford
  Crematorium
  Bristl 38 E5
Canford Heath Poole ... 15 J4
Canisbay Highld........... 231 L2
Canley Covtry................ 86 C7
Canley Crematorium
  Covtry 86 C7

Cann Dorset 27 K7
Canna Highld................ 198 C4
Cannich Highld............. 211 L7
Cannington Somset...... 25 K4
Canning Town Gt Lon... 45 H4
Cannock Staffs............... 85 H2
Cannock Chase Staffs... 99 M8
Cannon Bridge Herefs... 69 H6
Canonbie D & G 156 C6
Canon Frome Herefs 70 B5
Canon Pyon Herefs....... 69 J5
Canons Ashby Nhants... 73 H4
Canonstown Cnwll.......... 2 F4
Canterbury Kent............ 34 F3
Canterbury
  Cathedral Kent......... 34 F3
Cantley Norfk................ 93 H3
Canton Cardif................ 37 J5
Cantraywood Highld... 213 J5
Cantsfield Lancs.......... 130 C5
Canvey Island Essex 46 D4
Canwick Lincs............... 117 G7
Canworthy Water
  Cnwll 9 G6
Caol Highld 191 L2
Caolas Scalpaigh
  W Isls 232 e4
Caoles Ag & B 188 D6
Caonich Highld............ 201 G6
Capel Kent..................... 33 H4
Capel Surrey.................. 31 K4
Capel Bangor Cerdgn... 80 E7
Capel Coch IoA............. 108 F5
Capel Curig Conwy....... 96 A2
Capel Dewi Carmth....... 50 F2
Capel Dewi Cerdgn....... 66 B6
Capel-Dewi Cerdgn...... 80 E6
Capel Garmon Conwy... 96 C2
Capel Hendre Carmth... 51 H4
Capel Iwan Carmth....... 65 J7
Capel le Ferne Kent 35 H6
Capelles Guern............. 236 d2
Capel Parc IoA.............. 108 F4
Capel St Andrew
  Suffk 79 H5
Capel St Mary Suffk...... 78 C6
Capel Seion Cerdgn...... 80 E7
Capelulo Conwy........... 109 L6
Capenhurst Ches W..... 111 K6
Capheaton Nthumb...... 158 C6
Caplaw E Rens.............. 174 E6
Cappercleuch Border... 166 C5
Capton Devon.................. 7 J5
Caputh P & K................ 195 H2
Caradon Mining
  District Cnwll 5 K2
Carbeth Inn Stirlg....... 174 F3
Carbis Bay Cnwll............ 2 F4
Carbost Highld............. 208 F5
Carbost Highld............. 208 F7
Carbrook Sheff............. 115 G4
Carbrooke Norfk............ 91 L3
Car Colston Notts......... 102 B4
Carcroft Donc............... 124 E8
Cardenden Fife............. 186 C7
Cardhu Moray............... 214 F5
Cardiff Cardif................. 37 J5
Cardiff Airport V Glam... 37 G6
Cardiff Gate Services
  Cardif 37 K4
Cardiff West Services
  Cardif 37 H4
Cardigan Cerdgn........... 65 G5
Cardington Bed............. 74 F5
Cardington Shrops........ 83 K4
Cardinham Cnwll............ 5 H3
Cardrain D & G............. 144 D8
Cardrona Border.......... 166 D2
Cardross Ag & B.......... 174 C3
Cardross
  Crematorium
  Ag & B 174 C3
Cardryne D & G............ 144 D7
Cardurnock Cumb........ 147 L3
Careby Lincs.................. 88 E1
Careston Angus........... 196 E4

Carew Pembks................ 49 H6
Carew Cheriton
  Pembks...................... 49 H6
Carew Newton
  Pembks...................... 49 H6
Carey Herefs................. 54 E2
Carfin N Lans............... 175 K6
Carfraemill Border...... 178 B7
Cargate Green Norfk..... 93 H2
Cargenbridge D & G..... 155 G6
Cargill P & K................. 195 J8
Cargo Cumb.................. 148 C3
Cargreen Cnwll............... 6 C4
Carham Nthumb.......... 168 B2
Carhampton Somset..... 24 F3
Carharrack Cnwll............ 3 J3
Carie P & K.................. 193 K5
Carinish W Isls 233 c6
Carisbrooke IoW............ 16 F5
Cark Cumb.................... 129 H4
Carkeel Cnwll.................. 6 B4
Carlabhagh W Isls....... 232 e2
Carlbury Darltn........... 140 F4
Carlby Lincs.................. 88 F2
Carleen Cnwll.................. 3 G5
Carleton N York 122 E1
Carleton
  Crematorium
  Bpool 120 D3
Carleton Forehoe
  Norfk 92 C3
Carleton Rode Norfk..... 92 D5
Carleton St Peter
  Norfk 93 H3
Carlincraig Abers......... 216 D5
Carlingcott BaNES......... 39 G8
Carlisle Cumb............... 148 D4
Carlisle Airport Cumb... 148 E3
Carlisle Crematorium
  Cumb 148 C4
Carlops Border............. 177 G6
Carloway W Isls 232 e2
Carlton Barns.............. 124 B7
Carlton Bed................... 74 D4
Carlton Cambs.............. 76 F4
Carlton Leeds............... 123 L5
Carlton Leics................. 86 E3
Carlton N York 124 F5
Carlton N York 131 K3
Carlton N York 133 J3
Carlton Notts............... 101 L4
Carlton S on T 141 J3
Carlton Suffk................. 79 H2
Carlton Colville Suffk.... 93 K5
Carlton Curlieu Leics.... 87 K4
Carlton Green Cambs... 76 F4
Carlton Husthwaite
  N York 133 G4
Carlton-in-Cleveland
  N York 142 B6
Carlton in Lindrick
  Notts 115 L5
Carlton-le-Moorland
  Lincs 102 E2
Carlton Miniott
  N York 132 F4
Carlton-on-Trent
  Notts 116 D8
Carlton Scroop Lincs ... 102 F4
Carluke S Lans............. 175 L7
Carmacoup S Lans...... 164 E4
Carmarthen Carmth..... 50 E2
Carmel Carmth............. 51 H3
Carmel Flints 111 G6
Carmel Gwynd.............. 95 H2
Carmichael S Lans 165 H2
Carmountside
  Crematorium
  C Stke 99 K3
Carmunnock C Glas.... 175 G6
Carmyle C Glas............ 175 H6
Carmyllie Angus.......... 196 E7
Carnaby E R Yk............ 135 H6
Carnbee Fife................ 187 J6
Carnbo P & K............... 185 L6
Carn Brea Cnwll............. 3 H3

Carnbrogie Abers...........216 F8
Carndu Highld..............210 D8
Carnduff S Lans 164 D1
Carnell E Ayrs...............163 L3
Carnforth Lancs.............129 K5
Carn-gorm Highld..........200 E2
Carnhell Green Cnwll.......3 G4
Carnie Abers..................206 F4
Carnkie Cnwll....................3 H4
Carnkie Cnwll.....................3 J4
Carno Powys....................81 K4
Carnock Fife..................176 E1
Carnon Downs Cnwll........4 C7
Carnousie Abers.............216 C4
Carnoustie Angus..........187 J1
Carnwath S Lans............165 J1
Carol Green Solhll...........86 C7
Carperby N York.............131 J2
Carradale Ag & B...........161 K2
Carrbridge Highld..........203 L2
Carrefour Jersey.............236 c6
Carreglefn IoA...............108 E4
Carr Gate Wakefd...........123 L5
Carrhouse N Linc...........116 C1
Carrick Ag & B................172 F2
Carrick Castle Ag & B....183 H8
Carriden Falk.................176 D3
Carrington Mdloth..........177 J6
Carrington Traffd...........113 H3
Carrog Denbgs.................97 H4
Carron Falk....................176 B2
Carron Moray................214 F6
Carronbridge D & G.......154 F3
Carron Bridge Stirlg......175 K2
Carronshore Falk...........176 B2
Carr Shield Nthumb.......149 K5
Carrutherstown
    D & G.......................155 J7
Carruth House Inver......174 C5
Carrville Dur..................151 H6
Carsaig Ag & B..............181 H3
Carseriggan D & G.........145 G2
Carsethorn D & G..........147 H3
Carshalton Gt Lon...........44 F6
Carsington Derbys.........100 E2
Carskey Ag & B..............161 H7
Carsluith D & G.............145 K4
Carsphairn D & G..........153 L4
Carstairs S Lans.............165 H1
Carstairs Junction
    S Lans.......................165 J1
Carterton Oxon................56 F6
Carthew Cnwll....................4 F5
Carthorpe N York...........132 D3
Cartland S Lans..............165 G1
Cartmel Cumb................129 H4
Carway Carmth................50 F4
Cashe's Green Gloucs.....55 J6
Cassington Oxon..............57 J5
Cassop Colliery Dur.......151 J7
Castel Guern..................236 C3
Casterton Cumb.............130 C4
Castle Acre Norfk.............91 J1
Castle Ashby Nhants........74 C3
Castlebay W Isls.............233 b9
Castle Bolton N York......131 J2
Castle Bromwich
    Solhll........................85 K5
Castle Bytham Lincs.......103 G8
Castlebythe Pembks.......49 H2
Castle Caereinion
    Powys........................82 D3
Castle Camps Cambs......76 F6
Castle Carrock
    Cumb.......................148 F4
Castlecary Falk..............175 K3
Castle Cary Somset.........26 F5
Castle Combe Wilts.........39 J5
Castle Donington
    Leics.........................101 H6
Castle Douglas D & G....146 D3
Castle Eaton Swindn.......40 C2
Castle Eden Dur.............151 K7
Castleford Wakefd.........124 C5
Castle Frome Herefs.......70 C5
Castle Gresley Derbys....100 F8

Castle Hedingham
    Essex.........................77 H7
Castlehill Border.............166 C3
Castlehill Highld.............231 H2
Castle Hill Suffk...............78 D5
Castle Howard N York...133 L5
Castle Kennedy D & G...144 D3
Castle Lachlan Ag & B....182 E7
Castlemartin Pembks......48 F7
Castlemilk C Glas...........175 G6
Castlemorton Worcs........70 E6
Castlemorton
    Common Worcs..........70 E6
Castle O'er D & G...........156 A4
Castle Pulverbatch
    Shrops.......................83 H3
Castle Rising Norfk........105 G7
Castleside Dur...............150 D5
Castle Stuart Highld......213 H4
Castlethorpe M Keyn......74 B5
Castleton Border............156 E4
Castleton Derbys............114 D5
Castleton N York............142 E5
Castleton Newpt.............37 K4
Castleton Rochdl...........122 D7
Castletown Highld.........231 H3
Castletown IoM.............237 b7
Castletown Sundld........151 J4
Castley N York...............123 K2
Caston Norfk....................91 L4
Castor C Pete...................89 G4
Catacol N Ayrs................172 F7
Catcliffe Rothm..............115 H4
Catcomb Wilts..................40 A5
Catcott Somset.................26 B4
Catcott Burtle
    Somset.......................26 B3
Caterham Surrey.............32 C3
Catfield Norfk................107 H7
Catford Gt Lon.................45 G5
Catforth Lancs...............121 G4
Cathcart C Glas.............175 G6
Cathedine Powys.............53 H3
Catherington Hants.........30 B8
Catherston
    Leweston Dorset.........13 J4
Catisfield Hants...............17 G2
Catlodge Highld.............202 F6
Catmere End Essex.........76 C6
Catmore W Berk..............41 J4
Caton Lancs...................129 L6
Caton Green Lancs........129 L6
Catrine E Ayrs................164 B4
Catsfield E Susx..............20 E3
Catsgore Somset.............26 D6
Catshill Worcs..................85 G8
Cattadale Ag & B...........161 H7
Cattal N York.................133 G8
Cattawade Suffk..............62 D2
Catterall Lancs...............121 G3
Catterick N York.............141 G7
Catterick Bridge
    N York........................141 G7
Catterlen Cumb..............148 E7
Catterline Abers.............197 L2
Catterton N York............124 D2
Catteshall Surrey.............31 G3
Catthorpe Leics................87 G7
Cattistock Dorset.............14 B3
Catton N York................132 E4
Catton Nthumb..............149 L4
Catwick E R Yk...............126 E2
Catworth Cambs..............88 F8
Caudle Green Gloucs......55 L6
Caulcott Oxon..................57 K3
Cauldcots Angus............197 G6
Cauldhame Stirlg...........184 E8
Cauldmill Border............167 H6
Cauldon Staffs...............100 B3
Cauldwell Derbys.............86 B1
Caulkerbush D & G........147 G4
Caulside D & G...............156 D6
Caundle Marsh
    Dorset........................27 G8
Caunton Notts...............102 C1

Causeway End D & G....145 J3
Causeway End Essex......61 G4
Causewayend S Lans.....165 K3
Causewayhead Stirlg....185 G7
Causeyend Abers...........207 H2
Causey Park Bridge
    Nthumb......................158 F3
Cavendish Suffk..............77 J5
Cavenham Suffk..............77 H1
Caversfield Oxon..............57 L3
Caversham Readg...........42 B5
Caverswall Staffs............99 L4
Caverton Mill Border....167 M4
Cawdor Highld...............213 K4
Cawood N York..............124 E3
Cawsand Cnwll..................6 C5
Cawston Norfk...............106 D7
Cawthorne Barns..........123 K8
Caxton Cambs.................75 K3
Caynham Shrops.............83 K8
Caythorpe Lincs............102 F3
Caythorpe Notts............102 B4
Cayton N York................135 G3
Ceann a Bhaigh W Isls..233 b6
Ceannacroc Lodge
    Highld.......................201 K3
Cearsiadar W Isls..........232 f3
Cefn Newpt......................37 L3
Cefn-brith Conwy............96 E3
Cefn-bryn-brain
    Carmth.......................51 L3
Cefn Cribwr Brdgnd........36 D4
Cefneithin Carmth...........51 G3
Cefngorwydd Powys........67 J5
Cefn-mawr Wrexhm........97 L4
Cefn-y-pant Carmth.........49 K3
Cellardyke Fife..............187 J6
Cellarhead Staffs............99 L3
Cemaes IoA...................108 E3
Cemmaes Powys..............81 H3
Cemmaes Road
    Powys........................81 H3
Cenarth Cerdgn...............65 J6
Ceres Fife.......................186 F5
Cerne Abbas Dorset........14 C3
Cerney Wick Gloucs........40 B2
Cerrigydrudion
    Conwy........................96 E3
Ceunant Gwynd..............95 J1
Chaceley Gloucs..............55 J2
Chacewater Cnwll.............3 K3
Chackmore Bucks...........73 K7
Chacombe Nhants...........72 F5
Chadbury Worcs...............71 H5
Chadderton Oldham.......113 K1
Chaddesden Derbys......101 G5
Chaddesley Corbett
    Worcs.........................84 F8
Chaddlehanger
    Devon..........................6 C1
Chaddleworth W Berk.....41 H5
Chadlington Oxon............57 G4
Chadshunt Warwks.........72 D4
Chadwell Leics..............102 C7
Chadwell Heath
    Gt Lon.........................45 J3
Chadwell St Mary
    Thurr.........................45 M4
Chadwick Worcs..............70 E2
Chadwick End Solhll......86 B8
Chaffcombe Somset.........13 J1
Chagford Devon..............11 G7
Chailey E Susx................19 K2
Chainhurst Kent..............33 J4
Chaldon Surrey...............32 B3
Chaldon Herring
    Dorset........................14 E5
Chale IoW........................16 F6
Chale Green IoW..............16 F6
Chalfont Common
    Bucks.........................43 G3
Chalfont St Giles
    Bucks.........................43 G2
Chalfont St Peter
    Bucks.........................43 G3
Chalford Gloucs..............55 K7
Chalford Wilts.................27 K2
Chalgrove Oxon..............41 M2

Chalk Kent.......................46 A5
Chalkwell Kent................34 B2
Challacombe Devon.........23 L3
Challoch D & G..............145 H2
Challock Kent..................34 D5
Chalton C Beds................59 G3
Chalton Hants.................30 B7
Chalvey Slough................42 F4
Chalvington E Susx.........20 B4
Chandler's Cross
    Herts..........................43 H2
Chandler's Ford
    Hants.........................29 H7
Chanterlands
    Crematorium
    C KuH........................126 D4
Chantry Somset...............27 G3
Chantry Suffk..................78 D5
Chapel Fife....................186 D8
Chapel Allerton Leeds...123 L3
Chapel Allerton
    Somset.......................26 B2
Chapel Amble Cnwll.........4 F2
Chapel Brampton
    Nhants........................73 K2
Chapel Chorlton
    Staffs.........................99 J5
Chapelend Way Essex.....77 G6
Chapel-en-le-Frith
    Derbys.......................114 B5
Chapel Green Warwks.....72 F3
Chapel Haddlesey
    N York........................124 E5
Chapelhall N Lans..........175 K5
Chapel Hill Abers...........217 K7
Chapel Hill Lincs............103 K2
Chapel Hill Mons.............54 D7
Chapel Hill N York.........123 L2
Chapelhope Border........166 C5
Chapelknowe D & G......156 B7
Chapel Lawn Shrops.......82 F7
Chapel-le-Dale N York...130 E4
Chapel Leigh Somset......25 H5
Chapel of Garioch
    Abers........................206 D1
Chapel Rossan D & G....144 D6
Chapel Row W Berk........41 L6
Chapel St Leonards
    Lincs.........................119 H6
Chapel Stile Cumb.........137 K6
Chapelton Angus...........197 G6
Chapelton Devon............23 J6
Chapelton S Lans...........175 J8
Chapeltown Bl w D........121 L7
Chapeltown Moray........204 F2
Chapeltown Sheff..........115 G3
Chapmanslade Wilts......27 J2
Chapmans Well
    Devon..........................9 J6
Chapmore End Herts......60 B5
Chappel Essex..................61 L3
Chard Somset..................13 H2
Chard Junction
    Somset.......................13 J2
Chardleigh Green
    Somset.......................13 H1
Chardstock Devon...........13 H2
Charfield S Glos...............39 G3
Charing Kent...................34 C5
Charing
    Crematorium
    Kent............................34 C5
Charingworth Gloucs......71 L6
Charlbury Oxon...............57 G4
Charlcombe BaNES.........39 M5
Charlcutt Wilts.................39 M5
Charlecote Warwks..........72 C3
Charlemont Sandw..........85 H5
Charles Devon..................23 L5
Charleston Angus...........196 C7
Charlestown C Aber.......207 H5
Charlestown C Brad.......123 H3
Charlestown Calder.......122 E5
Charlestown Cnwll............5 G5
Charlestown Cnwll............5 G5
Charlestown Fife............176 E2

Charlestown Highld.....213 G5
Charlestown Highld.....219 J6
Charlestown Salfd........113 J2
Charles Tye Suffk.........78 B4
Charlesworth Derbys...114 A3
Charlinch Somset.........25 K4
Charlottetown Fife......186 E5
Charlton Gt Lon............45 H4
Charlton Nhants...........73 G7
Charlton Nthumb........157 K5
Charlton Oxon..............41 H3
Charlton Somset..........25 L6
Charlton Somset..........27 G2
Charlton W Susx...........18 B3
Charlton Wilts..............27 K6
Charlton Wilts..............39 L3
Charlton Worcs............71 H5
Charlton Wrekin...........83 L2
Charlton Abbots
  Gloucs.......................56 B3
Charlton Adam
  Somset.....................26 D5
Charlton All Saints
  Wilts.........................28 D6
Charlton Down
  Dorset......................14 D4
Charlton Horethorne
  Somset.....................26 F6
Charlton Kings Gloucs...55 L4
Charlton Mackrell
  Somset.....................26 D5
Charlton Marshall
  Dorset......................15 G2
Charlton Musgrove
  Somset.....................27 G5
Charlton-on-Otmoor
  Oxon........................57 K5
Charlton on the Hill
  Dorset......................15 G2
Charlton St Peter
  Wilts.........................28 C1
Charlwood Hants..........30 A5
Charlwood Surrey.........31 L3
Charminster Dorset......14 D4
Charmouth Dorset........13 J4
Charndon Bucks...........58 A3
Charney Bassett
  Oxon........................41 G2
Charnock Richard
  Lancs......................121 H7
Charnock Richard
  Crematorium
  Lancs......................121 H6
Charnock Richard
  Services Lancs.......121 H7
Charsfield Suffk...........78 F3
Charter Alley Hants........41 L8
Charterhall Border......179 G8
Charterhouse Somset...26 D1
Chartershall Stirlg.......175 K1
Chartham Kent.............34 E4
Chartham Hatch Kent...34 E4
Chartridge Bucks.........58 F7
Chart Sutton Kent........33 K4
Charvil Wokham...........42 C5
Charwelton Nhants.......73 G4
Chase Terrace Staffs....85 J2
Chasetown Staffs.........85 J2
Chastleton Oxon..........56 E3
Chasty Devon.................9 J4
Chatburn Lancs..........121 L2
Chatcull Staffs.............99 H5
Chatham Medway........46 C6
Chatham Green Essex...61 H5
Chathill Nthumb.........169 J4
Chatsworth House
  Derbys....................114 E7
Chattenden Medway....46 C5
Chatteris Cambs..........90 B6
Chatterton Lancs........122 B6
Chattisham Suffk.........78 C6
Chatto Border.............168 B5
Chatton Nthumb.........168 F4
Chawleigh Devon.........11 G3
Chawton Hants.............30 B4
Cheadle Staffs............100 A4

Cheadle Stockp...........113 K4
Cheadle Hulme
  Stockp....................113 K4
Cheam Gt Lon..............44 E7
Chearsley Bucks...........58 B6
Chebsey Staffs..............99 J6
Checkendon Oxon.........42 A4
Checkley Ches E...........99 G4
Checkley Staffs............100 B5
Chedburgh Suffk...........77 H3
Cheddar Somset...........26 C2
Cheddington Bucks........58 F4
Cheddleton Staffs..........99 L3
Cheddon Fitzpaine
  Somset.....................25 K6
Chedgrave Norfk...........93 H4
Chedington Dorset........13 L2
Chediston Suffk............93 H7
Chedworth Gloucs.........56 B5
Chedzoy Somset...........25 M4
Cheetham Hill Manch...113 J2
Cheldon Devon.............11 H3
Chelford Ches E...........113 J6
Chellaston C Derb.......101 G6
Chellington Bed...........74 D4
Chelmarsh Shrops........84 C5
Chelmondiston Suffk....78 E6
Chelmorton Derbys.....114 C7
Chelmsford Essex.........61 H6
Chelmsford
  Crematorium
  Essex.......................61 H6
Chelmsley Wood
  Solhll........................85 L6
Chelsea Gt Lon............44 F4
Chelsfield Gt Lon..........45 J7
Chelsworth Suffk.........77 L5
Cheltenham Gloucs......55 L4
Cheltenham
  Crematorium
  Gloucs......................55 L4
Chelveston Nhants........74 E1
Chelvey N Som.............38 C6
Chelwood BaNES..........38 F7
Chelwood Gate
  E Susx......................32 D6
Cheney Longville
  Shrops.....................83 H6
Chenies Bucks.............43 G2
Chepstow Mons...........38 D2
Cherhill Wilts................40 B6
Cherington Gloucs........55 K7
Cherington Warwks......72 C6
Cheriton Hants.............29 L5
Cheriton Kent...............35 G7
Cheriton Swans............50 F6
Cheriton Bishop
  Devon.......................11 H6
Cheriton Fitzpaine
  Devon.......................11 K4
Cheriton or
  Stackpole Elidor
  Pembks.....................49 G7
Cherrington Wrekin......98 F8
Cherry Burton E R Yk...126 B3
Cherry Hinton
  Cambs......................76 C3
Cherry Orchard
  Worcs.......................70 F4
Cherry Willingham
  Lincs.......................117 G6
Chertsey Surrey............43 H6
Cherwell Valley
  Services Oxon............57 K3
Cheselbourne Dorset....14 E3
Chesham Bucks............58 F7
Chesham Bury.............122 B7
Chesham Bois Bucks....58 F7
Cheshire Farm Ice
  Cream Ches W...........98 D2
Cheshunt Herts............60 B7
Chesil Beach Dorset.....14 B6
Cheslyn Hay Staffs.......85 H3
Chessets Wood
  Warwks.....................85 L8
Chessington Gt Lon......44 D7

Chessington World
  of Adventures
  Gt Lon......................44 D7
Chester Ches W..........112 B7
Chesterblade Somset...26 F3
Chester
  Crematorium
  Ches W....................111 L7
Chesterfield Derbys....115 G7
Chesterfield
  Crematorium
  Derbys....................115 H6
Chesterhill Mdloth.....177 K5
Chester-le-Street Dur...151 G5
Chester Moor Dur.......151 G5
Chesters Border..........167 J5
Chesters Border..........167 K7
Chester Services
  Ches W....................112 C6
Chesterton Cambs........76 C3
Chesterton Cambs........89 G4
Chesterton Gloucs........56 A7
Chesterton Oxon..........57 K4
Chesterton Shrops........84 D4
Chesterton Green
  Warwks.....................72 D3
Chesterwood
  Nthumb...................149 L2
Chester Zoo Ches W....112 B7
Chestfield Kent.............47 J6
Cheston Devon...............7 G4
Cheswardine Shrops.....99 G6
Cheswick Nthumb.......168 F1
Chetnole Dorset...........14 B2
Chettisham Cambs........90 D6
Chettle Dorset..............27 L8
Chetton Shrops............84 B5
Chetwynd Wrekin.........99 G7
Chetwynd Aston
  Wrekin......................99 H8
Cheveley Cambs...........76 F3
Chevening Kent.............32 E2
Chevington Suffk..........77 H3
Cheviot Hills..............168 A7
Chevithorne Devon......24 F7
Chew Magna BaNES......38 E7
Chew Stoke BaNES.......38 E7
Chewton Keynsham
  BaNES......................38 F6
Chewton Mendip
  Somset.....................26 E2
Chicheley M Keyn..........74 C5
Chichester W Susx........18 B5
Chichester
  Crematorium
  W Susx......................18 B4
Chickerell Dorset.........14 C6
Chicklade Wilts.............27 K4
Chidden Hants.............30 A7
Chiddingfold Surrey......30 F4
Chiddingly E Susx.........20 B3
Chiddingstone Kent......32 E4
Chiddingstone
  Causeway Kent..........32 F4
Chideock Dorset...........13 K4
Chidham W Susx..........17 L2
Chidswell Kirk.............123 K6
Chieveley W Berk..........41 J5
Chieveley Services
  W Berk.......................41 J6
Chignall St James
  Essex........................61 G6
Chignall Smealy Essex...61 G5
Chigwell Essex.............45 H2
Chigwell Row Essex......45 J2
Chilbolton Hants...........29 H4
Chilcomb Hants............29 J5
Chilcombe Dorset.........13 M4
Chilcompton Somset.....26 F2
Chilcote Leics..............86 C2
Childer Thornton
  Ches W....................111 K6
Child Okeford Dorset....27 J8
Childrey Oxon...............41 G3
Child's Ercall Shrops....98 F7
Childswickham Worcs...71 J6

Childwall Lpool...........112 B4
Chilfrome Dorset..........14 B3
Chilgrove W Susx..........18 A3
Chilham Kent................34 E4
Chillaton Devon............10 C8
Chillenden Kent............35 H4
Chillerton IoW...............16 F5
Chillesford Suffk...........79 H4
Chillington Devon............7 J7
Chillington Somset........13 K1
Chilmark Wilts..............27 L5
Chilmington Green
  Kent..........................34 C6
Chilson Oxon................56 F4
Chilsworthy Cnwll...........6 B2
Chilsworthy Devon..........9 J4
Chiltern Hills...............42 C2
Chilterns
  Crematorium
  Bucks........................42 F2
Chilthorne Domer
  Somset.....................26 D7
Chilton Bucks...............58 B5
Chilton Dur.................141 H2
Chilton Oxon................41 J4
Chilton Candover
  Hants........................29 L4
Chilton Cantelo
  Somset.....................26 E6
Chilton Foliat Wilts.......40 F6
Chilton Polden
  Somset.....................26 B4
Chilton Street Suffk......77 H5
Chilton Trinity
  Somset.....................25 L4
Chilwell Notts.............101 K5
Chilworth Hants...........29 H7
Chilworth Surrey...........31 G3
Chimney Oxon..............57 G7
Chineham Hants...........30 A1
Chingford Gt Lon..........45 G2
Chinley Derbys............114 B5
Chinnor Oxon...............58 C7
Chipnall Shrops............99 G6
Chippenham Cambs.....76 F1
Chippenham Wilts........39 L5
Chipperfield Herts........59 H7
Chipping Herts.............60 B2
Chipping Lancs...........121 J2
Chipping Campden
  Gloucs......................71 L6
Chipping Norton
  Oxon........................56 F3
Chipping Ongar Essex...60 E7
Chipping Sodbury
  S Glos.......................39 G4
Chipping Warden
  Nhants......................72 F5
Chipstable Somset........25 G6
Chipstead Kent.............32 E3
Chipstead Surrey..........32 B2
Chirbury Shrops............82 F4
Chirk Wrexhm...............97 L5
Chirnside Border.........179 H6
Chirnsidebridge
  Border.....................179 H7
Chirton Wilts................40 B8
Chisbury Wilts..............40 F6
Chiselborough
  Somset.....................26 C8
Chiseldon Swindn........40 D4
Chiselhampton Oxon....57 L7
Chisholme Border.......166 F6
Chislehurst Gt Lon........45 H6
Chislet Kent..................47 L6
Chisley Calder............122 F5
Chiswell Green Herts.....59 J6
Chiswick Gt Lon............44 E4
Chisworth Derbys.......113 M3
Chithurst W Susx..........30 D6
Chittering Cambs..........76 C1
Chitterne Wilts.............27 M3
Chittlehamholt
  Devon.......................23 K7
Chittlehampton
  Devon.......................23 K6

Chittoe Wilts 39 L6
Chivelstone Devon.......7 H7
Chivenor Devon...........23 H4
Chlenry D & G..........144 D3
Chobham Surrey 42 F7
Cholderton Wilts 28 E3
Cholesbury Bucks 58 F6
Chollerton Nthumb ...158 B7
Cholsey Oxon...............41 L3
Cholstrey Herefs 69 J3
Chop Gate N York 142 C7
Choppington
  Nthumb 159 G5
Chopwell Gatesd 150 E4
Chorley Ches E............98 E3
Chorley Lancs.............121 H6
Chorley Shrops 84 C6
Chorleywood Herts 43 H2
Chorleywood West
  Herts........................43 G2
Chorlton Ches E..........99 G3
Chorlton-cum-Hardy
  Manch 113 J3
Chorlton Lane Ches W...98 C3
Choulton Shrops 83 H5
Chrishall Essex 76 C6
Chrisswell Inver........173 L4
Christchurch Cambs ...90 C4
Christchurch Dorset ...15 M4
Christchurch Newpt ...37 M3
Christian Malford
  Wilts.........................39 L5
Christleton Ches W ...112 C7
Christon N Som 38 B8
Christon Bank
  Nthumb 169 J5
Christow Devon...........11 J7
Chudleigh Devon.........11 K8
Chudleigh Knighton
  Devon.........................7 J1
Chulmleigh Devon 11 G3
Church Lancs.............121 L5
Churcham Gloucs 55 H4
Church Aston Wrekin...99 H8
Church Brampton
  Nhants.......................73 K2
Church Broughton
  Derbys.....................100 D5
Church Cove Cnwll 3 J8
Church Crookham
  Hants........................30 D2
Churchdown Gloucs....55 K4
Church Eaton Staffs....99 J8
Church End C Beds 75 H6
Churchend Essex.........47 G2
Church End Essex 61 H3
Church End Gt Lon 44 E3
Church Enstone Oxon...57 G3
Church Fenton
  N York.....................124 D3
Churchfield Sandw......85 H5
Church Green Devon ..12 F3
Church Hanborough
  Oxon.........................57 H5
Church Houses
  N York.....................142 E7
Churchill Devon...........13 H3
Churchill N Som..........38 C7
Churchill Oxon.............56 F3
Churchill Worcs 71 G4
Churchill Worcs 84 F7
Churchinford Somset...25 K8
Churchover Warwks....87 G7

Church Preen Shrops 83 K4
Church Pulverbatch
  Shrops........................83 H3
Churchstanton
  Somset 25 J8
Churchstoke Powys.......82 F5
Churchstow Devon..........7 G6
Church Stowe Nhants 73 J3
Church Street Kent.......46 B5
Church Stretton
  Shrops........................83 J5
Church Warsop Notts...115 K7
Churston Ferrers
  Torbay 7 K5
Churt Surrey 30 D4
Churton Ches W 98 B2
Churwell Leeds 123 K5
Chwilog Gwynd............95 G5
Chyandour Cnwll............2 E5
Cilcain Flints 111 G7
Cilcennin Cerdgn.........66 C3
Cilfrew Neath...............52 B7
Cilfynydd Rhondd.........37 G3
Cilgerran Pembks.........65 H6
Cilmaengwyn Neath.....51 L4
Cilmery Powys..............67 L4
Cilsan Carmth...............51 H2
Ciltalgarth Gwynd.........96 D4
Cilycwm Carmth...........67 G6
Cimla Neath.................36 B2
Cinderford Gloucs.........54 F5
Cippenham Slough.......42 F4
Cirencester Gloucs.......56 A7
City Gt Lon....................45 G4
City Airport Gt Lon........45 H4
City of London
  Crematorium
  Gt Lon........................45 H3
Clabhach Ag & B........188 F5
Clachaig Ag & B..........173 J3
Clachan Ag & B...........172 C6
Clachan Ag & B...........182 A4
Clachan Ag & B...........191 G7
Clachan Highld............209 H6
Clachan-a-Luib W Isls...233 C6
Clachan Mor Ag & B....188 C6
Clachan na Luib W Isls...233 C6
Clachan of Campsie
  E Duns......................175 G3
Clachan-Seil Ag & B....181 M4
Clachnaharry Highld....213 G5
Clachtoll Highld..........224 C3
Clackavoid P & K........195 J4
Clacket Lane
  Services Surrey 32 D3
Clackmannan Clacks.....185 J8
Clackmarras Moray.....214 F3
Clacton-on-Sea Essex...62 E5
Cladich Ag & B...........182 F3
Cladswell Worcs 71 J3
Claggan Highld............190 E6
Claigan Highld............208 C4
Clanfield Hants.............30 B7
Clanfield Oxon..............56 F7
Clanville Hants.............28 F2
Clanville Somset...........26 F5
Claonaig Ag & B..........172 E6
Clapgate Herts.............60 C3
Clapham Bed...............74 F4
Clapham Gt Lon...........44 F5
Clapham N York..........130 E5
Clapham W Susx..........18 F4
Clapton Somset............13 K2
Clapton Somset............26 F2
Clapton-in-Gordano
  N Som.........................38 C5
Clapton-on-the-Hill
  Gloucs........................56 D4
Claravale Gatesd........150 E3
Clarbeston Pembks.......49 H3

Clarbeston Road
  Pembks 49 H4
Clarborough Notts 116 B5
Clare Suffk 77 H5
Clarebrand D & G.......146 D2
Clarencefield D & G....147 J2
Clarilaw Border...........167 H5
Clarkston E Rens 175 G6
Clashmore Highld.......223 G4
Clashmore Highld.......224 C3
Clashnessie Highld.....224 C3
Clashnoir Highld.........204 F2
Clathy P & K...............185 K4
Clathymore P & K.......185 L3
Clatt Abers.................205 L1
Clatter Powys...............81 L5
Clatworthy Somset......25 G5
Claughton Lancs.........121 G3
Claughton Lancs.........130 B6
Claughton Wirral........111 J4
Claverdon Warwks 71 L2
Claverham N Som........38 C6
Clavering Essex 60 D2
Claverley Shrops 84 E5
Claverton BaNES 39 H7
Clawdd-coch V Glam....37 G5
Clawdd-newydd
  Denbgs 97 G3
Clawton Devon 9 J5
Claxby Lincs................117 J3
Claxton N York 133 L7
Claxton Norfk 93 H3
Claybrooke Magna
  Leics..........................86 F5
Clay Coton Nhants 87 H7
Clay Cross Derbys......115 H8
Claydon Oxon..............72 F4
Claydon Suffk 78 D5
Claygate D & G...........156 D6
Claygate Kent...............33 J4
Claygate Surrey 44 D7
Clayhall Gt Lon............45 H3
Clayhanger Devon........24 F6
Clayhidon Devon..........25 J7
Clayhill E Susx.............21 G2
Clayock Highld............231 H4
Claypits Gloucs 55 H6
Claypole Lincs............102 D3
Clayton C Brad...........123 G4
Clayton Donc..............124 C8
Clayton W Susx 19 J3
Clayton-le-Moors
  Lancs........................121 L4
Clayton-le-Woods
  Lancs........................121 H6
Clayton West Kirk......123 K7
Clayworth Notts 116 B4
Cleadale Highld..........199 G7
Cleadon S Tyne..........151 J3
Clearbrook Devon..........6 D3
Clearwell Gloucs..........54 E6
Cleasby N York..........141 G5
Cleat Ork....................234 c8
Cleatlam Dur...............140 E4
Cleator Cumb.............136 D4
Cleator Moor Cumb....136 E4
Cleckheaton Kirk.........123 J5
Cleehill Shrops.............83 L7
Cleekhimin N Lans.....175 K6
Clee St Margaret
  Shrops........................83 L6
Cleethorpes NE Lin....127 H8
Cleeton St Mary
  Shrops........................84 B7
Cleeve N Som...............38 C7
Cleeve Oxon.................41 L4
Cleeve Hill Gloucs 55 M3
Cleeve Prior Worcs 71 J5
Cleghornie E Loth 178 D2
Clehonger Herefs 69 J6
Cleish P & K...............186 A7
Cleland N Lans...........175 L6
Clenamacrie Ag & B....182 C2
Clenchwarton Norfk...104 F7
Clenerty Abers............216 E3
Clent Worcs..................85 G7

Cleobury Mortimer
  Shrops 84 C7
Cleobury North
  Shrops 84 B6
Cleongart Ag & B........161 H3
Clephanton Highld......213 J4
Clerkhill D & G............156 A3
Cleuch-head D & G.....154 E3
Clevancy Wilts 40 B5
Clevedon N Som...........38 B6
Cleveleys Lancs...........120 D2
Cleverton Wilts.............39 L4
Clewer Somset..............26 C2
Cley next the Sea
  Norfk.........................106 C4
Cliburn Cumb.............138 E3
Cliddesden Hants.........29 M2
Cliffe Medway...............46 C5
Cliffe N York...............125 G4
Cliff End E Susx...........21 H3
Cliffe Woods Medway...46 C5
Clifford Herefs.............68 E5
Clifford Leeds.............124 C2
Clifford Chambers
  Warwks........................71 L4
Clifford's Mesne
  Gloucs.........................55 G4
Clifton Bristl................38 E5
Clifton C Beds.............75 H6
Clifton C Nott.............101 K5
Clifton C York............133 J8
Clifton Calder..............123 H6
Clifton Cumb..............138 D2
Clifton Derbys............100 D4
Clifton Devon...............23 J3
Clifton Donc...............115 K3
Clifton Lancs..............120 F4
Clifton N York.............123 J2
Clifton Oxon.................57 J2
Clifton Worcs................70 F5
Clifton Campville
  Staffs..........................86 B2
Clifton Hampden
  Oxon...........................41 K2
Clifton Reynes
  M Keyn........................74 C4
Clifton upon
  Dunsmore Warwks....87 G7
Clifton upon Teme
  Worcs..........................70 C3
Cliftonville Kent 35 K1
Climping W Susx..........18 D5
Clink Somset................27 H2
Clint N York................132 D7
Clinterty C Aber..........206 F3
Clint Green Norfk 92 B2
Clintmains Border.......167 J3
Clippesby Norfk 93 J2
Clipsham Rutlnd 88 D1
Clipston Nhants 87 K7
Clipston Notts............101 M5
Clipstone C Beds 58 F3
Clipstone Notts 115 L8
Clitheroe Lancs...........121 L3
Clive Shrops 98 D7
Cliveden Bucks 42 E4
Clixby Lincs................117 J2
Cloatley Wilts 39 M3
Clocaenog Denbgs.......97 G2
Clochan Moray............215 J3
Clodock Herefs............53 L3
Clola Abers.................217 J5
Clophill C Beds 74 F6
Clopton Nhants 88 F7
Clopton Suffk...............78 F4
Clopton Corner Suffk...78 F4
Clos du Valle Guern....236 d2
Closeburn D & G........154 F4
Closeburnmill D & G....154 F3
Closworth Somset 14 B1
Clothall Herts 59 L2
Clotton Ches W..........112 D8
Clough Foot Calder....122 D5
Clough Head Calder....123 G6
Cloughton N York.......143 K7
Clousta Shet...............235 c5

Clova Angus 196 B2
Clovelly Devon....22 E6
Clovenfords Border...167 G3
Clovulin Highld....191 K4
Clugston D & G....145 H4
Clun Shrops....82 F7
Clunas Highld....213 K5
Clunbury Shrops....83 G7
Clunderwen Carmth....49 J4
Clune Highld....203 J1
Clunes Highld....201 J7
Clungunford Shrops....83 H7
Clunie P & K....195 H7
Clunton Shrops....83 G7
Cluny Fife....186 D7
Clutton BaNES....38 F8
Clutton Ches W....98 C2
Clutton Hill BaNES....38 F8
Clydach Mons....53 K5
Clydach Swans....51 K5
Clydach Vale Rhondd....36 F2
Clydebank W Duns....174 F4
Clydebank Crematorium W Duns....174 E4
Clyffe Pypard Wilts....40 B5
Clynder Ag & B....174 A2
Clyne Neath....52 C7
Clynnog-fawr Gwynd....95 G3
Clyro Powys....68 E5
Clyst Honiton Devon....12 C4
Clyst Hydon Devon....12 D3
Clyst St George Devon....12 C5
Clyst St Lawrence Devon....12 D3
Clyst St Mary Devon....12 C4
Cnoc W Isls....232 g2
Cnwch Coch Cerdgn....80 F8
Coad's Green Cnwll....5 L1
Coalburn S Lans....164 F3
Coalburns Gatesd....150 E3
Coaley Gloucs....55 H7
Coalhill Essex....61 J7
Coalpit Heath S Glos....38 F4
Coalport Wrekin....84 C3
Coalsnaughton Clacks....185 J7
Coaltown of Balgonie Fife....186 E7
Coaltown of Wemyss Fife....186 E7
Coalville Leics....86 E2
Coanwood Nthumb....149 H3
Coat Somset....26 C7
Coatbridge N Lans....175 J5
Coatdyke N Lans....175 K5
Coate Swindn....40 D4
Coate Wilts....40 B7
Coates Cambs....89 K4
Coates Gloucs....55 L7
Coates Lincs....116 E5
Coates W Susx....18 D3
Cobbaton Devon....23 K6
Coberley Gloucs....55 L5
Cobham Kent....46 A6
Cobham Surrey....43 J7
Cobham Services Surrey....43 J8
Cobnash Herefs....69 J3
Cobo Guern....236 c2
Coburby Abers....217 H2
Cockayne Hatley C Beds....75 J5
Cock Bridge Abers....205 G4
Cockburnspath Border....179 G4
Cock Clarks Essex....61 K7
Cockenzie and Port Seton E Loth....177 L4
Cockerham Lancs....120 F1
Cockermouth Cumb....136 F2
Cockernhoe Herts....59 J4
Cockett Swans....51 J6

Cockfield Dur....140 E3
Cockfield Suffk....77 K4
Cockfosters Gt Lon....44 F2
Cock Green Essex....61 H4
Cocking W Susx....18 B3
Cocking Causeway W Susx....18 B2
Cockington Torbay....7 K3
Cocklake Somset....26 C2
Cockley Cley Norfk....91 H3
Cock Marling E Susx....21 H2
Cockpole Green Wokham....42 D4
Cockshutt Shrops....98 B6
Cockthorpe Norfk....106 B4
Cockwood Devon....12 C6
Cockyard Derbys....114 B5
Coddenham Suffk....78 D4
Coddington Herefs....70 C6
Coddington Notts....102 D2
Codford St Mary Wilts....27 L4
Codford St Peter Wilts....27 L4
Codicote Herts....59 K4
Codmore Hill W Susx....31 H7
Codnor Derbys....101 H3
Codrington S Glos....39 G5
Codsall Staffs....84 F3
Codsall Wood Staffs....84 F3
Coedpoeth Wrexhm....97 L3
Coed Talon Flints....97 L2
Coed-y-paen Mons....53 M7
Coffinswell Devon....7 K3
Cofton Devon....12 C6
Cofton Hackett Worcs....85 H7
Cogan V Glam....37 J5
Cogenhoe Nhants....74 B3
Coggeshall Essex....61 K4
Coignafearn Highld....203 H2
Coilacriech Abers....205 H6
Coilantogle Stirlg....184 D6
Coillore Highld....208 E6
Coity Brdgnd....36 E4
Col W Isls....232 g2
Colaboll Highld....225 L6
Colan Cnwll....4 D4
Colaton Raleigh Devon....12 D5
Colbost Highld....208 C5
Colburn N York....140 F7
Colby Cumb....138 F3
Colby IoM....237 b6
Colchester Essex....62 B3
Colchester Crematorium Essex....62 B4
Colchester Zoo Essex....62 A4
Cold Ash W Berk....41 K6
Cold Ashby Nhants....87 J7
Cold Ashton S Glos....39 H6
Cold Aston Gloucs....56 C4
Coldbackie Highld....229 J3
Cold Brayfield M Keyn....74 D4
Coldean Dr & H....19 J4
Coldeast Devon....7 J2
Colden Calder....122 E5
Colden Common Hants....29 J6
Cold Hanworth Lincs....117 G5
Coldharbour Surrey....31 J3
Cold Higham Nhants....73 J4
Coldingham Border....179 J5
Cold Kirby N York....133 H3
Coldmeece Staffs....99 J6
Cold Norton Essex....61 K7
Cold Overton Leics....88 B2
Coldred Kent....35 H5
Coldridge Devon....11 G4
Coldstream Border....168 C2
Coldwaltham W Susx....18 D3
Coldwell Herefs....69 H7
Coldwells Abers....217 H6
Cole Somset....26 F4
Colebatch Shrops....83 G6
Colebrook Devon....12 C2

Colebrooke Devon....11 H5
Coleby Lincs....102 F1
Coleby N Linc....125 L6
Coleford Devon....11 H5
Coleford Gloucs....54 E6
Coleford Somset....27 G2
Colegate End Norfk....92 E6
Colehill Dorset....15 J3
Coleman's Hatch E Susx....32 D6
Colemere Shrops....98 B6
Colemore Hants....30 B5
Colenden P & K....186 B2
Colerne Wilts....39 J6
Colesbourne Gloucs....56 A5
Coleshill Bucks....42 F2
Coleshill Oxon....40 E2
Coleshill Warwks....85 L5
Coley BaNES....26 E1
Colgate W Susx....31 L5
Colinsburgh Fife....187 H6
Colinton C Edin....177 H5
Colintraive Ag & B....173 H4
Colkirk Norfk....105 L7
Coll Ag & B....189 G5
Collace P & K....186 C2
Collafirth Shet....235 c3
Coll Airport Ag & B....188 F5
Collaton Devon....7 G7
Collaton St Mary Torbay....7 K4
College of Roseisle Moray....214 E2
College Town Br For....42 D7
Collessie Fife....186 E5
Collier Row Gt Lon....45 J2
Collier's End Herts....60 B4
Collier Street Kent....33 J4
Collieston Abers....217 K8
Collin D & G....155 H6
Collingbourne Ducis Wilts....28 E2
Collingbourne Kingston Wilts....28 E1
Collingham Leeds....124 B2
Collingham Notts....102 D1
Collington Herefs....70 B3
Collingtree Nhants....73 L4
Collins Green Warrtn....112 E3
Colliston Angus....196 F7
Colliton Devon....12 C2
Collyweston Nhants....88 E3
Colmonell S Ayrs....152 D5
Colmworth Bed....75 G3
Colnabaichin Abers....205 G4
Colnbrook Slough....43 G5
Colne Cambs....89 L7
Colne Lancs....122 D3
Colne Engaine Essex....61 K3
Colney Norfk....92 E3
Colney Heath Herts....59 K6
Coln Rogers Gloucs....56 B6
Coln St Aldwyns Gloucs....56 C6
Coln St Dennis Gloucs....56 B5
Colonsay Ag & B....180 E7
Colonsay Airport Ag & B....180 E8
Colpy Abers....216 C7
Colquhar Border....166 E2
Colsterworth Lincs....102 F7
Colston Bassett Notts....102 B5
Coltfield Moray....214 D2
Coltishall Norfk....106 F8
Colton Cumb....129 G3
Colton Leeds....124 B4
Colton N York....124 C2
Colton Norfk....92 D2
Colton Staffs....100 B7
Colt's Hill Kent....33 H4
Colvend D & G....146 F4
Colwall Herefs....70 D5
Colwell Nthumb....158 B6
Colwich Staffs....100 A7
Colwinston V Glam....36 E5
Colworth W Susx....18 C5

Colwyn Bay Conwy....110 B5
Colyford Devon....13 G4
Colyton Devon....13 G4
Combe Devon....57 H5
Combe W Berk....41 G7
Combe Down BaNES....39 H7
Combe Fishacre Devon....7 J3
Combe Florey Somset....25 J5
Combe Hay BaNES....39 G7
Combeinteignhead Devon....7 K2
Combe Martin Devon....23 J3
Combe Raleigh Devon....12 F3
Comberbach Ches W....112 F6
Comberford Staffs....85 L3
Comberton Cambs....75 L4
Comberton Herefs....69 K2
Combe St Nicholas Somset....13 H1
Combrook Warwks....72 C4
Combs Derbys....114 B6
Combs Suffk....78 C3
Combs Ford Suffk....78 C3
Combwich Somset....25 K3
Comers Abers....206 D4
Comhampton Worcs....70 E2
Commins Coch Powys....81 J3
Commondale N York....142 E5
Common End Cumb....136 D3
Common Moor Cnwll....5 K2
Compstall Stockp....113 L4
Compstonend D & G....146 B4
Compton Devon....7 K3
Compton Hants....29 J6
Compton Staffs....84 E6
Compton Surrey....30 F3
Compton W Berk....41 K4
Compton W Susx....30 C7
Compton Wilts....28 C2
Compton Abbas Dorset....27 K7
Compton Abdale Gloucs....56 B5
Compton Bassett Wilts....40 B6
Compton Beauchamp Oxon....40 F3
Compton Bishop Somset....26 B1
Compton Chamberlayne Wilts....28 B5
Compton Dando BaNES....38 F7
Compton Dundon Somset....26 C5
Compton Durville Somset....26 B7
Compton Greenfield S Glos....38 E4
Compton Martin BaNES....38 D8
Compton Pauncefoot Somset....26 F6
Compton Valence Dorset....14 B4
Comrie Fife....176 D1
Comrie P & K....185 G3
Conaglen House Highld....191 K3
Concha Highld....210 D8
Concraigie P & K....195 H7
Conderton Worcs....71 G6
Condicote Gloucs....56 D3
Condorrat N Lans....175 K4
Condover Shrops....83 J3
Coney Hill Gloucs....55 J4
Coneyhurst Common W Susx....31 J6
Coneysthorpe N York....133 L5
Coney Weston Suffk....91 L7
Congerstone Leics....86 D3
Congham Norfk....105 H7

Congleton Ches E......113 J8
Congresbury N Som......38 C7
Conheath D & G......147 H2
Conicavel Moray......214 B4
Coningsby Lincs......103 L2
Conington Cambs......75 K2
Conington Cambs......89 H6
Conisbrough Donc......115 K2
Conisholme Lincs......118 E3
Coniston Cumb......137 J7
Coniston E R Yk......126 E4
Coniston Cold N York......131 G8
Conistone N York......131 J6
Connah's Quay Flints......111 J7
Connel Ag & B......182 C1
Connel Park E Ayrs......164 C6
Connor Downs Cnwll......3 G4
Conon Bridge Highld......212 E4
Cononley N York......122 E2
Consall Staffs......99 M3
Consett Dur......150 E5
Constable Burton
    N York......132 B2
Constable Lee Lancs......122 B5
Constantine Cnwll......3 J5
Constantine Bay
    Cnwll......4 D2
Contin Highld......212 C3
Conwy Conwy......109 L6
Conwy Castle Conwy......109 L6
Conyer's Green Suffk......77 K2
Cooden E Susx......20 E4
Cookbury Devon......9 K4
Cookham W & M......42 E4
Cookham Dean W & M......42 E4
Cookham Rise W & M......42 E4
Cookhill Worcs......71 J3
Cookley Suffk......93 H7
Cookley Worcs......84 E7
Cookley Green Oxon......42 B3
Cookney Abers......207 G6
Cook's Green Essex......62 E4
Cooks Green Suffk......77 I4
Cooksmill Green
    Essex......61 G6
Coolham W Susx......31 J6
Cooling Medway......46 C5
Coombe Cnwll......4 E5
Coombe Devon......7 L2
Coombe Devon......12 E4
Coombe Gloucs......39 H2
Coombe Hants......30 A7
Coombe Abbey
    Warwks......86 E7
Coombe Bissett Wilts......28 C6
Coombe Cellars
    Devon......7 K2
Coombe Hill Gloucs......55 K3
Coombe Keynes
    Dorset......14 F5
Coombe Pafford
    Torbay......7 L3
Coombes W Susx......19 G4
Coombes-Moor Herefs......69 G2
Coopersale Common
    Essex......60 D7
Copdock Suffk......78 D6
Copford Green Essex......61 L4
Copgrove N York......132 E6
Copister Shet......235 d3
Cople Bed......75 G5
Copley Dur......140 D3
Copmanthorpe
    C York......124 E2
Copmere End Staffs......99 J6
Copp Lancs......120 F3
Coppenhall Staffs......99 K8
Copperhouse Cnwll......2 F4
Coppingford Cambs......89 H7
Copplestone Devon......11 H4
Coppull Lancs......121 H7
Copsale W Susx......31 K6
Copster Green Lancs......121 K4
Copston Magna
    Warwks......86 F5
Cop Street Kent......35 J3

Copt Hewick N York......132 E5
Copthorne W Susx......32 B5
Copt Oak Leics......86 F2
Copythorne Hants......28 F8
Corbets Tey Gt Lon......45 K3
Corbiere Jersey......236 a7
Corbridge Nthumb......150 C3
Corby Nhants......88 C5
Corby Glen Lincs......103 G7
Cordon N Ayrs......162 D4
Coreley Shrops......84 B8
Corfe Somset......25 K7
Corfe Castle Dorset......15 H6
Corfe Mullen Dorset......15 J3
Corfton Shrops......83 J6
Corgarff Abers......205 G4
Corhampton Hants......29 L7
Corley Warwks......86 C6
Corley Services
    Warwks......86 C6
Cormuir Angus......195 L3
Cornard Tye Suffk......77 K6
Cornforth Dur......151 H7
Cornhill Abers......216 B3
Cornhill-on-Tweed
    Nthumb......168 C2
Cornholme Calder......122 D5
Cornoigmore Ag & B......188 C6
Cornsay Dur......150 E6
Cornsay Colliery Dur......150 F6
Corntown Highld......212 E3
Corntown V Glam......36 E5
Cornwell Oxon......56 F3
Cornwood Devon......6 E4
Cornworthy Devon......7 J5
Corpach Highld......191 L2
Corpusty Norfk......106 D6
Corrachree Abers......205 K4
Corran Highld......191 K4
Corran Highld......200 C4
Corrie D & G......155 L5
Corrie N Ayrs......162 C2
Corriecravie N Ayrs......162 B5
Corriegills N Ayrs......162 D3
Corriegour Lodge
    Hotel Highld......201 K6
Corriemoille Highld......212 B2
Corrimony Highld......212 B7
Corringham Lincs......116 F4
Corringham Thurr......46 B4
Corris Gwynd......81 G2
Corris Uchaf Gwynd......81 G2
Corrow Ag & B......183 H7
Corry Highld......199 K1
Corscombe Devon......10 F5
Corscombe Dorset......13 M2
Corse Gloucs......55 H3
Corse Lawn Gloucs......55 J2
Corsham Wilts......39 K6
Corsindae Abers......206 D4
Corsley Wilts......27 J3
Corsley Heath Wilts......27 J3
Corsock D & G......154 D6
Corston BaNES......39 G7
Corston Wilts......39 L4
Corstorphine C Edin......177 G4
Cortachy Angus......196 C4
Corton Suffk......93 L4
Corton Wilts......27 L4
Corton Denham
    Somset......26 F6
Coruanan Highld......191 L3
Corwen Denbgs......97 G4
Coryton Devon......10 C7
Coryton Thurr......46 C4
Cosby Leics......87 G4
Coseley Dudley......85 G5
Cosgrove Nhants......73 L6
Cosham C Port......17 J2
Cosheston Pembks......49 G6
Coshieville P & K......194 C6
Cossall Notts......101 J4
Cossington Leics......87 H2
Cossington Somset......26 A4
Costessey Norfk......92 E2
Costock Notts......101 L7

Coston Leics......102 D7
Coston Norfk......92 C3
Cote Oxon......57 G7
Cotebrook Ches W......112 E7
Cotehill Cumb......148 E5
Cotes Leics......101 K7
Cotesbach Leics......87 G6
Cotford St Luke
    Somset......25 J6
Cotgrave Notts......101 M5
Cothal Abers......207 G3
Cotham Notts......102 C3
Cotherstone Dur......140 C4
Cothill Oxon......57 J7
Cotleigh Devon......13 G3
Cotmanhay Derbys......101 J4
Coton Cambs......76 B3
Coton Nhants......73 J1
Coton Staffs......99 J7
Coton Clanford Staffs......99 K7
Coton Hill Shrops......83 J2
Coton in the Elms
    Derbys......86 B1
Cotswolds......55 M6
Cotswold Wildlife
    Park & Gardens
    Oxon......56 E6
Cott Devon......7 H4
Cottam Lancs......121 G4
Cottam Notts......116 D5
Cottenham Cambs......76 C2
Cottered Herts......60 A3
Cotterstock Nhants......88 F5
Cottesbrooke Nhants......87 K8
Cottesmore Rutlnd......88 C2
Cottingham E R Yk......126 C4
Cottingham Nhants......88 B5
Cottingley C Brad......123 G3
Cottingley Hall
    Crematorium
    Leeds......123 K4
Cottisford Oxon......57 L2
Cotton Suffk......78 C2
Cottown Abers......206 E3
Cottown Abers......215 L8
Cottown of Gight
    Abers......216 F6
Cotts Devon......6 C3
Coughton Warwks......71 J3
Coulaghailtro Ag & B......172 C5
Coulags Highld......210 E5
Coull Abers......205 L5
Coulport Ag & B......173 L2
Coulsdon Gt Lon......32 B2
Coulston Wilts......27 L2
Coulter S Lans......165 K3
Coulton N York......133 K5
Coultra Fife......186 F3
Cound Shrops......83 L3
Coundon Dur......141 G2
Countersett N York......131 H2
Countess Wear Devon......12 B4
Countesthorpe Leics......87 H4
Countisbury Devon......24 B2
Coupar Angus P & K......195 K7
Coupland Nthumb......168 D3
Cour Ag & B......172 D8
Courteachan Highld......199 L6
Courteenhall Nhants......73 L4
Court Henry Carmth......51 H2
Courtsend Essex......47 G2
Courtway Somset......25 J5
Cousland Mdloth......177 K5
Cousley Wood E Susx......33 H6
Cove Ag & B......173 L2
Cove Border......179 G4
Cove Devon......24 E7
Cove Hants......30 E1
Cove Highld......219 J3
Cove Bay C Aber......207 H5
Covehithe Suffk......93 L6
Coven Staffs......85 G3
Coveney Cambs......90 C6
Covenham St
    Bartholomew
    Lincs......118 D3

Covenham St Mary
    Lincs......118 D3
Coventry Covtry......86 D7
Coventry Airport
    Warwks......86 D8
Coverack Cnwll......3 K7
Coverack Bridges
    Cnwll......3 H5
Coverham N York......131 L3
Covington Cambs......74 F1
Covington S Lans......165 J2
Cowan Bridge Lancs......130 C4
Cowbeech E Susx......20 C3
Cowbit Lincs......103 L8
Cowbridge V Glam......36 F5
Cowden Kent......32 E5
Cowdenbeath Fife......177 G1
Cowers Lane Derbys......100 F3
Cowes IoW......16 F3
Cowesby N York......133 G2
Cowfold W Susx......31 K6
Cowhill S Glos......38 E3
Cowie Stirlg......175 L1
Cowley Devon......11 K5
Cowley Gloucs......55 L5
Cowley Gt Lon......43 H4
Cowley Oxon......57 K7
Cowling Lancs......121 H6
Cowling N York......122 E2
Cowling N York......132 C3
Cowlinge Suffk......77 G4
Cowpen Nthumb......159 H5
Cowplain Hants......17 K1
Cowshill Dur......149 L6
Cowslip Green N Som......38 C7
Cowthorne N York......132 F8
Coxbank Ches E......98 F4
Coxbench Derbys......101 G4
Coxford Cnwll......8 F5
Coxford Norfk......105 K6
Coxheath Kent......33 J3
Coxhoe Dur......151 H7
Coxley Somset......26 D5
Coxley Wick Somset......26 D3
Coxtie Green Essex......45 K2
Coxwold N York......133 H4
Coychurch Brdgnd......36 E4
Coychurch
    Crematorium
    Brdgnd......36 E4
Coylton S Ayrs......163 K5
Coylumbridge Highld......203 L3
Coytrahen Brdgnd......36 D4
Crabbs Cross Worcs......71 J2
Crabtree W Susx......31 K6
Crackenthorpe Cumb......138 F3
Crackington Haven
    Cnwll......8 F5
Crackleybank Shrops......84 D2
Cracoe N York......131 J7
Craddock Devon......25 G8
Cradley Dudley......85 G6
Cradley Herefs......70 D5
Cradley Heath Sandw......85 G6
Cradoc Powys......52 F2
Crafthole Cnwll......6 B5
Craggan Highld......204 C1
Craghead Dur......150 F5
Cragside House &
    Garden Nthumb......158 D2
Crai Powys......52 D3
Craibstone Moray......215 L3
Craichie Angus......196 E6
Craig Angus......197 H5
Craig Highld......211 G4
Craigbank E Ayrs......164 C6
Craigburn Border......177 H7
Craigcleuch D & G......156 C5
Craigdam Abers......216 F7
Craigdhu Ag & B......182 B6
Craigearn Abers......206 D3
Craigellachie Moray......215 G5
Craigend P & K......186 B4
Craigend Rens......174 E4
Craigendoran Ag & B......174 C3
Craigends Rens......174 D5

Craighlaw D & G 145 G3
Craighouse Ag & B..........171 K5
Craigie P & K 195 H7
Craigie S Ayrs 163 K3
Craigiefold Abers 217 H2
Craigley D & G 146 D4
Craig Llangiwg Neath....51 K4
Craiglockhart C Edin 177 H4
Craigmillar C Edin 177 J4
Craigneston D & G 154 D5
Craigneuk N Lans 175 K5
Craigneuk N Lans 175 K6
Craignure Ag & B..........190 E8
Craigo Angus 197 H4
Craigrothie Fife.............186 F5
Craigruie Stirlg.............184 B4
Craigton Angus 196 E8
Craigton C Aber 206 F5
Craigton E Rens............174 F7
Craigton
   Crematorium
   C Glas...................174 F5
Craigton of Airlie
   Angus 196 B6
Crail Fife 187 K5
Crailing Border 167 L4
Craiselound N Linc.......116 C2
Crakehall N York 132 C2
Crambe N York..............133 L6
Cramlington Nthumb....159 G6
Cramond C Edin 177 G3
Cramond Bridge
   C Edin.....................177 G4
Cranage Ches E 113 H7
Cranberry Staffs 99 J5
Cranborne Dorset 28 B8
Cranbourne Br For........42 F5
Cranbrook Devon...........12 C4
Cranbrook Kent.............33 K6
Cranfield C Beds............74 D6
Cranford Gt Lon............43 J5
Cranford St Andrew
   Nhants......................88 D7
Cranford St John
   Nhants......................88 D7
Cranham Gloucs 55 K5
Crank St Hel.................112 D2
Cranleigh Surrey...........31 H4
Cranmore Somset..........26 F3
Cranoe Leics..................87 L4
Cransford Suffk..............79 G2
Cranshaws Border 178 E6
Crantock Cnwll................4 C4
Cranwell Lincs..............103 G3
Cranwich Norfk..............91 H4
Cranworth Norfk............92 B3
Craobh Haven Ag & B...182 A6
Crarae Ag & B................182 E7
Crask Inn Highld 225 L4
Crask of Aigas
   Highld.....................212 D6
Craster Nthumb 169 K5
Cratfield Suffk................93 G7
Crathes Abers 206 E6
Crathie Abers 205 G6
Crathie Highld...............202 E6
Crathorne N York 141 K5
Craven Arms Shrops......83 H6
Crawcrook Gatesd 150 E3
Crawford S Lans 165 J5
Crawfordjohn S Lans 165 G5
Crawley Hants 29 H4
Crawley Oxon.................57 G5
Crawley W Susx.............31 L4
Crawley Down W Susx...32 C5
Crawshawbooth
   Lancs......................122 B5
Crawton Abers 197 L1
Cray N York...................131 H4
Crayford Gt Lon.............45 K5
Crayke N York................133 H5
Crays Hill Essex.............46 B2
Creacombe Devon...........24 C7
Creagan Inn Ag & B.......191 J7
Creag Ghoraidh W Isls ..233 c7
Creagorry W Isls...........233 c7

Creaguaineach
   Lodge Highld............192 E3
Creaton Nhants 73 K1
Creca D & G..................155 M7
Credenhill Herefs 69 J5
Crediton Devon..............11 J5
Creebank D & G............153 H6
Creebridge D & G 145 J2
Creech Heathfield
   Somset 25 L6
Creech St Michael
   Somset 25 L6
Creed Cnwll.....................4 E6
Creekmouth Gt Lon........45 J4
Creeting St Mary
   Suffk........................78 D3
Creeton Lincs 103 G8
Creetown D & G............145 K3
Cregneash IoM 237 a7
Creich Fife 186 E3
Creigiau Cardif...............37 G4
Cremyll Cnwll...................6 C5
Cressage Shrops 83 L3
Cressbrook Derbys........114 D6
Cresselly Pembks 49 H6
Cressex Bucks 42 D3
Cressing Essex...............61 J4
Cresswell Nthumb 159 H4
Cresswell Pembks 49 H6
Cresswell Staffs.............99 L5
Creswell Derbys...........115 K6
Cretingham Suffk...........78 F3
Cretshengan Ag & B......172 C5
Crewe Ches E 99 G2
Crewe Ches W.................98 B2
Crewe Crematorium
   Ches E.......................99 G2
Crewe Green Ches E 99 G2
Crew Green Powys..........83 G1
Crewkerne Somset 13 K1
Crewton C Derb.............101 G5
Crianlarich Stirlg..........183 L3
Cribyn Cerdgn................66 C4
Criccieth Gwynd.............95 J5
Crich Derbys.................101 G2
Crichton Mdloth............177 K6
Crick Nhants..................87 H8
Crickadarn Powys...........68 C6
Cricket St Thomas
   Somset 13 J2
Crickhowell Powys.........53 K4
Cricklade Wilts...............40 C2
Cricklewood Gt Lon........44 E3
Crieff P & K 185 H3
Criggion Powys..............82 F1
Crigglestone Wakefd 123 L7
Crimond Abers 217 K3
Crimplesham Norfk 90 F3
Crimscote Warwks.........72 B5
Crinaglack Highld..........212 C6
Crinan Ag & B...............182 A8
Crindledyke N Lans 175 L6
Cringleford Norfk...........92 E3
Crinow Pembks 49 J5
Croachy Highld..............213 G8
Crockenhill Kent............45 J6
Crocker End Oxon...........42 B3
Crockernwell Devon.......11 H6
Crockerton Wilts............27 K3
Crocketford D & G 154 E7
Crockham Hill Kent........32 D3
Croeserw Neath.............36 D2
Croes-goch Pembks........48 D2
Croes-lan Cerdgn............65 L5
Croesor Gwynd...............95 L4
Croesyceiliog Carmth....50 E3
Croesyceiliog Torfn 37 L2
Croft Leics.....................87 G4
Croft Lincs....................104 E1
Croft Warrtn 112 F3
Croftamie Stirlg.............174 E2
Crofton Wakefd.............124 B6
Croft-on-Tees N York....141 H5
Croftown Highld............220 F5
Crofts Moray.................215 G4
Crofts of Dipple Moray...215 H3

Crofts of Savoch
   Abers 217 K3
Crofty Swans.................51 G6
Croggan Ag & B............181 L3
Croglin Cumb................148 F5
Croick Highld................222 B3
Cromarty Highld............223 H7
Crombie Fife.................176 E2
Cromdale Highld 214 D8
Cromer Herts 59 M3
Cromer Norfk................106 F4
Cromford Derbys...........100 F2
Cromhall S Glos.............39 G3
Cromor W Isls...............232 f3
Cromwell Notts.............102 D1
Cronberry E Ayrs...........164 C5
Crondall Hants...............30 C2
Cronton Knows.............112 C4
Crook Cumb.................138 C2
Crook Dur.....................150 E7
Crookedholm E Ayrs.....163 L3
Crookham Nthumb.......168 D2
Crookham W Berk.........41 K7
Crookham Village
   Hants........................30 C2
Crook Inn Border..........165 L4
Crooklands Cumb..........129 L3
Crook of Devon P & K ...185 L7
Cropredy Oxon...............72 F5
Cropston Leics...............87 G2
Cropthorne Worcs..........71 H5
Cropton N York.............134 B2
Cropwell Bishop
   Notts.......................102 B5
Cropwell Butler Notts...102 B5
Cros W Isls...................232 g1
Crosbost W Isls.............232 f3
Crosby Cumb.................147 J7
Crosby IoM...................237 c5
Crosby N Linc...............125 K7
Crosby Sefton...............111 J2
Crosby Garret Cumb.....139 G5
Crosby Ravensworth
   Cumb......................138 F4
Croscombe Somset........26 E3
Cross Somset.................26 B1
Crossaig Ag & B............172 E1
Crossapol Ag & B..........188 C2
Cross Ash Mons.............54 B4
Cross-at-Hand Kent.......33 K4
Crosscanonby Cumb......147 J6
Crossdale Street Norfk..106 F5
Cross Flatts C Brad........123 G3
Crossford Fife...............176 E2
Crossford S Lans...........175 L8
Crossgatehall E Loth....177 K5
Crossgates E Ayrs.........163 J1
Crossgates Fife.............176 F1
Cross Gates Leeds 124 B4
Crossgates N York.........134 F3
Crossgill Lancs..............129 L6
Cross Green Leeds.........123 L4
Cross Green Suffk..........77 K4
Cross Green Suffk..........78 B4
Cross Hands Carmth......51 H3
Crosshands E Ayrs.........163 L4
Crosshill Fife................186 C7
Crosshill S Ayrs.............163 J7
Crosshouse E Ayrs.........163 K2
Cross Houses Shrops.....83 K3
Cross in Hand E Susx.....20 B2
Cross Inn Cerdgn............65 L3
Cross Keys Ag & B.........174 C2
Crosskeys Caerph...........37 K3
Crosskirk Highld...........230 F2
Cross Lane IoW..............17 G4
Cross Lane Head
   Shrops.......................84 C4
Crosslee Rens................174 D5
Crossmichael D & G......146 C2
Cross of Jackston
   Abers 216 E7
Cross o' th' hands
   Derbys....................100 F4
Crossroads Abers..........206 B4
Crossroads Abers..........206 E6

Cross Street Suffk 92 E7
Crosston Angus 196 E5
Cross Town Ches E.........113 H5
Crossway Green Worcs....70 E2
Crossways Dorset 14 E5
Crosswell Pembks 64 F6
Crosthwaite Cumb.........129 J2
Croston Lancs 121 G6
Crostwick Norfk..............92 F1
Crouch End Gt Lon..........44 F3
Croucheston Wilts..........28 B6
Crouch Hill Dorset..........14 D1
Croughton Nhants 73 G7
Crovie Abers..................216 F2
Crowan Cnwll...................3 H4
Crowborough E Susx......32 F6
Crowcombe Somset........25 H4
Crowdecote Derbys........114 C7
Crowden Derbys............114 B2
Crow Edge Barns...........114 D2
Crowell Oxon..................58 C7
Crowfield Suffk...............78 D3
Crowhill E Loth..............178 F4
Crow Hill Herefs.............54 F3
Crowhurst E Susx...........20 F3
Crowhurst Surrey...........32 D4
Crowland Lincs...............89 J2
Crowland Suffk...............78 B1
Crowlas Cnwll...................2 F5
Crowle N Linc................125 J7
Crowle Worcs..................71 G4
Crowle Green Worcs.......71 G3
Crowmarsh Gifford
   Oxon.........................41 L3
Crown Corner Suffk........78 F1
Crownhill C Plym..............6 C4
Crownhill
   Crematorium
   M Keyn......................74 B6
Crownthorpe Norfk........92 C3
Crowntown Cnwll.............3 H5
Crows-an-Wra Cnwll........2 D5
Crowthorne Wokham......42 D7
Crowton Ches W............112 E6
Croxdale Dur.................151 G7
Croxden Staffs...............100 B5
Croxley Green Herts.......43 H2
Croxteth Lpool..............111 L3
Croxton Cambs...............75 J3
Croxton N Linc..............126 D7
Croxton Norfk.................91 K6
Croxton Norfk................106 B6
Croxton Staffs................99 H6
Croxton Kerrial Leics ...102 D6
Croy Highld...................213 J4
Croy N Lans...................175 J3
Croyde Devon.................23 G4
Croydon Cambs...............75 K5
Croydon Gt Lon..............44 F6
Croydon
   Crematorium
   Gt Lon.......................44 F6
Crubenmore Highld.......203 G7
Cruckmeole Shrops........83 H2
Cruckton Shrops............83 H2
Cruden Bay Abers.........217 K6
Crudgington Wrekin.......98 F8
Crudwell Wilts................39 L2
Crumlin Caerph..............37 K2
Crumplehorn Cnwll..........5 K5
Crumpsall Manch..........113 J2
Crundale Kent................34 E5
Crunwear Pembks...........49 K5
Crux Easton Hants.........29 H1
Crwbin Carmth...............50 F3
Cryers Hill Bucks............42 E2
Crymych Pembks............65 G7
Crynant Neath................52 C6
Crystal Palace Gt Lon....45 G5
Cuaig Highld.................209 L3
Cuan Ag & B.................181 L4
Cubbington Warwks.......72 D2
Cubert Cnwll....................4 C4
Cublington Bucks............58 D4
Cublington Herefs...........69 H6
Cuckfield W Susx............32 B7

Cucklington Somset 27 H6
Cuckney Notts.............115 K7
Cuddesdon Oxon 57 L7
Cuddington Bucks.......... 58 C5
Cuddington Ches W....112 E7
Cuddington Heath
    Ches W.....................98 C3
Cudham Gt Lon..............32 D2
Cudliptown Devon.......... 10 D8
Cudnell Bmouth 15 K3
Cudworth Barns..........124 B8
Cudworth Somset.......... 13 J1
Cuffley Herts.................59 M7
Cuil Highld 191 J5
Culbokie Highld 212 F3
Culburnie Highld 212 D6
Culcabock Highld 213 G5
Culcharry Highld 213 K4
Culcheth Warrtn..........112 F3
Culdrain Abers.............215 L7
Culduie Highld 209 L6
Culford Suffk.................77 J1
Culgaith Cumb 138 E2
Culham Oxon 41 J2
Culkein Highld.............224 C2
Culkein Drumbeg
    Highld.....................224 D2
Culkerton Gloucs..........39 L2
Cullen Moray 215 L2
Cullercoats N Tyne.....159 J7
Cullerlie Abers...........206 E5
Cullicudden Highld.....213 G3
Cullingworth C Brad....123 G3
Cuillin Hills Highld 199 G2
Cullipool Ag & B..........181 L5
Cullivoe Shet...............235 d2
Culloden Highld...........213 H5
Cullompton Devon.........12 C2
Cullompton Services
    Devon.....................12 D2
Culm Davy Devon..........25 H7
Culmington Shrops........83 J6
Culmstock Devon..........25 H8
Culnacraig Highld........224 C7
Culnaightrie D & G......146 D5
Culnaknock Highld.......209 H2
Culrain Highld.............222 D3
Culross Fife.................176 D2
Culroy S Ayrs.............163 H6
Culsalmond Abers.......216 C7
Culscadden D & G.......145 K5
Culshabbin D & G........145 G5
Culswick Shet.............235 b6
Cultercullen Abers.....207 H1
Cults C Aber................207 G5
Culverstone Green
    Kent.........................45 M7
Culverthorpe Lincs.....103 G4
Culworth Nhants..........73 G5
Culzean Castle &
    Country Park
    S Ayrs....................163 G7
Cumbernauld N Lans...175 K4
Cumbernauld Village
    N Lans....................175 K3
Cumberworth Lincs.....119 G6
Cuminestown Abers.....216 F4
Cumledge Border.........179 G6
Cummersdale Cumb....148 D4
Cummertrees D & G....147 K2
Cummingston Moray....214 E1
Cumnock E Ayrs..........164 B5
Cumnor Oxon 57 J7
Cumrew Cumb 148 F5
Cumrue D & G 155 J5
Cumwhinton Cumb......148 D4
Cumwhitton Cumb......148 E4
Cundall N York...........132 F5
Cunninghamhead
    N Ayrs....................163 J2
Cunningsburgh Shet...235 c7
Cupar Fife..................186 F4
Cupar Muir Fife..........186 F5
Curbar Derbys............114 E6
Curbridge Hants..........17 G1
Curbridge Oxon............57 G6

Curdridge Hants 29 K8
Curdworth Warwks.......85 L5
Curland Somset............25 L7
Curridge W Berk..........41 J6
Currie C Edin..............177 G5
Curry Mallet Somset.....25 L6
Curry Rivel Somset.......26 B6
Curtisden Green Kent....33 J5
Curtisknowle Devon........7 H5
Cury Cnwll.....................3 H6
Cushnie Abers.............205 L3
Cutcloy D & G 145 J7
Cutcombe Somset 24 E4
Cuthill Highld 223 G4
Cutnall Green Worcs......70 F2
Cutsdean Gloucs...........56 C3
Cutthorpe Derbys.......115 G6
Cuxham Oxon 42 A2
Cuxton Medway............46 B6
Cuxwold Lincs.............117 K2
Cwm Denbgs................110 E6
Cwmafan Neath 36 B3
Cwmaman Rhondd........52 F7
Cwmbach Carmth..........50 B1
Cwmbach Powys............68 D6
Cwmbach Rhondd.........52 F7
Cwmbach Llechrhyd
    Powys......................68 B4
Cwmbran Torfn.............37 L2
Cwmcarn Caerph..........37 K2
Cwmcarvan Mons.........54 C6
Cwm-cou Cerdgn..........65 J6
Cwm Crawnon Powys....53 H4
Cwmdare Rhondd.........52 F7
Cwmdu Powys...............53 J4
Cwmdu Swans..............51 J6
Cwmduad Carmth.........65 L7
Cwmfelin Brdgnd..........36 D3
Cwmfelin Myr Td..........53 H7
Cwmfelin Boeth
    Carmth....................49 K4
Cwmfelinfach Caerph....37 J3
Cwmffrwd Carmth.........50 E3
Cwmgiedd Powys.........52 C5
Cwmgorse Carmth.........51 K4
Cwmgwili Carmth.........51 H4
Cwmhiraeth Carmth......65 K6
Cwm Llinau Powys........81 J2
Cwmllynfell Neath.........51 L3
Cwmmawr Carmth........51 G3
Cwmparc Rhondd.........36 E2
Cwmpengraig
    Carmth....................65 K6
Cwmtillery Blae G........53 K6
Cwm-twrch Isaf
    Powys......................52 B6
Cwm-twrch Uchaf
    Powys......................51 L4
Cwm-y-glo Gwynd 109 H8
Cwmystwyth Cerdgn....81 H8
Cwrt-newydd Cerdgn....66 C5
Cyfarthfa Castle
    Museum Myr Td.......53 G6
Cylibebyll Neath...........51 L5
Cymer Neath................36 D2
Cymmer Rhondd...........36 F3
Cynonville Neath..........36 C2
Cynwyd Denbgs............97 G4
Cynwyl Elfed Carmth....65 L8

D

Daccombe Devon............7 K3
Dacre Cumb.................138 C2
Dacre N York...............132 B7
Dacre Banks N York....132 B6
Daddry Shield Dur.....149 M7
Dadford Bucks..............73 J6
Dadlington Leics..........86 E4
Dagenham Gt Lon.........45 J3
Daglingworth Gloucs....55 M6
Dagnall Bucks..............59 G5
Dailly S Ayrs..............152 F2

Dairsie Fife.................187 G4
Dalabrog W Isls..........233 b8
Dalavich Ag & B..........182 D5
Dalbeattie D & G.........146 E3
Dalby IoM...................237 b5
Dalby N York..............133 K5
Dalcapon P & K...........194 F5
Dalchalm Highld.........226 F7
Dalchreichart Highld...201 L3
Dalchruin P & K..........184 F4
Dalcrue P & K.............185 L2
Dalditch Devon.............12 D5
Daldowie
    Crematorium
    C Glas....................175 J6
Dale Derbys................101 H5
Dale Pembks.................48 D6
Dalelia Highld.............190 E3
Dalgarven N Ayrs........163 H1
Dalgety Bay Fife..........177 G2
Dalgig E Ayrs..............164 B6
Dalginross P & K..........185 G3
Dalguise P & K...........194 F6
Dalhalvaig Highld.......230 C5
Dalham Suffk................77 G3
Daliburgh W Isls.........233 b8
Dalkeith Mdloth...........177 K5
Dallas Moray..............214 D4
Dallinghoo Suffk...........78 F4
Dallington E Susx.........20 D2
Dallington Nhants.........73 K3
Dalmally Ag & B..........183 H3
Dalmary Stirlg.............184 C7
Dalmellington E Ayrs...153 K2
Dalmeny C Edin...........176 F3
Dalmore Highld...........222 F7
Dalmuir W Duns...........174 E4
Dalnabreck Highld.......190 E3
Dalnacardoch P & K....194 B3
Dalnahaitnach Highld...203 K2
Dalnaspidal P & K.......193 K2
Dalnawillan Lodge
    Highld.....................230 F7
Daloist P & K..............194 C5
Dalqueich P & K..........186 A6
Dalquhairn S Ayrs.......153 G3
Dalreavoch Lodge
    Highld.....................226 D6
Dalry N Ayrs...............174 B7
Dalrymple E Ayrs........163 J6
Dalserf S Lans............175 L7
Dalsmeran Ag & B......161 G6
Dalston Cumb.............148 C5
Dalston Gt Lon.............45 G3
Dalswinton D & G.......155 G5
Dalton D & G 155 K7
Dalton N York............132 F4
Dalton N York............140 E5
Dalton Nthumb............158 E7
Dalton-in-Furness
    Cumb......................128 F5
Dalton-le-Dale Dur......151 K5
Dalton-on-Tees
    N York....................141 H5
Dalton Piercy Hartpl....141 L2
Dalveich Stirlg.............184 D3
Dalwhinnie Highld.......202 F7
Dalwood Devon.............13 G3
Damerham Hants..........28 C7
Damgate Norfk..............93 J2
Damnaglaur D & G......144 D7
Danbury Essex..............61 J6
Danby N York.............142 F5
Danby Wiske N York....141 H7
Dandaleith Moray........215 G5
Danderhall Mdloth.......177 J4
Danebridge Ches E......113 L7
Dane End Herts............60 B4
Danehill E Susx............32 D7
Dane Hill S Leic...........87 H3
Dane Street Kent..........34 E4
Danshillock Abers.......216 D3
Danskine E Loth.........178 C5
Darenth Kent................45 K5
Daresbury Halton........112 E5
Darfield Barns............115 H1

Dargate Kent................34 E3
Darite Cnwll....................5 K3
Darlaston Wsall............85 H4
Darlaston Green Wsall...85 H4
Darley N York.............132 C7
Darley Abbey C Derb....101 G5
Darley Bridge Derbys...100 E1
Darley Dale Derbys.....114 F8
Darley Green Solhll......85 L8
Darleyhall Herts............59 J4
Darley Head N York.....132 B7
Darlingscott Warwks.....72 B6
Darlington Darltn.........141 H4
Darlington
    Crematorium
    Darltn....................141 G4
Darlton Notts..............116 C6
Darnick Border............167 H3
Darowen Powys............81 H3
Darra Abers................216 E5
Darracott Devon.............9 G2
Darracott Devon...........23 G4
Darras Hall Nthumb.....158 E7
Darrington Wakefd......124 D6
Darsham Suffk..............79 J1
Darshill Somset............26 E3
Dartford Kent...............45 K5
Dartington Devon...........7 H4
Dartmoor National
    Park Devon..............11 G8
Dartmouth Devon...........7 K5
Darton Barns..............123 L7
Darvel E Ayrs..............164 B2
Darwen Bl w D............121 K6
Datchet W & M.............43 G5
Datchworth Herts.........59 L4
Daubhill Bolton...........121 K8
Daugh of Kinnermony
    Moray....................214 F6
Dauntsey Wilts.............39 M4
Dava Highld................214 C6
Davenham Ches W......112 F7
Daventry Nhants...........73 H3
Davidson's Mains
    C Edin....................177 G4
Davidstow Cnwll.............8 F7
Davington D & G.........155 M2
Davington Hill Kent......34 D3
Daviot Abers...............216 E8
Daviot Highld.............213 H6
Daviot House Highld....213 H6
Davoch of Grange
    Moray....................215 K4
Dawesgreen Surrey......31 K3
Dawley Wrekin.............84 C2
Dawlish Devon..............12 B6
Dawlish Warren
    Devon.....................12 C6
Daybrook Notts...........101 L4
Daylesford Gloucs.........56 E3
Deal Kent.....................35 K4
Dean Cumb.................136 E3
Dean Devon....................7 H3
Dean Devon..................23 L2
Dean Hants..................29 K7
Dean Oxon...................57 G4
Dean Somset................26 F3
Dean Bottom Kent.........45 L6
Deanburnhaugh
    Border....................166 F6
Deancombe Devon..........7 G3
Dean Court Oxon..........57 J6
Deane Bolton..............121 K8
Deane Hants.................29 K2
Deanhead Kirk............122 F7
Deanland Dorset...........27 M7
Dean Prior Devon...........7 H3
Deanraw Nthumb........149 L3
Deans W Loth.............176 D5
Deanscales Cumb.......136 F2
Deanshanger Nhants....73 L6
Deanshaugh Moray.....215 H4
Deanston Stirlg...........184 F6
Dearham Cumb...........147 J7
Debach Suffk................78 F4
Debden Essex...............45 H2

Debden Essex 60 E2
Debenham Suffk 78 E2
Deblin's Green Worcs 70 E5
Dechmont W Loth 176 E4
Dechmont Road
W Loth 176 D4
Deddington Oxon 57 J2
Dedham Essex 62 C2
Dedworth W & M 42 F5
Deene Nhants 88 D5
Deenethorpe Nhants 88 D5
Deepcar Sheff 114 F3
Deeping Gate C Pete 89 G2
Deeping St James
Lincs 89 H2
Deeping St Nicholas
Lincs 89 J1
Deerhurst Gloucs 55 K3
Defford Worcs 71 G5
Defynnog Powys 52 E3
Deganwy Conwy 109 L5
Degnish Ag & B 182 A5
Deighton C York 124 F2
Deighton N York 141 J6
Deiniolen Gwynd 109 H8
Delabole Cnwll 8 E7
Delamere Ches W 112 E7
Delfrigs Abers 207 H2
Delliefure Highld 214 D7
Dell Quay W Susx 18 A5
Delnabo Moray 204 E3
Delnashaugh Inn
Moray 214 E7
Delny Highld 223 G6
Delph Oldham 122 E8
Delves Dur 150 E5
Dembleby Lincs 103 H5
Denaby Donc 115 J2
Denbigh Denbgs 110 E7
Denbrae Fife 186 F4
Denbury Devon 7 J3
Denby Derbys 101 H4
Denby Dale Kirk 123 J8
Denchworth Oxon 41 G3
Dendron Cumb 128 F5
Denfield P & K 185 K4
Denford Nhants 88 E7
Dengie Essex 62 B7
Denham Bucks 43 H3
Denham Suffk 77 H3
Denham Suffk 92 E8
Denham Green Bucks 43 H3
Denhead Abers 217 J4
Denhead Fife 187 G5
Denhead of Gray
C Dund 186 F2
Denholm Border 167 J5
Denholme C Brad 123 G4
Denmead Hants 30 A8
Denmore C Aber 207 H3
Dennington Suffk 79 G2
Denny Falk 175 L2
Dennyloanhead Falk ... 175 L3
Den of Lindores Fife 186 D4
Denshaw Oldham 122 E7
Denside Abers 206 F6
Densole Kent 35 G6
Denston Suffk 77 H4
Denstone Staffs 100 C4
Denstroude Kent 34 E3
Dent Cumb 130 D3
Denton Cambs 89 G6
Denton Darltn 140 F4
Denton E Susx 19 L5
Denton Kent 35 G5
Denton Lincs 102 E6
Denton N York 123 H2
Denton Nhants 74 B3
Denton Norfk 93 G5
Denton Tamesd 113 L3
Denver Norfk 90 E3
Denwick Nthumb 169 J6
Deopham Norfk 92 C4
Deopham Green
Norfk 92 C4
Depden Suffk 77 H3

Deptford Gt Lon 45 G4
Deptford Wilts 28 A4
Derby C Derb 101 G5
Derby Devon 23 J5
Derbyhaven IoM 237 b7
Derculich P & K 194 D5
Dereham Norfk 92 B2
Deri Caerph 53 H7
Derringstone Kent 35 G5
Derrington Staffs 99 K7
Derry Hill Wilts 39 L6
Derrythorpe N Linc 125 J8
Dersingham Norfk 105 H6
Dervaig Ag & B 189 K6
Derwen Denbgs 97 G3
Derwenlas Powys 80 F4
Derwent Valley Mills
Derbys 100 F2
Derwent Water
Cumb 137 J3
Desborough Nhants 88 B6
Desford Leics 86 F3
Deskford Moray 215 L3
Detling Kent 33 K2
Devauden Mons 54 C7
Devil's Bridge Cerdgn ... 81 G7
Devizes Wilts 40 A7
Devonport C Plym 6 C5
Devonside Clacks 185 J7
Devoran Cnwll 4 C7
Devoran & Perran
Cnwll 3 K4
Dewarton Mdloth 177 K5
Dewlish Dorset 14 E3
Dewsbury Kirk 123 K6
Dewsbury Moor
Crematorium Kirk ... 123 J6
Deytheur Powys 97 K8
Dial Post W Susx 18 F2
Dibden Hants 16 E2
Dibden Purlieu Hants ... 16 E2
Dickleburgh Norfk 92 E6
Didbrook Gloucs 56 B2
Didcot Oxon 41 K3
Diddington Cambs 75 H2
Diddlebury Shrops 83 K6
Didling W Susx 18 A3
Didmarton Gloucs 39 J3
Didsbury Manch 113 J3
Digby Lincs 103 H2
Digg Highld 218 C7
Diggle Oldham 122 F8
Digmoor Lancs 112 C1
Dihewyd Cerdgn 66 C4
Dilham Norfk 107 G7
Dilhorne Staffs 99 L4
Dill Hall Lancs 121 L4
Dillington Cambs 75 G2
Dilston Nthumb 150 B3
Dilton Wilts 27 K2
Dilton Marsh Wilts 27 J2
Dilwyn Herefs 69 H4
Dinas Gwynd 94 E5
Dinas Pembks 64 E6
Dinas-Mawddwy
Gwynd 81 J1
Dinas Powys V Glam 37 J6
Dinder Somset 26 E3
Dinedor Herefs 69 K6
Dingestow Mons 54 C6
Dingle Lpool 111 K4
Dingley Nhants 87 L6
Dingwall Highld 212 E3
Dinnet Abers 205 K5
Dinnington N u Ty 158 F7
Dinnington Rothm 115 K4
Dinnington Somset 26 B8
Dinorwic Gwynd 95 K1
Dinton Bucks 58 C5
Dinton Wilts 28 A5
Dinwoodie D & G 155 K4
Dinworthy Devon 9 J2
Dipford Somset 25 J6
Dippen Ag & B 161 K2
Dippen N Ayrs 162 D5
Dippertown Devon 10 C7

Dipple Moray 215 H3
Dipple S Ayrs 152 E2
Diptford Devon 7 G4
Dipton Dur 150 E4
Dirleton E Loth 178 B2
Dirt Pot Nthumb 149 L5
Diseworth Leics 101 J7
Dishforth N York 132 F5
Disley Ches E 113 L5
Diss Norfk 92 D7
Distington Cumb 136 D3
Distington Hall
Crematorium
Cumb 136 E3
Ditchampton Wilts 28 C5
Ditcheat Somset 26 F4
Ditchingham Norfk 93 G5
Ditchling E Susx 19 J3
Ditherington Shrops 83 K2
Ditteridge Wilts 39 J6
Dittisham Devon 7 K5
Ditton Kent 33 J2
Ditton Green Cambs 76 F3
Ditton Priors Shrops 83 L5
Dixton Mons 54 D5
Dobcross Oldham 113 M1
Dobwalls Cnwll 5 K3
Doccombe Devon 11 H7
Dochgarroch Highld 212 F6
Docking Norfk 105 J5
Docklow Herefs 69 L3
Dockray Cumb 137 L3
Doddinghurst Essex 60 F7
Doddington Cambs 90 B5
Doddington Kent 34 C4
Doddington Lincs 116 E7
Doddington Nthumb ... 168 E3
Doddington Shrops 84 B7
Doddiscombsleigh
Devon 11 K7
Dodd's Green Ches E 98 E4
Dodford Nhants 73 H3
Dodford Worcs 85 G8
Dodington S Glos 39 H4
Dodington Somset 25 J4
Dodleston Ches W 98 A1
Dodside E Rens 174 F7
Dodworth Barns 114 F1
Dogdyke Lincs 103 K2
Dogmersfield Hants 30 C2
Dolanog Powys 82 B2
Dolbenmaen Gwynd 95 J4
Dolfach Powys 81 K3
Dolfor Powys 82 C6
Dolgarrog Conwy 109 L7
Dolgellau Gwynd 96 B8
Doll Highld 226 F7
Dollar Clacks 185 K7
Dollarfield Clacks 185 K7
Dolphin Flints 111 H6
Dolphinholme Lancs 129 L8
Dolphinton S Lans 176 F8
Dolton Devon 10 E3
Dolwen Conwy 110 B6
Dolwyddelan Conwy 96 B3
Domgay Powys 97 L8
Doncaster Donc 115 L2
Doncaster North
Services Donc 125 G7
Donhead St Andrew
Wilts 27 K6
Donhead St Mary
Wilts 27 K6
Donibristle Fife 177 G2
Doniford Somset 25 G3
Donington Lincs 103 K5
Donington on Bain
Lincs 118 C5
Donington Park
Services Leics 101 J7
Donisthorpe Leics 86 C2
Donnington Gloucs 56 D3
Donnington Shrops 83 L2
Donnington W Berk 41 J6
Donnington W Susx 18 B5

Donnington Wrekin 84 C2
Donnington Wood
Wrekin 84 C2
Donyatt Somset 25 M8
Doonfoot S Ayrs 163 H5
Dorback Lodge
Highld 204 D3
Dorchester Dorset 14 D4
Dorchester Oxon 41 L2
Dordon Warwks 86 C4
Dore Sheff 114 F5
Dores Highld 212 F7
Dorking Surrey 31 K2
Dormans Land Surrey ... 32 D5
Dormington Herefs 69 L6
Dormston Worcs 71 H3
Dorney Bucks 42 F5
Dornie Highld 200 D1
Dornoch Highld 223 H4
Dornock D & G 147 M2
Dorrery Highld 230 F5
Dorridge Solhll 85 L8
Dorrington Lincs 103 H2
Dorrington Shrops 83 J3
Dorrington Shrops 99 G4
Dorsington Warwks 71 K4
Dorstone Herefs 69 G6
Dorton Bucks 58 B5
Douglas IoM 237 d6
Douglas S Lans 165 G4
Douglas and Angus
C Dund 187 G2
Douglas Borough
Crematorium IoM ... 237 d5
Douglas Pier Ag & B 183 H7
Douglastown Angus 196 C6
Douglas Water S Lans .. 165 G3
Douglas West S Lans ... 164 F3
Doulting Somset 26 F3
Dounby Ork 234 b5
Doune Highld 221 L2
Doune Stirlg 184 F6
Dounepark S Ayrs 152 E3
Dounie Highld 222 D4
Dousland Devon 6 D3
Dove Holes Derbys 114 B6
Dovenby Cumb 147 J7
Dover Kent 35 J6
Dover Castle Kent 35 J6
Dovercourt Essex 62 F2
Doverdale Worcs 70 F2
Doveridge Derbys 100 C5
Doversgreen Surrey 31 L2
Dowally P & K 194 F6
Dowdeswell Gloucs 55 M4
Dowlais Myr Td 53 G6
Dowland Devon 10 E3
Dowlish Wake
Somset 26 A8
Down Ampney
Gloucs 40 C2
Downderry Cnwll 5 L5
Downe Gt Lon 45 H7
Downend Gloucs 39 J2
Downend S Glos 38 F5
Downfield C Dund 186 F2
Downgate Cnwll 6 A2
Downham Essex 46 B2
Downham Gt Lon 45 H5
Downham Lancs 122 B2
Downham Market
Norfk 90 E3
Down Hatherley
Gloucs 55 K4
Downhead Somset 26 E6
Downhead Somset 27 G3
Downhill P & K 186 A2
Downholme N York 140 E7
Downies Abers 207 H6
Downley Bucks 42 D2
Down St Mary Devon 11 H4
Downs Crematorium
Br & H 19 J4
Downside Surrey 43 J8
Down Thomas Devon 6 D6
Downton Wilts 28 D6

Dowsby Lincs................103 J6
Doynton S Glos............39 G5
Draethen Caerph...........37 K3
Draffan S Lans.............164 F1
Drakeholes Notts..........116 B4
Drakemyre N Ayrs.........174 B7
Drakes Broughton
  Worcs 71 G5
Draughton N York.........131 K8
Draughton Nhants.........87 L7
Drax N York.................125 G5
Draycote Warwks..........72 F1
Draycott Derbys...........101 H6
Draycott Gloucs...........71 L7
Draycott Somset...........26 C2
Draycott in the Clay
  Staffs.......................100 D6
Draycott in the
  Moors Staffs.............99 M4
Drayton C Port.............17 J2
Drayton Leics...............88 B5
Drayton Norfk..............92 E2
Drayton Oxon...............41 J2
Drayton Oxon...............72 E6
Drayton Somset............26 B6
Drayton Worcs.............85 G7
Drayton Bassett
  Staffs.......................85 L4
Drayton Beauchamp
  Bucks......................58 E5
Drayton Manor Park
  Staffs.......................85 L4
Drayton Parslow
  Bucks......................58 D3
Drayton St Leonard
  Oxon.......................41 L2
Dreen Hill Pembks........48 F5
Drefach Carmth...........51 G3
Drefach Carmth...........65 K6
Drefach Cerdgn...........66 C5
Dreghorn N Ayrs...........163 J2
Drellingore Kent...........35 H6
Drem E Loth.................178 B3
Drewsteignton
  Devon.....................11 H6
Driffield E R Yk.............134 F7
Driffield Gloucs............56 B7
Drift Cnwll...................2 D5
Drigg Cumb.................136 E7
Drighlington Leeds........123 J5
Drimnin Highld.............190 B5
Drimpton Dorset...........13 K2
Drimsallie Highld..........191 J1
Dringhouses C York.......124 E2
Drinkstone Suffk..........77 L3
Drinkstone Green
  Suffk.......................77 L3
Drointon Staffs.............100 A6
Droitwich Worcs...........70 F2
Dron P & K..................186 B4
Dronfield Derbys...........115 G5
Drongan E Ayrs.............163 K5
Dronley Angus.............186 E1
Droop Dorset................14 E2
Droxford Hants.............29 L7
Droylsden Tamesd.........113 K2
Druid Denbgs...............97 G4
Druidston Pembks.........48 E4
Druimarbin Highld.........191 L3
Druimavuic Ag & B........191 K7
Druimdrishaig Ag & B....172 C4
Druimindarroch
  Highld.....................199 L7
Drum Ag & B................172 F3
Drum P & K..................185 L7
Drumalbin S Lans..........165 H2
Drumbeg Highld...........224 D3
Drumblade Abers..........216 B6
Drumbuie Highld...........210 B7
Drumburgh Cumb.........148 A3
Drumburn D & G...........146 F4
Drumchapel C Glas........174 F4
Drumchastle P & K........193 L5
Drumclog S Lans..........164 C2
Drumeldrie Fife............187 G6

Drumelzier Border.........165 M3
Drumfearn Highld.........199 L3
Drumfrennie Abers........206 D5
Drumgley Angus...........196 C6
Drumguish Highld.........203 J5
Drumin Moray..............214 E7
Drumjohn D & G...........153 L3
Drumlamford S Ayrs......153 G6
Drumlasie Abers...........206 C4
Drumleaning Cumb.......148 A5
Drumlemble Ag & B.......161 H5
Drumlithie Abers...........197 J1
Drummoddie D & G.......144 D7
Drummore D & G...........144 D7
Drummuir Moray...........215 J5
Drumnadrochit
  Highld.....................212 D7
Drumnagorrach
  Moray.....................215 L4
Drumpark D & G...........154 F6
Drumrunie Lodge
  Highld.....................224 E7
Drumshang S Ayrs.........163 G6
Drumuie Highld............209 G5
Drumuillie Highld..........204 B2
Drumvaich Stirlg...........184 E6
Drunzie P & K...............186 B5
Drybeck Cumb..............138 F4
Drybridge Moray...........215 K2
Drybridge N Ayrs...........163 J3
Drybrook Gloucs...........54 F4
Dryburgh Border...........167 J3
Dry Doddington Lincs 102 D3
Dry Drayton Cambs.......75 L3
Drymen Stirlg...............174 E2
Drymuir Abers..............217 G5
Drynoch Highld............208 F7
Dubford Abers..............216 F2
Duchally Highld............225 J5
Ducklington Oxon.........57 G6
Duddenhoe End
  Essex......................76 C7
Duddingston C Edin......177 J4
Duddington Nhants.......88 E4
Duddlestone Somset......25 K7
Duddo Nthumb.............168 D2
Duddon Ches W............112 D8
Dudleston Shrops.........97 M5
Dudleston Heath
  Shrops....................98 A5
Dudley Dudley..............85 G5
Dudley N Tyne..............159 G7
Dudley Port Sandw........85 G5
Dudsbury Dorset...........15 K3
Duffield Derbys............101 G4
Duffryn Neath..............36 C2
Dufftown Moray............215 H6
Duffus Moray...............214 E2
Dufton Cumb...............139 G3
Duggleby N York...........134 D6
Duirinish Highld............210 B7
Duisdalemore Highld......199 L3
Duisky Highld...............191 K2
Duke Street Suffk..........78 C6
Dukinfield Tamesd........113 L2
Dukinfield
  Crematorium
  Tamesd...................113 L2
Dulcote Somset............26 E3
Dulford Devon..............12 D2
Dull P & K....................194 C6
Dullatur N Lans.............175 K3
Dullingham Cambs........76 F3
Dulnain Bridge Highld....204 B1
Duloe Bed...................75 H3
Duloe Cnwll.................5 K4
Dulverton Somset.........24 E5
Dulwich Gt Lon.............45 G5
Dumbarton W Duns.......174 D4
Dumbleton Gloucs........71 H7
Dumfries D & G.............155 G6
Dumgoyne Stirlg...........174 F2
Dummer Hants..............29 L3
Dumpton Kent..............35 K2
Dun Angus...................197 G4
Dunalastair P & K..........193 L5

Dunan Ag & B..............173 K4
Dunan Highld...............209 J8
Dunan P & K................193 G5
Dunaverty Ag & B.........161 H7
Dunball Somset............25 L3
Dunbar E Loth..............178 E3
Dunbeath Highld..........227 L3
Dunbeg Ag & B.............182 C2
Dunblane Stirlg.............185 G6
Dunbog Fife.................186 E4
Duncanston Highld........212 F3
Duncanstone Abers.......216 B8
Dunchideock Devon......11 K7
Dunchurch Warwks.......72 F1
Duncow D & G..............155 G5
Duncrievie P & K...........186 B5
Duncton W Susx...........18 C3
Dundee C Dund.............186 F2
Dundee Airport
  C Dund....................186 F2
Dundee
  Crematorium
  C Dund....................186 F2
Dundon Somset............26 C5
Dundonald S Ayrs.........163 J3
Dundonnell Highld........220 E4
Dundraw Cumb.............147 L5
Dundreggan Highld.......201 L3
Dundrennan D & G........146 D5
Dundry N Som..............38 E6
Dunecht Abers.............206 E4
Dunfermline Fife...........176 F2
Dunfermline
  Crematorium Fife....176 F2
Dunfield Gloucs............40 C2
Dungavel S Lans...........164 D3
Dungeness Kent...........21 L3
Dunham Notts...............116 D6
Dunham-on-the-Hill
  Ches W....................112 C6
Dunhampton Worcs.......70 F2
Dunham Town Traffd......113 H4
Dunham
  Woodhouses
  Traffd......................113 G4
Dunholme Lincs............117 G5
Dunino Fife..................187 J5
Dunipace Falk..............175 L2
Dunkeld P & K..............195 G7
Dunkerton BaNES.........39 G8
Dunkeswell Devon.........12 E2
Dunkeswick N York........123 L2
Dunkirk Kent................34 E3
Dunkirk S Glos..............39 H4
Dunk's Green Kent.........33 G3
Dunlappie Angus...........196 F3
Dunley Worcs................70 E2
Dunlop E Ayrs...............174 D8
Dunmaglass Highld........202 F2
Dunmore Falk...............176 B1
Dunnet Highld..............231 J2
Dunnichen Angus..........196 E6
Dunning P & K..............185 L4
Dunnington C York........133 K8
Dunnington E R Yk........126 E1
Dunnington Warwks......71 J4
Dunoon Ag & B............173 K3
Dunphail Moray............214 C5
Dunragit D & G.............144 E4
Duns Border.................179 G7
Dunsby Lincs................103 J6
Dunscore D & G............154 F5
Dunscroft Donc............124 F8
Dunsdale R & Cl............142 D4
Dunsden Green Oxon.....42 C5
Dunsdon Devon............9 J3
Dunsfold Surrey...........31 G4
Dunsford Devon............11 J6
Dunshalt Fife................186 D5
Dunshillock Abers.........217 J5
Dunsill Notts................101 J1
Dunsley N York.............143 H5
Dunsley Staffs..............84 F6
Dunsmore Bucks...........58 E6
Dunsop Bridge Lancs.....121 K1
Dunstable C Beds..........59 G4

Dunstall Staffs..............100 D7
Dunstan Nthumb..........169 K5
Dunster Somset............24 F3
Duns Tew Oxon.............57 J3
Dunston Gatesd............151 G3
Dunston Lincs...............117 H8
Dunston Norfk..............92 F3
Dunston Staffs..............99 L8
Dunstone Devon...........6 E5
Dunstone Devon...........7 G2
Dunsville Donc..............124 F8
Dunswell E R Yk............126 D4
Dunsyre S Lans.............176 E8
Dunterton Devon...........6 B1
Duntisbourne
  Abbots Gloucs..........55 L6
Duntisbourne Rouse
  Gloucs.....................55 M6
Duntish Dorset..............14 D2
Duntocher W Duns........174 E4
Dunton Bucks...............58 D3
Dunton C Beds.............75 J5
Dunton Norfk................105 L6
Dunton Bassett Leics.....87 G5
Dunton Green Kent........32 F2
Duntulm Highld............218 C6
Dunure S Ayrs..............163 G6
Dunvant Swans............51 H6
Dunvegan Highld..........208 D5
Dunwich Suffk..............79 K1
Durgan Cnwll...............3 K5
Durham Dur.................151 G6
Durham Cathedral
  Dur.........................151 G6
Durham
  Crematorium Dur.....151 G6
Durham Services Dur....151 H7
Durham Tees Valley
  Airport S on T...........141 J5
Durisdeer D & G............154 F2
Durisdeermill D & G.......154 F2
Durleigh Somset...........25 L4
Durley Hants................29 K7
Durley Wilts..................40 D7
Durley Street Hants.......29 K7
Durlock Kent.................35 H3
Durlock Kent.................35 J2
Durness Highld.............228 F3
Durno Abers.................216 D8
Duror Highld.................191 K5
Durran Ag & B..............182 D5
Durrington W Susx........18 F5
Durrington Wilts...........28 D3
Durris Abers.................206 E6
Dursley Gloucs.............39 H2
Dursley Cross
  Gloucs.....................55 G4
Durston Somset............25 L4
Durweston Dorset.........15 G2
Duston Nhants..............73 K3
Duthil Highld................203 L1
Dutton Ches W..............112 E5
Duxford Cambs............76 C5
Duxford Oxon...............57 G7
Duxford IWM Cambs.....76 C5
Dwygyfylchi Conwy.......109 L6
Dwyran IoA..................108 F7
Dyce C Aber.................207 G3
Dyffryn Ardudwy
  Gwynd.....................95 K7
Dyffryn Cellwen
  Neath......................52 D6
Dyke Lincs...................103 J7
Dyke Moray..................214 B3
Dykehead Angus...........195 K5
Dykehead Angus...........196 C5
Dykehead N Lans..........176 B6
Dykehead Stirlg............184 D7
Dykelands Abers...........197 H3
Dykends Angus.............195 K5
Dykeside Abers.............216 D5
Dymchurch Kent...........34 E8
Dymock Gloucs.............55 G2
Dyrham S Glos..............39 H5
Dysart Fife...................186 E8
Dyserth Denbgs............110 E5

E

Eagland Hill Lancs 120 F2
Eagle Lincs.....................116 E7
Eaglescliffe S on T.........141 K4
Eaglesfield D & G........136 F2
Eaglesfield D & G...........155 M7
Eaglesham E Rens..........175 G7
Eagley Bolton 121 L7
Eakring Notts 102 A1
Ealand N Linc 125 J7
Ealing Gt Lon...................44 D4
Eals Nthumb 149 H4
Eamont Bridge Cumb..138 D2
Earby Lancs 122 D2
Eardington Shrops..........84 C5
Eardisland Herefs...........69 H3
Eardisley Herefs 68 F5
Eardiston Shrops............98 A7
Eardiston Worcs.............70 C2
Earith Cambs 89 L8
Earlestown St Hel 112 E3
Earley Wokham...............42 C6
Earlham Norfk.................92 E2
**Earlham
  Crematorium**
  Norfk.............................92 E2
Earlish Highld................208 F3
Earls Barton Nhants 74 C2
Earls Colne Essex...........61 K3
Earls Common Worcs 71 G3
Earl's Croome Worcs 70 F6
Earlsdon Covtry..............86 D7
Earlsferry Fife 187 H7
Earlsfield Gt Lon.............44 E5
Earlsford Abers 216 F7
Earlsheaton Kirk...........123 K6
Earl Shilton Leics............86 F4
Earl Soham Suffk............78 F2
Earl Sterndale Derbys...114 C7
Earlston Border 167 J2
Earlston E Ayrs..............163 K3
Earlswood Surrey............32 B4
Earlswood Warwks.........85 K8
Earnley W Susx 17 M3
Earsdon N Tyne 159 H7
Earsham Norfk................93 G5
Eartham W Susx 18 C4
Easby N York 142 C5
Easdale Ag & B..............181 L4
Easebourne W Susx 30 E6
Easenhall Warwks..........86 F7
Eashing Surrey................30 F3
Easington Bucks.............58 B6
Easington Dur 151 K6
Easington E R Yk............127 J6
Easington R & Cl............142 F4
Easington Colliery
  Dur 151 K6
Easington Lane
  Sundld 151 J5
Easingwold N York.........133 H5
Eassie and Nevay
  Angus 196 B7
East Aberthaw
  V Glam 37 G6
East Allington Devon......7 H6
East Anstey Devon.........24 D6
East Ashey IoW...............17 G6
East Ashling W Susx......17 M2
East Ayton N York 134 F3
East Barkwith Lincs......117 K5
East Barming Kent..........33 J3
East Barnby N York.......143 G5
East Barnet Gt Lon.........44 F2
East Barns E Loth 178 F3
East Barsham Norfk......105 L5
East Beckham Norfk.....106 E4
East Bedfont Gt Lon.......43 H5
East Bergholt Suffk........78 C7
East Bilney Norfk..........106 A8
East Blatchington
  E Susx 20 A5
East Boldon S Tyne 151 J3
East Boldre Hants 16 D3

Eastbourne Darltn 141 H4
Eastbourne E Susx 20 C5
**Eastbourne
  Crematorium**
  E Susx 20 D5
East Bradenham
  Norfk.............................91 L2
East Brent Somset.........25 M2
Eastbridge Suffk.............79 J2
East Bridgford Notts....102 B4
East Buckland Devon 23 L5
East Budleigh Devon......12 D5
Eastburn C Brad 122 F2
Eastbury Herts 43 J2
Eastbury W Berk.............41 G5
East Butterwick
  N Linc...........................116 D1
Eastby N York 131 J8
East Calder W Loth.......176 E5
East Carleton Norfk.......92 E3
East Carlton Leeds 123 J2
East Carlton Nhants......88 B5
**East Chaldon
  (Chaldon Herring)**
  Dorset 14 E5
East Challow Oxon.........41 G3
East Charleton Devon 7 H7
East Chelborough
  Dorset 14 A2
East Chiltington
  E Susx 19 K3
East Chinnock
  Somset 26 C8
East Chisenbury Wilts 28 C2
Eastchurch Kent 47 G5
East Clandon Surrey 31 H2
East Claydon Bucks........58 C3
East Coker Somset.........26 D8
Eastcombe Gloucs 55 K6
East Compton
  Somset 26 E3
East Cornworthy
  Devon 7 J5
Eastcote Gt Lon 43 J3
Eastcote Nhants 73 K4
Eastcote Solhll 85 L7
Eastcott Wilts 28 A1
East Cottingwith
  E R Yk 125 G3
Eastcourt Wilts 40 E7
East Cowes IoW..............16 F4
East Cowick E R Yk.......125 G6
East Cowton N York......141 H6
East Cranmore
  Somset 27 G3
East Dean E Susx 20 B6
East Dean Gloucs...........54 F4
East Dean Hants 28 F6
East Dean W Susx..........18 B3
**East Devon
  Crematorium**
  Devon 12 D4
East Drayton Notts.......116 C6
East Dulwich Gt Lon 45 G5
East Dundry N Som 38 E7
East Ella C KuH.............126 C5
Eastend Essex.................46 F2
East End Hants 16 D3
East End Hants 41 H7
East End Kent 33 L6
East End Oxon 57 H5
East End Somset 26 F3
Easter Balmoral
  Abers 205 G6
Easter Compton
  S Glos 38 E4
Easter Dalziel Highld 213 H4
Eastergate W Susx 18 C5
Easterhouse C Glas 175 J5
Easter Howgate
  Mdloth 177 H5
Easter Kinkell Highld....212 E4
Easter Moniack
  Highld 212 E5
Eastern Green Covtry...86 C7
Easter Ord Abers..........206 F4

Easter Pitkierie Fife......187 J6
Easter Skeld Shet.........235 c6
Easter Softlaw
  Border 168 A3
Easterton Wilts 28 A1
East Everleigh Wilts.......28 D2
East Farleigh Kent 33 J3
East Farndon Nhants.....87 K6
East Ferry Lincs 116 D2
Eastfield N Lans............176 B5
Eastfield N York............135 G3
East Fortune E Loth......178 C3
East Garston W Berk.....41 G5
Eastgate Dur 150 B7
Eastgate Norfk..............106 D7
East Goscote Leics.........87 J2
East Grafton Wilts..........40 E7
East Grinstead Wilts 28 E5
East Grinstead
  W Susx 32 D5
East Guldeford E Susx ...21 J2
East Haddon Nhants.......73 J2
East Hagbourne
  Oxon 41 K3
East Halton N Linc........126 E6
East Ham Gt Lon............45 H4
**Easthampstead Park
  Crematorium**
  Br For 42 D6
East Hampton Herefs.....69 H2
East Hanney Oxon 41 H2
East Hanningfield
  Essex.............................61 J7
East Hardwick
  Wakefd 124 C6
East Harling Norfk.........92 B6
East Harlsey N York.....141 K7
East Harnham Wilts........28 C5
East Harptree BaNES 26 E1
East Hartburn S on T....141 K4
East Harting W Susx 30 D7
East Hatch Wilts 27 L5
East Hatley Cambs.........75 K4
East Hauxwell N York...132 B2
East Haven Angus.........187 J1
East Heckington
  Lincs 103 K4
East Hedleyhope Dur...150 E6
East Helmsdale
  Highld 227 H5
East Hendred Oxon........41 J3
East Heslerton N York..134 E4
East Hoathly E Susx.......20 B3
East Holme Dorset 15 G5
Easthope Shrops............83 L4
Easthorpe Essex.............61 L4
East Horrington
  Somset 26 E3
East Horsley Surrey........31 H2
East Howe Bmouth........15 K4
East Huntspill Somset ...25 M3
East Ilsley W Berk..........41 J4
Eastington Devon...........11 H3
Eastington Gloucs..........55 H6
Eastington Gloucs..........56 C5
East Keal Lincs 118 E8
East Kennett Wilts..........40 C6
East Keswick Leeds 124 B2
East Kilbride S Lans......175 H7
East Kirkby Lincs..........118 D8
East Knighton Dorset....14 F5
East Knoyle Wilts 27 K5
East Lambrook
  Somset 26 B7
**East Lancashire
  Crematorium**
  Bury 122 B8
Eastlands D & G...........154 E7
East Langdon Kent.........35 J5
East Langton Leics.........87 K5
East Lavant W Susx 18 B4
East Lavington
  W Susx 18 C3
East Layton N York.......140 E5
Eastleach Martin
  Gloucs 56 D6

Eastleach Turville
  Gloucs 56 D6
East Leake Notts 101 K7
Eastleigh Devon 23 H5
Eastleigh Hants 29 J7
East Lexham Norfk......105 K8
Eastling Kent 34 C4
East Linton E Loth........178 D3
East Lockinge Oxon.......41 H3
**East London
  Crematorium**
  Gt Lon 45 H4
East Lound N Linc 116 C2
East Lulworth Dorset......15 G6
East Lutton N York.......134 E5
East Lydford Somset......26 E5
East Malling Kent 33 J2
East Marden W Susx 30 D8
East Markham Notts....116 C6
East Martin Hants 28 B7
East Marton N York.....122 D1
East Meon Hants 30 B6
East Mersea Essex.........62 C5
East Midlands Airport
  Leics 101 J7
East Molesey Surrey......43 J6
East Morden Dorset........15 G4
East Morton C Brad 123 G3
East Morton D & G......154 F3
East Ness N York..........133 L4
Eastney C Port...............17 J3
Eastnor Herefs 70 D6
East Norton Leics...........87 L4
Eastoft N Linc 125 J7
East Ogwell Devon..........7 J2
Easton Cambs.................75 G1
Easton Devon 11 G6
Easton Dorset 14 D7
Easton Hants 29 K5
Easton Lincs 102 F6
Easton Norfk...................92 D2
Easton Somset 26 D3
Easton Suffk....................79 G3
Easton Wilts 39 K6
Easton Grey Wilts 39 K3
Easton-in-Gordano
  N Som 38 D5
Easton Maudit
  Nhants...........................74 C3
Easton-on-the-Hill
  Nhants...........................88 E3
Easton Royal Wilts.........40 D7
East Orchard Dorset......27 J7
East Peckham Kent........33 H4
East Pennar Pembks 49 G6
East Pennard Somset.....26 E4
East Perry Cambs...........75 G2
East Portlemouth
  Devon 7 H7
East Prawle Devon 7 H8
East Preston W Susx......18 E5
East Putford Devon 9 K2
East Quantoxhead
  Somset 25 H3
East Rainton Sundld 151 H5
East Ravendale
  NE Lin 118 C2
East Raynham Norfk....105 L7
Eastrea Cambs................89 K4
**East Riding
  Crematorium**
  E R Yk 134 F5
Eastriggs D & G...........147 M2
East Rigton Leeds 124 B2
Eastrington E R Yk.......125 J4
Eastrop Swindn..............40 D2
East Rounton N York....141 K6
East Rudham Norfk......105 K6
East Runton Norfk.......106 E4
East Ruston Norfk.......107 H6
Eastry Kent 35 J4
East Saltoun E Loth 178 B5
East Sheen Gt Lon.........44 D5
East Shefford W Berk....41 H5
East Stockwith Lincs ...116 C3
East Stoke Dorset 15 G5

East Stoke Notts......102 C3
East Stour Dorset.....27 J6
East Stourmouth
  Kent...............35 H3
East Stowford Devon.....23 K6
East Stratton Hants.....29 K4
East Studdal Kent......35 J5
East Taphouse Cnwll...5 J3
East-the-Water
  Devon...............23 G6
East Thirston
  Nthumb...............158 F3
East Tilbury Thurr.....46 B5
East Tisted Hants......30 B5
East Torrington Lincs...117 J5
East Tuddenham
  Norfk................92 C2
East Tytherley Hants...28 F5
East Tytherton Wilts...39 L5
East Village Devon.....11 J4
Eastville Bristl.......38 E5
Eastville Lincs........104 C2
East Walton Norfk......91 G1
East Week Devon........10 F6
Eastwell Leics.........102 C6
East Wellow Hants......28 F7
East Wemyss Fife.......186 E7
East Whitburn W Loth...176 C5
Eastwick Herts.........60 C5
East Wickham Gt Lon....45 J5
East Williamston
  Pembks...............49 J6
East Winch Norfk.......91 G1
East Winterslow Wilts..28 E5
East Wittering W Susx..17 L3
East Witton N York.....131 L3
Eastwood Notts.........101 J3
Eastwood Sthend........46 D3
East Woodburn
  Nthumb...............158 A5
East Woodhay Hants.....41 H7
East Worldham Hants....30 C4
East Wretham Norfk.....91 K5
East Youlstone Devon...9 H2
Eathorpe Warwks........72 E2
Eaton Ches E...........113 K7
Eaton Ches W...........112 E8
Eaton Leics............102 D6
Eaton Norfk............92 E3
Eaton Notts............116 B6
Eaton Oxon.............57 H7
Eaton Shrops...........83 K5
Eaton Bray C Beds......58 F4
Eaton Constantine
  Shrops...............83 L3
Eaton Green C Beds.....58 F4
Eaton Hastings Oxon....56 E7
Eaton Mascott
  Shrops...............83 K3
Eaton Socon Cambs......75 H3
Eaton upon Tern
  Shrops...............98 F7
Ebberston N York.......134 D3
Ebbesborne Wake
  Wilts................27 M6
Ebbw Vale Blae G.......53 J6
Ebchester Dur..........150 D4
Ebford Devon...........12 C5
Ebley Gloucs...........55 J6
Ebnal Ches W...........98 C3
Ebrington Gloucs.......71 L6
Ecchinswell Hants......41 J8
Ecclaw Border..........178 F5
Ecclefechan D & G......155 L7
Eccles Border..........168 A2
Eccles Kent............46 B7
Eccles Salfd...........113 H2
Ecclesall Sheff........114 F5
Eccles Crematorium
  Salfd................113 H3
Ecclesfield Sheff......115 G3
Eccleshall Staffs......99 J6
Eccleshill C Brad......123 H4
Ecclesmachan W Loth....176 E4
Eccles Road Norfk......92 B5
Eccleston Ches W.......112 B8

Eccleston Lancs........121 G6
Eccleston St Hel.......112 C3
Echt Abers.............206 E4
Eckford Border.........167 L4
Eckington Derbys.......115 H5
Eckington Worcs........71 G6
Ecton Nhants...........74 B2
Edale Derbys...........114 C4
Eday Ork...............234 d4
Eday Airport Ork.......234 d4
Edburton W Susx........19 H4
Edderton Highld........222 F4
Eddleston Border.......177 H8
Eddlewood S Lans.......175 J7
Edenbridge Kent........32 D4
Edenfield Lancs........122 B6
Edenhall Cumb..........138 E2
Edenham Lincs..........103 H7
Eden Park Gt Lon.......45 G6
Eden Project Cnwll.....5 G5
Edensor Derbys.........114 E7
Edentaggart Ag & B.....183 K8
Edenthorpe Donc........115 L1
Edern Gwynd............94 E5
Edgbaston Birm.........85 J6
Edgcott Bucks..........58 B4
Edgcott Somset.........24 D4
Edge Gloucs............55 J6
Edgefield Norfk........106 C5
Edgefield Green
  Norfk................106 D5
Edgerton Kirk..........123 H6
Edgeworth Gloucs.......55 L6
Edgmond Wrekin.........99 G8
Edgton Shrops..........83 H6
Edgware Gt Lon.........44 D2
Edgworth Bl w D........121 L6
Edinbane Highld........208 E4
Edinburgh C Edin.......177 H4
Edinburgh Airport
  C Edin...............176 F4
Edinburgh Castle
  C Edin...............177 H4
Edinburgh Old & New
  Town C Edin..........177 H4
Edinburgh Royal
  Botanic Gardens
  C Edin...............177 H4
Edinburgh Zoo C Edin...177 G4
Edingale Staffs........86 B2
Edingham D & G.........146 E3
Edingley Notts.........102 A2
Edingthorpe Norfk......107 G6
Edingthorpe Green
  Norfk................107 G6
Edington Border........179 J7
Edington Nthumb........158 E5
Edington Somset........26 B4
Edington Wilts.........27 L2
Edington Burtle
  Somset...............26 B3
Edingworth Somset......26 A2
Edithmead Somset.......25 L2
Edith Weston Rutlnd....88 D3
Edlesborough Bucks.....58 F4
Edlingham Nthumb.......169 G7
Edlington Lincs........118 C7
Edmondsham Dorset......15 K1
Edmondsley Dur.........151 G5
Edmondthorpe Leics.....102 E8
Edmonton Gt Lon........45 G2
Edmundbyers Dur........150 C5
Ednam Border...........167 L2
Edradynate P & K.......194 D6
Edrom Border...........179 H7
Edstaston Shrops.......98 D6
Edstone Warwks.........71 L3
Edwalton Notts.........101 L5
Edwinstowe Notts.......115 L7
Edworth C Beds.........75 J6
Edwyn Ralph Herefs.....70 B3
Edzell Angus...........196 F3
Edzell Woods Abers.....197 G3
Efail-fach Neath.......36 B2
Efail Isaf Rhondd......37 G4
Efailnewydd Gwynd......94 F5

Efailwen Carmth........49 K3
Efenechtyd Denbgs......97 H2
Effgill D & G..........156 B4
Effingham Surrey.......31 J2
Efford Crematorium
  C Plym...............6 D4
Egerton Bolton.........121 K7
Egerton Kent...........34 B5
Eggborough N York......124 E5
Eggbuckland C Plym.....6 D4
Eggesford Devon........11 G3
Eggington C Beds.......58 F3
Egginton Derbys........100 E6
Egglescliffe S on T....141 K4
Eggleston Dur..........140 C3
Egham Surrey...........43 G6
Egleton Rutlnd.........88 C3
Eglingham Nthumb.......169 G5
Egloshayle Cnwll.......4 F2
Egloskerry Cnwll.......9 H7
Eglwysbach Conwy.......109 M7
Eglwys Cross Wrexhm....98 C4
Eglwyswrw Pembks.......65 G6
Egmanton Notts.........116 B7
Egremont Cumb..........136 D5
Egremont Wirral........111 K3
Egton N York...........143 G6
Egton Bridge N York....143 G6
Egypt Bucks............42 F3
Eigg Highld............199 G7
Eight Ash Green
  Essex................61 M3
Eilanreach Highld......200 C2
Eilean Donan Castle
  Highld...............200 D1
Elan Valley Powys......67 J2
Elan Village Powys.....67 K2
Elberton S Glos........38 E3
Elburton C Plym........6 D5
Elcombe Swindn.........40 C4
Eldersfield Worcs......55 H2
Elderslie Rens.........174 E5
Eldon Dur..............141 G2
Elfhill Abers..........206 F7
Elford Staffs..........85 L2
Elgin Moray............214 F2
Elgol Highld...........199 H3
Elie Fife..............187 H7
Ellm IoA...............108 D4
Eling Hants............29 G8
Elkesley Notts.........116 B6
Elkstone Gloucs........55 L5
Ella Abers.............216 C3
Ellacombe Torbay.......7 L3
Elland Calder..........123 G6
Ellary Ag & B..........172 C3
Ellastone Staffs.......100 C4
Ellel Lancs............129 K7
Ellemford Border.......178 F6
Ellenabeich Ag & B.....181 L4
Ellenhall Staffs.......99 J7
Ellen's Green Surrey...31 H4
Ellerbeck N York.......141 K7
Ellerby N York.........143 G4
Ellerdine Heath
  Wrekin...............98 F7
Elleric Ag & B.........191 K6
Ellerker E R Yk........125 L5
Ellerton E R Yk........125 G3
Ellerton N York........141 G7
Ellesborough Bucks.....58 D6
Ellesmere Shrops.......98 B5
Ellesmere Port
  Ches W...............111 L6
Ellingham Norfk........93 H5
Ellingham Nthumb.......169 H4
Ellingstring N York....132 B3
Ellington Cambs........75 H1
Ellington Nthumb.......159 G4
Elliots Green Somset...27 J3
Ellisfield Hants.......29 M3
Ellishader Highld......209 H2
Ellistown Leics........86 E2
Ellon Abers............217 H7
Ellonby Cumb...........148 D7

Elloughton E R Yk......126 B5
Ellwood Gloucs.........54 E6
Elm Cambs..............90 C3
Elmbridge Worcs........70 F2
Elmdon Essex...........76 C6
Elmdon Solhll..........85 L6
Elmers End Gt Lon......45 G6
Elmer's Green Lancs....112 D1
Elmesthorpe Leics......86 F4
Elmhurst Staffs........85 K2
Elmley Castle Worcs....71 H6
Elmley Lovett Worcs....70 F1
Elmore Gloucs..........55 H5
Elmore Back Gloucs.....55 H5
Elm Park Gt Lon........45 K3
Elmsett Suffk..........78 C5
Elmstead Market
  Essex................62 C3
Elmsted Kent...........34 F5
Elmstone Kent..........35 H3
Elmstone Hardwicke
  Gloucs...............55 K3
Elmswell E R Yk........134 F7
Elmswell Suffk.........78 B2
Elmton Derbys..........115 J6
Elphin Highld..........224 F6
Elphinstone E Loth.....177 K4
Elrick Abers...........206 F4
Elrig D & G............145 G5
Elrington Nthumb.......149 L3
Elsdon Nthumb..........158 B4
Elsenham Essex.........60 E3
Elsfield Oxon..........57 K6
Elsham N Linc..........126 C7
Elsing Norfk...........92 C1
Elslack N York.........122 D2
Elson Hants............17 H3
Elsrickle S Lans.......165 K2
Elstead Surrey.........30 E3
Elsted W Susx..........30 D7
Elsthorpe Lincs........103 H7
Elston Notts...........102 C3
Elstow Bed.............74 F5
Elstree Herts..........44 D2
Elstronwick E R Yk.....126 F4
Elswick Lancs..........120 F3
Elswick N u Ty.........151 G3
Elsworth Cambs.........75 K2
Elterwater Cumb........137 K6
Eltham Gt Lon..........45 H5
Eltham Crematorium
  Gt Lon...............45 J5
Eltisley Cambs.........75 J3
Elton Cambs............88 F5
Elton Ches W...........112 C6
Elton Derbys...........100 E1
Elton Herefs...........69 J1
Elton Notts............102 C5
Elton S on T...........141 J4
Eltringham Nthumb......150 D3
Elvanfoot S Lans.......165 J6
Elvaston Derbys........101 H6
Elveden Suffk..........91 J7
Elvetham Heath
  Hants................30 D1
Elvingston E Loth.....178 A4
Elvington C York.......125 G2
Elvington Kent.........35 H5
Elwick Hartpl..........141 K2
Elworth Ches E.........99 H1
Elworthy Somset........25 G4
Ely Cambs..............90 D7
Ely Cardif.............37 H5
Emberton M Keyn........74 C5
Embleton Cumb..........137 G2
Embleton Nthumb........169 J5
Embo Highld............223 H3
Emborough Somset.......26 E2
Embo Street Highld.....223 H3
Embsay N York..........131 J8
Emery Down Hants.......16 C2
Emley Kirk.............123 K7
Emmington Oxon.........58 C7
Emneth Norfk...........90 C3
Emneth Hungate
  Norfk................90 D3

Empingham Rutlnd 88 D2
Empshott Hants 30 C5
Emstrey
Crematorium
Shrops 83 K2
Emsworth Hants 17 K2
Enborne W Berk............41 H7
Enborne Row W Berk......41 H7
Enderby Leics 87 G4
Endmoor Cumb............129 L3
Endon Staffs................99 L2
Endon Bank Staffs........99 L2
Enfield Gt Lon 60 B7
Enfield Crematorium
Gt Lon......................60 B7
Enfield Lock Gt Lon......60 B7
Enfield Wash Gt Lon......60 B7
Enford Wilts 28 C2
Engine Common
S Glos......................39 G4
Englefield W Berk..........41 L6
Englefield Green
Surrey 43 G6
English Bicknor
Gloucs......................54 E5
Englishcombe BaNES ..39 G7
English Frankton
Shrops......................98 C6
Enham-Alamein
Hants 29 G2
Enmore Somset............25 K4
Enmore Green Dorset....27 J6
Ennerdale Bridge
Cumb 136 E4
Enochdhu P & K 195 G4
Ensay Ag & B............189 J6
Ensbury Bmouth..........15 K3
Ensdon Shrops............83 H1
Enstone Oxon..............57 G3
Enterkinfoot D & G......154 E2
Enville Staffs 84 E6
Eolaigearraidh W Isls....233 b9
Epney Gloucs 55 H5
Epperstone Notts........101 M3
Epping Essex................60 D7
Epping Green Essex......60 C6
Epping Upland Essex....60 C6
Eppleby N York............140 F5
Epsom Surrey..............44 E7
Epwell Oxon................72 D6
Epworth N Linc............116 C2
Erbistock Wrexhm 97 M4
Erdington Birm............85 K5
Eridge Green E Susx......32 F6
Erines Ag & B 172 E4
Eriska Ag & B............191 H7
Eriskay W Isls 233 c9
Eriswell Suffk..............91 G7
Erith Gt Lon 45 K4
Erlestoke Wilts............27 L2
Ermington Devon 6 F5
Erpingham Norfk..........106 E6
Errogie Highld............202 E2
Errol P & K 186 D3
Erskine Rens 174 E4
Ervie D & G 144 B2
Erwarton Suffk............78 F7
Erwood Powys..............68 C6
Eryholme N York..........141 H5
Eryrys Denbgs 97 J2
Escomb Dur 140 F2
Escrick N York 124 F2
Esgairgeiliog Powys......81 G3
Esh Dur 150 F6
Esher Surrey................43 J7
Eshott Nthumb............158 F3
Esh Winning Dur........150 F6
Eskadale Highld..........212 C6
Eskbank Mdloth..........177 J5
Eskdale Green Cumb....136 E4
Eskdalemuir D & G......156 A3
Esprick Lancs 120 E3
Essendine Rutlnd..........88 F2
Essendon Herts 59 L6
Essich Highld............213 G6
Essington Staffs 85 G3

Esslemont Abers 217 H7
Eston R & Cl..............142 C4
Etal Nthumb..............168 D2
Etchilhampton Wilts......40 B7
Etchingham E Susx......33 J7
Etchinghill Kent............34 F6
Etchinghill Staffs........100 B8
Eton W & M 42 F5
Eton Wick W & M........42 F5
Etruria C Stke..............99 K3
Etteridge Highld..........203 G6
Ettersgill Dur 139 K2
Ettiley Heath Ches E......99 G1
Ettingshall Wolves........85 G4
Ettington Warwks 72 C5
Etton C Pete................89 G3
Etton E R Yk..............126 B2
Ettrick Border 166 D6
Ettrickbridge Border....166 F4
Ettrickhill Border........166 C6
Etwall Derbys............100 F6
Euston Suffk................91 K7
Euxton Lancs 121 H6
Evanton Highld............212 F2
Evedon Lincs............103 H3
Evelix Highld............223 G4
Evenjobb Powys............68 F3
Evenley Nhants 73 H7
Evenlode Gloucs............56 E3
Evenwood Dur............140 E3
Evercreech Somset........26 F4
Everingham E R Yk 125 J3
Everleigh Wilts............28 D2
Eversholt C Beds..........59 G2
Evershot Dorset............14 B2
Eversley Hants............42 C7
Eversley Cross Hants....42 C7
Everthorpe E R Yk......125 L4
Everton C Beds............75 H4
Everton Hants............16 C4
Everton Lpool............111 K3
Everton Notts............116 B4
Evertown D & G..........156 C6
Evesbatch Herefs 70 C5
Evesham Worcs............71 J5
Evington C Leic............87 J3
Ewden Village Sheff 114 F3
Ewell Surrey................44 E7
Ewell Minnis Kent 35 H6
Ewelme Oxon 41 M3
Ewen Gloucs................40 A2
Ewenny V Glam............36 D5
Ewerby Lincs............103 J3
Ewhurst Surrey............31 H4
Ewhurst Green E Susx....20 F2
Ewhurst Green Surrey....31 H4
Ewloe Flints..............111 J7
Eworthy Devon............10 C6
Ewshot Hants..............30 D2
Ewyas Harold Herefs....54 B3
Exbourne Devon..........10 E4
Exbury Hants..............16 E3
Exebridge Somset........24 E6
Exelby N York............132 D3
Exeter Devon..............11 L6
Exeter Airport Devon....12 C4
Exeter & Devon
Crematorium
Devon....................12 B4
Exeter Services
Devon....................12 C4
Exford Somset............24 D4
Exfordsgreen Shrops....83 J3
Exhall Warwks............71 K4
Exhall Warwks............86 D6
Exlade Street Oxon......42 A4
Exminster Devon..........12 B5
Exmoor National
Park 24 D4
Exmouth Devon............12 C6
Exning Suffk................76 E2
Exton Devon..............12 C5
Exton Hants 29 L7
Exton Rutlnd..............88 D2
Exton Somset..............24 E5
Exwick Devon..............11 K6

Eyam Derbys..............114 E6
Eydon Nhants 73 G4
Eye C Pete..................89 J3
Eye Herefs..................69 J2
Eye Suffk....................92 D8
Eyemouth Border 179 K5
Eyeworth C Beds..........75 J5
Eyhorne Street Kent......33 L3
Eyke Suffk..................79 G4
Eynesbury Cambs........75 H3
Eynsford Kent..............45 K6
Eynsham Oxon............57 H6
Eype Dorset................13 L4
Eyre Highld..............208 F4
Eythorne Kent..............35 H5
Eyton Herefs................69 J3
Eyton Shrops..............98 C7
Eyton on Severn
Shrops....................83 L3
Eyton upon the
Weald Moors
Wrekin 84 B1

F

Faccombe Hants 41 H8
Faceby N York............141 L6
Fachwen Powys............82 B1
Faddiley Ches E............98 E3
Fadmoor N York..........133 K2
Faifley W Duns............174 F4
Failand N Som..............38 D6
Failford S Ayrs............163 L4
Failsworth Oldham 113 K2
Fairbourne Gwynd........80 E2
Fairburn N York..........124 D5
Fairfield Derbys..........114 B6
Fairfield Worcs............85 G7
Fairford Gloucs............56 D7
Fairgirth D & G..........146 F4
Fair Green Norfk..........90 F1
Fairhaven Lancs 120 D5
Fair Isle Shet............235 e7
Fairlands Surrey..........30 F2
Fairlie N Ayrs............173 L7
Fairlight E Susx............21 G4
Fairmile Devon 12 E3
Fairmile Surrey............43 J7
Fairmilee Border..........167 G3
Fair Oak Hants............29 J7
Fairoak Staffs..............99 H6
Fair Oak Green Hants....42 A7
Fairseat Kent..............45 L7
Fairstead Essex............61 J5
Fairstead Norfk..........105 G8
Fairwarp E Susx............32 E7
Fairwater Cardif..........37 H5
Fairy Cross Devon........22 F6
Fakenham Norfk........105 L6
Fakenham Magna
Suffk......................91 K7
Fala Mdloth..............177 L6
Fala Dam Mdloth........177 L6
Faldingworth Lincs......117 H5
Faldouet Jersey..........236 e7
Falfield S Glos............39 G2
Falkenham Suffk..........79 G6
Falkirk Falk................176 B3
Falkirk Crematorium
Falk........................176 B3
Falkirk Wheel Falk 176 A3
Falkland Fife..............186 D6
Fallburn S Lans..........165 J2
Fallin Stirlg................185 H8
Falladon Nthumb........169 J5
Fallowfield Manch........113 J3
Fallowfield Nthumb......150 B2
Falls of Blarghour
Ag & B 182 E5
Falmer E Susx............19 K4
Falmouth Cnwll............3 K5
Falnash Border..........156 D2
Falsgrave N York........134 F2

Falstone Nthumb........157 J5
Fanagmore Highld......228 B5
Fancott C Beds............59 G3
Fanellan Highld..........212 D5
Fangdale Beck N York..142 C7
Fangfoss E R Yk........134 B8
Fanmore Ag & B........189 K7
Fannich Lodge Highld..211 K2
Fans Border................167 J2
Far Bletchley M Keyn....74 C7
Farcet Cambs..............89 H5
Far Cotton Nhants........73 L3
Fareham Hants............17 H2
Far End Cumb............137 J7
Farewell Staffs............85 J2
Faringdon Oxon............40 F2
Farington Lancs..........121 H5
Farlam Cumb............148 F3
Farleigh N Som............38 D6
Farleigh Surrey............32 C2
Farleigh Hungerford
Somset....................39 J8
Farleigh Wallop
Hants......................29 L3
Farlesthorpe Lincs......119 G6
Farleton Cumb..........129 L4
Farleton Lancs..........130 B6
Farley Staffs..............100 B4
Farley Wilts................28 E5
Farley Green Surrey......31 H3
Farley Hill Wokham......42 C7
Farleys End Gloucs......55 H5
Farlington C Port..........17 J2
Farlington N York........133 J6
Farlow Shrops............84 B7
Farmborough BaNES....38 F7
Farmcote Gloucs..........56 B3
Farmers Carmth..........66 E5
Farmington Gloucs......56 C5
Farmoor Oxon............57 J6
Far Moor Wigan..........112 D2
Farmtown Moray........215 L4
Farnborough Gt Lon....45 H7
Farnborough Hants......30 E2
Farnborough W Berk....41 H4
Farnborough Warwks....72 E5
Farnborough Park
Hants......................30 E1
Farnborough Street
Hants......................30 E1
Farncombe Surrey........31 G3
Farndish Bed..............74 D2
Farndon Ches W..........98 B2
Farndon Notts..........102 C3
Farne Islands
Nthumb..................169 J2
Farnell Angus............197 G5
Farnham Dorset............27 L7
Farnham Essex............60 D3
Farnham N York..........132 E7
Farnham Suffk............79 H3
Farnham Surrey............30 D3
Farnham Common
Bucks....................42 F4
Farnham Royal Bucks....42 F4
Farningham Kent..........45 K6
Farnley Leeds............123 K4
Farnley N York..........123 J2
Farnley Tyas Kirk........123 H7
Farnsfield Notts........101 M2
Farnworth Bolton........113 G1
Farnworth Halton........112 D4
Far Oakridge Gloucs....55 L7
Farr Highld................203 K5
Farr Highld................213 G7
Farr Highld................229 L3
Farraline Highld..........202 E2
Farringdon Devon........12 C4
Farrington Gurney
BaNES....................26 F1
Far Sawrey Cumb........137 K7
Farthinghoe Nhants....73 G6
Farthingstone
Nhants....................73 H4
Fartown Kirk..............123 H6
Fartown Leeds............123 J4

Fasnacloich Ag & B..........191 K6
Fasnakyle Highld.............211 L8
Fassfern Highld 191 K2
Fatfield Sundld...............151 H4
Fauldhouse W Loth........176 C6
Faulkbourne Essex 61 L3
Faulkland Somset............27 H1
Fauls Shrops...................98 E6
Faversham Kent..............34 D3
Fawdington N York 132 F5
Fawdon N u Ty 151 G2
Fawkham Green Kent....45 L6
Fawler Oxon 57 G4
Fawley Bucks 42 C3
Fawley Hants..................16 F2
Fawley W Berk 41 H4
Faxfleet E R Yk 125 K5
Faygate W Susx 31 K5
Fazakerley Lpool............111 K3
Fazeley Staffs 85 L3
Fearby N York 132 B4
Fearn Highld 223 H6
Fearnan P & K 194 B7
Fearnbeg Highld 210 B3
Fearnmore Highld.........209 L3
Fearnoch Ag & B 172 F3
Featherstone Staffs.........85 G3
Featherstone Wakefd ...124 C6
Feckenham Worcs..........71 H3
Feering Essex 61 L4
Feetham N York 140 C7
Felbridge Surrey.............32 C5
Felbrigg Norfk 106 E5
Felcourt Surrey...............32 C5
Felindre Carmth 51 G2
Felindre Carmth 65 K6
Felindre Powys................82 D7
Felindre Swans 51 J5
Felindre Farchog
    Pembks 64 F6
Felingwm Isaf
    Carmth 51 G2
Felingwm Uchaf
    Carmth 51 G1
Felixkirk N York 133 G3
Felixstowe Suffk 79 G7
Felling Gatesd 151 G3
Felmersham Bed 74 E3
Felmingham Norfk 106 F6
Felpham W Susx 18 C5
Felsham Suffk 77 L3
Felsted Essex 61 G4
Feltham Gt Lon 43 J3
Felthamhill Surrey 43 H6
Felthorpe Norfk 106 E8
Felton Herefs 69 L5
Felton N Som 38 D7
Felton Nthumb...............158 F3
Felton Butler Shrops 98 B8
Feltwell Norfk.................91 G5
Fence Lancs...................122 C3
Fence Rothm 115 H4
Fencott Oxon...................57 L5
Fendike Corner Lincs.....104 D1
Fen Ditton Cambs..........76 C3
Fen Drayton Cambs.......75 L2
Feniscowles Bl w D.......121 J5
Feniton Devon.................12 E3
Fenland
    Crematorium
    Cambs 90 B5
Fenn Green Shrops........84 D6
Fenn Street Medway.....46 D5
Fenny Bentley Derbys..100 D3
Fenny Bridges Devon....12 E3
Fenny Compton
    Warwks 72 E4
Fenny Drayton Leics 86 D4
Fenstanton Cambs 75 K2
Fen Street Norfk 92 B4
Fenton C Stke 99 K4
Fenton Cambs 89 K7
Fenton Cumb.................148 E4
Fenton Lincs 102 E3
Fenton Lincs 116 D6
Fenton Notts 116 C5

Fenton Nthumb 168 E3
Fenton Barns E Loth.....178 B3
Fenwick Donc................124 F7
Fenwick E Ayrs 163 L2
Fenwick Nthumb 158 D7
Fenwick Nthumb 169 G2
Feock Cnwll 4 C7
Feolin Ferry Ag & B.....171 H4
Fergushill N Ayrs 163 J2
Feriniquarrie Highld 208 B4
Fermain Bay Guern......236 d3
Fern Angus 196 D4
Ferndale Rhondd 36 F2
Ferndown Dorset............15 K3
Ferness Highld 214 B5
Fernham Oxon 40 F3
Fernhill Heath Worcs....70 F3
Fernhurst W Susx...........30 E5
Fernie Fife 186 E4
Ferniegair S Lans...........175 K7
Fernilea Highld 208 F7
Fernilee Derbys 114 A5
Fernwood Notts 102 D3
Ferrensby N York 132 E7
Ferrindonald Highld 199 K4
Ferring W Susx................18 F5
Ferrybridge Services
    Wakefd 124 D6
Ferryden Angus 197 H5
Ferryhill Dur 141 H2
Ferry Point Highld 223 G4
Ferryside Carmth 50 D4
Ferrytown Highld 223 G4
Fersfield Norfk 92 C6
Fersit Highld 192 F2
Feshiebridge Highld.....203 K4
Fetcham Surrey...............31 J1
Fetlar Shet 235 e2
Fetterangus Abers........217 J4
Fettercairn Abers..........197 G2
Fewston N York 132 B8
Ffairfach Carmth 51 J2
Ffair Rhos Cerdgn 87 G2
Ffestiniog Gwynd 96 A4
Ffestiniog Railway
    Gwynd 95 L4
Fforest Carmth 51 H5
Fforest Fach Swans 51 J6
Ffostrasol Cerdgn 65 L5
Ffrith Flints 97 L2
Ffynnongroyw Flints ...111 G5
Fiag Lodge Highld 225 K3
Fickleshole Surrey..........32 C2
Fiddington Somset 25 K4
Fiddleford Dorset 27 J8
Fiddlers Green Cnwll 4 C5
Field Staffs...................100 A5
Field Dalling Norfk.......106 B5
Field Head Leics 86 F2
Fifehead Magdalen
    Dorset 27 H6
Fifehead Neville
    Dorset 14 E1
Fifehead St Quintin
    Dorset 14 E1
Fife Keith Moray...........215 J4
Fifield Oxon....................56 E4
Fifield W & M..................42 E5
Figheldean Wilts 28 D3
Filby Norfk......................93 K2
Filey N York 135 H4
Filgrave M Keyn..............74 C5
Filkins Oxon....................56 E6
Filleigh Devon.................23 K5
Fillingham Lincs 116 F4
Fillongley Warwks..........86 C6
Filton S Glos 38 E5
Fimber E R Yk...............134 D7
Finavon Angus 196 D5
Fincham Norfk 91 G3
Finchampstead
    Wokham 42 D7
Fincharn Ag & B 182 C6
Finchdean Hants 30 C8
Finchingfield Essex........61 G2
Finchley Gt Lon 44 F2

Findern Derbys..............100 F6
Findhorn Moray.............214 C2
Findhorn Bridge
    Highld 213 J8
Findochty Moray...........215 K2
Findo Gask P & K 185 L4
Findon Abers 207 H6
Findon W Susx.................18 F4
Findon Mains Highld....212 F3
Findrack House Abers..206 B4
Finedon Nhants 74 D1
Fingask P & K................186 C4
Fingest Bucks 42 C3
Finghall N York 132 B2
Fingland D & G 164 E6
Finglesham Kent 35 J4
Fingringhoe Essex 62 B4
Finlarig Stirlg 184 C1
Finmere Oxon.................57 M2
Finnart P & K 193 H5
Finningham Suffk 78 C1
Finningley Donc............116 A2
Finsbay W Isls 232 d5
Finstall Worcs..................71 H1
Finsthwaite Cumb.........129 H2
Finstock Oxon.................57 G5
Finstown Ork.................234 b6
Fintry Abers 216 E4
Fintry Stirlg 175 H2
Finzean Abers 206 B6
Fionnphort Ag & B.......180 D3
Fionnsbhagh W Isls......232 d5
Firbank Cumb................130 C2
Firbeck Rothm...............115 K4
Firby N York 132 D3
Firby N York 134 B6
Firle E Susx 19 M4
Firsby Lincs 118 F8
Fir Tree Dur 150 E7
Fishbourne IoW..............17 G4
Fishbourne W Susx........18 A5
Fishburn Dur 141 J2
Fishcross Clacks............185 J7
Fisherford Abers............216 C7
Fisherrow E Loth..........177 K4
Fisher's Pond Hants.......29 J7
Fisherton Highld 213 H4
Fisherton S Ayrs 163 H6
Fisherton de la Mere
    Wilts 27 M4
Fishguard Pembks 64 D6
Fishlake Donc................125 G7
Fishnish Pier Ag & B ...190 D7
Fishponds Bristl..............38 F5
Fishtoft Lincs 104 B4
Fishtoft Drove Lincs 104 A3
Fiskavaig Highld 208 E7
Fiskerton Lincs 117 H6
Fiskerton Notts 102 C3
Fittleton Wilts 28 D2
Fittleworth W Susx 18 D2
Fitz Shrops 98 C8
Fitzhead Somset 25 H5
Fitzwilliam Wakefd 124 C7
Five Ash Down E Susx..19 M2
Five Ashes E Susx...........32 F7
Fivehead Somset 26 A6
Fivelanes Cnwll................9 G8
Five Oak Green Kent.....33 H4
Five Oaks Jersey..........236 d7
Five Oaks W Susx...........31 H5
Five Roads Carmth 50 F4
Flackwell Heath
    Bucks 42 E3
Fladbury Worcs...............71 H5
Fladdabister Shet 235 c6
Flagg Derbys 114 D7
Flamborough E R Yk....135 K5
Flamborough Head
    E R Yk 135 K5
Flamingo Land
    Theme Park
    N York 134 B4
Flamstead Herts.............59 H5
Flansham W Susx...........18 C5
Flanshaw Wakefd.........123 L6

Flasby N York 131 H7
Flash Staffs....................114 A7
Flashader Highld 208 E4
Flaunden Herts................59 G7
Flawborough Notts.......102 C4
Flawith N York 133 G6
Flax Bourton N Som......38 D6
Flaxby N York 132 F7
Flaxley Gloucs.................55 G5
Flaxpool Somset 25 H4
Flaxton N York 133 K6
Fleckney Leics 87 J5
Flecknoe Warwks 73 G2
Fledborough Notts........116 D6
Fleet Dorset 14 C6
Fleet Hants 30 D2
Fleet Lincs 104 C7
Fleet Hargate Lincs.......104 C7
Fleet Services Hants 30 D1
Fleetwood Lancs...........120 D2
Flemingston V Glam......36 F6
Flemington S Lans.........175 H6
Flempton Suffk 77 J1
Fletchertown Cumb.......147 L6
Fletching E Susx 19 L2
Flexbury Cnwll..................9 G4
Flexford Surrey................30 F2
Flimby Cumb.................147 H7
Flimwell E Susx...............33 J6
Flint Flints 111 H6
Flintham Notts...............102 C4
Flinton E R Yk...............126 F4
Flitcham Norfk 105 H6
Flitton C Beds..................74 F7
Flitwick C Beds................74 F7
Flixborough N Linc 125 K7
Flixborough Stather
    N Linc 125 K7
Flixton N York 135 G4
Flixton Suffk 93 G6
Flixton Traffd 113 H3
Flockton Kirk 123 J7
Flockton Green Kirk......123 K7
Flodigarry Highld 218 C8
Flookburgh Cumb 129 H4
Flordon Norfk 92 E4
Flore Nhants 73 J3
Flowton Suffk 78 C5
Flushing Cnwll 3 L4
Fluxton Devon 12 E4
Flyford Flavell Worcs....71 H4
Fobbing Thurr 46 B4
Fochabers Moray 215 H3
Fochriw Caerph..............53 H6
Fockerby N Linc............125 K6
Foddington Somset........26 E5
Foel Powys 81 L2
Foggathorpe E R Yk.....125 H3
Fogo Border...................179 G8
Fogwatt Moray..............214 F3
Foindle Highld 228 B5
Folda Angus 195 J4
Fole Staffs.....................100 B5
Foleshill Covtry 86 D6
Folke Dorset....................26 F8
Folkestone Kent..............35 H7
Folkingham Lincs..........103 H5
Folkington E Susx 20 B5
Folksworth Cambs 89 G5
Folkton N York 135 G4
Folla Rule Abers 216 D7
Follifoot N York 132 E8
Folly Gate Devon 10 E5
Fonthill Bishop Wilts.....27 L5
Fonthill Gifford Wilts.....27 L5
Fontmell Magna
    Dorset 27 K7
Fontmell Parva
    Dorset 27 J8
Fontwell W Susx.............18 C4
Foolow Derbys 114 D6
Forbestown Abers........205 H3
Forcett N York 140 F5
Ford Ag & B 182 C6
Ford Bucks 58 C6
Ford Derbys 115 H5

Ford Devon 22 F6
Ford Gloucs 56 C3
Ford Nthumb 168 E2
Ford Somset 25 H5
Ford Staffs 100 B2
Ford W Susx 18 D5
Ford Wilts 39 J5
Fordcombe Kent 32 F5
Fordell Fife 177 G2
Forden Powys 82 E4
Ford End Essex 61 G5
Forder Green Devon 7 H3
Fordham Cambs 76 H1
Fordham Essex 61 L3
Fordham Norfk 90 E4
Fordingbridge Hants 28 D8
Fordon E R Yk 135 G4
Fordoun Abers 197 J2
Fordstreet Essex 61 L3
Ford Street Somset 25 J7
Fordwich Kent 35 G3
Fordyce Abers 216 B2
Forebridge Staffs 99 L7
Forest Guern 236 C4
Forest Chapel Ches E 113 L6
Forest Gate Gt Lon 45 H3
Forest Green Surrey 31 J3
Forest Hall N Tyne 151 G2
Forest Hill Gt Lon 45 G5
Forest Hill Oxon 57 L6
Forest Lane Head
  N York........................132 E7
Forest Mill Clacks.........185 K8
Forest of Dean
  Gloucs.........................54 F5
Forest Park
  Crematorium
  Gt Lon..........................45 J2
Forest Row E Susx 32 D6
Forestside W Susx 30 C8
Forfar Angus 196 D6
Forgandenny P & K 186 A4
Forge Hammer Torfn 37 L2
Forgie Moray 215 J4
Forgieside Moray 215 J4
Forgue Abers 216 B5
Formby Sefton 111 J1
Forncett End Norfk 92 D5
Forncett St Mary
  Norfk...........................92 E5
Forncett St Peter
  Norfk...........................92 E5
Fornham All Saints
  Suffk............................77 J2
Fornham St Martin
  Suffk............................77 J2
Fornighty Highld 213 L4
Forres Moray 214 C3
Forsbrook Staffs 99 L4
Forse Highld 227 M2
Forsinard Highld 230 C6
Fort Augustus Highld 202 B4
Forteviot P & K 185 L4
Forth S Lans 176 C7
Forthampton Gloucs.......55 K2
Fort Hommet Guern 236 C2
Fortingall P & K 194 B6
Fort le Marchant
  Guern 236 d1
Forton Hants 29 H3
Forton Lancs 121 G1
Forton Shrops 83 H1
Forton Somset 13 J2
Forton Staffs 99 H7
Fortrie Abers 216 C5
Fortrose Highld 213 H3
Fortuneswell Dorset 14 D7
Fort William Highld 191 L2
Forty Hill Gt Lon 60 B7
Fosbury Wilts 40 F8
Foscot Oxon 56 E4
Fosdyke Lincs 104 A5
Foss P & K 194 C5
Fossebridge Gloucs 55 K5
Foster Street Essex.........60 D6
Foston Derbys 100 D6

Foston Leics 87 H4
Foston Lincs 102 E4
Foston N York 133 L6
Foston on the Wolds
  E R Yk........................135 H7
Fotherby Lincs 118 D3
Fotheringhay Nhants......88 F5
Foula Shet 235 a6
Foulden Border 179 J7
Foulden Norfk 91 H4
Foul End Warwks 86 B4
Foulness Island Essex....47 G2
Foulon Vale
  Crematorium
  Guern 236 d3
Foulridge Lancs 122 D3
Foulsham Norfk 106 B7
Fountainhall Border 177 L8
Four Ashes Suffk 78 B1
Four Cabots Guern 236 c3
Four Crosses Powys 97 K8
Four Elms Kent 32 E4
Four Forks Somset 25 K4
Four Gotes Cambs 90 C1
Four Lanes Cnwll 3 J4
Four Marks Hants 30 A4
Four Mile Bridge IoA 108 C5
Four Oaks Solhll 86 B7
Fourpenny Highld 223 H3
Four Roads Carmth 50 F4
Four Throws Kent 33 K7
Fovant Wilts 28 A5
Foveran Abers 207 H2
Fowey Cnwll 5 H5
Fowlhall Kent 33 J4
Fowlis Angus 186 E2
Fowlis Wester P & K 185 J3
Fowlmere Cambs 76 B5
Fownhope Herefs 69 L7
Foxbar Rens 174 E6
Foxcote Somset 27 G1
Foxdale IoM 237 b5
Foxearth Essex 77 J5
Foxfield Cumb 128 F3
Foxhole Cnwll 4 F5
Foxholes N York 134 F5
Foxley Norfk 106 C7
Foxt Staffs 100 B3
Foxton Cambs 76 B5
Foxton Leics 87 K5
Foxton N York 141 K7
Foxwood Shrops 84 B7
Foy Herefs 54 E3
Foyers Highld 202 D2
Foynesfield Highld 213 L4
Fraddon Cnwll 4 E4
Fradley Staffs 85 L2
Fradswell Staffs 99 M6
Fraisthorpe E R Yk 135 J7
Framfield E Susx 20 A2
Framingham Earl
  Norfk...........................92 F3
Framingham Pigot
  Norfk...........................92 F3
Framlingham Suffk........79 G2
Frampton Dorset 14 C4
Frampton Lincs 104 B5
Frampton Cotterell
  S Glos.........................38 C4
Frampton Mansell
  Gloucs.........................55 L7
Frampton-on-Severn
  Gloucs.........................55 H6
Framsden Suffk 78 E3
Framwellgate Moor
  Dur 151 G6
Franche Worcs 84 E7
Frankby Wirral 111 H4
Frankley Worcs 85 H7
Frankley Services
  Worcs 85 H7
Frankton Warwks 72 E1
Frant E Susx 33 G6
Fraserburgh Abers 217 J2
Frating Essex 62 C4

Frating Green Essex 62 C4
Fratton C Port 17 J3
Freathy Cnwll 6 B5
Freckenham Suffk 76 F1
Freckleton Lancs 120 F5
Freeby Leics 102 D7
Freefolk Hants 29 J2
Freeland Oxon 57 H5
Freethorpe Norfk 93 J3
Freethorpe Common
  Norfk...........................93 J3
Freiston Lincs 104 B4
Fremington Devon 23 H5
Fremington N York 140 D7
Frenchay S Glos 38 F5
Frenich P & K 194 C5
Frensham Surrey 30 D3
Freshfield Sefton 120 C8
Freshford Wilts 39 H7
Freshwater IoW 16 D5
Fressingfield Suffk 92 F7
Freston Suffk 78 E6
Freswick Highld 231 L3
Fretherne Gloucs 55 G6
Frettenham Norfk 106 F8
Freuchie Fife 186 E6
Freystrop Pembks 49 G5
Friar Park Sandw 85 H4
Friday Bridge Cambs 90 C3
Friday Street Suffk 79 H3
Fridaythorpe E R Yk 134 D7
Friern Barnet Gt Lon 44 F2
Friesthorpe Lincs 117 H5
Frieston Lincs 102 F3
Frieth Bucks 42 D3
Frilford Oxon 41 H2
Frilsham W Berk 41 K5
Frimley Surrey 42 E8
Frindsbury Medway 46 C6
Fring Norfk 105 H5
Fringford Oxon 57 L3
Frinsted Kent 34 B4
Frinton-on-Sea Essex.....62 F4
Friockheim Angus........196 F6
Frisby on the
  Wreake Leics.............102 B8
Friskney Lincs 104 D2
Friston E Susx 20 B6
Friston Suffk 79 J3
Fritchley Derbys 101 G3
Fritham Hants 28 E8
Frithelstock Devon 23 G7
Frithelstock Stone
  Devon 23 G7
Frithville Lincs 104 A3
Frittenden Kent 33 K5
Frittiscombe Devon..........7 J6
Fritton Norfk 92 F5
Fritton Norfk 93 K4
Fritwell Oxon 57 K3
Frizinghall C Brad........123 H4
Frizington Cumb...........136 E4
Frocester Gloucs 55 H7
Frodesley Shrops 83 K3
Frodsham Ches W 112 D6
Frogden Border 168 B4
Frog End Cambs 76 B5
Froggatt Derbys 114 E6
Froghall Staffs 100 A3
Frogmore Devon 7 H7
Frognall Lincs 89 H2
Frog Pool Worcs 70 E2
Frogwell Cnwll 6 A3
Frolesworth Leics 87 G5
Frome Somset 27 H2
Frome St Quintin
  Dorset 14 B2
Fromes Hill Herefs 70 C5
Froncysyllte Denbgs 97 K4
Fron-goch Gwynd 96 D5
Fron Isaf Wrexhm 97 L4
Frosterley Dur 150 C7
Froxfield Wilts 40 F6
Froxfield Green Hants 30 B6
Fryern Hill Hants 29 H7
Fryerning Essex 61 G7

Fuinary Highld 190 C6
Fulbeck Lincs 102 F3
Fulbourn Cambs 76 D4
Fulbrook Oxon 56 E5
Fulflood Hants 29 J5
Fulford C York 124 F2
Fulford Somset 25 K5
Fulford Staffs 99 L5
Fulham Gt Lon 44 E5
Fulking W Susx 19 H4
Fullarton N Ayrs 163 H2
Fuller Street Essex 61 H5
Fullerton Hants 29 G4
Fulletby Lincs 118 D6
Fullready Warwks 72 C5
Full Sutton E R Yk 134 B7
Fullwood E Ayrs 174 E7
Fulmer Bucks 43 G4
Fulmodeston Norfk 106 B6
Fulnetby Lincs 117 H5
Fulney Lincs 103 L7
Fulstow Lincs 118 D3
Fulwell Sundld 151 J3
Fulwood Lancs 121 H4
Fulwood Sheff 114 F4
Fundenhall Norfk 92 D4
Funtington W Susx 17 L2
Funtullich P & K 184 F3
Furley Devon 13 H2
Furnace Ag & B 182 E7
Furnace Carmth 51 G5
Furness Vale Derbys 114 A5
Furneux Pelham
  Herts...........................60 C3
Furzley Hants 28 F7
Fyfield Essex 60 F6
Fyfield Hants 28 F3
Fyfield Oxon 57 H7
Fyfield Wilts 40 C6
Fyfield Wilts 40 D7
Fylingthorpe N York 143 J6
Fyning W Susx 30 D6
Fyvie Abers 216 E6

G

Gabroc Hill E Ayrs 174 E7
Gaddesby Leics 87 K2
Gaddesden Row
  Herts...........................59 H5
Gadgirth S Ayrs 163 K5
Gaer-llwyd Mons 38 C2
Gaerwen IoA 108 F7
Gailes N Ayrs 163 H3
Gailey Staffs 85 G2
Gainford Dur 140 F4
Gainsborough Lincs......116 D4
Gainsford End Essex......77 G7
Gairloch Highld 219 J6
Gairlochy Highld 201 J8
Gairneybridge P & K 186 B7
Gaitsgill Cumb 148 C5
Galashiels Border 167 G3
Galgate Lancs 129 K7
Galhampton Somset.......26 F5
Gallanachbeg Ag & B...182 B2
Gallanachmore
  Ag & B 182 B3
Gallatown Fife 186 E8
Galleywood Essex 61 H7
Gallovie Highld 202 E7
Galloway Forest
  Park 153 J5
Gallowfauld Angus 196 D7
Gallowhill P & K 186 B1
Galltair Highld 200 C2
Galmpton Devon 7 G7
Galmpton Torbay 7 K5
Galphay N York 132 C5
Galston E Ayrs 163 L3
Gamblesby Cumb 149 G6
Gamlingay Cambs 75 J4
Gamlingay Great
  Heath Cambs 75 J4

Gamrie Abers 216 F2
Gamston Notts 101 L5
Gamston Notts 116 B6
Ganavan Bay Ag & B.. 182 B2
Ganllwyd Gwynd 96 B7
Gannachy Angus 196 F3
Ganstead E R Yk 126 E4
Ganthorpe N York 133 L5
Ganton N York 134 F4
Garbity Moray 215 H4
Garboldisham Norfk..... 92 B7
Garbole I lighld............ 203 H1
Garchory Abers 205 G4
Gardeners Green
  Wokham...................... 42 D6
Gardenstown Abers 216 F2
Garden Village Sheff... 114 E2
Garderhouse Shet........ 235 c5
Gare Hill Somsct............ 27 H4
Garelochhead Ag & B .. 173 L1
Garford Oxon............ 41 H2
Garforth Leeds 124 B4
Gargrave N York............ 131 H8
Gargunnock Stirlg....... 184 F8
Garlic Street Norfk....... 92 E6
Garlieston D & G............ 145 K5
Garlinge Kent............ 35 J2
Garlinge Green Kent..... 34 F4
Garlogie Abers 206 E4
Garmond Abers 216 F4
Garmouth Moray............ 215 H2
Garmston Shrops 83 L3
Garn-Dolbenmaen
  Gwynd...................... 95 J4
Garnkirk N Lans 175 J5
Garrabost W Isls 232 g2
Garrallan E Ayrs 164 B5
Garras Cnwll............ 3 J6
Garreg Gwynd............ 95 K4
Garrigill Cumb 149 J6
Garroch D & G............ 153 M6
Garrochtrie D & G......... 144 D7
Garrochty Ag & D 173 J7
Garros Highld............ 209 H2
Garsdale Head Cumb .. 130 E2
Garsdon Wilts............ 39 L3
Garsington Oxon............ 57 L7
Garstang Lancs............ 121 G2
Garston Herts............ 59 J7
Garston Lpool............ 112 B5
Gartachossan Ag & B.... 171 G6
Gartcosh N Lans 175 J5
Garth Powys............ 67 K5
Garth Wrexhm............ 97 K4
Garthamlock C Glas 175 H5
Garthmyl Powys............ 82 E4
Garthorpe Leics............ 102 D7
Garthorpe N Linc............ 125 K6
Garth Penrhyncoch
  Cerdgn...................... 80 E6
Garth Row Cumb............ 138 D7
Gartly Abers............ 215 L7
Gartmore Stirlg............ 184 C7
Gartness N Lans............ 175 K5
Gartness Stirlg............ 174 F2
Gartocharn W Duns 174 D2
Garton-on-the-Wolds
  E R Yk...................... 134 F7
Gartymore Highld............ 227 H5
Garvald E Loth............ 178 D4
Garvan Highld............ 191 J2
Garvard Ag & B............ 171 G1
Garve Highld............ 212 B3
Garvellachs Ag & B..... 181 K5
Garvestone Norfk............ 92 B3
Garvock Inver............ 174 B4
Garway Herefs............ 54 C4
Garyvard W Isls............ 232 f3
Gasper Wilts............ 27 H5
Gastard Wilts............ 39 K6
Gasthorpe Norfk............ 91 L7
Gatcombe IoW............ 16 F5
Gate Burton Lincs............ 116 D5
Gateforth N York............ 124 E5

Gatehead E Ayrs............ 163 K3
Gate Helmsley N York.. 133 L7
Gatehouse Nthumb..... 157 K4
Gatehouse of Fleet
  D & G...................... 145 M4
Gateley Norfk............ 106 A7
Gatenby N York............ 132 E3
Gateshaw Border............ 168 B5
Gateshead Gatesd....... 151 G3
Gateside Angus............ 196 D7
Gateside E Rens............ 174 E6
Gateside Fife............ 186 C5
Gateside N Ayrs............ 174 C7
Gateslack D & G............ 154 F2
Gatley Stockp............ 113 J4
Gattonside Border............ 167 H3
Gatwick Airport
  W Susx...................... 32 B5
Gaulby Leics............ 87 K4
Gauldry Fife............ 186 F3
Gauldswell P & K......... 195 K6
Gautby Lincs............ 117 K6
Gavinton Border............ 179 G7
Gawcott Bucks............ 58 B2
Gawsworth Ches E....... 113 K7
Gawthrop Cumb............ 130 D3
Gawthwaite Cumb......... 129 G3
Gaydon Warwks............ 72 D4
Gayhurst M Keyn............ 74 B5
Gayle N York............ 131 G2
Gayles N York............ 140 E5
Gayton Nhants............ 73 K4
Gayton Norfk............ 105 H8
Gayton Staffs............ 99 M6
Gayton le Marsh Lincs.. 118 F5
Gayton Thorpe Norfk... 105 H8
Gaywood Norfk............ 105 G7
Gazeley Suffk............ 77 G2
Gearraidh Bhaird
  W Isls...................... 232 f3
Geary Highld............ 208 D3
Gedding Suffk............ 77 L3
Geddington Nhants..... 88 C6
Gedling Notts............ 101 L4
Gedney Lincs............ 104 C7
Gedney Broadgate
  Lincs...................... 104 C7
Gedney Drove End
  Lincs...................... 104 D6
Gedney Dyke Lincs...... 104 C7
Gedney Hill Lincs............ 89 L2
Geeston Rutlnd............ 88 E3
Geldeston Norfk............ 93 H5
Gellifor Denbgs............ 110 F8
Gelligaer Caerph............ 37 H2
Gellilydan Gwynd............ 95 M4
Gellinudd Neath............ 51 K5
Gellyburn P & K............ 195 H8
Gellywen Carmth............ 50 C2
Gelston D & G............ 146 D3
Gelston Lincs............ 102 E4
Gembling E R Yk............ 135 H7
Gentleshaw Staffs............ 85 J2
Georgefield D & G......... 156 B4
George Green Bucks..... 43 G4
Georgeham Devon............ 23 G4
Georgemas Junction
  Station Highld......... 231 H4
George Nympton
  Devon...................... 23 L6
Georth Ork............ 234 b5
Germansweek Devon.... 10 C6
Gerrans Cnwll............ 4 D8
Gerrards Cross Bucks.. 43 G3
Gerrick R & Cl............ 142 E5
Gestingthorpe Essex... 77 J6
Geuffordd Powys............ 82 E2
Gidea Park Gt Lon............ 45 K3
Giffnock E Rens............ 175 G6
Gifford E Loth............ 178 C5
Giffordtown Fife............ 186 E5
Giggleswick N York...... 130 F6
Gigha Ag & B............ 171 L7
Gilberdyke E R Yk........ 125 K5
Gilchriston E Loth........ 178 B5
Gilcrux Cumb............ 147 K7

Gildersome Leeds.......... 123 K5
Gildingwells Rothm..... 115 K4
Gilesgate Moor Dur..... 151 H6
Gileston V Glam............ 36 F6
Gilfach Caerph............ 53 J7
Gilfach Goch Brdgnd.... 36 F3
Gilfachrheda Cerdgn.... 65 L3
Gilgarran Cumb............ 136 E3
Gillamoor N York............ 133 K2
Gillen Highld............ 208 D3
Gillesbie D & G............ 155 K4
Gilling East N York............ 133 J4
Gillingham Dorset............ 27 J6
Gillingham Medway....... 46 C6
Gillingham Norfk............ 93 J5
Gilling West N York...... 140 F6
Gillock Highld............ 231 J4
Gills Highld............ 231 K2
Gilmanscleuch Border.. 166 E5
Gilmerton C Edin............ 177 J5
Gilmerton P & K............ 185 J3
Gilmonby Dur............ 140 C5
Gilmorton Leics............ 87 H6
Gilroes Crematorium
  C Leic...................... 87 H3
Gilsland Nthumb............ 149 G2
Gilston Border............ 177 L6
Gilston Herts............ 60 D5
Gilwern Mons............ 53 K5
Gimingham Norfk............ 107 G5
Gipping Suffk............ 78 C2
Gipsey Bridge Lincs...... 103 M3
Girdle Toll N Ayrs............ 163 J2
Girlsta Shet............ 235 c5
Girsby N York............ 141 J5
Girthon D & G............ 146 A4
Girton Cambs............ 76 B3
Girton Notts............ 116 D7
Girvan S Ayrs............ 152 E3
Gisburn Lancs............ 122 C2
Gisleham Suffk............ 93 K5
Gislingham Suffk............ 78 C1
Gissing Norfk............ 92 D6
Gittisham Dcvon............ 12 E3
Gladestry Powys............ 68 E4
Gladsmuir E Loth............ 177 M4
Glais Swans............ 51 K5
Glaisdale N York............ 143 G6
Glamis Angus............ 196 C6
Glanaman Carmth............ 51 J3
Glandford Norfk............ 106 C4
Glandwr Pembks............ 49 K2
Glandyfi Cerdgn............ 80 F4
Glanllynfi Brdgnd............ 36 D3
Glan-rhyd Powys............ 52 B6
Glanton Nthumb............ 169 G6
Glanvilles Wootton
  Dorset...................... 14 D2
Glan-y-don Flints............ 111 G5
Glapthorn Nhants............ 88 E5
Glapwell Derbys............ 115 J7
Glasbury Powys............ 68 D6
Glascwm Powys............ 68 D4
Glasfryn Conwy............ 96 E3
Glasgow D & G............ 175 G5
Glasgow Airport Rens.. 174 E5
Glasgow Science
  Centre C Glas............ 175 G5
Glasinfryn Gwynd............ 109 H7
Glasnacardoch Bay
  Highld...................... 199 L6
Glasnakille Highld......... 199 H3
Glassford S Lans............ 175 J8
Glasshouse Gloucs......... 55 G4
Glasshouses N York...... 132 B6
Glasson Cumb............ 148 A3
Glasson Lancs............ 129 K7
Glassonby Cumb............ 149 G7
Glasterlaw Angus............ 196 F6
Glaston Rutlnd............ 88 C4
Glastonbury Somset..... 26 D4
Glatton Cambs............ 89 H6
Glazebrook Warrtn......... 113 G3
Glazebury Warrtn............ 112 F3
Glazeley Shrops............ 84 C5
Gleaston Cumb............ 128 F5

Glebe Highld............ 202 D2
Gledhow Leeds............ 123 L3
Gledpark D & G............ 146 B5
Gledrid Shrops............ 97 L5
Glemsford Suffk............ 77 J5
Glenallachie Moray....... 215 G6
Glenancross Highld....... 199 K6
Glenaros House
  Ag & B...................... 190 B7
Glen Auldyn IoM............ 237 d3
Glenbarr Ag & B............ 161 H3
Glenbarry Abers............ 216 B3
Glenbeg Highld............ 190 C4
Glenbervie Abers............ 197 J1
Glenboig N Lans............ 175 J5
Glenborrodale Highld... 190 C4
Glenbranter Ag & B...... 183 G7
Glenbreck Border............ 165 K5
Glenbrittle House
  Highld...................... 198 F2
Glenbuck E Ayrs............ 164 E4
Glencally Angus............ 196 B4
Glencaple D & G............ 147 H2
Glencarron Lodge
  Highld...................... 211 G4
Glencarse P & K............ 186 C3
Glen Clunie Lodge
  Abers...................... 204 E8
Glencoe Highld............ 191 L5
Glencothe Border............ 165 L4
Glencraig Fife............ 186 C7
Glencrosh D & G............ 154 D4
Glendale Highld............ 208 B4
Glendaruel Ag & B........ 173 G2
Glendevon P & K............ 185 K6
Glendoe Lodge
  Highld...................... 202 C4
Glendoick P & K............ 186 C3
Glenduckie Fife............ 186 D4
Glenegedale Ag & B..... 170 F7
Glenelg Highld............ 200 C2
Glenerney Moray............ 214 C5
Glenfarg P & K............ 186 B5
Glenfield Leics............ 87 G3
Glenfinnan Highld......... 191 H1
Glenfintaig Lodge
  Highld...................... 201 K7
Glenfoot P & K............ 186 C4
Glenfyne Lodge
  Ag & B...................... 183 H4
Glengarnock N Ayrs...... 174 C7
Glengolly Highld............ 231 G3
Glengorm Castle
  Ag & B...................... 189 K5
Glengrasco Highld......... 209 G5
Glenholm Border............ 165 L3
Glenhoul D & G............ 154 A5
Glenisla Angus............ 195 K4
Glenkin Ag & B............ 173 K3
Glenkindie Abers............ 205 K3
Glenlivet Moray............ 214 F8
Glenlochar D & G............ 146 C3
Glenlomond P & K......... 186 C6
Glenluce D & G............ 144 E4
Glenmassen Ag & B..... 173 J2
Glenmavis N Lans............ 175 K5
Glen Maye IoM............ 237 b5
Glenmore Highld............ 209 G6
Glenmore Lodge
  Highld...................... 204 B4
Glen Nevis House
  Highld...................... 192 B3
Glenochil Clacks............ 185 H7
Glen Parva Leics............ 87 H4
Glenquiech Angus............ 196 C4
Glenralloch Ag & B....... 172 E5
Glenridding Cumb............ 137 L4
Glenrothes Fife............ 186 D7
Glenshero Lodge
  Highld...................... 202 E6
Glenstriven Ag & B...... 173 J3
Glentham Lincs............ 117 G4
Glen Trool Lodge
  D & G...................... 153 J6
Glentrool Village
  D & G...................... 153 H6

Glentruim House
Highld..................203 G6
Glentworth Lincs.........116 F6
Glenuig Highld............190 D2
Glenvarragill Highld......209 G6
Glen Vine IoM.............237 c5
Glenwhilly D & G..........152 E7
Glespin S Lans............164 F4
Glewstone Herefs.........54 E4
Clinton C Pete............89 H3
Glooston Leics............87 L4
Glossop Derbys...........114 B3
Gloster Hill Nthumb......159 G2
Gloucester Gloucs.........55 J4
Gloucester
  Crematorium
  Gloucs......................55 J5
Gloucester Services
  Gloucs.....................55 J5
Gloucestershire
  Airport Gloucs............55 K4
Glusburn N York..........122 F2
Glutt Lodge Highld.......227 H2
Glympton Oxon............57 H4
Glynarthen Cerdgn........65 K5
Glyn Ceiriog Wrexhm.....97 J5
Glynde E Susx.............19 L4
Glyndyfrdwy Denbgs......97 J4
Glynneath Neath..........52 D6
Glynn Valley
  Crematorium
  Cnwll.......................5 H3
Glyntaff
  Crematorium
  Rhondd.....................37 H3
Glyntawe Powys...........52 D5
Glynteg Carmth...........65 K6
Gnosall Staffs.............99 J7
Gnosall Heath Staffs......99 J7
Goadby Leics..............87 L4
Goadby Marwood
  Leics......................102 C7
Goatacre Wilts............40 A5
Goathill Dorset...........26 F7
Goathland N York........143 H6
Goathurst Somset.........25 K5
Gobowen Shrops..........97 L5
Godalming Surrey..........30 F3
Goddard's Green
  Kent.......................33 L6
Godmanchester
  Cambs.....................75 J1
Godmanstone Dorset.....14 C3
Godmersham Kent.........34 E5
Godney Somset............26 C3
Godolphin Cross
  Cnwll.......................3 G5
Godre'r-graig Neath.......51 L4
Godshill IoW...............17 G6
Godstone Surrey...........32 C3
Goetre Mons...............53 L6
Goff's Oak Herts..........60 B7
Gofilon Mons..............53 K5
Gogar C Edin.............177 G4
Goginan Cerdgn...........80 F7
Golan Gwynd...............95 J4
Golant Cnwll...............5 H5
Golberdon Cnwll............5 M2
Golborne Wigan..........112 E3
Golcar Kirk...............123 G7
Goldcliff Newpt............38 A4
Golden Green Kent.........33 H4
Golden Pot Hants.........30 B3
Golders Green Gt Lon.....44 E3
Golders Green
  Crematorium
  Gt Lon.....................44 E3
Goldhanger Essex.........61 L6
Goldington Bed............74 F4
Goldsborough N York....132 F7
Goldsborough N York....143 H4
Goldsithney Cnwll..........2 F5
Goldsworth Park
  Surrey.....................43 G8
Goldthorpe Barns........115 J2

Goldworthy Devon.........22 F6
Gollanfield Highld.........213 J4
Golspie Highld............223 N4
Gomeldon Wilts...........28 D4
Gomshall Surrey...........31 H2
Gonalston Notts..........102 B3
Gonerby Hill Foot
  Lincs......................102 E5
Gonfirth Shet.............235 c4
Good Easter Essex.........60 F5
Gooderstone Norfk........91 H3
Goodleigh Devon...........23 J5
Goodmanham E R Yk.....125 K2
Goodmayes Gt Lon.........45 J3
Goodnestone Kent.........34 D3
Goodnestone Kent.........35 H4
Goodrich Herefs...........54 E4
Goodrington Torbay.........7 K4
Goodshaw Lancs..........122 B5
Goodwick Pembks..........64 C6
Goodworth Clatford
  Hants......................29 G3
Goole E R Yk..............125 H5
Goom's Hill Worcs.........71 H4
Goonbell Cnwll..............3 J2
Goonhavern Cnwll...........3 K1
Goonvrea Cnwll.............3 J2
Goosecruives Abers......206 E8
Gooseford Devon...........11 G6
Goose Green Essex.........62 D3
Goose Green S Glos........38 F5
Gooseham Cnwll............9 G2
Goosey Oxon...............41 G3
Goosnargh Lancs.........121 H3
Goostrey Ches E..........113 H7
Gordano Services
  N Som.....................38 D5
Gordon Border............167 K2
Gordon Arms Hotel
  Border....................166 D4
Gordonstown Abers......216 B3
Gordonstown Abers......216 D6
Gorebridge Mdloth.......177 K6
Gorefield Cambs...........90 B2
Gores Wilts................40 C8
Gorey Jersey..............236 e7
Goring Oxon...............41 L4
Goring-by-Sea W Susx....18 F5
Gorleston on Sea
  Norfk......................93 L3
Gornal Wood
  Crematorium
  Dudley.....................85 G5
Gorrachie Abers.........216 E3
Gorran Churchtown
  Cnwll.......................4 F7
Gorran Haven Cnwll........4 F7
Gorsedd Flints...........111 G6
Gorse Hill Swindn.........40 D3
Gorseinon Swans..........51 H5
Gorsgoch Cerdgn..........66 C4
Gorslas Carmth............51 H3
Gorsley Gloucs............55 G3
Gorsley Common
  Herefs......................54 F3
Gorstan Highld...........212 B2
Gorsty Hill Staffs.........100 C6
Gorten Ag & B............181 L2
Gorthleck Highld.........202 E2
Gorton Manch............113 K3
Gosbeck Suffk.............78 D4
Gosberton Lincs..........103 L6
Gosfield Essex.............61 J3
Gosforth Cumb...........136 E6
Gosforth N u Ty..........151 G2
Gospel End Staffs.........84 F5
Gosport Hants.............17 H3
Gossington Gloucs.........55 H7
Gotham Notts.............101 K6
Gotherington Gloucs......55 L3
Gotton Somset............25 K5
Goudhurst Kent............33 J5
Goulceby Lincs...........118 C5
Gourdas Abers...........216 E6
Gourdie C Dund..........186 F2
Gourdon Abers...........197 K3

Gourock Inver............173 L3
Govan C Glas.............174 F5
Goveton Devon.............7 H6
Gowdall E R Yk...........124 F6
Gower Highld.............212 D3
Gower Swans..............51 G7
Gowerton Swans...........51 H6
Gowkhall Fife.............176 E1
Goxhill E R Yk............126 F2
Goxhill N Linc.............126 D6
Grabhair W Isls...........232 f3
Graffham W Susx..........18 C3
Grafham Cambs............75 H2
Grafham Surrey............31 G2
Grafton N York...........132 F6
Grafton Oxon..............56 F7
Grafton Shrops............98 B8
Grafton Worcs.............71 H6
Grafton Flyford
  Worcs......................71 G4
Grafton Regis Nhants......73 L5
Grafton Underwood
  Nhants.....................88 D7
Grafty Green Kent.........34 B5
Graig Conwy..............109 M6
Graig-fechan Denbgs.......97 J2
Grain Medway..............46 E5
Grainsby Lincs............118 C2
Grainthorpe Lincs........118 E3
Grampound Cnwll...........4 E6
Grampound Road
  Cnwll.......................4 E5
Gramsdal W Isls..........233 c6
Gramsdale W Isls.........233 c6
Granborough Bucks........58 C3
Granby Notts.............102 C5
Grandborough
  Warwks.....................72 F2
Grand Chemins
  Jersey....................236 d7
Grandes Rocques
  Guern.....................236 c2
Grandtully P & K.........194 E5
Grange Cumb.............137 H4
Grange Medway............46 D6
Grange P & K.............186 D3
Grange Crossroads
  Moray.....................215 K4
Grange Hall Moray........214 C3
Grangehall S Lans.........165 J2
Grange Hill Essex..........45 H2
Grangemill Derbys........100 E2
Grange Moor Kirk........123 J7
Grangemouth Falk.........176 C3
Grange of Lindores
  Fife......................186 D4
Grange-over-Sands
  Cumb......................129 J4
Grangepans Falk.........176 D3
Grangetown R & Cl........142 C3
Grangetown Sundld.......151 K4
Grange Villa Dur..........151 G4
Gransmoor E R Yk........135 H7
Granston Pembks..........64 C7
Grantchester Cambs.......76 B4
Grantham Lincs..........102 E5
Grantham
  Crematorium
  Lincs.....................102 F5
Granton C Edin...........177 H3
Grantown-on-Spey
  Highld....................214 D8
Grantshouse Border......179 G5
Grasby Lincs.............117 H1
Grasmere Cumb...........137 K5
Grasscroft Oldham.......113 L1
Grassendale Lpool........111 L4
Grassington N York.......131 J6
Grassmoor Derbys........115 H7
Grassthorpe Notts........116 C7
Grateley Hants............28 F3
Graveley Cambs............75 J2
Graveley Herts.............59 L3
Graveney Kent.............34 E3
Gravesend Kent............46 A5
Gravir W Isls.............232 f3

Grayingham Lincs.........116 F3
Grayrigg Cumb............138 E7
Grays Thurr................45 L4
Grayshott Hants...........30 E4
Grayswood Surrey.........30 E4
Greasbrough Rothm......115 H3
Greasby Wirral...........111 H4
Great Abington
  Cambs......................76 D5
Great Addington
  Nhants.....................88 D7
Great Alne Warwks........71 K3
Great Altcar Lancs.......111 K1
Great Amwell Herts........60 B5
Great Asby Cumb.........138 F5
Great Ashfield Suffk.......78 B2
Great Ayton N York......142 C5
Great Baddow Essex.......61 H6
Great Badminton
  S Glos......................39 J4
Great Bardfield Essex......61 G2
Great Barford Bed.........75 G4
Great Barr Sandw..........85 J3
Great Barrington
  Gloucs......................56 E5
Great Barrow Ches W.....112 C4
Great Barton Suffk........77 K2
Great Barugh N York.....134 B4
Great Bavington
  Nthumb....................158 C6
Great Bealings Suffk.......78 E5
Great Bedwyn Wilts........40 F7
Great Bentley Essex.......62 D4
Great Billing Nhants.......74 B3
Great Bircham Norfk......105 J6
Great Blakenham
  Suffk.......................78 D4
Great Blencow Cumb......138 C2
Great Bolas Wrekin........98 F7
Great Bookham
  Surrey......................31 J1
Great Bourton Oxon.......72 F5
Great Bowden Leics........87 L5
Great Bradley Suffk........76 F4
Great Braxted Essex.......61 K5
Great Bricett Suffk........78 C4
Great Brickhill Bucks......58 E3
Great Bridgeford
  Staffs......................99 K6
Great Brington
  Nhants......................73 J2
Great Bromley Essex.......62 C3
Great Broughton
  Cumb......................136 E2
Great Broughton
  N York....................142 C6
Great Budworth
  Ches W....................112 F6
Great Burdon Darltn......141 H4
Great Burstead Essex......46 B2
Great Busby N York......142 B6
Great Carlton Lincs......118 E4
Great Casterton
  Rutlnd......................88 E2
Great Chalfield Wilts.......39 K7
Great Chart Kent..........34 C6
Great Chatwell Staffs......84 E1
Great Chesterford
  Essex.......................76 D6
Great Cheverell Wilts......27 M1
Great Chishill Cambs......76 B6
Great Clacton Essex.......62 E5
Great Clifton Cumb.......136 E2
Great Coates NE Lin......126 F8
Great Comberton
  Worcs......................71 G6
Great Corby Cumb........148 C4
Great Cornard Suffk.......77 K6
Great Cowden E R Yk....126 F3
Great Coxwell Oxon.......40 F2
Great Cransley
  Nhants......................88 B7
Great Cressingham
  Norfk.......................91 J3
Great Crosthwaite
  Cumb......................137 J3

Great Cubley Derbys.....100 D5
Great Cumbrae
  Island N Ayrs.........173 K6
Great Dalby Leics.......87 L2
Great Doddington
  Nhants....................74 C2
Great Dunham Norfk......91 K1
Great Dunmow Essex.....61 G4
Great Durnford Wilts...28 C4
Great Easton Essex......60 F3
Great Easton Leics......88 B5
Great Eccleston Lancs.120 F3
Great Ellingham
  Norfk....................92 B4
Great Elm Somset.......27 H2
Great Everdon
  Nhants....................73 H3
Great Eversden
  Cambs....................75 L4
Great Fencote N York..132 D2
Great Finborough
  Suffk.....................78 B3
Greatford Lincs.........88 F2
Great Fransham
  Norfk....................91 K2
Great Gaddesden
  Herts.....................59 G5
Greatgate Staffs.......100 B4
Great Gidding Cambs....89 G6
Great Givendale
  E R Yk..................134 C8
Great Glemham Suffk....79 H3
Great Glen Leics........87 J4
Great Gonerby Lincs...102 E5
Great Gransden
  Cambs....................75 J4
Great Green Cambs......75 K5
Great Green Suffk.......77 K4
Great Habton N York...134 B4
Great Hale Lincs.......103 J4
Great Hallingbury
  Essex.....................60 E4
Greatham Hants.........30 C5
Greatham Hartpl.......141 L2
Greatham W Susx........18 E3
Great Hampden
  Bucks.....................58 D7
Great Harrowden
  Nhants....................74 C1
Great Harwood Lancs...121 L4
Great Haseley Oxon.....57 M7
Great Hatfield E R Yk..126 F3
Great Haywood Staffs...99 M7
Great Heck N York......124 E6
Great Henny Essex.......77 K6
Great Hinton Wilts.....39 K8
Great Hockham Norfk....91 L5
Great Holland Essex.....62 E4
Great Hollands Br For...42 E6
Great Horkesley
  Essex.....................62 B2
Great Hormead Herts....60 C3
Great Horton C Brad...123 H4
Great Horwood Bucks...58 C2
Great Houghton
  Barns....................115 H1
Great Houghton
  Nhants....................73 L3
Great Hucklow
  Derbys...................114 D6
Great Kelk E R Yk......135 H7
Great Kimble Bucks.....58 D6
Great Kingshill Bucks..42 E2
Great Langdale Cumb...137 J6
Great Langton N York..141 H7
Great Leighs Essex......61 H4
Great Limber Lincs....126 E8
Great Linford M Keyn...74 C6
Great Livermere Suffk..77 K1
Great Longstone
  Derbys...................114 D6
Great Lumley Dur......151 H5
Great Malvern Worcs....70 D5
Great Maplestead
  Essex.....................77 J7
Great Marton Bpool....120 D4

Great Massingham
  Norfk....................105 J7
Great Milton Oxon......57 L7
Great Missenden
  Bucks.....................58 E7
Great Mitton Lancs....121 K3
Great Mongeham
  Kent......................35 K4
Great Moulton Norfk....92 E5
Great Musgrave
  Cumb....................139 H4
Great Ness Shrops......98 B8
Great Notley Essex......61 H4
Great Oak Mons..........54 B6
Great Oakley Essex......62 E3
Great Oakley Nhants....88 C6
Great Offley Herts......59 J3
Great Ormside Cumb...139 G4
Great Orton Cumb......148 B4
Great Ouseburn
  N York...................133 G6
Great Oxendon
  Nhants....................87 K6
Great Oxney Green
  Essex.....................61 G6
Great Paxton Cambs.....75 H2
Great Plumpton
  Lancs....................120 E4
Great Plumstead
  Norfk.....................93 G2
Great Ponton Lincs....102 F6
Great Preston Leeds...124 B5
Great Raveley Cambs....89 J7
Great Rissington
  Gloucs....................56 D5
Great Rollright Oxon...56 F2
Great Ryburgh Norfk..106 A6
Great Ryton Shrops.....83 J3
Great Saling Essex......61 H3
Great Salkeld Cumb....148 F7
Great Sampford
  Essex.....................76 F7
Croat Saughall
  Ches W...................111 K7
Great Shefford
  W Berk....................41 G5
Great Shelford
  Cambs.....................76 C4
Great Smeaton
  N York...................141 H6
Great Snoring Norfk...105 M5
Great Somerford
  Wilts.....................39 L4
Great Soudley Shrops...99 G6
Great Stainton Darltn.141 H3
Great Stambridge
  Essex.....................46 E2
Great Staughton
  Cambs.....................75 G2
Great Steeping Lincs..118 F8
Great Stoke S Glos......38 F4
Greatstone-on-Sea
  Kent......................21 L2
Great Strickland
  Cumb....................138 D3
Great Stukeley
  Cambs.....................89 J8
Great Sturton Lincs...117 K6
Great Swinburne
  Nthumb..................158 B6
Great Tew Oxon.........57 H3
Great Tey Essex.........61 L3
Great Thurlow Suffk....76 F4
Great Torrington
  Devon.....................23 H7
Great Tosson Nthumb..158 C3
Great Totham Essex......61 K5
Great Totham Essex......61 L5
Great Urswick Cumb...129 G5
Great Wakering Essex...46 F3
Great Waldingfield
  Suffk.....................77 K5
Great Walsingham
  Norfk....................105 M5
Great Waltham Essex....61 H5
Great Warley Essex......45 L2

Great Washbourne
  Gloucs....................71 H7
Great Weeke Devon......11 G7
Great Weldon Nhants....88 D5
Great Wenham Suffk.....78 C6
Great Whittington
  Nthumb..................158 C7
Great Wigborough
  Essex.....................62 A5
Great Wilbraham
  Cambs.....................76 D3
Great Wishford Wilts...28 B4
Great Witcombe
  Gloucs....................55 K5
Great Witley Worcs......70 D2
Great Wolford
  Warwks....................72 B7
Greatworth Nhants......73 G6
Great Wratting Suffk...77 G5
Great Wymondley
  Herts.....................59 K3
Great Wyrley Staffs....85 H3
Great Yarmouth
  Norfk.....................93 L3
Great Yarmouth
  Crematorium
  Norfk.....................93 K3
Great Yeldham Essex....77 H6
Greenburn W Loth......176 C6
Green End Herts.........60 B2
Green End Herts.........60 B4
Greenfield Ag & B.....173 M1
Greenfield C Beds......74 F7
Greenfield Flints......111 H6
Greenfield Highld.....201 J5
Greenfield Oldham.....113 M2
Greenford Gt Lon.......43 J4
Greengairs N Lans.....175 K4
Greengates C Brad.....123 J3
Greenham Somset........25 G7
Green Hammerton
  N York...................133 G2
Greenhaugh Nthumb....157 K5
Greenhead Nthumb.....149 H3
Green Heath Staffs......85 H2
Greenhill D & G........155 J6
Greenhill Falk.........175 L3
Greenhill Kent..........47 K6
Greenhill S Lans.......165 H3
Greenhithe Kent.........45 L5
Greenholm E Ayrs......164 B3
Greenhouse Border.....167 H5
Greenhow Hill N York..131 L6
Greenland Highld......231 J3
Greenland Sheff.......115 H4
Greenlaw Border.......167 L1
Greenlea D & G.........155 H6
Greenloaning P & K....185 H6
Greenmount Bury.......122 B7
Greenock Inver........174 B3
Greenock
  Crematorium
  Inver....................174 B3
Greenodd Cumb.........129 G3
Green Ore Somset........26 E2
Green Quarter Cumb...138 C6
Greenshields S Lans...165 K2
Greenside Gatesd......150 E3
Greenside Kirk........123 H7
Greens Norton
  Nhants....................73 J4
Greenstead Green
  Essex.....................61 K3
Green Street Herts......59 K7
Green Street Herts......60 D4
Green Street Green
  Kent......................45 L6
Green Tye Herts.........60 C4
Greenway Somset........25 L6
Greenwich Gt Lon.......45 G4
Greenwich Maritime
  Gt Lon....................45 H4
Greet Gloucs............56 B3
Greete Shrops...........69 L1
Greetham Lincs........118 D7
Greetham Rutlnd........88 D2

Greetland Calder......123 G6
Greinton Somset........26 B4
Grenaby IoM............237 b6
Grendon Nhants.........74 C3
Grendon Warwks.........86 C4
Grendon Underwood
  Bucks.....................58 B4
Grenoside Sheff.......115 G3
Grenoside
  Crematorium
  Sheff....................114 F3
Greosabhagh W Isls....232 e4
Gresford Wrexhm........97 M2
Gresham Norfk.........106 E5
Greshornish House
  Hotel Highld.........208 E4
Gressenhall Norfk......91 L1
Gressenhall Green
  Norfk.....................91 L1
Gressingham Lancs....130 B5
Greta Bridge Dur......140 D5
Gretna D & G...........148 B2
Gretna Green D & G....148 B2
Gretna Services D & G.148 B2
Gretton Gloucs..........56 A2
Gretton Nhants.........88 C5
Gretton Shrops.........83 K4
Grewelthorpe N York..132 C4
Greyrigg D & G.........155 J4
Greys Green Oxon.......42 B4
Greysouthen Cumb.....136 E2
Greystoke Cumb........138 B2
Greystone Angus.......196 E7
Greywell Hants.........30 B2
Griff Warwks............86 D5
Griffithstown Torfn....53 L7
Grimeford Village
  Lancs....................121 J7
Grimesthorpe Sheff...115 G4
Grimethorpe Barns....124 C8
Grimley Worcs..........70 F3
Grimmet S Ayrs........163 H4
Grimoldby Lincs.......118 E4
Grimpo Shrops..........98 A7
Grimsargh Lancs.......121 H4
Grimsby NE Lin........127 G7
Grimsby
  Crematorium
  NE Lin...................118 C1
Grimscote Nhants.......73 J4
Grimscott Cnwll..........9 H4
Grimshader W Isls.....232 f3
Grimsthorpe Lincs....103 H7
Grimston Leics.........102 B7
Grimston Norfk........105 H7
Grimstone Dorset.......14 C4
Grimstone End Suffk....77 L2
Grindale E R Yk.......135 H5
Grindleford Derbys...114 E6
Grindleton Lancs.....121 L2
Grindley Brook
  Shrops....................98 D4
Grindlow Derbys.......114 D6
Grindon Staffs........100 B2
Gringley on the Hill
  Notts....................116 C4
Grinsdale Cumb........148 C4
Grinshill Shrops........98 D7
Grinton N York........140 D7
Griomaisiader W Isls..232 f3
Griomsaigh W Isls.....233 c6
Grishipoll Ag & B.....188 F4
Gristhorpe N York....135 H3
Griston Norfk..........91 L4
Gritley Ork.............234 d6
Grittenham Wilts.......40 B4
Grittleton Wilts........39 K4
Grizebeck Cumb........128 F3
Grizedale Cumb........137 K7
Groby Leics.............87 G3
Groes Conwy...........110 D8
Groes-faen Rhondd......37 G4
Groeslon Gwynd.........95 H2
Groes-Wen Caerph......37 H3
Grogarry W Isls.......233 b7
Grogport Ag & B.......161 K1

Groigearraidh W Isls 233 b7
Gronant Flints 110 F5
Groombridge E Susx....32 F5
Grosebay W Isls 232 e4
Grosmont Mons 54 B3
Grosmont N York.......143 H6
Groton Suffk 77 L6
Grouville Jersey 236 e7
Grove Notts.............116 C5
Grove Oxon 41 H3
Grove Green Kent 33 K3
Grove Park Gt Lon 45 H5
Grovesend Swans......51 H5
Gruinard Highld 219 L4
Gruinart Ag & B 170 F5
Grula Highld 208 F8
Gruline Ag & B........190 B7
Grundisburgh Suffk...78 F4
Gruting Shet 235 c5
Gualachulain Highld ...192 B7
Guardbridge Fife 187 G4
Guarlford Worcs.........70 E5
Guay P & K 194 F6
Guernsey Guern 236 c3
Guernsey Airport
  Guern 236 c3
Guestling Green
  E Susx 21 G3
Guestling Thorn
  E Susx 21 G3
Guestwick Norfk 106 C6
Guide Post Nthumb......159 G5
Guilden Morden
  Cambs 75 K5
Guilden Sutton
  Ches W 112 C7
Guildford Surrey..........31 G2
Guildford
  Crematorium
  Surrey 31 G3
Guildtown P & K 186 B2
Guilsborough Nhants...87 J8
Guilsfield Powys 82 E2
Guiltreehill S Ayrs 163 J7
Guineaford Devon 23 J4
Guisborough R & Cl ..142 D4
Guiseley Leeds 123 J3
Guist Norfk 106 B7
Guiting Power Gloucs...56 C3
Gullane E Loth..........178 B2
Gulval Cnwll 2 E5
Gulworthy Devon..........6 C2
Gumfreston Pembks 49 J7
Gumley Leics 87 K5
Gunby Lincs 102 E7
Gunby Lincs 118 F7
Gundleton Hants 29 L5
Gun Hill E Susx 20 C3
Gunn Devon 23 K5
Gunnerside N York 139 L7
Gunnerton Nthumb......158 A7
Gunness N Linc 125 K7
Gunnislake Cnwll..........6 C2
Gunnista Shet............235 d6
Gunthorpe N Linc......116 D3
Gunthorpe Norfk 106 B5
Gunthorpe Notts......102 B4
Gunwalloe Cnwll 3 H6
Gurnard IoW 16 F4
Gurney Slade Somset...26 F2
Gurnos Powys 52 B6
Gussage All Saints
  Dorset 15 J1
Gussage St Andrew
  Dorset 27 L8
Gussage St Michael
  Dorset 15 J1
Guston Kent 35 J5
Gutcher Shet............235 d2
Guthrie Angus...........196 F6
Guyhirn Cambs 90 B3
Guyzance Nthumb......158 F2
Gwaenysgor Flints....110 F5
Gwalchmai IoA 108 E6
Gwaun-Cae-Gurwen
  Carmth 51 K3

Gweek Cnwll 3 J6
Gwenddwr Powys.....68 B6
Gwennap Cnwll 3 J4
Gwennap Mining
  District Cnwll 3 K3
Gwent Crematorium
  Mons 37 L2
Gwernaffield Flints.....111 H7
Gwernesney Mons.....54 B7
Gwernogle Carmth 66 C7
Gwernymynydd
  Flints..................111 H8
Gwespyr Flints.........110 F5
Gwinear Cnwll............3 G4
Gwithian Cnwll 3 G3
Gwyddelwern
  Denbgs 97 G3
Gwyddgrug Carmth....66 B7
Gwytherin Conwy 96 D1

H

Habberley Shrops 83 H3
Habberley Worcs......84 E7
Habergham Lancs.....122 B4
Habertoft Lincs 119 G7
Habrough NE Lin 126 E7
Hacconby Lincs 103 J7
Haceby Lincs 103 G5
Hacheston Suffk........79 G3
Hackbridge Gt Lon 44 F6
Hackenthorpe Sheff...115 H5
Hackford Norfk..........92 C3
Hackforth N York 132 C2
Hackland Ork 234 c5
Hackleton Nhants 74 B4
Hacklinge Kent 35 J4
Hackness N York......134 F2
Hackney Gt Lon 45 G4
Hackthorn Lincs 117 G5
Hackthorpe Cumb 138 D3
Hadden Border 168 B3
Haddenham Bucks.....58 C6
Haddenham Cambs....90 C7
Haddington E Loth ...178 B4
Haddington Lincs.....116 E8
Haddiscoe Norfk 93 J4
Haddo Abers 216 F6
Haddon Cambs.........89 G5
Hadfield Derbys.......114 A3
Hadham Ford Herts....60 C4
Hadleigh Essex 46 D3
Hadleigh Suffk.........78 B6
Hadley Worcs...........70 F2
Hadley Wrekin 84 C2
Hadley End Staffs....100 C7
Hadley Wood Gt Lon ...44 E1
Hadlow Kent 33 H3
Hadlow Down E Susx...20 B2
Hadnall Shrops 98 D7
Hadrian's Wall
  Nthumb 150 B2
Hadstock Essex 76 D5
Hadzor Worcs 71 G3
Haggerston Nthumb...168 F2
Haggs Falk.............175 L3
Hagley Herefs 69 L6
Hagley Worcs...........85 G7
Hagworthingham
  Lincs 118 D7
Haile Cumb.............136 E5
Hailey Oxon 57 G5
Hailsham E Susx 20 C4
Hail Weston Cambs....75 H3
Hainault Gt Lon 45 J2
Hainford Norfk 106 F8
Hainton Lincs 117 K5
Haisthorpe E R Yk ...135 H6
Hakin Pembks 48 F6
Halam Notts............102 B2
Halbeath Fife 176 F1
Halberton Devon 24 F8
Halcro Highld 231 J4

Hale Cumb.............129 K4
Hale Halton 112 C5
Hale Hants 28 D7
Hale Surrey 30 D2
Hale Traffd 113 H4
Halebarns Traffd......113 H4
Hales Norfk 93 H4
Hales Staffs.............99 G5
Halesowen Dudley.....85 G6
Hales Place Kent 34 F3
Hale Street Kent........33 H4
Halesworth Suffk......93 H7
Halewood Knows 112 C4
Halford Devon 7 J2
Halford Warwks 72 C5
Halfpenny Green
  Staffs 84 E5
Halfway House
  Shrops 83 G2
Halfway Houses Kent...46 F5
Halifax Calder 123 G5
Halket E Ayrs 174 D7
Halkirk Highld 231 G4
Halkyn Flints 111 H7
Hall E Rens 174 D7
Halland E Susx 20 A3
Hallaton Leics 87 L4
Hallatrow BaNES 38 F8
Hallbankgate Cumb ..149 G3
Hall Dunnerdale
  Cumb 137 H7
Hallen S Glos 38 D4
Hallgarth Dur..........151 H6
Hall Glen Falk 176 B3
Hall Green Birm........85 K7
Hallin Highld 208 D3
Halling Medway 46 B7
Hallington Lincs.......118 D4
Hallington Nthumb...158 C6
Halliwell Bolton 121 K7
Halloughton Notts....102 B3
Hallow Worcs...........70 E3
Hall's Green Herts 59 L3
Hallyne Border 166 B2
Halmore Gloucs 55 G7
Halnaker W Susx 18 B4
Halsall Lancs 120 E7
Halse Hants 73 H6
Halse Somset 25 H5
Halsetown Cnwll 2 E4
Halsham E R Yk 127 G5
Halstead Essex 61 K2
Halstead Kent 45 J7
Halstead Leics 87 L3
Halstock Dorset 14 A2
Haltemprice
  Crematorium
  E R Yk 126 C4
Haltham Lincs 118 C8
Halton Bucks 58 E6
Halton Halton...........112 D5
Halton Lancs 129 K6
Halton Leeds 123 L4
Halton Nthumb 150 C2
Halton Wrexhm 97 L4
Halton East N York ...131 K8
Halton Gill N York 131 G4
Halton Holegate Lincs..118 F7
Halton Lea Gate
  Nthumb 149 H4
Halton Shields
  Nthumb 150 C2
Halton West N York...130 F8
Haltwhistle Nthumb...149 J3
Halvergate Norfk 93 J3
Halwell Devon 7 H5
Halwill Devon 10 C5
Halwill Junction
  Devon 10 C5
Ham Devon 13 G3
Ham Gloucs 55 G7
Ham Gt Lon 44 D5
Ham Kent................35 J4
Ham Somset 25 L6
Ham Wilts 41 G7
Hambleden Bucks 42 C3

Hambledon Hants 29 M7
Hambledon Surrey......30 F4
Hamble-le-Rice Hants...16 F2
Hambleton Lancs 120 E3
Hambleton N York 124 E4
Hambridge Somset.....26 B6
Hambrook W Susx 17 L2
Hameringham Lincs 118 D7
Hamerton Cambs.......89 G7
Ham Green Worcs 71 H2
Hamilton S Lans.......175 J7
Hamilton Services
  S Lans 175 J6
Hamlet Dorset 14 B2
Hammersmith Gt Lon ...44 E4
Hammerwich Staffs....85 J3
Hammoon Dorset 27 J8
Hamnavoe Shet 235 c6
Hampden Park E Susx...20 C5
Hampnett Gloucs 56 C5
Hampole Donc........124 D7
Hampreston Dorset....15 K3
Hampstead Gt Lon.....44 E3
Hampstead Norreys
  W Berk 41 K5
Hampsthwaite N York..132 C7
Hampton C Pete........89 H5
Hampton Gt Lon 43 J6
Hampton Kent...........47 K6
Hampton Shrops 84 D6
Hampton Swindn 40 D3
Hampton Worcs 71 H5
Hampton Bishop
  Herefs 69 L6
Hampton Court
  Palace Gt Lon 44 D6
Hampton Heath
  Ches W 98 D3
Hampton in Arden
  Solhll 86 B7
Hampton Lovett
  Worcs 70 F2
Hampton Lucy
  Warwks 72 B3
Hampton Magna
  Warwks 72 C2
Hampton Poyle Oxon...57 J5
Hampton Wick Gt Lon...44 D6
Hamptworth Wilts......28 E7
Hamsey E Susx 19 L3
Hamstall Ridware
  Staffs 100 C8
Hamstead Marshall
  W Berk 41 H7
Hamsterley Dur.........140 E2
Hamsterley Dur........150 E4
Hamstreet Kent.........34 D7
Ham Street Somset....26 D4
Hamworthy Poole 15 J4
Hanbury Staffs.........100 D6
Hanbury Worcs.........71 G2
Hanchurch Staffs 99 J4
Handa Island Highld ...228 A6
Hand and Pen Devon...12 D4
Handbridge Ches W....112 B7
Handcross W Susx......31 L5
Handforth Ches E 113 J5
Handley Ches W.........98 C2
Handley Derbys 101 G1
Handsworth Birm......85 J5
Handsworth Sheff 115 H4
Hanging Heaton Kirk...123 K6
Hanging Houghton
  Nhants 87 L8
Hanging Langford
  Wilts 28 B4
Hangleton Br & H......19 H4
Hanham S Glos.........38 F6
Hankelow Ches E......98 F5
Hankerton Wilts 39 L3
Hanley C Stke..........99 K3
Hanley Castle Worcs...70 E6
Hanley Child Worcs....70 B2
Hanley Swan Worcs...70 E6
Hanley William Worcs...70 C2
Hanlith N York..........131 G7

Hanmer Wrexhm 98 C4
Hannaford Devon 23 J5
Hannington Hants 29 K1
Hannington Nhants 74 B1
Hannington Swindn 40 D2
Hannington Wick
 Swindn 40 D2
Hanslope M Keyn 74 B5
Hanthorpe Lincs 103 H7
Hanwell Gt Lon 44 D4
Hanwell Oxon 72 E5
Hanwood Shrops 83 J2
Hanworth Gt Lon 43 J6
Hanworth Norfk 106 E5
Happendon S Lans 165 G3
Happendon Services
 S Lans 165 G3
Happisburgh Norfk 107 H6
Happisburgh
 Common Norfk 107 H6
Hapsford Ches W 112 C6
Hapton Lancs 122 B4
Hapton Norfk 92 E4
Harberton Devon 7 H4
Harbertonford Devon 7 H5
Harbledown Kent 34 F3
Harborne Birm 85 H6
Harborough Magna
 Warwks 86 F7
Harbottle Nthumb 158 B2
Harbourneford
 Devon 7 G4
Harbury Warwks 72 D3
Harby Leics 102 C6
Harby Notts 116 E7
Harcombe Devon 11 K8
Harcombe Devon 12 F4
Harcombe Bottom
 Devon 13 J4
Harden C Brad 123 G3
Harden Wsall 85 H4
Hardenhuish Wilts 39 K5
Hardgate Abers 206 E5
Hardgate D & G 146 E2
Hardgate W Duns 174 F4
Hardham W Susx 18 E3
Hardingham Norfk 92 C3
Hardingstone Nhants 73 L3
Hardington Somset 27 H2
Hardington
 Mandeville
 Somset 13 M1
Hardington Marsh
 Somset 13 M1
Hardington Moor
 Somset 26 D8
Hardisworthy Devon 22 C7
Hardley Hants 16 E2
Hardley Street Norfk 93 H4
Hardraw N York 131 G2
Hardstoft Derbys 115 H8
Hardway Hants 17 H3
Hardway Somset 27 G5
Hardwick Bucks 58 D4
Hardwick Cambs 75 L3
Hardwick Nhants 74 B1
Hardwick Norfk 92 F5
Hardwick Oxon 57 G6
Hardwick Oxon 57 L3
Hardwicke Gloucs 55 H5
Hardwicke Gloucs 55 K3
Hardwick Hall Dur 141 H2
Hardy's Green Essex 61 M4
Hare Croft C Brad 123 G4
Harefield Gt Lon 43 H3
Hare Green Essex 62 D3
Hare Hatch Wokham 42 D5
Harehill Derbys 100 D5
Harehills Leeds 123 L4
Harelaw Border 167 H5
Harelaw D & G 156 D6
Harescombe Gloucs 55 J6
Haresfield Gloucs 55 J6
Harestock Hants 29 J5
Hare Street Essex 60 C6
Hare Street Herts 60 C3

Harewood Leeds 123 L2
Harewood End
 Herefs 54 D3
Harford Devon 6 F4
Hargrave Ches W 98 C1
Hargrave Nhants 74 F1
Hargrave Suffk 77 H3
Harkstead Suffk 78 E7
Harlaston Staffs 86 B2
Harlaxton Lincs 102 E6
Harlech Gwynd 95 K6
Harlech Castle Gwynd 95 K6
Harlescott Shrops 83 K1
Harlesden Gt Lon 44 E4
Harlesthorpe Derbys 115 J6
Harleston Devon 7 J6
Harleston Norfk 92 F6
Harleston Suffk 78 B3
Harlestone Nhants 73 K2
Harle Syke Lancs 122 C4
Harley Rothm 115 G2
Harley Shrops 83 L3
Harlington C Beds 59 G2
Harlington Donc 115 J2
Harlington Gt Lon 43 H5
Harlosh Highld 208 D6
Harlow Essex 60 D6
Harlow Carr RHS
 N York 132 D8
Harlow Hill Nthumb 150 D2
Harlthorpe E R Yk 125 H3
Harlton Cambs 75 L4
Harlyn Cnwll 4 D2
Harman's Cross
 Dorset 15 J6
Harmby N York 131 L2
Harmer Green Herts 59 L5
Harmer Hill Shrops 98 C7
Harmston Lincs 116 F8
Harnage Shrops 83 L3
Harnhill Gloucs 56 B7
Harold Hill Gt Lon 45 K2
Haroldston West
 Pembks 48 E4
Haroldswick Shet 235 e1
Harold Wood Gt Lon 45 K3
Harome N York 133 K3
Harpenden Herts 59 J5
Harpford Devon 12 E4
Harpham E R Yk 135 H7
Harpley Norfk 105 J7
Harpley Worcs 70 C3
Harpole Nhants 73 K3
Harpsdale Highld 231 G4
Harpswell Lincs 116 F4
Harpurhey Manch 113 K2
Harraby Cumb 148 D4
Harracott Devon 23 J6
Harrapool Highld 199 K2
Harrietfield P & K 185 K2
Harrietsham Kent 33 L3
Harringay Gt Lon 44 F3
Harrington Cumb 136 D3
Harrington Lincs 118 E6
Harrington Nhants 87 L7
Harringworth Nhants 88 D4
Harris W Isls 232 d4
Harrogate N York 132 D8
Harrogate
 Crematorium
 N York 132 E8
Harrold Bed 74 D3
Harrow Gt Lon 44 D3
Harrowbarrow Cnwll 6 B2
Harrow Green Suffk 77 J4
Harrow on the Hill
 Gt Lon 44 D3
Harrow Weald Gt Lon 44 D2
Harston Cambs 76 B4
Harston Leics 102 D6
Harswell E R Yk 125 J3
Hart Hartpl 151 L7
Hartburn Nthumb 158 D5
Hartest Suffk 77 J4
Hartfield E Susx 32 E6
Hartford Cambs 89 J8

Hartford Ches W 112 F6
Hartfordbridge Hants 42 C8
Hartford End Essex 61 G4
Hartforth N York 140 F6
Hartgrove Dorset 27 J7
Harthill Ches W 98 D2
Harthill N Lans 176 B5
Harthill Rothm 115 J5
Hartington Derbys 100 C1
Hartland Devon 22 D6
Hartland Quay Devon 22 C6
Hartlebury Worcs 70 E1
Hartlepool Hartpl 151 L7
Hartlepool
 Crematorium
 Hartpl 142 B2
Hartley Cumb 139 H5
Hartley Kent 33 K6
Hartley Kent 45 L6
Hartley Wespall
 Hants 42 B8
Hartley Wintney
 Hants 30 C1
Hartlip Kent 46 D7
Harton N York 133 L6
Harton S Tyne 151 J2
Hartpury Gloucs 55 J3
Hartshead Kirk 123 J6
Hartshead Moor
 Services Calder 123 H5
Hartshill C Stke 99 K4
Hartshill Warwks 86 D5
Hartshorne Derbys 100 F7
Hartwell Nhants 73 L4
Hartwith N York 132 C6
Hartwood N Lans 175 L6
Hartwoodmyres
 Border 166 F4
Harvel Kent 46 A7
Harvington Worcs 71 J5
Harvington Worcs 84 F8
Harwell Notts 116 B3
Harwell Oxon 41 J3
Harwich Essex 62 F2
Harwood Dale N York 143 K7
Harwood Park
 Crematorium
 Herts 59 L4
Harworth Notts 115 L3
Hasbury Dudley 85 G6
Hascombe Surrey 31 G4
Haselbech Nhants 87 K7
Haselbury Plucknett
 Somset 13 L1
Haseley Warwks 72 B2
Haselor Warwks 71 K3
Hasfield Gloucs 55 J3
Haskayne Lancs 120 E8
Hasketon Suffk 78 F4
Haslemere Surrey 30 E5
Haslingden Lancs 122 B6
Haslingfield Cambs 76 B4
Haslington Ches E 99 G2
Hassingham Norfk 93 H3
Hassocks W Susx 19 J3
Hassop Derbys 114 E6
Haster Highld 231 K5
Hastingleigh Kent 34 E5
Hastings E Susx 21 G4
Hastings Borough
 Crematorium
 E Susx 21 G3
Hastingwood Essex 60 D6
Hastoe Herts 58 F6
Haswell Dur 151 J6
Haswell Plough Dur 151 J6
Hatch Beauchamp
 Somset 25 L7
Hatch End Gt Lon 43 J3
Hatchmere Ches W 112 D6
Hatcliffe NE Lin 117 K2
Hatfield Donc 125 G8
Hatfield Herefs 69 L3
Hatfield Herts 59 L6
Hatfield Broad Oak
 Essex 60 E5

Hatfield Heath Essex 60 E5
Hatfield Peverel
 Essex 61 J5
Hatfield Woodhouse
 Donc 125 G8
Hatford Oxon 41 G2
Hatherden Hants 29 G2
Hatherleigh Devon 10 D4
Hathern Leics 101 J7
Hatherop Gloucs 56 D6
Hathersage Derbys 114 E5
Hathersage Booths
 Derbys 114 E5
Hatherton Ches E 99 G3
Hatherton Staffs 85 G2
Hatley St George
 Cambs 75 K4
Hatt Cnwll 6 B4
Hattersley Tamesd 113 M3
Hatton Abers 217 K6
Hatton Angus 196 D7
Hatton Derbys 100 E6
Hatton Gt Lon 43 J5
Hatton Lincs 117 K6
Hatton Shrops 83 J5
Hatton Warrtn 112 E5
Hatton Warwks 72 B2
Hatton of Fintray
 Abers 206 F3
Haugh E Ayrs 163 L4
Haugham Lincs 118 D5
Haughhead E Duns 175 G3
Haughley Suffk 78 B3
Haughley Green Suffk 78 B2
Haugh of Glass Moray 215 J6
Haugh of Urr D & G 146 E2
Haughs of Kinnaird
 Angus 197 G5
Haughton Shrops 98 B6
Haughton Staffs 99 K7
Haughton le Skerne
 Darltn 141 H4
Haughton Moss
 Ches E 98 E2
Haultwick Herts 60 B4
Haunton Staffs 86 B2
Hautes Croix Jersey 236 c5
Hauxton Cambs 76 B4
Havant Hants 17 K2
Havant Crematorium
 Hants 17 K2
Havenstreet IoW 17 G4
Havercroft Wakefd 124 B7
Haverfordwest
 Pembks 48 F4
Haverhill Suffk 76 F5
Haverigg Cumb 128 E4
Havering-atte-
 Bower Gt Lon 45 K2
Haversham M Keyn 74 B6
Haverthwaite Cumb 129 H3
Havyat N Som 38 C7
Hawarden Flints 111 J7
Hawbush Green
 Essex 61 J4
Hawen Cerdgn 65 K5
Hawes N York 131 G2
Hawe's Green Norfk 92 F4
Hawford Worcs 70 E3
Hawick Border 167 G6
Hawkchurch Devon 13 J3
Hawkedon Suffk 77 H4
Hawkeridge Wilts 27 K2
Hawkesbury S Glos 39 H3
Hawkesbury Upton
 S Glos 39 H3
Hawkhurst Kent 33 K6
Hawkinge Kent 35 G6
Hawkinge
 Crematorium
 Kent 35 G6
Hawkley Hants 30 C5
Hawkridge Somset 24 D5
Hawkshead Cumb 137 K7
Hawkshead Hill
 Cumb 137 K7

Hawksland S Lans 165 G2
Hawkstone Shrops 98 E6
Hawkswick N York 131 H5
Hawksworth Leeds 123 H3
Hawksworth Notts 102 C4
Hawkwell Essex 46 E2
Hawley Hants 42 E8
Hawling Gloucs 56 B4
Hawnby N York 133 H2
Haworth C Brad 122 F3
Hawstead Suffk 77 J3
Hawthorn Dur 151 K5
Hawthorn Hill Lincs 103 K2
Hawton Notts 102 C3
Haxby C York 133 J7
Haxey N Linc 116 C2
Haycombe
  Crematorium
  BaNES 39 G7
Haydock St Hel 112 E3
Haydon Bridge
  Nthumb 149 L3
Haydon Wick Swindn 40 C3
Hayes Gt Lon 43 J4
Hayes Gt Lon 45 H6
Hayes End Gt Lon 43 H4
Hayfield Ag & B 182 F3
Hayfield Derbys 114 B4
Hayhillock Angus 196 E7
Hayle Cnwll 2 F4
Hayle Port Cnwll 2 F4
Hayley Green Dudley 85 G6
Hayling Island Hants 17 K3
Hayne Devon 11 H7
Haynes (Church End)
  C Beds 74 F6
Haynes (Northwood
  End) C Beds 75 G6
Haynes (Silver End)
  C Beds 75 G6
Haynes (West End)
  C Beds 74 F6
Hay-on-Wye Powys 68 E6
Hayscastle Pembks 48 F3
Hayscastle Cross
  Pembks 48 F3
Hay Street Herts 60 C3
Hayton Cumb 147 K6
Hayton Cumb 148 E4
Hayton E R Yk 125 J2
Hayton Notts 116 B5
Haytor Vale Devon 7 H1
Haytown Devon 9 K3
Haywards Heath
  W Susx 19 J2
Haywood Donc 124 E7
Hazelbank S Lans 165 G1
Hazelbury Bryan
  Dorset 14 E2
Hazeleigh Essex 61 K7
Hazel Grove Stockp 113 L4
Hazelton Walls Fife 186 E6
Hazelwood Derbys 101 G4
Hazlemere Bucks 42 E2
Hazlerigg N u Ty 159 G7
Hazleton Gloucs 56 B4
Heacham Norfk 105 G5
Headbourne Worthy
  Hants 29 J5
Headcorn Kent 33 L4
Headingley Leeds 123 K4
Headington Oxon 57 K6
Headlam Dur 140 F4
Headlesscross N Lans 176 B6
Headless Cross Worcs 71 J2
Headley Hants 30 D4
Headley Hants 41 K7
Headley Surrey 31 K1
Headley Down Hants 30 D4
Headon Notts 116 C6
Heads Nook Cumb 148 E4
Heage Derbys 101 G3
Healaugh N York 124 D2
Healaugh N York 140 C7
Heale Somset 25 K7

Heale Somset 26 B6
Healey N York 132 B4
Healeyfield Dur 150 D5
Healing NE Lin 126 F7
Heamoor Cnwll 2 E5
Heanor Derbys 101 H3
Heanton
  Punchardon
  Devon 23 H4
Heapham Lincs 116 E4
Heart of England
  Crematorium
  Warwks 86 E5
Heart of Scotland
  Services N Lans 176 B5
Heasley Mill Devon 24 B5
Heast Highld 199 K2
Heath Derbys 115 J7
Heath Wakefd 123 L6
Heath and Reach
  C Beds 58 F3
Heathcote Derbys 100 D1
Heather Leics 86 E2
Heathfield E Susx 20 C2
Heathfield Somset 25 J6
Heath Green Worcs 71 J1
Heath Hall D & G 155 H6
Heath Hayes &
  Wimblebury Staffs 85 H2
Heath Hill Shrops 84 D2
Heathrow Airport
  Gt Lon 43 H5
Heathton Shrops 84 E5
Heath Town Wolves 85 G4
Heatley Warrtn 113 G4
Heaton C Brad 123 H4
Heaton N u Ty 151 G2
Heaton Staffs 113 L8
Heaton's Bridge
  Lancs 120 E7
Heaverham Kent 33 G2
Heavitree Devon 12 B4
Hebburn S Tyne 151 H3
Hebden N York 131 J6
Hebden Bridge Calder 122 E5
Hebing End Herts 60 A4
Hebron Carmth 49 K3
Hebron Nthumb 158 F4
Heckfield Hants 42 B7
Heckfield Green Suffk 92 E7
Heckfordbridge
  Essex 61 M4
Heckington Lincs 103 J4
Heckmondwike Kirk 123 J5
Heddington Wilts 39 M6
Heddon-on-the-Wall
  Nthumb 150 E2
Hedenham Norfk 93 G5
Hedge End Hants 29 J8
Hedgerley Bucks 42 F3
Hedging Somset 25 L5
Hedley on the Hill
  Nthumb 150 D3
Hednesford Staffs 85 H2
Hedon E R Yk 126 F5
Hedsor Bucks 42 E3
Heglibister Shet 235 c5
Heighington Darltn 141 G3
Heighington Lincs 117 G7
Heightonington Worcs 70 D1
Heiton Border 167 L4
Hele Devon 12 C2
Hele Devon 23 H3
Helensburgh Ag & B 174 B2
Helenton S Ayrs 163 K3
Helford Cnwll 3 K6
Helford Passage
  Cnwll 3 K6
Helhoughton Norfk 105 K7
Helions Bumpstead
  Essex 76 F6
Helland Cnwll 5 G2
Hellescott Cnwll 9 H6
Hellesdon Norfk 92 E2
Hellidon Nhants 73 G3
Hellifield N York 131 G7

Hellingly E Susx 20 C4
Helmdon Nhants 73 H5
Helme Kirk 123 G7
Helmingham Suffk 78 E2
Helmsdale Highld 227 H5
Helmshore Lancs 122 B6
Helmsley N York 133 J3
Helperby N York 133 G5
Helperthorpe N York 134 E3
Helpringham Lincs 103 J4
Helpston C Pete 89 G3
Helsby Ches W 112 C6
Helston Cnwll 3 H5
Helstone Cnwll 8 E8
Helton Cumb 138 D3
Hemel Hempstead
  Herts 59 H6
Hemerdon Devon 6 E4
Hemingbrough
  N York 125 G4
Hemingby Lincs 118 C6
Hemingford Abbots
  Cambs 75 K1
Hemingford Grey
  Cambs 75 K1
Hemingstone Suffk 78 D4
Hemington Leics 101 J6
Hemington Nhants 88 F6
Hemington Somset 27 G2
Hemley Suffk 79 G6
Hemlington Middsb 142 B4
Hempnall Norfk 92 F5
Hempnall Green
  Norfk 92 F5
Hempriggs Moray 214 D2
Hempstead Essex 76 F6
Hempstead Norfk 106 D5
Hempstead Norfk 107 J4
Hempton Norfk 105 L6
Hempton Oxon 57 H2
Hemsby Norfk 107 K8
Hemswell Lincs 116 F4
Hemswell Cliff Lincs 116 F4
Hemsworth Wakefd 124 C7
Hemyock Devon 25 H8
Hendon Gt Lon 44 E3
Hendon Sundld 151 K4
Hendon
  Crematorium
  Gt Lon 44 E2
Hendy Carmth 51 H5
Henfield W Susx 19 G3
Hengoed Caerph 37 J2
Hengoed Powys 68 E4
Hengrave Suffk 77 J2
Henham Essex 60 E3
Heniarth Powys 82 C2
Henlade Somset 25 L6
Henley Dorset 14 D2
Henley Somset 26 B5
Henley Suffk 78 E4
Henley W Susx 30 E6
Henley-in-Arden
  Warwks 71 L2
Henley-on-Thames
  Oxon 42 C4
Henley's Down E Susx 20 E3
Henllan Cerdgn 65 K6
Henllan Denbgs 110 E7
Henllys Torfn 37 K3
Henlow C Beds 75 H6
Hennock Devon 11 J8
Henny Street Essex 77 K6
Henryd Conwy 109 L6
Henry's Moat (Castell
  Hendre) Pembks 49 H3
Hensall N York 124 F5
Henshaw Nthumb 149 K3
Hensingham Cumb 136 D4
Henstead Suffk 93 K6
Hensting Hants 29 J6
Henstridge Somset 27 G7
Henstridge Ash
  Somset 27 G7
Henton Oxon 58 C7
Henton Somset 26 C3

Henwick Worcs 70 E4
Henwood Cnwll 5 L2
Heol-y-Cyw Brdgnd 36 E4
Hepple Nthumb 158 C2
Hepscott Nthumb 158 F5
Heptonstall Calder 122 E5
Hepworth Kirk 114 D1
Hepworth Suffk 92 B8
Herbrandston
  Pembks 48 E6
Hereford Herefs 69 K6
Hereford
  Crematorium
  Herefs 69 J6
Hereson Kent 35 K2
Heribusta Highld 218 B7
Heriot Border 177 L7
Hermiston C Edin 177 G4
Hermitage Border 156 E3
Hermitage Dorset 14 C2
Hermitage W Berk 41 J5
Hermon Carmth 65 K7
Hermon Pembks 49 L2
Herne Kent 47 K6
Herne Bay Kent 47 K6
Herne Hill Gt Lon 44 F5
Herne Pound Kent 33 H3
Hernhill Kent 34 E3
Herodsfoot Cnwll 5 K4
Heronsford S Ayrs 152 D5
Herriard Hants 30 A3
Herringfleet Suffk 93 K4
Herringswell Suffk 77 G1
Herringthorpe Rothm 115 J3
Herrington Sundld 151 J4
Hersden Kent 35 G3
Hersham Surrey 43 J7
Herstmonceux E Susx 20 D3
Herston Ork 234 c7
Hertford Herts 60 B5
Hertford Heath Herts 60 B5
Hertingfordbury
  Herts 60 A5
Hesketh Bank Lancs 120 F5
Hesketh Lane Lancs 121 J3
Hesket Newmarket
  Cumb 148 C7
Hesleden Dur 151 K8
Heslington C York 124 F1
Hessay C York 133 H8
Hessenford Cnwll 5 L4
Hessett Suffk 77 L3
Hessle E R Yk 126 C5
Hessle Wakefd 124 C6
Hest Bank Lancs 129 K6
Heston Gt Lon 43 J5
Heston Services
  Gt Lon 43 J5
Hestwall Ork 234 b5
Heswall Wirral 111 J5
Hethe Oxon 57 L3
Hethersett Norfk 92 D3
Hethersgill Cumb 148 E2
Hett Dur 151 G7
Hetton N York 131 H7
Hetton-le-Hole
  Sundld 151 J3
Heugh Nthumb 158 D7
Heughhead Abers 205 J3
Heugh Head Border 179 H6
Heveningham Suffk 93 G8
Hever Kent 32 E4
Heversham Cumb 129 K3
Hevingham Norfk 106 E7
Hewas Water Cnwll 4 F6
Hewelsfield Gloucs 54 E7
Hewish Somset 13 K2
Hewood Dorset 13 J2
Hexham Nthumb 150 B3
Hextable Kent 45 K6
Hexthorpe Donc 115 K2
Hexton Herts 59 J2
Hexworthy Cnwll 9 K8
Hexworthy Devon 6 F2
Heybridge Essex 61 G7
Heybridge Essex 61 K6

Heybrook Bay Devon 6 D6
Heydon Cambs 76 B6
Heydon Norfk......106 D6
Heydour Lincs......103 G5
Heylipoll Ag & B......188 C7
Heylor Shet......235 c3
Heysham Lancs......129 J7
Heyshott W Susx......18 B3
Heytesbury Wilts......27 L3
Heythrop Oxon......57 G3
Heywood Rochdl......122 C7
Heywood Wilts......27 K2
Hibaldstow N Linc......116 F2
Hickleton Donc......115 J1
Hickling Norfk......107 J7
Hickling Notts......102 B6
Hickling Green Norfk......107 J7
Hickstead W Susx......31 L7
Hidcote Bartrim
  Gloucs......71 L6
Hidcote Boyce
  Gloucs......71 L6
High Ackworth
  Wakefd......124 C6
Higham Barns......114 F1
Higham Derbys......101 H2
Higham Kent......33 G4
Higham Kent......46 B5
Higham Lancs......122 B3
Higham Suffk......77 H2
Higham Suffk......78 B7
Higham Ferrers
  Nhants......74 D2
Higham Gobion
  C Beds......59 J2
Higham Hill Gt Lon......45 G3
Higham on the Hill
  Leics......86 E4
Highampton Devon......10 C4
Highams Park Gt Lon......45 H2
High Ardwell D & G......144 C6
High Auldgirth D & G......154 F5
High Bankhill Cumb......148 F6
High Beach Essex......60 C7
High Bentham N York......130 C5
High Bickington
  Devon......23 J7
High Biggins Cumb......130 B4
High Blantyre S Lans......175 J6
High Bonnybridge
  Falk......175 L3
High Bray Devon......23 L5
Highbridge Somset......25 L3
Highbrook W Susx......32 C7
High Brooms Kent......33 G5
Highburton Kirk......123 J7
Highbury Gt Lon......44 F3
Highbury Somset......27 G2
High Casterton Cumb......130 C4
High Catton E R Yk......133 L8
Highclere Hants......41 H8
Highcliffe Dorset......16 B4
High Coniscliffe
  Darltn......141 G4
High Crosby Cumb......148 E3
High Cross E Ayrs......163 K1
High Cross Hants......30 B6
High Cross Herts......60 B4
High Cross Warwks......71 L2
High Drummore
  D & G......144 D7
High Easter Essex......60 F5
High Ellington N York......132 B3
Higher Ansty Dorset......14 E2
Higher Bartle Lancs......121 G4
Higher
  Bockhampton
  Dorset......14 D4
Higher Brixham
  Torbay......7 L5
High Ercall Wrekin......98 E8
Higher Chillington
  Somset......13 K1
Higher Folds Wigan......113 G2
Higher Gabwell
  Devon......7 L3

Higher Heysham
  Lancs......129 J7
Higher Irlam Salfd......113 G3
Higher Kinnerton
  Flints......97 L1
Higher Muddiford
  Devon......23 J4
Higher Penwortham
  Lancs......121 G5
Higher Prestacott
  Devon......9 K5
Higher Town Cnwll......4 C6
Higher Town Cnwll......4 F4
Higher Town IoS......2 b1
Higher Walton Lancs......121 H5
Higher Walton Warrtn......112 E4
Higher Wambrook
  Somset......13 H2
Higher Waterston
  Dorset......14 D4
Higher Wheelton
  Lancs......121 J6
Higher Whitley
  Ches W......112 F5
Higher Wincham
  Ches W......113 G6
Higher Wraxhall
  Dorset......14 B3
Higher Wych Ches W......98 C4
High Etherley Dur......140 F2
Highfield Gatesd......150 E3
Highfield N Ayrs......174 C7
High Garrett Essex......61 J3
Highgate Gt Lon......44 F3
High Grantley N York......132 C5
High Green Norfk......92 D3
High Green Norfk......92 E5
High Green Sheff......115 G3
High Halden Kent......34 B7
High Halstow
  Medway......46 C5
High Ham Somset......26 B5
High Hauxley
  Nthumb......159 G2
High Hawsker N York......143 J5
High Hesket Cumb......148 E6
High Hoyland Barns......123 K8
High Hurstwood
  E Susx......32 E7
High Hutton N York......134 B5
High Ireby Cumb......147 M7
High Kilburn N York......133 H4
High Lands Dur......140 E3
Highlane Derbys......115 H5
High Lane Stockp......113 L4
High Lanes Cnwll......3 G4
Highleadon Gloucs......55 H4
High Legh Ches E......113 G5
Highleigh W Susx......18 A6
High Leven S on T......141 K5
Highley Shrops......84 D6
High Littleton BaNES......38 F8
High Lorton Cumb......137 G3
High Marnham Notts......116 D7
High Melton Donc......115 K2
High Mickley Nthumb......150 D3
Highmoor Oxon......42 B4
Highmoor Cross Oxon......42 B4
Highnam Gloucs......55 H4
High Newport Sundld......151 J4
High Newton Cumb......129 J3
High Nibthwaite
  Cumb......129 G2
High Offley Staffs......99 H7
High Ongar Essex......60 E7
High Onn Staffs......84 E1
High Park Corner
  Essex......62 C4
High Pennyvenie
  E Ayrs......163 L7
High Roding Essex......60 F4
High Salvington
  W Susx......18 F4

High Spen Gatesd......150 E3
Highsted Kent......34 B3
High Street Cnwll......4 F5
Highstreet Kent......34 E3
Highstreet Green
  Surrey......31 G4
Hightae D & G......155 J6
Hightown Sefton......111 J2
Hightown Green
  Suffk......77 L4
High Toynton Lincs......118 C7
High Valleyfield Fife......176 D2
Highweek Devon......7 J2
Highwood Hill Gt Lon......44 E2
Highworth Swindn......40 D2
High Wray Cumb......137 K7
High Wych Herts......60 D5
High Wycombe Bucks......42 E2
Hilborough Norfk......91 I4
Hilcott Wilts......40 C8
Hildenborough Kent......32 F4
Hilden Park Kent......33 G4
Hildersham Cambs......76 D5
Hilderstone Staffs......99 L5
Hilderthorpe E R Yk......135 J6
Hilgay Norfk......90 E4
Hill S Glos......38 F2
Hill Warwks......72 F2
Hillam N York......124 D5
Hill Brow Hants......30 C6
Hillbutts Dorset......15 J3
Hill Chorlton Staffs......99 H5
Hillclifflane Derbys......100 F3
Hill Common Somset......25 H6
Hilldyke Lincs......104 B3
Hillend Fife......176 F2
Hill End Fife......185 L7
Hill End Gloucs......70 F6
Hillend Mdloth......177 H5
Hillend N Lans......175 L5
Hillesden Bucks......58 B3
Hillesley Gloucs......39 H3
Hillfarrance Somset......25 J6
Hill Green Kent......46 D7
Hillhead Abers......216 B7
Hill Head Hants......17 G2
Hillhead S Lans......165 J2
Hillhead of Cocklaw
  Abers......217 K5
Hilliclay Highld......231 H3
Hillingdon Gt Lon......43 H4
Hillington C Glas......174 F5
Hillington Norfk......105 H7
Hillmorton Warwks......87 G8
Hill of Beath Fife......176 F1
Hill of Fearn Highld......223 H5
Hillowton D & G......146 D3
Hill Ridware Staffs......100 B8
Hillside Abers......207 H5
Hillside Angus......197 H4
Hill Side Kirk......123 H6
Hills Town Derbys......115 J7
Hillstreet Hants......29 G7
Hillswick Shet......235 c3
Hill Top Wakefd......123 L7
Hillwell Shet......235 c8
Hilmarton Wilts......40 A5
Hilperton Wilts......39 K8
Hilsea C Port......17 J2
Hilston E R Yk......127 G4
Hilton Border......179 H7
Hilton Cambs......75 K2
Hilton Cumb......139 G3
Hilton Derbys......100 E6
Hilton Dorset......14 E2
Hilton Dur......140 F3
Hilton Highld......223 J6
Hilton S on T......141 K5
Hilton Shrops......84 D4
Hilton Park Services
  Staffs......85 G3
Himbleton Worcs......71 G3
Himley Staffs......84 F5
Hincaster Cumb......129 L3
Hinchley Wood
  Surrey......44 D6

Hinckley Leics......86 E5
Hinderclay Suffk......92 B7
Hinderwell N York......143 G4
Hindhead Surrey......30 E4
Hindley Wigan......112 F1
Hindlip Worcs......70 F3
Hindolveston Norfk......106 C6
Hindon Wilts......27 K5
Hindringham Norfk......106 B5
Hingham Norfk......92 B3
Hinstock Shrops......99 G7
Hintlesham Suffk......78 C5
Hinton Herefs......69 G6
Hinton S Glos......39 G5
Hinton Shrops......83 H2
Hinton Ampner Hants......29 L6
Hinton Blewett
  BaNES......26 E1
Hinton Charterhouse
  BaNES......39 H8
Hinton-in-the-
  Hedges Nhants......73 H6
Hinton Martell Dorset......15 J2
Hinton on the Green
  Worcs......71 H6
Hinton Parva Swindn......40 E4
Hinton St George
  Somset......26 B8
Hinton St Mary
  Dorset......27 H7
Hinton Waldrist Oxon......57 G7
Hints Staffs......85 L3
Hinwick Bed......74 D3
Hinxhill Kent......34 D6
Hinxton Cambs......76 C5
Hinxworth Herts......75 J6
Hipperholme Calder......123 H5
Hipswell N York......140 F7
Hirn Abers......206 D5
Hirnant Powys......97 G7
Hirst Nthumb......159 G5
Hirst Courtney N York......124 F5
Hirwaun Rhondd......52 F6
Hiscott Devon......23 J6
Histon Cambs......76 B2
Hitcham Suffk......78 B4
Hitcham Causeway
  Suffk......78 B4
Hitcham Street Suffk......78 B4
Hitchin Herts......59 K3
Hither Green Gt Lon......45 H5
Hittisleigh Devon......11 H5
Hive E R Yk......125 J4
Hixon Staffs......100 A7
Hoaden Kent......35 H3
Hoar Cross Staffs......100 C7
Hoarwithy Herefs......54 D3
Hoath Kent......47 K7
Hobarris Shrops......82 F7
Hobkirk Border......167 J7
Hobson Dur......150 F4
Hoby Leics......102 A8
Hockering Norfk......92 C2
Hockerton Notts......102 B2
Hockley Essex......46 D2
Hockley Heath Solhll......85 L8
Hockliffe C Beds......58 F3
Hockwold cum
  Wilton Norfk......91 G6
Hockworthy Devon......25 G7
Hoddesdon Herts......60 B6
Hoddlesden Bl w D......121 L6
Hoddom Cross D & G......155 L7
Hoddom Mains D & G......155 K7
Hodgeston Pembks......49 H7
Hodnet Shrops......98 E6
Hodsock Notts......115 L4
Hodsoll Street Kent......45 M7
Hodson Swindn......40 D4
Hodthorpe Derbys......115 K6
Hoe Norfk......92 B1
Hogben's Hill Kent......34 D4
Hoggeston Bucks......58 D3
Hoggrill's End Warwks......86 B5
Hoghton Lancs......121 J5
Hognaston Derbys......100 E3

Hogsthorpe Lincs..........119 H6
Holbeach Lincs 104 B7
Holbeach Bank Lincs 104 B6
Holbeach Clough
   Lincs 104 B6
Holbeach Drove Lincs 89 K2
Holbeach Hurn Lincs 104 C6
Holbeach St Johns
   Lincs 104 B8
Holbeach St Mark's
   Lincs 104 B6
Holbeach St
   Matthew Lincs....104 C6
Holbeck Notts..............115 K6
Holberrow Green
   Worcs 71 H3
Holbeton Devon 6 F5
Holborn Gt Lon 44 F4
Holbrook Derbys..........101 G4
Holbrook Suffk 78 E6
Holbrooks Covtry............86 D6
Holbury Hants..............16 E2
Holcombe Devon 12 B7
Holcombe Somset..........26 F2
Holcombe Rogus
   Devon 25 G7
Holcot Nhants................73 L1
Holden Lancs..............122 B1
Holdenby Nhants..........73 K2
Holder's Green Essex....61 G3
Holdgate Shrops 83 L5
Holdingham Lincs........103 H3
Holditch Dorset 13 J2
Holemoor Devon 10 B4
Holford Somset..............25 J3
Holgate C York............124 E1
Holker Cumb................129 H4
Holkham Norfk............105 L4
Hollacombe Devon 9 K4
Holland Fen Lincs........103 L3
Holland-on-Sea
   Essex 62 E5
Hollandstoun Ork 234 e3
Hollee D & G 148 A2
Hollesley Suffk..............79 H5
Hollicombe Torbay..........7 K4
Hollingbourne Kent......33 L3
Hollingbury Br & H......19 J4
Hollingdon Bucks........58 E3
Hollington Derbys........100 E5
Hollington Staffs..........100 B5
Hollingworth Tamesd....114 A3
Hollinsclough Staffs......114 B7
Hollins End Sheff........115 G5
Hollins Green Warrtn ...113 G4
Hollinswood Wrekin....84 C2
Hollinwood
   Crematorium
     Oldham......................113 K2
Hollocombe Devon 10 F3
Holloway Derbys..........100 F2
Holloway Gt Lon............44 F3
Hollowell Nhants..........73 K1
Hollowmoor Heath
   Ches W 112 C7
Hollows D & G 156 C6
Hollybush Caerph..........53 J7
Hollybush E Ayrs..........163 K6
Hollybush Herefs..........70 D6
Hollym E R Yk..............127 H5
Holmbridge Kirk..........114 C1
Holmbury St Mary
   Surrey 31 J3
Holmbush Cnwll..............5 G5
Holmcroft Staffs............99 K7
Holme Cambs................89 H6
Holme Cumb................129 L4
Holme Kirk..................114 C1
Holme N York..............132 E3
Holme Notts................102 D2
Holme Chapel Lancs....122 C5
Holme Hale Norfk..........91 K3
Holme Lacy Herefs........69 L7
Holme Marsh Herefs....69 G4
Holme next the Sea
   Norfk 105 H4

Holme on the Wolds
   E R Yk........................126 B2
Holme Pierrepont
   Notts..........................101 L5
Holmer Herefs 69 K6
Holmer Green Bucks....42 E2
Holme St Cuthbert
   Cumb 147 J5
Holmes Chapel
   Ches E 113 H7
Holmesfield Derbys......114 F6
Holmeswood Lancs......120 F6
Holmethorpe Surrey....32 B3
Holme upon
   Spalding Moor
     E R Yk........................125 J3
Holmewood Derbys......115 H7
Holmfirth Kirk..............123 H8
Holmhead E Ayrs..........164 B5
Holmpton E R Yk..........127 J5
Holmrook Cumb..........136 E7
Holmsford Bridge
   Crematorium
     N Ayrs 163 J2
Holmside Dur..............150 F5
Holne Devon 7 G3
Holnicote Somset..........24 E3
Holsworthy Devon..........9 J4
Holsworthy Beacon
   Devon 9 K3
Holt Dorset 15 J2
Holt Norfk..................106 C5
Holt Wilts 39 K7
Holt Worcs 70 E3
Holt Wrexhm................98 B2
Holtby C York..............133 K8
Holt End Worcs..............71 J1
Holt Heath Worcs..........70 E2
Holton Oxon..................57 L6
Holton Somset..............27 G6
Holton Suffk..................93 J7
Holton cum
   Beckering Lincs 117 J5
Holton le Clay Lincs 118 C2
Holton le Moor Lincs 117 H3
Holton St Mary Suffk....78 C6
Holwell Dorset..............14 D1
Holwell Herts 59 K2
Holwell Leics..............102 B7
Holwell Oxon................56 E6
Holwick Dur................139 K2
Holybourne Hants..........30 B4
Holyhead IoA 108 C5
Holy Island IoA............108 C5
Holy Island Nthumb....169 H2
Holy Island Nthumb....169 H2
Holymoorside Derbys....115 G7
Holyport W & M............42 E5
Holystone Nthumb......158 B2
Holytown N Lans........175 K6
Holytown
   Crematorium
     N Lans........................175 K6
Holywell C Beds............59 G5
Holywell Cambs............75 L1
Holywell Cnwll................4 B4
Holywell Dorset............14 B2
Holywell Flints............111 G6
Holywell Green
   Calder 123 G6
Holywell Lake Somset....25 H7
Holywell Row Suffk......91 G7
Holywood D & G..........155 G6
Holywood Village
   D & G 155 G6
Homer Shrops................84 B3
Homer Green Sefton 111 K2
Homersfield Suffk..........93 G6
Homington Wilts..........28 C6
Honeybourne Worcs......71 K5
Honeychurch Devon......10 F4
Honeystreet Wilts..........40 C7
Honey Tye Suffk............77 L7
Honiley Warwks 86 B8
Honing Norfk..............107 G6
Honingham Norfk........92 D2

Honington Lincs..........102 F4
Honington Suffk............91 K8
Honington Warwks 72 C6
Honiton Devon 12 F3
Honley Kirk..................123 H7
Honor Oak
   Crematorium
     Gt Lon 45 G5
Hooe C Plym....................6 D5
Hooe E Susx..................20 E4
Hoo Green Ches E 113 G5
Hoohill Bpool..............120 D3
Hook Gt Lon..................44 D7
Hook Hants....................30 B1
Hook Pembks................49 G5
Hook Wilts....................40 B4
Hooke Dorset................14 A3
Hook Green Kent..........33 H6
Hook Green Kent..........45 L6
Hook Norton Oxon........57 G2
Hookway Devon............11 K5
Hooley Surrey................32 B3
Hoo St Werburgh
   Medway 46 C5
Hooton Levitt Rothm....115 K3
Hooton Pagnell Donc...124 D8
Hooton Roberts
   Rothm 115 J3
Hope Derbys................114 D5
Hope Devon 7 G7
Hope Flints..................97 L2
Hope Staffs..................100 C2
Hope Bagot Shrops......83 L8
Hope Bowdler Shrops....83 J5
Hopehouse Border 166 D6
Hopeman Moray..........214 E1
Hope Mansell Herefs....54 F4
Hopesay Shrops............83 H6
Hope under Dinmore
   Herefs 69 K4
Hopgrove C York..........133 K8
Hopperton N York........132 F7
Hopstone Shrops..........84 D5
Hopton Derbys............100 E2
Hopton Staffs................99 L7
Hopton Suffk................92 B7
Hopton Cangeford
   Shrops 83 K7
Hopton Castle Shrops....83 G7
Hoptonheath Shrops....83 H7
Hopton on Sea Norfk....93 L4
Hopton Wafers
   Shrops 84 B7
Hopwas Staffs..............85 L3
Hopwood Worcs............85 J7
Hopwood Park
   Services Worcs..........85 J8
Horam E Susx................20 C3
Horbling Lincs..............103 J5
Horbury Wakefd..........123 K6
Horden Dur..................151 K6
Hordle Hants................16 C4
Hordley Shrops..............98 B6
Horfield Bristl................38 E5
Horham Suffk................92 E8
Horkesley Heath
   Essex 62 B3
Horkstow N Linc..........126 B6
Horley Oxon..................72 E5
Horley Surrey................32 B5
Hornblotton Green
   Somset..........................26 E5
Hornby Lancs..............130 B5
Hornby N York............132 C2
Hornby N York............141 J6
Horncastle Lincs..........118 C7
Hornchurch Gt Lon......45 K3
Horncliffe Nthumb......179 J7
Horndean Border........179 J7
Horndean Hants..........30 B8
Horndon Devon 10 D8
Horndon on the Hill
   Thurr 46 A4
Horne Surrey................32 C4
Horner Somset..............24 D3

Horning Norfk..............107 H8
Horninghold Leics........88 B4
Horninglow Staffs........100 E7
Horningsea Cambs........76 C3
Horningsham Wilts......27 J3
Horningtoft Norfk........105 M7
Horns Cross Devon........22 F6
Hornsea E R Yk............126 F2
Hornsey Gt Lon..............44 F3
Hornton Oxon................72 E5
Horra Shet....................235 d2
Horrabridge Devon..........6 D2
Horringer Suffk..............77 J3
Horrocksford Lancs......121 L2
Horsebridge Devon..........6 B2
Horsebridge E Susx......20 C4
Horsebridge Hants........29 G5
Horsehay Wrekin..........84 C3
Horseheath Cambs........76 E5
Horsehouse N York......131 K4
Horsell Surrey................43 G8
Horseman's Green
   Wrexhm......................98 C4
Horsey Norfk..............107 K7
Horsey Somset..............25 L4
Horsford Norfk..............92 E1
Horsforth Leeds..........123 J3
Horsham W Susx............31 K5
Horsham Worcs..............70 D3
Horsham St Faith
   Norfk 92 E1
Horsington Lincs..........117 K7
Horsington Somset........27 G6
Horsley Derbys..............101 G4
Horsley Gloucs..............39 J2
Horsley Nthumb..........150 D2
Horsley Nthumb..........157 L3
Horsleycross Street
   Essex 62 D3
Horsleyhill Border........167 H5
Horsley Woodhouse
   Derbys 101 H4
Horsmonden Kent........33 J5
Horspath Oxon..............57 L6
Horstead Norfk..........106 F8
Horsted Keynes
   W Susx..........................32 C7
Horton Bucks................58 F4
Horton Dorset..............15 J2
Horton Lancs..............122 C1
Horton Nhants..............74 B4
Horton S Glos................39 H4
Horton Somset..............25 L7
Horton Staffs................99 L2
Horton Swans..............50 F7
Horton W & M..............43 G5
Horton Wilts................40 B7
Horton Wrekin..............84 C1
Horton-cum-Studley
   Oxon............................57 L5
Horton Green
   Ches W 98 C3
Horton-in-
   Ribblesdale
     N York........................130 F5
Horton Kirby Kent........45 K6
Horwich Bolton 121 J7
Horwood Devon............23 H6
Hoscote Border............166 F6
Hose Leics..................102 B6
Hosh P & K..................185 H3
Hoswick Shet..............235 C7
Hotham E R Yk............125 L4
Hothfield Kent..............34 C5
Hoton Leics..................101 L7
Hough Ches E................99 G3
Hougham Lincs............102 E4
Hough Green Halton....112 C4
Hough-on-the-Hill
   Lincs 102 F3
Houghton Cambs..........75 K1
Houghton Hants..........29 G5
Houghton Pembks........49 G6
Houghton W Susx........18 D4
Houghton Conquest
   C Beds 74 F6

Houghton Green
  E Susx 21 H2
Houghton-le-Spring
  Sundld 151 H5
Houghton on the Hill
  Leics 87 J3
Houghton Regis
  C Beds 59 G4
Houghton St Giles
  Norfk 105 L5
Hound Green Hants 42 B8
Houndslow Border 178 D8
Houndwood Border 179 H5
Hounslow Gt Lon 43 J5
Househill Highld 213 L4
Houses Hill Kirk 123 J6
Housieside Abers 207 G1
Houston Rens 174 D5
Houstry Highld 227 K2
Houton Ork 234 b6
Hove Br & H 19 J5
Hoveringham Notts 102 B3
Hoveton Norfk 107 G8
Hovingham N York 133 K4
How Caple Herefs 54 E3
Howden E R Yk 125 H5
Howden-le-Wear Dur ...150 E7
Howe Highld 231 K3
Howe N York 132 E4
Howe Norfk 92 F4
Howe Bridge
   Crematorium
   Wigan 112 F2
Howe Green Essex 61 J2
Howegreen Essex 61 K7
Howell Lincs 103 J4
Howe of Teuchar
   Abers 216 E5
Howes D & G 147 L2
Howe Street Essex 61 H5
Howe Street Essex 77 G7
Howey Powys 68 B3
Howgate Cumb 136 D3
Howgate Mdloth 177 H6
Howick Nthumb 169 K5
Howlett End Essex 76 E7
Howley Somset 13 H1
How Mill Cumb 148 E4
Howmore W Isls 233 b7
Hownam Border 168 B5
Howsham N Linc 117 H2
Howsham N York 133 L6
Howtel Nthumb 168 D3
Howwood Rens 174 D6
Hoxne Suffk 92 E7
Hoy Ork 234 b7
Hoylake Wirral 111 H4
Hoyland Nether
   Barns 115 G2
Hoyland Swaine
   Barns 114 E1
Hubberston Pembks 48 E6
Huby N York 123 K2
Huby N York 133 J6
Hucclecote Gloucs 55 K4
Hucking Kent 33 L2
Hucknall Notts 101 K3
Huddersfield Kirk 123 H7
Huddersfield
   Crematorium Kirk ...123 H6
Huddington Worcs 71 G3
Hudswell N York 140 E7
Huggate E R Yk 134 D7
Hughenden Valley
   Bucks 42 E2
Hughley Shrops 83 L4
Hugh Town IoS 2 b2
Huish Devon 10 D3
Huish Wilts 40 C7
Huish Champflower
   Somset 25 G5
Huish Episcopi
   Somset 26 B6
Hulcott Bucks 58 D5
Hulham Devon 12 C5
Hulland Derbys 100 E3

Hulland Ward Derbys 100 E3
Hullavington Wilts 39 K4
Hullbridge Essex 46 D2
Hull, Kingston upon
   C KuH 126 D5
Hulme Manch 113 J3
Hulme Staffs 99 L4
Hulme Warrtn 112 E4
Hulme End Staffs 100 C2
Hulme Walfield
   Ches E 113 J7
Hulverstone IoW 16 E5
Hulver Street Suffk 93 K6
Humberside Airport
   N Linc 126 D7
Humberston NE Lin 118 D1
Humberstone C Leic 87 J3
Humbie E Loth 178 B5
Humbleton E R Yk 126 F4
Humby Lincs 103 G6
Hume Border 167 L2
Humshaugh Nthumb 158 A7
Huna Highld 231 L2
Huncote Leics 87 G4
Hundalee Border 167 K5
Hunderthwaite Dur 140 C3
Hundleby Lincs 118 E7
Hundleton Pembks 49 G7
Hundon Suffk 77 G5
Hundred House
   Powys 68 C4
Hungarton Leics 87 K3
Hungerford Somset 25 G4
Hungerford W Berk 41 G6
Hungerford
   Newtown W Berk 41 G6
Hungerstone Herefs 69 J7
Hunmanby N York 135 H4
Hunningham
   Warwks 72 D2
Hunsbury Hill Nhants 73 K3
Hunsdon Herts 60 C5
Hunsingore N York 132 F8
Hunslet Leeds 123 L4
Hunsonby Cumb 149 G7
Hunstanton Norfk 105 G4
Hunstanworth Dur 150 B5
Hunsterson Ches E 99 G4
Hunston Suffk 77 J2
Hunston W Susx 18 B5
Hunstrete BaNES 38 F7
Hunsworth Kirk 123 J5
Hunter's Quay Ag & B ..173 K3
Huntham Somset 25 M6
Hunthill Lodge Angus ...196 D3
Huntingdon Cambs 89 J8
Huntingfield Suffk 93 G8
Huntington C York 133 J7
Huntington Ches W 112 B8
Huntington E Loth 178 B4
Huntington Herefs 68 E4
Huntington Staffs 85 H2
Huntley Gloucs 55 G4
Huntly Abers 215 L6
Hunton Kent 33 J4
Hunton N York 132 B2
Huntscott Somset 24 E3
Huntsham Devon 24 F7
Huntshaw Devon 23 H6
Huntspill Somset 25 L3
Huntstile Somset 25 K5
Huntworth Somset 25 L4
Hunwick Dur 140 F2
Hunworth Norfk 106 C5
Hurdcott Wilts 28 D5
Hurdsfield Ches E 113 L6
Hurley W & M 42 D4
Hurley Warwks 86 B4
Hurley Common
   Warwks 86 B4
Hurlford E Ayrs 163 L3
Hurn Dorset 15 L3
Hursley Hants 29 H6
Hurst Wokham 42 C5
Hurstbourne Priors
   Hants 29 H3

Hurstbourne Tarrant
   Hants 29 G2
Hurst Green E Susx 33 J7
Hurst Green Essex 62 C5
Hurst Green Lancs 121 K3
Hurst Green Surrey 32 D3
Hurstpierpoint
   W Susx 19 J3
Hurstwood Lancs 122 C4
Hurtiso Ork 234 c6
Hurworth-on-Tees
   Darltn 141 H5
Hurworth Place
   Darltn 141 H5
Husbands Bosworth
   Leics 87 J6
Husborne Crawley
   C Beds 74 D7
Hushwaite N York 133 H4
Hutcliffe Wood
   Crematorium
   Sheff 115 G5
Huthwaite Notts 101 J2
Huttoft Lincs 119 G6
Hutton Border 179 J7
Hutton E R Yk 134 F8
Hutton Essex 45 M2
Hutton Lancs 121 G5
Hutton N Som 37 M8
Hutton Buscel N York ...134 F3
Hutton Conyers
   N York 132 E5
Hutton Cranswick
   E R Yk 126 C1
Hutton End Cumb 148 D7
Hutton Henry Dur 151 K7
Hutton-le-Hole
   N York 133 L2
Hutton Lowcross
   R & Cl 142 D4
Hutton Magna Dur 140 E5
Hutton Roof Cumb 130 B4
Hutton Roof Cumb 148 C7
Hutton Rudby N York ...141 K6
Hutton Sessay N York ...133 G4
Hutton Wandesley
   N York 124 D1
Huxham Devon 12 B3
Huxley Ches W 98 D1
Huyton Knows 112 C4
Hycemoor Cumb 128 D2
Hyde Tamesd 113 L3
Hyde Heath Bucks 58 F7
Hyde Lea Staffs 99 K8
Hylands House &
   Park Essex 61 G7
Hyndford Bridge
   S Lans 165 H2
Hynish Ag & B 188 C8
Hyssington Powys 82 F5
Hythe Essex 62 B3
Hythe Hants 16 E2
Hythe Kent 34 F7
Hythe End W & M 43 G6

I

Ibberton Dorset 14 E2
Ible Derbys 100 E2
Ibsley Hants 15 L1
Ibstock Leics 86 E2
Ibstone Bucks 42 C2
Ibthorpe Hants 29 G2
Iburndale N York 143 H5
Ibworth Hants 29 K1
Ichrachan Ag & B 182 E2
Ickburgh Norfk 91 J4
Ickenham Gt Lon 43 H3
Ickford Bucks 57 M6
Ickham Kent 35 G3
Ickleford Herts 59 K2
Icklesham E Susx 21 H3
Ickleton Cambs 76 C5
Icklingham Suffk 91 H8

Ickornshaw N York 122 E2
Ickwell Green C Beds 75 G5
Icomb Gloucs 56 E4
Idbury Oxon 56 E4
Iddesleigh Devon 10 E3
Ide Devon 11 K6
Ideford Devon 7 K1
Ide Hill Kent 32 E3
Iden E Susx 21 H2
Iden Green Kent 33 J5
Iden Green Kent 33 K6
Idle C Brad 123 H3
Idless Cnwll 4 C6
Idlicote Warwks 72 C5
Idmiston Wilts 28 D4
Idole Carmth 50 E3
Idridgehay Derbys 100 F3
Idrigill Highld 208 F2
Idstone Oxon 40 E4
Iffley Oxon 57 K7
Ifield W Susx 31 L4
Ifold W Susx 31 G5
Iford Bmouth 15 L4
Iford E Susx 19 L4
Ifton Mons 38 C3
Ightfield Shrops 98 E5
Ightham Kent 33 G2
Ilam Staffs 100 C3
Ilchester Somset 26 D6
Ilderton Nthumb 168 F5
Ilford Gt Lon 45 H3
Ilford Somset 26 A7
Ilfracombe Devon 23 H2
Ilkeston Derbys 101 J4
Ilketshall St Andrew
   Suffk 93 H6
Ilketshall St
   Margaret Suffk 93 H6
Ilkley C Brad 123 G2
Illand Cnwll 5 L1
Illey Dudley 85 H7
Illogan Cnwll 3 H3
Illston on the Hill
   Leics 87 K4
Ilmer Bucks 58 C6
Ilmington Warwks 72 B5
Ilminster Somset 26 A8
Ilsington Devon 7 H2
Ilston Swans 51 H7
Ilton N York 132 B4
Ilton Somset 25 M7
Imachar N Ayrs 161 L2
Immingham NE Lin 126 F7
Immingham Dock
   NE Lin 126 F7
Impington Cambs 76 C2
Ince Ches W 112 C6
Ince Blundell Sefton 111 K2
Ince-in-Makerfield
   Wigan 112 E1
Inchbae Lodge Hotel
   Highld 221 K7
Inchbare Angus 196 F4
Inchberry Moray 215 G4
Incheril Highld 211 G3
Inchinnan Rens 174 E5
Inchlaggan Highld 201 J5
Inchmichael P & K 186 D3
Inchnacardoch Hotel
   Highld 202 B3
Inchnadamph Highld 224 F4
Inchture P & K 186 D2
Inchvuilt Highld 211 K6
Inchyra P & K 186 C4
Indian Queens Cnwll 4 E4
Ingatestone Essex 61 G7
Ingbirchworth Barns 114 E1
Ingestre Staffs 99 L7
Ingham Lincs 116 F5
Ingham Norfk 107 H7
Ingham Suffk 77 J1
Ingham Corner
   Norfk 107 H6
Ingleby Derbys 101 G6
Ingleby Arncliffe
   N York 141 K6

Ingleby Barwick
S on T 141 K4
Ingleby Greenhow
N York.................................142 C6
Ingleigh Green Devon 10 E4
Inglesbatch BaNES.............39 G7
Inglesham Swindn...............56 D7
Ingleston D & G.................147 G2
Ingleton Dur.......................140 F3
Ingleton N York..................130 D5
Inglewhite Lancs................121 H3
Ingoe Nthumb.....................158 C7
Ingol Lancs.........................121 G4
Ingoldisthorpe Norfk.........105 G6
Ingoldmells Lincs...............119 H7
Ingoldsby Lincs..................103 G6
Ingram Nthumb...................168 F6
Ingrave Essex......................45 M2
Ingrow C Brad....................122 F3
Ings Cumb..........................138 C7
Ingst S Glos.........................38 E3
Ingthorpe Rutlnd.................88 E2
Ingworth Norfk...................106 E6
Inkberrow Worcs.................71 H3
Inkhorn Abers.....................217 H6
Inkpen W Berk.....................41 G7
Inkstack Highld...................231 J2
Innellan Ag & B..................173 K4
Innerleithen Border............166 E3
Innerleven Fife...................186 F7
Innermessan D & G............144 C3
Innerwick E Loth................178 F4
Innesmill Moray..................215 G2
Insch Abers........................216 C8
Insh Highld.........................203 J5
Inskip Lancs........................120 F3
Instow Devon.......................23 G5
Intake Sheff........................115 H5
Inver Abers.........................204 F6
Inver Highld........................223 J5
Inver P & K.........................194 F7
Inverailort Highld...............190 F1
Inveralligin Highld..............210 C3
Inverallochy Abers..............217 K2
Inveran Highld....................222 D2
Inveraray Ag & B................182 F5
Inverarish Highld................209 J7
Inverarity Angus.................196 D7
Inverarnan Stirlg................183 K4
Inverasdale Highld..............219 J4
Inverbeg Ag & B.................183 K7
Inverbervie Abers...............197 K2
Inver-boyndie Abers............216 C2
Invercreran House
Hotel Ag & B....................191 K6
Inverdruie Highld................203 L3
Inveresk E Loth...................177 K4
Inveresragan Ag & B 182 E1
Inverey Abers.....................204 D7
Inverfarigaig Highld 202 D2
Inverfolla Ag & B................191 J7
Invergarry Highld................201 L5
Invergeldie P & K................184 F2
Invergloy Highld..................201 K7
Invergordon Highld.............222 F7
Invergowrie P & K...............186 F2
Inverguseran Highld............200 B4
Inverhadden P & K..............193 L5
Inverherive Hotel
Stirlg...............................183 L3
Inverie Highld.....................200 B5
Inverinan Ag & B................182 E4
Inverinate Highld................200 E2
Inverkeilor Angus................197 K2
Inverkeithing Fife...............176 F2
Inverkeithny Abers..............216 C5
Inverkip Inver.....................173 L4
Inverkirkaig Highld.............224 C4
Inverlael Highld..................220 F4
Inverlair Highld...................192 E1
Inverliever Lodge
Ag & B.............................182 C6
Inverlochy Ag & B...............183 H2
Invermark Angus.................196 D1
Invermoriston Highld...........202 C3
Invernaver Highld................229 L4

Inverness Highld.................213 G5
Inverness Airport
Highld.............................213 J4
Inverness Crematorium
Highld..............................212 F5
Invernoaden Ag & B............183 G7
Inveroran Hotel
Ag & B.............................192 D7
Inverquharity Angus............196 C5
Inverquhomery
Abers................................217 J5
Inverroy Highld...................201 K8
Inversanda Highld...............191 J4
Invershiel Highld.................200 E2
Invershin Highld..................222 D3
Inversnaid Hotel
Stirlg...............................183 K5
Inverugie Abers...................217 L5
Inveruglas Ag & B...............183 K5
Inveruglass Highld..............203 J5
Inverurie Abers...................206 E2
Inwardleigh Devon...............10 E5
Inworth Essex......................61 L4
Iochdar W Isls....................233 b7
Iona Ag & B........................180 D3
Iping W Susx........................30 D6
Ipplepen Devon......................7 J3
Ipsden Oxon.........................41 M4
Ipstones Staffs....................100 A3
Ipswich Suffk.......................78 E5
Ipswich Crematorium
Suffk................................78 E5
Irby Wirral..........................111 J5
Irby in the Marsh
Lincs................................118 F8
Irby upon Humber
NE Lin..............................117 K1
Irchester Nhants..................74 D2
Ireby Cumb.........................147 M7
Ireby Lancs.........................130 C4
Ireleth Cumb.......................128 F4
Ireshopeburn Dur...............149 L7
Irnham Lincs.......................103 G7
Iron Acton S Glos.................39 G4
Ironbridge Wrekin...............84 C3
Ironbridge Gorge
Wrekin............................84 C3
Ironmacannie D & G............154 B6
Ironville Derbys..................101 H3
Irstead Norfk......................107 H7
Irthington Cumb.................148 E3
Irthlingborough
Nhants..............................74 D1
Irton N York........................134 F3
Irvine N Ayrs......................163 H2
Isauld Highld......................230 E3
Isbister Shet.......................235 C2
Isbister Shet.......................235 d4
Isfield E Susx.......................19 L3
Isham Nhants........................88 C8
Isington Hants......................30 C3
Islay Ag & B.......................171 G4
Isle Abbotts Somset.............26 A7
Isle Brewers Somset.............26 A7
Isleham Cambs.....................90 F8
Isle of Dogs Gt Lon..............45 G4
Isle of Grain Medway............46 E5
Isle of Lewis W Isls..............232 f2
Isle of Man IoM...................237 C4
Isle of Man
Ronaldsway
Airport IoM....................237 b7
Isle of Mull Ag & B..............181 J1
Isle of Purbeck
Dorset.............................15 J5
Isle of Sheppey Kent............46 F6
Isle of Skye Highld..............208 F6
Isle of Thanet Kent...............35 J2
Isle of Walney Cumb............128 E6
Isle of Whithorn
D & G...............................145 K7

Isle of Wight IoW..................17 G5
Isle of Wight Crematorium IoW....17 G4
Isleornsay Highld.................199 L3
Isles of Scilly IoS....................2 b1
Isles of Scilly St
Mary's Airport IoS...........2 b2
Islesteps D & G...................155 G7
Islet Village Guern..............236 d2
Isleworth Gt Lon..................44 D5
Isley Walton Leics...............101 H7
Islibhig W Isls....................232 d3
Islington Gt Lon....................44 F3
Islip Nhants..........................88 E7
Islip Oxon............................57 K5
Islivig W Isls.......................232 d3
Isombridge Wrekin...............83 L2
Itchen Abbas Hants..............29 K5
Itchen Stoke Hants...............29 K5
Itchingfield W Susx...............31 J5
Itteringham Norfk...............106 D6
Itton Mons...........................38 C2
Itton Common Mons.............38 C2
Ivegill Cumb........................148 D6
Iver Bucks............................43 G4
Iver Heath Bucks..................43 G4
Iveston Dur.........................150 E5
Ivinghoe Bucks......................58 F5
Ivinghoe Aston Bucks............58 F4
Ivington Herefs....................69 J3
Ivybridge Devon.....................6 F5
Ivychurch Kent.....................21 K1
Ivy Hatch Kent.....................33 G3
Iwade Kent...........................46 E6
Iwerne Courtney or Shroton Dorset.............27 K8
Iwerne Minster
Dorset..............................27 K8
Ixworth Suffk.......................77 L1
Ixworth Thorpe Suffk...........91 K8

Jack-in-the-Green
Devon...............................12 C4
Jackton S Lans...................175 G7
Jacobstow Cnwll....................9 G5
Jacobstowe Devon................10 E4
Jameston Pembks.................49 H7
Jamestown Highld................212 D3
Jamestown W Duns...............174 D3
Janetstown Highld................227 L3
Janetstown Highld................231 L5
Jardine Hall D & G...............155 J5
Jarrow S Tyne......................151 H3
Jasper's Green Essex.............61 H3
Jawcraig Falk......................175 L4
Jaywick Essex.......................62 D5
Jedburgh Border.................167 K5
Jeffreyston Pembks................49 J6
Jemimaville Highld..............213 H2
Jerbourg Guern...................236 d4
Jersey Jersey......................236 c6
Jersey Airport Jersey........236 b7
Jersey Crematorium
Jersey..............................236 c7
Jesmond N u Ty...................151 G2
Jevington E Susx...................20 B5
Jockey End Herts..................59 H5
Johnby Cumb.......................148 D7
John Lennon Airport
Lpool..............................112 B5
John o' Groats Highld...........231 L2
Johnshaven Abers................197 J3
Johnston Pembks...................48 F5
Johnstone D & G..................155 M3
Johnstone Rens...................174 D5
Johnstonebridge
D & G...............................155 J4
Johnstown Carmth................50 E2
Johnstown Wrexhm...............97 L4
Joppa C Edin.......................177 J4
Joppa Cerdgn.......................66 D2
Joppa S Ayrs.......................163 K5

Jordanston Pembks...............64 C7
Joyden's Wood Kent.............45 K5
Juniper Nthumb...................150 B3
Juniper Green C Edin...........177 G5
Jura Ag & B.........................171 J2
Jurassic Coast Devon 13 H4
Jurby IoM...........................237 C2

K

Kaber Cumb........................139 H5
Kaimend S Lans..................165 J1
Kames Ag & B.....................173 G4
Kames E Ayrs......................164 D4
Kea Cnwll...............................4 C7
Keadby N Linc.....................125 K7
Keal Cotes Lincs..................104 B1
Kearsley Bolton...................113 H1
Kearsney Kent......................35 H6
Kearstwick Cumb.................130 B4
Kedington Suffk....................77 G5
Kedleston Derbys................100 F4
Keelby Lincs........................126 E8
Keele Staffs...........................99 J4
Keele Services Staffs 99 J4
Keelham C Brad...................123 G4
Keeston Pembks....................48 F4
Keevil Wilts...........................39 L8
Kegworth Leics...................101 J7
Kehelland Cnwll.....................3 G3
Keig Abers..........................206 B2
Keighley C Brad..................122 F3
Keighley Crematorium
C Brad.............................122 F3
Keilarsbrae Clacks..............185 J8
Keillour P & K.....................185 K3
Keiloch Abers.....................204 E6
Keils Ag & B.......................171 K5
Keinton Mandeville
Somset..............................26 D5
Keir Mill D & G...................154 E4
Keisley Cumb......................139 G3
Keiss Highld.......................231 L4
Keith Moray........................215 J4
Keithick P & K.....................195 K8
Keithock Angus...................196 F4
Keithtown Highld.................212 E3
Kelbrook Lancs....................122 D2
Kelby Lincs.........................103 G4
Keld N York........................139 K6
Kelfield N York....................124 F3
Kelham Notts......................102 C2
Kelhead D & G.....................147 K2
Kellamergh Lancs................120 E5
Kellas Angus........................187 G1
Kellas Moray.......................214 E4
Kellaton Devon........................7 J7
Kelleth Cumb......................138 E6
Kelling Norfk.......................106 C4
Kellington N York.................124 E5
Kelloe Dur...........................151 J7
Kelloholm D & G..................164 E6
Kelly Devon............................9 K8
Kelmarsh Nhants..................87 K7
Kelmscott Oxon....................56 E7
Kelsale Suffk.........................79 H2
Kelsall Ches W.....................112 D7
Kelshall Herts.......................75 K7
Kelsick Cumb.......................147 L5
Kelso Border.......................167 L3
Kelstedge Derbys................115 G8
Kelstern Lincs.....................118 C4
Kelston BaNES......................39 G6
Keltneyburn P & K...............194 B6
Kelton D & G.......................155 H7
Kelty Fife............................186 B8
Kelvedon Essex.....................61 K4
Kelvedon Hatch
Essex...............................60 F7
Kelynack Cnwll......................2 C5
Kemback Fife......................187 G4
Kemberton Shrops................84 D3
Kemble Gloucs......................39 M2
Kemerton Worcs....................71 G6

Kemeys Commander
Mons 53 M6
Kemnay Abers 206 E3
Kempley Gloucs 54 F3
Kempley Green
Gloucs 55 G3
Kempsey Worcs 70 F5
Kempsford Gloucs 40 D2
Kempshott Hants 29 L2
Kempston Bed 74 F5
Kempton Shrops 83 G6
Kemp Town Br & H 19 J5
Kemsing Kent 32 F2
Kenardington Kent 34 C7
Kenchester Herefs 69 J6
Kencot Oxon 56 E6
Kendal Cumb 129 L2
Kenfig Brdgnd 36 C4
Kenilworth Warwks 72 C1
Kenley Gt Lon 32 B2
Kenley Shrops 83 L4
Kenmore Highld 210 B3
Kenmore P & K 194 B7
Kenn Devon 11 L7
Kenn N Som 38 B6
Kennacraig Ag & B 172 C6
Kennall Vale Cnwll 3 J4
Kennerleigh Devon 11 J4
Kennessee Green
Sefton 111 L2
Kennet Clacks 176 C1
Kennethmont Abers 215 L8
Kennett Cambs 77 G2
Kennford Devon 11 L7
Kenninghall Norfk 92 C6
Kennington Kent 34 D5
Kennington Oxon 57 K7
Kennoway Fife 186 F6
Kenny Somset 25 L7
Kennyhill Suffk 90 F7
Kennythorpe N York ... 134 C6
Kenovay Ag & B 188 C6
Kensaleyre Highld 208 F4
Kensington Gt Lon 44 E4
Kensington Palace
Gt Lon 44 E4
Kensworth Common
C Beds 59 G4
Kentallen Highld 191 K5
Kent and Sussex
Crematorium
Kent 33 G5
Kentchurch Herefs 54 B3
Kentford Suffk 77 G2
Kent International
Airport Kent 35 J2
Kentisbeare Devon 12 D2
Kentisbury Devon 23 K3
Kentish Town Gt Lon 44 F3
Kentmere Cumb 138 C6
Kenton Devon 12 B5
Kenton Gt Lon 44 D3
Kenton N u Ty 150 F2
Kenton Suffk 78 E2
Kentra Highld 190 D3
Kent's Green Gloucs 55 H4
Kent's Oak Hants 28 F6
Kenwyn Cnwll 4 C6
Keoldale Highld 228 F3
Keppoch Highld 200 D1
Kepwick N York 133 G2
Keresley Covtry 86 D6
Kerrera Ag & B 182 B2
Kerris Cnwll 2 D5
Kerry Powys 82 D5
Kerrycroy Ag & B 173 J6
Kersall Notts 116 B8
Kersbrook Devon 12 D5
Kersey Suffk 78 B5
Kershader W Isls 232 f3
Kerswell Devon 12 D2
Kerswell Green Worcs ... 70 F5
Kesgrave Suffk 78 F5
Kessingland Suffk 93 L6
Kestle Cnwll 4 F6
Kestle Mill Cnwll 4 D4

Keston Gt Lon 45 H7
Keswick Cumb 137 J3
Keswick Norfk 92 E3
Kettering Nhants 88 C7
Kettering
Crematorium
Nhants 88 C7
Ketteringham Norfk 92 E3
Kettins P & K 195 K8
Kettlebaston Suffk 77 L4
Kettlebridge Fife 186 E6
Kettlebrook Staffs 86 B3
Kettleburgh Suffk 78 F3
Kettleholm D & G 155 K6
Kettleshulme Ches E ... 113 M5
Kettlesing N York 132 C7
Kettlesing Bottom
N York 132 C7
Kettlestone Norfk 106 A6
Kettlethorpe Lincs 116 D6
Kettletoft Ork 234 d4
Kettlewell N York 131 H5
Ketton Rutlnd 88 E3
Kew Gt Lon 44 D5
Kew Royal Botanic
Gardens Gt Lon 44 D5
Kewstoke N Som 37 M7
Kexby C York 125 G1
Kexby Lincs 116 E4
Key Green Ches E 113 K8
Keyham Leics 87 J3
Keyhaven Hants 16 C4
Keyingham E R Yk 127 G5
Keymer W Susx 19 J3
Keynsham BaNES 38 F6
Keysoe Bed 74 F3
Keysoe Row Bed 74 F3
Keyston Cambs 88 F7
Keyworth Notts 101 L6
Kibblesworth Gatesd .. 151 G4
Kibworth
Beauchamp Leics 87 K5
Kibworth Harcourt
Leics 87 K5
Kidbrooke Gt Lon 45 H5
Kidderminster Worcs ... 84 E7
Kidlington Oxon 57 J5
Kidmore End Oxon 42 B5
Kidsdale D & G 145 J7
Kidsgrove Staffs 99 J3
Kidwelly Carmth 50 E4
Kiel Crofts Ag & B 191 H8
Kielder Nthumb 157 G4
Kiells Ag & B 171 H5
Kilbarchan Rens 174 D5
Kilbeg Highld 199 K4
Kilberry Ag & B 172 C5
Kilbirnie N Ayrs 174 C7
Kilbride Ag & B 172 C3
Kilbride Ag & B 173 H5
Kilbuiack Moray 214 D3
Kilburn Derbys 101 G4
Kilburn Gt Lon 44 E4
Kilburn N York 133 H4
Kilby Leics 87 J4
Kilchamaig Ag & B 172 D6
Kilchattan Ag & B 173 J7
Kilchattan Ag & B 180 E7
Kilcheran Ag & B 191 G8
Kilchoan Highld 189 L4
Kilchoman Ag & B 170 D5
Kilchrenan Ag & B 182 E3
Kilconquhar Fife 187 H6
Kilcot Gloucs 55 G3
Kilcoy Highld 212 E4
Kilcreggan Ag & B 173 L3
Kildale N York 142 D5
Kildalloig Ag & B 161 J5
Kildary Highld 223 G6
Kildavaig Ag & B 173 G5
Kildavanan Ag & B 173 H5
Kildonan Highld 227 G4
Kildonan N Ayrs 162 D5
Kildonan Lodge
Highld 226 F4
Kildonnan Highld 199 G7

Kildrochet House
D & G 144 C4
Kildrummy Abers 205 K2
Kildwick N York 122 F2
Kilfinan Ag & B 172 F3
Kilfinnan Highld 201 K6
Kilgetty Pembks 49 J6
Kilgrammie S Ayrs ... 152 F2
Kilgwrrwg Common
Mons 38 C2
Kilham E R Yk 135 G6
Kilkenneth Ag & B 188 B7
Kilkenzie Ag & B 161 H4
Kilkerran Ag & B 161 J5
Kilkhampton Cnwll 9 H3
Killamarsh Derbys 115 J5
Killay Swans 51 H6
Killearn Stirlg 174 F2
Killen Highld 213 G3
Killerby Darltn 140 F3
Killerton Devon 12 C3
Killichonan P & K 193 J5
Killiechonate Highld .. 192 D1
Killiechronan Ag & B .. 190 B7
Killiecrankie P & K ... 194 E4
Killilan Highld 210 E7
Killimster Highld 231 K4
Killin Stirlg 184 C2
Killinghall N York 132 D7
Killington Cumb 130 C2
Killington Lake
Services Cumb 130 B2
Killingworth N Tyne ... 159 G7
Killochyett Border 167 G1
Kilmacolm Inver 174 C4
Kilmahog Stirlg 184 D5
Kilmahumaig Ag & B .. 182 A8
Kilmaluag Highld 218 C6
Kilmany Fife 186 F3
Kilmarnock E Ayrs ... 163 K2
Kilmartin Ag & B 182 B7
Kilmaurs E Ayrs 163 K2
Kilmelford Ag & B 182 B5
Kilmersdon Somset ... 27 G2
Kilmeston Hants 29 L6
Kilmichael Ag & B 161 H5
Kilmichael Glassary
Ag & B 182 B8
Kilmichael of
Inverlussa Ag & B ... 172 D2
Kilmington Devon 13 H3
Kilmington Wilts 27 H4
Kilmington Common
Wilts 27 H4
Kilmington Street
Wilts 27 H4
Kilmorack Highld 212 D5
Kilmore Ag & B 182 C3
Kilmore Highld 199 K4
Kilmory Ag & B 172 C4
Kilmory Highld 190 B3
Kilmory N Ayrs 162 B5
Kilmuir Highld 208 D5
Kilmuir Highld 213 G4
Kilmuir Highld 218 B7
Kilmun Ag & B 173 K3
Kilnave Ag & B 170 F4
Kilncadzow S Lans ... 176 B8
Kilndown Kent 33 J6
Kilninver Ag & B 182 B3
Kilnsea E R Yk 127 J7
Kilnsey N York 131 H6
Kilnwick E R Yk 126 C1
Kiloran Ag & B 180 E7
Kilpatrick N Ayrs 162 A4
Kilpeck Herefs 54 C3
Kilpin E R Yk 125 J5
Kilrenny Fife 187 J6
Kilsby Nhants 73 H1
Kilspindie P & K 186 C3
Kilstay D & G 144 D7
Kilsyth N Lans 175 J3
Kiltarlity Highld 212 D6
Kilton R & Cl 142 E4
Kilton Thorpe R & Cl . 142 E4

Kilvaxter Highld 218 B7
Kilve Somset 25 H3
Kilvington Notts 102 D4
Kilwinning N Ayrs 163 H2
Kimberley Norfk 92 C3
Kimberley Notts 101 J4
Kimberworth Rothm .. 115 H3
Kimblesworth Dur ... 151 G5
Kimbolton Cambs 75 G2
Kimbolton Herefs 69 K3
Kimcote Leics 87 H6
Kimmeridge Dorset .. 15 H6
Kimpton Hants 28 E3
Kimpton Herts 59 K4
Kinbrace Highld 226 F3
Kinbuck Stirlg 185 G6
Kincaple Fife 187 G4
Kincardine Fife 176 C2
Kincardine Highld ... 222 E4
Kincardine O'Neil
Abers 206 B5
Kinclaven P & K 195 J8
Kincorth C Aber 207 H5
Kincorth House
Moray 214 C3
Kincraig Highld 203 K4
Kincraigie P & K 194 F6
Kindallachan P & K .. 194 F6
Kinerarach Ag & B .. 172 B7
Kineton Gloucs 56 C3
Kineton Warwks 72 D4
Kinfauns P & K 186 C3
Kingarth Ag & B 173 J6
Kingcausie Abers ... 207 G5
Kingcoed Mons 54 B6
Kingerby Lincs 117 H3
Kingham Oxon 56 E3
Kingholm Quay D & G 155 G7
Kinghorn Fife 177 H2
Kinglassie Fife 186 D7
Kingoldrum Angus .. 196 B5
Kingoodie P & K ... 186 E2
Kingsand Cnwll 6 C5
Kingsbarns Fife 187 K5
Kingsbridge Devon ... 7 H5
Kingsbridge Somset .. 24 F4
King's Bromley Staffs . 85 K1
Kingsburgh Highld .. 208 F4
Kingsbury Gt Lon ... 44 D3
Kingsbury Warwks .. 86 B4
Kingsbury Episcopi
Somset 26 B7
King's Caple Herefs .. 54 E3
Kingsclere Hants 41 K8
King's Cliffe Nhants .. 88 E4
Kingscote Gloucs 39 J2
Kingscott Devon 23 H7
King's Coughton
Warwks 71 J3
Kingscross N Ayrs .. 162 D4
Kingsdon Somset ... 26 D6
Kingsdown Kent 35 K5
Kingsdown Swindn .. 40 D3
Kingsdown Wilts 39 J6
Kingsdown
Crematorium
Swindn 40 D3
Kingseat Fife 176 F1
Kingsey Bucks 58 C6
Kingsfold W Susx ... 31 K4
Kingsford C Aber ... 206 F4
Kingsford E Ayrs ... 174 E8
Kingsgate Kent 35 K1
Kingshall Street Suffk 77 K3
King's Heath Birm ... 85 J7
Kings Hill Kent 33 H3
King's Hill Wsall ... 85 H4
Kings House Hotel
Highld 192 D5
Kingshouse Hotel
Stirlg 184 C4
Kingskerswell Devon .. 7 K3
Kingskettle Fife 186 E5
Kingsland Herefs ... 69 J3
Kingsland IoA 108 C5
Kings Langley Herts .. 59 H7

Kingsley Ches W 112 D6
Kingsley Hants...............30 C4
Kingsley Staffs..............100 A3
Kingsley Green
  W Susx 30 E5
Kingsley Park Nhants....73 L3
King's Lynn Norfk.........104 F8
Kings Meaburn Cumb ..138 E3
King's Mills Guern.........236 C3
Kingsmuir Angus...........196 D6
Kings Muir Border 166 C2
Kingsmuir Fife..............187 J5
Kingsnorth Kent.............34 D6
King's Norton Birm........85 J7
King's Norton Leics........87 K4
Kings Nympton
  Devon 23 L7
King's Pyon Herefs 69 J4
Kings Ripton Cambs 89 J7
King's Somborne
  Hants 29 G5
King's Stag Dorset 14 D1
King's Stanley Gloucs 55 J7
King's Sutton Nhants 72 F7
Kingstanding Birm 85 J4
Kingsteignton Devon 7 K2
Kingsthorne Herefs 54 D2
Kingsthorpe Nhants 73 L2
Kingston Cambs 75 L4
Kingston Cnwll 6 A2
Kingston Devon 6 F6
Kingston Dorset 14 E1
Kingston Dorset 15 H6
Kingston E Loth 178 C3
Kingston IoW 16 F6
Kingston Kent 35 G4
Kingston Bagpuize
  Oxon.............................57 H7
Kingston Blount
  Oxon.............................58 C7
Kingston Deverill
  Wilts..............................27 J4
Kingstone Herefs 69 H7
Kingstone Somset..........26 B8
Kingstone Staffs...........100 B6
Kingston Lacy House
  & Gardens Dorset......15 J3
Kingston Lisle Oxon......40 F3
Kingston near Lewes
  E Susx 19 K4
Kingston on Soar
  Notts...........................101 J6
Kingston on Spey
  Moray..........................215 H2
Kingston Russell
  Dorset 14 B4
Kingston St Mary
  Somset 25 K5
Kingston Seymour
  N Som 38 B6
Kingston upon Hull
  C KuH..........................126 D5
Kingston upon
  Thames Gt Lon......44 D6
Kingston upon
  Thames
  Crematorium
  Gt Lon...........................44 D6
King's Walden Herts 59 K4
Kingswear Devon.............7 K5
Kingswells C Aber 207 G4
Kings Weston Bristl......38 D5
Kingswinford Dudley 84 F5
Kingswood Bucks 58 B4
Kingswood Gloucs 39 H3
Kingswood S Glos 38 F5
Kingswood Somset........25 H4
Kingswood Surrey 31 L1
Kingswood Warwks 71 L1
Kingswood Common
  Staffs 84 E3
Kings Worthy Hants........29 J5
Kingthorpe Lincs 117 J6
Kington Herefs...............68 F3
Kington S Glos 38 F3
Kington Worcs................71 H4

Kington Langley Wilts 39 L5
Kington Magna
  Dorset 27 H6
Kington St Michael
  Wilts..............................39 K5
Kingussie Highld...........203 H5
Kingweston Somset.......26 D5
Kinharrachie Abers 217 H7
Kinharvie D & G 147 G2
Kinkell Bridge P & K.....185 J4
Kinknockie Abers..........217 J6
Kinleith C Edin 177 G5
Kinlet Shrops.................84 C7
Kinloch Highld 198 F5
Kinloch Highld 225 H2
Kinloch Highld 229 H5
Kinloch P & K 195 J7
Kinlochard Stirlg 184 B6
Kinlochbervie Highld....228 C4
Kinlocheil Highld 191 J1
Kinlochewe Highld........210 F3
Kinloch Hourn Highld...200 E4
Kinlochlaggan Highld....202 E7
Kinlochleven Highld 192 C4
Kinlochmoidart
  Highld..........................190 E2
Kinlochnanuagh
  Highld..........................200 B8
Kinloch Rannoch
  P & K 193 L5
Kinloss Moray...............214 C3
Kinmel Bay Conwy 110 D5
Kinmuck Abers..............206 F2
Kinmundy Abers 207 G2
Kinnabus Ag & B..........160 B2
Kinnadie Abers 217 H5
Kinnaird P & K..............194 F5
Kinneff Abers................197 K2
Kinnelhead D & G 155 H2
Kinnell Angus...............196 F6
Kinnerley Shrops............97 M7
Kinnersley Herefs..........69 G5
Kinnersley Worcs 70 F5
Kinnerton Powys............68 E2
Kinnesswood P & K 186 C6
Kinnordy Angus............196 B5
Kinoulton Notts 102 B6
Kinross P & K................186 B6
Kinrossie P & K.............186 C2
Kinross Services
  P & K 186 B6
Kinsham Herefs..............69 G2
Kinsham Worcs...............71 G7
Kinsley Wakefd.............124 C7
Kinson Bmouth...............15 K3
Kintail Highld 200 F2
Kintbury W Berk............41 G6
Kintessack Moray..........214 B3
Kintillo P & K................186 B4
Kinton Herefs.................83 H8
Kinton Shrops................98 A8
Kintore Abers................206 E3
Kintour Ag & B..............171 H7
Kintra Ag & B................170 F8
Kintra Ag & B................180 D3
Kintraw Ag & B.............182 B6
Kintyre Ag & B..............161 J2
Kinveachy Highld..........203 L2
Kinver Staffs...................84 E6
Kippax Leeds................124 C4
Kippen Stirlg 184 E7
Kippford or Scaur
  D & G...........................146 E4
Kipping's Cross Kent 33 H5
Kirbister Ork 234 b6
Kirby Bedon Norfk.........93 G3
Kirby Bellars Leics.......102 B8
Kirby Cane Norfk...........93 H5
Kirby Cross Essex 62 E4
Kirby Fields Leics..........87 G3
Kirby Grindalythe
  N York.........................134 D6
Kirby Hill N York...........132 F5
Kirby Hill N York...........140 E6
Kirby Knowle N York ...133 G3
Kirby le Soken Essex.....62 F4

Kirby Misperton
  N York.........................134 B4
Kirby Muxloe Leics.........87 G3
Kirby Underdale
  E R Yk..........................134 C7
Kirby Wiske N York......132 E3
Kirdford W Susx.............31 G6
Kirk Highld 231 K4
Kirkabister Shet............235 d6
Kirkandrews D & G.......146 A5
Kirkandrews upon
  Eden Cumb 148 C4
Kirkbampton Cumb 148 B4
Kirkbean D & G 147 G3
Kirk Bramwith Donc....124 F7
Kirkbride Cumb............147 M4
Kirkbuddo Angus..........196 E7
Kirkburn Border 166 D2
Kirkburn E R Yk............134 F7
Kirkburton Kirk............123 J7
Kirkby Knows...............111 L2
Kirkby Lincs..................117 H3
Kirkby N York 142 C6
Kirkby Fleetham
  N York.........................141 G7
Kirkby Green Lincs.......103 H2
Kirkby in Ashfield
  Notts 101 J2
Kirkby-in-Furness
  Cumb 128 F3
Kirkby la Thorpe
  Lincs...........................103 J4
Kirkby Lonsdale
  Cumb 130 B4
Kirkby Malham
  N York.........................131 G7
Kirkby Mallory Leics.....86 F4
Kirkby Malzeard
  N York.........................132 C5
Kirkbymoorside
  N York.........................133 L3
Kirkby on Bain Lincs....118 C8
Kirkby Overblow
  N York.........................123 L2
Kirkby Stephen
  Cumb 139 H5
Kirkby Thore Cumb......138 F3
Kirkby Underwood
  Lincs...........................103 H6
Kirkby Wharf N York....124 D3
Kirkcaldy Fife 186 D8
Kirkcaldy
  Crematorium Fife....186 D8
Kirkcambeck Cumb......148 F2
Kirkchrist D & G...........146 B5
Kirkcolm D & G 144 B2
Kirkconnel D & G 164 E6
Kirkconnell D & G 147 G2
Kirkcowan D & G 145 G3
Kirkcudbright D & G 146 B5
Kirkdale Lpool..............111 K3
Kirk Deighton N York...124 B1
Kirk Ella E R Yk............126 C5
Kirkfieldbank S Lans....165 G2
Kirkgunzeon D & G 146 F2
Kirk Hallam Derbys......101 J4
Kirkham Lancs..............120 F4
Kirkham N York 134 B6
Kirkhamgate Wakefd...123 K6
Kirk Hammerton
  N York.........................133 G7
Kirkhaugh Nthumb......149 H5
Kirkheaton Kirk............123 H6
Kirkheaton Nthumb.....158 C6
Kirkhill Highld 212 E5
Kirkhope S Lans 165 J7
Kirkibost Highld...........199 H2
Kirkinch P & K..............195 L7
Kirkinner D & G 145 J5
Kirkintilloch E Duns....175 H4
Kirk Ireton Derbys.......100 E3
Kirkland Cumb.............136 E4
Kirkland D & G.............154 E4
Kirkland D & G.............155 H4
Kirkland D & G.............164 E6
Kirk Langley Derbys.....100 F5

Kirkleatham R & Cl......142 D3
Kirklevington S on T....141 K5
Kirkley Suffk...................93 L5
Kirklington N York 132 D4
Kirklington Notts 102 B2
Kirklinton Cumb..........148 D2
Kirkliston C Edin..........176 F4
Kirkmabreck D & G 145 K4
Kirkmaiden D & G........144 D7
Kirk Merrington Dur....141 G2
Kirk Michael IoM 237 C4
Kirkmichael P & K 195 H4
Kirkmichael S Ayrs......163 J7
Kirkmuirhill S Lans......164 F2
Kirknewton Nthumb....168 D4
Kirknewton W Loth 176 F5
Kirkney Abers...............215 L7
Kirk of Shotts N Lans...175 L5
Kirkoswald Cumb.........148 F6
Kirkoswald S Ayrs........163 G7
Kirkpatrick D & G.........154 F4
Kirkpatrick Durham
  D & G...........................154 D7
Kirkpatrick-Fleming
  D & G...........................156 B7
Kirk Sandall Donc........124 F8
Kirksanton Cumb.........128 D4
Kirk Smeaton N York...124 D7
Kirkstall Leeds.............123 K4
Kirkstead Lincs 103 K1
Kirkstile Abers.............215 L7
Kirkstile D & G.............156 C4
Kirkstyle Highld 231 L2
Kirkthorpe Wakefd......124 B6
Kirkton Abers...............206 C1
Kirkton D & G...............155 G6
Kirkton Fife..................186 F3
Kirkton Highld 210 C8
Kirkton Highld 210 D6
Kirkton P & K...............185 K4
Kirkton Manor Border..166 C2
Kirkton of Airlie
  Angus.........................195 L6
Kirkton of
  Auchterhouse
  Angus.........................196 B8
Kirkton of Barevan
  Highld..........................213 K5
Kirkton of Collace
  P & K 186 C2
Kirkton of
  Glenbuchat Abers....205 J3
Kirkton of Logie
  Buchan Abers...........217 J7
Kirkton of Menmuir
  Angus.........................196 E4
Kirkton of Monikie
  Angus.........................196 E8
Kirkton of Rayne
  Abers..........................216 D7
Kirkton of Skene
  Abers..........................206 F4
Kirkton of
  Strathmartine
  Angus.........................186 F1
Kirkton of Tealing
  Angus.........................196 C8
Kirkton of Tough
  Abers..........................206 C3
Kirktown Abers.............217 J2
Kirktown Abers.............217 K4
Kirktown of Alvah
  Abers..........................216 D3
Kirktown of Bourtie
  Abers..........................206 F1
Kirktown of
  Fetteresso Abers......206 F7
Kirktown of
  Mortlach Moray.......215 H6
Kirktown of Slains
  Abers..........................217 K8
Kirkurd Border.............165 M1
Kirkwall Ork 234 c6
Kirkwall Airport Ork....234 c6
Kirkwhelpington
  Nthumb......................158 C5

Kirk Yetholm Border.....168 C4
Kirmington N Linc........126 D7
Kirmond le Mire Lincs..117 K3
Kirn Ag & B................173 K3
Kirriemuir Angus.........196 C5
Kirstead Green Norfk.....93 G4
Kirtlebridge D & G.......155 M7
Kirtling Cambs.............77 G3
Kirtling Green Cambs....76 F4
Kirtlington Oxon...........57 J4
Kirtomy Highld...........229 M3
Kirton Lincs................104 A5
Kirton Notts................116 B7
Kirton Suffk.................78 F6
Kirtonhill W Duns........174 D4
Kirton in Lindsey
   N Linc...................116 F2
Kirwaugh D & G..........145 J4
Kishorn I lighld...........210 C6
Kislingbury Nhants........73 K3
Kittisford Somset..........25 G6
Kittybrewster C Aber...207 H4
Kivernoll Herefs............54 C2
Kiveton Park Rothm....115 J5
Knaith Lincs................116 D5
Knap Corner Dorset.......27 J6
Knaphill Surrey.............42 F8
Knapp Somset................25 L6
Knapton C York............124 E1
Knapton N York...........134 D4
Knapton Norfk............107 G5
Knapwell Cambs............75 K2
Knaresborough
   N York...................132 E7
Knarsdale Nthumb.......149 H4
Knaven Abers..............217 G5
Knayton N York...........132 F2
Knebworth Herts...........59 L4
Knedlington E R Yk.....125 H5
Kneesall Notts.............116 B8
Kneesworth Cambs........75 L5
Kneeton Notts.............102 B4
Knelston Swans.............50 F7
Knenhall Staffs.............99 L5
Knightcote Warwks........72 E4
Knightley Staffs............99 J7
Knighton C Leic............87 H4
Knighton Dorset............14 C1
Knighton Powys.............82 F8
Knighton Somset...........25 J3
Knighton Staffs.............99 G4
Knighton Staffs.............99 H6
Knighton on Teme
   Worcs......................70 B1
Knightwick Worcs..........70 D4
Knill Herefs...................68 F3
Knipton Leics...............102 D6
Kniveton Derbys...........100 E3
Knock Cumb.................138 F2
Knock Highld...............199 K4
Knock Moray................215 L4
Knock W Isls...............232 g2
Knockally Highld..........227 K3
Knockan Highld...........224 F6
Knockando Moray........214 F6
Knockbain Highld........212 E5
Knockbain Highld........212 F3
Knock Castle N Ayrs....173 L5
Knockdee Highld.........231 H4
Knockdow Ag & B........173 J4
Knockdown Wilts...........39 J3
Knockeen S Ayrs.........153 G3
Knockenkelly N Ayrs....162 D4
Knockentiber E Ayrs....163 K2
Knockholt Kent.............32 E2
Knockholt Pound
   Kent........................32 E2
Knockin Shrops.............97 M7
Knockinlaw E Ayrs......163 K2
Knocknain D & G.........144 B3
Knockrome Ag & B......171 K4
Knocksharry IoM.........237 b4
Knocksheen D & G.......153 M5
Knockvennie Smithy
   D & G.....................154 D7
Knodishall Suffk...........79 J3

Knodishall Common
   Suffk.......................79 J3
Knole Somset.................26 C6
Knolls Green Ches E.....113 J5
Knolton Wrexhm............98 B5
Knook Wilts...................27 L3
Knossington Leics..........88 B2
Knott End-on-Sea
   Lancs.....................120 E2
Knotting Bed.................74 E2
Knotting Green Bed......74 E3
Knottingley Wakefd.....124 D5
Knotty Ash Lpool........112 B3
Knowbury Shrops..........83 L7
Knowe D & G...............153 G7
Knowehead D & G.......154 A4
Knoweside S Ayrs........163 G6
Knowle Bristl................38 E6
Knowle Devon................11 H5
Knowle Devon................12 C2
Knowle Devon................12 D6
Knowle Devon................23 H4
Knowle Shrops..............83 L8
Knowle Solhll................85 L7
Knowle Somset..............24 E3
Knowlefield Cumb.......148 D4
Knowle Green Lancs....121 J3
Knowle St Giles
   Somset......................13 J1
Knowl Hill W & M..........42 D4
Knowsley Knows.........112 C3
Knowsley Safari Park
   Knows....................112 C3
Knowstone Devon..........24 C6
Knox Bridge Kent..........33 K5
Knucklas Powys.............82 F8
Knuston Nhants.............74 D2
Knutsford Ches E.........113 H5
Knutsford Services
   Ches E...................113 G6
Krumlin Calder............122 F6
Kuggar Cnwll..................3 J7
Kyleakin Highld...........200 B1
Kyle of Lochalsh
   Highld...................210 B8
Kylerhea Highld...........200 B2
Kylesku Highld............224 F2
Kylesmorar Highld.......200 C6
Kyles Scalpay W Isls....232 e4
Kylestrome Highld.......224 F2
Kynnersley Wrekin........84 C1
Kyrewood Worcs...........69 L2

L

La Bellieuse Guern......236 d3
Lacasaigh W Isls.........232 f3
Lacasdal W Isls...........232 f2
Laceby NE Lin.............117 K1
Lacey Green Bucks........58 D7
Lach Dennis Ches W....113 G6
Lackford Suffk...............77 H1
Lackford Green Suffk....77 H1
Lacock Wilts..................39 K6
Ladbroke Warwks..........72 E3
Laddingford Kent..........33 J4
Ladock Cnwll...................4 D5
Lady Ork....................234 d4
Ladybank Fife.............186 E5
Ladygill S Lans...........165 H4
Lady Hall Cumb...........128 E3
Ladykirk Border...........179 J8
Ladywood Birm............85 J6
Ladywood Worcs...........70 F3
La Fontenelle Guern....236 e1
La Fosse Guern...........236 d4
Lag D & G...................154 F5
Laga Highld................190 D4
Lagavulin Ag & B........160 C1
Lagg N Ayrs...............162 B5
Laggan Highld.............201 L6
Laggan Highld.............202 F6
Lagganlia Highld.........203 K5
La Greve Guern...........236 d2

La Greve de Lecq
   Jersey...................236 b5
La Hougue Bie Jersey..236 d7
La Houguette Guern....236 b3
Laid Highld.................228 F4
Laide Highld...............219 L3
Laig Highld.................199 G7
Leigh Clunch E Ayrs...174 E8
Leigh Fenwick E Ayrs..163 L2
Leigh Glenmuir E Ayrs.164 C5
Laighstonehall S Lans..175 J7
Laindon Essex..............46 B3
Lairg Highld................225 M7
Laisterdyke C Brad......123 J4
Lake IoW.......................17 H5
Lake Wilts.....................28 C4
Lake District National
   Park Cumb..............137 H5
Lakenheath Suffk..........91 G6
Lakesend Norfk.............90 D4
Laleston Brdgnd............36 D4
Lamarsh Essex..............77 K7
Lamas Norfk................106 F7
Lambden Border..........167 L2
Lamberhurst Kent..........33 H6
Lamberhurst Down
   Kent........................33 H6
Lamberton Border.......179 K6
Lambeth Gt Lon............44 F4
Lambeth
   Crematorium
   Gt Lon.....................44 F5
Lambfair Green Suffk....77 G4
Lambley Notts.............101 M4
Lambley Nthumb.........149 H4
Lambourn W Berk.........40 F5
Lambourne End
   Essex......................45 J2
Lambs Green W Susx....31 L4
Lamerton Devon..............6 C1
Lamesley Gatesd.........151 G4
Lamington S Lans........165 J3
Lamlash N Ayrs...........162 C3
Lamonby Cumb...........148 D7
Lamorna Cnwll................2 E6
Lamorran Cnwll..............4 D7
Lampeter Cerdgn..........66 D5
Lampeter Velfrey
   Pembks....................49 K5
Lamphey Pembks..........49 H7
Lamplugh Cumb..........136 F3
Lamport Nhants............87 L8
Lamyatt Somset............26 F4
Lanark S Lans.............165 G2
Lancaster Lancs...........129 K7
Lancaster &
   Morecambe
   Crematorium
   Lancs.....................129 K6
Lancaster Services
   Lancs.....................121 G1
Lanchester Dur...........150 F5
Lancing W Susx.............19 G5
L'Ancresse Guern........236 d1
Landbeach Cambs.........76 C2
Landcross Devon............23 G6
Landerberry Abers......206 E4
Landford Wilts...............28 E7
Land-hallow Highld.....227 L2
Landican
   Crematorium
   Wirral....................111 J4
Landimore Swans..........50 F6
Landkey Devon..............23 J5
Landore Swans..............51 J6
Landrake Cnwll...............6 B4
Land's End Airport
   Cnwll........................2 C5
Landulph Cnwll...............6 C4
Lane Cnwll......................4 C4
Laneast Cnwll.................9 G7
Lane End Bucks.............42 D3
Lane End Wilts..............27 J3
Lane Ends Derbys.......100 E5
Laneham Notts............116 D6
Lane Head Dur............140 E5

Lanehead Dur.............149 L6
Langaller Somset..........25 K6
Langar Notts...............102 B5
Langbank Rens...........174 D4
Langbar N York...........123 G1
Langcliffe N York........130 F6
Langdale End N York...134 E2
Langdown Hants...........16 E2
Langdyke Fife..............186 E6
Langenhoe Essex..........62 B4
Langford C Beds............75 H6
Langford Devon............12 D2
Langford Essex.............61 K6
Langford Notts............102 D2
Langford Oxon..............56 E7
Langford Budville
   Somset......................25 H6
Langham Essex.............62 B2
Langham Norfk............106 D4
Langham Rutlnd............88 B2
Langham Suffk..............77 L1
Langho Lancs..............121 K4
Langholm D & G..........156 C5
Langlee Border............167 H3
Langley Hants...............16 F3
Langley Herts................59 K4
Langley Kent.................33 K3
Langley Nthumb..........149 L3
Langley Slough.............43 G5
Langley Somset.............25 G5
Langley W Susx.............30 D5
Langley Warwks............71 L3
Langley Burrell Wilts....39 L5
Langley Green Essex.....61 L4
Langley Marsh
   Somset......................25 G5
Langley Park Dur.........150 F6
Langley Street Norfk....93 H3
Langley Upper Green
   Essex......................76 C7
Langney E Susx.............20 D5
Langold Notts..............115 L4
Langore Cnwll..................9 J7
Langport Somset...........26 B6
Langrick Lincs.............103 L3
Langridge BaNES...........39 H6
Langrigg Cumb............147 K5
Langrish Hants..............30 D6
Langsett Barns............114 E2
Langside P & K............185 G5
Langstone Hants............17 K2
Langthorne N York.......132 C2
Langthorpe N York.......132 F6
Langthwaite N York.....140 C6
Langtoft E R Yk..........134 F6
Langtoft Lincs...............89 G2
Langton Dur................140 F4
Langton Lincs..............118 C7
Langton Lincs..............118 E7
Langton N York...........134 C6
Langton by Wragby
   Lincs.....................117 J6
Langton Green Kent......32 F5
Langton Herring
   Dorset......................14 C6
Langton Matravers
   Dorset......................15 J6
Langtree Devon............10 C2
Langwathby Cumb.......148 F7
Langwell House
   Highld...................227 K4
Langwith Derbys.........115 K7
Langwith Junction
   Derbys...................115 K7
Langworth Lincs..........117 H6
Lanhydrock House &
   Gardens Cnwll............5 H3
Lanivet Cnwll..................5 G3
Lanlivery Cnwll...............5 G4
Lanner Cnwll...................3 J4
Lanreath Cnwll................5 J4
Lansallos Cnwll...............5 J5
Lanteglos Cnwll..............8 E7
Lanteglos Highway
   Cnwll........................5 J5
Lanton Border.............167 J5

Lanton Nthumb............168 D3
La Passee Guern............236 d2
Lapford Devon............11 H3
Laphroaig Ag & B............160 C1
Lapley Staffs............84 F2
La Pulente Jersey............236 a7
Lapworth Warwks............71 L1
Larachbeg Highld............190 E6
Larbert Falk............176 B3
Largie Abers............216 B3
Largiemore Ag & B............172 F2
Largoward Fife............187 H5
Largs N Ayrs............173 L6
Largybeg N Ayrs............162 D5
Largymore N Ayrs............162 D4
Larkfield Inver............173 L4
Larkfield Kent............33 J2
Larkhall S Lans............175 K7
Larkhill Wilts............28 C3
Larling Norfk............92 B5
La Rocque Jersey............236 e8
La Rousaillerie Guern............236 d2
Lartington Dur............140 C4
Lasham Hants............30 A3
Lasswade Mdloth............177 J5
Lastingham N York............133 L2
Latchingdon Essex............61 L7
Latchley Cnwll............6 B2
Lathbury M Keyn............74 C5
Latheron Highld............227 L2
Latheronwheel
    Highld............227 L3
Lathones Fife............187 H5
Latimer Bucks............59 G7
Latteridge S Glos............38 F4
Lattiford Somset............27 G6
Latton Wilts............40 C2
Lauder Border............178 C8
Laugharne Carmth............50 C4
Laughterton Lincs............116 D6
Laughton E Susx............20 A3
Laughton Leics............87 J5
Laughton Lincs............103 H6
Laughton Lincs............116 D3
Laughton-en-le-
    Morthen Rothm............115 K4
Launcells Cnwll............9 H4
Launceston Cnwll............9 J7
Launton Oxon............57 L4
Laurencekirk Abers............197 H3
Laurieston D & G............146 B3
Laurieston Falk............176 B3
Lavendon M Keyn............74 D4
Lavenham Suffk............77 K5
Lavernock V Glam............37 J6
Laversdale Cumb............148 E3
Laverstock Wilts............28 D5
Laverstoke Hants............29 J2
Laverton Gloucs............71 J7
Laverton N York............132 C5
Laverton Somset............27 H2
La Villette Guern............236 d4
Lavister Wrexhm............98 A2
Law S Lans............175 L7
Lawers P & K............193 L7
Lawford Essex............62 C2
Lawford Somset............25 H4
Law Hill S Lans............175 L7
Lawhitton Cnwll............9 J7
Lawkland N York............130 E6
Lawns Wood
    Crematorium
        Leeds............123 K3
Lawrenny Pembks............49 H6
Lawshall Suffk............77 K4
Laxay W Isls............232 f3
Laxdale W Isls............232 f2
Laxey IoM............237 d4
Laxfield Suffk............93 G8
Laxford Bridge Highld............228 C6
Laxo Shet............235 d4
Laxton E R Yk............125 J5
Laxton Nhants............88 D4
Laxton Notts............116 B7
Laycock C Brad............122 F3
Layer Breton Essex............61 M4

Layer-de-la-Haye
    Essex............62 A4
Layer Marney Essex............61 L4
Layham Suffk............78 B6
Laymore Dorset............13 K2
Laytham E R Yk............125 H3
Lazonby Cumb............148 F6
Lea Derbys............101 G2
Lea Herefs............54 F4
Lea Lincs............116 D4
Lea Shrops............83 G5
Lea Wilts............39 L3
Leachkin Highld............212 F5
Leadburn Border............177 H7
Leadenham Lincs............102 F3
Leaden Roding Essex............60 F5
Leadgate Dur............150 E5
Leadhills S Lans............165 G6
Leafield Oxon............56 F5
Leagrave Luton............59 H4
Leake Common Side
    Lincs............104 C3
Lealholm N York............142 F5
Lealt Highld............209 H3
Lea Marston Warwks............86 B5
Leamington Hastings
    Warwks............72 F2
Leamington Spa
    Warwks............72 D2
Leap Cross E Susx............20 C4
Leasgill Cumb............129 K3
Leasingham Lincs............103 H3
Leasingthorne Dur............141 G2
Leatherhead Surrey............31 K1
Leathley N York............123 J2
Leaton Shrops............98 C8
Leaveland Kent............34 D4
Leavenheath Suffk............77 L6
Leavening N York............134 C6
Leaves Green Gt Lon............45 H7
Lebberston N York............135 G3
Le Bigard Guern............236 c4
Le Bourg Guern............236 c4
Le Bourg Jersey............236 e8
Lechlade on Thames
    Gloucs............56 E7
Lecht Gruinart Ag & B............170 E5
Leck Lancs............130 C4
Leckbuie P & K............193 L7
Leckford Hants............29 G4
Leckhampstead
    Bucks............73 K6
Leckhampstead
    W Berk............41 H5
Leckhampstead
    Thicket W Berk............41 H5
Leckhampton Gloucs............55 L4
Leckmelm Highld............220 F4
Leconfield E R Yk............126 C2
Ledaig Ag & B............191 H8
Ledburn Bucks............58 E4
Ledbury Herefs............70 C6
Ledgemoor Herefs............69 H4
Ledmore Junction
    Highld............224 F6
Ledsham Leeds............124 C4
Ledston Leeds............124 C5
Ledwell Oxon............57 H3
Lee Devon............23 H3
Lee Gt Lon............45 H5
Leebotwood Shrops............83 J4
Lee Brockhurst
    Shrops............98 D6
Leece Cumb............128 F5
Lee Chapel Essex............46 B3
Lee Clump Bucks............58 E6
Leeds Kent............33 L3
Leeds Leeds............123 K4
Leeds Bradford
    Airport Leeds............123 J3
Leeds Castle Kent............33 L3
Leedstown Cnwll............3 G4
Leek Staffs............99 M2
Leek Wootton
    Warwks............72 C2
Lee Mill Devon............6 E5

Leeming N York............132 D2
Leeming Bar N York............132 D2
Lee-on-the-Solent
    Hants............17 G3
Lees Derbys............100 E5
Lees Oldham............113 L2
Lees Green Derbys............100 E5
Leesthorpe Leics............87 L2
Leeswood Flints............97 K1
Leetown P & K............186 C3
Leftwich Ches W............112 F6
Legbourne Lincs............118 E5
Legerwood Border............167 J2
Legoland W & M............42 F5
Le Gron Guern............236 c3
Legsby Lincs............117 J4
Le Haguais Jersey............236 d8
Le Hocq Jersey............236 d8
Leicester C Leic............87 H3
Leicester Forest East
    Leics............87 G3
Leicester Forest East
    Services Leics............87 G3
Leigh Dorset............14 C2
Leigh Gloucs............55 K3
Leigh Kent............32 F4
Leigh Surrey............31 L3
Leigh Wigan............112 F2
Leigh Wilts............40 B3
Leigh Worcs............70 D4
Leigh Beck Essex............46 D4
Leigh Delamere Wilts............39 K5
Leigh Delamere
    Services Wilts............39 K5
Leigh Green Kent............34 B7
Leigh Knoweglass
    S Lans............175 H7
Leigh-on-Sea Sthend............46 D3
Leigh Park Dorset............15 J3
Leigh Sinton Worcs............70 D4
Leighswood Wsall............85 J3
Leighterton Gloucs............39 J3
Leighton Powys............82 E3
Leighton Shrops............84 B3
Leighton Bromswold
    Cambs............89 G7
Leighton Buzzard
    C Beds............58 F3
Leigh upon Mendip
    Somset............27 G3
Leigh Woods N Som............38 E6
Leinthall Earls Herefs............69 J2
Leinthall Starkes
    Herefs............69 J1
Leintwardine Herefs............83 H8
Leire Leics............87 G5
Leiston Suffk............79 J3
Leith C Edin............177 H3
Leitholm Border............168 B1
Lelant Cnwll............2 F4
Lelley E R Yk............126 F4
Lelley Suffk............126 F4
Lempitlaw Border............168 B3
Lemreway W Isls............232 f3
Lemsford Herts............59 L5
Lenchwick Worcs............71 J5
Lendalfoot S Ayrs............152 D4
Lendrick Stirlg............184 C6
Lendrum Terrace
    Abers............217 L6
Lenham Kent............34 B4
Lenham Heath Kent............34 B5
Lenie Highld............202 D1
Lennel Border............168 C2
Lennox Plunton
    D & G............146 A5
Lennoxtown E Duns............175 H3
Lenton C Nott............101 K5
Lenton Lincs............103 G6
Lenwade Norfk............106 D8
Lenzie E Duns............175 H4
Leochel-Cushnie
    Abers............205 L4
Leominster Herefs............69 K3
Leonard Stanley
    Gloucs............55 J7
Leoville Jersey............236 b6

Lephin Highld............208 B4
Leppington N York............134 B7
Lepton Kirk............123 J7
Lerags Ag & B............182 B3
L'Erée Guern............236 b3
Lerryn Cnwll............5 J4
Lerwick Shet............235 d6
Les Arquets Guern............236 b3
Lesbury Nthumb............169 J6
Les Hubits Guern............236 d3
Leslie Abers............206 B1
Leslie Fife............186 D6
Les Lohiers Guern............236 c3
Lesmahagow S Lans............164 F2
Les Murchez Guern............236 c4
Lesnewth Cnwll............8 F5
Les Nicolles Guern............236 c4
Les Quartiers Guern............236 d2
Les Quennevais
    Jersey............236 b7
Les Sages Guern............236 b3
Lessingham Norfk............107 H6
Lessonhall Cumb............147 L5
Les Villets Guern............236 c4
Leswalt D & G............144 B3
L'Etacq Jersey............236 a6
Letchmore Heath
    Herts............43 J2
Letchworth Garden
    City Herts............59 L2
Letcombe Bassett
    Oxon............41 G4
Letcombe Regis Oxon............41 G3
Letham Angus............196 E6
Letham Border............167 K7
Letham Falk............176 B2
Letham Fife............186 E4
Letham Grange
    Angus............197 G7
Lethendy P & K............195 H7
Lethenty Abers............206 B2
Lethenty Abers............216 F6
Letheringham Suffk............78 F3
Letheringsett Norfk............106 C5
Letterewe Highld............219 L7
Letterfearn Highld............200 D2
Letterfinlay Lodge
    Hotel Highld............201 K6
Lettermorar Highld............199 M7
Letters Highld............220 F4
Lettershaw S Lans............165 H5
Letterston Pembks............48 F2
Lettoch Highld............204 C2
Lettoch Highld............214 D7
Letton Herefs............69 G5
Letty Green Herts............59 M5
Letwell Rothm............115 K4
Leuchars Fife............187 G3
Leumrabhagh W Isls............232 f3
Leurbost W Isls............232 f3
Levedale Staffs............84 F1
Leven E R Yk............126 D2
Leven Fife............186 F7
Levens Cumb............129 K3
Levens Green Herts............60 B4
Levenshulme Manch............113 K3
Levenwick Shet............235 c7
Leverburgh W Isls............232 d5
Leverington Cambs............90 C2
Leverstock Green
    Herts............59 H6
Leverton Lincs............104 C3
Le Villocq Guern............236 c2
Levington Suffk............78 F6
Levisham N York............134 C2
Lew Oxon............56 F6
Lewannick Cnwll............9 H8
Lewdown Devon............10 C7
Lewes E Susx............19 L4
Leweston Pembks............48 F3
Lewisham Gt Lon............45 G5
Lewisham
    Crematorium
        Gt Lon............45 H5
Lewiston Highld............212 D8
Lewistown Brdgnd............36 E3

Lewknor Oxon 42 B2
Lewson Street Kent 34 C3
Lewtrenchard Devon 10 C7
Lexden Essex 62 A3
Lexworthy Somset 25 K4
Leybourne Kent 33 H2
Leyburn N York 131 L2
Leygreen Herts 59 K3
Ley Hill Bucks 59 G7
Leyland Lancs 121 H6
Leylodge Abers 206 E3
Leys Abers 217 J4
Leys P & K 195 K8
Leysdown-on-Sea
  Kent 47 G6
Leysmill Angus 196 F6
Leys of Cossans
  Angus 196 C6
Leysters Herefs 69 L2
Leyton Gt Lon 45 G3
Leytonstone Gt Lon 45 H3
Lezant Cnwll 5 M1
Lhanbryde Moray 215 G3
Libanus Powys 52 F3
Libberton S Lans 165 J2
Liberton C Edin 177 J4
Lichfield Staffs 85 K2
Lickey Worcs 85 H7
Lickey End Worcs 85 H8
Lickfold W Susx 30 F6
Liddesdale Highld 190 F4
Liddington Swindn 40 E4
Lidgate Suffk 77 G3
Lidlington C Beds 74 E6
Liff Angus 186 E2
Lifford Birm 85 J7
Lifton Devon 9 K7
Liftondown Devon 9 K7
Lighthorne Warwks 72 D4
Lighthorne Heath
  Warwks 72 D4
Lightwater Surrey 42 F7
Lightwater Valley
  Theme Park
  N York 132 D4
Lilbourne Nhants 87 H7
Lilleshall Wrekin 84 D1
Lilley Herts 59 J3
Lilliesleaf Border 167 H4
Lillingstone Dayrell
  Bucks 73 K6
Lillingstone Lovell
  Bucks 73 K6
Lillington Dorset 26 F8
Lilliput Poole 15 K4
Lilstock Somset 25 J3
Limbury Luton 59 H3
Limekilnburn S Lans 175 J7
Limekilns Fife 176 E2
Limerigg Falk 176 B4
Limerstone IoW 16 E6
Lime Street Worcs 55 J2
Limington Somset 26 D6
Limmerhaugh E Ayrs 164 C4
Limpenhoe Norfk 93 H3
Limpley Stoke Wilts 39 H7
Limpsfield Surrey 32 D3
Limpsfield Chart
  Surrey 32 D3
Linby Notts 101 K3
Linchmere W Susx 30 E5
Lincluden D & G 155 G6
Lincoln Lincs 116 F7
Lincoln Crematorium
  Lincs 117 G7
Lincomb Worcs 70 E2
Lindale Cumb 129 J4
Lindal in Furness
  Cumb 128 F4
Lindfield W Susx 32 C7
Lindford Hants 30 D4
Lindley Kirk 123 G6
Lindores Fife 186 D4
Lindridge Worcs 70 C2
Lindsell Essex 61 G3
Lindsey Suffk 77 L5

Lindsey Tye Suffk 78 B5
Lingdale R & Cl 142 E4
Lingen Herefs 69 G2
Lingfield Surrey 32 C4
Lingwood Norfk 93 H2
Linicro Highld 218 D7
Linkend Worcs 55 J2
Linkenholt Hants 41 G8
Linkinhorne Cnwll 5 L2
Linktown Fife 177 J1
Linkwood Moray 214 F3
Linley Shrops 83 G5
Linley Green Herefs 70 C4
Linlithgow W Loth 176 D3
Linsidemore Highld 222 D2
Linslade C Beds 58 E3
Linstead Parva Suffk 93 G7
Linstock Cumb 148 D4
Linthurst Worcs 85 H8
Linthwaite Kirk 123 G7
Lintlaw Border 179 H6
Lintmill Moray 215 L2
Linton Border 168 B4
Linton Cambs 76 E5
Linton Derbys 86 C1
Linton Herefs 54 F3
Linton Kent 33 K3
Linton Leeds 124 B2
Linton N York 131 J6
Linton Hill Herefs 54 F3
Linton-on-Ouse
  N York 133 G7
Linwood Lincs 117 J4
Linwood Rens 174 E5
Lionacleit W Isls 233 b7
Lional W Isls 232 g1
Liphook Hants 30 D5
Liscard Wirral 111 J3
Liscombe Somset 24 D5
Liskeard Cnwll 5 K3
Lismore Ag & B 191 G2
Liss Hants 30 C5
Lissett E R Yk 135 H7
Lissington Lincs 117 J5
Lisvane Cardif 37 J4
Liswerry Newpt 37 M3
Litcham Norfk 105 L8
Litchborough Nhants 73 J4
Litchfield Hants 29 J2
Litherland Sefton 111 K2
Litlington Cambs 75 K6
Litlington E Susx 20 B5
Little Abington
  Cambs 76 D5
Little Addington
  Nhants 88 D8
Little Airies D & G 145 J5
Little Alne Warwks 71 K3
Little Altcar Sefton 111 J1
Little Amwell Herts 60 B5
Little Aston Staffs 85 K4
Little Ayton N York 142 C5
Little Baddow Essex 61 J6
Little Badminton
  S Glos 39 J4
Little Bampton Cumb 148 A4
Little Bardfield Essex 61 G2
Little Barford Bed 75 H3
Little Barningham
  Norfk 106 D5
Little Barrington
  Gloucs 56 D5
Little Barrow Ches W 112 C7
Little Bavington
  Nthumb 158 C6
Little Bedwyn Wilts 40 F7
Little Bentley Essex 62 D3
Little Berkhamsted
  Herts 59 M6
Little Billing Nhants 74 B3
Little Billington
  C Beds 58 F4
Little Birch Herefs 54 D2
Little Blakenham
  Suffk 78 D5
Little Blencow Cumb 148 E7

Little Bognor W Susx 31 G7
Little Bollington
  Ches E 113 G4
Little Bookham
  Surrey 31 J1
Littleborough Notts 116 D5
Littleborough Rochdl 122 D7
Littlebourne Kent 35 G3
Little Bourton Oxon 72 F5
Little Braxted Essex 61 K5
Little Brechin Angus 196 F4
Littlebredy Dorset 14 B5
Little Brickhill M Keyn 58 E2
Little Brington
  Nhants 73 J2
Little Bromley Essex 62 C3
Little Budworth
  Ches W 112 E7
Littleburn Highld 212 F4
Little Burstead Essex 46 A2
Littlebury Essex 76 D6
Littlebury Green
  Essex 76 C6
Little Bytham Lincs 103 G8
Little Carlton Lincs 118 E4
Little Casterton
  Rutlnd 88 E2
Little Cawthorpe
  Lincs 118 E5
Little Chalfont Bucks 43 G2
Little Chart Kent 34 C5
Little Chesterford
  Essex 76 D6
Little Cheverell Wilts 27 M2
Little Chishill Cambs 76 B6
Little Clacton Essex 62 E4
Little Clifton Cumb 136 E2
Little Comberton
  Worcs 71 G5
Little Common E Susx ... 20 E4
Little Compton
  Warwks 56 E3
Little Cornard Suffk 77 K6
Little Cowarne Herefs 69 L4
Little Coxwell Oxon 40 F2
Little Crakehall
  N York 132 C2
Little Cressingham
  Norfk 91 K4
Little Crosby Sefton 111 K2
Little Cubley Derbys 100 D5
Little Dalby Leics 87 L2
Littledean Gloucs 54 F5
Little Dewchurch
  Herefs 54 D2
Little Ditton Cambs 76 F3
Little Downham
  Cambs 90 D6
Little Driffield E R Yk ... 134 F7
Little Dunham Norfk 91 K2
Little Dunkeld P & K 195 G7
Little Dunmow Essex 61 G4
Little Durnford Wilts 28 C5
Little Easton Essex 60 F3
Little Eaton Derbys 101 G4
Little Ellingham Norfk 92 B4
Little Everdon Nhants 73 H3
Little Eversden
  Cambs 75 L4
Little Faringdon Oxon 56 E7
Little Fencote N York ... 132 D2
Little Fenton N York 124 D4
Little Fransham
  Norfk 91 K2
Little Gaddesden
  Herts 59 G5
Little Glemham Suffk 79 H3
Little Gorsley Herefs 55 G3
Little Gransden
  Cambs 75 J4
Little Green Somset 27 G2
Little Hadham Herts 60 C4
Little Hale Lincs 103 J4
Little Hallam Derbys 101 J4
Little Hallingbury
  Essex 60 D4

Littleham Devon 12 D6
Littleham Devon 23 G6
Littlehampton W Susx ... 18 D5
Little Harrowden
  Nhants 74 C1
Little Haseley Oxon 57 M7
Little Haven Pembks 48 E5
Littlehaven W Susx 31 K5
Little Hay Staffs 85 K3
Little Haywood Staffs ... 100 A7
Littlehempston
  Devon 7 J4
Little Hereford Herefs 69 K2
Little Horkesley Essex 62 A2
Little Hormead Herts 60 C3
Little Horsted E Susx 19 M3
Little Horton C Brad 123 H4
Little Horwood Bucks 58 C2
Little Houghton
  Barns 115 H1
Little Houghton
  Nhants 74 B3
Little Hucklow Derbys .. 114 D5
Little Hutton N York 133 G4
Little Irchester
  Nhants 74 C2
Little Keyford Somset 27 H3
Little Kimble Bucks 58 D6
Little Kineton Warwks 72 D4
Little Kingshill Bucks 58 E7
Little Knox D & G 146 E3
Little Langdale Cumb ... 137 J6
Little Langford Wilts 28 B4
Little Leigh Ches W 112 F6
Little Leighs Essex 61 H5
Little Lever Bolton 121 L8
Little Linford M Keyn 74 B5
Little Load Somset 26 C6
Little London E Susx 20 C2
Little London Hants 29 G2
Little London Hants 41 L8
Little Longstone
  Derbys 114 D6
Little Maplestead
  Essex 77 J7
Little Marcle Herefs 70 C7
Little Marlow Bucks 42 E3
Little Massingham
  Norfk 105 J7
Little Melton Norfk 92 E3
Littlemill Abers 205 H6
Littlemill Highld 213 L4
Little Mill Mons 53 L7
Little Milton Oxon 57 L7
Little Missenden
  Bucks 58 F7
Littlemore Oxon 57 K7
Little Musgrave
  Cumb 139 H5
Little Ness Shrops 98 B8
Little Newcastle
  Pembks 49 G2
Little Newsham Dur 140 E4
Little Norton Somset 26 C7
Little Oakley Essex 62 F3
Little Oakley Nhants 88 C6
Little Orton Cumb 148 C4
Littleover C Derb 101 G5
Little Packington
  Warwks 86 B6
Little Paxton Cambs 75 H3
Little Petherick Cnwll 4 E2
Little Plumstead
  Norfk 93 G2
Little Ponton Lincs 102 F6
Littleport Cambs 90 E6
Little Preston Nhants 73 H4
Little Raveley Cambs 89 J7
Little Reedness E R Yk . 125 J6
Little Ribston N York ... 132 F8
Little Rissington
  Gloucs 56 D4
Little Rollright Oxon 56 F3
Little Ryburgh Norfk 106 A6
Little Salkeld Cumb 148 F7
Little Sampford Essex ... 76 F7

Little Saughall
  Ches W 111 K7
Little Saxham Suffk 77 H2
Little Scatwell Highld ...212 B3
Little Shelford Cambs....76 C4
Little Singleton Lancs ...120 E3
Little Skipwith N York...125 G3
Little Smeaton N York...124 D6
Little Snoring Norfk......106 A6
Little Sodbury S Glos 39 H4
Little Somborne
  Hants 29 G5
Little Somerford Wilts....39 L4
Little Soudley Shrops 99 G6
Little Stainton Darltn...141 J3
Little Stanney Ches W ..112 B6
Little Staughton Bed.....75 G3
Little Steeping Lincs ...118 F8
Little Stoke Staffs..........99 K6
Littlestone-on-Sea
  Kent 21 L2
Little Stonham Suffk 78 D3
Little Stretton Leics 87 J4
Little Stretton Shrops....83 J5
Little Strickland
  Cumb 138 E4
Little Stukeley Cambs ...89 H7
Little Sugnall Staffs........99 J6
Little Swinburne
  Nthumb 158 B6
Little Sypland D & G....146 C4
Little Tew Oxon 57 G3
Little Tey Essex 61 L4
Little Thetford Cambs....90 D7
Little Thorpe Dur 151 K6
Littlethorpe Leics 87 G4
Littlethorpe N York 132 E5
Little Thurlow Suffk.......76 F4
Little Thurrock Thurr.....45 L4
Littleton Angus..............196 B6
Littleton Ches W...........112 C7
Littleton D & G..............146 B4
Littleton Hants................29 J5
Littleton Somset 26 C5
Littleton Surrey 43 H6
Littleton Drew Wilts 39 J4
Littleton-on-Severn
  S Glos 38 E3
Littleton Pannell
  Wilts 27 M2
Little Torrington
  Devon 10 D2
Littletown Dur...............151 H6
Little Town Lancs 121 K4
Little Urswick Cumb....128 F5
Little Wakering
  Essex 46 F3
Little Walden Essex........76 D6
Little Waldingfield
  Suffk 77 K5
Little Walsingham
  Norfk 105 M5
Little Waltham Essex......61 H5
Little Weighton
  E R Yk 126 B4
Little Weldon Nhants.....88 D5
Little Wenlock Wrekin ...84 B3
Little Weston Somset 26 F6
Little Whitefield IoW 17 H4
Littlewick Green
  W & M.........................42 D4
Little Wilbraham
  Cambs 76 D3
Little Witcombe
  Gloucs 55 K5
Little Witley Worcs.........70 D2
Little Wittenham
  Oxon 41 K2
Little Wolford Warwks ...72 C7
Little Woodcote
  Gt Lon 44 F7
Littleworth Oxon 40 F2
Littleworth Staffs............99 L7
Littleworth Worcs...........70 F4
Little Wymington
  Bed 74 D2

Little Wymondley
  Herts 59 K3
Little Wyrley Staffs 85 H3
Little Yeldham Essex 77 H6
Littley Green Essex 61 H4
Litton Derbys 114 D6
Litton N York 131 G5
Litton Somset 26 E1
Litton Cheney Dorset 14 A4
Liurbost W Isls..............232 f3
Liverpool Lpool.............111 K4
Liverpool Maritime
  Mercantile City
  Lpool 111 K4
Liversedge Kirk.............123 J5
Liverton Devon.................7 J2
Liverton R & Cl.............142 F4
Livingston W Loth 176 E5
Livingston Village
  W Loth 176 E5
Lixwm Flints 111 G7
Lizard Cnwll......................3 J8
Llanaelhaearn Gwynd....95 G4
Llanafan Cerdgn.............66 F1
Llanafan-Fawr Powys 67 L4
Llanallgo IoA 109 G4
Llanarmon Dyffryn
  Ceiriog Wrexhm.........97 J6
Llanarmon-yn-Ial
  Denbgs........................97 J2
Llanarth Cerdgn.............65 L3
Llanarth Mons 54 B5
Llanarthne Carmth 51 G2
Llanasa Flints 110 F5
Llanbadarn Fawr
  Cerdgn........................80 E7
Llanbadarn Fynydd
  Powys 82 C7
Llanbadoc Mons 54 B7
Llanbeder Newpt 38 B3
Llanbedr Gwynd 95 K7
Llanbedr Powys 53 K4
Llanbedr-Dyffryn-
  Clwyd Denbgs.............97 H2
Llanbedrgoch IoA 109 G5
Llanbedrog Gwynd..........94 F6
Llanbedr-y-Cennin
  Conwy 109 L7
Llanberis Gwynd 95 K1
Llanbethery V Glam 37 G6
Llanbister Powys 82 C8
Llanblethian V Glam........36 F5
Llanboidy Carmth 49 L3
Llanbradach Caerph 37 J3
Llanbrynmair Powys........81 J3
Llancadle V Glam 37 G6
Llancarfan V Glam 37 G6
Llancloudy Herefs...........54 D4
Llandaff Cardif................37 J5
Llandanwg Gwynd...........95 K6
Llanddaniel Fab IoA......109 G7
Llanddarog Carmth 51 G3
Llanddeiniol Cerdgn........66 D1
Llanddeiniolen
  Gwynd 109 H7
Llanddderfel Gwynd........96 F5
Llanddeusant IoA...........108 D4
Llanddew Powys 53 G2
Llanddewi Swans............50 F7
Llanddewi Brefi
  Cerdgn........................66 F4
Llanddewi
  Rhydderch Mons 53 M5
Llanddewi Velfrey
  Pembks........................49 K4
Llanddewi
  Ystradenni Powys.....68 C2
Llanddoget Conwy........109 M8
Llanddona IoA 109 H5
Llanddowror Carmth.......50 B3
Llanddulas Conwy.........110 C6
Llanddwywe Gwynd........95 K7
Llanddyfnan IoA 109 G5
Llandefaelog-Tre'r-
  Graig Powys 53 H3
Llandefalle Powys 68 C7

Llandegfan IoA.............109 H6
Llandegla Denbgs 97 J3
Llandegley Powys 68 D2
Llandegveth Mons..........37 M2
Llandeilo Carmth.............51 J2
Llandeilo Graban
  Powys 68 C5
Llandeloy Pembks...........48 E3
Llandenny Mons..............54 B7
Llandevaud Newpt 38 B3
Llandevenny Mons 38 B3
Llandinam Powys.............82 B5
Llandissilio Pembks........49 J3
Llandogo Mons 54 D7
Llandough V Glam 36 F6
Llandough V Glam 37 J5
Llandovery Carmth..........67 G7
Llandow V Glam 36 E5
Llandre Carmth 66 F6
Llandre Cerdgn 80 E6
Llandre Isaf Pembks 49 J2
Llandrillo Denbgs 97 G5
Llandrillo-yn-Rhos
  Conwy 110 B5
Llandrindod Wells
  Powys 68 B3
Llandrinio Powys 97 L8
Llandudno Conwy.........109 L5
Llandudno Junction
  Conwy 109 M6
Llandulas Powys 67 J6
Llandwrog Gwynd...........95 H2
Llandybie Carmth............51 J3
Llandyfaelog Carmth.......50 E3
Llandyfriog Cerdgn 65 K6
Llandygai Gwynd...........109 H7
Llandygwydd Cerdgn......65 H5
Llandyrnog Denbgs 110 F8
Llandyssil Powys 82 E4
Llandysul Cerdgn 65 L6
Llanedeyrn Cardif 37 K4
Llaneglwys Powys...........68 B6
Llanegryn Gwynd 80 D3
Llanegwad Carmth 51 G2
Llaneilian IoA 108 F3
Llanelian-yn-Rhôs
  Conwy 110 B6
Llanelidan Denbgs 97 H3
Llanelieu Powys...............68 D7
Llanellen Mons 53 L5
Llanelli Carmth................51 G5
Llanelli Crematorium
  Carmth 51 G5
Llanelltyd Gwynd............96 A8
Llanelwedd Powys 68 B4
Llanenddwyn Gwynd.......95 K7
Llanengan Gwynd 94 E6
Llanerchymedd IoA.......108 E5
Llanerfyl Powys 82 B2
Llanfachraeth IoA..........108 D5
Llanfachreth Gwynd........96 B7
Llanfaelog IoA 108 D6
Llanfaelrhys Gwynd........94 D6
Llanfaethlu IoA..............108 D4
Llanfair Gwynd................95 K6
Llanfair Caereinion
  Powys 82 C3
Llanfair Clydogau
  Cerdgn........................66 E4
Llanfair Dyffryn
  Clwyd Denbgs.............97 H2
Llanfairfechan Conwy...109 K6
Llanfairpwllgwyngyll
  IoA 109 G6
Llanfair Talhaiarn
  Conwy 110 C7
Llanfair Waterdine
  Shrops 82 E7
Llanfairynghornwy
  IoA 108 D4
Llanfair-yn-Neubwll
  IoA 108 C6
Llanfallteg Carmth..........49 K4
Llanfallteg West
  Carmth 49 K4
Llanfarian Cerdgn 80 D7

Llanfechain Powys..........97 J7
Llanfechell IoA...............108 E3
Llanferres Denbgs...........97 J1
Llanfihangel-ar-arth
  Carmth 66 B6
Llanfihangel Glyn
  Myfyr Conwy 96 F3
Llanfihangel Nant
  Bran Powys 67 K7
Llanfihangel
  Rhydithon Powys......68 D2
Llanfihangel Rogiet
  Mons 38 C3
Llanfihangel-y-
  Creuddyn Cerdgn.....80 F7
Llanfihangel-yng-
  Ngwynfa Powys........82 C1
Llanfihangel yn
  Nhowyn IoA.............108 D6
Llanfihangel-y-
  traethau Gwynd 95 K5
Llanfilo Powys.................53 H2
Llanfoist Mons 53 L5
Llanfor Gwynd 96 E5
Llanfrechfa Torfn............37 L2
Llanfrynach Powys 53 G3
Llanfwrog Denbgs 97 H2
Llanfwrog IoA................108 C5
Llanfyllin Powys 97 H8
Llanfynydd Carmth..........66 D8
Llanfynydd Flints 97 L2
Llanfyrnach Pembks.......49 L2
Llangadfan Powys 81 L2
Llangadog Carmth 66 F8
Llangadwaladr IoA 108 E7
Llangaffo IoA.................108 F7
Llangammarch Wells
  Powys 67 K5
Llangan V Glam 36 E5
Llangarron Herefs...........54 D4
Llangathen Carmth..........51 H2
Llangattock Powys 53 K4
Llangattock Lingoed
  Mons 54 A4
Llangedwyn Powys..........97 J7
Llangefni IoA 108 F6
Llangeinor Brdgnd..........36 E3
Llangeitho Cerdgn 66 E3
Llangeler Carmth 65 L6
Llangelynin Gwynd 80 D3
Llangendeirne
  Carmth 50 F3
Llangennech Carmth.......51 H5
Llangennith Swans..........50 E7
Llangernyw Conwy.........110 B7
Llangian Gwynd 94 E6
Llangloffan Pembks.........64 C7
Llanglydwen Carmth.......49 K3
Llangoed IoA.................109 J5
Llangollen Denbgs 97 K4
Llangolman Pembks........49 J3
Llangors Powys 53 H3
Llangower Gwynd 96 D6
Llangrannog Cerdgn........65 K4
Llangristiolus IoA...........108 F6
Llangrove Herefs.............54 D4
Llangunllo Powys 68 E1
Llangunnor Carmth.........50 E2
Llangurig Powys 81 K7
Llangwm Conwy..............96 F4
Llangwm Mons 54 B7
Llangwm Pembks 49 G5
Llangwnnadl Gwynd........94 D6
Llangwyryfon Cerdgn......66 D1
Llangybi Cerdgn 66 E4
Llangybi Gwynd 95 G4
Llangybi Mons 38 A2
Llangynhafal Denbgs.....110 F8
Llangynidr Powys 53 J4
Llangynin Carmth............50 B2
Llangynog Carmth............50 D3
Llangynog Powys 97 G7
Llangynwyd Brdgnd.........36 D3
Llanhamlach Powys.........53 H3
Llanharan Rhondd...........36 F4
Llanharry Rhondd...........36 F4

Llanhennock Mons 38 A2
Llanhilleth Blae G......53 K7
Llanidloes Powys.........81 K6
Llaniestyn Gwynd........94 E5
Llanigon Powys 68 E6
Llanilar Cerdgn 80 E8
Llanilid Rhondd...........36 F4
Llanina Cerdgn 65 L3
Llanishen Cardif..........37 J4
Llanishen Mons 54 C7
Llanllechid Gwynd........109 J7
Llanllowell Mons 54 B7
Llanllugan Powys..........82 B3
Llanllwch Carmth..........50 E2
Llanllwchaiarn Powys 82 C5
Llanllwni Carmth 66 C6
Llanllyfni Gwynd...........95 H3
Llanmadoc Swans 50 F6
Llanmaes V Glam 36 F6
Llanmartin Newpt.........38 B3
Llanmiloe Carmth..........50 B4
Llannefydd Conwy........110 D7
Llannon Carmth............51 G4
Llannor Gwynd..............94 F5
Llanon Cerdgn 66 C2
Llanover Mons 53 L6
Llanpumsaint Carmth 65 L8
Llanrhaeadr-ym-
     Mochnant Powys 97 H7
Llanrhian Pembks 48 D2
Llanrhidian Swans 50 F6
Llanrhychwyn Conwy 96 B1
Llanrhyddlad IoA 108 D4
Llanrhystud Cerdgn.......66 C1
Llanrug Gwynd.............109 G8
Llanrumney Cardif........37 K4
Llanrwst Conwy...........96 C1
Llansadurnen Carmth 50 C4
Llansadwrn Carmth 66 F7
Llansadwrn IoA 109 H6
Llansaint Carmth...........50 E4
Llansamlet Swans 51 K6
Llansanffraid Glan
     Conwy Conwy........109 M6
Llansannan Conwy........110 C7
Llansantffraed Powys 53 H4
Llansantffraed-
     Cwmdeuddwr
     Powys 67 L2
Llansantffraed-in-
     Elvel Powys 68 C4
Llansantffraid
     Cerdgn 66 C2
Llansantffraid-ym-
     Mechain Powys 97 K7
Llansawel Carmth 66 E7
Llansilin Powys 97 K6
Llansoy Mons...............54 C7
Llanspyddid Powys........52 F3
Llanstadwell Pembks 48 F6
Llansteffan Carmth........50 D4
Llanteg Pembks............49 K5
Llanthewy Skirrid
     Mons 53 M5
Llanthony Mons 53 L3
Llantilio-Crossenny
     Mons 54 B5
Llantilio Pertholey
     Mons 53 L5
Llantrisant Mons...........38 B2
Llantrisant Rhondd........37 G4
Llantrithyd V Glam 37 G6
Llantwit Fardre
     Rhondd 37 G3
Llantwit Major V Glam...36 F6
Llanuwchllyn Gwynd......96 D6
Llanvaches Newpt.........38 B3
Llanvair Discoed
     Mons 38 C3
Llanvapley Mons 54 A5
Llanvetherine Mons 54 A5
Llanvihangel
     Crucorney Mons 53 L4
Llanwddyn Powys.........96 F8
Llanwenog Cerdgn 66 C5

Llanwern Newpt...........38 A3
Llanwinio Carmth.........50 C1
Llanwnda Gwynd.........95 H2
Llanwnda Pembks........64 C6
Llanwnnen Cerdgn 66 C5
Llanwnog Powys..........82 B5
Llanwrda Carmth 66 F7
Llanwrin Powys 81 H3
Llanwrthwl Powys........67 L2
Llanwrtyd Wells
     Powys 67 J5
Llanwyddelan Powys 82 C4
Llanyblodwel Shrops....97 K7
Llanybri Carmth............50 D3
Llanybydder Carmth 66 C5
Llanycefn Pembks.........49 J3
Llanychaer Bridge
     Pembks 64 D7
Llanymawddwy
     Gwynd 96 D8
Llanymynech Powys.....97 K7
Llanynghenedl IoA 108 D5
Llanynys Denbgs........110 F8
Llanyre Powys..............68 B3
Llanystumdwy
     Gwynd 95 H5
Llanywern Powys..........53 H3
Llawhaden Pembks 49 H4
Llawryglyn Powys.........81 K5
Llay Wrexhm 97 M2
Llechrhyd Caerph.........53 H6
Llechryd Cerdgn..........65 H5
Lledrod Cerdgn...........66 E1
Lleyn Peninsula
     Gwynd 94 E5
Llithfaen Gwynd...........94 F4
Lloc Flints...................111 G6
Llowes Powys 68 D6
Llwydcoed Rhondd.......52 F6
Llwydcoed
     Crematorium
     Rhondd 52 F6
Llwydiarth Powys..........82 B1
Llwyncelyn Cerdgn........66 B3
Llwyndafydd Cerdgn 65 L4
Llwyngwril Gwynd.........80 D2
Llwynmawr Wrexhm.....97 K5
Llwynypia Rhondd........36 F2
Llynclys Shrops............97 L7
Llynfaes IoA 108 E5
Llysfaen Conwy 110 B6
Llyswen Powys 68 C6
Llysworney V Glam 36 E5
Llys-y-frân Pembks......49 H3
Llywel Powys 52 D3
Loan Falk 176 C3
Loanhead Mdloth.........177 J5
Loaningfoot D & G........147 G4
Loans S Ayrs................163 J3
Lobhillcross Devon 10 C7
Lochailort Highld..........200 B8
Lochaline Highld...........190 D7
Lochans D & G.............144 C4
Locharbriggs D & G......155 H6
Lochavich Ag & B.........182 D4
Lochawe Ag & B 183 G2
Loch Baghasdail
     W Isls 233 c8
Lochboisdale W Isls......233 c8
Lochbuie Ag & B..........181 J3
Lochcarron Highld........210 D6
Lochdon Ag & B...........181 L2
Lochdonhead Ag & B....181 L2
Lochead Ag & B 172 D3
Lochearnhead Stirlg.....184 D3
Lochee C Dund 186 F2
Locheilside Station
     Highld 191 K2
Lochend Highld............212 F6
Locheport W Isls..........233 c6
Loch Euphoirt W Isls....233 c6
Lochfoot D & G............154 F7
Lochgair Ag & B...........172 F1
Lochgelly Fife...............186 C8
Lochgilphead Ag & B....172 E2
Lochgoilhead Ag & B ...183 H6

Lochieheads Fife..........186 D5
Lochill Moray................215 G2
Lochindorb Lodge
     Highld 214 B7
Lochinver Highld 224 D4
Loch Lomond and
     The Trossachs
     National Park 184 A5
Lochluichart Highld 211 L2
Lochmaben D & G........155 J5
Lochmaddy W Isls.......233 c6
Loch Maree Hotel
     Highld 219 L7
Loch nam Madadh
     W Isls 233 c6
Loch Ness Highld........202 E1
Lochore Fife.................186 C7
Lochranza N Ayrs.........172 F7
Lochside Abers.............197 H4
Lochside D & G............155 G6
Lochside Highld 213 J4
Lochslin Highld.............223 J5
Lochton S Ayrs.............152 F6
Lochty Angus...............196 E4
Lochty Fife...................187 H5
Lochuisge Highld..........190 F5
Lochwinnoch Rens........174 C6
Lochwood D & G 155 J3
Lockengate Cnwll..........5 G4
Lockerbie D & G...........155 K5
Lockeridge Wilts...........40 C6
Lockerley Hants............28 F6
Locking N Som 38 A8
Locking Stumps
     Warrtn 112 F3
Lockington E R Yk........126 B2
Lockleywood Shrops.....99 G6
Locksbottom Gt Lon......45 H6
Locks Heath Hants........17 G2
Lockton N York.............134 C2
Loddington Leics..........87 L3
Loddington Nhants........88 B7
Loddiswell Devon..........7 G6
Loddon Norfk 93 H4
Lode Cambs.................76 D3
Lode Heath Solhll.........85 L7
Loders Dorset 13 L4
Lodge Hill
     Crematorium
     Birm......................85 H6
Lodsworth W Susx 30 F6
Lofthouse Leeds...........123 L5
Lofthouse N York 151 L5
Lofthouse Gate
     Wakefd 123 L5
Loftus R & Cl 142 F4
Logan E Ayrs................164 C5
Loganlea W Loth 176 C6
Loggerheads Staffs.......99 G5
Logie Angus.................197 H4
Logie Fife....................186 F4
Logie Moray.................214 C4
Logie Coldstone
     Abers....................205 K4
Logie Newton Abers......216 C6
Logie Pert Angus.........197 G4
Logierait P & K.............194 F6
Logierieve Abers...........217 H8
Login Carmth 49 K3
Lolworth Cambs...........75 L2
Lonbain Highld 209 L4
Londesborough
     E R Yk 125 K2
London Gt Lon 44 F4
London Apprentice
     Cnwll.....................4 F6
London Colney Herts.....59 K7
Londonderry N York......132 D3
London Gateway
     Services Ag & B......44 D2
Londonthorpe Lincs......102 F5
London Zoo ZSL
     Gt Lon...................44 F4
Londubh Highld............219 K5
Lonemore Highld 219 J6
Long Ashton N Som......38 D6

Long Bank Worcs 84 D8
Long Bennington
     Lincs 102 D4
Longbenton N Tyne......151 G2
Longborough Gloucs.....56 D3
Long Bredy Dorset........14 B4
Longbridge Birm..........85 H7
Longbridge Deverill
     Wilts.....................27 K4
Long Buckby Nhants......73 J2
Longburton Dorset........26 F8
Long Clawson Leics......102 B6
Longcliffe Derbys..........100 E2
Longcombe Devon 7 J4
Long Compton Staffs 99 J7
Long Compton
     Warwks 56 F2
Longcot Oxon 40 F3
Long Crendon Bucks.....58 B6
Long Crichel Dorset......15 J1
Longden Shrops 83 J3
Long Ditton Surrey........44 D6
Longdon Staffs 85 J2
Longdon Worcs 70 E7
Longdon Green Staffs....85 J2
Longdon upon Tern
     Wrekin 84 B1
Longdown Devon 11 K6
Longdowns Cnwll..........3 J4
Long Duckmanton
     Derbys 115 H7
Long Eaton Derbys 101 J5
Longfield Kent..............45 L6
Longford Covtry...........86 D6
Longford Derbys 100 F5
Longford Gloucs...........55 J4
Longford Shrops 98 F5
Longford Wrekin 99 G8
Longforgan P & K.........186 E2
Longformacus
     Border 178 E6
Longframlington
     Nthumb 158 E3
Long Green Ches W.....112 C7
Longham Dorset 15 K3
Longham Norfk............91 L1
Long Hanborough
     Oxon.....................57 H5
Longhaven Abers..........217 L6
Longhirst Nthumb 158 F4
Longhope Gloucs..........55 G4
Longhope Ork...............234 b7
Longhorsley Nthumb.....158 E4
Longhoughton
     Nthumb 169 J6
Long Itchington
     Warwks 72 E2
Longlane Derbys 100 E5
Long Lawford
     Warwks 86 F7
Longleat Safari &
     Adventure Park
     Wilts.....................27 J3
Longlevens Gloucs........55 J4
Longleys P & K.............195 L7
Long Load Somset.......26 C6
Longmanhill Abers........216 E2
Long Marston Herts......58 E5
Long Marston N York....124 D1
Long Marston Warwks...71 L5
Long Marton Cumb.......138 F3
Long Melford Suffk.......77 J5
Longmoor Camp
     Hants....................30 C5
Longmorn Moray..........214 F3
Longmoss Ches E.........113 K6
Long Newnton Gloucs...39 K3
Longnewton Border......167 J4
Long Newton E Loth.....178 B5
Longnewton S on T.......141 J4
Longney Gloucs............55 H5
Longniddry E Loth 177 L3
Longnor Shrops............83 J4
Longnor Staffs.............114 C8
Longparish Hants..........29 H3
Long Preston N York 130 F7

Longridge Lancs 121 J3
Longridge W Loth 176 C5
Longriggend N Lans 175 L4
Long Riston E R Yk 126 E3
Longrock Cnwll 2 E5
Longsdon Staffs 99 L2
Longside Abers 217 K5
Longstanton Cambs 76 B2
Longstock Hants 29 G4
Longstowe Cambs 75 K4
Long Stratton Norfk 92 E5
Long Street M Keyn 74 B5
Longstreet Wilts 28 C2
Long Sutton Hants 30 C3
Long Sutton Lincs 104 C7
Long Sutton Somset 26 C6
Longthorpe C Pete 89 H4
Long Thurlow Suffk 78 B2
Longthwaite Cumb 138 B3
Longton C Stke 99 K4
Longton Lancs 121 G5
Longtown Cumb 148 C2
Longtown Herefs 53 L3
Longueville Jersey 236 d7
Longville in the Dale
Shrops 83 K5
Long Waste Wrekin 84 B1
Long Whatton Leics 101 J7
Longwick Bucks 58 C6
Long Wittenham
Oxon 41 K2
Longwitton Nthumb 158 D4
Longwood D & G 146 C3
Longworth Oxon 57 G7
Longyester E Loth 178 C5
Lonmay Abers 217 J3
Lonmore Highld 208 D5
Looe Cnwll 5 K5
Loose Kent 33 K3
Loosley Row Bucks 58 D7
Lootcherbrae Abers 216 B4
Lopen Somset 26 B8
Loppington Shrops 98 C6
Lords Wood Medway 46 C7
Lornty P & K 195 J6
Loscoe Derbys 101 H3
Lossiemouth Moray 214 F1
Lostock Gralam
Ches W 113 G6
Lostock Green
Ches W 113 G6
Lostwithiel Cnwll 5 H4
Lothbeg Highld 227 G6
Lothersdale N York 122 E2
Lothmore Highld 227 G6
Loudwater Bucks 42 E3
Loughborough
Leics 101 K8
Loughborough
Crematorium
Leics 101 K8
Loughor Swans 51 H6
Loughton Essex 45 H2
Loughton M Keyn 74 B6
Lound Lincs 103 H8
Lound Notts 116 B4
Lound Suffk 93 K4
Lount Leics 101 G8
Louth Lincs 118 D4
Lovedean Hants 30 B8
Lover Wilts 28 E7
Loversall Donc 115 L2
Loves Green Essex 61 G6
Loveston Pembks 49 J5
Lovington Somset 26 E5
Low Ackworth
Wakefd 124 C6
Low Barbeth D & G 144 B2
Low Bentham N York ...130 C5
Low Biggins Cumb 130 B4
Low Borrowbridge
Cumb 138 E6
Low Bradfield Sheff 114 E3
Low Bradley N York 122 F2
Low Burnham N Linc ...116 C2
Lowca Cumb 136 D3
Low Catton E R Yk 133 L8

Low Crosby Cumb 148 D3
Lowdham Notts 102 A3
Low Dinsdale Darltn 141 J5
Lower Aisholt Somset 25 J4
Lower Ansty Dorset 14 E2
Lower Apperley
Gloucs 55 J3
Lower Ashton Devon 11 J7
Lower Assendon
Oxon 42 C4
Lower Bartle Lancs 121 G4
Lower Basildon
W Berk 41 L5
Lower Beeding
W Susx 31 L6
Lower Benefield
Nhants 88 E5
Lower Bentley Worcs 71 H2
Lower Boddington
Nhants 72 F4
Lower Bourne Surrey 30 D3
Lower Brailes Warwks ...72 C6
Lower Breakish
Highld 199 L2
Lower Broadheath
Worcs 70 E3
Lower Broxwood
Herefs 69 G4
Lower Bullingham
Herefs 69 K6
Lower Burgate Hants ...28 D7
Lower Caldecote
C Beds 75 H5
Lower Chapel Powys 68 B7
Lower Chicksgrove
Wilts 27 L5
Lower Chute Wilts 28 F2
Lower Clapton Gt Lon ...45 G3
Lower Clent Worcs 85 G7
Lower Cumberworth
Kirk 123 J8
Lower Dean Bed 74 F2
Lower Diabaig Highld ...210 C3
Lower Dicker E Susx 20 B4
Lower Down Shrops 83 G6
Lower Dunsforth
N York 133 G6
Lower Egleton Herefs 70 B5
Lower End M Keyn 74 D6
Lower Eythorne Kent 35 H5
Lower Failand N Som 38 D5
Lower Farringdon
Hants 30 B4
Lower Feltham
Gt Lon 43 H6
Lower Froyle Hants 30 C3
Lower Gabwell Devon 7 L2
Lower Gledfield
Highld 222 D4
Lower Godney
Somset 26 C3
Lower Gravenhurst
C Beds 75 G7
Lower Green Kent 32 F5
Lower Green Kent 33 G5
Lower Halliford
Surrey 43 H6
Lower Halstow Kent 46 E6
Lower Hamworthy
Poole 15 J4
Lower Hardres Kent 34 F4
Lower Hartwell Bucks 58 C5
Lower Hergest Herefs 68 F4
Lower Heyford Oxon 57 J3
Lower Houses Kirk 123 H7
Lower Killeyan Ag & B ..160 A2
Lower Langford
N Som 38 C7
Lower Largo Fife 187 G6
Lower Leigh Staffs 100 A5
Lower Loxhore
Devon 23 K4
Lower Lydbrook
Gloucs 54 E5
Lower Lye Herefs 69 H2

Lower Machen Newpt 37 K3
Lower Merridge
Somset 25 J4
Lower Middleton
Cheney Nhants 73 G6
Lower Moor Worcs 71 H5
Lower Morton S Glos 38 F3
Lower Nazeing Essex 60 C6
Lower Penarth
V Glam 37 J6
Lower Penn Staffs 84 F4
Lower Peover Ches E 113 H6
Lower Quinton
Warwks 71 L5
Lower Raydon Suffk 78 C6
Lower Roadwater
Somset 25 G4
Lower Seagry Wilts 39 L4
Lower Shelton C Beds 74 E6
Lower Shiplake Oxon 42 C4
Lower Shuckburgh
Warwks 72 F3
Lower Slaughter
Gloucs 56 D4
Lower Standen Kent 35 H6
Lower Stanton St
Quintin Wilts 39 L4
Lower Stoke Medway 46 D5
Lower Stone Gloucs 38 F2
Lower Stow Bedon
Norfk 91 L5
Lower Street Norfk 106 F5
Lower Street Suffk 78 D4
Lower Swanwick
Hants 16 F1
Lower Swell Gloucs 56 D3
Lower Tean Staffs 100 A5
Lower Town Devon 7 G2
Lower Town Pembks 64 D6
Lower Upcott Devon 11 K8
Lower Upham Hants 29 K7
Lower Weare Somset 26 B2
Lower Welson Herefs 68 F4
Lower Westmancote
Worcs 71 G6
Lower Whatley
Somset 27 H3
Lower Whitley
Ches W 112 E5
Lower Wield Hants 29 M4
Lower Willington
E Susx 20 C5
Lower Withington
Ches E 113 J7
Lower Woodford
Wilts 28 C4
Lower Wraxhall
Dorset 14 B3
Lowesby Leics 87 K3
Lowestoft Suffk 93 L5
Loweswater Cumb 137 G3
Low Fell Gatesd 151 G3
Lowfield Heath
W Susx 31 L4
Low Gartachorrans
Stirlg 174 E2
Low Grantley N York 132 C5
Low Ham Somset 26 B5
Low Harrogate
N York 132 D7
Low Hesket Cumb 148 E5
Low Hutton N York 134 B6
Lowick Nhants 88 E7
Lowick Nthumb 168 F2
Lowick Green Cumb 129 G3
Low Lorton Cumb 137 G3
Low Marnham Notts 116 D7
Low Mill N York 142 E7
Low Moorsley Sundld ...151 H5
Low Moresby Cumb 136 D3
Low Newton Cumb 129 J3
Low Row Cumb 149 G3
Low Row N York 138 B7
Low Salchrie D & G 144 B2
Low Santon N Linc 125 L7
Lowsonford Warwks 71 L2

Low Tharston Norfk 92 E4
Lowther Cumb 138 D3
Lowthorpe E R Yk 135 G7
Lowton Somset 25 J7
Low Torry Fife 176 D2
Low Worsall N York 141 J5
Low Wray Cumb 137 K6
Loxbeare Devon 11 L2
Loxhill Surrey 31 G4
Loxhore Devon 23 K4
Loxley Warwks 72 C4
Loxton N Som 26 A1
Loxwood W Susx 31 H5
Loyal Lodge Highld 229 J6
Lubenham Leics 87 K6
Luccombe Somset 24 E3
Luccombe Village
IoW 17 H6
Lucker Nthumb 169 H4
Luckett Cnwll 6 B2
Lucking Street Essex 77 J7
Luckington Wilts 39 J4
Lucklawhill Fife 187 G3
Luckwell Bridge
Somset 24 E4
Lucton Herefs 69 J2
Ludag W Isls 233 b9
Ludborough Lincs 118 D3
Ludbrook Devon 6 F5
Ludchurch Pembks 49 K5
Luddenden Calder 122 F5
Luddenden Foot
Calder 122 F5
Luddesdown Kent 46 A6
Luddington N Linc 125 J7
Luddington Warwks 71 L4
Luddington in the
Brook Nhants 89 G6
Ludford Lincs 117 K4
Ludford Shrops 83 K8
Ludgershall Bucks 58 A4
Ludgershall Wilts 28 E2
Ludgvan Cnwll 2 E5
Ludham Norfk 107 H8
Ludlow Shrops 83 K7
Ludney Somset 26 B8
Ludwell Wilts 27 K6
Ludworth Dur 151 J6
Luffness E Loth 178 B3
Lugar E Ayrs 164 C5
Luggate Burn E Loth ...178 D4
Luggiebank N Lans 175 K4
Lugton E Ayrs 174 D7
Lugwardine Herefs 69 K6
Luib Highld 209 J8
Luing Ag & B 181 L5
Lulham Herefs 69 H6
Lullington Derbys 86 B2
Lullington Somset 27 H2
Lulsgate Bottom
N Som 38 D7
Lulsley Worcs 70 D4
Lumb Calder 122 F6
Lumby N York 124 D4
Lumloch E Duns 175 H4
Lumphanan Abers 206 B4
Lumphinnans Fife 186 C8
Lumsden Abers 205 K2
Lunan Angus 197 H6
Lunanhead Angus 196 D6
Luncarty P & K 186 A2
Lund E R Yk 126 B2
Lund N York 125 G4
Lundie Angus 186 E1
Lundin Links Fife 187 G6
Lundin Mill Fife 187 G6
Lundy Devon 22 B3
Lunga Ag & B 181 L5
Lunna Shet 235 d4
Lunsford Kent 33 J2
Lunsford's Cross
E Susx 20 E4
Lunt Sefton 111 K2
Luppitt Devon 12 F2
Lupset Wakefd 123 L6
Lupton Cumb 129 L4

Lurgashall W Susx 30 F6
Lurley Devon 11 L2
Luscombe Devon 7 J4
Luss Ag & B 183 L8
Lussagiven Ag & B 171 L2
Lusta Highld 208 D3
Lustleigh Devon 11 H8
Luston Herefs 69 J2
Luthermuir Abers 197 G3
Luthrie Fife 186 E4
Luton Devon 7 K1
Luton Devon 12 D2
Luton Luton 59 H4
Luton Medway 46 C6
Luton Airport Luton 59 J4
Lutterworth Leics 87 G6
Lutton Devon 6 E4
Lutton Devon 7 G4
Lutton Lincs 104 C7
Lutton Nhants 89 G6
Luxborough Somset 24 F4
Luxulyan Cnwll 5 G4
Luxulyan Valley Cnwll 5 G4
Lybster Highld 231 J7
Lydbury North
    Shrops 83 G6
Lydd Kent 21 K2
Lydd Airport Kent 21 L2
Lydden Kent 35 H5
Lydden Kent 35 K2
Lyddington Rutlnd 88 C4
Lydeard St Lawrence
    Somset 25 H5
Lydford Devon 10 D7
Lydford on Fosse
    Somset 26 E5
Lydgate Calder 122 D5
Lydham Shrops 83 G5
Lydiard Millicent Wilts 40 C3
Lydiard Tregoze
    Swindn 40 C4
Lydiate Sefton 111 K2
Lydiate Ash Worcs 85 H7
Lydlinch Dorset 27 I10
Lydney Gloucs 54 F7
Lydstep Pembks 49 J7
Lye Dudley 85 G6
Lye Green E Susx 32 F6
Lye Green Warwks 71 L2
Lye's Green Wilts 27 J3
Lyford Oxon 41 H2
Lymbridge Green
    Kent 34 F6
Lyme Regis Dorset 13 J4
Lyminge Kent 34 F6
Lymington Hants 16 C4
Lyminster W Susx 18 D5
Lymm Warrtn 113 G4
Lymm Services
    Warrtn 112 F4
Lympne Kent 34 F7
Lympsham Somset 25 M1
Lympstone Devon 12 C5
Lynchat Highld 203 J5
Lynch Green Norfk 92 D3
Lyndhurst Hants 16 C2
Lyndon Rutlnd 88 C3
Lyne Border 166 B2
Lyne Surrey 43 G7
Lyneal Shrops 98 C6
Lyneham Oxon 56 F4
Lyneham Wilts 40 A5
Lynemouth Nthumb 159 H4
Lyne of Skene Abers 206 E4
Lyness Ork 234 b7
Lyng Norfk 106 C8
Lyng Somset 25 M5
Lynmouth Devon 23 L2
Lynsted Kent 34 C3
Lynton Devon 23 L2
Lyon's Gate Dorset 14 C2
Lyonshall Herefs 69 G4
Lytchett Matravers
    Dorset 15 H4
Lytchett Minster
    Dorset 15 H4

Lyth Highld 231 K3
Lytham Lancs 120 E5
Lytham St Anne's
    Lancs 120 D5
Lythe N York 143 H5
Lythmore Highld 230 F3

M

Mabe Burnthouse
    Cnwll 3 K4
Mablethorpe Lincs 119 G4
Macclesfield Ches E 113 K6
Macclesfield
    Crematorium
    Ches E 113 K6
Macduff Abers 216 D2
Macharioch Ag & B 161 J7
Machen Caerph 37 K3
Machrie N Ayrs 162 A3
Machrihanish Ag & B 161 G5
Machrins Ag & B 180 E8
Machynlleth Powys 81 G4
Machynys Carmth 51 G5
Mackworth Derbys 100 F5
Macmerry E Loth 177 L4
Madderty P & K 185 K3
Maddiston Falk 176 C3
Madeley Staffs 99 H4
Madeley Wrekin 84 C3
Madingley Cambs 76 B3
Madley Herefs 69 H6
Madresfield Worcs 70 E5
Madron Cnwll 2 E5
Maenclochog Pembks 49 J3
Maendy V Glam 36 F5
Maentwrog Gwynd 95 L4
Maen-y-groes Cerdgn 65 L3
Maer Staffs 99 H5
Maerdy Rhondd 36 F2
Maesbrook Shrops 97 L7
Maesbury Shrops 97 L7
Maesbury Marsh
    Shrops 97 L7
Maesllyn Cerdgn 65 K5
Maesteg Brdgnd 36 D3
Maesybont Carmth 51 H3
Maesycwmmer
    Caerph 37 J2
Maggieknockater
    Moray 215 H5
Magham Down
    E Susx 20 C4
Maghull Sefton 111 K2
Magna Park Leics 87 G6
Magor Mons 38 B3
Magor Services Mons 38 B3
Maidenbower W Susx 32 B6
Maiden Bradley Wilts 27 J4
Maidencombe Torbay 7 L3
Maidenhayne Devon 13 H4
Maiden Head N Som 38 E6
Maidenhead W & M 42 E4
Maiden Newton
    Dorset 14 B3
Maidens S Ayrs 163 G7
Maiden's Green
    Br For 42 E5
Maiden Wells Pembks 49 G7
Maidford Nhants 73 H4
Maids Moreton Bucks 73 K7
Maidstone Kent 33 K3
Maidstone Services
    Kent 33 L3
Maidwell Nhants 87 L7
Mail Shet 235 d6
Maindee Newpt 37 L3
Mainland Ork 234 c6
Mainland Shet 235 c5
Mainsforth Dur 141 H2
Mains of Balhall
    Angus 196 E4
Mains of Balnakettle
    Abers 197 G2

Mains of Dalvey
    Highld 214 D7
Mains of Haulkerton
    Abers 197 H2
Mains of Lesmoir
    Abers 215 K8
Mains of Melgunds
    Angus 196 E5
Mainsriddle D & G 147 G4
Mainstone Shrops 82 F6
Maisemore Gloucs 55 J4
Malborough Devon 7 G7
Maldon Essex 61 K6
Malham N York 131 G6
Maligar Highld 209 G2
Mallaig Highld 199 L6
Mallaigvaig Highld 199 L5
Malleny Mills C Edin 177 G5
Malltraeth IoA 108 E7
Mallwyd Gwynd 81 J2
Malmesbury Wilts 39 L3
Malmsmead Devon 24 C2
Malpas Ches W 98 C3
Malpas Cnwll 4 D7
Malpas Newpt 37 L3
Maltby Rothm 115 K3
Maltby S on T 141 L5
Maltby le Marsh Lincs 118 F5
Maltman's Hill Kent 34 B6
Malton N York 134 C5
Malvern Hills 70 D5
Malvern Link Worcs 70 E5
Malvern Wells Worcs 70 D6
Mamble Worcs 70 C1
Mamhilad Mons 53 L7
Manaccan Cnwll 3 K6
Manafon Powys 82 C3
Manais W Isls 232 d5
Manaton Devon 11 H8
Manby Lincs 118 E4
Mancetter Warwks 86 D4
Manchester Manch 113 J3
Manchester Airport
    Manch 113 J5
Manchester
    Cathedral Salfd 113 J2
Mancot Flints 111 K7
Mandally Highld 201 L5
Manea Cambs 90 C5
Maney Birm 85 K4
Manfield N York 140 F4
Mangotsfield S Glos 38 F5
Manish W Isls 232 d5
Manley Ches W 112 D7
Manmoel Caerph 53 J7
Mannel Ag & B 188 C7
Manningford
    Bohune Wilts 40 C8
Manningford Bruce
    Wilts 40 C8
Manningham C Brad 123 H4
Manning's Heath
    W Susx 31 K5
Mannington Dorset 15 K2
Manningtree Essex 62 D2
Mannofield C Aber 207 H4
Manorbier Pembks 49 H7
Manorbier Newton
    Pembks 49 H7
Manorhill Border 167 K3
Manorowen Pembks 64 C7
Manor Park Gt Lon 45 H3
Manor Park
    Crematorium
    Gt Lon 45 H3
Mansell Gamage
    Herefs 69 H5
Mansell Lacy Herefs 69 H5
Mansfield E Ayrs 164 C6
Mansfield Notts 101 K1
Mansfield & District
    Crematorium
    Notts 101 K2
Mansfield
    Woodhouse Notts 115 K8
Manston Dorset 27 J7

Manston Kent 35 J2
Manston Leeds 124 B4
Manswood Dorset 15 J2
Manthorpe Lincs 88 F1
Manton N Linc 116 F2
Manton Rutlnd 88 C3
Manton Wilts 40 D6
Manuden Essex 60 D3
Maperton Somset 26 F6
Maplebeck Notts 102 B1
Mapledurham Oxon 42 A5
Mapledurwell Hants 30 B2
Maplehurst W Susx 31 K6
Maplescombe Kent 45 K7
Mapleton Derbys 100 D3
Mapperley Derbys 101 H4
Mapperley Park
    C Nott 101 L4
Mapperton Dorset 13 L3
Mappleborough
    Green Warwks 71 J2
Mappleton E R Yk 126 F2
Mapplewell Barns 123 L7
Mappowder Dorset 14 E2
Marazanvose Cnwll 4 C5
Marazion Cnwll 2 F5
Marbury Ches E 98 E4
March Cambs 90 B4
March S Lans 165 J6
Marcham Oxon 41 J2
Marchamley Shrops 98 E6
Marchington Staffs 100 C6
Marchros Gwynd 94 F7
Marchwiel Wrexhm 98 A3
Marchwood Hants 16 D1
Marcross V Glam 36 E6
Marden Herefs 69 K5
Marden Kent 33 J4
Marden Wilts 40 C8
Marden Thorn Kent 33 K5
Mardy Mons 53 L5
Mareham le Fen Lincs 103 L1
Mareham on the Hill
    Lincs 118 C7
Marehill W Susx 18 E3
Maresfield E Susx 19 M2
Marfleet C KuH 126 E5
Marford Wrexhm 98 A2
Margam Neath 36 B3
Margam
    Crematorium
    Neath 36 C4
Margaret Marsh
    Dorset 27 J7
Margaretting Essex 61 G7
Margaretting Tye
    Essex 61 G7
Margate Kent 35 K1
Margnaheglish N Ayrs 162 D3
Margrie D & G 145 M5
Margrove Park R & Cl 142 E4
Marham Norfk 91 G2
Marhamchurch Cnwll 9 G4
Marholm C Pete 89 G3
Mariansleigh Devon 24 B6
Marine Town Kent 46 F5
Marionburgh Abers 206 D4
Marishader Highld 209 H2
Maristow Devon 6 C3
Marjoriebanks D & G 155 J5
Mark Somset 26 B2
Markbeech Kent 32 E5
Markby Lincs 119 G5
Mark Cross E Susx 33 G6
Markeaton
    Crematorium
    C Derb 100 F5
Market Bosworth
    Leics 86 E3
Market Deeping Lincs 89 G2
Market Drayton
    Shrops 98 F5
Market Harborough
    Leics 87 K6
Market Lavington
    Wilts 28 A1

Market Overton
Rutlnd 88 C1
Market Rasen Lincs...117 J4
Market Stainton Lincs..118 C5
Market Warsop Notts..115 K7
Market Weighton
E R Yk 125 K3
Market Weston Suffk 92 B7
Markfield Leics 86 F2
Markham Caerph 53 J7
Markham Moor Notts ..116 B6
Markinch Fife 186 E6
Markington N York 132 D6
Markle E Loth 178 C3
Marksbury BaNES.........38 F7
Marks Tey Essex 61 L4
Markyate Herts 59 H5
Marlborough Wilts........40 D6
Marlcliff Warwks 71 K4
Marldon Devon................7 K3
Marlesford Suffk 79 G3
Marlingford Norfk 92 D2
Marloes Pembks 48 D5
Marlow Bucks 42 D3
Marlow Bottom
Bucks 42 D3
Marlpit Hill Kent 32 D4
Marnhull Dorset 27 H7
Marple Stockp.............113 L4
Marr Donc 115 K1
Marrick N York 140 D7
Marsden Kirk 122 F7
Marsden S Tyne 151 J3
Marshalswick Herts 59 K6
Marsham Norfk 106 E7
Marsh Baldon Oxon 57 K7
Marshborough Kent.......35 J3
Marshbrook Shrops........83 J5
Marshchapel Lincs 118 E2
Marsh Farm Luton 59 H3
Marshfield Newpt 37 K4
Marshfield S Glos...........39 H5
Marshgate Cnwll 8 F6
Marsh Gibbon Bucks 57 M4
Marsh Green Devon 12 D4
Marsh Green Kent 32 D4
Marshland St James
Norfk 90 D2
Marsh Lane Derbys 115 H5
Marsh Street Somset......24 F3
Marshwood Dorset.........13 J3
Marske N York.............140 D6
Marske-by-the-Sea
R & Cl.........................142 D3
Marston Herefs 69 G3
Marston Lincs 102 E4
Marston Oxon 57 K6
Marston Staffs 99 L6
Marston Wilts 27 L1
Marston Green Solhll......85 L6
Marston Magna
Somset 26 E6
Marston Meysey Wilts....40 C2
**Marston
Montgomery**
Derbys 100 C5
Marston Moretaine
C Beds 74 E6
Marston on Dove
Derbys 100 E6
Marston St Lawrence
Nhants 73 G6
Marston Trussell
Nhants 87 K6
Marstow Herefs 54 D4
Marsworth Bucks 58 F7
Marten Wilts 40 F7
Martham Norfk 107 J8
Martin Hants 28 B7
Martin Kent 35 J6
Martin Lincs 103 J1
Martinhoe Devon 23 L2
Martin Hussingtree
Worcs 70 F3
Martinstown Dorset.......14 C5
Martlesham Suffk 78 F5

Martlesham Heath
Suffk 78 F5
Martletwy Pembks 49 H5
Martley Worcs 70 D3
Martock Somset 26 C7
Marton Ches E 113 J7
Marton E R Yk 126 F3
Marton Lincs 116 D5
Marton Middsb 142 B4
Marton N York 132 F6
Marton N York 134 B3
Marton Shrops..............82 F3
Marton Warwks.............72 E2
Marton-le-Moor
N York 132 E5
Martyr Worthy Hants 29 K5
Marwell Wildlife
Hants 29 J6
Marwick Ork 234 b5
Marwood Devon 23 H4
Marybank Highld..........212 D4
Maryburgh Highld.........212 E3
Maryculter Abers 207 G5
Marygold Border 179 G6
Maryhill C Glas 175 G4
Maryhill
Crematorium
C Glas 175 G4
Marykirk Abers 197 H3
Marylebone Gt Lon 44 F4
Marylebone Wigan.......121 H8
Marypark Moray 214 F6
Maryport Cumb 147 H7
Maryport D & G 144 D7
Marystow Devon 10 C7
Mary Tavy Devon 6 D1
Maryton Angus 197 H5
Marywell Abers 206 B6
Marywell Abers 207 H5
Marywell Angus 197 G7
Masham N York 132 C4
Masongill N York 130 C4
Masonhill
Crematorium
S Ayrs 163 J5
Mastin Moor Derbys 115 J6
Matching Green
Essex 60 E5
Matching Tye Essex 60 E5
Matfen Nthumb 158 C7
Matfield Kent 33 H5
Mathern Mons 38 D3
Mathon Herefs..............70 D5
Mathry Pembks 48 E2
Matlask Norfk 106 D5
Matlock Derbys............100 F1
Matlock Bath Derbys 100 F2
Matson Gloucs 55 J5
Mattersey Notts...........116 B4
Mattingley Hants 42 B8
Mattishall Norfk 92 C2
Mattishall Burgh
Norfk 92 C2
Mauchline E Ayrs.........163 L4
Maud Abers 217 H5
Maufant Jersey 236 d6
Maugersbury Gloucs 56 D3
Maughold IoM 237 e3
Mauld Highld...............212 C6
Maulden C Beds 74 F6
Maulds Meaburn
Cumb 138 F4
Maunby N York 132 E3
Maundown Somset 25 G5
Mautby Norfk 93 K2
Mavesyn Ridware
Staffs 85 J1
Mavis Enderby Lincs....118 E7
Mawbray Cumb 147 J5
Mawdesley Lancs 121 G7
Mawdlam Brdgnd 36 C4
Mawgan Cnwll 3 J6
Mawgan Porth Cnwll 4 D3
Mawla Cnwll 3 J3
Mawnan Cnwll 3 K5
Mawnan Smith Cnwll 3 K5

Mawsley Nhants............88 B7
Maxey C Pete 89 G2
Maxstoke Warwks 86 B6
Maxton Border 167 J4
Maxton Kent 35 J6
Maxwell Town D & G 155 G6
Maxworthy Cnwll 9 H6
May Bank Staffs.............99 J3
Maybole S Ayrs 163 H7
Maybury Surrey 43 G8
Mayfield E Susx 33 G7
Mayfield Mdloth 177 K5
Mayfield Staffs.............100 D4
Mayford Surrey 31 G1
May Hill Gloucs 55 G4
Mayland Essex 61 L7
Maylandsea Essex 61 L7
Maynard's Green
E Susx 20 C3
Maypole Green Norfk 93 J4
Maypole Green Suffk.....77 K3
Meadgate BaNES...........39 G8
Meadle Bucks 58 D6
Meadowfield Dur..........151 G6
Meadwell Devon 9 K8
Meanwood Leeds..........123 K3
Meare Somset 26 C3
Meare Green Somset 25 L6
Meare Green Somset 25 M6
Mearns E Rens 174 F7
Mears Ashby Nhants......74 B2
Measham Leics 86 D2
Meathop Cumb 129 J4
Meavy Devon 6 D3
Medbourne Leics 88 B5
Meddon Devon 9 H2
Meden Vale Notts 115 L7
Medmenham Bucks........42 D4
Medomsley Dur............150 E4
Medstead Hants 30 A4
Medway
Crematorium
Kent 46 C7
Meerbrook Staffs 99 M1
Meesden Herts 60 C2
Meeth Devon 10 E3
Meeting House Hill
Norfk 107 G6
Meidrim Carmth 50 C2
Meifod Powys 82 D2
Meigle P & K................195 L7
Meikle Carco D & G 164 F6
Meikle Earnock S Lans..175 J7
Meikle Kilmory
Ag & B 173 H6
Meikle Obney P & K.....195 G8
Meikleour P & K...........195 J7
Meikle Wartle Abers 216 D7
Meinciau Carmth...........50 F4
Meir C Stke 99 L4
Melbourn Cambs...........75 L5
Melbourne Derbys 101 G7
Melbourne E R Yk........125 H2
Melbury Abbas
Dorset 27 K7
Melbury Bubb Dorset....14 B2
Melbury Osmond
Dorset 14 B2
Melchbourne Bed 74 E2
Melcombe Bingham
Dorset 14 E3
Meldon Devon 10 E6
Meldon Nthumb 158 E5
Meldreth Cambs............75 L5
Meldrum Stirlg.............184 F7
Melfort Ag & B.............182 B5
Meliden Denbgs...........110 E5
Melin-y-wig Denbgs 97 G3
Melkinthorpe Cumb......138 D3
Melkridge Nthumb 149 J3
Melksham Wilts 39 K7
Melling Lancs 130 B5
Melling Sefton 111 L2
Mellis Suffk 92 C8

Mellon Charles Highld...219 K3
Mellon Udrigle Highld...219 K3
Mellor Lancs 121 J4
Mellor Stockp 113 M4
Mellor Brook Lancs 121 J4
Mells Somset 27 G2
Melmerby Cumb 149 G7
Melmerby N York 131 K3
Melmerby N York 132 E4
Melness Highld 229 J3
Melplash Dorset 13 L3
Melrose Border 167 H3
Melsetter Ork...............234 b7
Melsonby N York 140 F5
Meltham Kirk 123 G7
Melton E R Yk..............126 B5
Melton Suffk 79 G4
Melton Constable
Norfk 106 C6
Melton Mowbray
Leics 102 C8
Melton Ross N Linc 126 D7
Melvaig Highld.............219 H4
Melverley Shrops 83 G1
Melvich Highld.............230 C3
Membury Devon 13 H2
Memsie Abers 217 H2
Memus Angus 196 C5
Menai Bridge IoA 109 H6
Mendham Suffk.............92 F6
Mendip Crematorium
Somset 26 E3
Mendip Hills 26 D2
Mendlesham Suffk.........78 D2
Mendlesham Green
Suffk 78 D2
Menheniot Cnwll 5 L4
Mennock D & G.............164 F7
Menston C Brad 123 H2
Menstrie Clacks...........185 H7
Mentmore Bucks 58 E4
Meoble Highld..............200 C7
Meole Brace Shrops......83 J2
Meonstoke Hants..........29 L7
Meopham Kent 45 M6
Mepal Cambs 90 B7
Meppershall C Beds.......75 G7
Mere Ches E 113 G5
Mere Wilts 27 J5
Mere Brow Lancs.........120 F6
Mereclough Lancs........122 C4
Mereworth Kent 33 H3
Meriden Solhll...............86 B6
Merkadale Highld 208 F7
Merley Poole 15 J3
Merrion Pembks 48 F7
Merriott Somset 26 C8
Merrow Surrey 31 G2
Merry Hill Herts 43 J2
Merryhill Wolves 84 F4
Merrymeet Cnwll 5 L3
Mersea Island Essex 62 B5
Mersham Kent 34 E6
Merstham Surrey 32 B3
Merston W Susx 18 B5
Merstone IoW 17 G5
Merthyr Cynog
Powys 67 L6
Merthyr Mawr
Brdgnd 36 D5
Merthyr Tydfil Myr Td....53 G6
Merthyr Vale Myr Td......53 G7
Merton Devon 10 D3
Merton Gt Lon 44 E6
Merton Norfk 91 K4
Merton Oxon 57 L4
Meshaw Devon 24 B7
Messing Essex...............61 L4
Messingham N Linc......116 E2
Metfield Suffk 93 G7
Metherell Cnwll 6 B3
Metheringham Lincs 103 H1
Methil Fife 186 F7
Methilhill Fife...............186 F7

Methlick Abers.............217 G6
Methven P & K.............185 L3
Methwold Norfk............91 G4
Methwold Hythe
  Norfk.....................91 G4
Mettingham Suffk.........93 H5
Metton Norfk..............106 E5
Mevagissey Cnwll..........4 F6
Mexborough Donc 115 J2
Mey Highld.................231 K2
Meyllteyrn Gwynd........94 D6
Meysey Hampton
  Gloucs....................56 C7
Miabhig W Isls.............232 d2
Miavaig W Isls..............232 d2
Michaelchurch Herefs....54 D3
Michaelchurch
  Escley Herefs 69 G7
Michaelstone-y-
  Fedw Newpt 37 K4
Michaelston-le-Pit
  V Glam....................37 J5
Michaelstow Cnwll.........5 G1
Michaelwood
  Services Gloucs.........39 G2
Micheldever Hants.........29 K4
Micheldever Station
  Hants......................29 K3
Michelmersh Hants.......29 G6
Mickfield Suffk............78 D3
Micklebring Donc........115 K3
Mickleby N York...........143 G5
Micklefield Leeds 124 C4
Mickleham Surrey..........31 K2
Mickleover C Derb.......100 F5
Mickleton Dur.............140 B3
Mickleton Gloucs..........71 L5
Mickletown Leeds.......124 B5
Mickle Trafford
  Ches W....................112 C7
Mickley N York............132 C4
Mickley Square
  Nthumb..................150 D3
Mid Ardlaw Abers........217 H2
Midbea Ork................234 c4
Mid Beltie Abers 206 C5
Mid Calder W Loth.......176 E5
Mid Clyth Highld..........231 K4
Mid Culbeuchly Abers ..216 C3
Middle Aston Oxon 57 J3
Middle Barton Oxon 57 H3
Middlebie D & G...........155 L6
Middlebridge P & K......194 D3
Middle Chinnock
  Somset....................26 C8
Middle Claydon Bucks...58 B3
Middleham N York.......131 L3
Middle Handley
  Derbys...................115 H6
Middlehill Wilts............39 J6
Middlehope Shrops.......83 K5
Middle Kames Ag & B...172 F1
Middle Littleton
  Worcs......................71 J5
Middlemarsh Dorset.....14 C2
Middle Mayfield
  Staffs.....................100 C4
Middle Rasen Lincs 117 H4
Middle Rocombe
  Devon.......................7 K2
Middlesbrough
  Middsb...................141 L4
Middleshaw Cumb.......129 L2
Middlesmoor N York....131 K5
Middle Stoke Medway...46 D5
Middlestone Dur..........141 G2
Middlestown Wakefd...123 K6
Middlethird Border......167 K2
Middleton Ag & B........188 B7
Middleton Derbys.......100 F2
Middleton Derbys.......114 D8
Middleton Essex..........77 K6
Middleton Hants..........29 H3
Middleton Herefs.........69 K1
Middleton Leeds 123 L5
Middleton N York.......123 G2

Middleton N York 134 B3
Middleton Nhants.........88 B5
Middleton Norfk...........90 F1
Middleton Nthumb.......158 D5
Middleton P & K..........186 B6
Middleton Rochdl.......113 K1
Middleton Shrops.........83 K7
Middleton Suffk...........79 J2
Middleton Swans..........50 E7
Middleton Warwks........85 L4
Middleton Cheney
  Nhants.....................73 G6
Middleton
  Crematorium
  Rochdl....................113 K1
Middleton-in-
  Teesdale Dur............139 L3
Middleton Moor Suffk...79 J2
Middleton One Row
  Darltn.....................141 J5
Middleton-on-Sea
  W Susx....................18 C5
Middleton on the Hill
  Herefs.....................69 K2
Middleton on the
  Wolds E R Yk 125 L2
Middleton Park
  C Aber....................207 H3
Middleton
  Quernhow N York....132 E4
Middleton St George
  Darltn.....................141 J5
Middleton Scriven
  Shrops.....................84 C6
Middleton Stoney
  Oxon.......................57 K4
Middleton Tyas
  N York....................141 G6
Middle Town IoS...........2 a2
Middletown Powys........82 F2
Middle Tysoe Warwks...72 D5
Middle Wallop Hants.....28 F4
Middlewich Ches E.......113 G7
Middle Winterslow
  Wilts.......................28 E5
Middlewood Cnwll.........5 L2
Middle Woodford
  Wilts.......................28 C4
Middlewood Green
  Suffk.......................78 D3
Middleyard E Ayrs......163 M3
Middlezoy Somset........26 B5
Midford BaNES.............39 H7
Midgham W Berk..........41 K6
Midgley Calder...........122 F5
Midgley Wakefd.........123 K7
Midhopestones Sheff...114 E2
Midhurst W Susx..........30 E6
Mid Lavant W Susx.......18 B4
Midlem Border............167 H4
Mid Mains Highld........212 C6
Midpark Ag & B...........173 H6
Midsomer Norton
  BaNES.....................26 F1
Midtown Highld...........229 J4
Mid Warwickshire
  Crematorium
  Warwks....................72 C3
Mid Yell Shet.............235 d3
Migvie Abers..............205 K4
Milborne Port Somset...26 F7
Milborne St Andrew
  Dorset.....................14 F3
Milborne Wick
  Somset....................26 F7
Milbourne Nthumb.....158 E6
Milbourne Wilts...........39 L3
Milburn Cumb.............138 F2
Milbury Heath S Glos....38 F3
Milby N York..............132 F6
Milcombe Oxon............72 E7
Milden Suffk................77 L5
Mildenhall Suffk...........91 G8
Mildenhall Wilts...........40 E6
Mileham Norfk............105 L8
Mile Oak Br & H...........19 H4

Milesmark Fife............176 E2
Miles Platting Manch...113 J2
Mile Town Kent...........46 F5
Milfield Nthumb.........168 D3
Milford Derbys............101 G4
Milford Devon..............22 C6
Milford Staffs..............99 L7
Milford Surrey.............30 F3
Milford Haven
  Pembks....................48 F6
Milford on Sea Hants...16 C4
Milkwall Gloucs............54 E6
Millais Jersey.............236 a5
Milland W Susx............30 D5
Mill Bank Calder........122 F6
Millbreck Abers..........217 J3
Millbridge Surrey.........30 D3
Millbrook C Beds..........74 E6
Millbrook C Sotn..........29 G8
Millbrook Cnwll.............6 B5
Millbrook Jersey.........236 c7
Millbuie Abers............206 F4
Millbuie Highld...........212 E4
Millcorner E Susx.........21 G2
Millcraig Highld..........222 E7
Milldale Staffs............100 C2
Mill End Bucks............42 C4
Mill End Herts.............60 B2
Millerhill Mdloth.........177 J4
Miller's Dale Derbys...114 C6
Millerston C Glas........175 H5
Mill Green Cambs.........76 F5
Mill Green Essex..........61 G7
Mill Green Lincs.........103 L7
Mill Green Suffk...........77 L6
Mill Green Suffk...........78 B3
Mill Green Suffk...........78 D3
Millhalf Herefs.............68 F5
Millheugh S Lans.........175 K7
Mill Hill Gt Lon............44 E2
Millhouse Ag & B........173 G4
Millhousebridge
  D & G......................155 K5
Millhouse Green
  Barns.....................114 E2
Millhouses Sheff.........115 G5
Milliken Park Rens......174 D6
Millington E R Yk.........125 J1
Millmeece Staffs..........99 J5
Mill of Drummond
  P & K......................185 H4
Mill of Haldane
  W Duns....................174 D2
Millom Cumb.............128 E4
Millport N Ayrs...........173 K7
Mill Street Suffk...........78 C1
Millthrop Cumb..........130 C2
Milltimber C Aber.......207 G5
Milltown Abers..........205 G4
Milltown Abers..........205 K3
Milltown D & G...........156 C6
Milltown Devon...........23 J4
Milltown of
  Campfield Abers 206 C5
Milltown of Edinvillie
  Moray.....................215 G6
Milltown of Learney
  Abers......................206 C5
Milnathort P & K.........186 B6
Milngavie E Duns........175 G4
Milnrow Rochdl..........122 D7
Milnthorpe Cumb........129 K3
Milovaig Highld..........208 B4
Milson Shrops.............84 B8
Milstead Kent.............34 B3
Milston Wilts..............28 D3
Milthorpe Nhants.........73 H5
Milton Cambs..............76 C2
Milton Cumb..............148 F3
Milton D & G..............144 F4
Milton D & G..............154 E3
Milton Derbys............100 F7
Milton Highld.............209 L5
Milton Highld.............212 D7
Milton Highld.............212 E4

Milton Highld.............223 G6
Milton Highld.............231 L5
Milton Inver..............174 C5
Milton Kent.................46 A5
Milton Moray.............204 E2
Milton Moray.............215 L2
Milton N Som.............37 M7
Milton Notts..............116 B6
Milton Oxon...............41 J3
Milton Oxon...............72 F7
Milton P & K..............195 G4
Milton Pembks............49 H6
Milton Somset.............26 C6
Milton Stirlg..............184 B6
Milton W Duns...........174 D4
Milton Abbas Dorset....14 F3
Milton Abbot Devon......9 K8
Milton Bridge Mdloth...177 H5
Milton Bryan C Beds....58 F3
Milton Clevedon
  Somset....................26 F4
Milton Combe Devon.....6 D3
Milton Damerel
  Devon.......................9 K3
Milton Ernest Bed........74 E4
Milton Green Ches W....98 C2
Milton Hill Oxon..........41 J3
Milton Keynes M Keyn..74 C6
Milton Lilbourne Wilts..40 D7
Milton Malsor Nhants...73 K4
Milton Morenish
  P & K......................184 D1
Milton of
  Auchinhove Abers...206 B5
Milton of Balgonie
  Fife........................186 E7
Milton of Buchanan
  Stirlg.....................174 E1
Milton of Campsie
  E Duns....................175 H3
Milton of Leys Highld...213 G6
Milton of Murtle
  C Aber....................207 G5
Milton of Tullich
  Abers......................205 J6
Milton on Stour
  Dorset.....................27 J5
Milton Regis Kent.........46 E6
Milton-under-
  Wychwood Oxon......56 E4
Milverton Somset.........25 H6
Milverton Warwks........72 C2
Milwich Staffs.............99 L6
Minard Ag & B............182 D7
Minchinhampton
  Gloucs.....................55 K7
Minehead Somset........24 F3
Minera Wrexhm...........97 L3
Minety Wilts...............40 A3
Minffordd Gwynd.........95 K5
Mingarrypark Highld....190 D3
Miningsby Lincs.........118 D8
Minions Cnwll...............5 L2
Minishant S Ayrs........163 J6
Minllyn Gwynd.............81 J2
Minnigaff D & G..........145 J2
Minnonie Abers..........216 E3
Minskip N York...........132 F6
Minstead Hants...........16 C1
Minsted W Susx...........30 D7
Minster Kent...............35 J2
Minster Kent...............46 F5
Minsterley Shrops........83 G3
Minster Lovell Oxon......56 F5
Minsterworth Gloucs....55 H5
Minterne Magna
  Dorset.....................14 C2
Minting Lincs.............117 K6
Mintlaw Abers............217 J5
Mintlyn
  Crematorium
  Norfk.....................105 G8
Minto Border.............167 H5
Minton Shrops............83 H5
Mirehouse Cumb.........136 D4
Mireland Highld..........231 K4

Mirfield Kirk............123 J6
Miserden Gloucs.............55 L6
Miskin Rhondd.............37 G4
Misson Notts.............116 B3
Misterton Leics.............87 G6
Misterton Notts.............116 C3
Misterton Somset.............13 L2
Mistley Essex.............62 D2
Mitcham Gt Lon.............44 F6
Mitcheldean Gloucs.............54 H4
Mitchell Cnwll.............4 D5
Mitchellslacks D & G.............155 G3
Mitchel Troy Mons.............54 C6
Mitford Nthumb.............158 F5
Mithian Cnwll.............3 J2
Mixbury Oxon.............73 H7
Mobberley Ches E.............113 H5
Mobberley Staffs.............100 A4
Mochdre Powys.............82 B5
Mochrum D & G.............145 H5
Mockbeggar Kent.............33 J4
Mockerkin Cumb.............136 F3
Modbury Devon.............6 F5
Moddershall Staffs.............99 L5
Moelfre IoA.............109 G4
Moelfre Powys.............97 J6
Moffat D & G.............155 J2
Moggerhanger
C Beds.............75 G5
Moira Leics.............86 C1
Molash Kent.............34 D4
Mol-chlach Highld.............199 G3
Mold Flints.............111 H8
Moldgreen Kirk.............123 H7
Molehill Green Essex.............60 E3
Molescroft E R Yk.............126 C3
Molesworth Cambs.............88 F7
Molland Devon.............24 C5
Mollington Ches W.............111 L7
Mollington Oxon.............72 F5
Mollinsburn N Lans.............175 J4
Mondynes Abers.............197 J1
Monewden Suffk.............78 F3
Moneydie P & K.............185 M2
Moniaive D & G.............154 D4
Monifieth Angus.............187 H2
Monikie Angus.............196 E8
Monimail Fife.............186 E5
Monken Hadley
Gt Lon.............44 E1
Monk Fryston N York.............124 D5
Monkhide Herefs.............70 B5
Monkhill Cumb.............148 C3
Monkhopton Shrops.............84 B5
Monkland Herefs.............69 J3
Monkleigh Devon.............23 G7
Monknash V Glam.............36 E6
Monkokehampton
Devon.............10 E4
Monkseaton N Tyne.............159 H7
Monks Eleigh Suffk.............77 L5
Monk's Gate W Susx.............31 K6
Monks Heath Ches E.............113 J6
Monk Sherborne
Hants.............29 L1
Monksilver Somset.............25 G4
Monks Kirby Warwks.............86 F6
Monk Soham Suffk.............78 E2
Monks Risborough
Bucks.............58 D6
Monksthorpe Lincs.............118 F7
Monk Street Essex.............60 F3
Monkswood Mons.............53 M7
Monkton Devon.............12 F2
Monkton Kent.............47 M6
Monkton S Ayrs.............163 J4
Monkton S Tyne.............151 H3
Monkton Combe
BaNES.............39 H7
Monkton Deverill
Wilts.............27 J4
Monkton Farleigh
Wilts.............39 J7
Monkton Heathfield
Somset.............25 K6
Monkton Wyld Dorset.............13 J3

Monkwearmouth
Sundld.............151 J4
Monkwood Hants.............30 A5
Monmore Green
Wolves.............85 G4
Monmouth Mons.............54 D5
Monnington on Wye
Herefs.............69 G5
Monreith D & G.............145 H6
Montacute Somset.............26 D7
Montford Shrops.............83 H1
Montford Bridge
Shrops.............83 H1
Montgarrie Abers.............206 B2
Montgomery Powys.............82 E4
Montrose Angus.............197 H5
Mont Saint Guern.............236 b3
Monxton Hants.............28 F3
Monyash Derbys.............114 D7
Monymusk Abers.............206 D3
Monzie P & K.............185 H3
Moodiesburn N Lans.............175 J4
Moonzie Fife.............186 E4
Moor Allerton Leeds.............123 L3
Moorby Lincs.............118 D8
Moor Crichel Dorset.............15 J2
Moordown Bmouth.............15 K4
Moore Halton.............112 E5
Moor End Calder.............122 F5
Moorends Donc.............125 G7
Moorhead C Brad.............123 H3
Moorhouse Cumb.............148 B4
Moorhouse Notts.............116 C7
Moorhouse Bank
Surrey.............32 D3
Moorlinch Somset.............26 B4
Moor Monkton
N York.............133 H7
Moorsholm R & Cl.............142 E4
Moorside Dorset.............27 H7
Moorswater Cnwll.............5 K3
Moorthorpe Wakefd.............124 C7
Moortown Leeds.............123 K3
Moortown Lincs.............117 H7
Morangie Highld.............223 G5
Morar Highld.............199 L6
Moray Crematorium
Moray.............215 J3
Morborne Cambs.............89 G5
Morchard Bishop
Devon.............11 H4
Morcombelake
Dorset.............13 K4
Morcott Rutlnd.............88 D4
Morda Shrops.............97 L6
Morden Dorset.............15 H4
Morden Gt Lon.............44 E6
Mordiford Herefs.............69 L6
Mordon Dur.............141 H2
More Shrops.............83 G5
Morebath Devon.............24 E6
Morebattle Border.............168 B4
Morecambe Lancs.............129 J6
Moredon Swindn.............40 C3
Morefield Highld.............220 E3
Morehall Kent.............35 G7
Moreleigh Devon.............7 H5
Morenish P & K.............184 D1
Morestead Hants.............29 K6
Moreton Dorset.............14 F4
Moreton Essex.............60 E6
Moreton Herefs.............69 K2
Moreton Oxon.............58 B6
Moreton Wirral.............111 J4
Moreton Corbet
Shrops.............98 E7
Moretonhampstead
Devon.............11 H7
Moreton-in-Marsh
Gloucs.............56 D2
Moreton Jeffries
Herefs.............69 L5
Moreton Morrell
Warwks.............72 C4
Moreton on Lugg
Herefs.............69 K5

Moreton Pinkney
Nhants.............73 H5
Moreton Say Shrops.............98 F5
Moreton Valence
Gloucs.............55 H6
Morfa Nefyn Gwynd.............94 E4
Morham E Loth.............178 C4
Morland Cumb.............138 E3
Morley Ches E.............113 J5
Morley Derbys.............101 H4
Morley Leeds.............123 K5
Morley Green Ches E.............113 J5
Morley St Botolph
Norfk.............92 C4
Morningside C Edin.............177 H4
Morningside N Lans.............175 L7
Morningthorpe Norfk.............92 F5
Morpeth Nthumb.............158 F5
Morphie Abers.............197 H4
Morrey Staffs.............100 C8
Morriston Swans.............51 J6
Morston Norfk.............106 B4
Mortehoe Devon.............23 G3
Morthen Rothm.............115 J4
Mortimer W Berk.............41 M7
Mortimer West End
Hants.............41 M7
Mortlake Gt Lon.............44 E5
Mortlake
Crematorium
Gt Lon.............44 D5
Morton Cumb.............148 C4
Morton Derbys.............101 H1
Morton Lincs.............103 H7
Morton Lincs.............116 D3
Morton Notts.............102 B3
Morton Shrops.............97 L7
Mortonhall
Crematorium
C Edin.............177 H5
Morton-on-Swale
N York.............132 E2
Morton on the Hill
Norfk.............92 D1
Morvah Cnwll.............2 D4
Morvich Highld.............200 E2
Morville Shrops.............84 C5
Morwenstow Cnwll.............9 G2
Mosborough Sheff.............115 H5
Moscow E Ayrs.............163 L2
Moseley Birm.............85 J6
Moseley Wolves.............85 G4
Moseley Worcs.............70 E3
Moss Ag & B.............188 B7
Moss Donc.............124 F7
Mossat Abers.............205 K2
Mossbank Shet.............235 d4
Moss Bank St Hel.............112 D3
Mossbay Cumb.............136 D2
Mossblown S Ayrs.............163 K4
Mossburnford Border.............167 K6
Mossdale D & G.............154 B7
Mossdale E Ayrs.............153 K2
Moss Edge Lancs.............120 F2
Mossend N Lans.............175 K6
Mossley Tamesd.............113 L2
Mosspaul Hotel
Border.............156 D3
Moss-side Highld.............213 K4
Mosstodloch Moray.............215 H3
Mossyard D & G.............145 L5
Mossy Lea Lancs.............121 H7
Mosterton Dorset.............13 L2
Moston Manch.............113 K2
Mostyn Flints.............111 G5
Motcombe Dorset.............27 J6
Mothecombe Devon.............6 F6
Motherby Cumb.............138 B2
Motherwell N Lans.............175 K6
Motspur Park Gt Lon.............44 E6
Mottingham Gt Lon.............45 H5
Mottisfont Hants.............28 F6
Mottistone IoW.............16 E5
Mottram in
Longdendale
Tamesd.............113 M3

Mottram St Andrew
Ches E.............113 K5
Mouilpied Guern.............236 c3
Mouldsworth Ches W.............112 D7
Moulin P & K.............194 E4
Moulsecoomb Br & H.............19 J4
Moulsford Oxon.............41 L4
Moulsoe M Keyn.............74 C6
Moultavie Highld.............222 E7
Moulton Ches W.............112 F7
Moulton Lincs.............104 A7
Moulton N York.............141 G6
Moulton Nhants.............73 L2
Moulton Suffk.............77 G2
Moulton V Glam.............37 G6
Moulton Chapel Lincs.............103 M8
Moulton St Mary
Norfk.............93 H3
Moulton Seas End
Lincs.............104 A6
Mount Cnwll.............5 J3
Mountain C Brad.............123 G4
Mountain Ash
Rhondd.............53 G7
Mountain Cross
Border.............176 F8
Mount Ambrose
Cnwll.............3 J3
Mount Bures Essex.............61 L2
Mountfield E Susx.............20 E2
Mountgerald House
Highld.............212 E3
Mount Hawke Cnwll.............3 J2
Mountjoy Cnwll.............4 D4
Mount Lothian
Mdloth.............177 H6
Mountnessing Essex.............60 F8
Mounton Mons.............38 D2
Mount Pleasant Derbys.............101 G3
Mount Pleasant Suffk.............77 G5
Mountsett
Crematorium Dur.............150 E4
Mountsorrel Leics.............87 H2
Mount Tabor Calder.............122 F5
Mousehill Surrey.............30 F3
Mousehole Cnwll.............2 E6
Mouswald D & G.............155 J7
Mow Cop Ches E.............99 J2
Mowhaugh Border.............168 B5
Mowsley Leics.............87 J5
Moy Highld.............202 C8
Moy Highld.............213 J7
Moyle Highld.............200 D2
Moylegrove Pembks.............64 F5
Muasdale Ag & B.............161 H2
Muchalls Abers.............207 G6
Much Birch Herefs.............54 D3
Much Cowarne Herefs.............70 B5
Much Dewchurch
Herefs.............54 C2
Muchelney Somset.............26 B6
Muchelney Ham
Somset.............26 C6
Much Hadham Herts.............60 C4
Much Hoole Lancs.............120 F6
Muchlarnick Cnwll.............5 K5
Much Marcle Herefs.............54 F2
Much Wenlock
Shrops.............84 B4
Muck Highld.............189 K1
Muckleburgh
Collection Norfk.............106 D4
Mucklestone Staffs.............99 G5
Muckton Lincs.............118 E5
Muddiford Devon.............23 J4
Muddles Green E Susx.............20 B3
Mudeford Dorset.............16 A4
Mudford Somset.............26 E7
Mudford Sock Somset.............26 E7
Mugdock Stirlg.............175 G3
Mugeary Highld.............209 G6
Mugginton Derbys.............100 F4
Muirden Abers.............216 D4
Muirdrum Angus.............196 F8
Muiresk Abers.............216 D5
Muirhead Angus.............186 E1

Muirhead Fife 186 E6
Muirhead N Lans 175 J4
Muirkirk E Ayrs...........164 D4
Muirmill Stirlg 175 J2
Muir of Fowlis Abers ...206 B3
Muir of Miltonduff
  Moray 214 E3
Muir of Ord Highld 212 E4
Muirshearlich Highld ...192 B1
Muirtack Abers 217 J6
Muirton P & K 185 J5
Muirton Mains Highld...212 C4
Muirton of Ardblair
  P & K.....................195 J7
Muker N York 139 K7
Mulbarton Norfk 92 E4
Mulben Moray.............215 H4
Mull Ag & B.................181 J1
Mullion Cnwll 3 H7
Mullion Cove Cnwll 3 H7
Mumby Lincs 119 G6
Munderfield Row
  Herefs.....................70 B4
Munderfield Stocks
  Herefs.....................70 B4
Mundesley Norfk 107 G5
Mundford Norfk 91 H5
Mundham Norfk 93 G4
Mundon Hill Essex.......61 K7
Mungrisdale Cumb 137 K2
Munlochy Highld 213 G4
Munnoch N Ayrs 174 B8
Munsley Herefs.............70 B6
Munslow Shrops...........83 K6
Murchington Devon 11 G7
Murcott Oxon 57 L5
Murkle Highld 231 H2
Murlaggan Highld 200 F6
Murroes Angus 187 G1
Murrow Cambs............89 L3
Mursley Bucks.............58 D3
Murthill Angus 196 D5
Murthly P & K.............195 H8
Murton C York 133 K8
Murton Cumb.............139 G3
Murton Dur................151 J5
Murton Nthumb 179 K8
Musbury Devon 13 H4
Musselburgh E Loth ...177 K4
Muston Leics..............102 D5
Muston N York 135 H4
Muswell Hill Gt Lon 44 F3
Mutehill D & G 146 C5
Mutford Suffk 93 K6
Muthill P & K.............185 H4
Mybster Highld 231 H5
Myddfai Carmth 52 B3
Myddle Shrops............98 C7
Mydroilyn Cerdgn 66 B4
Mylor Cnwll 4 C8
Mylor Bridge Cnwll 4 C8
Mynachlog ddu
  Pembks...................49 K2
Mynydd-bach Mons 38 C2
Mynydd-Bach Swans 51 J6
Mynyddgarreg
  Carmth 50 E4
Mynydd Isa Flints 111 J8
Myrebird Abers...........206 E5
Myredykes Border 157 G3
Mytchett Surrey 30 E1
Mytholm Calder 122 E5
Mytholmroyd Calder ...122 F5
Myton-on-Swale
  N York....................132 F6

N

Naast Highld...............219 J5
Na Buirgh W Isls..........232 d4
Naburn N York...........124 F2
Nab Wood
  Crematorium
  C Brad....................123 H3

Nackington Kent...........34 F4
Nacton Suffk................78 F6
Nafferton E R Yk........135 G7
Nailbourne Somset 25 K5
Nailsea N Som.............38 C6
Nailstone Leics............86 E3
Nailsworth Gloucs........55 J7
Nairn Highld...............213 K3
Nannerch Flints 111 G7
Nanpantan Leics..........87 G1
Nanpean Cnwll 4 F5
Nanstallon Cnwll 5 G3
Nanternis Cerdgn........65 L3
Nantgaredig Carmth 50 F2
Nantglyn Denbgs.........96 F1
Nantmel Powys 68 B2
Nantmor Gwynd..........95 K4
Nant Peris Gwynd........95 K2
Nantwich Ches E..........98 F3
Nantyglo Blae G..........53 J6
Nant-y-moel Brdgnd 36 E2
Naphill Bucks.............42 D2
Napton on the Hill
  Warwks...................72 F3
Narberth Pembks.........49 J4
Narborough Leics........87 G4
Narborough Norfk........91 H2
Nasareth Gwynd..........95 H3
Naseby Nhants...........87 K7
Nash Bucks................73 L7
Nash Newpt.................37 M4
Nash Shrops...............69 L1
Nassington Nhants......88 F4
Nateby Cumb.............139 H6
Nateby Lancs............120 F2
National Memorial
  Arboretum Staffs 85 L1
National Motor
  Museum
  (Beaulieu) Hants.......16 E2
National Space
  Science Centre
  C Leic.....................87 H3
Natland Cumb 129 L2
Naughton Suffk...........78 B5
Naunton Gloucs..........56 C4
Naunton Worcs 70 F6
Naunton Beauchamp
  Worcs 71 G4
Navenby Lincs 103 G2
Navestock Essex 45 K1
Navestock Side Essex ..60 F8
Navidale House
  Hotel Highld 227 J5
Navity Highld 213 J2
Nawton N York 133 K3
Nayland Suffk.............77 L7
Nazeing Essex 60 C6
Neap Shet..................235 d5
Near Cotton Staffs......100 B4
Near Sawrey Cumb 137 K7
Neasden Gt Lon..........44 E3
Neasham Darltn.........141 H5
Neath Neath................51 L6
Neatham Hants 30 C4
Neatishead Norfk.......107 H7
Nebo Cerdgn...............66 D2
Nebo Conwy................96 C2
Nebo Gwynd...............95 H3
Nebo IoA..................108 F4
Necton Norfk...............91 K2
Nedd Highld..............224 D3
Nedging Suffk.............78 B5
Nedging Tye Suffk.......78 B4
Needham Norfk...........92 F6
Needham Lake &
  Nature Reserve
  Suffk.....................78 C4
Needham Market
  Suffk.....................78 C4
Needingworth Cambs....75 L1
Neen Savage Shrops....84 C7
Neen Sollars Shrops....84 B8
Neenton Shrops..........84 B6
Nefyn Gwynd 94 E4
Neilston E Rens...........174 E6

Nelson Caerph 37 H2
Nelson Lancs 122 C3
Nemphlar S Lans........165 G1
Nempnett Thrubwell
  BaNES 38 D7
Nenthead Cumb.........149 K6
Nenthorn Border........167 K2
Nercwys Flints 97 K1
Nereabolls Ag & B.......170 E7
Nerston S Lans..........175 H6
Nesbit Nthumb 168 E3
Nesfield N York 123 G1
Nesscliffe Shrops.........98 B8
Neston Ches W 111 J6
Neston Wilts...............39 K6
Netchwood Shrops.......84 B5
Nether Alderley
  Ches E....................113 J6
Netheravon Wilts........28 D2
Nether Blainslie
  Border....................167 H2
Netherbrae Abers.......216 F3
Nether Broughton
  Leics.....................102 B7
Netherburn S Lans......175 L8
Netherbury Dorset 13 L3
Netherby N York 123 L2
Nether Cerne Dorset 14 C3
Nethercleuch D & G.....155 K5
Nether Compton
  Dorset 26 E7
Nether Crimond
  Abers 206 F2
Nether Dallachy
  Moray 215 H2
Netherend Gloucs.......54 E7
Netherfield E Susx.......20 E2
Nether Fingland
  S Lans....................165 H7
Netherhampton Wilts 28 C5
Nether Handwick
  Angus 196 B7
Nether Haugh Rothm...115 H3
Netherhay Dorset 13 K2
Nether Headon Notts...116 C6
Nether Heage
  Derbys....................101 G3
Nether Heyford
  Nhants....................73 J3
Nether Howcleugh
  S Lans....................165 K6
Nether Kellet Lancs.....129 K6
Nether Kinmundy
  Abers 217 K5
Nether Langwith
  Notts.....................115 K7
Netherlaw D & G.........146 C6
Netherley Abers 207 G6
Nethermill D & G.........155 H5
Nethermuir Abers.......217 G5
Netherne-on-the-Hill
  Surrey 32 B3
Netheroyd Hill Kirk 123 H6
Nether Padley Derbys...114 E6
Netherplace E Rens....174 F7
Nether Poppleton
  C York....................133 J8
Netherseal Derbys.......86 C2
Nether Silton N York....133 G2
Nether Stowey
  Somset 25 J4
Netherthong Kirk........123 H8
Netherton Angus 196 E6
Netherton Devon 7 K2
Netherton Dudley 85 G6
Netherton Kirk...........123 H7
Netherton N Lans 175 K7
Netherton Nthumb......168 E7
Netherton P & K..........195 J6
Netherton Stirlg 175 G3
Netherton Wakefd 123 K6
Nethertown Cumb.......136 D5
Nethertown Highld......231 L1
Nethertown Staffs.......100 C8
Netherurd Border 165 L1
Nether Wallop Hants....28 F4

Nether Wasdale
  Cumb 136 F6
Nether Westcote
  Gloucs....................56 E4
Nether Whitacre
  Warwks...................86 B5
Nether Whitecleuch
  S Lans....................165 G5
Nether Winchendon
  Bucks.....................58 B5
Netherwitton
  Nthumb..................158 D4
Nethy Bridge Highld.....204 B2
Netley Hants 16 F2
Netley Marsh Hants.....29 G8
Nettlebed Oxon 42 B3
Nettlebridge Somset.....26 F2
Nettlecombe Dorset 13 M4
Nettleden Herts...........59 G6
Nettleham Lincs 117 G6
Nettlestead Kent..........33 H3
Nettlestead Green
  Kent......................33 H3
Nettlestone IoW 17 H4
Nettlesworth Dur 151 G5
Nettleton Lincs 117 J2
Nettleton Wilts 39 J5
Netton Wilts 28 C4
Nevern Pembks...........64 F6
Nevill Holt Leics 88 B5
New Abbey D & G........147 G2
New Aberdour Abers....217 G2
New Addington
  Gt Lon 45 G7
Newall Leeds.............123 J2
New Alresford Hants 29 L5
New Alyth P & K 195 K6
Newark Ork................234 e4
Newark-on-Trent
  Notts.....................102 D2
Newarthill N Lans.......175 K6
New Ash Green Kent 45 L6
New Balderton Notts...102 D3
New Barn Kent 45 L6
New Barnet Gt Lon......44 F2
Newbattle Mdloth.......177 J3
New Bewick Nthumb....169 G5
Newbie D & G............147 L5
Newbiggin Cumb.......138 C2
Newbiggin Cumb.......138 F2
Newbiggin Cumb.......148 F5
Newbiggin Dur 139 K2
Newbiggin N York 131 J3
Newbiggin-by-the-
  Sea Nthumb...........159 H5
Newbigging Angus......187 H1
Newbigging Angus......195 L7
Newbigging Angus......196 C8
Newbigging S Lans......165 K1
Newbiggin-on-Lune
  Cumb 139 G6
New Bilton Warwks.......86 F7
Newbold Derbys.........115 G6
Newbold on Avon
  Warwks...................86 F7
Newbold on Stour
  Warwks...................72 B5
Newbold Pacey
  Warwks...................72 C3
Newbold Verdon
  Leics......................86 F3
New Bolingbroke
  Lincs......................104 A2
Newborough C Pete.....89 H3
Newborough IoA 108 E7
Newborough Staffs.....100 C7
New Boultham Lincs....116 F7
Newbourne Suffk.........78 F6
New Bradwell M Keyn....74 B6
New Brampton
  Derbys....................115 G7
New Brancepeth Dur...151 G6
Newbridge C Edin.......176 F4
Newbridge Caerph.......37 K2
Newbridge Cnwll 2 D5
Newbridge D & G........155 G6

Newbridge Hants............28 F7
Newbridge IoW..............16 E5
Newbridge Green
Worcs......................70 E6
Newbridge on Wye
Powys.....................67 L3
New Brighton Wirral....111 J3
Newbrough Nthumb...149 L2
New Buckenham
Norfk.......................92 C5
Newbuildings Devon....11 J4
Newburgh Abers..........207 J1
Newburgh Abers..........217 H3
Newburgh Fife............186 D4
Newburgh Lancs..........121 G7
Newburgh Priory
N York.....................133 H4
Newburn N u Ty..........150 F2
Newbury Somset..........27 G2
Newbury W Berk..........41 J6
Newbury Park Gt Lon....45 J3
Newby Cumb...............138 E3
Newby Lancs...............122 B2
Newby N York..............130 D5
Newby N York..............142 B5
Newby Bridge Cumb....129 H3
Newby East Cumb........148 E4
New Byth Abers...........216 F4
Newby West Cumb.......148 C4
Newcastle Mons............54 C5
Newcastle Shrops..........82 E6
Newcastle Airport
Nthumb...................158 F7
Newcastle Emlyn
Carmth....................65 J6
Newcastleton Border....156 E5
Newcastle-under-
Lyme Staffs..............99 J4
Newcastle upon
Tyne N u Ty.............151 G3
Newchapel Pembks.......65 H6
Newchapel Surrey.........32 C5
Newchurch IoW............17 G5
Newchurch Kent............34 E7
Newchurch Mons...........38 C2
Newchurch Powys..........68 E4
Newchurch Staffs.........100 D7
New Costessey Norfk.....92 E2
Newcraighall C Edin.....177 J4
New Crofton Wakefd....124 B6
New Cross Gt Lon..........45 G5
New Cross Somset.........26 B7
New Cumnock
E Ayrs....................164 C6
New Deer Abers...........217 G5
New Denham Bucks........43 H4
Newdigate Surrey.........31 K3
New Duston Nhants.......73 K3
New Earswick C York....133 J7
New Edlington Donc.....115 K2
New Elgin Moray..........214 F3
New Ellerby E R Yk......126 E3
Newell Green Br For......42 E6
New Eltham Gt Lon........45 H5
New End Worcs.............71 J3
Newenden Kent.............33 L7
New England C Pete......89 H4
Newent Gloucs..............55 G3
Newfield Dur...............150 F7
Newfield Highld...........223 H6
New Fletton C Pete........89 H4
New Forest National
Park......................16 C2
Newgale Pembks...........48 E3
New Galloway D & G....154 B6
Newgate Street Herts...59 M6
New Gilston Fife..........187 G5
New Grimsby IoS.............2 a1
Newhall Ches E.............98 E4
New Hartley Nthumb....159 H6
Newhaven C Edin.........177 H3
Newhaven E Susx..........19 L5
New Haw Surrey...........43 H7
New Hedges Pembks......49 J6
New Holland N Linc.....126 D5
Newholm N York...........143 H5

New Houghton
Derbys...................115 J7
New Houghton Norfk ..105 J6
Newhouse N Lans.........175 L6
New Hutton Cumb........130 B2
Newick E Susx...............19 L2
Newington Kent............35 G7
Newington Kent............46 E6
Newington Oxon............41 L2
New Inn Carmth.............66 B6
New Inn Torfn...............53 L7
New Invention
Shrops.....................82 F7
New Lakenham Norfk.....92 F3
New Lanark S Lans.......165 G2
New Lanark Village
S Lans.....................165 G2
Newland C KuH............126 D4
Newland Gloucs............54 D6
Newland N York...........125 G5
Newland Somset............24 C4
Newland Worcs..............70 E5
Newlandrig Mdloth.......177 K6
Newlands Border..........156 E4
Newlands Nthumb........150 D4
Newlands of
Dundurcas Moray ..215 G4
New Langholm D & G...156 C5
New Leake Lincs..........104 C2
New Leeds Abers..........217 J4
New Lodge Barns.........123 L8
New Longton Lancs......121 G5
New Luce D & G...........144 E3
Newlyn Cnwll.................2 E5
Newmachar Abers........207 G2
Newmains N Lans.........175 L6
New Malden Gt Lon.......44 E6
Newman's Green
Suffk.......................77 K5
Newmarket Suffk..........76 F2
Newmarket W Isls.........232 f2
New Marske R & Cl.......142 D3
New Marston Oxon.........57 K6
New Mill Abers.............206 E8
Newmill Border.............167 G7
New Mill Cnwll...............2 E4
Newmill Kirk................123 H8
Newmill Moray.............215 K4
Newmillerdam
Wakefd...................123 L7
Newmill of Inshewan
Angus.....................196 C4
Newmills C Edin...........177 G5
New Mills Derbys.........113 M4
Newmills Fife...............176 D2
Newmills Mons..............54 D6
New Mills Powys............82 C4
Newmiln P & K.............186 B2
Newmilns E Ayrs..........164 B2
New Milton Hants..........16 B4
New Mistley Essex..........62 D2
New Moat Pembks..........49 H3
Newney Green Essex......61 G6
Newnham Gloucs...........55 G5
Newnham Hants.............30 B2
Newnham Herts.............75 J6
Newnham Kent.............34 C3
Newnham Nhants..........73 H3
Newnham Worcs............70 B2
New Ollerton Notts......116 A7
New Pitsligo Abers.......217 G3
Newport Cnwll................9 J7
Newport E R Yk............125 K4
Newport Essex.............76 D7
Newport Gloucs............39 G2
Newport Highld...........227 K4
Newport IoW................16 F5
Newport Newpt............37 L3
Newport Pembks............64 E6
Newport Wrekin............99 H8
Newport-on-Tay Fife ...187 G2
Newport Pagnell
M Keyn....................74 C5
Newport Pagnell
Services M Keyn......74 C5
New Prestwick S Ayrs...163 J4

New Quay Cerdgn..........65 L3
Newquay Cnwll..............4 C4
Newquay Airport
Cnwll........................4 D3
New Rackheath
Norfk.......................93 G2
New Radnor Powys........68 E3
New Ridley Nthumb......150 D3
New Romney Kent..........21 L2
New Rossington
Donc.....................115 L2
New Sauchie Clacks.....185 J7
Newseat Abers.............216 D7
Newsham Lancs...........121 G4
Newsham N York...........132 E3
Newsham N York...........140 E5
Newsham Nthumb.........159 H6
New Sharlston
Wakefd....................124 B6
Newsholme E R Yk........125 H5
New Silksworth
Sundld....................151 J4
Newsome Kirk..............123 H7
New Somerby Lincs......102 F5
New Southgate
Crematorium
Gt Lon....................44 F2
Newstead Border..........167 H3
Newstead Notts...........101 K3
Newstead Nthumb........169 H4
New Stevenston
N Lans....................175 K6
Newthorpe Notts..........101 J4
Newton Ag & B............182 F7
Newton Border.............167 J5
Newton Brdgnd.............36 C5
Newton C Beds.............75 J5
Newton Cambs..............76 B5
Newton Cambs..............90 B1
Newton Ches W.............98 D1
Newton Ches W............112 B7
Newton Cumb..............128 F5
Newton Derbys............101 H2
Newton Herefs.............53 M2
Newton Herefs.............69 K4
Newton Highld............212 F4
Newton Highld............213 H5
Newton Highld............213 J2
Newton Highld............231 L5
Newton Lincs..............103 H5
Newton Mdloth...........177 J4
Newton Moray............214 E2
Newton Moray............215 H2
Newton Nhants.............88 C6
Newton Norfk...............91 J1
Newton Notts.............102 B4
Newton Nthumb..........150 C3
Newton S Lans............165 H3
Newton S Lans............175 H6
Newton Staffs............100 B7
Newton Suffk................77 K6
Newton W Loth...........176 E3
Newton Warwks............87 G7
Newton Abbot Devon......7 K2
Newton Arlosh
Cumb.....................147 L4
Newton Aycliffe Dur 141 G3
Newton Bewley
Hartpl....................141 K2
Newton Blossomville
M Keyn.....................74 D4
Newton Bromswold
Nhants.....................74 E2
Newton Burgoland
Leics.......................86 D2
Newton-by-the-Sea
Nthumb..................169 J4
Newton by Toft Lincs ...117 H4
Newton Ferrers
Devon.......................6 E6
Newton Ferry W Isls....232 c5
Newton Flotman
Norfk.......................92 E4
Newtongrange
Mdloth....................177 J5
Newton Green Mons......38 D3

Newton Harcourt
Leics.......................87 J4
Newton Heath Manch...113 K2
Newtonhill Abers..........207 G6
Newton-in-Bowland
Lancs....................121 K1
Newton Kyme N York ...124 C2
Newton-le-Willows
N York....................132 C2
Newton-le-Willows
St Hel....................112 E3
Newtonloan Mdloth......177 J5
Newton Longville
Bucks.......................58 D2
Newton Mearns
E Rens....................174 F7
Newtonmill Angus.......196 F4
Newtonmore Highld......203 H5
Newton Morrell
N York....................141 G5
Newton of
Balcanquhal P & K..186 B5
Newton of Balcormo
Fife.......................187 H6
Newton on Ouse
N York....................133 H7
Newton-on-
Rawcliffe N York.....134 C2
Newton-on-the-
Moor Nthumb..........158 F2
Newton on Trent
Lincs.......................116 D6
Newton Poppleford
Devon......................12 E4
Newton Purcell Oxon.....57 L3
Newton Regis
Warwks....................86 C3
Newton Reigny
Cumb.....................138 C2
Newton St Cyres
Devon......................11 K5
Newton St Faith
Norfk.......................92 F1
Newton St Loe BaNES...39 G7
Newton St Petrock
Devon.......................9 K3
Newton Solney
Derbys....................100 F7
Newton Stacey Hants....29 H4
Newton Stewart
D & G.....................145 J3
Newton Tony Wilts........28 E4
Newton Tracey
Devon......................23 H6
Newton under
Roseberry R & Cl....142 C5
Newton upon
Derwent E R Yk.......125 H2
Newton Valence
Hants.......................30 B5
Newton Wamphray
D & G.....................155 K3
Newton with Scales
Lancs....................120 F4
Newtown Cumb...........147 J5
Newtown Cumb...........148 E3
Newtown D & G...........164 F7
Newtown Devon............12 D3
Newtown Devon............24 B6
New Town Dorset..........27 L7
New Town Dorset..........27 M7
New Town E Susx..........19 M2
Newtown Gloucs............54 F7
Newtown Hants............29 L8
Newtown Herefs............70 B5
Newtown Herefs............70 C6
Newtown Highld..........202 B4
Newtown IoW................16 E4
Newtown Nthumb.........168 F4
Newtown Poole............15 K4
Newtown Powys.............82 C5
Newtown Shrops............98 B7
Newtown Shrops............98 C6
Newtown Somset...........25 L8
Newtown Staffs.............99 K1
Newtown Wigan...........112 E1

Newtown Worcs 70 F4
Newtown Linford
Leics.........................87 G2
Newtown of
Beltrees Rens 174 D6
Newtown St
Boswells Border 167 J3
New Tredegar Caerph 53 H7
New Trows S Lans 164 F2
Newtyle Angus..........195 L7
New Walsoken
Cambs 90 C2
New Waltham NE Lin....118 C1
New Winton E Loth....177 L4
Newyork Ag & B.......182 D5
New York Lincs 103 L2
Neyland Pembks 49 G6
Nicholashayne Devon ..25 H7
Nicholaston Swans.....51 G7
Nidd N York 132 D7
Nigg C Aber 207 H5
Nigg Highld...............223 H6
Nigg Ferry Highld.....223 H7
Ninebanks Nthumb 149 K4
Nine Elms Swindn......40 C3
Ninfield E Susx 20 E3
Ningwood IoW 16 E5
Nisbet Border...........167 K4
Nisbet Hill Border 179 G7
Niton IoW...................17 F6
Nitshill C Glas..........174 F6
Nocton Lincs 117 H8
Noke Oxon...................57 K5
Nolton Pembks 48 E4
Nolton Haven
Pembks 48 E4
No Man's Heath
Ches W 98 D3
No Man's Heath
Warwks 86 C2
Nomansland Devon 11 J3
Nomansland Wilts.....28 E7
Noneley Shrops 98 C6
Nonington Kent 35 H4
Nook Cumb................129 L3
Norbiton Gt Lon.........44 D6
Norbury Ches E..........98 E3
Norbury Derbys........100 C4
Norbury Gt Lon..........44 F6
Norbury Shrops..........83 G5
Norbury Staffs 99 H7
Norchard Worcs 70 F2
Nordelph Norfk 90 D4
Nordley Shrops..........84 C4
Norfolk Broads Norfk....93 K2
Norham Nthumb 179 J8
Norley Ches W 112 E6
Norleywood Hants......16 D3
Normanby Lincs 117 G4
Normanby N Linc......125 K7
Normanby N York 133 K3
Normanby R & Cl.......142 C4
Normanby le Wold
Lincs 117 J5
Normandy Surrey.......30 F2
Norman's Green
Devon......................12 D2
Normanton C Derb ...101 G5
Normanton Leics......102 D4
Normanton Lincs......102 F4
Normanton Notts.....102 B2
Normanton Wakefd....124 B6
Normanton le Heath
Leics 86 D2
Normanton on Soar
Notts 101 K7
Normanton on the
Wolds Notts..........101 L6
Normanton on Trent
Notts 116 C4
Norris Green Lpool....111 L3
Norris Hill Leics........86 D1
Norristhorpe Kirk 123 J6
Northall Bucks 58 F4
Northallerton N York ...141 J7
Northam C Sotn 29 H8

Northam Devon...............23 G5
Northampton Nhants....73 L3
Northampton Worcs 70 E2
Northampton
Services Nhants......73 K3
North Anston Rothm....115 K5
North Ascot Br For......42 E6
North Aston Oxon......57 J3
Northaw Herts............59 L7
Northay Somset........13 H1
North Baddesley
Hants......................29 H7
North Ballachulish
Highld....................191 L4
North Barrow Somset....26 E5
North Barsham Norfk..105 L5
North Benfleet Essex 46 C3
North Bersted W Susx....18 C5
North Berwick E Loth....178 C2
North Boarhunt
Hants......................17 H1
Northborough C Pete....89 H3
Northbourne Kent......35 J4
North Bovey Devon....11 H7
North Bradley Wilts....27 J1
North Brentor Devon....10 C8
North Brewham
Somset....................27 G4
Northbrook Hants......29 K4
North Buckland
Devon......................23 G4
North Burlingham
Norfk.......................93 H2
North Cadbury
Somset....................26 F6
North Carlton Lincs....116 F6
North Carlton Notts....115 L4
North Cave E R Yk......125 K4
North Cerney Gloucs 56 A6
North Chailey E Susx....19 K2
Northchapel W Susx....30 F5
North Charford Hants....28 D7
North Charlton
Nthumb 169 H5
North Cheam Gt Lon....44 E6
North Cheriton
Somset....................27 G6
North Chideock
Dorset.....................13 K4
Northchurch Herts......58 F6
North Cliffe E R Yk......125 K3
North Clifton Notts....116 D6
North Cockerington
Lincs 118 E4
North Connel Ag & B....182 C1
North Cornelly
Brdgnd....................36 C4
North Cotes Lincs......118 E2
Northcott Devon..........9 J6
Northcourt Oxon.........57 J7
North Cove Suffk........93 K5
North Cowton N York....141 G6
North Crawley
M Keyn....................74 D5
North Creake Norfk....105 K5
North Curry Somset....25 L6
North Dalton E R Yk....125 L1
North Deighton
N York 124 B1
North Devon
Crematorium
Devon......................23 H5
Northdown Kent........35 K2
North Downs 34 B4
North Duffield N York...125 G3
North Duntulm
Highld....................218 C6
North East Surrey
Crematorium
Gt Lon.....................44 E6
North Elmham Norfk...106 B7
North Elmsall Wakefd...124 D7
North End C Port.......17 J3
North End Essex 61 G4
North End Hants.......28 C7
North End Nhants......74 D2

North End W Susx.......18 D5
Northend Warwks.......72 E4
Northenden Manch....113 J4
North Erradale Highld...219 H5
North Evington C Leic....87 J3
North Fambridge
Essex......................61 K7
North Ferriby E R Yk....126 B5
Northfield Birm...........85 H7
Northfield C Aber......207 G4
Northfield E R Yk.......126 C5
Northfields Lincs........88 E2
Northfleet Kent..........45 M5
North Frodingham
E R Yk.....................135 H8
North Gorley Hants.....15 M1
North Green Suffk......79 G3
North Greetwell Lincs ..117 G6
North Grimston
N York 134 C6
North Haven Shet......235 e7
North Hayling Hants....17 K2
North Hill Cnwll............5 L1
North Hillingdon
Gt Lon.....................43 H4
North Hinksey
Village Oxon...........57 J6
North Holmwood
Surrey.....................31 K3
North Huish Devon.......7 G5
North Hykeham Lincs...116 F7
Northiam E Susx..........21 G2
Northill C Beds.............75 G5
Northington Hants......29 K4
North Kelsey Lincs......117 H2
North Kessock Highld....213 G5
North Killingholme
N Linc.....................126 E6
North Kilvington
N York 132 F3
North Kilworth Leics....87 H6
North Kyme Lincs......103 J3
North Landing E R Yk...135 K5
Northlands Lincs.......104 B2
Northleach Gloucs......56 C5
North Lee Bucks........58 D6
Northleigh Devon......12 F3
North Leigh Oxon......57 H5
North Leverton with
Habblesthorpe
Notts 116 C5
Northlew Devon..........10 D5
North Littleton Worcs....71 J5
North Lopham Norfk....92 C6
North Luffenham
Rutlnd.....................88 D3
North Marden W Susx....30 D7
North Marston Bucks....58 C4
North Middleton
Mdloth....................177 K6
North Millbrex Abers....216 F5
North Milmain D & G....144 C4
North Molton Devon....24 B5
North Moreton Oxon....41 K3
Northmuir Angus......196 C5
North Mundham
W Susx....................18 B5
North Muskham
Notts 102 D2
North Newbald E R Yk...125 L3
North Newington
Oxon.......................72 E6
North Newnton Wilts....40 C8
North Newton
Somset....................25 L5
Northney Hants..........17 K2
North Nibley Gloucs....39 H7
Northolt Gt Lon..........43 J4
Northop Flints..........111 H7
Northop Hall Flints....111 J7
North Ormesby
Middsb....................142 B4
North Ormsby Lincs....118 C3
Northorpe Kirk 123 J6
Northorpe Lincs.......103 K5

Northorpe Lincs 116 E3
North Otterington
N York 132 E2
North Owersby Lincs....117 H3
Northowram Calder 123 G5
North Perrott Somset 13 L1
North Petherton
Somset....................25 L5
North Petherwin
Cnwll.........................9 H6
North Pickenham
Norfk.......................91 J3
North Piddle Worcs 71 G4
North Poorton Dorset....13 M3
Northport Dorset.......15 H5
North Queensferry
Fife 176 F3
North Raceby Lincs....103 G3
Northrepps Norfk......106 F5
North Reston Lincs....118 E5
North Rigton N York....123 K1
North Rode Ches E....113 K7
North Ronaldsay Ork....234 e3
North Ronaldsay
Airport Ork............234 e3
North Runcton Norfk....90 F1
North Scarle Lincs......116 D7
North Shian Ag & B....191 H7
North Shields N Tyne....151 J2
North Shoebury
Sthend....................46 F3
North Shore Bpool....120 D3
North Side C Pete........89 K4
North Somercotes
Lincs 118 F3
North Stainley N York...132 D4
North Stifford Thurr....45 L4
North Stoke BaNES....39 G6
North Stoke Oxon........41 L3
North Stoke W Susx....18 D4
North Street Kent.......34 D3
North Street W Berk....41 M6
North Sunderland
Nthumb 169 J3
North Tamerton
Cnwll.........................9 J5
North Tawton Devon....10 F4
North Third Stirlg......175 K1
North Thoresby Lincs...118 D2
Northton W Isls........232 d5
North Town Devon......10 D3
North Town Somset....26 E3
North Town W & M......42 E4
North Tuddenham
Norfk.......................92 C2
North Uist W Isls......233 b6
Northumberland
National Park
Nthumb 157 L3
North Walsham Norfk..107 G6
North Waltham
Hants......................29 K3
North Warnborough
Hants......................30 B2
North Weald Bassett
Essex......................60 D7
North Wheatley
Notts 116 C5
Northwich Ches W......112 F6
Northwick Worcs 70 E3
North Widcombe
BaNES.....................38 E8
North Willingham
Lincs 117 K4
North Wingfield
Derbys....................115 H8
North Witham Lincs....102 F7
Northwold Norfk........91 H4
Northwood Gt Lon......43 H3
Northwood IoW 16 F4
Northwood Shrops....98 C6
Northwood Green
Gloucs....................55 G5
North Wootton
Dorset.....................26 F8
North Wootton Norfk..105 G7

North Wootton
Somset 26 E3
North Wraxall Wilts....39 J5
North York Moors
National Park 142 F6
Norton Donc 124 E7
Norton E Susx 19 M5
Norton Gloucs..............55 J3
Norton Halton 112 D5
Norton Nhants............73 H2
Norton Notts 115 L6
Norton Powys...............68 F2
Norton S on T............141 K3
Norton Shrops.............84 D4
Norton Suffk................77 L2
Norton W Susx............18 C4
Norton Wilts................39 K4
Norton Worcs...............70 F4
Norton Worcs...............71 J5
Norton Bavant Wilts....27 K3
Norton Bridge Staffs....99 K6
Norton Canes Staffs....85 H2
Norton Canes
Services 85 H3
Norton Canon Herefs....69 H5
Norton Disney Lincs...102 E2
Norton Fitzwarren
Somset 25 J6
Norton Green IoW......16 D5
Norton Hawkfield
BaNES 38 E7
Norton Heath Essex....60 F6
Norton in Hales
Shrops 99 G5
Norton-Juxta-
Twycross Leics.........86 D3
Norton-le-Clay
N York.......................132 F5
Norton Lindsey
Warwks 72 B2
Norton Little Green
Suffk...........................77 L2
Norton Malreward
BaNES 38 E7
Norton-on-Derwent
N York.......................134 C5
Norton St Philip
Somset 27 H1
Norton Subcourse
Norfk............................93 J4
Norton sub Hamdon
Somset 26 C7
Norwell Notts 102 C1
Norwell Woodhouse
Notts 116 B8
Norwich Norfk..............92 F2
Norwich Airport Norfk...92 E2
Norwich (St Faith)
Crematorium
Norfk...........................92 F1
Norwick Shet.............235 e1
Norwood Clacks 185 J8
Norwood Green
Gt Lon 43 J5
Norwood Hill Surrey.......31 L3
Noss Mayo Devon 6 E6
Nosterfield N York....132 D4
Nostie Highld 210 D8
Notgrove Gloucs 56 C4
Nottage Brdgnd 36 C5
Nottingham C Nott....101 L5
Notton Wakefd 123 L7
Notton Wilts................39 K6
Noutard's Green
Worcs 70 E2
Nuffield Oxon 42 A3
Nunburnholme
E R Yk 125 K2
Nuneaton Warwks......86 D5
Nunhead Gt Lon 45 G5
Nun Monkton N York....133 H7
Nunney Somset 27 G3
Nunnington N York....133 K4
Nunsthorpe NE Lin....127 G8
Nunthorpe C York 124 F1
Nunthorpe Middsb....142 C4

Nunthorpe Village
Middsb......................142 C5
Nunton Wilts................28 D6
Nunwick N York 132 E5
Nursling Hants.............29 G7
Nutbourne W Susx........17 L2
Nutbourne W Susx........18 E3
Nutfield Surrey.............32 B3
Nuthall Notts..............101 K4
Nuthampstead Herts....76 B7
Nuthurst W Susx..........31 K6
Nutley E Susx................32 D7
Nuttall Bury................122 B7
Nybster Highld...........231 L3
Nyetimber W Susx........18 B6
Nyewood W Susx.........30 D6
Nymans W Susx............31 L5
Nymet Rowland
Devon 11 G4
Nymet Tracey Devon....11 G5
Nympsfield Gloucs......55 J7
Nynehead Somset.......25 H6
Nyton W Susx................18 C5

O

Oadby Leics 87 J4
Oad Street Kent............34 B3
Oakamoor Staffs 100 B4
Oakbank W Loth.........176 E5
Oak Cross Devon 10 D5
Oakdale Caerph............37 J2
Oake Somset 25 J6
Oaken Staffs.................84 F3
Oakenclough Lancs....121 H2
Oakengates Wrekin 84 C2
Oakenshaw Dur..........150 F7
Oakenshaw Kirk 123 H5
Oakford Cerdgn 66 B3
Oakford Devon 24 E6
Oakham Rutlnd............88 C2
Oakhanger Hants.........30 C4
Oakhill Somset.............26 F3
Oakington Cambs.........76 B2
Oakle Street Gloucs....55 H4
Oakley Bed....................74 E4
Oakley Bucks.................57 M5
Oakley Fife..................176 D1
Oakley Hants.................29 K2
Oakley Suffk.................92 E7
Oakridge Lynch
Gloucs........................55 K7
Oaksey Wilts................39 M2
Oakthorpe Leics...........86 D2
Oakwood C Derb.........101 G5
Oakworth C Brad 122 F3
Oare Kent 34 D3
Oare Somset 24 C3
Oare Wilts 40 D7
Oasby Lincs 103 G5
Oath Somset 26 B6
Oathlaw Angus...........196 D5
Oatlands Park Surrey....43 H7
Oban Ag & B 182 B2
Oban Airport Ag & B....182 C1
Obley Shrops................83 G7
Obney P & K................195 G8
Oborne Dorset 26 F7
Occold Suffk.................78 D1
Occumster Highld.......231 J7
Ochiltree E Ayrs..........163 L5
Ockbrook Derbys........101 H5
Ockham Surrey.............31 H1
Ockle Highld 190 B3
Ockley Surrey................31 J4
Ocle Pychard Herefs....69 L5
Odcombe Somset..........26 D7
Odd Down BaNES.........39 H7
Oddingley Worcs...........71 G3
Oddington Gloucs........56 E3
Oddington Oxon...........57 K5
Odell Bed......................74 D3
Odiham Hants...............30 C2
Odsal C Brad...............123 H5

Odsey Cambs................75 K6
Odstock Wilts...............28 D6
Odstone Leics..............86 E3
Offchurch Warwks.......72 D2
Offenham Worcs...........71 J5
Offerton Stockp..........113 K4
Offham E Susx 19 L3
Offham Kent..................33 H2
Offham W Susx 18 D4
Offord Cluny Cambs....75 J2
Offord D'Arcy Cambs....75 J2
Offton Suffk..................78 C5
Offwell Devon...............12 F3
Ogbourne Maizey
Wilts...........................40 D6
Ogbourne St Andrew
Wilts...........................40 D6
Ogbourne St George
Wilts...........................40 D5
Ogle Nthumb 158 E6
Oglet Lpool 112 C5
Ogmore V Glam 36 D5
Ogmore-by-Sea
V Glam 36 D5
Ogmore Vale Brdgnd....36 E3
Okeford Fitzpaine
Dorset 14 F1
Okehampton Devon......10 E5
Oker Side Derbys........100 F1
Okewood Hill Surrey......31 J4
Old Nhants....................87 L8
Old Aberdeen C Aber...207 H4
Old Alresford Hants......29 L5
Oldany Highld..............224 D2
Old Auchenbrack
D & G 154 D3
Old Basford C Nott......101 K4
Old Basing Hants..........30 A2
Old Beetley Norfk.......106 A8
Oldberrow Warwks........71 K2
Old Bewick Nthumb 169 G5
Old Bolingbroke Lincs...118 E8
Old Bramhope Leeds...123 J2
Old Brampton Derbys...115 G6
Old Bridge of Urr
D & G 146 D2
Old Buckenham
Norfk............................92 C5
Old Burghclere Hants....41 J8
Oldbury Sandw.............85 H5
Oldbury Shrops.............84 C5
Oldbury Warwks............86 C5
Oldbury-on-Severn
S Glos..........................38 E2
Oldbury on the Hill
Gloucs........................39 J3
Old Byland N York 133 H3
Old Cantley Donc........115 L2
Oldcastle Mons............53 L3
Old Catton Norfk..........92 F2
Old Clee NE Lin..........127 G8
Old Cleeve Somset........25 G3
Old Clipstone Notts....115 L8
Old Colwyn Conwy.....110 B6
Oldcotes Notts............115 L4
Old Dailly S Ayrs.........152 F3
Old Dalby Leics 102 A7
Old Deer Abers...........217 J5
Old Edlington Donc....115 K3
Old Ellerby E R Yk......126 E3
Old Felixstowe Suffk....79 G7
Oldfield Worcs 70 E2
Old Fletton C Pete........89 H4
Oldford Somset 27 H2
Old Forge Herefs..........54 E4
Old Grimsby IoS.............2 a1
Old Hall Green Herts....60 B4
Oldham Oldham...........113 L1
Oldhamstocks E Loth...178 F4
Old Harlow Essex 60 D5
Old Hunstanton
Norfk..........................105 G4
Old Hutt Cambs............89 K7
Old Hutton Cumb.......130 B2
Old Inns Services
N Lans.......................175 K3

Old Kilpatrick W Duns...174 E4
Old Knebworth Herts....59 L4
Old Lakenham Norfk.....92 F3
Oldland S Glos..............38 F6
Old Langho Lancs.......121 K4
Old Leake Lincs..........104 C3
Old Malton N York......134 C5
Oldmeldrum Abers......216 F8
Oldmill Cnwll..................6 B2
Old Milverton Warwks...72 C2
Oldmixon N Som..........37 M8
Old Newton Suffk.........78 C3
Old Radnor Powys.........68 E3
Old Rayne Abers..........216 D8
Old Romney Kent..........21 K2
Old Shoreham W Susx....19 G4
Oldshoremore Highld...228 C4
Old Sodbury S Glos.......39 H4
Old Somerby Lincs......102 F5
Oldstead N York..........133 H4
Old Stratford Nhants....73 L6
Old Struan P & K.........194 C4
Old Swinford Dudley....84 F6
Old Thirsk N York.......132 F3
Old Town Cumb...........130 B3
Old Town E Susx 20 C5
Old Town IoS..................2 b2
Old Trafford Traffd......113 J3
Oldwall Cumb..............148 E3
Oldwalls Swans............50 F6
Old Warden C Beds.......75 G5
Old Weston Cambs.......89 G7
Old Wick Highld..........231 L5
Old Windsor W & M......43 G5
Old Wives Lees Kent.....34 E4
Old Woking Surrey........43 G8
Olgrinmore Highld......231 G5
Olive Green Staffs.......100 C8
Oliver's Battery Hants....29 J6
Ollaberry Shet.............235 C3
Ollach Highld...............209 H6
Ollerton Ches E...........113 H6
Ollerton Notts.............116 A7
Ollerton Shrops............98 F7
Olney M Keyn................74 C4
Olrig House Highld.....231 H3
Olton Solhll...................85 K6
Olveston S Glos.............38 E3
Ombersley Worcs..........70 E2
Ompton Notts.............116 B7
Onchan IoM.................237 d5
Onecote Staffs.............100 B2
Onibury Shrops.............83 J7
Onich Highld...............191 K4
Onllwyn Neath..............52 C6
Onneley Staffs 99 H4
Onslow Green Essex.....61 G4
Onslow Village Surrey....31 G2
Onston Ches W............112 E6
Opinan Highld.............219 H6
Orbliston Moray..........215 G3
Orbost Highld..............208 D5
Orby Lincs 119 G7
Orchard Portman
Somset 25 K6
Orcheston Wilts............28 B3
Orcop Herefs 54 C3
Orcop Hill Herefs 54 C3
Ord Abers....................216 C3
Ordhead Abers............206 C3
Ordie Abers.................205 K5
Ordiequish Moray.......215 H3
Ordsall Notts...............116 B5
Ore E Susx 21 G4
Orford Suffk..................79 J4
Orford Warrtn.............112 E4
Organford Dorset.........15 H4
Orkney Islands Ork.....234 c6
Orkney Neolithic Ork....234 b6
Orlestone Kent..............34 D7
Orleton Herefs..............69 J2
Orleton Worcs...............70 C2
Orlingbury Nhants........74 C1
Ormesby R & Cl..........142 C4
Ormesby St
Margaret Norfk.......93 K1

Ormesby St Michael
Norfk 93 K1
Ormiscaig Highld...........219 K4
Ormiston E Loth 177 L4
Ormsaigmore Highld....189 L4
Ormsary Ag & B.............172 C4
Ormskirk Lancs 120 F8
Oronsay Ag & B.............171 G2
Orphir Ork 234 b6
Orpington Gt Lon 45 J6
Orrell Sefton..................111 K3
Orrell Wigan 112 D2
Orroland D & G 146 D5
Orsett Thurr 45 M4
Orslow Staffs 84 E1
Orston Notts 102 C4
Orton Cumb 138 F5
Orton Nhants 88 B7
Orton Staffs 84 F4
Orton Longueville
C Pete............................89 H4
Orton-on-the-Hill
Leics...............................86 C3
Orton Waterville
C Pete............................89 H4
Orwell Cambs 75 L4
Osbaldeston Lancs........121 J4
Osbaldwick C York 124 F1
Osbaston Leics 86 E3
Osbaston Shrops 97 L7
Osborne House IoW 17 G4
Osbournby Lincs 103 H5
Oscroft Ches W.............112 D7
Ose Highld 208 E6
Osgathorpe Leics 101 H8
Osgodby Lincs 117 H3
Osgodby N York.............124 F4
Osgodby N York.............135 G3
Oskaig Highld 209 H6
Oskamull Ag & B...........189 L7
Osmaston Derbys...........100 D4
Osmington Dorset 14 D5
Osmington Mills
Dorset 14 E6
Osmondthorpe Leeds ..123 L4
Osmotherley N York 141 K7
Osney Oxon.....................57 J6
Ospringe Kent.................34 D3
Ossett Wakefd 123 K6
Ossington Notts 116 C8
Osterley Gt Lon...............44 D5
Oswaldkirk N York 133 K4
Oswaldtwistle
Lancs............................121 L5
Oswestry Shrops 97 L6
Otford Kent.....................32 F2
Otham Kent.....................33 K3
Othery Somset 26 B5
Otley Leeds 123 J2
Otley Suffk.......................78 E4
Otterbourne Hants 29 J6
Otterburn N York 131 G7
Otterburn Nthumb 157 M4
Otter Ferry Ag & B........172 F2
Otterham Cnwll.................8 F6
Otterhampton
Somset...........................25 K3
Otternish W Isls 232 c5
Ottershaw Surrey............43 G7
Otterswick Shet 235 d3
Otterton Devon 12 E5
Ottery St Mary Devon ...12 E4
Ottinge Kent....................34 F6
Ottringham E R Yk 127 G5
Oughterside Cumb....147 K6
Oughtibridge Sheff.......114 F3
Oughtrington Warrtn ...113 G4
Oulston N York...............133 H5
Oulton Cumb 147 M5
Oulton Norfk 106 D6
Oulton Staffs 99 K5
Oulton Suffk 93 L5
Oulton Broad Suffk.........93 L5
Oulton Street Norfk......106 D6
Oundle Nhants 88 F6
Ounsdale Staffs 84 F5

Our Dynamic Earth
C Edin 177 H4
Ousby Cumb 149 G7
Ousden Suffk 77 G3
Ousefleet E R Yk 125 K6
Ouston Dur 151 G4
Outgate Cumb 137 K7
Outhgill Cumb 139 H6
Outhill Warwks 71 K2
Outlane Kirk 123 G6
Out Rawcliffe Lancs......120 E3
Outwell Norfk 90 D3
Outwood Surrey...............32 B4
Outwoods Staffs 99 H8
Ouzlewell Green
Leeds 123 L5
Over Cambs 75 L1
Overbury Worcs 71 G6
Overcombe Dorset 14 D6
Over Compton Dorset.....26 E7
Overdale
Crematorium
Bolton 121 K8
Over Haddon Derbys 114 D7
Over Kellet Lancs 129 L5
Over Kiddington
Oxon...............................57 H4
Overleigh Somset............26 C4
Over Norton Oxon 56 F3
Over Peover Ches E 113 H6
Overpool Ches W............111 L6
Overscaig Hotel
Highld 225 J4
Overseal Derbys 86 C1
Over Silton N York.........133 G2
Oversland Kent................34 E3
Overstone Nhants............74 B2
Over Stowey Somset 25 J4
Overstrand Norfk...........106 F4
Over Stratton Somset.....26 B7
Overthorpe Nhants..........72 F6
Overton C Aber...............207 G3
Overton Hants 29 K2
Overton Lancs 129 J7
Overton N York 133 H7
Overton Shrops 69 K1
Overton Swans 50 F7
Overton Wakefd 123 K7
Overton Wrexhm 98 A4
Overtown N Lans 175 L7
Over Wallop Hants 28 F4
Over Whitacre
Warwks 86 B5
Over Worton Oxon...........57 H3
Oving Bucks 58 C4
Oving W Susx 18 B5
Ovingdean Br & H............19 K5
Ovingham Nthumb.........150 D3
Ovington Dur 140 E4
Ovington Essex................77 H6
Ovington Hants 29 K5
Ovington Norfk 91 K3
Ovington Nthumb..........150 D3
Ower Hants 28 F7
Owermoigne Dorset.......14 E5
Owlerton Sheff...............115 G4
Owlsmoor Br For.............42 D7
Owlswick Bucks...............58 C6
Owmby Lincs 117 G2
Owmby Lincs 117 H1
Owslebury Hants.............29 K6
Owston Donc 124 E7
Owston Leics 88 B3
Owston Ferry N Linc......116 D2
Owstwick E R Yk.............127 G4
Owthorne E R Yk.............127 H5
Owthorpe Notts.............102 A5
Owton Manor Hartpl 141 L2
Oxborough Norfk.............91 G3
Oxcombe Lincs 118 D6
Oxenholme Cumb..........129 L2
Oxenhope C Brad...........122 F4
Oxen Park Cumb............129 G3
Oxenpill Somset 26 C3
Oxenton Gloucs 55 L2
Oxenwood Wilts 40 F8

Oxford Oxon 57 K6
Oxford Airport Oxon 57 J5
Oxford Crematorium
Oxon...............................57 K6
Oxford Services Oxon....57 L6
Oxhey Herts 43 J2
Oxhill Warwks 72 C5
Oxley Wolves 84 F3
Oxley Green Essex...........61 L5
Oxlode Cambs..................90 C6
Oxnam Border 167 L5
Oxnead Norfk 106 F7
Oxshott Surrey 43 J7
Oxspring Barns 114 F2
Oxted Surrey....................32 C3
Oxton Border 178 B7
Oxton N York 124 D2
Oxton Notts 101 M3
Oxwich Swans 51 G7
Oxwich Green Swans.......50 F7
Oykel Bridge Hotel
Highld 221 K2
Oyne Abers 206 D1
Oystermouth Swans........51 H7

P

Pabail W Isls 232 g2
Packington Leics 86 D1
Padanaram Angus..........196 C6
Padbury Bucks 58 B2
Paddington Gt Lon..........44 F4
Paddlesworth Kent..........35 G6
Paddlesworth Kent..........46 B7
Paddock Wood Kent........33 H4
Padiham Lancs 122 B4
Padside N York 132 B7
Padstow Cnwll....................4 E2
Padworth W Berk..............41 L7
Pagham W Susx................18 B6
Paglesham Essex..............46 F2
Paignton Torbay 7 K4
Pailton Warwks 86 F6
Painscastle Powys 68 D5
Painshawfield
Nthumb 150 D3
Painsthorpe E R Yk 134 C7
Painswick Gloucs 55 K6
Painter's Forstal Kent......34 D3
Paisley Rens 174 F5
Paisley Woodside
Crematorium
Rens..............................174 E5
Pakefield Suffk 93 L5
Pakenham Suffk................77 L2
Paley Street W & M..........42 E5
Palfrey Wsall 85 H4
Palgrave Suffk 92 D7
Pallington Dorset..............14 E4
Palmerston E Ayrs..........163 L5
Palnackie D & G..............146 E4
Palnure D & G 145 J3
Palterton Derbys.............115 J7
Pamber End Hants............41 L8
Pamber Green Hants........41 L8
Pamber Heath Hants.........41 L7
Pamington Gloucs 55 L2
Pamphill Dorset................15 J3
Pampisford Cambs 76 C5
Panbride Angus...............187 J1
Pancrasweek Devon 9 H4
Pandy Mons 53 M4
Pandy Tudur Conwy 110 B8
Panfield Essex 61 H3
Pangbourne W Berk..........41 M5
Pangdean W Susx 19 J4
Pannal N York 123 L1
Pannal Ash N York..........132 D8
Pannanich Wells
Hotel Abers...................205 J6
Pant Shrops 97 L7
Pantasaph Flints.............111 G6
Pant-ffrwyth Brdgnd.......36 E4
Pant Glas Gwynd 95 H3

Pantglas Powys 81 G4
Panton Lincs 117 K5
Pant-y-dwr Powys 81 L8
Pant-y-mwyn Flints.........111 H8
Panxworth Norfk...............93 H2
Papa Westray Airport
Ork...............................234 c3
Papcastle Cumb 136 F2
Papigoe Highld 231 L5
Papple E Loth 178 D4
Papplewick Notts 101 K3
Papworth Everard
Cambs 75 K3
Papworth St Agnes
Cambs 75 J2
Par Cnwll.............................5 G5
Parbold Lancs 121 G7
Parbrook Somset 26 E4
Parc Gwynd 96 D5
Parc Gwyn
Crematorium
Pembks 49 K5
Parc Seymour Newpt.......38 B3
Pardshaw Cumb 136 F3
Parham Suffk 79 G3
Park D & G 154 F4
Park Nthumb 149 H3
Park Corner Oxon 42 B3
Park Crematorium
Lancs............................120 E5
Parkend Gloucs 54 E6
Parkers Green Kent 33 G4
Park Farm Kent.................34 D6
Parkgate Ches W..............111 J6
Parkgate D & G................155 H4
Park Gate Hants 17 G2
Park Gate Leeds 123 J3
Parkgate Surrey 31 K3
Parkgrove
Crematorium
Angus...........................196 F6
Parkhall W Duns 174 E4
Parkham Devon 22 F6
Parkmill Swans 51 G7
Park Royal Gt Lon............44 D4
Parkside Dur 151 K5
Parkside N Lans 175 L6
Parkstone Poole 15 J4
Park Street Herts 59 J6
Park Wood
Crematorium
Calder 123 G6
Parndon Essex 60 C6
Parndon Wood
Crematorium
Essex.............................60 C6
Parracombe Devon 23 L3
Parson Drove Cambs........89 L2
Parson's Heath Essex.......62 B3
Partick C Glas 174 F5
Partington Traffd 113 G3
Partney Lincs 118 F7
Parton Cumb 136 D3
Partridge Green
W Susx............................19 G2
Parwich Derbys 100 D2
Passenham Nhants............73 L6
Paston Norfk 107 G5
Patcham Br & H.................19 J4
Patching W Susx................18 E4
Patchway S Glos................38 E4
Pateley Bridge N York....132 B6
Pathhead Fife 186 E8
Pathhead Mdloth 177 K5
Path of Condie P & K.....185 M5
Patna E Ayrs....................163 K7
Patney Wilts 40 B8
Patrick IoM 237 b5
Patrick Brompton
N York...........................132 C2
Patricroft Salfd 113 H2
Patrington E R Yk...........127 H6
Patrington Haven
E R Yk 127 H6
Patrixbourne Kent............35 G4
Patterdale Cumb.............137 L4

Pattingham Staffs..........84 E4
Pattishall Nhants..........73 J4
Pattiswick Green
 Essex..........61 K3
Paul Cnwll..........2 E5
Paulerspury Nhants..........73 K5
Paull E R Yk..........126 E5
Paul's Dene Wilts..........28 C5
Paulton BaNES..........26 F1
Pauperhaugh
 Nthumb..........158 D3
Pavenham Bed..........74 E4
Pawlett Somset..........25 L3
Paxford Gloucs..........71 L6
Paxton Border..........179 J7
Payhembury Devon..........12 E3
Paythorne Lancs..........122 C1
Peacehaven E Susx..........19 L5
Peak District National
 Park..........114 D3
Peak Forest Derbys..........114 C5
Peakirk C Pete..........89 H3
Peasedown St John
 BaNES..........39 G8
Peaseland Green
 Norfk..........92 C1
Peasemore W Berk..........41 J5
Peasenhall Suffk..........79 H2
Pease Pottage
 W Susx..........31 L5
Peaslake Surrey..........31 H3
Peasley Cross St Hel..........112 D3
Peasmarsh E Susx..........21 H2
Peathill Abers..........217 H2
Peat Inn Fife..........187 G5
Peatling Magna Leics..........87 H5
Peatling Parva Leics..........87 H5
Pebmarsh Essex..........77 J7
Pebworth Worcs..........71 K5
Pecket Well Calder..........122 E5
Peckforton Ches E..........98 D2
Peckham Gt Lon..........45 G5
Peckleton Leics..........86 F4
Pedlinge Kent..........34 F7
Pedmore Dudley..........85 G6
Pedwell Somset..........26 B4
Peebles Border..........166 C2
Peel IoM..........237 b4
Peene Kent..........35 G6
Pegsdon C Beds..........59 J2
Pegswood Nthumb..........159 G5
Pegwell Kent..........35 K2
Peinchorran Highld..........209 H7
Peinlich Highld..........208 F3
Peldon Essex..........62 B5
Pelsall Wsall..........85 H3
Pelton Dur..........151 G4
Pelynt Cnwll..........5 K5
Pemberton Carmth..........51 G5
Pemberton Wigan..........112 D2
Pembrey Carmth..........50 E5
Pembridge Herefs..........69 H3
Pembroke Pembks..........49 G7
Pembroke Dock
 Pembks..........49 G6
Pembrokeshire Coast
 National Park
 Pembks..........48 E4
Pembury Kent..........33 G5
Pen-allt Herefs..........54 E3
Penallt Mons..........54 D6
Penally Pembks..........49 J7
Penarth V Glam..........37 J6
Pen-bont
 Rhydybeddau
 Cerdgn..........80 F6
Penbryn Cerdgn..........65 J4
Pencader Carmth..........66 B7
Pencaitland E Loth..........177 L5
Pencarnisiog IoA..........108 D6
Pencarreg Carmth..........66 C5
Pencelli Powys..........53 H3
Penclawdd Swans..........51 G6
Pencoed Brdgnd..........36 E4
Pencombe Herefs..........69 L4
Pencraig Herefs..........54 E4

Pencraig Powys..........97 G6
Pendeen Cnwll..........2 C4
Penderyn Rhondd..........52 E6
Pendine Carmth..........50 B4
Pendlebury Salfd..........113 H2
Pendleton Lancs..........121 L3
Pendock Worcs..........55 H2
Pendoggett Cnwll..........8 D8
Pendomer Somset..........13 M1
Pendoylan V Glam..........37 G5
Penegoes Powys..........81 G4
Pen-ffordd Pembks..........49 J3
Pengam Caerph..........37 J2
Pengam Cardif..........37 K5
Penge Gt Lon..........45 G6
Pengelly Cnwll..........8 E7
Penhallow Cnwll..........3 K2
Penhalvean Cnwll..........3 J4
Penhill Swindn..........40 D3
Penhow Newpt..........38 B3
Penicuik Mdloth..........177 H6
Penifiler Highld..........209 G6
Peninver Ag & B..........161 J4
Penistone Barns..........114 E2
Penkill S Ayrs..........152 F3
Penkridge Staffs..........85 G2
Penley Wrexhm..........98 B4
Penllyn V Glam..........36 F5
Penmachno Conwy..........96 C3
Penmaen Caerph..........37 J2
Penmaen Swans..........51 G7
Penmaenmawr
 Conwy..........109 K6
Penmaenpool Gwynd..........95 M8
Penmark V Glam..........37 G6
Penmount
 Crematorium
 Cnwll..........4 C6
Penmynydd IoA..........109 G6
Penn Bucks..........42 F2
Pennal Gwynd..........80 F4
Pennan Abers..........216 F2
Pennant Powys..........81 J4
Pennerley Shrops..........83 G4
Pennines..........122 E4
Pennington Cumb..........128 F4
Pennorth Powys..........53 H3
Penn Street Bucks..........42 F2
Penny Bridge Cumb..........129 G3
Pennycross Ag & B..........181 G3
Pennyghael Ag & B..........181 H3
Pennyglen S Ayrs..........163 H7
Pennymoor Devon..........11 K3
Pennywell Sundld..........151 J4
Penparc Cerdgn..........65 H5
Penperlleni Mons..........53 L6
Penpoll Cnwll..........5 J5
Penponds Cnwll..........3 H4
Penpont D & G..........154 E4
Pen-rhiw Pembks..........65 H6
Penrhiwceiber
 Rhondd..........37 G2
Pen Rhiwfawr Neath..........51 L4
Penrhiw-llan Cerdgn..........65 K6
Penrhiw-pal Cerdgn..........65 K5
Penrhos Gwynd..........94 F5
Penrhos Mons..........54 B5
Penrhyn Bay Conwy..........110 A5
Penrhyndeudraeth
 Gwynd..........95 K5
Penrice Swans..........50 F7
Penrioch N Ayrs..........161 L1
Penrith Cumb..........138 D2
Penrose Cnwll..........4 D2
Penruddock Cumb..........138 D2
Penryn Cnwll..........3 K4
Pensarn Conwy..........110 C5
Pensax Worcs..........70 C2
Penselwood Somset..........27 H5
Pensford BaNES..........38 F7
Pensham Worcs..........71 G5
Penshaw Sundld..........151 H4
Penshurst Kent..........32 F4
Pensilva Cnwll..........5 L2
Pentewan Cnwll..........4 F6
Pentir Gwynd..........109 H7

Pentire Cnwll..........4 C4
Pentlow Essex..........77 J5
Pentney Norfk..........91 G2
Pentonbridge Cumb..........156 D6
Penton Mewsey
 Hants..........29 G3
Pentraeth IoA..........109 G5
Pentre Mons..........54 B7
Pentre Rhondd..........36 F2
Pentre Shrops..........98 A8
Pentrebach Myr Td..........53 G7
Pentre-bach Powys..........52 E2
Pentre Berw IoA..........108 F6
Pentrebychan
 Crematorium
 Wrexhm..........97 L3
Pentre-celyn Denbgs..........97 J2
Pentre-celyn Powys..........81 J3
Pentre-chwyth
 Swans..........51 J6
Pentre-cwrt Carmth..........65 L6
Pentredwr Denbgs..........97 J3
Pentrefelin Gwynd..........95 J5
Pentrefoelas Conwy..........96 D3
Pentregat Cerdgn..........65 K4
Pentre-Gwenlais
 Carmth..........51 H3
Pentre Hodrey
 Shrops..........83 G7
Pentre Llanrhaeadr
 Denbgs..........110 F8
Pentre Meyrick
 V Glam..........36 E5
Pentre-tafarn-y-
 fedw Conwy..........96 C1
Pentrich Derbys..........101 G3
Pentridge Dorset..........28 B7
Pen-twyn Mons..........54 D6
Pentwynmaur
 Caerph..........37 J2
Pentyrch Cardif..........37 H4
Penwithick Cnwll..........5 G5
Penybanc Carmth..........51 H2
Penybont Powys..........68 C2
Pen-y-bont Powys..........97 K7
Pen-y-bont-fawr
 Powys..........97 G7
Pen-y-bryn Pembks..........65 G6
Penycae Wrexhm..........97 L4
Pen-y-clawdd Mons..........54 C6
Pen-y-coedcae
 Rhondd..........37 G3
Pen-y-cwn Pembks..........48 E3
Pen-y-felin Flints..........111 G7
Penyffordd Flints..........97 L1
Pen-y-Garnedd
 Powys..........97 H7
Pen-y-graig Gwynd..........94 D5
Penygraig Rhondd..........36 F3
Penygroes Carmth..........51 H3
Penygroes Gwynd..........95 H2
Pen-y-Mynydd
 Carmth..........50 F5
Penymynydd Flints..........97 L1
Penysarn IoA..........108 F4
Pen-y-stryt Denbgs..........97 J3
Penywaun Rhondd..........52 F6
Penzance Cnwll..........2 E5
Peopleton Worcs..........71 G4
Peplow Shrops..........98 F7
Perceton N Ayrs..........163 J2
Percyhorner Abers..........217 H2
Perelle Guern..........236 B3
Perham Down Wilts..........28 E2
Periton Somset..........24 E3
Perivale Gt Lon..........44 D4
Perkins Village
 Devon..........12 B4
Perlethorpe Notts..........115 M7
Perranarworthal
 Cnwll..........3 K4
Perranporth Cnwll..........3 K1
Perranuthnoe Cnwll..........2 F5
Perranwell Cnwll..........3 K4
Perranzabuloe Cnwll..........3 K2
Perry Barr Birm..........85 J5

Perry Barr
 Crematorium
 Birm..........85 J5
Perry Green Wilts..........39 L3
Pershall Staffs..........99 J6
Pershore Worcs..........71 G5
Pertenhall Bed..........74 F2
Perth P & K..........186 B3
Perth Crematorium
 P & K..........186 A3
Perthy Shrops..........98 A5
Perton Herefs..........69 L6
Perton Staffs..........84 F4
Peterborough C Pete..........89 H4
Peterborough
 Crematorium
 C Pete..........89 H3
Peterborough
 Services Cambs..........89 G5
Peterchurch Herefs..........69 G6
Peterculter C Aber..........206 F5
Peterhead Abers..........217 L5
Peterlee Dur..........151 K6
Petersfield Hants..........30 C6
Peter's Green Herts..........59 J4
Petersham Gt Lon..........44 D5
Peters Marland
 Devon..........10 C3
Peterstone
 Wentlooge Newpt..........37 K4
Peterston-super-Ely
 V Glam..........37 G5
Peterstow Herefs..........54 E3
Peter Tavy Devon..........6 D1
Petham Kent..........34 F4
Petherwin Gate Cnwll..........9 H6
Petrockstow Devon..........10 D3
Pett E Susx..........21 H3
Pettaugh Suffk..........78 E3
Petterden Angus..........196 C7
Pettinain S Lans..........165 J2
Pettistree Suffk..........79 G4
Petton Devon..........24 F6
Petts Wood Gt Lon..........45 J6
Pettycur Fife..........177 H2
Pettymuk Abers..........207 G1
Petworth W Susx..........31 G6
Pevensey E Susx..........20 D5
Pevensey Bay E Susx..........20 D5
Pewsey Wilts..........40 D7
Phepson Worcs..........71 G3
Philham Devon..........22 D6
Philiphaugh Border..........166 F4
Phillack Cnwll..........2 F4
Philleigh Cnwll..........4 D7
Philpstoun W Loth..........176 E3
Phoenix Green
 Hants..........30 C1
Phones Highld..........203 G6
Pibsbury Somset..........26 C6
Pickburn Donc..........115 K1
Pickering N York..........134 C3
Pickford Covtry..........86 C6
Pickhill N York..........132 E3
Picklescott Shrops..........83 J4
Pickmere Ches E..........113 G6
Pickney Somset..........25 J5
Pickwell Leics..........87 L2
Pickworth Lincs..........103 H5
Pickworth Rutlnd..........88 E2
Picton Ches W..........112 B7
Picton N York..........141 K5
Piddinghoe E Susx..........19 L5
Piddington Nhants..........74 B4
Piddington Oxon..........57 M5
Piddlehinton Dorset..........14 D3
Piddletrenthide
 Dorset..........14 D3
Pidley Cambs..........89 K7
Piercebridge Darltn..........140 F4
Pierowall Ork..........234 c3
Pilgrims Hatch Essex..........45 L2
Pilham Lincs..........116 E3
Pillaton Cnwll..........6 A3
Pillerton Hersey
 Warwks..........72 C5

Pillerton Priors
Warwks.....................72 C5
Pilley Barns.................115 G2
Pilley Hants..................16 D3
Pilling Lancs................120 E2
Pilning S Glos...............38 D4
Pilsbury Derbys.............114 C8
Pilsdon Dorset..............13 K3
Pilsley Derbys..............101 H1
Pilsley Derbys..............114 E7
Pilson Green Norfk........93 H2
Piltdown E Susx.............19 L2
Pilton Devon.................23 J5
Pilton Nhants................88 E6
Pilton Rutlnd................88 D3
Pilton Somset...............26 E3
Pimperne Dorset............15 G1
Pinchbeck Lincs.............103 L7
Pin Green Herts..............59 L3
Pinhoe Devon.................12 C4
Pinley Green Warwks.......72 B2
Pinminnoch S Ayrs.........152 E4
Pinmore S Ayrs.............152 E4
Pinn Devon....................12 E5
Pinner Gt Lon................43 J3
Pinner Green Gt Lon.......43 J3
Pinvin Worcs.................71 G5
Pinwherry S Ayrs...........152 E5
Pinxton Derbys.............101 J2
Pipe and Lyde Herefs......69 K5
Pipe Aston Herefs..........69 J1
Pipe Gate Shrops...........99 G4
Piperhill Highld.............213 K4
Pipewell Nhants.............88 B6
Pirbright Surrey.............30 F1
Pirnie Border................167 K4
Pirnmill N Ayrs.............161 L1
Pirton Herts.................59 J2
Pishill Oxon..................42 B3
Pistyll Gwynd................94 F4
Pitagowan P & K............194 C3
Pitblae Abers...............217 J2
Pitcairngreen P & K.......185 M3
Pitcalnie Highld............223 H6
Pitcaple Abers.............206 D1
Pitcarity Angus............196 B4
Pitchcombe Gloucs..........55 J6
Pitchcott Bucks.............58 C4
Pitchford Shrops............83 K3
Pitch Green Bucks..........58 C7
Pitchroy Moray.............214 E6
Pitcombe Somset............26 F5
Pitcox E Loth...............178 E4
Pitfichie Abers.............206 D3
Pitglassie Abers............216 D5
Pitgrudy Highld.............223 H3
Pitlessie Fife..............186 E5
Pitlochry P & K.............194 E5
Pitmachie Abers............216 C8
Pitmain Highld.............203 H5
Pitmedden Abers............217 G8
Pitmedden Garden
Abers.....................217 G8
Pitminster Somset..........25 K7
Pitmuies Angus.............196 F6
Pitmunie Abers.............206 C3
Pitney Somset...............26 C5
Pitroddie P & K.............186 C3
Pitscottie Fife.............187 G5
Pitsea Essex.................46 C3
Pitsford Nhants.............73 L2
Pitstone Bucks...............58 F5
Pittarrow Abers............197 H2
Pittenweem Fife............187 J6
Pitteuchar Fife.............186 D7
Pittington Dur..............151 H6
Pittodrie House
Hotel Abers..............206 D1
Pitton Wilts..................28 E5
Pittulie Abers..............217 H2
Pity Me Dur.................151 G5
Pixham Surrey................31 K2
Plains N Lans...............175 L5
Plaish Shrops................83 K4
Plaistow Gt Lon.............45 H4
Plaistow W Susx.............31 G5

Plaitford Hants.............28 F7
Platt Kent.....................33 G2
Plawsworth Dur............151 G5
Plaxtol Kent..................33 G3
Playden E Susx..............21 H2
Playford Suffk...............78 F5
Play Hatch Oxon............42 C5
Playing Place Cnwll..........4 C7
Playley Green Gloucs......55 H2
Plealey Shrops...............83 H3
Plean Stirlg.................175 L2
Pleasance Fife..............186 D5
Pleasington Bl w D..........121 J5
Pleasington
Crematorium
Bl w D....................121 J5
Pleasley Derbys.............115 J8
Pleinheaume Guern.........236 d2
Plemont Jersey.............236 a5
Plemstall Ches W............112 C7
Pleshey Essex................61 G5
Plockton Highld............210 C7
Plowden Shrops..............83 H6
Pluckley Kent................34 B5
Pluckley Thorne Kent......34 B5
Plumbland Cumb............147 K6
Plumley Ches E.............113 G6
Plumpton Cumb.............148 E7
Plumpton E Susx.............19 K3
Plumpton Nhants............73 H5
Plumpton Green
E Susx.....................19 K3
Plumstead Gt Lon...........45 J4
Plumstead Norfk...........106 D5
Plumtree Notts.............101 L6
Plungar Leics...............102 C5
Plurenden Kent..............34 C7
Plush Dorset.................14 D3
Plwmp Cerdgn...............65 K4
Plymouth C Plym.............6 C5
Plymouth Airport
C Plym......................6 D4
Plympton C Plym.............6 D5
Plymstock C Plym...........6 D5
Plymtree Devon.............12 D2
Pockley N York.............133 K3
Pocklington E R Yk........125 J2
Podimore Somset............26 D6
Podington Bed...............74 D3
Podmore Staffs..............99 H5
Pointon Lincs...............103 J6
Pokesdown Bmouth..........15 L4
Polbain Highld.............224 B6
Polbathic Cnwll..............6 A4
Polbeth W Loth............176 D5
Poldark Mine Cnwll...........3 H5
Polebrook Nhants............88 F6
Polegate E Susx.............20 C5
Polesden Lacey
Surrey.....................31 J2
Polesworth Warwks.........86 C3
Polglass Highld............224 C6
Polgooth Cnwll................4 F5
Polgown D & G..............154 C2
Poling W Susx................18 E5
Poling Corner W Susx......18 E5
Polkerris Cnwll................5 H5
Pollington E R Yk..........124 F6
Polloch Highld..............190 F3
Pollokshaws C Glas........175 G6
Pollokshields C Glas.......175 G5
Polmassick Cnwll.............4 F6
Polmont Falk................176 C3
Polnish Highld..............200 B8
Polperro Cnwll................5 K5
Polruan Cnwll..................5 H5
Polstead Suffk...............78 B6
Poltalloch Ag & B..........182 B7
Poltimore Devon.............12 C3
Polton Mdloth..............177 J5
Polwarth Border...........178 F7
Polyphant Cnwll..............9 H7
Polzeath Cnwll................4 E1
Pomathorn Mdloth.........177 H6
Pondersbridge
Cambs......................89 J5

Ponders End Gt Lon........45 G2
Ponsanooth Cnwll.............3 K4
Ponsworthy Devon...........7 G2
Pont Abraham
Services Carmth.........51 H4
Pontac Jersey...............236 e8
Pontantwn Carmth.........50 F3
Pontardawe Neath..........51 K5
Pontarddulais Swans.......51 H5
Pont-ar-gothi Carmth......51 G2
Pontarsais Carmth..........66 B8
Pontblyddyn Flints..........97 L1
Pontcysyllte
Aqueduct
Wrexhm....................97 L4
Pontefract Wakefd..........124 C6
Pontefract
Crematorium
Wakefd.....................124 C6
Ponteland Nthumb..........158 F7
Ponterwyd Cerdgn...........81 G7
Pontesbury Shrops..........83 H3
Pontesford Shrops..........83 H3
Pontfadog Wrexhm...........97 K5
Pontfaen Pembks.............64 E7
Pont-faen Powys..............67 L7
Pontgarreg Cerdgn..........65 K4
Ponthenry Carmth..........50 F4
Ponthir Torfn.................37 M2
Ponthirwaun Cerdgn........65 J5
Pontllanfraith Caerph......37 J2
Pontlliw Swans...............51 H5
Pontlottyn Caerph...........53 H6
Pontlyfni Gwynd..............95 G3
Pontneddfechan
Neath......................52 D6
Pontnewydd Torfn...........37 L2
Pontrhydfendigaid
Cerdgn.....................67 G2
Pont-rhyd-y-fen
Neath......................36 C2
Pontrhydygroes
Cerdgn.....................81 G8
Pontrilas Herefs.............54 B5
Pont Robert Powys..........82 C2
Pontshaen Cerdgn...........66 B5
Pontsticill Myr Td...........53 G5
Pontwelly Carmth............65 L6
Pontyates Carmth...........50 F4
Pontyberem Carmth.........51 G4
Pontybodkin Flints..........97 L2
Pontyclun Rhondd...........37 G4
Pontycymer Brdgnd.........36 D3
Pont-y-pant Conwy..........96 B2
Pontypool Torfn.............53 L7
Pontypridd Rhondd.........37 G3
Pontywaun Caerph...........37 K2
Pool Cnwll......................3 H3
Pool Leeds....................123 J2
Poole Poole....................15 J4
Poole Crematorium
Poole.......................15 J3
Poole Keynes Gloucs.......39 M2
Poolewe Highld.............219 K5
Pooley Bridge Cumb.......138 C3
Poolfold Staffs...............99 K1
Poolhill Gloucs...............55 G3
Pool of Muckhart
Clacks.....................185 L7
Pool Street Essex...........77 H6
Poplar Gt Lon.................45 G4
Porchfield IoW................16 F4
Poringland Norfk.............92 F3
Porkellis Cnwll.................3 J5
Porlock Somset...............24 D3
Porlock Weir Somset.......24 D2
Portachoillan Ag & B......172 C6
Port-an-Eorna Highld.....210 B7
Port Appin Ag & B.........191 H7
Port Askaig Ag & B........171 H5
Portavadie Ag & B.........172 F4
Port Bannatyne
Ag & B....................173 J5
Portbury N Som..............38 D5
Port Carlisle Cumb........147 M3
Port Charlotte Ag & B....170 E6

Portchester Hants..........17 H2
Portchester
Crematorium
Hants......................17 H2
Port Driseach Ag & B.....173 G4
Port Ellen Ag & B..........160 C1
Port Elphinstone
Abers.....................206 E2
Portencalzie D & G........152 B7
Portencross N Ayrs........173 K8
Port Erin IoM................237 a6
Portesham Dorset...........14 B5
Portessie Moray............215 K2
Port Eynon Swans...........50 F7
Portfield Gate
Pembks.....................48 F4
Portgate Devon...............10 B7
Port Gaverne Cnwll..........8 D8
Port Glasgow Inver........174 C4
Portgordon Moray..........215 J2
Portgower Highld..........227 H5
Porth Cnwll......................4 C4
Porth Rhondd..................36 F3
Porthallow Cnwll..............3 K6
Porthallow Cnwll..............5 K5
Porthcawl Brdgnd...........36 C5
Porthcothan Cnwll............4 D2
Porthcurno Cnwll.............2 C6
Port Henderson
Highld.....................219 H6
Porthgain Pembks...........64 A7
Porthgwarra Cnwll...........2 C6
Porthkerry V Glam..........37 G6
Porthleven Cnwll..............3 H6
Porthmadog Gwynd..........95 K5
Porth Navas Cnwll............3 K5
Porthoustock Cnwll..........3 K6
Porthpean Cnwll...............5 G5
Porthtowan Cnwll.............3 J2
Porthyrhyd Carmth...........51 G3
Portincaple Ag & B.........183 J8
Portinfer Jersey.............236 a5
Portington E R Yk..........125 J4
Portinnisherrich
Ag & B....................182 D5
Portinscale Cumb...........137 H3
Port Isaac Cnwll...............8 D8
Portishead N Som............38 C5
Portknockie Moray.........215 K2
Portland Dorset...............14 D7
Portlethen Abers............207 H6
Portling D & G...............146 F4
Portloe Cnwll...................4 E7
Port Logan D & G..........144 D6
Portmahomack
Highld.....................223 K5
Portmeirion Gwynd..........95 K5
Portmellon Cnwll..............4 F6
Port Mor Highld............189 K1
Portnacroish Ag & B.......191 H6
Portnaguran W Isls........232 g2
Portnahaven Ag & B.......170 D7
Portnalong Highld..........208 F7
Port nan Giuran
W Isls.....................232 g2
Port nan Long W Isls......232 c5
Port Nis W Isls..............232 g1
Portobello C Edin..........177 J4
Portobello Wolves...........85 G4
Port of Menteith
Stirlg......................184 D6
Port of Ness W Isls........232 g1
Porton Wilts...................28 D4
Portpatrick D & G..........144 B4
Port Quin Cnwll................8 C8
Port Ramsay Ag & B......191 H7
Portreath Cnwll................3 H3
Portreath Harbour
Cnwll........................3 H3
Portree Highld..............209 G5
Port St Mary IoM...........237 b7
Portscatho Cnwll..............4 D8
Portsea C Port................17 J3
Portskerra Highld..........230 C3
Portskewett Mons...........38 D3
Portslade Br & H............19 H4

Portslade-by-Sea
Br & H.....................19 H5
Portslogan D & G 144 B3
Portsmouth C Port.......17 J3
Portsmouth Calder......122 D5
Portsmouth
Dockyard C Port.......17 J3
Port Soderick IoM.......237 c6
Portsonachan Hotel
Ag & B....................182 F3
Portsoy Abers.............216 B2
Port Sunlight Wirral....111 K5
Portswood C Sotn........29 H8
Port Talbot Neath........36 B3
Portuairk Highld..........189 K3
Portway Worcs............85 J8
Port Wemyss Ag & B....170 D7
Port William D & G 145 H6
Portwrinkle Cnwll...........6 A5
Portyerrock D & G 145 K7
Poslingford Suffk.........77 H5
Posso Border..............166 B3
Postbridge Devon.........10 F8
Postcombe Oxon..........58 B7
Postling Kent...............34 F6
Postwick Norfk............93 G2
Potarch Abers.............206 B6
Potten End Herts..........59 G6
Potter Brompton
N York....................134 F4
Potterhanworth
Lincs.....................117 H7
Potterhanworth
Booths Lincs........117 H7
Potter Heigham
Norfk.....................107 J8
Potterne Wilts............39 M8
Potterne Wick Wilts.....39 M8
Potters Bar Herts.........59 L7
Potters Crouch Herts....59 J6
Potters Green Covtry....86 D6
Potters Marston Leics...87 G4
Potterspury Nhants.......73 L6
Potterton Abers..........207 H3
Potto N York...............141 L6
Potton C Beds..............75 J5
Pott Shrigley Ches E....113 L5
Poughill Cnwll...............9 G4
Poughill Devon............11 K3
Poulner Hants.............15 M2
Poulshot Wilts.............39 L7
Poulton Gloucs............56 C7
Poulton-le-Fylde Lancs..120 D3
Poundbury Dorset.........14 D4
Poundffald Swans.........51 H6
Pound Green E Susx......20 B2
Pound Green Suffk........77 G4
Pound Hill W Susx.........32 B5
Poundon Bucks............57 M3
Poundsgate Devon..........7 G2
Poundstock Cnwll..........9 G5
Pouton D & G..............145 K5
Povey Cross Surrey.......31 L3
Powburn Nthumb.........168 F6
Powderham Devon........12 C5
Powerstock Dorset.......13 M3
Powfoot D & G.............147 K2
Powick Worcs..............70 E4
Powmill P & K..............185 L7
Poxwell Dorset.............14 E5
Poyle Slough...............43 G5
Poynings W Susx...........19 H4
Poyntington Dorset.......26 F7
Poynton Ches E...........113 L5
Poynton Green
Wrekin....................98 E8
Praa Sands Cnwll...........3 G5
Pratt's Bottom Gt Lon...45 J7
Praze-an-Beeble
Cnwll.......................3 H4
Prees Shrops...............98 D5
Preesall Lancs............120 E2
Prees Green Shrops.......98 E6
Prees Heath Shrops.......98 E5
Prees Higher Heath
Shrops....................98 E5

Pren-gwyn Cerdgn.......65 L5
Prenteg Gwynd............95 K4
Prescot Knows...........112 C3
Prescott Devon............25 H8
Presnerb Angus..........195 J3
Prestatyn Denbgs.......110 E5
Prestbury Ches E.........113 K6
Prestbury Gloucs.........55 L4
Presteigne Powys.........69 G2
Prestleigh Somset.........26 F4
Preston Border............179 G6
Preston Br & H.............19 J4
Preston Devon..............7 K2
Preston Dorset............14 D5
Preston E R Yk...........126 F4
Preston Gloucs............56 B7
Preston Herts..............59 K3
Preston Kent...............34 D3
Preston Kent...............35 H3
Preston Lancs.............121 H4
Preston Nthumb..........169 H4
Preston Rutlnd.............88 C3
Preston Somset............25 H4
Preston Suffk...............77 L4
Preston Torbay..............7 K4
Preston Wilts..............40 B5
Preston Bagot
Warwks...................71 L2
Preston Bissett Bucks....58 A3
Preston Bowyer
Somset...................25 H6
Preston Brockhurst
Shrops....................98 D7
Preston Brook Halton ..112 E5
Preston Candover
Hants.....................29 L3
Preston Capes
Nhants....................73 H4
**Preston
Crematorium**
Lancs....................121 H4
Preston Green
Warwks...................71 L2
Preston Gubbals
Shrops....................98 C8
Preston on Stour
Warwks...................72 B4
Preston on the Hill
Halton...................112 E5
Preston on Wye
Herefs.....................69 H6
Prestonpans E Loth.....177 K4
Preston Patrick
Cumb.....................129 L3
Preston Plucknett
Somset...................26 D7
Preston-under-Scar
N York...................131 K2
**Preston upon the
Weald Moors**
Wrekin...................84 C1
Preston Wynne
Herefs.....................69 L5
Prestwich Bury...........113 J1
Prestwick S Ayrs.........163 J4
Prestwick Airport
S Ayrs...................163 J4
Prestwood Bucks..........58 E7
Prickwillow Cambs........90 E6
Priddy Somset.............26 D2
Priest Hutton Lancs.....129 L5
Priestland E Ayrs........164 B2
Priest Weston Shrops....82 F4
Primrosehill Border.....179 G6
Primsidemill Border.....168 B4
Princes Risborough
Bucks.....................58 D7
Princethorpe Warwks....72 E1
Princetown Devon..........6 E2
Priors Hardwick
Warwks...................72 F4
Priorslee Wrekin...........84 C2
Priors Marston
Warwks...................72 F3
Priors Norton Gloucs....55 K3
Priory Vale Swindn......40 C3

Priston BaNES.............39 G7
Prittlewell Sthend.........46 E3
Privett Hants...............30 B6
Prixford Devon.............23 J4
Probus Cnwll.................4 E6
Prora E Loth...............178 C3
Prospect Cumb...........147 K6
Prospidnick Cnwll...........3 H5
Protstonhill Abers........216 F2
Prudhoe Nthumb.........150 D3
Publow BaNES.............38 F7
Puckeridge Herts.........60 C4
Puckington Somset.......26 B7
Pucklechurch S Glos.....39 G5
Puddington Ches W.....111 K6
Puddington Devon.........11 J3
Puddletown Dorset.......14 E4
Pudsey Leeds.............123 J4
Pulborough W Susx......18 E3
Pulford Ches W............98 A2
Pulham Dorset..............14 D2
Pulham Market Norfk....92 E6
Pulham St Mary
Norfk.....................92 E6
Pulloxhill C Beds..........74 F7
Pumpherston W Loth....176 E4
Pumsaint Carmth..........66 E6
Puncheston Pembks.......49 G2
Puncknowle Dorset.......14 A5
Punnett's Town
E Susx....................20 C2
Purbrook Hants............17 J2
Purfleet Thurr..............45 K4
Puriton Somset............25 L3
Purleigh Essex.............61 K7
Purley Gt Lon..............44 F7
Purley W Berk.............42 A5
Purse Caundle Dorset....27 G7
Purtington Somset.......13 K2
Purton Gloucs..............54 F6
Purton Gloucs..............55 G7
Purton Wilts...............40 C3
Purton Stoke Wilts.......40 C3
Pury End Nhants..........73 K5
Pusey Oxon................41 G2
Putley Herefs..............70 B6
Putley Green Herefs.....70 B6
Putney Gt Lon..............44 E5
**Putney Vale
Crematorium**
Gt Lon...................44 E5
Puttenham Surrey.........30 F2
Puxley Nhants..............73 L6
Puxton N Som.............38 B7
Pwll Carmth................50 F5
Pwll-glâs Denbgs.........97 H2
Pwllgloyw Powys..........68 B7
Pwllheli Gwynd............94 F5
Pwllmeyric Mons..........38 D2
Pwll Trap Carmth..........50 C3
Pwll-y-glaw Neath.........36 C2
Pye Bridge Derbys......101 H3
Pyecombe W Susx........19 J3
Pyle Brdgnd................36 C4
Pyleigh Somset............25 H5
Pylle Somset...............26 E4
Pymoor Cambs............90 C6
Pymore Dorset............13 L4
Pyrford Surrey.............43 H8
Pyrton Oxon................42 B2
Pytchley Nhants..........88 C8
Pyworthy Devon...........9 J4

Quadring Lincs...........103 L6
Quadring Eaudike
Lincs....................103 L5
Quainton Bucks...........58 C4
Quantock Hills
Somset...................25 J4
Quarff Shet...............235 c6
Quarley Hants.............28 F3
Quarndon Derbys........101 G4

Quarrier's Village
Inver.....................174 C5
Quarrington Lincs........103 H4
Quarrington Hill Dur ...151 H7
Quarry Bank Dudley......85 G6
Quarrywood Moray......214 E2
Quarter N Ayrs...........173 L6
Quarter S Lans............175 J7
Quatford Shrops...........84 D5
Quatt Shrops................84 D6
Quebec Dur................150 F6
Quedgeley Gloucs.........55 J5
Queen Adelaide
Cambs.....................90 E7
Queenborough Kent......46 E5
Queen Camel Somset....26 E6
Queen Charlton
BaNES....................38 F6
**Queen Elizabeth
Forest Park** Stirlg....184 B6
Queenhill Worcs...........70 F6
Queen Oak Dorset.......27 H5
Queen's Bower IoW......17 H5
Queensbury C Brad.....123 G4
Queensferry Flints.......111 K7
Queenslie C Glas.........175 H5
Queenzieburn N Lans...175 J3
Quendon Essex............60 E3
Queniborough Leics......87 J2
Quenington Gloucs.......56 C7
Queslett Birm..............85 J4
Quethiock Cnwll.............5 L3
Quidenham Norfk.........92 B6
Quidhampton Wilts.......28 C5
Quinton Nhants............73 L4
Quintrell Downs
Cnwll.......................4 D4
Quixwood Border........179 G5
Quoig P & K...............185 H3
Quorn Leics................87 H1
Quothquan S Lans........165 J2
Quoyburray Ork..........234 c6
Quoyloo Ork...............234 b5

R

Raasay Highld............209 J5
Rachan Mill Border.....165 L3
Rachub Gwynd............109 J7
Rackenford Devon.........24 D7
Rackham W Susx..........18 E3
Rackheath Norfk..........93 G1
Racks D & G...............155 H7
Rackwick Ork.............234 a7
Radbourne Derbys.......100 F5
Radcliffe Bury............113 H1
Radcliffe on Trent
Notts....................101 M5
Radclive Bucks.............73 J7
Raddery Highld...........213 H3
Radernie Fife.............187 G5
Radford Covtry............86 D7
Radford Semele
Warwks...................72 D2
Radlett Herts..............59 K7
Radley Oxon................57 K7
Radley Green Essex......60 F6
Radnage Bucks............42 C2
Radstock BaNES...........27 G1
Radstone Nhants..........73 H6
Radway Warwks...........72 D5
Radwell Bed................74 E3
Radwell Herts..............75 J7
Radwinter Essex...........76 E6
Radyr Cardif................37 H4
Rafford Moray............214 C3
**RAF Museum
Cosford** Shrops.......84 E3
**RAF Museum
Hendon** Gt Lon.........44 E3
Ragdale Leics.............102 A8
Raglan Mons...............54 B6
Ragnall Notts.............116 D6
Raigbeg Highld...........213 J8

Rainbow Hill Worcs........70 F4
Rainford St Hel............112 C2
Rainham Gt Lon............45 K4
Rainham Medway..........46 D6
Rainhill St Hel.............112 C4
Rainhill Stoops St Hel...112 D4
Rainow Ches E.............113 L6
Rainsbrook
  Crematorium
  Warwks....................87 G8
Rainton N York............132 E4
Rainworth Notts..........101 L2
Rait P & K...................186 D3
Raithby Lincs..............118 D5
Raithby Lincs..............118 E7
Rake Hants...................30 D5
Ralia Highld................203 H5
Ramasaig Highld..........208 B5
Rame Cnwll....................3 J4
Rame Cnwll.....................6 B6
Rampisham Dorset........14 B3
Rampside Cumb...........128 F6
Rampton Cambs............76 B2
Rampton Notts.............116 D5
Ramsbottom Bury........122 B6
Ramsbury Wilts.............40 F6
Ramscraigs Highld.......227 K3
Ramsdean Hants...........30 B6
Ramsdell Hants............41 L8
Ramsden Oxon..............57 G5
Ramsden Bellhouse
  Essex.......................46 B2
Ramsey Cambs.............89 K6
Ramsey Essex..............62 E2
Ramsey IoM................237 c3
Ramsey Forty Foot
  Cambs......................89 K6
Ramsey Heights
  Cambs......................89 J6
Ramsey Island Essex....61 M6
Ramsey Island
  Pembks....................48 B3
Ramsey Mereside
  Cambs......................89 K5
Ramsey St Mary's
  Cambs......................89 J6
Ramsgate Kent.............35 K2
Ramsgill N York...........131 L5
Ramshope Nthumb.......157 J2
Ramshorn Staffs..........100 B4
Ramsnest Common
  Surrey......................30 F5
Ranby Lincs................118 B5
Ranby Notts................116 A5
Rand Lincs..................117 J5
Randalls Park
  Crematorium
  Surrey......................44 D8
Randwick Gloucs...........55 J6
Ranfurly Rens.............174 D5
Rangemore Staffs........100 D7
Rangeworthy S Glos......39 G3
Rankinston E Ayrs........163 L6
Rannoch Station
  P & K.....................193 G5
Ranscombe Somset........24 E3
Ranskill Notts.............116 A4
Ranton Staffs................99 J7
Ranton Green Staffs......99 J7
Ranworth Norfk............93 H1
Raploch Stirlg.............185 G7
Rapness Ork................234 c4
Rascarrel D & G...........146 D5
Rashfield Ag & B.........173 K2
Rashwood Worcs...........71 G2
Raskelf N York............133 G5
Rastrick Calder...........123 H6
Ratagan Highld...........200 E2
Ratby Leics..................87 G3
Ratcliffe Culey Leics.....86 D4
Ratcliffe on Soar
  Notts.....................101 J6
Ratcliffe on the
  Wreake Leics............87 J1
Rathen Abers..............217 J3
Rathillet Fife.............186 F3

Rathmell N York..........130 F7
Ratho C Edin...............176 F4
Ratho Station C Edin....176 F4
Rathven Moray............215 K2
Ratley Warwks..............72 E5
Ratling Kent.................35 H4
Ratlinghope Shrops........83 H4
Rattar Highld..............231 J2
Rattery Devon.................7 H4
Rattlesden Suffk............77 L3
Ratton Village E Susx....20 C5
Rattray P & K..............195 J7
Raunds Nhants..............88 E8
Ravenfield Rothm.........115 J3
Ravenglass Cumb.........136 F7
Raveningham Norfk.......93 H4
Ravenscar N York.........143 K6
Ravenscraig N Lans......175 K6
Ravensden Bed..............74 F4
Ravenshead Notts........101 K2
Ravensthorpe Kirk......123 J6
Ravensthorpe Nhants....73 J1
Ravenstone Leics..........86 E2
Ravenstone M Keyn........74 B4
Ravenstonedale
  Cumb.....................139 G6
Ravenstruther S Lans....165 H1
Ravensworth N York.....140 E5
Rawcliffe C York.........133 J8
Rawcliffe E R Yk.........125 G6
Rawdon Leeds.............123 J3
Rawdon
  Crematorium
  Leeds....................123 J3
Rawling Street Kent......34 B3
Rawmarsh Rothm.........115 H3
Rawreth Essex..............46 C2
Rawridge Devon............12 F2
Rawtenstall Lancs.......122 B6
Raydon Suffk................78 C6
Rayleigh Essex..............46 D2
Rayne Essex..................61 H4
Raynes Park Gt Lon.......44 E6
Reach Cambs................76 E2
Read Lancs.................122 B4
Reading Readg..............42 B5
Reading
  Crematorium
  Readg......................42 B5
Reading Services
  W Berk.....................42 A6
Reading Street Kent......34 B8
Reading Street Kent......35 K2
Reagill Cumb..............138 E4
Realwa Cnwll................3 G4
Rearquhar Highld........223 G3
Rearsby Leics...............87 J2
Reay Highld................230 D3
Reculver Kent..............47 L6
Red Ball Devon.............25 H7
Redberth Pembks..........49 J6
Redbourn Herts............59 J5
Redbourne N Linc.........116 F2
Redbrook Gloucs...........54 D6
Redbrook Wrexhm..........98 D4
Redbrook Street Kent....34 C7
Redburn Highld...........213 L5
Redcar R & Cl..............142 D3
Redcastle D & G..........146 E2
Redcastle Highld.........212 E4
Redding Falk..............176 C3
Reddingmuirhead
  Falk......................176 C3
Redditch Worcs............71 J2
Redditch
  Crematorium
  Worcs......................71 J2
Rede Suffk..................77 J4
Redenhall Norfk...........92 F6
Redesmouth Nthumb....157 L5
Redford Abers............197 J3
Redford Angus............196 F7
Redford W Susx............30 E6
Redfordgreen Border....166 E6
Redgorton P & K..........186 A2
Redgrave Suffk.............92 C7

Redhill Abers..............206 E4
Red Hill Bmouth...........15 K4
Redhill Herts................59 M2
Redhill N Som...............38 D7
Redhill Surrey..............32 B3
Redisham Suffk............93 J6
Redland Bristl..............38 E5
Redland Ork................234 b5
Redlingfield Suffk..........78 E1
Redlingfield Green
  Suffk.......................78 E1
Red Lodge Suffk............77 G1
Redlynch Somset...........27 G5
Redlynch Wilts..............28 D7
Redmarley Worcs...........70 D2
Redmarley D'Abitot
  Gloucs.....................55 H2
Redmarshall S on T......141 J3
Redmile Leics..............102 D5
Redmire N York...........131 K2
Redmyre Abers.............197 J2
Rednal Shrops...............98 A6
Redpath Border...........167 J3
Redpoint Highld..........219 H7
Red Roses Carmth.........49 L5
Red Row Nthumb.........159 G3
Redruth Cnwll................3 J3
Redstone P & K............186 C1
Red Wharf Bay IoA......109 G5
Redwick Newpt..............38 B4
Redwick S Glos.............38 D3
Redworth Darltn.........141 G3
Reed Herts...................75 L7
Reedham Norfk.............93 J3
Reedness E R Yk..........125 J6
Reeds Holme Lancs......122 B5
Reepham Lincs.............117 H6
Reepham Norfk...........106 D7
Reeth N York..............140 C7
Reeves Green Solhll......86 C7
Regil N Som.................38 D7
Reiff Highld...............224 B5
Reigate Surrey..............31 L2
Reighton N York..........135 I4
Reisque Abers.............207 G2
Reiss Highld...............231 L5
Relubbus Cnwll..............2 F5
Relugas Moray.............214 B5
Remenham Wokham......42 C4
Remenham Hill
  Wokham....................42 C4
Rempstone Notts.........101 L7
Rendcomb Gloucs..........56 A6
Rendham Suffk.............79 H2
Rendlesham Suffk.........79 H4
Renfrew Rens..............174 F5
Renhold Bed................74 F4
Renishaw Derbys.........115 J6
Rennington Nthumb....169 J5
Renton W Duns............174 D3
Renwick Cumb............149 G6
Repps Norfk.................93 J1
Repton Derbys............100 F6
Resaurie Highld..........213 H5
Resipole Highld..........190 E4
Reskadinnick Cnwll........3 H3
Resolis Highld............213 G2
Resolven Neath.............52 C7
Rest and be thankful
  Ag & B...................183 J6
Reston Border.............179 H6
Reswallie Angus...........196 E6
Retford Notts..............116 B5
Rettendon Essex............61 J7
Revesby Lincs.............103 M1
Rewe Devon..................12 B3
Rew Street IoW.............16 F4
Reydon Suffk................93 K7
Reymerston Norfk.........92 B3
Reynalton Pembks.........49 J5
Reynoldston Swans.......50 F7
Rezare Cnwll...................6 A1
Rhandirmwyn
  Carmth.....................67 H5
Rhayader Powys............67 L2
Rheindown Highld.......212 D5

Rhes-y-cae Flints.........111 G7
Rhewl Denbgs..............97 H1
Rhewl Denbgs..............97 J4
Rhicarn Highld............224 D4
Rhiconich Highld.........228 C5
Rhicullen Highld.........222 F6
Rhigos Rhondd.............52 E6
Rhireavach Highld.......220 D3
Rhives Highld.............223 H2
Rhiwbina Cardif............37 J4
Rhiwderyn Newpt..........37 K3
Rhiwlas Gwynd...........109 H7
Rhoden Green Kent........33 H4
Rhodes Minnis Kent......34 G6
Rhodiad-y-brenin
  Pembks....................48 C3
Rhonehouse D & G.......146 C3
Rhoose V Glam..............37 G6
Rhos Carmth.................65 L7
Rhos Neath..................51 L5
Rhoscolyn IoA.............108 C6
Rhoscrowther
  Pembks....................48 F6
Rhosesmor Flints.........111 H7
Rhosgoch Powys............68 D5
Rhoshill Pembks...........65 H6
Rhoshirwaun Gwynd......94 D6
Rhoslefain Gwynd..........80 D3
Rhosllanerchrugog
  Wrexhm....................97 L3
Rhosmeirch IoA...........108 F6
Rhosneigr IoA.............108 D6
Rhosnesni Wrexhm........97 M3
Rhôs-on-Sea Conwy......110 B5
Rhossili Swans..............50 E7
Rhostryfan Gwynd.........95 H2
Rhostyllen Wrexhm........97 L3
Rhosybol IoA..............108 F4
Rhos-y-gwaliau
  Gwynd......................96 E5
Rhosymedre Wrexhm......97 L4
Rhu Ag & B................174 B2
Rhualt Denbgs.............110 F6
Rhubodach Ag & B.......173 H4
Rhuddlan Denbgs.........110 E6
Rhunahaorine Ag & B...172 C8
Rhyd Gwynd.................95 L4
Rhydargaeau Carmth......50 F1
Rhydcymerau
  Carmth.....................66 D6
Rhyd-Ddu Gwynd...........95 K3
Rhydlewis Cerdgn..........65 K5
Rhydowen Cerdgn..........66 B5
Rhyd-uchaf Gwynd.........96 D5
Rhyd-y-clafdy Gwynd.....94 F5
Rhyd-y-foel Conwy.......110 C6
Rhydyfro Neath.............51 K4
Rhyd-y-groes Gwynd....109 H7
Rhyd-y pennau
  Cerdgn......................80 E6
Rhyl Denbgs...............110 D5
Rhymney Caerph............53 H6
Rhynd P & K...............186 B4
Rhynie Abers..............215 L8
Rhynie Highld.............223 J5
Ribbesford Worcs..........84 D8
Ribbleton Lancs...........121 H4
Ribchester Lancs.........121 H4
Riby Lincs.................126 F8
Riccall N York.............124 F3
Riccarton Border.........156 F3
Riccarton E Ayrs.........163 K3
Richards Castle
  Herefs......................69 J1
Richmond Gt Lon..........44 D5
Richmond N York.........140 F6
Richmond Sheff...........115 H4
Richmond Fort Guern...236 b3
Rickerscote Staffs........99 L7
Rickford N Som.............38 C8
Rickham Devon...............7 H7
Rickinghall Suffk..........92 C7
Rickling Green Essex....60 E3
Rickmansworth Herts....43 H2
Riddell Border.............167 H4
Riddlecombe Devon......10 F3

Riddlesden C Brad.........123 G3
Ridge Dorset 15 H5
Ridge Herts 59 K7
Ridge Wilts 27 L5
Ridge Lane Warwks 86 C4
Ridgeway Derbys 115 H5
Ridgewell Essex................77 G6
Ridgewood E Susx 19 M2
Ridgmont C Beds 74 E7
Riding Mill Nthumb.........150 C3
Ridlington Norfk 107 H6
Ridlington Rutlnd..............88 B3
Ridsdale Nthumb.............158 A5
Rievaulx N York 133 J3
Rigg D & G 148 B2
Riggend N Lans 175 K4
Righoul Highld 213 K4
Rigsby Lincs 118 F6
Rigside S Lans 165 G3
Riley Green Lancs 121 J5
Rilla Mill Cnwll 5 L2
Rillington N York 134 D5
Rimington Lancs 122 B2
Rimpton Somset 26 E6
Rimswell E R Yk..............127 H5
Rinaston Pembks 49 G3
Rindleford Shrops............84 D4
Ringford D & G 146 C4
Ringland Norfk 92 D2
Ringmer E Susx 19 L3
Ringmore Devon 6 F6
Ringmore Devon 7 L2
Ringorm Moray................215 G5
Ringsfield Suffk 93 J5
Ringsfield Corner
  Suffk 93 J6
Ringshall Herts 59 G5
Ringshall Suffk 78 C4
Ringshall Stocks
  Suffk 78 C4
Ringstead Nhants 88 E7
Ringstead Norfk 105 H4
Ringwood Hants 15 L2
Ringwould Kent 35 K5
Ripe E Susx 20 B4
Ripley Derbys 101 H3
Ripley Hants 15 M3
Ripley N York...................132 D7
Ripley Surrey 31 H1
Riplington Hants 30 A6
Ripon N York 132 D5
Rippingale Lincs 103 H6
Ripple Kent.......................35 J5
Ripple Worcs 70 F6
Ripponden Calder 122 F6
Risabus Ag & B................160 B2
Risbury Herefs 69 K4
Risby Suffk 77 H2
Risca Caerph 37 K3
Rise E R Yk 126 E3
Risegate Lincs 103 K6
Riseley Bed 74 F3
Riseley Wokham 42 B7
Rishangles Suffk 78 E2
Rishton Lancs 121 L4
Rishworth Calder 122 F6
Risley Derbys 101 J5
Risley Warrtn 112 K3
Risplith N York 132 C5
River Kent.........................35 J6
River W Susx 30 F6
Riverford Highld 212 E4
Riverhead Kent 32 F3
Rivington Lancs...............121 J7
Rivington Services
  Lancs 121 J7
Roade Nhants 73 L4
Roadmeetings S Lans 176 B7
Roadside E Ayrs 164 B5
Roadside Highld 231 H4
Roadwater Somset............25 G4
Roag Highld 208 D5
Roan of Craigoch
  S Ayrs 153 G2
Roath Cardif 37 J5
Roberton Border 166 F6

Roberton S Lans 165 H4
Robertsbridge E Susx.......20 E2
Roberttown Kirk 123 J6
Robeston Wathen
  Pembks 49 J4
Robgill Tower D & G.......155 M7
Robin Hood
  Crematorium
  Solhll 85 K7
Robin Hood
  Doncaster
  Sheffield Airport
  Donc 115 M2
Robin Hood's Bay
  N York...........................143 K6
Roborough Devon 6 D4
Roborough Devon 10 E2
Roby Knows 112 B4
Rocester Staffs 100 C5
Roch Pembks 48 E3
Rochdale Rochdl 122 D7
Rochdale
  Crematorium
  Rochdl 122 C7
Roche Cnwll 4 F4
Rochester Medway 46 C6
Rochester Nthumb...........157 L3
Rochford Essex 46 E3
Rochford Worcs 70 B2
Rock Cnwll 4 E2
Rock Nthumb 169 J5
Rock Worcs 70 D1
Rockbeare Devon 12 C4
Rockbourne Hants 28 C7
Rockcliffe Cumb 148 C3
Rockcliffe D & G 146 E4
Rockend Torbay...................7 L4
Rock Ferry Wirral 111 K4
Rockfield Highld 223 K5
Rockfield Mons 54 C5
Rockford Devon 24 B2
Rockhampton S Glos 38 F2
Rockhill Shrops 82 F7
Rockingham Nhants...........88 C5
Rockland All Saints
  Norfk 92 B4
Rockland St Mary
  Norfk 93 G3
Rockland St Peter
  Norfk 92 B4
Rockley Notts 116 B6
Rockville Ag & B 173 L1
Rockwell End Bucks 42 D3
Rodborough Gloucs...........55 J6
Rodbourne Swindn............40 C4
Rodbourne Wilts 39 L4
Rodden Dorset 14 B5
Rode Somset 27 J2
Rode Heath Ches E 99 J2
Rodel W Isls 232 d5
Roden Wrekin 83 L1
Rodhuish Somset 24 F4
Rodington Wrekin..............83 L1
Rodington Heath
  Wrekin...........................83 L1
Rodley Gloucs 55 H5
Rodmarton Gloucs.............39 L2
Rodmell E Susx 19 L4
Rodmersham Kent 34 B3
Rodmersham Green
  Kent...............................34 B3
Rodney Stoke Somset........26 C2
Rodsley Derbys 100 D4
Roecliffe N York 132 E6
Roe Green Herts 59 K6
Roe Green Herts 75 K7
Roehampton Gt Lon 44 E5
Roffey W Susx 31 K5
Rogart Highld 226 C7
Rogate W Susx 30 D6
Rogerstone Newpt.............37 L3
Roghadal W Isls 232 d5
Rogiet Mons 38 C3
Roke Oxon 41 L2
Roker Sundld 151 J3
Rollesby Norfk 93 J1

Rolleston Leics..................87 K4
Rolleston Notts 102 C3
Rolleston on Dove
  Staffs 100 E6
Rolston E R Yk.................126 F2
Rolvenden Kent 33 L6
Rolvenden Layne
  Kent...............................33 L7
Romaldkirk Dur...............140 C3
Romanby N York 132 E2
Romanno Bridge
  Border 177 G8
Romansleigh Devon 24 B7
Romesdal Highld 208 F4
Romford Dorset 15 K1
Romford Gt Lon.................45 K3
Romiley Stockp................113 L4
Romsey Hants 29 G6
Romsley Shrops.................84 D6
Romsley Worcs 85 G7
Rona Highld......................209 K3
Ronachan Ag & B 172 C7
Rookhope Dur 150 B6
Rookley IoW......................17 G5
Rooks Bridge Somset........26 A2
Rooks Nest Somset............25 H5
Rookwith N York 132 C3
Roos E R Yk.....................127 G4
Roothams Green Bed.........75 G3
Ropley Hants 29 M5
Ropley Dean Hants 29 L5
Ropsley Lincs 103 G5
Rora Abers 217 K4
Rorrington Shrops 82 F4
Rosarie Moray..................215 J4
Rose Cnwll 3 K1
Rose Ash Devon 24 C6
Rosebank S Lans..............175 L2
Rosebush Pembks 49 J2
Rosedale Abbey
  N York...........................142 F7
Rose Green Essex 61 L3
Rose Green Suffk...............77 L5
Rose Green Suffk...............77 L6
Rose Green W Susx 18 B5
Rosehall Highld 225 K7
Rosehearty Abers 217 H2
Rose Hill Lancs 122 C4
Roseisle Moray.................214 E2
Roselands E Susx...............20 C5
Rosemarket Pembks 49 G5
Rosemarkie Highld 213 H3
Rosemary Lane
  Devon 25 J7
Rosemount P & K.............195 J7
Rosenannon Cnwll..............4 E3
Rosewell Mdloth 177 J6
Roseworth S on T 141 K3
Rosgill Cumb....................138 D4
Roskhill Highld 208 D5
Rosley Cumb....................148 B6
Roslin Mdloth 177 H5
Rosliston Derbys 86 B1
Rosneath Ag & B 174 B2
Ross D & G 146 B6
Rossett Wrexhm 98 A2
Rossett Green N York 132 D8
Rossington Donc 115 L2
Rossland Rens 174 E4
Ross-on-Wye Herefs..........54 E4
Roster Highld 231 J7
Rostherne Ches E.............113 H5
Rosthwaite Cumb.............137 H4
Roston Derbys 100 C4
Rosyth Fife.......................176 F2
Rothbury Nthumb.............158 D2
Rotherby Leics...................87 J1
Rotherfield E Susx 32 F7
Rotherfield Greys
  Oxon 42 B4
Rotherfield Peppard
  Oxon 42 B4
Rotherham Rothm 115 H3
Rotherham
  Crematorium
  Rothm 115 J3

Rothersthorpe
  Nhants............................73 K3
Rotherwick Hants 30 B1
Rothes Moray...................215 G4
Rothesay Ag & B 173 J5
Rothiebrisbane Abers.......216 E6
Rothiemay Moray..............215 M5
Rothiemurchus
  Lodge Highld..................204 B4
Rothiemurchus
  Visitor Centre
  Highld............................203 L3
Rothienorman Abers........216 D7
Rothley Leics.....................87 H2
Rothmaise Abers..............216 D7
Rothwell Leeds 123 L5
Rothwell Lincs 117 J2
Rothwell Nhants 88 B7
Rottal Lodge Angus...........196 B3
Rottingdean Br & H 19 K5
Rottington Cumb 136 D5
Roucan D & G 155 H6
Roucan Loch
  Crematorium
  D & G 155 H6
Rougham Norfk 105 K7
Rougham Suffk 77 K3
Rough Common Kent 34 F3
Roughpark Abers 205 H3
Roughton Lincs 118 C8
Roughton Norfk................106 F5
Roughton Shrops 84 D5
Roundbush Green
  Essex 60 F5
Round Green Luton 59 J4
Roundham Somset.............13 K1
Roundhay Leeds 123 L3
Roundway Wilts 40 A7
Roundyhill Angus..............196 C6
Rousay Ork.......................234 c4
Rousdon Devon 13 H4
Rousham Oxon 57 J3
Rous Lench Worcs.............71 H4
Routenburn N Ayrs 173 L6
Routh E R Yk...................126 D3
Row Cumb 129 K2
Rowanburn D & G 156 D6
Rowardennan Stirlg 183 L7
Rowarth Derbys 114 A4
Rowberrow Somset 38 C8
Rowde Wilts 39 L7
Rowen Conwy...................109 L6
Rowfoot Nthumb 149 H3
Rowhedge Essex 62 B4
Rowington Warwks...........72 B2
Rowland Derbys 114 E6
Rowland's Castle
  Hants 17 K1
Rowland's Gill Gatesd......150 E4
Rowledge Surrey 30 D3
Rowley Dur 150 D5
Rowley Regis Sandw..........85 H6
Rowley Regis
  Crematorium
  Sandw 85 G6
Rowlstone Herefs 54 A3
Rowly Surrey.....................31 H4
Rowner Hants 17 H3
Rowney Green Worcs.........71 J1
Rownhams Hants...............29 G7
Rownhams Services
  Hants 29 H7
Rowrah Cumb 136 E4
Rowsham Bucks 58 D4
Rowsley Derbys 114 E7
Rowston Lincs 103 H2
Rowton Ches W................112 C8
Rowton Wrekin..................98 E8
Roxburgh Border 167 L4
Roxby N Lincs 125 L6
Roxton Bed 75 G4
Roxwell Essex 61 G6
Royal Leamington
  Spa Warwks 72 D2
Royal Sutton
  Coldfield Birm.................85 K4

Royal Tunbridge
Wells Kent 33 G5
Royal Wootton
Bassett Wilts 40 B4
Royal Yacht
Britannia C Edin 177 H3
Roy Bridge Highld 192 D1
Roydon Essex 60 C6
Roydon Norfk 92 D7
Roydon Norfk 105 H7
Roydon Hamlet Essex 60 L6
Royston Barns 124 B7
Royston Herts 75 L6
Royton Oldham 122 D8
Rozel Jersey 236 e6
Ruabon Wrexhm 97 L4
Ruaig Ag & B 188 D6
Ruan Lanihorne Cnwll 4 D7
Ruan Major Cnwll 3 J7
Ruan Minor Cnwll 3 J7
Ruardean Gloucs 54 F4
Ruardean Hill Gloucs 54 F5
Ruardean Woodside
Gloucs 54 F5
Rubery Birm 85 H7
Rubha Ban W Isls 233 c9
Ruckhall Herefs 69 J6
Ruckinge Kent 34 D7
Ruckley Shrops 83 K4
Rudby N York 141 L6
Rudchester Nthumb 150 E2
Ruddington Notts 101 L6
Rudge Somset 27 J2
Rudgeway S Glos 38 F3
Rudgwick W Susx 31 H5
Rudheath Ches W 112 F6
Rudley Green Essex 61 K7
Rudloe Wilts 39 J6
Rudry Caerph 37 J3
Rudston E R Yk 135 H6
Rudyard Staffs 99 L2
Ruecastle Border 167 J5
Rufford Lancs 120 F7
Rufford Abbey Notts 115 M0
Rufforth C York 124 D1
Rugby Warwks 87 G7
Rugeley Staffs 100 B8
Ruishton Somset 25 K6
Ruislip Gt Lon 43 H3
Rùm Highld 198 F5
Rumbach Moray 215 J4
Rumbling Bridge
P & K 185 L7
Rumburgh Suffk 93 H7
Rumford Cnwll 4 D2
Rumford Falk 176 C3
Rumney Cardif 37 K5
Runcorn Halton 112 D5
Runcton W Susx 18 B5
Runcton Holme Norfk 90 E2
Runfold Surrey 30 E3
Runhall Norfk 92 C3
Runham Norfk 93 K2
Runnington Somset 25 H6
Runswick N York 143 G4
Runtaleave Angus 195 L3
Runway Visitor Park
Manch 113 J5
Runwell Essex 46 C2
Ruscombe Wokham 42 D5
Rushall Herefs 70 B7
Rushall Norfk 92 E6
Rushall Wilts 28 C1
Rushbrooke Suffk 77 K3
Rushbury Shrops 83 K5
Rushden Herts 60 A2
Rushden Nhants 74 D2
Rushenden Kent 46 E5
Rushford Norfk 91 K7
Rush Green Essex 62 E5
Rush Green Gt Lon 45 K3
Rush Green Warrtn 113 G4
Rushlake Green
E Susx 20 D3
Rushmere Suffk 93 K6
Rushmoor Surrey 30 E4

Rushock Worcs 70 F1
Rusholme Manch 113 J3
Rushton Nhants 88 B6
Rushton Spencer
Staffs 113 L8
Rushwick Worcs 70 E4
Rushyford Dur 141 G2
Ruskie Stirlg 184 D7
Ruskington Lincs 103 H3
Rusland Cross Cumb 129 H2
Rusper W Susx 31 K4
Ruspidge Gloucs 54 F5
Russell's Water Oxon 42 B3
Russ Hill Surrey 31 L4
Rusthall Kent 32 F5
Rustington W Susx 18 E5
Ruston N York 134 E3
Ruston Parva E R Yk 135 G6
Ruswarp N York 143 H5
Rutherford Border 167 K4
Rutherglen S Lans 175 H6
Ruthernbridge Cnwll 4 F3
Ruthin Denbgs 97 H2
Ruthrieston C Aber 207 H4
Ruthven Abers 215 L5
Ruthven Angus 195 L6
Ruthven Highld 203 H5
Ruthvoes Cnwll 4 E4
Ruthwell D & G 147 J2
Ruyton-XI-Towns
Shrops 98 B7
Ryal Nthumb 158 C7
Ryall Dorset 13 K4
Ryall Worcs 70 F6
Ryarsh Kent 33 H2
Rydal Cumb 137 K6
Ryde IoW 17 H4
Rye E Susx 21 H2
Rye Foreign E Susx 21 H2
Rye Street Worcs 70 D7
Ryhall Rutlnd 88 F2
Ryhill Wakefd 124 B7
Ryhope Sundld 151 K4
Ryland Lincs 117 G5
Rylands Notts 101 K5
Rylstone N York 131 H7
Ryme Intrinseca
Dorset 14 B1
Ryther N York 124 E3
Ryton Gatesd 150 E3
Ryton Shrops 84 D3
Ryton-on-Dunsmore
Warwks 86 E8

S

Sabden Lancs 122 B3
Sacombe Herts 60 B4
Sacriston Dur 151 G5
Sadberge Darltn 141 H4
Saddell Ag & B 161 K3
Saddington Leics 87 J5
Saddle Bow Norfk 90 E1
Saddlescombe
W Susx 19 H4
Saffron Walden Essex 76 D6
Sageston Pembks 49 H6
Saham Hills Norfk 91 K3
Saham Toney Norfk 91 K3
Saighton Ches W 98 C1
St Abbs Border 179 J5
St Agnes Border 178 E5
St Agnes Cnwll 3 J2
St Agnes IoS 2 a2
St Agnes Mining
District Cnwll 3 J2
St Albans Herts 59 J6
St Allen Cnwll 4 C5
St Andrew Guern 236 c3
St Andrews Fife 187 H4
St Andrews Botanic
Garden Fife 187 H4
St Andrew's Major
V Glam 37 H6

St Andrews Well
Dorset 13 L4
St Anne's Lancs 120 D5
St Ann's D & G 155 J4
St Ann's Chapel Cnwll 6 B2
St Ann's Chapel
Devon 6 F6
St Anthony Cnwll 3 K6
St Anthony's Hill
E Susx 20 D5
St Arvans Mons 38 D2
St Asaph Denbgs 110 E6
St Athan V Glam 36 F6
St Aubin Jersey 236 b7
St Austell Cnwll 4 F5
St Bees Cumb 136 D5
St Blazey Cnwll 5 G5
St Boswells Border 167 J3
St Brelade Jersey 236 b7
St Brelade's Bay
Jersey 236 b7
St Breock Cnwll 4 F2
St Breward Cnwll 5 H1
St Briavels Gloucs 54 E6
St Bride's Major
V Glam 36 D5
St Brides-super-Ely
V Glam 37 H5
St Brides Wentlooge
Newpt 37 L4
St Budeaux C Plym 6 C4
Saintbury Gloucs 71 K6
St Buryan Cnwll 2 D6
St Catherines Ag & B ... 183 G6
St Chloe Gloucs 55 J7
St Clears Carmth 50 C3
St Cleer Cnwll 5 K3
St Clement Cnwll 4 D6
St Clement Jersey 236 e8
St Clether Cnwll 5 G7
St Colmac Ag & B 173 H5
St Columb Major
Cnwll 4 F3
St Columb Minor
Cnwll 4 D4
St Columb Road Cnwll 4 E4
St Combs Abers 217 K2
St Cross South
Elmham Suffk 93 G6
St Cyrus Abers 197 J4
St David's P & K 185 K4
St Davids Pembks 48 C3
St David's Cathedral
Pembks 48 C3
St Day Cnwll 3 J4
St Dennis Cnwll 4 E4
St Dogmaels
Pembks 65 G5
St Dominick Cnwll 6 B3
St Donats V Glam 36 E6
St Endellion Cnwll 4 F1
St Enoder Cnwll 4 D4
St Erme Cnwll 4 D6
St Erney Cnwll 6 B4
St Erth Cnwll 2 F4
St Erth Praze Cnwll 3 G4
St Ervan Cnwll 4 D2
St Eval Cnwll 4 D3
St Ewe Cnwll 4 F6
St Fagans Cardif 37 H5
St Fagans: National
History Museum
Cardif 37 H5
St Fergus Abers 217 K4
St Fillans P & K 184 F3
St Florence Pembks 49 J7
St Gennys Cnwll 8 F5
St George Conwy 110 D6
St Georges N Som 38 B7
St George's V Glam 37 H5
St Germans Cnwll 6 A4
St Giles in the Wood
Devon 23 H7
St Giles-on-the-
Heath Devon 9 K6
St Harmon Powys 81 L8

St Helen Auckland
Dur 140 F2
St Helens IoW 17 J5
St Helens St Hel 112 D3
St Helens
Crematorium
St Hel 112 C3
St Helier C Lon 44 E6
St Helier Jersey 236 d7
St Hilary Cnwll 2 F5
St Hilary V Glam 36 F5
St Ippollitts Herts 59 K3
St Ishmael's Pembks 48 E6
St Issey Cnwll 4 E2
St Ive Cnwll 5 L3
St Ives Cambs 75 K1
St Ives Cnwll 2 F3
St James's End
Nhants 73 L3
St James South
Elmham Suffk 93 G7
St Jidgey Cnwll 4 E3
St John Cnwll 6 B5
St John Jersey 236 c6
St John's IoM 237 D5
St Johns Kent 32 F3
St Johns Surrey 43 G8
St Johns Worcs 70 E4
St John's Chapel
Devon 23 H5
St John's Chapel Dur ... 149 M7
St John's Fen End
Norfk 90 D2
St John's Kirk S Lans ... 165 J3
St John's Town of
Dalry D & G 154 B6
St John's Wood
Gt Lon 44 F4
St Jude's IoM 237 d3
St Just Cnwll 2 C5
St Just-in-Roseland
Cnwll 4 D8
St Just Mining
District Cnwll 2 D5
St Katherines Abers 216 E7
St Keverne Cnwll 3 K6
St Kew Cnwll 5 G1
St Kew Highway
Cnwll 5 G2
St Keyne Cnwll 5 K4
St Lawrence Essex 62 A6
St Lawrence IoW 17 G6
St Lawrence Jersey 236 c6
St Lawrence Kent 35 K2
St Leonards Bucks 58 E6
St Leonards Dorset 15 L2
St Leonards E Susx 20 F4
St Levan Cnwll 2 C6
St Lythans V Glam 37 H6
St Mabyn Cnwll 5 G2
St Madoes P & K 186 C3
St Margarets Herefs 69 G7
St Margarets Herts 60 B5
St Margaret's at
Cliffe Kent 35 K5
St Margaret's Hope
Ork 234 c7
St Margaret South
Elmham Suffk 93 G6
St Marks IoM 237 c6
St Martin Cnwll 3 J6
St Martin Cnwll 5 K5
St Martin Guern 236 d3
St Martin Jersey 236 e6
St Martin's IoS 2 b1
St Martin's P & K 186 B2
St Martins Shrops 97 L5
St Mary Jersey 236 b6
St Mary Bourne
Hants 29 H2
St Mary Church
V Glam 36 F6
St Mary Cray Gt Lon 45 J6
St Mary in the Marsh
Kent 21 L1

St Marylebone
Crematorium
Gt Lon 44 E3
St Mary's IoS 2 b1
St Mary's Ork 234 c6
St Mary's Bay Kent............21 L1
St Mary's Hoo
Medway 46 D5
St Maughans Green
Mons 54 C5
St Mawes Cnwll 3 L5
St Mawgan Cnwll 4 D3
St Mellion Cnwll 6 B3
St Mellons Cardif 37 K4
St Merryn Cnwll 4 D2
St Michael Caerhays
Cnwll 4 F7
St Michael Church
Somset 25 L5
St Michael Penkevil
Cnwll 4 D7
St Michaels Kent..............34 B7
St Michaels Worcs 69 L2
St Michael's Mount
Cnwll 2 F5
St Michael's on Wyre
Lancs 120 F3
St Minver Cnwll 4 F1
St Monans Fife 187 H6
St Neot Cnwll 5 J3
St Neots Cambs 75 H3
St Newlyn East Cnwll........4 C5
St Nicholas Pembks 64 C7
St Nicholas V Glam 37 H5
St Nicholas at Wade
Kent..............................47 L6
St Ninians Stirlg 185 G8
St Olaves Norfk................93 J4
St Osyth Essex 62 D5
St Ouen Jersey 236 b6
St Owens Cross
Herefs 54 D3
St Paul's Cray Gt Lon 45 J6
St Paul's Walden
Herts..............................59 K4
St Peter Jersey 236 b6
St Peter Port Guern 236 d3
St Peter's Guern 236 b3
St Peter's Kent................35 K2
St Pinnock Cnwll 5 J3
St Quivox S Ayrs............163 J5
St Sampson Guern 236 d2
St Saviour Guern 236 c3
St Saviour Jersey 236 d7
St Stephen Cnwll 4 E5
St Stephens Cnwll 6 B4
St Stephens Cnwll 9 J7
St Teath Cnwll 8 E8
St Tudy Cnwll 5 G1
St Twynnells
Pembks 48 F7
St Veep Cnwll 5 J5
St Vigeans Angus 197 G7
St Wenn Cnwll 4 F3
St Weonards Herefs........54 D3
Salcey Forest Nhants 74 B4
Salcombe Devon 7 H7
Salcombe Regis
Devon 12 F5
Salcott-cum-Virley
Essex 61 M5
Sale Traffd......................113 H3
Saleby Lincs....................118 F5
Sale Green Worcs 71 G3
Salehurst E Susx 20 F2
Salem Cerdgn 80 F6
Salen Ag & B 190 C7
Salen Highld 190 D4
Salford C Beds 74 D6
Salford Oxon....................56 F3
Salford Salfd 113 J2
Salford Priors Warwks....71 J4
Salfords Surrey................32 B4
Salhouse Norfk................93 G1
Saline Fife........................185 L8
Salisbury Wilts 28 C5

Salisbury
Crematorium
Wilts 28 D5
Salisbury Plain Wilts 28 B3
Salkeld Dykes Cumb.....148 F7
Salle Norfk......................106 D7
Salmonby Lincs 118 D6
Salperton Gloucs 56 B4
Salsburgh N Lans..........175 L5
Salt Staffs..........................99 L6
Saltaire C Brad 123 H3
Saltaire C Brad 123 H3
Saltash Cnwll......................6 B4
Saltburn Highld 223 G7
Saltburn-by-the-Sea
R & Cl 142 E3
Saltby Leics....................102 D7
Saltcoats N Ayrs............163 G2
Saltdean Br & H 19 K5
Salterbeck Cumb 136 D3
Salterforth Lancs 122 D2
Salterton Wilts................28 C4
Saltfleet Lincs 118 F3
Saltfleetby All Saints
Lincs 118 F4
Saltfleetby St
Clement Lincs 118 F3
Saltfleetby St Peter
Lincs 118 F4
Saltford BaNES 39 G6
Salthouse Norfk............106 C4
Saltmarshe E R Yk 125 J5
Saltney Flints 111 L8
Salton N York 133 L4
Saltrens Devon 23 G6
Saltwell
Crematorium
Gatesd 151 G3
Saltwood Kent..................34 F7
Salvington W Susx 18 F5
Salwarpe Worcs 70 F3
Salway Ash Dorset..........13 L3
Sambourne Warwks........71 J3
Sambrook Wrekin 99 G7
Sampford Arundel
Somset 25 H7
Sampford Brett
Somset 25 G3
Sampford Courtenay
Devon 10 F5
Sampford Moor
Somset 25 H7
Sampford Peverell
Devon 25 G8
Sampford Spiney
Devon 6 D2
Samsonlane Ork 234 d5
Samuelston E Loth........178 B4
Sanaigmore Ag & B.......170 E4
Sancreed Cnwll..................2 D5
Sancton E R Yk..............125 L3
Sandaig Highld 199 L5
Sandal Magna
Wakefd 123 L6
Sandavore Highld 199 G7
Sanday Ork......................234 d4
Sanday Airport Ork....234 d4
Sandbach Ches E............99 H1
Sandbach Services
Ches E 99 H1
Sandbank Ag & B 173 K3
Sandbanks Poole 15 K5
Sandend Abers 216 B2
Sanderstead
Gt Lon............................45 G7
Sandford Cumb..............139 G4
Sandford Devon 11 J4
Sandford Dorset..............15 H5
Sandford Hants 15 M3
Sandford IoW....................17 G5
Sandford N Som..............38 B8
Sandford S Lans............164 E2
Sandford-on-Thames
Oxon 57 K7
Sandford Orcas
Dorset 26 F7

Sandford St Martin
Oxon 57 H3
Sandgate Kent..................35 G7
Sandhaven Abers............217 H2
Sandhead D & G 144 D5
Sand Hills Leeds............124 B3
Sandhills Oxon..................57 K6
Sandhills Surrey..............30 F4
Sandhoe Nthumb..........150 B2
Sandhole Ag & B............182 E7
Sand Hole E R Yk 125 J3
Sandholme E R Yk..........125 J4
Sandhurst Br For............42 D7
Sandhurst Gloucs 55 J4
Sandhurst Kent................33 K7
Sandhutton N York 132 F3
Sand Hutton N York......133 L7
Sandiacre Derbys..........101 J5
Sandilands Lincs 119 G5
Sandleheath Hants 28 C7
Sandleigh Oxon 57 J7
Sandley Dorset 27 H6
Sandness Shet 235 b5
Sandon Essex 61 H6
Sandon Herts....................75 K7
Sandon Staffs 99 L6
Sandon Bank Staffs 99 L6
Sandown IoW 17 H5
Sandplace Cnwll 5 K4
Sandridge Herts 59 K6
Sandringham Norfk........105 H6
Sandsend N York 143 H5
Sandtoft N Linc 125 H8
Sandway Kent..................34 B5
Sandwich Kent..................35 J3
Sandwick Shet 235 c7
Sandwick W Isls 232 g2
Sandwith Cumb 136 D4
Sandy C Beds 75 H5
Sandyford D & G 155 L4
Sandygate Devon 7 K2
Sandygate IoM 237 d3
Sandyhills D & G 146 F4
Sandylands Lancs..........129 J6
Sandy Lane Wilts 39 L6
Sandy Park Devon 11 G6
Sangobeg Highld............228 F3
Sangomore Highld 228 F3
Sankyn's Green
Worcs 70 E2
Sanna Bay Highld 189 K3
Sanndabhaig W Isls......232 g2
Sannox N Ayrs................162 C1
Sanquhar D & G 164 F7
Santon Bridge Cumb....136 F6
Santon Downham
Suffk 91 J6
Sapcote Leics 86 F5
Sapey Common
Herefs 70 C2
Sapiston Suffk..................91 K7
Sapperton Gloucs............55 L7
Sapperton Lincs 103 G5
Saracen's Head Lincs....104 B6
Sarclet Highld 231 L6
Sarisbury Hants 17 G2
Sarn Gwynd 94 D6
Sarn Powys......................81 K4
Sarn Powys......................82 E5
Sarnau Cerdgn................65 K4
Sarnau Powys..................82 E1
Sarn Park Services
Brdgnd 36 D4
Saron Carmth..................51 H3
Saron Gwynd 109 G7
Sarratt Herts 59 H7
Sarre Kent........................47 L6
Sarsden Oxon 56 F4
Satley Dur........................150 E6
Satterleigh Devon............23 L6
Satterthwaite Cumb......129 H2
Sauchen Abers 206 D3
Saucher P & K 186 C2
Sauchieburn Abers........197 G3
Saul Gloucs 55 H6
Saundby Notts................116 C4

Saundersfoot
Pembks 49 K6
Saunderton Bucks 58 C7
Saunton Devon................23 G4
Sausthorpe Lincs 118 E7
Savile Town Kirk 123 K6
Sawbridge Warwks 73 G2
Sawbridgeworth
Herts..............................60 D5
Sawdon N York 134 E3
Sawley Lancs..................122 B2
Sawley N York 132 C6
Sawston Cambs 76 C5
Sawtry Cambs 89 H6
Saxby Leics 102 D8
Saxby Lincs 117 G2
Saxby All Saints
N Linc 126 B7
Saxelbye Leics................102 B7
Saxham Street Suffk........78 C3
Saxilby Lincs 116 E6
Saxlingham Norfk 106 B5
Saxlingham Green
Norfk..............................92 F4
Saxlingham
Nethergate Norfk......92 F4
Saxlingham Thorpe
Norfk..............................92 E4
Saxmundham Suffk........79 H2
Saxondale Notts 102 B4
Saxon Street Cambs........76 F3
Saxtead Suffk..................78 F2
Saxtead Green Suffk........78 F2
Saxtead Little Green
Suffk 78 F2
Saxthorpe Norfk............106 D6
Saxton N York 124 D3
Sayers Common
W Susx............................19 H3
Scackleton N York 133 K5
Scafell Pike Cumb..........137 H5
Scaftworth Notts 116 A3
Scagglethorpe N York ..134 C5
Scalasaig Ag & B............180 E8
Scalby E R Yk 125 K5
Scalby N York 134 F2
Scaldwell Nhants 73 L1
Scaleby Cumb 148 D3
Scalebyhill Cumb 148 D3
Scales Cumb 129 G5
Scales Cumb 137 K2
Scalford Leics 102 C7
Scaling N York 142 F4
Scalloway Shet 235 c6
Scalpay Highld 209 J7
Scamblesby Lincs..........118 C5
Scamodale Highld..........191 G2
Scampston N York 134 D4
Scampton Lincs 116 F5
Scaniport Highld 212 F6
Scapegoat Hill Kirk........123 G7
Scarba Ag & B 181 K6
Scarborough N York 135 G2
Scarcewater Cnwll............4 E5
Scarcliffe Derbys 115 J7
Scarcroft Leeds 124 B3
Scarfskerry Highld 231 J2
Scarinish Ag & B............188 D7
Scarisbrick Lancs 120 E7
Scarning Norfk 91 L2
Scarrington Notts..........102 B4
Scartho NE Lin 118 C1
Scatsta Airport Shet....235 c4
Scawby N Linc................116 F1
Scawsby Donc................115 K1
Scawthorpe Donc..........115 K1
Scawton N York 133 H3
Scayne's Hill W Susx......19 K2
Scethrog Powys 53 H3
Scholar Green Ches E......99 J2
Scholemoor
Crematorium
C Brad 123 H4
Scholes Kirk 123 H8
Scholes Leeds 124 B3
Scholes Rothm 115 H3

Scholes Wigan............112 E1
Scissett Kirk................123 K7
Scleddau Pembks.... 64 C7
Scofton Notts..............115 L5
Scole Norfk..................92 D7
Scone P & K...............186 B3
Sconser Highld...........209 H7
Scoonie Fife................186 F6
Scopwick Lincs...........103 H2
Scoraig Highld 220 C3
Scorborough E R Yk....126 C2
Scorrier Cnwll...............3 J3
Scorton Lancs.............121 G2
Scorton N York...........141 G7
Scotby Cumb...............148 D4
Scotch Corner N York....140 F6
Scotforth Lancs...........129 K7
Scothern Lincs.............117 G6
Scotlandwell P & K....186 C6
Scotscalder Station
   Highld.....................231 G4
Scot's Gap Nthumb.......158 C5
Scotsmill Abers...........206 B2
Scotstoun C Glas.......174 F5
Scotswood N u Ty.......150 F3
Scotter Lancs..............116 E2
Scotterthorpe Lincs....116 E2
Scottish Seabird
   Centre E Loth..........178 C2
Scottish Wool Centre
   Stirlg.......................184 C7
Scotton Lincs..............116 E2
Scotton N York............132 E7
Scotton N York............140 F7
Scoulton Norfk.............92 D4
Scourie Highld............228 B6
Scourie More Highld....228 B6
Scousburgh Shet.........235 C7
Scrabster Highld.........231 G2
Scraesburgh Border....167 K5
Scrane End Lincs........104 C4
Scraptoft Leics.............87 J3
Scratby Norfk...............93 K1
Scrayingham N York....155 L7
Scredington Lincs.......103 H4
Scremby Lincs.............118 F7
Scremerston Nthumb..179 L8
Screveton Notts..........102 B4
Scriven N York............132 E7
Scrooby Notts............115 M4
Scropton Derbys.........100 D6
Scrub Hill Lincs...........103 L2
Scruton N York............132 D2
Scullomie Highld.........229 J4
Sculthorpe Norfk.........105 L6
Scunthorpe N Linc......125 K7
Seaborough Dorset.......13 K2
Seabrook Kent.............35 G7
Seaburn Sundld..........151 J3
Seacroft Leeds...........124 B4
Seafield Highld...........209 G5
Seafield W Loth..........176 D5
Seafield
   Crematorium
   C Edin....................177 J4
Seaford E Susx...........20 A6
Seaforth Sefton..........111 K3
Seagrave Leics...........101 L8
Seaham Dur................151 K5
Seahouses Nthumb....169 J3
Seal Kent....................32 F2
Sealand Flints............111 K7
Seale Surrey................30 E2
Seamer N York...........134 F3
Seamer N York...........142 B5
Seamill N Ayrs...........173 L8
Sea Palling Norfk.......107 J6
Searby Lincs...............117 H1
Seasalter Kent.............47 H6
Seascale Cumb...........136 E6
Seathwaite Cumb.......137 H7
Seatoller Cumb...........137 H4
Seaton Cnwll.................5 L5
Seaton Cumb..............136 D2
Seaton Devon...............13 G4
Seaton E R Yk............126 E2

Seaton Kent.................35 G3
Seaton Nthumb...........159 H6
Seaton Rutlnd..............88 C4
Seaton Carew Hartpl ..142 B2
Seaton Delaval
   Nthumb...................159 H6
Seaton Ross E R Yk 125 J3
Seaton Sluice
   Nthumb...................159 H6
Seatown Dorset...........13 K4
Seave Green N York....142 C7
Seaview IoW................17 J4
Seaville Cumb.............147 K4
Seavington St Mary
   Somset.....................26 B7
Seavington St
   Michael Somset........26 B7
Sebergham Cumb.......148 C6
Seckington Warwks.....86 C3
Sedbergh Cumb..........130 C2
Sedbury Gloucs............38 D2
Sedbusk N York..........131 G2
Sedgeberrow Worcs......71 H6
Sedgebrook Lincs.......102 D5
Sedgefield Dur............141 J2
Sedgeford Norfk..........105 H5
Sedgehill Wilts.............27 K5
Sedgemoor Services
   Somset.....................26 A2
Sedgley Dudley............85 G5
Sedgwick Cumb..........129 L3
Sedlescombe E Susx....20 F3
Sedrup Bucks...............58 D5
Seend Wilts..................39 L7
Seend Cleeve Wilts......39 L7
Seer Green Bucks.........42 F3
Seething Norfk.............93 G4
Sefton Sefton.............111 K2
Seighford Staffs...........99 K7
Seion Gwynd..............109 H7
Seisdon Staffs.............84 E4
Selattyn Shrops............97 K5
Selborne Hants............30 C5
Selby N York...............124 F4
Selham W Susx............30 F7
Selhurst Gt Lon............45 G6
Selkirk Border............167 G4
Sellack Herefs.............54 E3
Sellafirth Shet............235 d2
Sellindge Kent.............34 E6
Selling Kent.................34 D4
Sells Green Wilts.........39 L7
Selly Oak Birm............85 J6
Selmeston E Susx........20 B4
Selsdon Gt Lon............45 G7
Selsey Gloucs..............55 J7
Selsey W Susx.............18 B6
Selside N York...........130 E4
Selsted Kent................35 G5
Selston Notts.............101 J2
Selworthy Somset........24 E3
Semer Suffk.................78 B5
Semington Wilts..........39 K7
Semley Wilts................27 K6
Send Surrey.................31 G1
Senghenydd Caerph....37 H3
Sennen Cnwll.................2 C6
Sennen Cove Cnwll.......2 C6
Sennybridge Powys.....52 E3
Sessay N York............133 G4
Setchey Norfk..............90 F2
Seton Mains E Loth....177 L4
Settle N York..............130 F6
Settrington N York......134 C5
Sevenhampton
   Gloucs......................56 B4
Sevenhampton
   Swindn.....................40 E3
Seven Hills
   Crematorium
   Suffk........................78 F6
Seven Kings Gt Lon.....45 J3
Sevenoaks Kent..........32 F3
Sevenoaks Weald
   Kent........................32 F3
Seven Sisters Neath....52 C6

Seven Star Green
   Essex.......................61 M3
Severn Beach S Glos 38 D4
Severn Stoke Worcs.....70 F5
Severn View Services
   S Glos.......................38 E3
Sevington Kent.............34 D6
Sewards End Essex......76 E6
Sewell C Beds..............59 G4
Sewerby E R Yk..........135 J5
Seworgan Cnwll.............3 J5
Sewstern Leics...........102 E7
Sgiogarstaigh W Isls ...232 g1
Shabbington Bucks......58 A6
Shackerstone Leics......86 D3
Shackleford Surrey.......30 F3
Shader W Isls..............232 f1
Shadforth Dur.............151 H6
Shadingfield Suffk........93 J6
Shadoxhurst Kent.........34 C7
Shadwell Norfk.............91 L6
Shaftenhoe End
   Herts........................76 B6
Shaftesbury Dorset......27 K6
Shafton Barns............124 B7
Shakerley Wigan.........113 G2
Shalbourne Wilts..........40 F7
Shalden Hants.............30 B3
Shaldon Devon...............7 L2
Shalfleet IoW...............16 E5
Shalford Essex............61 H3
Shalford Surrey...........31 G3
Shalford Green Essex....61 H3
Shalmsford Street
   Kent........................34 E4
Shalstone Bucks..........73 J7
Shamley Green
   Surrey......................31 G3
Shandford Angus........196 D4
Shandon Ag & B..........174 B2
Shandwick Highld.......223 J6
Shangton Leics.............87 K4
Shanklin IoW................17 H6
Shap Cumb.................138 E4
Shapinsay Ork............234 c5
Shapwick Dorset..........15 H3
Shapwick Somset.........26 B4
Shardlow Derbys.........101 H6
Shareshill Staffs...........85 G3
Sharlston Wakefd........124 B6
Sharnbrook Bed...........74 E3
Sharnford Leics............86 F5
Sharoe Green Lancs....121 G4
Sharow N York...........132 E5
Sharpenhoe C Beds......59 H2
Sharperton Nthumb....158 B2
Sharpness Gloucs.........54 F7
Sharrington Norfk.......106 C5
Shatterford Worcs........84 E7
Shaugh Prior Devon......6 D3
Shavington Ches E.......99 G3
Shaw Oldham.............122 D8
Shaw W Berk................41 J6
Shaw Wilts....................39 K7
Shawbirch Wrekin........84 B2
Shawbost W Isls.........232 e2
Shawbury Shrops.........98 E7
Shawell Leics...............87 G7
Shawford Hants............29 J6
Shawhead D & G........154 F6
Shaw Mills N York......132 C6
Shawsburn S Lans......175 K7
Shearington D & G......147 H2
Shearsby Leics.............87 J5
Shearston Somset.........25 L5
Shebbear Devon...........10 C3
Shebdon Staffs.............99 H7
Shebster Highld..........230 E3
Sheddens E Rens........175 G6
Shedfield Hants............29 K8
Sheen Staffs...............100 C1
Sheepridge Kirk..........123 H6
Sheepscar Leeds........123 L4
Sheepscombe Gloucs....55 K6
Sheepstor Devon...........6 E3
Sheepwash Devon.......10 C4

Sheepy Magna Leics....86 D3
Sheepy Parva Leics......86 D3
Sheering Essex............60 E5
Sheerness Kent............46 F5
Sheerwater Surrey.......43 H7
Sheet Hants.................30 C6
Sheffield Sheff...........115 G4
Sheffield City Road
   Crematorium
   Sheff.......................115 G4
Sheffield Park E Susx....19 L2
Shefford C Beds...........75 G6
Sheigra Highld...........228 B4
Sheinton Shrops..........83 L3
Shelderton Shrops........83 H7
Sheldon Birm...............85 L6
Sheldon Derbys..........114 D7
Sheldon Devon............12 E2
Sheldwich Kent............34 D4
Shelfanger Norfk.........92 D6
Shelford Notts............102 A4
Shelley Kirk................123 J7
Shelley Suffk...............78 B6
Shellingford Oxon........40 F2
Shellow Bowells
   Essex.......................60 F6
Shelsley Beauchamp
   Worcs.......................70 D2
Shelsley Walsh Worcs....70 C2
Shelton Bed.................74 F2
Shelton Norfk...............92 F5
Shelton Notts.............102 C4
Shelton Under
   Harley Staffs............99 J5
Shelve Shrops..............83 G4
Shelwick Herefs...........69 K6
Shenfield Essex...........45 L2
Shenington Oxon.........72 D6
Shenley Herts..............59 K7
Shenley Brook End
   M Keyn.....................74 B7
Shenley Church End
   M Keyn.....................74 B7
Shenmore Herefs.........69 H6
Shennanton D & G 145 H3
Shenstone Staffs.........85 K3
Shenstone Worcs.........84 F8
Shenton Leics..............86 F4
Shenval Moray...........214 F7
Shephall Herts.............59 L4
Shepherd's Bush
   Gt Lon......................44 E4
Shepherdswell Kent......35 H5
Shepley Kirk...............123 J8
Shepperton Surrey.......43 H6
Shepreth Cambs..........76 B5
Shepshed Leics..........101 J8
Shepton Beauchamp
   Somset.....................26 B7
Shepton Mallet
   Somset.....................26 F3
Shepton Montague
   Somset.....................27 G5
Shepway Kent.............33 K3
Sheraton Dur.............151 K7
Sherborne Dorset........26 F7
Sherborne Gloucs........56 D5
Sherborne Somset.......26 E1
Sherborne St John
   Hants........................29 L1
Sherbourne Warwks....72 C3
Sherburn Dur.............151 H6
Sherburn N York.........134 E4
Sherburn Hill Dur.........151 H6
Sherburn in Elmet
   N York.....................124 D4
Shere Surrey................31 H2
Shereford Norfk..........105 L6
Sherfield English
   Hants........................28 F6
Sherfield on Loddon
   Hants........................42 B8
Sherford Devon.............7 H6
Sheriffhales Shrops.....84 D2
Sheriff Hutton N York..133 K6
Sheringham Norfk.......106 E4

Sherington M Keyn..............74 C5
Shernborne Norfk........105 H6
Sherrington Wilts...........27 L4
Sherston Wilts................39 J3
Sherwood C Nott..........101 K4
Sherwood Forest
Notts...........................101 L1
Sherwood Forest
Crematorium
Notts.........................116 A7
Shetland Islands Shet...235 c5
Shettleston C Glas.........175 H5
Shevington Wigan........121 H8
Sheviock Cnwll..................6 B5
Shibden Head C Brad...123 G5
Shide IoW.........................16 F5
Shidlaw Nthumb............168 B2
Shiel Bridge Highld......200 E2
Shieldaig Highld............210 C4
Shieldhill D & G.............155 H5
Shieldhill Falk...............176 B3
Shieldhill House
Hotel S Lans..............165 J2
Shields N Lans...............175 K7
Shielfoot Highld............190 D3
Shielhill Angus..............196 C5
Shielhill Inver................173 L4
Shifnal Shrops................84 D2
Shilbottle Nthumb.........169 J7
Shildon Dur...................141 G3
Shillford E Rens.............174 E6
Shillingford Devon..........24 F6
Shillingford Oxon............41 L2
Shillingford Abbot
Devon.........................11 K6
Shillingford St
George Devon.............11 K7
Shillingstone Dorset.......14 F1
Shillington C Beds..........75 G7
Shilton Oxon....................56 E6
Shilton Warwks...............86 E6
Shimpling Norfk...............92 D6
Shimpling Suffk...............77 J4
Shimpling Street
Suffk...........................77 K4
Shincliffe Dur................151 H6
Shiney Row Sundld........151 H4
Shinfield Wokham...........42 B6
Shinness Highld.............225 L5
Shipbourne Kent..............33 G3
Shipdham Norfk...............91 L3
Shipham Somset.............38 C8
Shiphay Torbay.................7 K3
Shiplake Oxon..................42 C5
Shipley C Brad...............123 H3
Shipley W Susx................31 J6
Shipley Bridge Surrey.....32 B5
Shipmeadow Suffk...........93 H5
Shippon Oxon...................41 J2
Shipston-on-Stour
Warwks.......................72 B6
Shipton Gloucs................56 B4
Shipton N York..............133 H7
Shipton Shrops...............83 L5
Shipton Bellinger
Hants..........................28 E3
Shipton Gorge Dorset....13 L4
Shipton Green W Susx...17 L3
Shipton Moyne
Gloucs........................39 K3
Shipton-on-Cherwell
Oxon...........................57 J5
Shiptonthorpe E R Yk...125 K2
Shipton-under-
Wychwood Oxon.....56 F4
Shirburn Oxon..................42 B2
Shirdley Hill Lancs........120 E7
Shirebrook Derbys.........115 K7
Shiregreen Sheff...........115 G3
Shirehampton Bristl........38 D5
Shiremoor N Tyne.........159 H7
Shirenewton Mons...........38 C2
Shireoaks Notts.............115 K5
Shirland Derbys.............101 H2
Shirley C Sotn.................29 H8
Shirley Derbys...............100 E4

Shirley Gt Lon.................45 G6
Shirley Solhll..................85 K7
Shirrell Heath Hants......29 L8
Shirvan Ag & B..............172 E2
Shirwell Devon................23 J4
Shiskine N Ayrs.............162 B4
Shobdon Herefs..............69 H3
Shobrooke Devon............11 K5
Shoby Leics...................102 B7
Shocklach Ches W...........98 C3
Shoeburyness Sthend.....46 F3
Sholden Kent...................35 K4
Sholing C Sotn.................16 F1
Shop Cnwll........................9 G2
Shoreditch Gt Lon...........45 G4
Shoreditch Somset..........25 K6
Shoreham Kent................45 K7
Shoreham Airport
W Susx......................19 G5
Shoreham-by-Sea
W Susx......................19 H5
Shorley Hants..................29 L6
Shorne Kent.....................46 B6
Shortgate E Susx.............20 A3
Shortlanesend Cnwll.........4 C6
Shortlees E Ayrs............163 K3
Shortstown Bed................74 F5
Shorwell IoW...................16 F5
Shoscombe BaNES..........27 G1
Shotesham Norfk..............92 F4
Shotgate Essex................46 C2
Shotley Suffk...................78 F7
Shotley Bridge Dur........150 D4
Shotley Gate Suffk..........78 F7
Shotley Street Suffk........78 F7
Shottenden Kent..............34 D4
Shottermill Surrey...........30 E4
Shottery Warwks.............71 L4
Shotteswell Warwks.........72 E5
Shottisham Suffk.............79 G5
Shottlegate Derbys........100 F3
Shotton Dur...................151 K6
Shotton Flints................111 J7
Shotton Colliery Dur.....151 J6
Shotts N Lans................176 B6
Shotwick Ches W...........111 K6
Shougle Moray...............214 F4
Shouldham Norfk.............90 F2
Shouldham Thorpe
Norfk...........................90 F2
Shoulton Worcs................70 E3
Shrawardine Shrops........83 H1
Shrawley Worcs................70 E2
Shrewley Warwks.............72 B2
Shrewsbury Shrops.........83 J2
Shrewton Wilts................28 B3
Shripney W Susx.............18 C5
Shrivenham Oxon............40 E3
Shropham Norfk...............92 B5
Shucknall Herefs.............69 L6
Shudy Camps Cambs.......76 E5
Shuna Ag & B.................181 M5
Shurdington Gloucs..........55 L4
Shurlock Row W & M......42 D5
Shurrery Highld..............230 F4
Shurrery Lodge
Highld.......................230 F4
Shurton Somset...............25 J3
Shustoke Warwks.............86 B5
Shute Devon.....................11 K5
Shute Devon.....................13 G3
Shutford Oxon..................72 E6
Shut Heath Staffs.............99 K7
Shuthonger Gloucs..........70 F7
Shutlanger Nhants............73 K4
Shuttington Warwks.........86 B3
Shuttlewood Derbys.......115 J6
Shuttleworth Bury..........122 B6
Siabost W Isls................232 e2
Siadar W Isls.................232 f1
Sibbertoft Nhants............87 K6
Sibford Ferris Oxon.........72 D6
Sibford Gower Oxon.........72 D6
Sible Hedingham
Essex...........................77 H7
Sibley's Green Essex.......60 F3
Sibsey Lincs..................104 B3

Sibson Cambs..................89 G4
Sibson Leics....................86 D4
Sibster Highld................231 K5
Sibthorpe Notts.............102 C4
Sibthorpe Notts.............116 B6
Sibton Suffk.....................79 H1
Sicklesmere Suffk............77 K3
Sicklinghall N York........124 B2
Sidbury Devon.................12 E4
Sidbury Shrops................84 C6
Sidcot N Som...................38 B8
Sidcup Gt Lon..................45 J5
Siddington Ches E..........113 J7
Siddington Gloucs............56 B7
Sidestrand Norfk............106 F4
Sidford Devon.................12 E4
Sidlesham W Susx...........18 B6
Sidley E Susx...................20 E4
Sidmouth Devon..............12 E5
Sigglesthorne E R Yk.....126 E2
Sigingstone V Glam..........36 F6
Silchester Hants..............41 L7
Sileby Leics....................87 H1
Silecroft Cumb...............128 D3
Silfield Norfk...................92 D4
Silkstone Barns..............114 F1
Silkstone Common
Barns.........................114 F1
Silk Willoughby Lincs...103 H4
Silloth Cumb..................147 K4
Silpho N York.................134 E2
Silsden C Brad...............122 F2
Silsoe C Beds...................74 F7
Silton Dorset....................27 H5
Silverburn Mdloth...........177 G6
Silverdale Lancs.............129 K4
Silverdale Staffs...............99 J3
Silver End Essex..............61 K4
Silverford Abers.............216 E2
Silverstone Nhants...........73 J5
Silverton Devon...............12 B2
Silvington Shrops.............84 B7
Simonburn Nthumb........157 L7
Simonsbath Somset.........24 B4
Simonstone Lancs..........122 B4
Simprim Border..............168 C1
Simpson M Keyn..............74 C7
Simpson Cross
Pembks.......................48 F4
Sinclair's Hill Border.....179 G7
Sinclairston E Ayrs........163 L6
Sinderby N York.............132 E3
Sinderland Green
Traffd.........................113 G4
Sindlesham Wokham.......42 B6
Sinfin C Derb.................101 G6
Singleton Kent.................34 D6
Singleton Lancs..............120 E3
Singleton W Susx.............18 B3
Singlewell Kent................46 A6
Sinnarhard Abers..........205 K3
Sinnington N York..........134 B3
Sinton Worcs....................70 E3
Sinton Worcs....................70 F2
Sinton Green Worcs.........70 E3
Sissinghurst Kent............33 K5
Siston S Glos....................39 G5
Sithney Cnwll.....................3 H5
Sittingbourne Kent..........34 B3
Six Ashes Shrops.............84 E5
Sixhills Lincs..................117 K4
Six Mile Bottom
Cambs.........................76 E3
Sixpenny Handley
Dorset.........................27 M7
Six Rues Jersey.............236 c6
Skaill Ork......................234 d6
Skara Brae Ork..............234 b5
Skares E Ayrs.................164 B6
Skateraw Abers.............207 G6
Skateraw E Loth............178 F4
Skeabost Highld............208 F5
Skeeby N York................140 F6
Skeffington Leics............87 L3
Skeffling E R Yk.............127 J6
Skegby Notts.................101 J1

Skegby Notts.................116 C7
Skegness Lincs..............119 H8
Skelbo Highld................223 H3
Skelbo Street Highld.....223 H3
Skelbrooke Donc...........124 D7
Skeldyke Lincs...............104 B5
Skellingthorpe Lincs.....116 F6
Skellow Donc.................124 E7
Skelmanthorpe Kirk......123 J7
Skelmersdale Lancs......112 C1
Skelmorlie N Ayrs.........173 L5
Skelpick Highld..............229 L4
Skelston D & G..............154 E5
Skelton C York...............133 J7
Skelton Cumb.................148 D7
Skelton E R Yk...............125 H5
Skelton N York...............132 E5
Skelton R & Cl...............142 E4
Skelwith Bridge
Cumb.........................137 K6
Skendleby Lincs.............118 F7
Skene House Abers.......206 E4
Skenfrith Mons................54 C4
Skerne E R Yk................135 G7
Skerray Highld...............229 K3
Skerricha Highld............228 C5
Skerton Lancs................129 K6
Sketchley Leics................86 E5
Sketty Swans....................51 J6
Skewsby N York.............133 K5
Skiall Highld..................230 E1
Skidby E R Yk................126 C4
Skigersta W Isls............232 g1
Skilgate Somset...............24 F6
Skillington Lincs............102 E7
Skinburness Cumb........147 K4
Skinflats Falk.................176 B2
Skinidin Highld..............208 C5
Skipness Ag & B............172 F6
Skipper's Bridge
D & G.........................156 C5
Skipsea E R Yk...............135 J8
Skipton N York...............122 E1
Skipton-on-Swale
N York.........................132 E4
Skipwith N York.............125 G3
Skirlaugh E R Yk............126 E3
Skirling Border..............165 L2
Skirmett Bucks................42 C3
Skirpenbeck E R Yk.......134 B7
Skirwith Cumb...............149 G2
Skirza Highld.................231 L2
Skokholm Island
Pembks.......................48 C6
Skomer Island
Pembks.......................48 C5
Skulamus Highld............199 K2
Skye Green Essex............61 L4
Skye of Curr Highld......204 B1
Slack Calder..................122 E5
Slacks of Cairnbanno
Abers.........................216 F5
Slad Gloucs.....................55 K6
Slade Devon.....................23 H3
Slade Green Gt Lon.........45 K5
Slade Hooton Rothm.....115 K4
Slaggyford Nthumb.......149 H4
Slaidburn Lancs.............130 D8
Slaithwaite Kirk............123 G7
Slaley Nthumb...............150 B4
Slamannan Falk............176 B4
Slapton Bucks.................58 F4
Slapton Devon...................7 J6
Slapton Nhants................73 J5
Slaugham W Susx............31 L5
Slaughterford Wilts........39 J5
Slawston Leics.................87 L5
Sleaford Hants................30 D4
Sleaford Lincs................103 H4
Sleagill Cumb.................138 E4
Sleapford Wrekin.............84 B1
Sleasdairidh Highld.......222 E3
Sledmere E R Yk............134 E6
Sleetbeck Cumb.............156 E6
Sleights N York..............143 H5
Slickly Highld.................231 K3

Sliddery N Ayrs..............162 B5
Sligachan Highld............209 G7
Sligrachan Ag & B.........173 K1
Slimbridge Gloucs.........55 H7
Slimbridge Wetland
    Centre Gloucs...........55 G6
Slindon Staffs................99 J6
Slindon W Susx.............18 C4
Slinfold W Susx.............31 J5
Slingsby N York.............133 L4
Slip End C Beds............59 H4
Slip End Herts..............75 K6
Slipton Nhants..............88 D7
Slitting Mill Staffs.........100 B8
Slockavullin Ag & B......182 B7
Sloncombe Devon..........11 H7
Sloothby Lincs..............119 G7
Slough Slough...............43 G4
Slough Crematorium
    Bucks......................43 G4
Slough Green Somset.....25 L7
Slumbay Highld............210 D6
Slyne Lancs..................129 K6
Smailholm Border.........167 K3
Smallburgh Norfk.........107 G7
Small Dole W Susx........19 G3
Smalley Derbys..............101 H4
Smallfield Surrey...........32 B5
Small Heath Birm..........85 K6
Small Hythe Kent...........34 B8
Smallridge Devon...........13 H3
Smallworth Norfk..........92 B7
Smannell Hants.............29 G2
Smarden Kent................34 B6
Smarden Bell Kent.........34 B6
Smart's Hill Kent...........32 F5
Smearisary Highld.........190 D2
Smeatharpe Devon.........12 F1
Smeeth Kent.................34 E6
Smeeton Westerby
    Leics.......................87 K5
Smerral Highld..............227 L2
Smestow Staffs.............84 F5
Smethwick Sandw..........85 H6
Smisby Derbys...............101 G8
Smithfield Cumb...........148 D2
Smith's Green Essex.......76 F6
Smithstown Highld........219 J6
Smithton Highld............213 H5
Smoo Highld.................228 F3
Smythe's Green Essex....61 L4
Snade D & G................154 E5
Snailbeach Shrops.........83 G3
Snailwell Cambs............76 F2
Snainton N York............134 E3
Snaith E R Yk................124 F6
Snape N York................132 D3
Snape Suffk..................79 H3
Snape Street Suffk........79 H3
Snaresbrook Gt Lon.......45 H3
Snarestone Leics...........86 D2
Snarford Lincs...............117 H5
Snargate Kent...............34 D8
Snave Kent....................34 D8
Sneaton N York.............143 H5
Snelland Lincs...............117 H5
Snelston Derbys............100 D4
Snetterton Norfk...........92 B5
Snettisham Norfk..........105 G5
Snitter Nthumb.............158 C2
Snitterby Lincs..............117 G3
Snitterfield Warwks.......72 B3
Snitton Shrops..............83 L7
Snodland Kent...............46 B7
Snowdon Gwynd...........95 K2
Snowdonia National
    Park.......................96 C6
Snow End Herts.............60 C2
Snowshill Gloucs...........71 K7
Soake Hants..................17 J1
Soay Highld..................199 G3
Soberton Hants.............29 L7
Soberton Heath
    Hants......................29 L8
Sockburn Darltn............141 J5
Soham Cambs...............90 E8

Solas W Isls..................232 C5
Soldridge Hants.............29 M4
Sole Street Kent............34 E5
Sole Street Kent............46 A6
Solihull Solhll................85 L7
Sollers Dilwyn Herefs....69 H4
Sollers Hope Herefs.......54 E2
Solva Pembks................48 D3
Solwaybank D & G........156 B6
Somerby Leics...............87 L2
Somerby Lincs...............117 H1
Somercotes Derbys........101 H2
Somerford Dorset..........15 M4
Somerford Keynes
    Gloucs....................40 A2
Somerley W Susx...........17 M3
Somerleyton Suffk.........93 K4
Somersal Herbert
    Derbys....................100 C5
Somersby Lincs.............118 D6
Somersham Cambs.........89 L7
Somersham Suffk..........78 C5
Somerton Oxon.............57 J3
Somerton Somset..........26 C5
Somerton Suffk.............77 J4
Sompting W Susx..........19 G5
Sonning Wokham...........42 C5
Sonning Common
    Oxon......................42 B4
Sopley Hants.................15 M3
Sopworth Wilts..............39 J3
Sorbie D & G.................145 J5
Sordale Highld...............231 G3
Sorisdale Ag & B...........189 H4
Sorn E Ayrs..................164 R4
Sortat Highld.................231 K3
Sotby Lincs...................117 K5
Sotterley Suffk..............93 J6
Soughton Flints.............111 H7
Soulbury Bucks.............58 E3
Soulby Cumb.................139 H5
Souldern Oxon..............57 K2
Souldrop Bed................74 E3
Sound Ches E................98 F3
Sound Muir Moray.........215 H4
Soundwell S Glos...........38 F5
Sourton Devon..............10 D6
Soutergate Cumb...........128 F3
South Acre Norfk...........91 J2
South Alkham Kent.........35 H6
Southall Gt Lon.............43 J4
South Allington
    Devon.....................7 J7
South Alloa Falk............185 J8
Southam Gloucs............55 L3
Southam Warwks...........72 E3
South Ambersham
    W Susx....................30 E7
Southampton C Sotn......29 H8
Southampton Airport
    Hants......................29 J7
Southampton
    Crematorium
    Hants......................29 H7
South Anston Rothm......115 K5
South Ashford Kent........34 D6
South Baddesley
    Hants......................16 D3
South Ballachulish
    Highld.....................191 K5
South Bank C York.........124 F1
South Barrow
    Somset....................26 E5
South Beddington
    Gt Lon.....................44 F7
South Benfleet Essex.....46 C3
South Bersted W Susx....18 C5
Southborough Gt Lon.....45 H6
Southborough Kent........33 G5
Southbourne Bmouth.....15 L4
Southbourne W Susx......17 L2
South Bramwith
    Donc.......................124 F7
South Brent Devon.........7 G4
South Brewham
    Somset....................27 G4

South Bristol
    Crematorium
    Bristl......................38 E6
South Broomhill
    Nthumb...................159 G3
Southburgh Norfk.........92 B3
South Burlingham
    Norfk......................93 H3
Southburn E R Yk..........134 F8
South Cadbury
    Somset....................26 F6
South Carlton Lincs.......116 F6
South Carlton Notts......115 L5
South Cave E R Yk.........125 L4
South Cerney Gloucs......40 B2
South Chailey E Susx.....19 K3
South Charlton
    Nthumb...................169 H5
South Cheriton
    Somset....................27 G6
South Church Dur..........140 F2
Southchurch Sthend.......46 E3
South Cliffe E R Yk.........125 K4
South Clifton Notts.......116 D7
South Cockerington
    Lincs.......................118 E4
South Cornelly
    Brdgnd....................36 C4
Southcott Cnwll............9 G5
Southcott Devon............11 H8
Southcourt Bucks.........58 D5
South Cove Suffk...........93 K7
South Creake Norfk.......105 K5
South Croxton Leics.......87 K2
South Dalton E R Yk......126 B2
South Darenth Kent.......45 K6
South Downs
    National Park...........19 K4
South Duffield N York.....125 G4
Southease E Susx..........19 L5
South Elkington Lincs.....118 D4
South Elmsall Wakefd.....124 D7
Southend Ag & B...........161 H7
Southend Airport
    Essex......................46 E3
Southend
    Crematorium
    Sthend....................46 E3
Southend-on-Sea
    Sthend....................46 E3
Southerndown
    V Glam....................36 D5
Southerness D & G........147 G4
South Erradale Highld....219 H7
Southerton Devon..........12 D4
Southery Norfk..............90 E5
South Essex
    Crematorium
    Gt Lon.....................45 L3
South Fambridge
    Essex......................46 E2
South Ferriby N Linc......126 B6
South Field E R Yk.........126 C5
Southfield Falk..............175 L4
Southfleet Kent.............45 L5
Southgate Gt Lon..........44 F2
Southgate Swans..........51 G7
South Gorley Hants.......15 M1
South Gosforth
    N u Ty.....................151 G2
South Green Essex.........46 B2
South Green Kent..........33 L2
South Green Norfk.........92 C2
South Gyle C Edin..........177 G4
South Hanningfield
    Essex......................61 H8
South Harting W Susx....30 C7
South Hayling Hants......17 K3
South Heath Bucks........58 E7
South Heighton
    E Susx.....................19 L5
South Hetton Dur..........151 J6
South Hiendley
    Wakefd....................124 D7
South Hill Cnwll.............5 M2
South Hinksey Oxon.......57 K7

South Holmwood
    Surrey.....................31 K3
South Hornchurch
    Gt Lon.....................45 K4
South Huish Devon.........7 G7
South Hykeham Lincs.....116 F8
South Hylton Sundld......151 J4
Southill C Beds..............75 H6
Southington Hants.........29 J2
South Kelsey Lincs.........117 H2
South Kessock Highld.....213 G5
South Killingholme
    N Linc......................126 E7
South Kilvington
    N York.....................132 F3
South Kilworth Leics.......87 H6
South Kirkby Wakefd......124 C7
South Kyme Lincs...........103 K3
South Lanarkshire
    Crematorium
    S Lans.....................175 J7
Southleigh Devon...........12 F4
South Leigh Oxon...........57 H6
South Leverton Notts......116 C5
South Littleton Worcs.....71 J5
South London
    Crematorium
    Gt Lon.....................44 F6
South Lopham Norfk......92 C7
South Luffenham
    Rutlnd.....................88 D3
South Malling E Susx.....19 L4
South Marston
    Swindn....................40 D3
South Merstham
    Surrey.....................32 B3
South Milford N York......124 D4
South Milton Devon........7 G7
South Mimms Herts.......59 L7
South Mimms
    Services Herts..........59 L7
Southminster Essex.......62 A7
South Molton Devon.......23 L6
South Moor Dur............150 F7
Southmoor Oxon............41 H2
South Moreton Oxon......41 K3
Southmuir Angus...........196 C5
South Mundham
    W Susx....................18 B5
South Newbald
    E R Yk.....................125 L4
South Newington
    Oxon......................57 H2
South Newton Wilts.......28 C4
South Normanton
    Derbys....................101 H2
South Norwood
    Gt Lon.....................45 G6
South Ockendon
    Thurr......................45 L4
Southoe Cambs.............75 H2
Southolt Suffk...............78 E2
South Ormsby Lincs.......118 E6
Southorpe C Pete..........88 F3
South Otterington
    N York.....................132 E3
Southover Dorset..........14 C4
South Owersby Lincs......117 H3
Southowram Calder.......123 G5
South Park Surrey..........31 L2
South Perrott
    Dorset.....................13 L2
South Petherton
    Somset....................26 B7
South Petherwin
    Cnwll......................9 J8
South Pickenham
    Norfk......................91 J3
South Pill Cnwll.............6 B4
South Pool Devon..........7 H7
South Poorton
    Dorset.....................13 M3
Southport Sefton...........120 D6
Southport
    Crematorium
    Lancs......................120 E7

South Queensferry
  C Edin **176** F3
South Rauceby Lincs ...**103** G4
South Raynham
  Norfk **105** L7
Southrepps Norfk **106** F5
South Reston Lincs **118** E5
Southrey Lincs **117** J7
South Ronaldsay Ork ..**234** C7
Southrop Gloucs **56** D7
Southrope Hants **30** A3
South Runcton Norfk **90** F2
South Scarle Notts **116** D8
Southsea C Port **17** J3
South Shian Ag & B **191** H7
South Shields S Tyne ...**151** J2
South Shields
  Crematorium
  S Tyne **151** J3
South Shore Bpool **120** D4
Southside Dur **140** E2
South Stainley N York ..**132** D6
South Stoke BaNES **39** H7
South Stoke Oxon **41** L4
South Stoke W Susx **18** D4
South Street Kent **34** E3
South Street Kent **47** J6
South Tarbrax S Lans ...**176** D7
South Tawton Devon **10** F6
South Tehidy Cnwll **3** H3
South Thoresby Lincs ..**118** E6
Southtown Norfk **93** L3
South Uist W Isls **233** c8
Southwaite Cumb **148** D6
Southwaite Services
  Cumb **148** D6
South Walsham
  Norfk **93** H2
Southwark Gt Lon **44** F4
South Warnborough
  Hants **30** B3
Southwater W Susx **31** J6
South Weald Essex **45** L2
Southwell Notts **102** B2
South West
  Middlesex
  Crematorium
  Gt Lon **43** J5
South Weston Oxon **42** B2
Southwick Hants **17** J2
Southwick Nhants **88** E5
Southwick Sundld **151** J4
Southwick W Susx **19** H5
Southwick Wilts **27** J1
South Widcombe
  BaNES **38** E8
South Wigston Leics **87** H4
South Willesborough
  Kent **34** D6
South Willingham
  Lincs **117** K5
South Wingfield
  Derbys **101** G2
South Witham Lincs **102** F8
Southwold Suffk **93** K7
South Woodham
  Ferrers Essex **61** J7
South Wootton Norfk ..**105** G7
South Wraxall Wilts **39** J7
South Zeal Devon **10** F6
Sowerby Calder **122** F6
Sowerby N York **132** F4
Sowerby Bridge
  Calder **122** F5
Sowood Calder **123** G6
Sowton Devon **6** D3
Sowton Devon **12** C4
Soyland Town Calder ..**122** F6
Spain's End Essex **76** F6
Spalding Lincs **103** L7
Spaldington E R Yk **125** H4
Spaldwick Cambs **89** G8
Spalford Notts **116** D7
Spanby Lincs **103** H5
Sparham Norfk **106** C8
Spark Bridge Cumb **129** G3

Sparkford Somset **26** E6
Sparkhill Birm **85** K6
Sparkwell Devon **6** E4
Sparrowpit Derbys **114** C5
Sparrows Green
  E Susx **33** H6
Sparsholt Hants **29** H5
Sparsholt Oxon **41** G3
Spaunton N York **133** L2
Spaxton Somset **25** K4
Spean Bridge Highld ...**201** K8
Spearywell Hants **28** F6
Speen Bucks **58** D7
Speen W Berk **41** J6
Speeton N York **135** J5
Speke Lpool **112** C5
Speldhurst Kent **32** F5
Spellbrook Herts **60** D4
Spencers Wood
  Wokham **42** B6
Spen Green Ches E **99** J1
Spennithorne N York....**131** L2
Spennymoor Dur **151** G7
Spetchley Worcs **70** F4
Spetisbury Dorset **15** G3
Spexhall Suffk **93** H7
Spey Bay Moray **215** H2
Speybridge Highld **204** C1
Speyview Moray **215** G6
Spilsby Lincs **118** E7
Spinkhill Derbys **115** J5
Spinningdale Highld ...**222** F4
Spital Hill Donc **115** L3
Spital E Loth **178** B3
Spital Highld **231** H5
Spittal Nthumb **179** L7
Spittal Pembks **49** G3
Spittalfield P & K **195** H7
Spittal of Glenmuick
  Abers **205** G7
Spittal of Glenshee
  P & K **195** H3
Spittal-on-Rule
  Border **167** J5
Spixworth Norfk **92** F1
Splatt Devon **10** E4
Splayne's Green
  E Susx **19** L2
Splottlands Cardif **37** K5
Spofforth N York **124** B1
Spondon C Derb **101** H5
Spooner Row Norfk **92** D4
Sporle Norfk **91** J2
Spott E Loth **178** E4
Spottiswoode Border...**178** D7
Spratton Nhants **73** K1
Spreakley Surrey **30** D3
Spreyton Devon **11** G5
Spriddlestone Devon **6** D5
Spridlington Lincs **117** G5
Springburn C Glas **175** G5
Springfield D & G **148** B2
Springfield Essex **61** H6
Springfield Fife **186** E5
Springholm D & G **154** E7
Springside N Ayrs **163** J2
Springthorpe Lincs **116** E4
Springwell Sundld **151** H4
Springwood
  Crematorium
  Lpool **112** B4
Sproatley E R Yk **126** F4
Sproston Green
  Ches W **113** G7
Sprotbrough Donc **115** K2
Sproughton Suffk **78** D5
Sprouston Border **168** A3
Sprowston Norfk **92** F2
Sproxton Leics **102** D7
Sproxton N York **133** J3
Spurstow Ches E **98** D2
Spyway Dorset **14** A4
Stableford Shrops **84** D4
Stacey Bank Sheff.......**114** F4
Stackhouse N York **130** F6
Stackpole Pembks **49** G7

Staddiscombe C Plym **6** D5
Stadhampton Oxon **57** L7
Stadhlaigearraidh
  W Isls **233** b7
Staffield Cumb **148** F6
Staffin Highld **218** D7
Stafford Staffs **99** L7
Stafford
  Crematorium
  Staffs **99** L7
Stafford Services
  (Northbound)
  Staffs **99** K6
Stafford Services
  (Southbound)
  Staffs **99** K6
Stagsden Bed **74** E5
Stainburn Cumb **136** E2
Stainby Lincs **102** E7
Staincross Barns **123** L7
Staindrop Dur **140** E3
Staines-upon-
  Thames Surrey **43** G6
Stainforth Donc **124** F7
Stainforth N York **130** F6
Staining Lancs **120** D4
Stainland Calder **123** G6
Stainsacre N York **143** J5
Stainton Cumb **129** L3
Stainton Cumb **138** C2
Stainton Donc **115** K3
Stainton Dur **140** D4
Stainton Middsb **141** L4
Stainton by
  Langworth Lincs **117** H6
Staintondale N York **143** K7
Stainton le Vale Lincs ..**117** K3
Stainton with
  Adgarley Cumb **128** F5
Stair E Ayrs **163** K5
Stairhaven D & G **144** E4
Staithes N York **143** G4
Stakeford Nthumb **159** G5
Stakes Hants **17** K2
Stalbridge Dorset **27** G7
Stalbridge Weston
  Dorset **27** G7
Stalham Norfk **107** H7
Stalisfield Green Kent ..**34** C4
Stallen Dorset **26** E7
Stallingborough
  NE Lin **126** F7
Stalmine Lancs **120** E2
Stalybridge Tamesd ...**113** L2
Stambourne Essex........**77** G6
Stambourne Green
  Essex **77** G6
Stamford Lincs **88** E3
Stamford Nthumb **169** J5
Stamford Bridge
  Ches W **112** C7
Stamford Bridge
  E R Yk **133** L7
Stamfordham
  Nthumb **158** D7
Stamford Hill Gt Lon **45** G3
Stanbridge C Beds **58** F3
Stanbury C Brad **122** F3
Stand N Lans **175** K5
Standburn Falk **176** C4
Standeford Staffs..........**85** G3
Standen Kent **33** L5
Standerwick Somset **27** J2
Standford Hants **30** D4
Standingstone Cumb...**147** J7
Standish Wigan **121** H7
Standlake Oxon **57** H7
Standon Hants **29** H6
Standon Herts **60** C4
Standon Staffs **99** J5
Stane N Lans **176** B6
Stanfield Norfk **105** M7
Stanford C Beds **75** H4
Stanford Kent **34** F6
Stanford Bishop
  Herefs **70** C4

Stanford Bridge
  Worcs **70** C2
Stanford Dingley
  W Berk **41** L6
Stanford in the Vale
  Oxon **41** G2
Stanford le Hope
  Thurr **46** B4
Stanford on Avon
  Nhants **87** H7
Stanford on Soar
  Notts **101** K7
Stanford on Teme
  Worcs **70** C2
Stanfree Derbys **115** J6
Stanghow R & Cl **142** E4
Stanground C Pete **89** H4
Stanhoe Norfk **105** J5
Stanhope Border **165** L4
Stanhope Dur **150** C6
Stanhope Kent **34** D6
Stanion Nhants **88** D6
Stanley Derbys **101** H4
Stanley Dur **150** F4
Stanley P & K **186** B2
Stanley Staffs **99** L3
Stanley Crook Dur **150** E7
Stanley Pontlarge
  Gloucs **55** M3
Stanmer Br & H.............**19** K4
Stanmore Gt Lon **44** D2
Stanmore Hants **29** J5
Stannersburn
  Nthumb **157** J5
Stanningfield Suffk.......**77** K3
Stannington Nthumb...**158** F6
Stannington Sheff **114** F4
Stannington Station
  Nthumb **158** F5
Stansbatch Herefs **69** G3
Stansfield Suffk **77** H4
Stanstead Suffk **77** J5
Stanstead Abbotts
  Herts **60** C5
Stansted Kent **45** L7
Stansted Airport
  Essex **60** E4
Stansted
  Mountfitchet
  Essex **60** E3
Stanton Gloucs **71** J7
Stanton Nthumb **158** E4
Stanton Staffs **100** C4
Stanton Suffk **91** L8
Stanton by Bridge
  Derbys **101** G6
Stanton by Dale
  Derbys **101** J5
Stanton Drew BaNES **38** E7
Stanton Fitzwarren
  Swindn **40** D3
Stanton Harcourt
  Oxon **57** H6
Stanton in Peak
  Derbys **114** E8
Stanton Lacy Shrops ...**83** K7
Stanton Lees Derbys....**114** E8
Stanton Long Shrops ...**83** L5
Stanton on the
  Wolds Notts **101** M6
Stanton Prior BaNES **39** G7
Stanton St Bernard
  Wilts **40** C7
Stanton St John Oxon ..**57** L6
Stanton St Quintin
  Wilts **39** K4
Stanton Street Suffk **77** L2
Stanton under
  Bardon Leics **86** F2
Stanton upon Hine
  Heath Shrops **98** E7
Stanton Wick BaNES **38** E7
Stanway Essex **61** M3
Stanway Gloucs **56** B2
Stanwell Surrey **43** H5
Stanwick Nhants **74** E1

Stanwix Cumb............148 D4
Staoinebrig W Isls 233 b8
Stape N York 143 G7
Stapeley Ches E.............99 G3
Stapenhill Staffs 100 E7
Staple Kent..................35 H4
Staple Cross Devon....25 G7
Staple Cross E Susx....20 F2
Staplefield W Susx......32 B7
Staple Fitzpaine
    Somset....................25 K7
Stapleford Cambs........76 C4
Stapleford Herts 60 A5
Stapleford Leics 102 D8
Stapleford Lincs 102 E2
Stapleford Notts 101 J5
Stapleford Wilts 28 B4
Stapleford Abbotts
    Essex......................45 K2
Staplegrove Somset.....25 K6
Staplehay Somset........25 K6
Staplehurst Kent..........33 K5
Staplestreet Kent.........34 E3
Stapleton Herefs 69 G2
Stapleton Leics 86 E4
Stapleton N York 141 G5
Stapleton Shrops 83 J3
Stapleton Somset 26 C7
Stapley Somset 25 J8
Staploe Bed 75 G3
Staplow Herefs 70 C6
Star Fife 186 E6
Star Pembks 65 H7
Star Somset 38 C8
Starbeck N York 132 F7
Starbotton N York 131 H5
Starcross Devon 12 C6
Stareton Warwks 72 D1
Starlings Green Essex ...60 D2
Starston Norfk 92 F6
Startforth Dur 140 D4
Startley Wilts 39 L4
Statenborough Kent 35 J4
Statham Warrtn...........112 F4
Stathe Somset 26 A5
Stathern Leics 102 C6
Staughton Green
    Cambs.....................75 G2
Staunton Gloucs 54 D5
Staunton Gloucs 55 H3
Staunton on Arrow
    Herefs....................69 G3
Staunton on Wye
    Herefs....................69 G5
Staveley Cumb 129 H3
Staveley Cumb 138 C7
Staveley Derbys 115 H6
Staveley N York 132 E6
Staverton Devon 7 J3
Staverton Gloucs 55 K4
Staverton Nhants 73 G3
Staverton Wilts 39 J7
Stawell Somset 26 A4
Stawley Somset 25 G6
Staxigoe Highld 231 L5
Staxton N York 134 F4
Staynall Lancs 120 E2
Stean N York 131 K5
Stearsby N York 133 J5
Steart Somset 25 L3
Stebbing Essex 61 G3
Stedham W Susx...........30 E6
Steelend Fife 185 L8
Steele Road Border.....156 F4
Steen's Bridge Herefs...69 K3
Steep Hants 30 C6
Steep Lane Calder 122 F5
Steeple Essex 61 M7
Steeple Ashton Wilts ...27 K1
Steeple Aston Oxon.....57 J3
Steeple Bumpstead
    Essex......................76 F6
Steeple Claydon
    Bucks.....................58 B3
Steeple Gidding
    Cambs.....................89 G7

Steeple Langford
    Wilts......................28 B4
Steeple Morden
    Cambs.....................75 K6
Steeton C Brad 122 F2
Stein Highld...............208 D3
Stelling Minnis Kent.....34 F5
Stembridge Somset.......26 B7
Stenalees Cnwll.............4 F4
Stenhouse D & G 154 D4
Stenhousemuir Falk 176 B2
Stenscholl Highld 218 D7
Stenson Fields Derbys...101 G6
Stenton E Loth............178 D4
Steornabhagh W Isls 232 f2
Stepaside Pembks..........49 K6
Stepford D & G 154 E5
Stepney Gt Lon 45 G4
Steppingley C Beds.......74 E7
Stepps N Lans 175 H5
Sternfield Suffk 79 H3
Stert Wilts 40 B8
Stetchworth Cambs 76 F3
Stevenage Herts 59 L3
Stevenston N Ayrs 163 H2
Steventon Hants 29 K2
Steventon Oxon 41 J3
Steventon End Essex.....76 E6
Stevington Bed 74 E4
Stewartby Bed 74 E6
Stewartfield S Lans......175 H7
Stewarton E Ayrs 163 K1
Stewkley Bucks 58 D3
Stewley Somset 25 L7
Steyning W Susx..........19 G4
Steynton Pembks...........48 F6
Stibb Cnwll 9 G3
Stibbard Norfk............106 B6
Stibb Cross Devon 10 C2
Stibb Green Wilts..........40 E7
Stibbington Cambs........88 F4
Stichill Border 167 L2
Sticker Cnwll.................4 F5
Stickford Lincs 104 B1
Sticklepath Devon 10 F6
Stickney Lincs 104 B2
Stiffkey Norfk 106 A4
Stilligarry W Isls 233 b7
Stillingfleet N York 124 F3
Stillington N York 133 J6
Stillington S on T.........141 J3
Stilton Cambs 89 H5
Stinchcombe Gloucs......55 G7
Stinsford Dorset...........14 D4
Stiperstones Shrops 83 G4
Stirchley Wrekin 84 C3
Stirling Abers 217 L6
Stirling Stirlg 185 G8
Stirling Castle Stirlg 185 G8
Stirling Services Stirlg ...175 L2
Stirtloe Cambs 75 H2
Stirton N York 131 H8
Stisted Essex 61 J3
Stithians Cnwll 3 J4
Stivichall Covtry 86 D7
Stixwould Lincs 117 K7
Stoak Ches W 112 B6
Stobo Border 166 B2
Stoborough Dorset........15 H5
Stobs Castle Border 167 G7
Stobswood Nthumb......158 F3
Stock Essex 61 H7
Stock N Som 38 C7
Stockbridge Hants 29 G4
Stockbriggs S Lans......164 F3
Stockbury Kent 46 D7
Stockcross W Berk 41 H6
Stockerston Leics.........88 B4
Stock Green Worcs 71 H3
Stocking Herefs 54 F2
Stockingford Warwks....86 D5
Stocking Pelham
    Herts.....................60 D3
Stockland Devon 13 G2
Stockland Bristol
    Somset....................25 K3

Stockleigh English
    Devon....................11 K4
Stockleigh Pomeroy
    Devon....................11 K4
Stockley Wilts 39 M6
Stocklinch Somset 26 B7
Stockport Stockp 113 K4
Stockport
    Crematorium
    Stockp..................113 K4
Stocksbridge Sheff 114 E2
Stocksfield Nthumb 150 D3
Stockton Herefs 69 K3
Stockton Norfk 93 H5
Stockton Shrops 84 C4
Stockton Warwks 72 E2
Stockton Wilts 27 M4
Stockton Wrekin 84 D1
Stockton Heath
    Warrtn 112 E4
Stockton-on-Tees
    S on T 141 K4
Stockton on Teme
    Worcs.....................70 C2
Stockton on the
    Forest C York 133 K7
Stockwood Bristl..........38 F6
Stockwood Dorset........14 B2
Stock Wood Worcs........71 H3
Stodmarsh Kent 35 G3
Stody Norfk 106 C5
Stoer Highld 224 C3
Stoford Somset 26 E8
Stoford Wilts 28 B4
Stogumber Somset........25 H4
Stogursey Somset..........25 J3
Stoke Covtry 86 D7
Stoke Devon 22 C6
Stoke Hants 17 K3
Stoke Hants 29 H2
Stoke Medway 46 D5
Stoke Abbott Dorset 13 L3
Stoke Albany Nhants.....88 B5
Stoke Ash Suffk 78 D1
Stoke Bardolph Notts ...101 M4
Stoke Bliss Worcs 70 B2
Stoke Bruerne
    Nhants...................73 L4
Stoke by Clare Suffk 77 G5
Stoke-by-Nayland
    Suffk.....................78 B7
Stoke Canon Devon 12 B3
Stoke Charity Hants......29 J4
Stoke Cross Herefs.......70 B4
Stoke D'Abernon
    Surrey....................43 J8
Stoke Doyle Nhants 88 E6
Stoke Dry Rutlnd 88 C4
Stoke Edith Herefs 69 L6
Stoke Farthing Wilts......28 B6
Stoke Ferry Norfk 91 G4
Stoke Fleming Devon......7 K6
Stokeford Dorset 15 G5
Stoke Gabriel Devon......7 J4
Stoke Gifford S Glos......38 F4
Stoke Golding Leics 86 E4
Stoke Goldington
    M Keyn....................74 B5
Stokeham Notts...........116 C6
Stoke Hammond
    Bucks.....................58 E3
Stoke Holy Cross
    Norfk.....................92 F3
Stokeinteignhead
    Devon......................7 L2
Stoke Lacy Herefs.........70 B5
Stoke Lyne Oxon 57 K3
Stoke Mandeville
    Bucks.....................58 D6
Stokenchurch Bucks......42 C2
Stoke Newington
    Gt Lon....................45 G3
Stokenham Devon 7 J7
Stoke-on-Trent C Stke...99 K3
Stoke Orchard Gloucs....55 K3

Stoke Poges Bucks 42 F4
Stoke Prior Herefs 69 K3
Stoke Prior Worcs 71 G2
Stoke Rivers Devon 23 K4
Stoke Rochford Lincs....102 F6
Stoke Row Oxon 42 B4
Stoke St Gregory
    Somset....................25 M6
Stoke St Mary Somset ...25 K6
Stoke St Michael
    Somset....................26 F3
Stoke St Milborough
    Shrops....................83 L6
Stokesby Norfk 93 J2
Stokesley N York 142 B5
Stoke sub Hamdon
    Somset....................26 C7
Stoke Talmage Oxon 58 B7
Stoke Trister Somset 27 H5
Stoke upon Tern
    Shrops....................98 F6
Stoke-upon-Trent
    C Stke.....................99 K4
Stolford Somset 25 K3
Stondon Massey
    Essex......................60 F7
Stone Bucks 58 C5
Stone Gloucs 39 G2
Stone Rothm...............115 K4
Stone Staffs 99 K5
Stone Worcs 84 F7
Stone Allerton
    Somset....................26 B1
Ston Easton Somset 26 F2
Stonebridge N Som 38 B7
Stonebridge Warwks 86 B6
Stonebroom Derbys 101 H2
Stone Cross Kent...........35 J4
Stonecrouch Kent..........33 J6
Stoneferry C KuH 126 D4
Stonefield Castle
    Hotel Ag & B.........172 E4
Stonegate E Susx 33 H7
Stonegrave N York 133 K4
Stonehaven Abers 207 G7
Stonehenge Wilts 28 C3
Stonehouse C Plym 6 C5
Stonehouse Gloucs 55 J6
Stonehouse S Lans......175 K8
Stone in Oxney Kent 21 J1
Stoneleigh Warwks 86 D8
Stonesby Leics 102 D7
Stonesfield Oxon 57 H4
Stones Green Essex 62 E3
Stone Street Kent 33 G3
Stone Street Suffk 93 H6
Stonewells Moray 215 G2
Stoneybridge W Isls 233 b8
Stoneyburn W Loth 176 D5
Stoneygate C Leic 87 H3
Stoneykirk D & G 144 C4
Stoney Middleton
    Derbys..................114 E6
Stoney Stanton Leics.....86 F4
Stoney Stoke Somset 27 G5
Stoney Stratton
    Somset....................26 F4
Stoneywood C Aber 207 G3
Stoneywood Falk 175 L2
Stonham Aspal Suffk 78 D3
Stonnall Staffs 85 J3
Stonor Oxon 42 B3
Stonton Wyville Leics 87 K4
Stony Houghton
    Derbys..................115 J7
Stony Stratford
    M Keyn....................73 L6
Stoodleigh Devon 23 K5
Stoodleigh Devon 24 E7
Stop 24 Services Kent....34 F7
Stopham W Susx 18 D2
Stopsley Luton 59 J3
Stornoway W Isls 232 f2
Stornoway Airport
    W Isls...................232 g2
Storrington W Susx......18 E3

Storth Cumb 129 K4
Storwood E R Yk 125 H2
Stotfield Moray............ 214 F1
Stotfold C Beds 75 J7
Stottesdon Shrops........ 84 C6
Stoughton Leics 87 J3
Stoughton Surrey 31 G2
Stoughton W Susx 17 L1
Stoulton Worcs 70 F4
Stourbridge Dudley 84 F6
Stourbridge
  Crematorium
  Dudley 84 F6
Stourhead Wilts............. 27 H5
Stourpaine Dorset 15 G1
Stourport-on-Severn
  Worcs 70 E1
Stour Provost Dorset 27 H6
Stour Row Dorset 27 J7
Stourton Staffs............. 84 F6
Stourton Warwks 72 C6
Stourton Wilts 27 H5
Stourton Caundle
  Dorset 27 G7
Stove Shet.................... 235 C7
Stoven Suffk 93 J6
Stow Border................. 167 G1
Stow Lincs 116 E5
Stow Bardolph Norfk 90 F3
Stow Bedon Norfk 91 L4
Stowbridge Norfk.......... 90 E3
Stow-cum-Quy
  Cambs 76 D3
Stowe Shrops................. 82 F8
Stowe by Chartley
  Staffs 100 A6
Stowell Somset............... 27 G6
Stowey BaNES 38 E7
Stowford Devon............... 10 C7
Stowlangtoft Suffk........ 77 L2
Stow Longa Cambs......... 75 G1
Stow Maries Essex 61 K7
Stowmarket Suffk 78 C3
Stow-on-the-Wold
  Gloucs 56 D3
Stowting Kent 34 F6
Stowting Common
  Kent 34 F6
Stowupland Suffk 78 C3
Straanruie Highld......... 204 B3
Strachan Abers 206 D6
Strachur Ag & B........... 182 F6
Stradbroke Suffk........... 92 F8
Stradishall Suffk 77 H4
Stradsett Norfk 90 F3
Stragglethorpe Lincs... 102 E3
Straiton Mdloth 177 H5
Straiton S Ayrs 153 H2
Straloch Abers 207 G2
Straloch P & K 195 G4
Stramshall Staffs 100 B5
Strang IoM 237 C5
Strangeways Salfd........ 113 J2
Strangford Herefs......... 54 E3
Stranraer D & G 144 C3
Stratfield Mortimer
  W Berk 42 A7
Stratfield Saye Hants 42 B7
Stratfield Turgis
  Hants 42 B7
Stratford Gt Lon 45 H3
Stratford St Andrew
  Suffk 79 H3
Stratford St Mary
  Suffk 78 C7
Stratford Tony Wilts 28 C6
Stratford-upon-Avon
  Warwks 72 B4
Strath Highld................ 219 J5
Strathan Highld............ 224 D4
Strathan Highld............ 229 J3
Strathaven S Lans 164 D1
Strathblane Stirlg........ 175 G3
Strathcanaird Highld... 220 F2
Strathcarron Highld 210 E6
Strathcoil Ag & B.......... 181 K2

Strathdon Abers............ 205 H3
Strathkinness Fife 187 G4
Strathloanhead
  W Loth 176 C4
Strathmashie House
  Highld......................... 202 F6
Strathmiglo Fife............ 186 C5
Strathpeffer Highld 212 D3
Strathtay P & K............. 194 E5
Strathwhillan N Ayrs ... 162 D3
Strathy Highld............. 230 B3
Strathy Inn Highld........ 230 B3
Strathyre Stirlg............ 184 C4
Stratton Cnwll 9 G4
Stratton Dorset 14 C4
Stratton Gloucs............. 56 A7
Stratton Audley Oxon 57 L3
Stratton-on-the-
  Fosse Somset............... 26 F2
Stratton St Margaret
  Swindn 40 D3
Stratton St Michael
  Norfk 92 E5
Stratton Strawless
  Norfk 106 F7
Streat E Susx 19 K3
Streatham Gt Lon.......... 44 F5
Streatley C Beds............ 59 H3
Streatley W Berk 41 L4
Street Devon.................. 12 F5
Street Somset................ 26 C4
Street Ashton
  Warwks 86 F6
Street Dinas Shrops...... 97 M5
Street End Kent............. 34 F4
Street End W Susx 18 A5
Streethay Staffs............ 85 K2
Streetlam N York 141 H7
Streetly
  Crematorium
  Wsall 85 J4
Streetly End Cambs 76 E5
Street on the Fosse
  Somset 26 F4
Strelitz P & K 186 C1
Strelley Notts............... 101 K4
Strensall C York 133 K7
Strensham Services
  (northbound)
  Worcs 70 F6
Strensham Services
  (southbound)
  Worcs 70 F6
Stretcholt Somset......... 25 L3
Strete Devon.................... 7 J6
Stretford Traffd 113 H3
Strethall Essex.............. 76 C6
Stretham Cambs............ 90 D8
Strettington W Susx 18 B4
Stretton Derbys........... 101 H1
Stretton Rutlnd.............. 88 D1
Stretton Staffs............... 84 F2
Stretton Staffs............. 100 E7
Stretton Warrtn........... 112 F5
Stretton Grandison
  Herefs.......................... 70 B5
Stretton-on-
  Dunsmore Warwks.... 86 E8
Stretton on Fosse
  Warwks 72 B6
Stretton Sugwas
  Herefs.......................... 69 J6
Stretton under Fosse
  Warwks 86 F7
Stretton Westwood
  Shrops 83 L4
Strichen Abers 217 H4
Stringston Somset........ 25 J3
Strixton Nhants............ 74 C3
Stroat Gloucs................ 38 E2
Stroma Highld.............. 231 L1
Stromeferry Highld 210 D7
Stromness Ork............. 234 b6
Stronachlachar Stirlg .. 183 L5
Stronafian Ag & B......... 173 H3
Stronchrubie Highld.... 224 F5

Strone Ag & B 173 L3
Strone Highld............... 192 B1
Strone Highld............... 212 E8
Stronenaba Highld....... 201 J8
Stronmilchan Ag & B... 183 G2
Stronsay Ork................ 234 d5
Stronsay Airport Ork ... 234 d5
Strontian Highld.......... 191 G4
Strood Medway.............. 46 B6
Stroud Gloucs................ 55 J6
Stroud Hants.................. 30 B6
Stroud Green Gloucs..... 55 J6
Stroxton Lincs............. 102 E6
Struan Highld.............. 208 E6
Struan P & K 194 C4
Strumpshaw Norfk........ 93 H3
Strutherhill S Lans...... 175 K7
Struthers Fife.............. 186 F5
Struy Highld................ 212 B6
Stuartfield Abers......... 217 H5
Stubbington Hants........ 17 G2
Stubbins Lancs............ 122 B6
Stubton Lincs.............. 102 E3
Stuckton Hants.............. 28 D8
Studham C Beds............ 59 G5
Studland Dorset............ 15 J6
Studley Warwks 71 J2
Studley Wilts................. 39 L6
Studley Roger N York... 132 D5
Studley Royal N York ... 132 D5
Studley Royal Park &
  Fountains Abbey
  N York 132 D5
Stuntney Cambs............ 90 D7
Sturmer Essex............... 77 G5
Sturminster
  Common Dorset......... 27 H8
Sturminster Marshall
  Dorset 15 H3
Sturminster Newton
  Dorset 27 H8
Sturry Kent................... 35 G3
Sturton N Linc............. 116 F2
Sturton by Stow
  Lincs 116 E5
Sturton le Steeple
  Notts 116 C5
Stuston Suffk................ 92 D7
Stutton N York............. 124 D3
Stutton Suffk................. 78 D7
Styal Ches E................. 113 J5
Stynie Moray............... 215 H3
Styrrup Notts............... 115 L4
Succoth Ag & B............ 183 K6
Suckley Worcs............... 70 C4
Sudborough Nhants....... 88 D6
Sudbourne Suffk........... 79 J4
Sudbrook Lincs............ 102 F4
Sudbrook Mons............. 38 D3
Sudbrooke Lincs........... 117 G6
Sudbury Derbys........... 100 D6
Sudbury Gt Lon............. 44 D3
Sudbury Suffk................ 77 K6
Suffield N York............ 134 F2
Suffield Norfk.............. 106 F6
Sugnall Staffs................ 99 H6
Sugwas Pool Herefs...... 69 J6
Suisnish Highld........... 199 J3
Sulby IoM.................... 237 d3
Sulgrave Nhants............ 73 G5
Sulham W Berk.............. 41 M5
Sulhamstead W Berk..... 41 M6
Sullom Shet................. 235 C4
Sullom Voe Shet........... 235 C4
Sully V Glam................. 37 J6
Sumburgh Airport
  Shet 235 c8
Summerbridge
  N York 132 C6
Summercourt Cnwll........ 4 D5
Summerfield Norfk...... 105 J5
Summerhill Pembks...... 49 K6
Summerhouse Darltn... 140 F4
Summersdale W Susx.... 18 B4
Summerseat Bury........ 122 B7
Summertown Oxon........ 57 K6

Sunbury-on-Thames
  Surrey........................... 43 J6
Sundaywell D & G 154 E5
Sunderland Ag & B...... 170 E6
Sunderland Cumb........ 147 L7
Sunderland Lancs........ 129 J7
Sunderland Sundld...... 151 J4
Sunderland Bridge
  Dur............................. 151 G7
Sunderland
  Crematorium
  Sundld........................ 151 J4
Sundhope Border........ 166 E4
Sundon Park Luton....... 59 H3
Sundridge Kent 32 E3
Sunningdale W & M...... 42 F6
Sunninghill W & M........ 42 F6
Sunningwell Oxon......... 57 J7
Sunniside Dur............. 150 E7
Sunniside Gatesd........ 150 F3
Sunnyhill C Derb......... 101 G6
Sunnyhurst Bl w D...... 121 K6
Sunnylaw Stirlg........... 185 G7
Sunnymead Oxon.......... 57 J6
Surbiton Gt Lon............ 44 D6
Surfleet Lincs.............. 103 L6
Surlingham Norfk......... 93 G3
Surrex Essex................. 61 L4
Surrey & Sussex
  Crematorium
  W Susx........................ 32 B5
Sustead Norfk.............. 106 E5
Susworth Lincs............ 116 D2
Sutcombe Devon............. 9 J3
Sutcombemill Devon...... 9 J3
Sutterby Lincs.............. 118 E6
Sutterton Lincs............ 103 M5
Sutton C Beds............... 75 J5
Sutton C Pete............... 89 G4
Sutton Cambs............... 90 C7
Sutton Devon.................. 7 G7
Sutton E Susx 20 A5
Sutton Gt Lon................ 44 E7
Sutton Kent................... 35 J5
Sutton N York.............. 124 D5
Sutton Norfk............... 107 H7
Sutton Notts................ 102 C5
Sutton Oxon.................. 57 H6
Sutton Shrops.............. 84 D6
Sutton Staffs................. 99 H7
Sutton Suffk.................. 79 G5
Sutton W Susx.............. 18 D3
Sutton at Hone Kent..... 45 K6
Sutton Bassett
  Nhants.......................... 87 L5
Sutton Benger Wilts...... 39 L5
Sutton Bonington
  Notts 101 K7
Sutton Bridge Lincs..... 104 D7
Sutton Cheney Leics..... 86 E4
Sutton Coldfield Birm... 85 K4
Sutton Coldfield
  Crematorium
  Birm............................. 85 K4
Sutton Courtenay
  Oxon............................. 41 J2
Sutton cum Lound
  Notts 116 B5
Sutton Green Surrey...... 31 G1
Sutton Howgrave
  N York 132 D4
Sutton in Ashfield
  Notts 101 J2
Sutton-in-Craven
  N York 122 F2
Sutton Maddock
  Shrops 84 C3
Sutton Mallet Somset.... 26 A4
Sutton Mandeville
  Wilts............................. 27 M5
Sutton Montis
  Somset 26 F6
Sutton-on-Hull C KuH... 126 E4
Sutton on Sea Lincs..... 119 G5
Sutton-on-the-
  Forest N York 133 J6

Sutton on the Hill
Derbys 100 E5
Sutton on Trent
Notts 116 D7
Sutton St Edmund
Lincs 89 L2
Sutton St James Lincs .. 104 C8
Sutton St Nicholas
Herefs 69 K5
Sutton Scotney Hants 29 J4
Sutton-under-Brailes
Warwks 72 C6
Sutton-under-Whitestonecliffe
N York 133 G3
Sutton upon Derwent E R Yk 125 G2
Sutton Valence Kent 33 L4
Sutton Veny Wilts 27 K3
Sutton Waldron
Dorset 27 K7
Sutton Weaver
Ches W 112 D5
Sutton Wick BaNES 38 E8
Sutton Wick Oxon 41 J2
Swaby Lincs 118 E6
Swadlincote Derbys 100 F8
Swaffham Norfk 91 J2
Swaffham Bulbeck
Cambs 76 D3
Swaffham Prior
Cambs 76 E2
Swafield Norfk 107 G6
Swainby N York 141 L6
Swainsthorpe Norfk 92 F4
Swainswick BaNES 39 H6
Swalcliffe Oxon 72 E6
Swalecliffe Kent 47 J6
Swallow Lincs 117 K2
Swallow Beck Lincs 116 F7
Swallowcliffe Wilts 27 L6
Swallowfield
Wokham 42 B7
Swanage Dorset 15 J6
Swanbourne Bucks 58 D3
Swan Green Ches W 113 G6
Swanland E R Yk 126 B5
Swanley Kent 45 K6
Swanley Village Kent 45 K6
Swanmore Hants 29 L7
Swannington Leics 86 E1
Swannington Norfk 106 D8
Swanpool Garden Suburb Lincs 116 F7
Swanscombe Kent 45 L5
Swansea Swans 51 J6
Swansea Airport
Swans 51 H7
Swansea Crematorium
Swans 51 J5
Swansea West Services Swans 51 J5
Swanton Abbot
Norfk 106 F7
Swanton Morley
Norfk 92 B1
Swanton Novers
Norfk 106 B6
Swanwick Derbys 101 H2
Swanwick Hants 17 G1
Swanwick Crematorium
Derbys 101 H2
Swarby Lincs 103 H4
Swardeston Norfk 92 E3
Swarkestone Derbys 101 G6
Swarland Nthumb 158 F2
Swarraton Hants 29 K4
Swarthmoor Cumb 129 G4
Swaton Lincs 103 J5
Swavesey Cambs 75 L2
Sway Hants 16 C3
Swayfield Lincs 103 G7
Swaythling C Sotn 29 H7
Sweetham Devon 11 K5

Sweethaws E Susx 32 E7
Sweets Cnwll 8 F5
Sweetshouse Cnwll 5 H4
Swefling Suffk 79 H2
Swepstone Leics 86 D2
Swerford Oxon 57 G2
Swettenham Ches E 113 J7
Swilland Suffk 78 E4
Swillington Leeds 124 B4
Swimbridge Devon 23 K5
Swimbridge Newland Devon 23 J5
Swinbrook Oxon 56 F5
Swincliffe N York 132 C7
Swinderby Lincs 116 E8
Swindon Gloucs 55 L3
Swindon Staffs 84 F5
Swindon Swindn 40 D4
Swine E R Yk 126 E4
Swinefleet E R Yk 125 H6
Swineshead Bed 74 F2
Swineshead Lincs 103 L4
Swiney Highld 227 M2
Swinford Leics 87 H7
Swingfield Minnis
Kent 35 G6
Swingfield Street
Kent 35 H6
Swingleton Green
Suffk 77 L5
Swinhoe Nthumb 169 J4
Swinithwaite N York 131 K2
Swinside Cumb 137 H3
Swinstead Lincs 103 G7
Swinton Bordor 179 H8
Swinton N York 132 C4
Swinton N York 134 B5
Swinton Rothm 115 J2
Swinton Salfd 113 H2
Swithland Leics 87 G2
Swordale Highld 212 E2
Swordland Highld 200 B6
Swordly Highld 229 M3
Swynnerton Staffs 99 J5
Swyre Dorset 13 M5
Sychtyn Powys 81 L3
Syde Gloucs 55 L5
Sydenham Gt Lon 45 G5
Sydenham Oxon 58 B7
Sydenham Damerel
Devon 6 B2
Syderstone Norfk 105 K6
Sydling St Nicholas
Dorset 14 C3
Sydmonton Hants 41 J8
Syerston Notts 102 C3
Sykehouse Donc 124 F6
Symbister Shet 235 d4
Symington S Ayrs 163 J3
Symington S Lans 165 J3
Symondsbury Dorset 13 K4
Symonds Yat Herefs 54 E5
Syre Highld 229 L6
Syreford Gloucs 56 B4
Syresham Nhants 73 J6
Syston Leics 87 J2
Syston Lincs 102 F4
Sytchampton Worcs 70 E2
Sywell Nhants 74 B2

Tackley Oxon 57 J4
Tacolneston Norfk 92 D4
Tadcaster N York 124 D2
Taddington Derbys 114 C7
Tadley Hants 41 L7
Tadlow Cambs 75 K5
Tadmarton Oxon 72 E6
Tadworth Surrey 44 E8
Taff's Well Rhondd 37 H4
Taibach Neath 36 B3
Tain Highld 223 G5
Tain Highld 231 J3

Tairbeart W Isls 232 e4
Takeley Essex 60 F4
Takeley Street Essex 60 E4
Talaton Devon 12 D3
Talbenny Pembks 48 E5
Taleford Devon 12 E3
Talerddig Powys 81 K4
Talgarreg Cerdgn 65 L4
Talgarth Powys 68 D7
Talisker Highld 208 E7
Talke Staffs 99 J2
Talkin Cumb 148 F4
Talladale Highld 219 L7
Talla Linnfoots
Border 165 M5
Tallaminnock S Ayrs 153 J3
Tallarn Green
Wrexhm 98 C4
Tallentire Cumb 147 K7
Talley Carmth 66 E7
Tallington Lincs 88 F2
Talmine Highld 229 J3
Talog Carmth 50 D1
Talsarn Cerdgn 66 D4
Talsarnau Gwynd 95 K5
Talskiddy Cnwll 4 E3
Talwrn IoA 109 G6
Tal-y-bont Cerdgn 80 E5
Tal-y-Bont Conwy 109 L7
Tal-y-bont Gwynd 95 K7
Tal-y-bont Gwynd 109 J7
Talybont-on-Usk
Powys 53 H4
Tal-y-Cafn Conwy 109 M7
Tal y coed Mons 54 B5
Talysarn Gwynd 95 H2
Tamar Valley Mining District Devon 6 C3
Tamerton Foliot
C Plym 6 C4
Tamworth Staffs 86 B3
Tamworth Services
Warwks 86 B4
Tandridge Surrey 32 C3
Tanfield Dur 150 F4
Tanfield Lea Dur 150 F4
Tangley Hants 28 F2
Tangmere W Susx 18 B4
Tangusdale W Isls 233 b9
Tankerness Ork 234 c6
Tankersley Barns 115 G2
Tankerton Kent 47 J6
Tannach Highld 231 K6
Tannachie Abers 206 E8
Tannadice Angus 196 D5
Tanner's Green Worcs 85 J8
Tannington Suffk 78 F2
Tannochside N Lans 175 J6
Tansley Derbys 100 F1
Tansor Nhants 88 F5
Tantobie Dur 150 F4
Tanworth in Arden
Warwks 71 K1
Tan-y-groes Cerdgn 65 J5
Taobh Tuath W Isls 232 d5
Taplow Bucks 42 E4
Tarbert Ag & B 172 B7
Tarbert Ag & B 172 E5
Tarbert W Isls 232 e4
Tarbet Ag & B 183 K6
Tarbet Highld 200 B6
Tarbet Highld 228 B5
Tarbolton S Ayrs 163 K4
Tarbrax S Lans 176 D7
Tardebigge Worcs 71 H2
Tarfside Angus 196 D1
Tarland Abers 205 K4
Tarleton Lancs 120 F6
Tarlton Gloucs 55 L7
Tarnock Somset 26 B2
Tarporley Ches W 112 D8
Tarrant Crawford
Dorset 15 H2
Tarrant Gunville
Dorset 27 L8
Tarrant Hinton Dorset 15 H1

Tarrant Keyneston
Dorset 15 H2
Tarrant Launceston
Dorset 15 H1
Tarrant Monkton
Dorset 15 H2
Tarrant Rawston
Dorset 15 H2
Tarrant Rushton
Dorset 15 H2
Tarring Neville E Susx 19 L5
Tarrington Herefs 70 B6
Tarskavaig Highld 199 J4
Tarves Abers 217 G7
Tarvin Ches W 112 C7
Tasburgh Norfk 92 E4
Tatenhill Staffs 100 D7
Tathwell Lincs 118 D5
Tatsfield Surrey 32 D2
Tattenhall Ches W 98 C2
Tatterford Norfk 105 K6
Tattersett Norfk 105 K6
Tattershall Lincs 103 K2
Tattershall Thorpe
Lincs 103 L1
Tattingstone Suffk 78 D6
Tattingstone White Horse Suffk 78 D6
Tatton Park Ches E 113 H5
Tatworth Somset 13 J2
Tauchers Moray 215 J4
Taunton Somset 25 K6
Taunton Deane Crematorium
Somset 25 J6
Taunton Deane Services Somset 25 J7
Taverham Norfk 92 E2
Tavernspite Pembks 49 K5
Tavistock Devon 6 C2
Tavistock Devon 6 C2
Taw Green Devon 10 F5
Tawstock Devon 23 J5
Taxal Derbys 114 A5
Taychreggan Hotel
Ag & B 182 F3
Tay Forest Park P & K .. 194 C4
Tayinloan Ag & B 161 H1
Taynton Gloucs 55 G4
Taynton Oxon 56 E5
Taynuilt Ag & B 182 E2
Tayport Fife 187 G2
Tayvallich Ag & B 172 C2
Tealby Lincs 117 J4
Tealing Angus 196 C8
Team Valley Gatesd 151 G3
Teangue Highld 199 K4
Teanord Highld 212 F2
Tebay Cumb 138 E6
Tebay Services Cumb .. 138 E6
Tebworth C Beds 59 G3
Tedburn St Mary
Devon 11 J6
Teddington Gloucs 55 L2
Teddington Gt Lon 44 D6
Tedstone Delamere
Herefs 70 C3
Tedstone Wafer
Herefs 70 C3
Teesside Crematorium
Middsb 141 L4
Teeton Nhants 73 K1
Teffont Evias Wilts 27 M5
Teffont Magna Wilts 27 M5
Tegryn Pembks 65 H7
Teigh Rutlnd 88 C1
Teigngrace Devon 7 K2
Teignmouth Devon 12 B7
Teindside Border 166 F7
Telford Wrekin 84 C2
Telford Crematorium
Wrekin 84 D2
Telford Services
Shrops 84 D2
Tellisford Somset 27 J1

Telscombe E Susx.............19 L5
Tempar P & K.................193 L5
Templand D & G..............155 D5
Temple Cnwll....................5 J2
Temple Mdloth................177 J6
Temple Bar Cerdgn............66 C4
Temple Cloud BaNES.........38 F8
Templecombe
  Somset...........................27 G6
Temple Ewell Kent...........35 H5
Temple Grafton
  Warwks..........................71 K4
Temple Guiting
  Gloucs...........................56 C3
Temple Hirst N York.......124 F5
Temple Normanton
  Derbys..........................115 H7
Temple of Fiddes
  Abers............................197 K1
Temple Sowerby
  Cumb............................138 E2
Templeton Devon.............11 K3
Templeton Pembks...........49 J5
Templetown Dur.............150 E5
Tempsford C Beds............75 H4
Tenbury Wells Worcs.......69 L2
Tenby Pembks.................49 J7
Tendring Essex................62 D3
Tendring Green Essex......62 D3
Tendring Heath Essex......62 D3
Ten Mile Bank Norfk........90 E4
Tenterden Kent...............34 B7
Terling Essex..................61 J5
Ternhill Shrops...............98 F6
Terregles D & G.............155 G6
Terrington N York..........133 K5
Terrington St
  Clement Norfk............104 E7
Terrington St John
  Norfk..............................90 D2
Teston Kent....................33 J3
Testwood Hants...............29 G8
Tetbury Gloucs................39 K2
Tetchill Shrops...............98 B6
Tetcott Devon...................9 J5
Tetford Lincs.................118 D6
Tetney Lincs..................118 D2
Tetsworth Oxon..............58 B7
Tettenhall Wolves...........84 F4
Teversal Notts...............101 J1
Teversham Cambs............76 C3
Teviothead Border..........156 D2
Tewin Herts...................59 L5
Tewkesbury Gloucs..........55 K2
Teynham Kent.................34 C3
Thackley C Brad.............123 H3
Thainstone Abers...........206 E2
Thakeham W Susx............18 F3
Thame Oxon.....................58 B6
Thames Ditton Surrey......44 D6
Thamesmead Gt Lon.........45 J4
Thamesport Medway..........46 E5
Thanet Crematorium
  Kent..............................35 K2
Thanington Kent..............34 F4
Thankerton S Lans..........165 J2
Tharston Norfk................92 E5
Thatcham W Berk.............41 K6
Thaxted Essex.................60 F2
Theakston N York...........132 D3
Thealby N Linc...............125 K6
Theale Somset.................26 C3
Theale W Berk.................41 M6
Thearne E R Yk...............126 D3
The Beeches Gloucs..........56 B7
Theberton Suffk..............79 J2
The Braes Highld............209 H7
The Brunt E Loth............178 E4
The Bungalow IoM...........237 d4
The Burf Worcs................70 E2
The Butts Gloucs.............55 K5
The City Bucks................42 C2
The Common Wilts............28 E5
The Counties
  Crematorium
  Nhants...........................73 K3

Theddingworth Leics........87 J6
Theddlethorpe All
  Saints Lincs................118 F4
Theddlethorpe St
  Helen Lincs................119 G4
The Den N Ayrs..............174 C7
The Forest of Dean
  Crematorium
  Gloucs...........................54 F5
The Forstal Kent..............34 D6
The Garden of
  England
  Crematorium
  Kent..............................46 E6
The Green Cumb..............128 E3
The Green Essex...............61 J4
The Green N York.............143 G6
The Green Wilts...............27 K5
The Headland Hartpl.......151 M7
The Hill Cumb.................128 E3
The Lee Bucks.................58 E6
The Lhen IoM.................237 d2
The Linn
  Crematorium
  E Rens..........................175 G4
Thelnetham Suffk............92 B7
The Lochs Moray.............215 G2
Thelveton Norfk..............92 E7
Thelwall Warrtn.............112 F4
The Manchester
  Crematorium
  Manch...........................113 J3
Themelthorpe Norfk........106 C7
The Moor Kent.................33 K7
The Mumbles Swans..........51 J7
The Murray S Lans..........175 H7
The Neuk Abers..............206 D5
Thenford Nhants..............73 G6
The Park
  Crematorium
  Hants.............................30 E2
The Reddings Gloucs........55 K4
Therfield Herts...............75 L6
The Rose Hill
  Crematorium
  Donc............................115 L2
The Ross P & K..............185 G3
The Stocks Kent...............21 H1
The Strand Wilts..............39 L8
Thetford Norfk................91 K6
Thetford Forest Park
  ....91.... J5
The Vale
  Crematorium
  Luton.............................59 J3
Theydon Bois Essex.........60 D7
Thickwood Wilts..............39 J5
Thimbleby Lincs.............118 C7
Thimbleby N York...........141 K7
Thingwall Wirral...........111 J5
Thirkleby N York...........133 G4
Thirlby N York...............133 G3
Thirlestane Border.........178 C8
Thirn N York..................132 C3
Thirsk N York.................132 F3
Thistleton Lancs............120 E3
Thistleton Rutlnd...........102 E8
Thistley Green Suffk........90 F7
Thixendale N York..........134 C7
Thockrington
  Nthumb.........................158 B6
Tholomas Drove
  Cambs............................90 B3
Tholthorpe N York..........133 G6
Thomastown Abers...........216 B6
Thompson Norfk................91 K4
Thoralby N York..............131 J3
Thoresway Lincs.............117 K3
Thorganby Lincs.............117 K3
Thorganby N York...........125 G3
Thorgill N York..............142 E7
Thorington Suffk.............93 J8
Thorington Street
  Suffk.............................78 B7
Thorlby N York...............131 H8
Thorley Herts...................60 D4

Thorley Street IoW..........16 D5
Thormanby N York...........133 G5
Thornaby-on-Tees
  S on T...........................141 K4
Thornage Norfk................106 C5
Thornborough Bucks.........73 L7
Thornborough N York......132 D4
Thornbury C Brad............123 J4
Thornbury Devon................9 K3
Thornbury Herefs.............70 B3
Thornbury S Glos.............38 F3
Thornby Nhants................87 J7
Thorncliff Staffs...........100 A2
Thorncliffe
  Crematorium
  Cumb............................128 E5
Thorncombe Dorset...........13 J2
Thorndon Suffk................78 D1
Thorndon Cross
  Devon.............................10 D6
Thorne Donc...................125 G7
Thorner Leeds.................124 B3
Thorne St Margaret
  Somset...........................25 H7
Thorney C Pete................89 K3
Thorney Notts.................116 E6
Thorney Somset................26 B6
Thorney Hill Hants...........16 A3
Thorney Island
  W Susx............................17 L2
Thornfalcon Somset..........25 L6
Thornford Dorset..............26 E8
Thorngrafton
  Nthumb.........................149 K2
Thorngumbald E R Yk......125 F5
Thornham Norfk..............105 H4
Thornham Magna
  Suffk.............................78 D1
Thornham Parva
  Suffk.............................92 D8
Thornhaugh C Pete...........88 F4
Thornhill C Sotn...............29 J8
Thornhill Cumb...............136 D5
Thornhill D & G...............154 F3
Thornhill Derbys.............114 D5
Thornhill Kirk.................123 K6
Thornhill Stirlg..............184 E7
Thornhill
  Crematorium
  Cardif.............................37 J4
Thornholme E R Yk..........135 H6
Thornicombe Dorset..........15 G2
Thornington Nthumb........168 D3
Thornley Dur..................150 E7
Thornley Dur..................151 J6
Thornliebank E Rens.......174 F6
Thorns Suffk....................77 G4
Thornsett Derbys............114 A4
Thornthwaite Cumb.........137 H3
Thornthwaite N York.......132 B7
Thornton Angus..............196 C6
Thornton Bucks................73 L7
Thornton C Brad.............123 G4
Thornton E R Yk.............125 H2
Thornton Fife.................186 E7
Thornton Lancs...............120 D3
Thornton Leics.................86 F3
Thornton Middsb............141 L4
Thornton Nthumb............179 K8
Thornton Curtis
  N Linc..........................126 D6
Thornton Garden
  of Rest
  Crematorium
  Sefton...........................111 K2
Thorntonhall S Lans.......175 G7
Thornton Heath
  Gt Lon............................44 F6
Thornton Hough
  Wirral............................111 J5
Thornton-in-Craven
  N York...........................122 D2
Thornton in Lonsdale
  N York...........................130 D5
Thornton-le-Beans
  N York...........................132 F2

Thornton-le-Clay
  N York...........................133 L6
Thornton-le-Dale
  N York...........................134 C3
Thornton le Moor
  Lincs............................117 H3
Thornton-le-Moor
  N York...........................132 F2
Thornton-le-Moors
  Ches W..........................112 C6
Thornton-le-Street
  N York...........................132 F3
Thorntonloch E Loth.......178 F4
Thornton Rust N York.....131 H2
Thornton Steward
  N York...........................132 B3
Thornton Watlass
  N York...........................132 C3
Thornydykes Border.......178 D8
Thornythwaite Cumb.......137 L3
Thoroton Notts...............102 C4
Thorp Arch Leeds...........124 C2
Thorpe Derbys................100 D3
Thorpe E R Yk.................126 B2
Thorpe N York................131 J6
Thorpe Notts..................102 C3
Thorpe Surrey..................43 G6
Thorpe Abbotts
  Norfk.............................92 E7
Thorpe Arnold Leics.......102 C7
Thorpe Audlin
  Wakefd..........................124 D7
Thorpe Bassett
  N York...........................134 D5
Thorpe Bay Sthend...........46 E3
Thorpe by Water
  Rutlnd............................88 C4
Thorpe Constantine
  Staffs.............................86 C2
Thorpe End Norfk............93 G2
Thorpe Green Essex.........62 E4
Thorpe Green Suffk..........77 L4
Thorpe Hesley Rothm.......115 G3
Thorpe in Balne Donc.....124 F7
Thorpe Langton Leics......87 L5
Thorpe Lea Surrey............43 G6
Thorpe-le-Soken
  Essex.............................62 E4
Thorpe le Street
  E R Yk..........................125 K2
Thorpe Malsor
  Nhants............................88 B7
Thorpe Mandeville
  Nhants............................73 G5
Thorpe Market Norfk......106 F5
Thorpe Marriot Norfk......92 E1
Thorpe Morieux Suffk.......77 L4
Thorpeness Suffk.............79 K3
Thorpe on the Hill
  Lincs............................116 E7
Thorpe Park Surrey..........43 G6
Thorpe St Andrew
  Norfk.............................92 F2
Thorpe St Peter Lincs.....104 D1
Thorpe Salvin Rothm.......115 K5
Thorpe Satchville
  Leics.............................87 K2
Thorpe Thewles
  S on T...........................141 J3
Thorpe Tilney Lincs.........103 J2
Thorpe Underwood
  N York...........................133 G7
Thorpe Waterville
  Nhants............................88 E7
Thorpe Willoughby
  N York...........................124 E4
Thorrington Essex............62 C4
Thorverton Devon.............11 L4
Thrandeston Suffk............92 D7
Thrapston Nhants.............88 E7
Threapwood Ches W..........98 C4
Threapwood Staffs..........100 B4
Threave S Ayrs................163 J7
Three Bridges W Susx......32 B5
Three Chimneys Kent........33 L5
Three Cocks Powys............68 D6

Three Counties
   Crematorium
      Essex **61** J3
Three Crosses Swans **51** H6
Three Cups Corner
   E Susx **20** D2
Threekingham Lincs.... **103** H5
Three Leg Cross
   E Susx **33** H6
Three Legged Cross
   Dorset **15** K2
Three Mile Cross
   Wokham **42** B6
Threemilestone Cnwll **3** K3
Three Miletown
   W Loth **176** E3
Three Oaks E Susx **21** G3
Threlkeld Cumb.......... **137** J3
Threshers Bush Essex...**60** D6
Threshfield N York **131** J6
Thrigby Norfk **93** K2
Thringstone Leics......... **86** E1
Thrintoft N York **132** D2
Thriplow Cambs **76** B5
Throcking Herts **60** B3
Throckley N u Ty **150** E2
Throckmorton Worcs..... **71** H4
Throop Bmouth.............. **15** L4
Thropton Nthumb **158** C2
Throsk Stirlg **176** B1
Throughgate D & G...... **154** F5
Throwleigh Devon **11** G6
Throwley Forstal
   Kent **34** C4
Thrumpton Notts.......... **101** J8
Thrumster Highld........ **231** L6
Thrunscoe NE Lin **127** H8
Thrupp Gloucs **55** K7
Thrussington Leics......... **87** J1
Thruxton Hants **28** F3
Thruxton Herefs **69** J7
Thrybergh Rothm **115** J3
Thulston Derbys.......... **101** H6
Thundersley Essex **46** C3
Thurcaston Leics **87** H2
Thurcroft Rothm......... **115** J4
Thurgarton Norfk........ **106** E5
Thurgarton Notts **102** B3
Thurgoland Barns **114** F2
Thurlaston Leics **87** G4
Thurlaston Warwks **72** F1
Thurlbear Somset **25** K7
Thurlby Lincs **89** G1
Thurlby Lincs.............. **102** E1
Thurlby Lincs.............. **119** G6
Thurleigh Bed **74** F3
Thurlestone Devon **7** G7
Thurloxton Somset........ **25** L5
Thurlstone Barns........ **114** E2
Thurlton Norfk **93** J4
Thurmaston Leics **87** H2
Thurnby Leics **87** J3
Thurne Norfk **93** J1
Thurnham Kent **33** K2
Thurning Nhants **88** F6
Thurning Norfk........... **106** C6
Thurnscoe Barns **115** J1
Thurrock Services
   Thurr **45** L4
Thursby Cumb.............. **148** B5
Thursford Norfk.......... **106** B5
Thursley Surrey **30** E4
Thurso Highld............. **231** G2
Thurstaston Wirral **111** H5
Thurston Suffk **77** L2
Thurstonfield Cumb..... **148** B4
Thurstonland Kirk **123** H7
Thurton Norfk **93** G4
Thurvaston Derbys...... **100** E5
Thuxton Norfk **92** B3
Thwaite N York **139** K7
Thwaite Suffk **78** D2
Thwaite Head Cumb ... **129** H2
Thwaite St Mary
   Norfk **93** G4
Thwing E R Yk **135** G5

Tibbermore P & K........ **185** L3
Tibbers D & G **154** E3
Tibberton Gloucs........... **55** H4
Tibberton Worcs........... **70** F3
Tibberton Wrekin **99** G7
Tibbie Shiels Inn
   Border **166** C5
Tibenham Norfk............ **92** D5
Tibshelf Derbys........... **101** H1
Tibshelf Services
   Derbys **101** H1
Tibthorpe E R Yk........ **134** E7
Ticehurst E Susx **33** H7
Tichborne Hants........... **29** L5
Tickencote Rutlnd.......... **88** E2
Tickenham N Som.......... **38** C6
Tickhill Donc **115** L3
Ticklerton Shrops.......... **83** J5
Ticknall Derbys........... **101** G7
Tickton E R Yk **126** D3
Tidcombe Wilts............. **40** F8
Tiddington Oxon **57** M6
Tiddington Warwks....... **72** B4
Tidebrook E Susx.......... **33** G7
Tideford Cnwll **6** A4
Tidenham Gloucs........... **38** E2
Tideswell Derbys......... **114** D6
Tidmarsh W Berk **41** M5
Tidmington Warwks....... **72** C6
Tidworth Wilts **28** E2
Tiers Cross Pembks **48** F5
Tiffield Nhants **73** K4
Tigerton Angus........... **196** E4
Tigh a Ghearraidh
   W Isls **233** b6
Tigharry W Isls **233** b6
Tighnabruaich Ag & B...**173** G4
Tigley Devon **7** H4
Tilbrook Cambs **74** F2
Tilbury Thurr **45** M5
Tile Hill Covtry **86** C7
Tilehurst Readg **42** A5
Tilford Surrey **30** E3
Tilgate W Susx **31** L4
Tilham Street Somset..... **26** E4
Tillicoultry Clacks....... **185** J7
Tillietudlem S Lans...... **164** F1
Tillingham Essex............ **62** B7
Tillington Herefs **69** J5
Tillington W Susx **30** F6
Tillington Common
   Herefs **69** J5
Tillybirloch Abers....... **206** D4
Tillyfourie Abers......... **206** C3
Tillygreig Abers.......... **207** G2
Tillyrie P & K **186** B6
Tilmanstone Kent **35** J4
Tilney All Saints Norfk..**104** F8
Tilney High End Norfk..**104** E8
Tilney St Lawrence
   Norfk **90** D2
Tilshead Wilts............... **28** B2
Tilstock Shrops............. **98** D5
Tilston Ches W **98** C3
Tilstone Fearnall
   Ches W **98** E1
Tilsworth C Beds **59** G3
Tilton on the Hill Leics...**87** L3
Tiltups End Gloucs......... **39** J2
Timberland Lincs......... **103** J2
Timbersbrook Ches E....**113** K8
Timberscombe
   Somset **24** E3
Timble N York **132** B8
Timpanheck D & G...... **156** B7
Timperley Traffd.......... **113** H4
Timsbury BaNES **38** F8
Timsbury Hants **29** G6
Timsgarry W Isls **232** d2
Timsgearraidh W Isls ...**232** d2
Timworth Suffk **77** J2
Timworth Green
   Suffk **77** J2
Tincleton Dorset............ **14** E4
Tindale Cumb **149** G3
Tindale Crescent Dur ...**140** F2

Tingewick Bucks........... **58** A2
Tingrith C Beds **59** G2
Tingwall Airport Shet.... **235** c6
Tingwell Ork................ **234** c5
Tinhay Devon **9** K7
Tinsley Sheff **115** H4
Tinsley Green W Susx..... **32** B5
Tintagel Cnwll **8** E7
Tintern Parva Mons........ **54** D7
Tintinhull Somset........... **26** D7
Tintwistle Derbys......... **114** A3
Tinwald D & G **155** H5
Tinwell Rutlnd............... **88** E3
Tipton Sandw **85** G5
Tipton St John Devon..... **12** E4
Tiptree Essex................. **61** L5
Tiptree Heath Essex....... **61** L5
Tirabad Powys **67** J6
Tiree Ag & B................ **188** D7
Tiree Airport Ag & B.....**188** C7
Tiretigan Ag & B.......... **172** C6
Tirley Gloucs................. **55** J3
Tiroran Ag & B............ **181** G2
Tirphil Caerph **53** H7
Tirril Cumb................. **138** D2
Tisbury Wilts **27** L5
Tissington Derbys........ **100** D3
Titchberry Devon **22** C6
Titchfield Hants............. **17** G2
Titchmarsh Nhants......... **88** E7
Titchwell Norfk............ **105** J4
Tithby Notts **102** B5
Titley Herefs................. **69** G3
Titsey Surrey **32** D3
Titson Cnwll **9** H5
Tittensor Staffs.............. **99** K5
Tittleshall Norfk **105** L7
Titton Worcs **70** E1
Tiverton Ches W **98** D1
Tiverton Devon **24** E8
Tivetshall St
   Margaret Norfk **92** E6
Tivetshall St Mary
   Norfk **92** E6
Tixall Staffs **99** L7
Tixover Rutlnd............... **88** E4
Toab Shet **235** c8
Tobermory Ag & B........ **189** L5
Toberonochy Ag & B.....**181** L5
Tobha Mor W Isls **233** b7
Tocher Abers............... **216** D7
Tochieneal Moray......... **215** L2
Tockenham Wilts............ **40** B4
Tockholes Bl w D **121** K6
Tockington S Glos **38** E3
Tockwith N York **133** G8
Todber Dorset................ **27** J7
Toddington C Beds **59** G3
Toddington Gloucs.......... **56** B2
Toddington Services
   C Beds **59** G3
Todenham Gloucs **72** B7
Todhills Angus............. **196** C8
Todhills Services
   Cumb **148** C3
Todmorden Calder **122** D5
Todwick Rothm **115** J5
Toft Cambs **75** L4
Toft Lincs **88** F1
Toft Shet **235** c3
Toft Hill Dur............... **140** E2
Toft Monks Norfk **93** J4
Toft next Newton
   Lincs **117** H4
Toftrees Norfk **105** L6
Togston Nthumb........... **159** G2
Tokavaig Highld........... **199** J3
Tokers Green Oxon **42** B5
Tolastadh W Isls **232** g2
Tolland Somset **25** H5
Tollard Royal Wilts......... **27** L7
Toll Bar Donc **124** E8
Toller Fratrum Dorset..... **14** B3
Toller Porcorum
   Dorset **14** B3
Tollerton N York **133** H6

Tollerton Notts............ **101** L5
Tollesbury Essex **62** A6
Tolleshunt D'Arcy
   Essex **61** L5
Tolleshunt Knights
   Essex **61** L5
Tolleshunt Major
   Essex **61** L5
Tolpuddle Dorset........... **14** E4
Tolsta W Isls **232** g2
Tolworth Gt Lon **44** D6
Tomatin Highld............ **213** J8
Tomchrasky Highld....... **201** K3
Tomdoun Highld.......... **201** H5
Tomich Highld............. **211** L8
Tomich Highld............. **212** E5
Tomich Highld............. **222** F7
Tomich Highld............. **226** A7
Tomintoul Moray......... **204** E2
Tomnacross Highld....... **212** D6
Tomnavoulin Moray...... **204** F1
Tonbridge Kent **33** G4
Tondu Brdgnd............... **36** D4
Tonedale Somset............ **25** H6
Tong C Brad **123** J4
Tong Kent **34** C4
Tong Shrops.................. **84** E3
Tonge Leics................. **101** H7
Tongham Surrey............ **30** E2
Tongland D & G........... **146** C4
Tong Norton Shrops....... **84** E2
Tongue Highld.............. **229** J4
Tongwynlais Cardif........ **37** H4
Tonmawr Neath **36** C2
Tonna Neath **52** D7
Tonwell Herts **60** B5
Tonypandy Rhondd........ **36** F3
Tonyrefail Rhondd......... **36** F3
Toot Baldon Oxon **57** K7
Toot Hill Essex **60** E7
Toothill Swindn **40** C4
Tooting Gt Lon **44** F5
Tooting Bec Gt Lon **44** F5
Topcliffe N York **152** F4
Topcroft Norfk **92** F5
Topcroft Street Norfk..... **92** F5
Toppesfield Essex **77** G6
Toprow Norfk **92** E4
Topsham Devon **12** C5
Torbeg N Ayrs **162** A4
Torboll Highld.............. **223** G2
Torbreck Highld........... **213** G6
Torbryan Devon **7** J3
Torcastle Highld.......... **192** B2
Torcross Devon **7** J7
Tore Highld................. **212** F4
Torinturk Ag & B.......... **172** D5
Torksey Lincs **116** D5
Tormarton S Glos **39** H5
Tormore N Ayrs **161** M3
Tornagrain Highld......... **213** J4
Tornaveen Abers.......... **206** C4
Torness Highld............. **212** E8
Toronto Dur................. **140** F2
Torpenhow Cumb......... **147** L6
Torphichen W Loth **176** C4
Torphins Abers............ **206** C5
Torpoint Cnwll **6** C5
Torquay Torbay **7** L3
Torquay
   Crematorium
      Torbay......................... **7** K3
Torquhan Border.......... **177** L8
Torran Highld.............. **209** J5
Torrance E Duns **175** H4
Torranyard N Ayrs....... **163** J1
Torridon Highld........... **210** D3
Torridon House
   Highld **210** D3
Torrin Highld............... **199** J2
Torrisdale Ag & B......... **161** K3
Torrisdale Highld......... **229** K3
Torrish Highld............. **227** G5
Torrisholme Lancs........ **129** K6
Torrobull Highld.......... **226** A7
Torry C Aber **207** H4

Torryburn Fife 176 D2
Torteval Guern. 236 b4
Torthorwald D & G 155 H6
Tortington W Susx 18 D5
Torton Worcs 84 E8
Tortworth S Glos 39 G2
Torvaig Highld 209 H5
Torver Cumb 137 J7
Torwood Falk 175 L2
Torwoodlee Border 167 G2
Torworth Notts 116 A4
Toscaig Highld 209 L6
Toseland Cambs 75 J3
Tosside Lancs 130 E7
Tostock Suffk 77 L2
Totaig Highld................ 208 C4
Tote Highld 208 F5
Tote Highld 209 H3
Totland IoW 16 D5
Totley Sheff 114 F5
Totnes Devon 7 J4
Toton Notts 101 J5
Totronald Ag & B 188 F5
Totscore Highld 208 F2
Tottenham Gt Lon 45 G3
Tottenhill Norfk 90 F2
Totteridge Gt Lon 44 E2
Totternhoe C Beds 59 G4
Tottington Bury 122 B7
Totton Hants 29 G8
Toulton Somset 25 J5
Toulvaddie Highld 223 J5
Tovil Kent 33 K3
Toward Ag & B 173 K5
Toward Quay Ag & B 173 J5
Towcester Nhants 73 K5
Towednack Cnwll 2 E4
Tower of London
    Gt Lon 45 G4
Towersey Oxon 58 B6
Towie Abers 205 K3
Tow Law Dur 150 E6
Town End Cambs 90 B4
Townend W Duns 174 D3
Townhead Barns 114 D2
Townhead D & G 155 H4
Townhead of
    Greenlaw D & G 146 C4
Townhill Fife 176 F1
Town Littleworth
    E Susx 19 L3
Towns End Hants 41 K8
Townshend Cnwll 3 G5
Town Street Suffk 91 H6
Town Yetholm Border.. 168 B4
Towthorpe C York 133 K7
Towton N York 124 D3
Towyn Conwy 110 D5
Toxteth Lpool 111 K4
Toynton All Saints
    Lincs 118 E8
Toy's Hill Kent 32 E3
Trabboch E Ayrs 163 K5
Trabbochburn E Ayrs... 163 L5
Tradespark Highld 213 K3
Trallong Powys 52 E3
Tranent E Loth 177 L4
Tranmere Wirral 111 J4
Trantelbeg Highld 230 C5
Trantlemore Highld 230 C5
Trapp Carmth 51 J2
Traprain E Loth 178 D4
Traquair Border 166 E3
Trawden Lancs............. 122 D3
Trawsfynydd Gwynd 96 A5
Trealaw Rhondd 36 F3
Treales Lancs 120 F4
Trearddur Bay IoA 108 C5
Treaslane Highld 208 F4
Trebetherick Cnwll......... 4 E1
Treborough Somset...... 24 F4
Trebullett Cnwll 5 M1
Treburley Cnwll 6 A1
Trecastle Powys 52 D3
Trecwn Pembks 64 D7
Trecynon Rhondd 52 F7

Tredegar Blae G 53 H6
Tredington Gloucs........ 55 K3
Tredington Warwks 72 C5
Tredunnock Mons........ 38 B2
Treen Cnwll..................... 2 D6
Treeton Rothm 115 H4
Trefasser Pembks......... 64 C6
Trefecca Powys 53 H2
Trefeglwys Powys........ 81 L5
Treffgarne Pembks 49 G3
Treffgarne Owen
    Pembks 48 E3
Trefforest Rhondd 37 G3
Trefilan Cerdgn............. 66 D3
Trefin Pembks 64 B7
Trefnant Denbgs......... 110 E7
Trefonen Shrops........... 97 K6
Trefor Gwynd 94 F4
Trefriw Conwy 109 L8
Tregadillett Cnwll 9 H7
Tregare Mons............... 54 B6
Tregaron Cerdgn.......... 66 F3
Tregarth Gwynd.......... 109 H7
Tregeare Cnwll................ 9 H7
Tregeiriog Wrexhm 97 J5
Tregele IoA 108 D3
Treglemais Pembks...... 48 D2
Tregonetha Cnwll............ 4 E3
Tregonning &
    Gwinear Mining
    District Cnwll 3 G5
Tregony Cnwll................. 4 E6
Tregorrick Cnwll.............. 4 F5
Tregoyd Powys.............. 68 E6
Tre-groes Cerdgn......... 65 L5
Tregynon Powys........... 82 C4
Tre-gynwr Carmth 50 E2
Trehafod Rhondd.......... 37 G3
Trehan Cnwll................... 6 B4
Treharris Myr Td 37 H2
Treherbert Rhondd........ 52 E7
Trekenner Cnwll.............. 6 A1
Treknow Cnwll................. 8 D7
Trelawnyd Flints......... 110 F5
Trelech Carmth 65 J7
Treleddyd-fawr
    Pembks 48 C2
Trelewis Myr Td 37 H2
Trelights Cnwll................ 8 C8
Trelill Cnwll 5 G1
Trellech Mons 54 D6
Trelogan Flints............ 110 F5
Tremadog Gwynd.......... 95 K4
Tremail Cnwll 8 F7
Tremain Cerdgn............. 65 H5
Tremaine Cnwll................ 9 G6
Tremar Cnwll................... 5 K3
Trematon Cnwll............... 6 B4
Tremeirchion Denbgs.. 110 F6
Trenance Cnwll................ 4 D3
Trenance Cnwll................ 4 E2
Trench Wrekin 84 C2
Trenear Cnwll.................. 3 H5
Treneglos Cnwll.............. 9 G7
Trent Dorset 26 E7
Trentham C Stke........... 99 K4
Trentishoe Devon......... 23 K2
Treoes V Glam 36 E5
Treorchy Rhondd........... 36 E2
Trequite Cnwll................. 5 G1
Trerhyngyll V Glam 36 F5
Trerulefoot Cnwll............ 5 M4
Tresaith Cerdgn............. 65 J4
Tresco IoS 2 a1
Trescowe Cnwll.............. 3 G5
Tresean Cnwll................. 4 C4
Tresham Gloucs 39 H3
Treshnish Isles Ag & B.. 189 G7
Tresillian Cnwll................ 4 D6
Treskinnick Cross
    Cnwll........................ 9 G5
Tresmeer Cnwll............... 9 G7
Tresparrett Cnwll............ 8 F6
Tressait P & K 194 C4
Tresta Shet 235 c5
Tresta Shet 235 e3

Treswell Notts 116 C5
Treswithian Downs
    Crematorium
    Cnwll......................... 3 H3
Tre Taliesin Cerdgn 80 E5
Trethevey Cnwll.............. 8 E6
Trethewey Cnwll............. 2 C6
Trethurgy Cnwll............... 5 G5
Tretire Herefs 54 D4
Tretower Powys 53 J4
Treuddyn Flints............ 97 K2
Trevalga Cnwll................ 8 E6
Trevalyn Wrexhm 98 B2
Trevarrian Cnwll............. 4 D3
Treveal Cnwll.................. 4 C4
Treveighan Cnwll............ 8 E8
Trevellas Downs
    Cnwll........................ 3 J2
Trevelmond Cnwll........... 5 K3
Treverva Cnwll................ 3 K5
Trevescan Cnwll............. 2 C6
Treviscoe Cnwll.............. 4 E5
Trevone Cnwll 4 D2
Trevor Wrexhm 97 L4
Trewalder Cnwll.............. 8 E7
Trewarmett Cnwll........... 8 E7
Trewavas Mining
    District Cnwll 3 G6
Trewen Cnwll.................. 9 H7
Trewint Cnwll.................. 9 G8
Trewithian Cnwll............ 4 D7
Trewoon Cnwll................ 4 F5
Treyford W Susx 30 D7
Trimdon Dur 151 J7
Trimdon Colliery Dur... 151 J7
Trimdon Grange Dur ... 151 J7
Trimingham Norfk 107 G5
Trimley St Martin
    Suffk 78 F6
Trimley St Mary Suffk... 79 G7
Trimsaran Carmth 50 F5
Trimstone Devon.......... 23 H3
Trinafour P & K 194 B4
Tring Herts 58 F5
Trinity Angus............... 196 F4
Trinity Jersey............. 236 d6
Trinity Gask P & K...... 185 K4
Triscombe Somset 25 J4
Trislaig Highld 191 L2
Trispen Cnwll.................. 4 D5
Tritlington Nthumb 158 F4
Trochry P & K 194 F7
Troedyraur Cerdgn...... 65 K5
Troedyrhiw Myr Td 53 G7
Trois Bois Jersey....... 236 c6
Troon Cnwll 3 H4
Troon S Ayrs 163 H3
Tropical World
    Roundhay Park
    Leeds 123 L3
Trossachs Stirlg 184 B5
Trossachs Pier Stirlg.. 184 B6
Troston Suffk 91 K8
Trotshill Worcs 70 F4
Trottiscliffe Kent.......... 33 H2
Trotton W Susx 30 D6
Troutbeck Cumb 137 L6
Troutbeck Bridge
    Cumb 137 L7
Troway Derbys............ 115 H5
Trowbridge Wilts.......... 39 J8
Trowell Notts 101 J4
Trowell Services
    Notts 101 J4
Trowse Newton
    Norfk 92 F3
Trudoxhill Somset........ 27 H3
Trull Somset 25 K6
Trumpan Highld 208 C3
Trumpet Herefs 70 B6
Trumpington Cambs.... 76 C4
Trunch Norfk............... 107 G5
Truro Cnwll 4 C6
Trusham Devon 11 K7
Trusley Derbys............ 100 E5
Trusthorpe Lincs......... 119 G5

Trysull Staffs................ 84 F5
Tubney Oxon................ 57 H7
Tuckenhay Devon 7 J5
Tuckhill Shrops 84 E6
Tuckingmill Cnwll 3 H3
Tuckingmill Wilts.......... 27 L5
Tuckton Bmouth........... 15 L4
Tuddenham Suffk 77 G1
Tuddenham Suffk 78 E5
Tudeley Kent................ 33 G4
Tudhoe Dur 151 G7
Tudweiliog Gwynd 94 D5
Tuffley Gloucs 55 J5
Tufton Hants 29 J3
Tufton Pembks 49 H2
Tugby Leics................. 87 L4
Tugford Shrops............ 83 L6
Tughall Nthumb 169 J4
Tullibody Clacks........ 185 H7
Tullich Highld 212 F8
Tullich Highld 223 J6
Tulliemet P & K 194 F5
Tulloch Abers 216 F7
Tullochgorm Ag & B.. 182 D7
Tulloch Station
    Highld 192 F1
Tullymurdoch P & K.... 195 J5
Tullynessle Abers 206 B2
Tulse Hill Gt Lon 44 F5
Tumble Carmth 51 G3
Tumby Lincs............... 103 L1
Tumby Woodside
    Lincs 103 L2
Tummel Bridge P & K.. 194 B5
Tunbridge Wells Kent.... 33 G5
Tundergarth D & G..... 155 L6
Tunley BaNES............. 39 G8
Tunstall C Stke............ 99 K3
Tunstall E R Yk 127 H4
Tunstall Kent............... 34 B3
Tunstall Lancs 130 B5
Tunstall N York........... 140 F7
Tunstall Norfk.............. 93 J2
Tunstall Staffs............. 99 H6
Tunstall Suffk.............. 79 H4
Tunstall Sundld.......... 151 J4
Tunstead Derbys........ 114 C6
Tunstead Norfk.......... 107 G7
Tunstead Milton
    Derbys 114 B5
Turgis Green Hants 42 B8
Turkdean Gloucs......... 56 C4
Tur Langton Leics 87 K5
Turleigh Wilts 39 J7
Turnastone Herefs...... 69 G7
Turnberry S Ayrs....... 152 E2
Turnditch Derbys........ 100 F3
Turner's Hill W Susx.... 32 C6
Turnhouse C Edin...... 177 G4
Turnworth Dorset......... 14 F2
Turriff Abers 216 D4
Turton Bottoms
    Bl w D 121 L7
Turves Cambs 89 L4
Turvey Bed 74 D4
Turville Bucks.............. 42 C3
Turweston Bucks......... 73 H6
Tushielaw Inn Border.. 166 D5
Tutbury Staffs............ 100 E6
Tutshill Gloucs............. 38 D2
Tuttington Norfk......... 106 F6
Tuxford Notts 116 C7
Twatt Ork 234 b5
Twatt Shet................. 235 c5
Twechar E Duns......... 175 J3
Tweedbank Border..... 167 H3
Tweedmouth
    Nthumb 179 K7
Tweedsmuir Border... 165 L4
Twelveheads Cnwll........ 3 K3
Twemlow Green
    Ches E 113 H7
Twenty Lincs.............. 103 J7
Twerton BaNES........... 39 G7
Twickenham Gt Lon..... 44 D5
Twigworth Gloucs........ 55 J4

Twineham W Susx 19 H2
Twinstead Essex 77 J6
Twitchen Devon 24 C5
Two Dales Derbys 114 F8
Two Gates Staffs 86 B4
Twycross Leics 86 D3
Twycross Zoo Leics 86 C3
Twyford Bucks 58 A3
Twyford Hants 29 J6
Twyford Leics 87 K2
Twyford Norfk 106 B7
Twyford Wokham 42 C5
Twynholm D & G 146 B4
Twyning Green
    Gloucs 70 F6
Twynllanan Carmth 51 L2
Twywell Nhants 88 D7
Tyberton Herefs 69 H6
Tycroes Carmth 51 H4
Tycrwyn Powys 97 H8
Tydd Gote Lincs 104 D8
Tydd St Giles Cambs 90 B1
Tydd St Mary Lincs 104 C8
Tye Green Essex 76 E7
Tyldesley Wigan 113 G2
Tyler Hill Kent 34 F3
Tylorstown Rhondd 36 F2
Ty-nant Conwy 96 F4
Tyndrum Stirlg 183 K2
Ty'n-dwr Denbgs 97 K4
Tynemouth N Tyne 151 J2
Tynemouth
    Crematorium
    N Tyne 151 J2
Tyninghame E Loth 178 D3
Tynron D & G 154 E4
Tynygraig Cerdgn 66 F1
Ty'n-y-Groes Conwy ...109 L7
Tyn-y-nant Rhondd 37 G4
Tyringham M Keyn 74 C5
Tythegston Brdgnd 36 D5
Tytherington Ches E 113 K6
Tytherington S Glos 38 F3
Tytherington Wilts 27 K3
Tytherleigh Devon 13 H2
Tytherton Lucas Wilts 39 L5
Tywardreath Cnwll 5 H5
Tywyn Gwynd 80 D4

U

Ubbeston Green
    Suffk 79 G1
Ubley BaNES 38 D8
Uckfield E Susx 19 M2
Uckinghall Worcs 70 F6
Uckington Gloucs 55 K3
Uddingston S Lans 175 J6
Uddington S Lans 165 G3
Udimore E Susx 21 H2
Udny Green Abers 207 G1
Udny Station Abers 207 G1
Uffculme Devon 25 G8
Uffington Lincs 88 F3
Uffington Oxon 40 F3
Uffington Shrops 83 K2
Ufford C Pete 89 G3
Ufford Suffk 79 G4
Ufton Warwks 72 E3
Ufton Nervet W Berk 41 M6
Ugadale Ag & B 161 K4
Ugborough Devon 7 G5
Uggeshall Suffk 93 J7
Ugglebarnby N York 143 H5
Ughill Sheff 114 E4
Ugley Essex 60 E3
Ugley Green Essex 60 E3
Ugthorpe N York 143 G5
Uibhist A Deas W Isls ..233 c8
Uibhist A Tuath W Isls ..233 b6
Uig Ag & B 188 F5
Uig Highld 208 C4
Uig Highld 208 F2
Uig W Isls 232 d2

Uigshader Highld 209 G5
Uisken Ag & B 180 E4
Ulbster Highld 231 K7
Ulceby Lincs 118 F6
Ulceby N Linc 126 D7
Ulceby Skitter N Linc ..126 E7
Ulcombe Kent 33 L4
Uldale Cumb 147 M7
Uley Gloucs 55 H7
Ulgham Nthumb 159 G4
Ullapool Highld 220 E3
Ullenhall Warwks 71 K2
Ulleskelf N York 124 D3
Ullesthorpe Leics 87 G6
Ulley Rothm 115 J4
Ullingswick Herefs 69 L4
Ullinish Lodge Hotel
    Highld 208 E6
Ullock Cumb 136 E3
Ullswater Cumb 138 B3
Ullswater Steamers
    Cumb 137 L4
Ulpha Cumb 128 E2
Ulrome E R Yk 135 J7
Ulsta Shet 235 d3
Ulva Ag & B 189 K7
Ulverston Cumb 129 G4
Ulwell Dorset 15 J6
Ulzieside D & G 164 F7
Umberleigh Devon 23 J6
Unapool Highld 224 F2
Underbarrow Cumb 129 K2
Under Burnmouth
    Border 156 E5
Undercliffe C Brad 123 J4
Underdale Shrops 83 K2
Under River Kent 32 F3
Underwood Notts 101 J3
Undy Mons 38 C3
Union Mills IoM 237 C5
Unst Shet 235 d1
Unstone Derbys 115 G6
Upavon Wilts 28 C1
Upchurch Kent 46 D6
Upcott Devon 24 B5
Up Exe Devon 12 B2
Upgate Norfk 106 D8
Uphall Dorset 14 B2
Uphall W Loth 176 E4
Upham Devon 11 K3
Upham Hants 29 K7
Uphampton Herefs   69 H2
Uphampton Worcs 70 E2
Uphill N Som 37 L8
Up Holland Lancs 112 D1
Uplawmoor E Rens 174 E7
Upleadon Gloucs 55 H3
Upleatham R & Cl 142 D4
Uploders Dorset 13 L4
Uplowman Devon 24 F7
Uplyme Devon 13 H4
Up Marden W Susx 30 D8
Upminster Gt Lon 45 K3
Up Mudford Somset 26 E7
Up Nately Hants 30 B2
Upottery Devon 12 F2
Upper Affcot Shrops 83 J6
Upper Ardchronie
    Highld 222 E4
Upper Arley Worcs 84 D7
Upper Basildon
    W Berk 41 L5
Upper Beeding
    W Susx 19 G4
Upper Benefield
    Nhants 88 E5
Upper Bentley Worcs 71 H2
Upper Bighouse
    Highld 230 C4
Upper Boddington
    Nhants 72 F4
Upper Brailes Warwks ...72 C6
Upper Breakish
    Highld 199 L2
Upper Broadheath
    Worcs 70 E4

Upper Broughton
    Notts 102 B7
Upper Bucklebury
    W Berk 41 K6
Upper Burgate Hants 28 D7
Upperby Cumb 148 D4
Upper Caldecote
    C Beds 75 H5
Upper Chapel Powys 67 L6
Upper Chicksgrove
    Wilts 27 L5
Upper Chute Wilts 28 F2
Upper Clapton Gt Lon 45 G3
Upper Clatford Hants 29 G3
Upper Cound Shrops 83 K3
Upper Cumberworth
    Kirk 123 J8
Upper Dallachy
    Moray 215 H2
Upper Deal Kent 35 K4
Upper Dean Bed 74 F2
Upper Denby Kirk 114 E1
Upper Dicker E Susx 20 B4
Upper Dounreay
    Highld 230 E3
Upper Dovercourt
    Essex 62 F2
Upper Drumbane
    Stirlg 184 E6
Upper Dunsforth
    N York 133 G6
Upper Eashing Surrey ...30 F3
Upper Eathie Highld 213 J2
Upper Egleton Herefs 70 B5
Upper Elkstone Staffs ..100 B2
Upper Ellastone
    Staffs 100 C4
Upper Farringdon
    Hants 30 B4
Upper Framilode
    Gloucs 55 H6
Upper Froyle Hants 30 C3
Upperglen Highld 208 E4
Upper Godney
    Somset 26 C3
Upper Gravenhurst
    C Beds 75 G7
Upper Green W Berk 41 G7
Upper Grove
    Common Herefs 54 E3
Upper Hale Surrey 30 D2
Upper Halliford
    Surrey 43 H6
Upper Hambleton
    Rutlnd 88 C3
Upper Harbledown
    Kent 34 F3
Upper Hartfield
    E Susx 32 E6
Upper Hatherley
    Gloucs 55 L4
Upper Heaton Kirk 123 H6
Upper Helmsley
    N York 133 L7
Upper Hergest Herefs 68 F4
Upper Heyford
    Nhants 73 J3
Upper Heyford Oxon 57 J3
Upper Hill Herefs 69 J4
Upper Hopton Kirk 123 J6
Upper Hulme Staffs 100 A1
Upper Inglesham
    Swindn 40 D2
Upper Killay Swans 51 H6
Upper Kinchrackine
    Ag & B 183 G2
Upper Lambourn
    W Berk 40 F4
Upper Landywood
    Staffs 85 H3
Upper Langford
    N Som 38 C7
Upper Langwith
    Derbys 115 K7
Upper Largo Fife 187 G6
Upper Leigh Staffs 100 A5

Upper Lochton Abers ...206 D6
Upper Longdon Staffs 85 J2
Upper & Lower
    Stondon C Beds 75 H7
Upper Lybster Highld ..231 J7
Upper Lydbrook
    Gloucs 54 E5
Upper Lye Herefs 69 H2
Uppermill Oldham 113 M1
Upper Milton Worcs 84 E8
Upper Minety Wilts 40 A3
Upper Mulben Moray ...215 H4
Upper Netchwood
    Shrops 83 L5
Upper Nobut Staffs 100 B5
Upper Norwood
    W Susx 18 C3
Upper Poppleton
    C York 133 H8
Upper Ratley Hants 28 F6
Upper Rissington
    Gloucs 56 D4
Upper Rochford
    Worcs 70 B2
Upper Ruscoe D & G ...145 L3
Upper Sapey Herefs 70 C2
Upper Seagry Wilts 39 L4
Upper Shelton C Beds ...74 E5
Upper Sheringham
    Norfk 106 D4
Upper Skelmorlie
    N Ayrs 173 L5
Upper Slaughter
    Gloucs 56 D4
Upper Soudley Gloucs ...54 F6
Upper Standen Kent 35 H6
Upper Stoke Norfk 92 F3
Upper Stowe Nhants 73 J3
Upper Street Norfk 28 D7
Upper Street Norfk 93 H1
Upper Street Norfk 107 G8
Upper Street Suffk 77 H4
Upper Street Suffk 78 D4
Upper Sundon C Beds ...59 H3
Upper Swell Gloucs 56 D3
Upper Tasburgh
    Norfk 92 E4
Upper Tean Staffs 100 A5
Upperthong Kirk 123 H8
Upperton W Susx 30 F6
Upper Town Herefs 69 L5
Upper Town Highld 231 L1
Upper Town N Som 38 D7
Upper Town Suffk 77 K2
Upper Tumble
    Carmth 51 G3
Upper Tysoe Warwks 72 D5
Upper Victoria Angus ...187 J1
Upper Wardington
    Oxon 72 F5
Upper Welland Worcs 70 D6
Upper Wellingham
    E Susx 19 L3
Upper Weybread
    Suffk 92 F7
Upper Wield Hants 29 L4
Upper Winchendon
    Bucks 58 C5
Upper Woodford
    Wilts 28 C4
Upper Wraxall Wilts 39 J5
Uppingham Rutlnd 88 C4
Uppington Shrops 83 L2
Upsall N York 133 G3
Upsettlington Border 168 C1
Upshire Essex 60 C7
Up Somborne Hants 29 H5
Upstreet Kent 35 G3
Upton Bucks 58 C5
Upton C Pete 89 G4
Upton Cambs 89 H7
Upton Ches W 112 B7
Upton Cnwll 5 L2
Upton Devon 7 G7
Upton Devon 12 E2
Upton Dorset 14 E5

Upton Dorset 15 J4
Upton Halton 112 C4
Upton Hants 29 G5
Upton Hants 29 G7
Upton Leics 86 D4
Upton Lincs 116 E4
Upton Norfk 93 H2
Upton Notts 102 B2
Upton Notts 116 C6
Upton Oxon 41 K3
Upton Slough 43 G5
Upton Somset 24 F5
Upton Somset 26 C4
Upton Wakefd 124 D7
Upton Wirral 111 J4
Upton Bishop Herefs 54 F3
Upton Cheyney S Glos ..39 G6
Upton Cressett
Shrops 84 B5
Upton Grey Hants 30 B2
Upton Hellions Devon 11 J4
Upton Lovell Wilts 27 L4
Upton Magna Shrops 83 K2
Upton Noble Somset 27 G4
Upton Pyne Devon 11 L5
Upton St Leonards
Gloucs 55 K5
Upton Scudamore
Wilts 27 K2
Upton Snodsbury
Worcs 71 G4
Upton-upon-Severn
Worcs 70 F6
Upton Warren Worcs......71 G2
Upwaltham W Susx......18 C3
Upwell Norfk 90 C3
Upwood Cambs 89 J6
Urchfont Wilts 40 B8
Urmston Traffd 113 H3
Urquhart Moray...............215 G2
Urquhart Castle
Highld 212 E8
Urra N York 142 C6
Urray Highld 212 D4
Usan Angus 197 H5
Ushaw Moor Dur............151 G6
Usk Mons 54 B7
Usselby Lincs 117 H3
Usworth Sundld 151 H4
Utkinton Ches W 112 D7
Utley C Brad 122 F3
Uton Devon 11 J5
Utterby Lincs 118 D3
Uxbridge Gt Lon 43 H4
Uyeasound Shet............235 d2
Uzmaston Pembks......49 G5

Vidlin Shet 235 d4
Viewfield Moray 215 G2
Viewpark N Lans 175 J6
Vigo Kent 45 M7
Village de Putron
Guern 236 d3
Ville la Bas Jersey 236 a5
Villiaze Guern 236 c5
Vines Cross E Susx......20 C3
Vinters Park
Crematorium
Kent 33 K2
Virginia Water Surrey.....43 G6
Virginstow Devon 9 K6
Vobster Somset 27 G2
Voe Shet 235 C4
Vowchurch Herefs 69 G7

Waberthwaite Cumb ...128 D2
Wackerfield Dur............140 E3
Wacton Norfk 92 E5
Wadborough Worcs ...70 F5
Waddesdon Bucks 58 C5
Waddesdon Manor
Bucks 58 B5
Waddeton Devon 7 K4
Waddingham Lincs 117 G3
Waddington Lancs.........121 L2
Waddington Lincs.........116 F8
Wadebridge Cnwll............4 F2
Wadeford Somset 13 H1
Wadenhoe Nhants 88 E6
Wadesmill Herts 60 B4
Wadhurst E Susx 33 H6
Wadshelf Derbys 114 F7
Wadworth Donc............115 K3
Wainfleet All Saints
Lincs 104 D2
Wainfleet St Mary
Lincs 104 D2
Wainhouse Corner
Cnwll 9 G5
Wainscott Medway.........46 C6
Wainstalls Calder............122 F5
Waitby Cumb 139 H5
Waithe Lincs 118 C2
Wakefield Wakefd 123 L6
Wakefield
Crematorium
Wakefd 123 L7
Wakehurst Place
W Susx 32 C6
Wakerley Nhants............88 D4
Wakes Colne Essex......61 L3
Walberswick Suffk 93 K8
Walberton W Susx.........18 C4
Walbutt D & G 146 D2
Walcombe Somset 26 D3
Walcot Lincs 103 H5
Walcot Shrops 83 L2
Walcot Swindn 40 D4
Walcote Leics 87 H6
Walcot Green Norfk......92 D7
Walcott Lincs 103 J2
Walcott Norfk 107 H6
Walden Stubbs
N York 124 E6
Walderslade
Medway 46 C7
Walderton W Susx.........17 L1
Walditch Dorset 13 L4
Waldridge Dur...............151 G5
Waldringfield Suffk.........79 G5
Waldron E Susx 20 B2
Wales Rothm 115 J5
Wales Somset 26 E6
Walesby Lincs 117 J3
Walesby Notts 116 B7
Wales Millennium
Centre Cardif............37 J5
Walford Herefs 54 E4
Walford Herefs 83 H8

Walford Heath
Shrops 98 C8
Walgherton Ches E.......99 G3
Walgrave Nhants............74 B1
Walkden Salfd...............113 G2
Walker N u Ty...............151 H3
Walkerburn Border......166 E3
Walkeringham Notts......116 C3
Walkerith Lincs 116 C3
Walkern Herts 59 M3
Walkerton Fife 186 D6
Walkford Dorset 16 B4
Walkhampton Devon 6 D2
Walkington E R Yk..........126 B3
Walkley Sheff 115 G4
Walk Mill Lancs...............122 C5
Walkwood Worcs............71 J2
Wall Nthumb 150 A2
Wall Staffs 85 K3
Wallacetown S Ayrs......153 G2
Wallacetown S Ayrs......163 J5
Wallands Park E Susx......19 L4
Wallasey Wirral 111 J3
Wallingford Oxon............41 L3
Wallington Gt Lon 44 F6
Wallington Hants 17 H2
Wallington Herts 75 K7
Wallisdown Poole 15 K4
Walls Shet 235 b5
Wallsend N Tyne 151 H2
Wallyford E Loth 177 K4
Walmer Kent 35 K5
Walmer Bridge Lancs...121 G5
Walmley Birm 85 K5
Walpole Suffk 93 H8
Walpole Cross Keys
Norfk 104 E8
Walpole Highway
Norfk 90 D2
Walpole St Andrew
Norfk 104 D8
Walpole St Peter
Norfk 90 C1
Walsall Wsall...............85 H4
Walsden Calder...............122 D6
Walsgrave on Sowe
Covtry 86 E7
Walsham le Willows
Suffk 78 B1
Walshford N York 132 F8
Walsoken Norfk...............90 C2
Walston S Lans...............165 K1
Walsworth Herts 59 K3
Walter's Ash Bucks......42 D2
Waltham Kent...............34 E5
Waltham NE Lin 118 C2
Waltham Abbey
Essex 60 C7
Waltham Chase Hants...29 K7
Waltham Cross Herts...60 B7
Waltham on the
Wolds Leics...............102 D7
Waltham St
Lawrence W & M......42 D5
Walthamstow Gt Lon......45 G3
Walton Cumb...............148 F3
Walton Derbys 115 G7
Walton Leeds 124 C2
Walton Leics 87 H6
Walton M Keyn...............74 C7
Walton Powys 68 F3
Walton Somset 26 C4
Walton Suffk 79 G7
Walton W Susx...............17 M2
Walton Wakefd 123 L6
Walton Wrekin 98 E8
Walton Cardiff Gloucs...55 K2
Walton East Pembks......49 H3
Walton-in-Gordano
N Som 38 B5
Walton Lea
Crematorium
Warrtn 112 E4
Walton-le-Dale Lancs...121 H5
Walton-on-Thames
Surrey 43 J6

Walton-on-the-Hill
Staffs 99 L7
Walton on the Hill
Surrey 31 L1
Walton on the Naze
Essex 62 F4
Walton on the Wolds
Leics 101 L8
Walton-on-Trent
Derbys 100 E8
Walton Park N Som 38 B6
Walton West Pembks ...48 E5
Waltonwrays
Crematorium
N York 122 E1
Walworth Darltn...............141 G4
Walworth Gt Lon 45 G4
Walwyn's Castle
Pembks 48 E5
Wambrook Somset........13 H2
Wanborough Surrey......30 F2
Wanborough Swindn......40 E4
Wandsworth Gt Lon 44 E5
Wangford Suffk...............93 K7
Wanlip Leics 87 H2
Wanlockhead D & G......165 G6
Wannock E Susx 20 C5
Wansford C Pete...............88 F4
Wansford E R Yk...............135 G7
Wanshurst Green
Kent 33 K4
Wanstead Gt Lon...........45 H3
Wanstrow Somset 27 G3
Wanswell Gloucs 55 G7
Wantage Oxon...............41 H3
Wappenbury Warwks ...72 E2
Wappenham Nhants......73 J5
Warbleton E Susx...............20 C3
Warborough Oxon...........41 L2
Warboys Cambs 89 K7
Warbreck Bpool 120 D3
Warbstow Cnwll 9 G6
Warburton Traffd...............113 G4
Warcop Cumb...............139 H4
Warden Nthumb 150 A2
Wardington Oxon 72 F5
Wardle Ches E...............98 E2
Wardle Rochdl 122 D6
Wardley Gatesd 151 H3
Wardley Rutlnd...............88 B4
Wardlow Derbys...............114 D6
Wardy Hill Cambs...........90 C6
Ware Herts 60 B5
Wareham Dorset...............15 H5
Warehorne Kent...............34 D7
Warenford Nthumb...169 H4
Wareside Herts 60 C5
Waresley Cambs 75 J4
Warfield Br For...............42 E6
Warfleet Devon 7 K6
Wargrave Wokham 42 C5
Warham All Saints
Norfk 105 M4
Warham St Mary
Norfk 105 M4
Wark Nthumb 157 L6
Wark Nthumb 168 C2
Warkleigh Devon...............23 K6
Warkton Nhants 88 C7
Warkworth Nhants......72 F6
Warkworth Nthumb...159 G2
Warlaby N York...............132 E2
Warleggan Cnwll...............5 J3
Warley Town Calder......122 F5
Warlingham Surrey......32 C2
Warmfield Wakefd 124 B6
Warmingham Ches E......99 G1
Warmington Nhants......88 F5
Warmington Warwks...72 E5
Warminster Wilts 27 K3
Warmley S Glos...............38 F5
Warmsworth Donc......115 K2
Warmwell Dorset 14 E5
Warner Bros Studio
Tour Herts...............59 H7
Warnford Hants...............29 L6

Warnham W Susx 31 J5
Warningcamp W Susx 18 D4
Warninglid W Susx 31 L6
Warren Ches E 113 K7
Warren Pembks 48 F7
Warren Row W & M 42 D4
Warren Street Kent 34 C4
Warrington M Keyn 74 C4
Warrington Warrtn 112 E4
Warriston C Edin 177 H4
Warriston
   Crematorium
   C Edin 177 H3
Warsash Hants 16 F2
Warslow Staffs 100 C2
Warter E R Yk 125 K1
Warthermaske N York .. 132 C4
Warthill N York 133 K7
Wartling E Susx 20 D4
Wartnaby Leics 102 B7
Warton Lancs 120 E5
Warton Lancs 129 K5
Warton Warwks 86 C3
Warwick Warwks 72 C2
Warwick Bridge
   Cumb 148 E4
Warwick Castle
   Warwks 72 C2
Warwick Services
   Warwks 72 D3
Wasbister Ork 234 c4
Wasdale Head Cumb 137 G5
Washaway Cnwll 5 G2
Washbourne Devon 7 J5
Washbrook Suffk 78 D6
Washfield Devon 11 L2
Washford Somset 25 G3
Washford Pyne
   Devon 11 J3
Washingborough
   Lincs 117 G7
Washington Sundld 151 H4
Washington W Susx 18 F3
Washington Services
   Gatesd 151 H4
Wasperton Warwks 72 C3
Wass N York 133 H4
Watchet Somset 25 G3
Watchfield Oxon 40 E3
Watchgate Cumb 138 D7
Water Devon 11 H8
Waterbeach Cambs 76 C2
Waterbeach W Susx 18 B4
Waterbeck D & G 155 M6
Water End E R Yk 125 J3
Waterfall Staffs 100 B3
Waterfoot E Rens 175 G2
Waterford Herts 60 A5
Waterheads Border 177 H7
Waterhouses Staffs 100 B3
Wateringbury Kent 33 H3
Waterloo Highld 199 K2
Waterloo N Lans 175 L7
Waterloo P & K 195 G8
Waterloo Pembks 49 G6
Waterloo Sefton 111 K2
Waterlooville Hants 17 J1
Watermillock Cumb 138 C3
Water Newton
   Cambs 89 G4
Water Orton Warwks 85 L5
Waterperry Oxon 57 L6
Waterrow Somset 25 G6
Watersfield W Susx 18 D3
Waterside Bl w D 121 K5
Waterside E Ayrs 163 K7
Waterside E Ayrs 163 L2
Waterside E Duns 175 J4
Waterstein Highld 208 B5
Waterstock Oxon 57 M6
Waterston Pembks 48 F6
Water Stratford
   Bucks 73 J7
Waters Upton Wrekin 98 F8
Watford Herts 43 J2

Watford Nhants 73 H2
Watford Gap
   Services Nhants 73 H2
Wath N York 132 B6
Wath N York 132 E4
Wath upon Dearne
   Rothm 115 H2
Watlington Norfk 90 E2
Watlington Oxon 42 B2
Watten Highld 231 J5
Wattisfield Suffk 92 B8
Wattisham Suffk 78 B4
Watton Dorset 13 L4
Watton E R Yk 126 C1
Watton Norfk 91 K4
Watton-at-Stone
   Herts 60 A4
Wattston N Lans 175 K4
Wattsville Caerph 37 J3
Waulkmill Abers 206 C6
Waunarlwydd Swans 51 H6
Waunfawr Cerdgn 80 E6
Waunfawr Gwynd 95 J2
Wavendon M Keyn 74 C6
Waverbridge Cumb 147 L5
Waverton Ches W 112 C8
Waverton Cumb 147 L5
Wawne E R Yk 126 D3
Waxham Norfk 107 J7
Wayford Somset 13 K2
Waytown Dorset 13 L3
Way Village Devon 11 K3
Weacombe Somset 25 H4
Weald Oxon 56 F7
Wealdstone Gt Lon 44 D3
Weardley Leeds 123 K2
Weare Somset 26 B2
Weare Giffard Devon 23 G6
Wearhead Dur 149 L6
Wearne Somset 26 B5
Wear Valley
   Crematorium Dur 141 G2
Weasenham All
   Saints Norfk 105 K7
Weasenham St Peter
   Norfk 105 K7
Weaste Salfd 113 J2
Weaverham Ches W 112 E6
Weaverthorpe N York .. 134 F5
Webheath Worcs 71 H2
Wedderlairs Abers 216 F7
Weddington Warwks 86 D5
Wedhampton Wilts 40 B8
Wedmore Somset 26 C2
Wednesbury Sandw 85 H4
Wednesfield Wolves 85 G4
Weedon Bucks 58 D4
Weedon Nhants 73 J3
Weedon Lois Nhants 73 H5
Weeford Staffs 85 K3
Weeke Hants 29 J5
Weekley Nhants 88 C7
Week St Mary Cnwll 9 H5
Weel E R Yk 126 D3
Weeley Essex 62 D4
Weeley Crematorium
   Essex 62 D4
Weeley Heath Essex 62 D4
Weem P & K 194 D6
Weethley Warwks 71 J4
Weeting Norfk 91 H5
Weeton E R Yk 127 H6
Weeton Lancs 120 E4
Weeton N York 123 K2
Weetwood Leeds 123 K3
Weir Lancs 122 C5
Weir Quay Devon 6 C3
Weisdale Shet 235 c5
Welborne Norfk 92 C2
Welbourn Lincs 102 F2
Welburn N York 133 L6
Welbury N York 141 J6
Welby Lincs 102 F5
Welcombe Devon 22 C7
Welford Nhants 87 J7
Welford W Berk 41 H5

Welford-on-Avon
   Warwks 71 K4
Welham Leics 87 L5
Welham Notts 116 B5
Welham Green Herts 59 L6
Well Hants 30 C3
Well Lincs 118 F6
Well N York 132 D3
Welland Worcs 70 E6
Wellbank Angus 196 D8
Wellesbourne Warwks ... 72 C4
Well Head Herts 59 K3
Welling Gt Lon 45 J5
Wellingborough
   Nhants 74 C2
Wellingham Norfk 105 L7
Wellingore Lincs 103 G2
Wellington Cumb 136 F6
Wellington Herefs 69 K5
Wellington Somset 25 H7
Wellington Wrekin 84 B2
Wellington Heath
   Herefs 70 C6
Wellow BaNES 39 H8
Wellow IoW 16 E5
Wellow Notts 116 A7
Wells Somset 26 D3
Wells-next-the-sea
   Norfk 105 L4
Wellstye Green Essex 61 G4
Welltree P & K 185 K3
Wellwood Fife 176 E2
Welney Norfk 90 D5
Welshampton Shrops 98 C5
Welsh Frankton
   Shrops 98 A6
Welsh Newton Herefs 54 D4
Welshpool Powys 82 E3
Welsh St Donats
   V Glam 36 F5
Welton Cumb 148 C6
Welton E R Yk 126 B5
Welton Lincs 117 G5
Welton Nhants 73 H2
Welton le Marsh Lincs .. 119 G7
Welton le Wold Lincs ... 118 C4
Welwick E R Yk 127 H6
Welwyn Herts 59 L5
Welwyn Garden City
   Herts 59 L5
Wem Shrops 98 D6
Wembdon Somset 25 L4
Wembley Gt Lon 44 D3
Wembury Devon 6 D6
Wemworthy Devon 10 F3
Wemyss Bay Inver 173 L4
Wendens Ambo Essex ... 76 D7
Wendlebury Oxon 57 K4
Wendling Norfk 91 L2
Wendover Bucks 58 E6
Wendron Cnwll 3 H5
Wendron Mining
   District Cnwll 3 J5
Wendy Cambs 75 K5
Wenhaston Suffk 93 J7
Wennington Cambs 89 J7
Wennington Gt Lon 45 K4
Wennington Lancs 130 C5
Wensley Derbys 100 E1
Wensley N York 131 K2
Wentbridge Wakefd 124 D6
Wentnor Shrops 83 H5
Wentworth Cambs 90 C7
Wentworth Rothm 115 G2
Wenvoe V Glam 37 H6
Weobley Herefs 69 H4
Wepham W Susx 18 E4
Wereham Norfk 90 F3
Werrington C Pete 89 H3
Werrington Cnwll 9 J7
Wervin Ches W 112 B6
Wesham Lancs 120 F4
Wessex Vale
   Crematorium
   Hants 29 J7
Wessington Derbys 101 G2

West Acre Norfk 91 H1
West Alvington
   Devon 7 G6
West Anstey Devon 24 D6
West Ashby Lincs 118 C6
West Ashling W Susx 17 M2
West Ashton Wilts 27 K1
West Auckland Dur 140 F3
West Ayton N York 134 F3
West Bagborough
   Somset 25 J5
West Bank Halton 112 D5
West Barkwith Lincs 117 K5
West Barnby N York 143 G5
West Barns E Loth 178 E3
West Barsham Norfk 105 L5
West Bay Dorset 13 L4
West Beckham Norfk ... 106 D5
West Bedfont Surrey 43 H5
Westbere Kent 35 G3
West Bergholt Essex 62 A3
West Berkshire
   Crematorium
   W Berk 41 K6
West Bexington
   Dorset 14 A5
West Bilney Norfk 91 G1
West Blatchington
   Br & H 19 J4
West Boldon S Tyne 151 J3
Westborough Lincs 102 D4
Westbourne Bmouth 15 K4
Westbourne W Susx 17 L2
West Bowling C Brad ... 123 H4
West Bradenham
   Norfk 91 K2
West Bradford Lancs 121 L2
West Bradley Somset 26 E4
West Bretton Wakefd .. 123 K7
West Bridgford Notts ... 101 L5
West Bromwich
   Sandw 85 H5
West Bromwich
   Crematorium
   Sandw 85 H5
Westbrook Kent 35 J2
Westbrook W Berk 41 H6
West Buckland Devon 23 K5
West Buckland
   Somset 25 J7
West Burton N York 131 J3
Westbury Bucks 73 J7
Westbury Shrops 83 G2
Westbury Wilts 27 K2
Westbury Leigh Wilts 27 K2
Westbury on Severn
   Gloucs 55 G5
Westbury-on-Trym
   Bristl 38 E5
Westbury-sub-
   Mendip Somset 26 D2
West Butterwick
   N Linc 116 D1
Westby Lancs 120 E4
West Byfleet Surrey 43 H7
West Cairngaan
   D & G 144 D8
West Caister Norfk 93 K2
West Calder W Loth 176 D5
West Camel Somset 26 E6
West Chaldon Dorset 14 E5
West Challow Oxon 41 G3
West Charleton
   Devon 7 H7
West Chiltington
   W Susx 18 E3
West Chinnock
   Somset 26 C8
West Clandon Surrey 31 H2
West Cliffe Kent 35 J5
Westcliff-on-Sea
   Sthend 46 E3
West Coker Somset 26 D8
Westcombe Somset 27 G4
West Compton
   Somset 26 E3

West Compton
  Abbas Dorset 14 B4
Westcote Gloucs............56 E4
Westcote Barton
  Oxon.........................57 H3
Westcott Bucks..............58 B5
Westcott Devon 12 C2
Westcott Surrey 31 J2
West Cottingwith
  N York.....................125 G3
Westcourt Wilts............40 E7
West Cowick E R Yk ..124 F6
West Cross Swans............51 H7
West Curthwaite
  Cumb....................148 B5
Westdean E Susx............20 B5
West Dean W Susx..........18 B3
West Dean Wilts 28 E6
West Deeping Lincs 89 G2
West Derby Lpool.........111 L3
West Dereham Norfk ...90 F4
West Down Devon 23 H3
Westdowns Cnwll 8 E7
West Drayton Gt Lon 43 H4
West Drayton Notts 116 B6
West Dunnet Highld 231 J2
West Ella E R Yk 126 C5
West End Bed 74 E4
West End Hants 29 J8
West End N Som............38 C6
West End Norfk 93 K2
West End Surrey 42 F7
West End Wilts 27 M6
West End Green
  Hants 42 A7
Wester Aberchalder
  Highld....................202 E2
Westerdale Highld 231 G5
Westerdale N York 142 E6
Westerfield Suffk 78 E5
Westergate W Susx........18 C5
Westerham Kent............32 D3
Westerhope N u Ty 150 F2
Westerland Devon 7 K4
Westerleigh S Glos 39 G4
Westerleigh
  Crematorium
  S Glos.......................39 G5
Western Isles W Isls......232 d5
Wester Ochiltree
  W Loth....................176 D4
Wester Pitkierie Fife ..187 J6
Wester Ross Highld....220 C5
Westerton of Rossie
  Angus 197 G5
Westerwick Shet.........235 c6
West Farleigh Kent........33 J3
West Farndon Nhants ..73 G4
West Felton Shrops 97 M7
Westfield BaNES 26 F2
Westfield Cumb 136 D2
Westfield E Susx............21 G3
Westfield Highld.........230 F3
Westfield N Lans.........175 J4
Westfield Norfk............92 B2
Westfield W Loth........176 C4
Westfields of Rattray
  P & K.......................195 J6
Westgate Dur 150 A7
Westgate N Linc 125 J8
Westgate on Sea
  Kent.........................35 J2
West Grafton Wilts........40 E7
West Green Hants 30 C1
West Grimstead Wilts ..28 E6
West Grinstead
  W Susx......................31 K6
West Haddlesey
  N York.....................124 E5
West Haddon Nhants ..73 J1
West Hagbourne
  Oxon.........................41 K3
West Hagley Worcs........84 F7
Westhall Suffk...............93 J7
West Hallam Derbys.....101 H4
West Halton N Linc 125 L6

Westham Dorset 14 C6
Westham E Susx............20 D5
West Ham Gt Lon...........45 H4
Westham Somset...........26 B3
Westhampnett
  W Susx......................18 B4
West Handley Derbys...115 H6
West Hanney Oxon.........41 H2
West Hanningfield
  Essex 61 H7
West Harnham Wilts.....28 C5
West Harptree BaNES.....38 E8
West Harting W Susx......30 C7
West Hatch Somset 25 L7
West Hatch Wilts 27 L5
West Haven Angus........187 J1
Westhay Somset 26 C3
West Heath Birm............85 J7
West Helmsdale
  Highld....................227 H5
West Hendred Oxon 41 H3
West Hertfordshire
  Crematorium
  Herts.........................59 J7
West Heslerton
  N York.....................134 E4
West Hewish N Som.......38 B7
Westhide Herefs............69 L5
Westhill Abers 206 F4
West Hill Devon 12 D4
West Hoathly W Susx....32 C6
West Holme Dorset.......15 G5
Westhope Herefs 69 J4
Westhope Shrops..........83 J6
West Horndon Essex 45 M3
Westhorpe Lincs..........103 L6
Westhorpe Suffk 78 C2
West Horrington
  Somset 26 E3
West Horsley Surrey 31 H2
West Hougham Kent.....35 H6
Westhoughton
  Bolton 112 F1
Westhouse N York.......130 D5
Westhouses Derbys....101 H2
West Howe Bmouth 15 K4
Westhumble Surrey.......31 K2
West Huntingtower
  P & K 185 M3
West Huntspill
  Somset 25 L3
West Hythe Kent...........34 F7
West Ilsley W Berk........41 J4
West Itchenor W Susx ...17 L3
West Kennett Wilts.......40 C6
West Kilbride N Ayrs ..173 L8
West Kingsdown
  Kent.........................45 L7
West Kington Wilts 39 J5
West Kirby Wirral.........111 H4
West Knapton N York ..134 D4
West Knighton
  Dorset 14 D5
West Knoyle Wilts 27 K5
Westlake Devon 6 F5
West Lambrook
  Somset 26 B7
West Langdon Kent......35 J5
West Lavington
  W Susx......................30 E7
West Lavington Wilts ...28 A2
West Layton N York 140 E5
West Leake Notts.........101 K7
Westleigh Devon 23 G5
Westleigh Devon 25 G7
West Leigh Somset 25 H5
Westleton Suffk 79 J2
West Lexham Norfk.......91 J1
Westley Suffk 77 J2
Westley Waterless
  Cambs 76 E3
West Lilling N York 133 K6
Westlington Bucks.......58 C6
West Linton Border.....176 F7
Westlinton Cumb........148 D3
West Littleton S Glos ...39 H5

West Lockinge Oxon......41 H3
West London
  Crematorium
  Gt Lon.......................44 E4
West Lulworth Dorset....14 F6
West Lutton N York......134 E5
West Lydford Somset 26 E5
West Lyng Somset..........25 L5
West Lynn Norfk..........104 F7
West Malling Kent..........33 H2
West Malvern Worcs......70 D5
West Marden W Susx.....30 C8
West Markham Notts....116 B6
Westmarsh Kent............35 H3
West Marsh NE Lin 127 G8
West Marton N York ...122 D1
West Melbury Dorset....27 K7
West Meon Hants 29 M6
West Mersea Essex 62 B5
Westmeston E Susx 19 K3
West Midland Safari
  Park Worcs................84 E7
Westmill Herts..............60 B3
West Milton Dorset 13 L3
Westminster Gt Lon......44 F4
West Minster Kent 46 E5
Westminster Abbey
  & Palace Gt Lon 44 F4
West Molesey Surrey.....43 J6
West Monkton
  Somset 25 K5
West Moors Dorset 15 K2
West Morden Dorset 15 G4
West Morriston
  Border 167 J2
West Mudford
  Somset 26 E7
Westmuir Angus.........196 B5
West Ness N York 133 L4
Westnewton Cumb 147 K6
West Newton E R Yk ...126 F3
West Newton Norfk.....105 H6
West Newton Somset...25 L5
West Norwood
  Gt Lon.......................44 F5
West Norwood
  Crematorium
  Gt Lon.......................44 F5
Westoe S Tyne.............151 J2
West Ogwell Devon 7 J2
Weston BaNES 39 G6
Weston Ches E..............99 G3
Weston Devon 12 E3
Weston Devon 12 F5
Weston Hants 30 B6
Weston Herts 59 L3
Weston Lincs................103 M7
Weston N York 123 H2
Weston Nhants 73 H5
Weston Notts................116 C7
Weston Shrops 83 L5
Weston Shrops 97 L6
Weston Staffs................99 L6
Weston W Berk 41 H5
Weston Beggard
  Herefs 69 L6
Westonbirt Gloucs 39 J3
Weston by Welland
  Nhants 87 L5
Weston Colville
  Cambs 76 E4
Weston Corbett
  Hants 30 B3
Weston Coyney
  C Stke 99 L4
Weston Favell Nhants ...73 L3
Weston Green Cambs....76 F4
Weston Heath Shrops ...84 D2
Westoning C Beds...........59 G2
Weston-in-Gordano
  N Som 38 C5
Weston Jones Staffs 99 H7
Weston Longville
  Norfk 92 D1
Weston Lullingfields
  Shrops 98 B7

Weston Mill
  Crematorium
  C Plym 6 C4
Weston-on-the-
  Green Oxon 57 K4
Weston Park Staffs 84 E2
Weston Patrick Hants ...30 B3
Weston Rhyn Shrops....97 L5
Weston-sub-Edge
  Gloucs 71 K6
Weston-super-Mare
  N Som 37 L7
Weston-super-Mare
  Crematorium
  N Som 38 A7
Weston Turville Bucks...58 D6
Weston-under-Lizard
  Staffs 84 E2
Weston under
  Penyard Herefs 54 F4
Weston-under-
  Redcastle Shrops ...98 E6
Weston under
  Wetherley Warwks ...72 D1
Weston Underwood
  Derbys 100 F4
Weston Underwood
  M Keyn 74 C4
Weston-upon-Trent
  Derbys 101 H6
Westonzoyland
  Somset 25 M4
West Orchard Dorset....27 J7
West Overton Wilts.......40 C6
Westow N York 134 B6
West Park Abers 206 E5
West Parley Dorset........15 K3
West Peckham Kent.......33 H3
West Pelton Dur...........151 G4
West Pennard
  Somset 26 D4
West Pentire Cnwll 4 B4
West Perry Cambs 75 G2
West Porlock Somset 24 D3
Westport Somset 26 B7
West Putford Devon........9 K2
West Quantoxhead
  Somset 25 H3
Westquarter Falk 176 B3
West Rainton Dur........151 H5
West Rasen Lincs.........117 H4
Westray Ork................234 c3
Westray Airport Ork 234 c3
West Raynham Norfk...105 L7
Westrigg W Loth.........176 B5
West Road
  Crematorium
  N u Ty 150 F2
Westrop Swindn 40 D2
West Rounton N York ..141 K6
West Row Suffk............90 F7
West Rudham Norfk....105 K6
West Runton Norfk.....106 E4
Westruther Border 178 D7
Westry Cambs..............90 B4
West Saltoun E Loth ...178 B5
West Sandford Devon...11 J4
West Sandwick Shet....235 d3
West Scrafton N York ..131 K3
West Stafford Dorset 14 D4
West Stockwith
  Notts......................116 C3
West Stoke W Susx.......17 M2
West Stour Dorset.........27 H6
West Stourmouth
  Kent.........................35 H3
West Stow Suffk............77 J1
West Stowell Wilts 40 C7
West Street Suffk...........78 B1
West Suffolk
  Crematorium
  Suffk 77 J2
West Tanfield N York ...132 D4
West Taphouse Cnwll 5 J3
West Tarbert Ag & B ...172 E5
West Tarring W Susx 18 F5

West Thirston
Nthumb 158 F3
West Thorney W Susx.....17 L3
West Thorpe Notts 101 L7
West Thurrock Thurr.....45 L4
West Tilbury Thurr.......46 A4
West Tisted Hants 29 M5
West Torrington Lincs...117 J5
West Town Hants 17 K3
West Town N Som.........38 C6
West Tytherley Hants....28 F5
West Walton Norfk.......90 C2
West Walton
Highway Norfk.........90 C2
Westward Cumb...........148 B6
Westward Ho! Devon 23 G5
Westwell Kent 34 D5
Westwell Oxon 56 E6
Westwell Leacon
Kent..........................34 C5
West Wellow Hants 28 F7
West Wemberry
Devon.........................6 D6
West Wemyss Fife 186 E7
Westwick Cambs...........76 B2
West Wickham
Cambs 76 E5
West Wickham Gt Lon ...45 G6
West Williamston
Pembks 49 H6
West Wiltshire
Crematorium
Wilts...........................39 K7
West Winch Norfk........90 F1
West Winterslow
Wilts...........................28 E5
West Wittering
W Susx.........................17 L3
West Witton N York 131 K2
Westwood Devon 12 C3
Westwood Kent 35 K2
Westwood Wilts 39 J8
West Woodburn
Nthumb 157 M5
West Woodhay
W Berk 41 H7
Westwoodside N Linc ..116 C2
West worldham
Hants 30 C4
West Worthing
W Susx.........................18 F5
West Wratting Cambs ...76 E4
Wetheral Cumb...........148 E4
Wetherby Leeds 124 B2
Wetherby Services
N York 124 C1
Wetherden Suffk..........78 B3
Wetheringsett Suffk......78 D2
Wethersfield Essex 61 H2
Wetherup Street
Suffk...........................78 D2
Wetley Rocks Staffs......99 L3
Wettenhall Ches E.........98 F1
Wetton Staffs..............100 C2
Wetwang E R Yk...........134 E7
Wetwood Staffs............99 H5
Wexcombe Wilts 40 F8
Weybourne Norfk........106 D4
Weybourne Surrey........30 D2
Weybread Suffk............92 F7
Weybread Street
Suffk...........................92 F7
weybridge Surrey 43 H7
Weycroft Devon...........13 H3
Weydale Highld 231 H3
Weyhill Hants 28 F3
Weymouth Dorset 14 D6
Weymouth
Crematorium
Dorset 14 C6
Whaddon Bucks...........74 B7
Whaddon Cambs...........75 L5
Whaddon Gloucs 55 J5
Whaddon Wilts 28 D6
Whaddon Wilts 39 K7
Whaley Derbys.............115 K7

Whaley Bridge
Derbys......................114 A5
Whaley Thorns
Derbys......................115 K7
Whaligoe Highld..........231 K7
Whalley Lancs.............121 L4
Whalsay Shet...............235 d4
Whalton Nthumb.........158 E6
Whaplode Lincs...........104 A7
Whaplode Drove
Lincs...........................89 K2
Wharf Warwks.............72 E4
Wharfe N York............130 E5
Wharles Lancs.............120 F4
Wharley End C Beds.....74 D5
Wharncliffe Side
Sheff 114 F3
Wharram-le-Street
N York.......................134 D6
Wharton Herefs............69 K4
Whashton N York.........140 E6
Whasset Cumb............129 L4
Whatcote Warwks 72 C5
Whateley Warwks..........86 B4
Whatfield Suffk.............78 B5
Whatley Somset............13 J2
Whatley Somset............27 G3
Whatlington E Susx.......20 F3
Whatton Notts............102 C5
Whauphill D & G...........145 J5
Wheal Peevor Cnwll 3 J3
Wheatacre Norfk..........93 K5
Wheathampstead
Herts..........................59 K5
Wheatley Hants............30 C4
Wheatley Oxon.............57 L6
Wheatley Hill Dur.........151 J6
Wheatley Hills Donc.....115 L1
Wheaton Aston Staffs....84 F2
Wheddon Cross
Somset.......................24 E4
Wheelock Ches E..........99 H2
Wheelton Lancs...........121 J6
Wheldrake C York........125 G2
Whelford Gloucs...........56 D7
Whelpley Hill Bucks......59 G6
Whempstead Herts 60 A4
Whenby N York............133 K5
Whepstead Suffk...........77 J3
Wherstead Suffk...........78 E6
Wherwell Hants............29 H3
Wheston Derbys..........114 C6
Whetsted Kent.............33 H4
Whetstone Leics...........87 G4
Whicham Cumb............128 D3
Whichford Warwks........72 C7
Whickham Gatesd........150 F3
Whiddon Down
Devon.........................11 G6
Whigstreet Angus........196 D7
Whilton Nhants.............73 J2
Whimple Devon............12 D3
Whimpwell Green
Norfk.........................107 H6
Whinburgh Norfk..........92 B2
Whinnie Liggate
D & G.........................146 C4
Whinnyfold Abers........217 K7
Whippingham IoW.........17 G4
Whipsnade C Beds.........59 G4
Whipsnade Zoo ZSL
C Beds........................59 G4
Whipton Devon.............12 B4
Whisby Lincs................116 E7
Whissendine Rutlnd......88 B2
Whissonsett Norfk.......105 L7
Whistlefield Ag & B......183 J8
Whistlefield Inn
Ag & B.......................183 G8
Whistley Green
Wokham......................42 C5
Whiston Knows...........112 C3
Whiston Nhants............74 B3
Whiston Rothm...........115 H4
Whiston Staffs..............84 F2
Whiston Staffs.............100 B3

Whitbeck Cumb...........128 D3
Whitbourne Herefs.......70 D3
Whitburn S Tyne..........151 J3
Whitburn W Loth.........176 C5
Whitby N York.............143 J5
Whitchester Border.....178 F6
Whitchurch BaNES........38 F6
Whitchurch Bucks.........58 D4
Whitchurch Cardif.........37 J4
Whitchurch Devon..........6 D2
Whitchurch Hants.........29 J2
Whitchurch Herefs........54 D4
Whitchurch Oxon..........41 M5
Whitchurch Pembks......48 D3
Whitchurch Shrops........98 D4
Whitchurch
Canonicorum
Dorset 13 K4
Whitchurch Hill Oxon....41 M5
Whitcombe Dorset........14 D5
Whitcot Shrops.............83 H5
Whitcott Keysett
Shrops........................82 F6
Whiteacre Heath
Warwks.......................86 B5
White Ball Somset........25 H7
Whitebridge Highld......202 D3
Whitebrook Mons..........54 D6
Whitecairns Abers.......207 H2
Whitechapel Gt Lon......45 G4
White Chapel Lancs.....121 H3
Whitecliffe Gloucs........54 E6
White Colne Essex........61 L3
Whitecraig E Loth........177 K4
Whitecrook D & G........144 E4
White Cross Cnwll..........3 H6
Whitecross Falk...........176 C3
Whiteface Highld.........222 F4
Whitefarland N Ayrs.....161 L2
Whitefaulds S Ayrs......163 H7
Whitefield Bury...........113 J1
Whitefield Somset........25 G5
Whiteford Abers..........206 D1
Whitegate Ches W........112 F7
Whitehall Ork..............234 d5
Whitehaven Cumb........136 D4
Whitehill and Bordon
Hants..........................30 C5
Whitehills Abers..........216 C2
Whitehouse Abers.......206 C3
Whitehouse Ag & B......172 D6
Whitekirk E Loth..........178 D3
White Lackington
Dorset 14 D3
Whitelackington
Somset.......................26 B7
White Ladies Aston
Worcs.........................71 G4
Whiteleaf Bucks...........58 D6
Whiteley Hants.............17 G1
Whiteley Bank IoW........17 G6
Whitemire Moray.........214 B4
Whitemoor C Nott.......101 K4
Whitemoor Cnwll...........4 F4
Whiteness Shet...........235 c6
White Notley Essex.......61 J4
Whiteparish Wilts.........28 E6
White Pit Lincs............118 E6
Whiterashes Abers......206 F2
White Roding Essex.......60 E5
Whiterow Highld.........231 L5
Whiterow Moray.........214 C3
Whiteshill Gloucs..........55 J6
Whitesmith E Susx........20 B3
Whitestaunton
Somset.......................13 H1
Whitestone Cross
Devon.........................11 K6
White Waltham
W & M.........................42 D5
Whitewell Lancs..........121 K2
Whitfield C Dund.........187 G2
Whitfield Kent..............35 J5
Whitfield Nhants...........73 H6
Whitfield Nthumb........149 K4
Whitfield S Glos...........38 F3

Whitford Devon............13 G4
Whitford Flints............111 G5
Whitgift E R Yk............125 J6
Whitgreave Staffs.........99 K6
Whithorn D & G...........145 J6
Whiting Bay N Ayrs......162 D4
Whitkirk Leeds............124 B4
Whitland Carmth...........49 L4
Whitlaw Border............167 G6
Whitletts S Ayrs...........163 J5
Whitley N York............124 E6
Whitley Readg...............42 B6
Whitley Sheff...............115 G3
Whitley Wilts................39 K6
Whitley Bay N Tyne.....159 J7
Whitley Bay
Crematorium
N Tyne......................159 H7
Whitley Chapel
Nthumb.....................150 B4
Whitley Lower Kirk......123 J6
Whitminster Gloucs......55 H6
Whitmore Staffs............99 J4
Whitnage Devon............25 G7
Whitnash Warwks..........72 D2
Whitney-on-Wye
Herefs........................68 F5
Whitsbury Hants..........28 C7
Whitsome Border.........179 H7
Whitson Newpt.............38 B4
Whitstable Kent............47 J6
Whitstone Cnwll............9 H5
Whittingham
Nthumb.....................168 F6
Whittingslow Shrops.....83 H5
Whittington Derbys.....115 G6
Whittington Gloucs.......56 A4
Whittington Lancs........130 B4
Whittington Norfk.........91 G4
Whittington Shrops........97 L6
Whittington Staffs.........84 F6
Whittington Staffs.........85 L2
Whittington Warwks......86 C4
Whittington Worcs........70 D4
Whittlebury Nhants.......73 K5
Whittle-le-Woods
Lancs........................121 H6
Whittlesey Cambs..........89 J4
Whittlesford Cambs.......76 C5
Whitton N Linc............125 L5
Whitton Nthumb..........158 D3
Whitton Powys..............68 F2
Whitton S on T............141 J3
Whitton Shrops.............83 L8
Whittonstall Nthumb....150 D4
Whitway Hants..............41 J8
Whitwell Derbys..........115 K6
Whitwell Herts..............59 K4
Whitwell IoW................17 G6
Whitwell N York...........141 G7
Whitwell Rutlnd.............88 D2
Whitwell-on-the-Hill
N York.......................133 L6
Whitwell Street Norfk..106 D7
Whitwick Leics.............86 E1
Whitworth Lancs.........122 D6
Whixall Shrops.............98 D5
Whixley N York............133 G7
Whorlton Dur..............140 E4
Whyle Herefs................69 L3
Whyteleafe Surrey.........32 C2
Wibsey C Brad.............123 H4
Wibtoft Warwks............86 F6
Wichenford Worcs........70 D3
Wichling Kent...............34 B4
Wick Bmouth................15 L4
Wick Highld................231 L5
Wick S Glos..................39 G5
Wick V Glam................36 E6
Wick W Susx................18 D5
Wick Worcs..................71 G5
Wicken Cambs..............76 E1
Wicken Nhants.............73 L6
Wicken Bonhunt
Essex.........................60 D2
Wickenby Lincs...........117 H5

Wicken Green Village
Norfk.....................105 K6
Wickersley Rothm.......115 J3
Wicker Street Green
Suffk.........................77 L6
Wickford Essex...............46 C2
Wickham Hants.............17 H1
Wickham W Berk..........41 H6
Wickham Bishops
Essex..........................61 K5
Wickhambreaux Kent...35 G3
Wickhambrook Suffk....77 H4
Wickhamford Worcs....71 J6
Wickham Green Suffk...78 D2
Wickham Market
Suffk.........................79 G4
Wickhampton Norfk.....93 J3
Wickham St Paul
Essex.........................77 J7
Wickham Skeith Suffk...78 C2
Wickham Street Suffk...78 C1
Wick John o' Groats
Airport Highld.........231 L5
Wicklewood Norfk........92 C3
Wickmere Norfk..........106 E5
Wick St Lawrence
N Som........................38 A7
Wicksteed Park
Nhants........................88 C7
Wickwar S Glos............39 G3
Widdington Essex.........60 E2
Widdrington Nthumb..159 G3
Widdrington Station
Nthumb.....................159 G4
Widecombe in the
Moor Devon................7 G1
Widegates Cnwll............5 L4
Widemouth Bay
Cnwll..........................9 G4
Wide Open N Tyne........159 G7
Widford Essex...............61 H6
Widford Herts...............60 C5
Widmer End Bucks........42 E2
Widmerpool Notts.......101 M6
Widmore Gt Lon............45 H6
Widnes Halton............112 D5
Widnes Crematorium
Halton......................112 D4
Widworthy Devon.........13 G3
Wigan Wigan...............112 E1
Wigan Crematorium
Wigan.......................112 E2
Wigborough Somset....26 C7
Wiggaton Devon...........12 E4
Wiggenhall St
Germans Norfk..........90 E2
Wiggenhall St Mary
Magdalen Norfk..........90 E2
Wiggenhall St Mary
the Virgin Norfk.........90 E2
Wigginton C York........133 J7
Wigginton Herts...........58 F6
Wigginton Oxon...........57 H2
Wigginton Staffs..........86 B3
Wigglesworth N York..130 F7
Wiggonby Cumb..........148 B4
Wighill N York.............124 D2
Wighton Norfk............105 M4
Wightwick Wolves.........84 F4
Wigley Hants................29 G7
Wigmore Herefs............69 H2
Wigmore Medway..........46 D6
Wigsley Notts..............116 E7
Wigsthorpe Nhants.......88 F6
Wigston Leics................87 H4
Wigston Parva Leics......86 F5
Wigthorpe Notts..........115 L5
Wigtoft Lincs..............103 L5
Wigton Cumb..............148 A5
Wigtown D & G............145 J4
Wike Leeds..................123 L3
Wilbarston Nhants........88 B5
Wilberfoss E R Yk........125 H1
Wilburton Cambs..........90 C7
Wilby Nhants................74 C2
Wilby Norfk..................92 B5

Wilby Suffk..................78 F1
Wilcot Wilts.................40 C7
Wilcott Shrops..............98 B8
Wildboarclough
Ches E.....................113 M7
Wilden Bed..................75 G4
Wilden Worcs...............84 E8
Wildmanbridge
S Lans......................175 L2
Wildmoor Worcs...........85 G7
Wildsworth Lincs.........116 D3
Wilford Hill
Crematorium
Notts.......................101 L5
Wilkesley Ches E............98 F4
Wilkhaven Highld........223 K4
Wilkieston W Loth.......176 F5
Willand Devon...............12 D1
Willaston Ches E............99 G3
Willaston Ches W.........111 K6
Willen M Keyn...............74 C6
Willenhall Covtry..........86 D7
Willenhall Wsall............85 H4
Willerby E R Yk...........126 C4
Willerby N York...........134 F4
Willersey Gloucs...........71 K6
Willersley Herefs...........68 F5
Willesborough Kent......34 D6
Willesborough Lees
Kent..........................34 D6
Willesden Gt Lon...........44 E3
Willesley Wilts..............39 J3
Willett Somset..............25 H5
Willey Shrops...............84 C4
Willey Warwks..............86 F6
Willey Green Surrey......30 F2
Williamscot Oxon..........72 F5
Willian Herts.................59 L2
Willingale Essex............60 F6
Willingdon E Susx.........20 C5
Willingham Cambs........76 B1
Willingham by Stow
Lincs.......................116 E5
Willington Bed.............75 G4
Willington Derbys........100 F6
Willington Dur............150 F7
Willington Kent............33 K3
Willington Warwks.......72 C6
Willington Quay
N Tyne.....................151 H2
Willitoft E R Yk..........125 H4
Williton Somset............25 H4
Willoughby Lincs.........119 G6
Willoughby Warwks......73 G2
Willoughby-on-the-
Wolds Notts............101 M7
Willoughby
Waterleys Leics........87 H5
Willoughton Lincs.......116 F3
Willows Green Essex.....61 H4
Willtown Somset...........26 B6
Wilmcote Warwks.........71 L3
Wilmington Devon.........13 G3
Wilmington E Susx........20 B5
Wilmington Kent...........45 K5
Wilmslow Ches E.........113 J5
Wilpshire Lancs...........121 K4
Wilsden C Brad...........123 G3
Wilsford Lincs.............103 G4
Wilsford Wilts..............28 C4
Wilsford Wilts..............40 C8
Wilshaw Kirk..............123 G8
Wilsill N York..............132 B6
Wilson Leics...............101 H7
Wilsontown S Lans......176 C7
Wilstead Bed................74 F5
Wilsthorpe Lincs...........88 F2
Wilstone Herts..............58 E5
Wilton Herefs...............54 E3
Wilton N York..............134 D3
Wilton R & Cl..............142 C4
Wilton Wilts.................28 C5
Wilton Wilts.................40 E7
Wilton Dean Border.....167 G6
Wimbish Green Essex...76 E7
Wimbledon Gt Lon.......44 E6

Wimblington Cambs.....90 B5
Wimboldsley Ches W..113 G8
Wimborne Minster
Dorset.......................15 J3
Wimborne St Giles
Dorset......................28 B8
Wimbotsham Norfk.......90 E3
Wimpole Cambs............75 L4
Wimpstone Warwks.......72 B5
Wincanton Somset.......27 G5
Winchburgh W Loth....176 E4
Winchcombe Gloucs.....56 A3
Winchelsea E Susx........21 H3
Winchester Hants.........29 J5
Winchester Services
Hants........................29 K4
Winchet Hill Kent.........33 J5
Winchfield Hants...........30 C1
Winchmore Hill Bucks..42 F2
Winchmore Hill
Gt Lon......................44 F2
Wincle Ches E.............113 L7
Wincobank Sheff.........115 G3
Windermere Cumb.......137 L7
Windermere
Steamboats &
Museum Cumb.........137 L7
Winderton Warwks.......72 D6
Windhill Highld...........212 E5
Windlesham Surrey.......42 F7
Windmill Cnwll...............4 D2
Windmill Hill E Susx.....20 D4
Windmill Hill Somset....25 L7
Windrush Gloucs...........56 D5
Windsole Abers...........216 B3
Windsor W & M............42 F5
Windsor Castle W & M..42 F5
Windsoredge Gloucs.....55 J7
Windsor Green Suffk.....77 K4
Windy Arbour
Warwks......................72 C1
Windygates Fife..........186 E7
Wineham W Susx..........31 L7
Winestead E R Yk........127 G5
Winfarthing Norfk........92 D6
Winford IoW.................17 G5
Winford N Som.............38 D7
Winforton Herefs..........68 F5
Winfrith Newburgh
Dorset......................14 F5
Wing Bucks..................58 E4
Wing Rutlnd.................88 C3
Wingate Dur...............151 J7
Wingerworth Derbys...115 G7
Wingfield C Beds..........59 G3
Wingfield Suffk.............92 F7
Wingfield Wilts.............27 J1
Wingham Kent..............35 H3
Wingrave Bucks............58 E4
Winkburn Notts..........102 B2
Winkfield Br For...........42 E6
Winkfield Row Br For....42 E6
Winkhill Staffs............100 B3
Winkleigh Devon...........10 F4
Winksley N York..........132 C5
Winlaton Gatesd.........150 F3
Winless Highld............231 K5
Winmarleigh Lancs.....120 F2
Winnall Hants..............29 J5
Winnersh Wokham.......42 C6
Winnington Ches W....112 F6
Winscombe N Som........38 B8
Winsford Ches W.........112 F7
Winsford Somset..........24 E4
Winsham Somset..........13 J2
Winshill Staffs............100 F7
Winshwen Swans..........51 K6
Winskill Cumb.............149 G7
Winsley Wilts...............39 J7
Winslow Bucks.............58 C3
Winson Gloucs.............56 C6
Winsor Hants...............28 F8
Winster Cumb.............129 J2
Winster Derbys............100 E1
Winston Dur...............140 E4
Winston Suffk...............78 E3

Winstone Gloucs..........55 L6
Winswell Devon............10 D3
Winterborne Came
Dorset......................14 D5
Winterborne
Clenston Dorset........14 F2
Winterborne
Houghton Dorset.....14 F2
Winterborne
Kingston Dorset......15 G3
Winterborne
Monkton Dorset.......14 D5
Winterborne
Stickland Dorset.......14 F2
Winterborne
Whitechurch
Dorset......................14 F3
Winterborne Zelston
Dorset......................15 G3
Winterbourne S Glos....38 F4
Winterbourne W Berk...41 J6
Winterbourne Abbas
Dorset......................14 C4
Winterbourne
Bassett Wilts............40 C5
Winterbourne
Dauntsey Wilts........28 D4
Winterbourne Earls
Wilts........................28 D5
Winterbourne
Gunner Wilts...........28 D4
Winterbourne
Monkton Wilts..........40 C6
Winterbourne
Steepleton Dorset....14 C4
Winterbourne Stoke
Wilts........................28 B3
Winterburn N York......131 H7
Winteringham
N Linc......................125 L6
Winterley Ches E...........99 H2
Winterslow Wilts...........28 E5
Winterton N Linc.........125 L6
Winterton-on-Sea
Norfk......................107 K8
Winthorpe Notts.........102 D2
Winton Bmouth.............15 K4
Winton Cumb..............139 H5
Wintringham N York....134 D5
Winwick Cambs............89 G7
Winwick Nhants............87 J8
Winwick Warrtn...........112 E3
Wirksworth Derbys......100 F2
Wirral.........................111 J4
Wirswall Ches E............98 D4
Wisbech Cambs............90 C2
Wisbech St Mary
Cambs......................90 B2
Wisborough Green
W Susx......................31 H6
Wiseman's Bridge
Pembks.....................49 K6
Wiseton Notts.............116 B4
Wishaw N Lans...........175 L7
Wishaw Warwks............85 L5
Wisley Garden RHS
Surrey.......................43 H8
Wispington Lincs.........117 K6
Wissett Suffk................93 H7
Wissington Suffk..........62 A2
Wistanstow Shrops.......83 H6
Wistanswick Shrops......98 F6
Wistaston Ches E..........99 G2
Wiston Pembks.............49 H4
Wiston S Lans.............165 J3
Wiston W Susx..............18 F3
Wistow Cambs.............89 K7
Wistow N York............124 F4
Wiswell Lancs..............121 L3
Witcham Cambs............90 C7
Witchampton Dorset.....15 J2
Witchford Cambs..........90 C7
Witcombe Somset........26 C6
Witham Essex...............61 K5
Witham Friary
Somset......................27 H3

Witham on the Hill
Lincs **88** F1
Withcall Lincs................**118** C5
Withdean Br & H **19** J4
Witherenden Hill
E Susx **33** H7
Witheridge Devon..........**11** J3
Witherley Leics...............**86** D4
Withern Lincs................**118** F5
Withernsea E R Yk........**127** H5
Withernwick E R Yk.......**126** F3
Withersdale Street
Suffk **92** F7
Withersfield Suffk..........**76** F5
Witherslack Cumb.........**129** J3
Withiel Cnwll **4** F3
Withiel Florey Somset....**24** F5
Withington Gloucs..........**56** B5
Withington Herefs..........**69** I5
Withington Manch........**113** J3
Withington Shrops..........**83** L2
Withington Staffs.........**100** B5
Withleigh Devon **11** K3
Withnell Lancs..............**121** J6
Withybed Green
Worcs **85** H8
Withybrook Warwks **86** E6
Withycombe Somset......**24** F3
Withyham E Susx...........**32** E6
Withypool Somset **24** D4
Withywood Bristl............**38** E6
Witley Surrey..................**30** F4
Witnesham Suffk **78** E4
Witney Oxon **57** G6
Wittering C Pete **88** F3
Wittersham Kent **21** H1
Witton Birm **85** J5
Witton Norfk..................**93** G2
Witton Norfk.................**107** H6
Witton Gilbert Dur.......**151** G5
Witton le Wear Dur **140** E2
Witton Park Dur...........**140** F2
Wiveliscombe Somset ...**25** G5
Wivelrod Hants...............**30** A4
Wivelsfield E Susx **19** K2
Wivelsfield Green
E Susx **19** K2
Wivenhoe Essex **62** C4
Wiveton Norfk...............**106** C4
Wix Essex.......................**62** E3
Wixford Warwks **71** K4
Wixoe Suffk.....................**77** G6
Woburn C Beds...............**58** F2
Woburn Abbey
C Beds..........................**58** F2
Woburn Sands
M Keyn **74** D7
Woking Surrey **43** G8
Woking
Crematorium
Surrey **42** F8
Wokingham Wokham **42** D6
Woldingham Surrey........**32** C3
Wold Newton E R Yk....**135** G5
Wold Newton NE Lin....**118** C3
Wolfclyde S Lans...........**165** K3
Wolferton Norfk...........**105** G6
Wolfhill P & K **186** B2
Wolf's Castle Pembks **49** G3
Wolfsdale Pembks **48** F3
Wollaston Dudley............**84** F6
Wollaston Nhants...........**74** C2
Wollaston Shrops............**83** G2
Wollaton C Nott............**101** K4
Wollaton Hall & Park
C Nott.........................**101** K5
Wollerton Shrops............**98** F6
Wollescote Dudley...........**85** G6
Wolseley Bridge
Staffs **100** A7
Wolsingham Dur...........**150** D7
Wolstanton Staffs...........**99** J3
Wolston Warwks **86** E7
Wolvercote Oxon............**57** J6
Wolverhampton
Wolves...........................**85** G4

Wolverhampton
Halfpenny Green
Airport Staffs **84** E5
Wolverley Worcs............**84** E7
Wolverton Hants............**41** K8
Wolverton M Keyn **74** B6
Wolverton Warwks..........**72** B3
Wolverton Wilts.............**27** H5
Wolvesnewton Mons......**54** C7
Wolvey Warwks **86** E6
Wolvey Heath
Warwks..........................**86** E5
Wolviston S on T **141** K3
Wombleton N York........**133** K3
Wombourne Staffs..........**84** F5
Wombwell Barns...........**115** H2
Womenswold Kent...........**35** G5
Womersley N York.........**124** E6
Wonersh Surrey...............**31** G3
Wonford Devon...............**12** B4
Wonston Dorset **14** E2
Wonston Hants...............**29** J4
Wooburn Bucks...............**42** E3
Wooburn Green
Bucks............................**42** E3
Woodacott Devon..............**9** K4
Woodall Rothm.............**115** J5
Woodall Services
Rothm.........................**115** J5
Woodbastwick Norfk......**93** G1
Wood Bevington
Warwks..........................**71** J4
Woodborough Notts....**101** M3
Woodborough Wilts........**40** C7
Woodbridge Suffk...........**78** F5
Woodbury Devon............**12** C5
Woodbury Salterton
Devon **12** C5
Woodchester Gloucs......**55** J7
Woodchurch Kent...........**34** C7
Woodcombe Somset........**24** E3
Woodcote Gt Lon...........**44** F7
Woodcote Oxon.............**41** M4
Woodcroft Gloucs...........**38** D2
Wood Dalling Norfk.....**106** C6
Woodditton Cambs.........**76** F3
Woodeaton Oxon............**57** K5
Wood End Gt Lon...........**43** J4
Wood End Herts.............**60** B3
Woodend Highld...........**190** F4
Woodend Nhants.............**73** H5
Woodend W Loth...........**176** C4
Woodend W Susx............**17** M2
Wood End Warwks..........**71** K1
Wood Enderby Lincs.....**118** C8
Woodfalls Wilts...............**28** D7
Woodford Cnwll **9** G3
Woodford Gloucs............**39** G2
Woodford Gt Lon...........**45** H2
Woodford Nhants............**88** D7
Woodford Stockp.........**113** K5
Woodford Bridge
Gt Lon..........................**45** H2
Woodford Halse
Nhants...........................**73** G4
Woodford Wells
Gt Lon..........................**45** H2
Woodgate Birm...............**85** H6
Woodgate Devon.............**25** H7
Woodgate W Susx...........**18** C5
Woodgate Worcs.............**71** H2
Wood Green Gt Lon........**44** F2
Woodgreen Hants............**28** D7
Woodhall N York............**131** J2
Woodhall Spa Lincs......**117** K8
Woodham Bucks..............**58** B4
Woodham Surrey.............**43** H7
Woodham Ferrers
Essex **61** J7
Woodham Mortimer
Essex **61** K6
Woodham Walter
Essex **61** K6
Wood Hayes Wolves **85** G3
Woodhead Abers **216** E6

Woodhill Shrops **84** D6
Woodhill Somset **26** A6
Woodhorn Nthumb.......**159** H4
Woodhouse Leeds **123** K4
Woodhouse Leics............**87** G1
Woodhouse Sheff..........**115** H4
Woodhouse Wakefd......**124** B6
Woodhouse Eaves
Leics.............................**87** G2
Woodhouselee
Mdloth........................**177** H5
Woodhouselees
D & G **156** D6
Woodhouses Staffs.......**100** D8
Woodhurst Cambs...........**89** K7
Woodingdean Br & H......**19** K5
Woodkirk Leeds.............**123** K5
Woodland Abers............**207** G2
Woodland Devon................**6** F5
Woodland Devon................**7** J3
Woodland Dur...............**140** D2
Woodland S Ayrs...........**152** E3
Woodlands Abers...........**206** E6
Woodlands Donc...........**124** E8
Woodlands Dorset...........**15** K2
Woodlands Hants............**16** C1
Woodlands N York.........**132** E8
Woodlands (Coleshill)
Crematorium
Warwks..........................**85** L5
Woodlands Park
W & M...........................**42** E5
Woodlands
(Scarborough)
Crematorium
N York **134** F3
Woodlands
(Scunthorpe)
Crematorium
N Linc **125** K7
Woodleigh Devon **7** H6
Woodley Wokham **42** C5
Woodmancote
Gloucs...........................**39** H2
Woodmancote
Gloucs...........................**55** L3
Woodmancote
Gloucs...........................**56** A6
Woodmancote
W Susx...........................**17** L2
Woodmancote
W Susx...........................**19** H3
Woodmancott Hants.......**29** K3
Woodmansey E R Yk......**126** C3
Woodmansgreen
W Susx...........................**30** E6
Woodmansterne
Surrey............................**32** B2
Woodmanton Devon........**12** C5
Woodnesborough
Kent...............................**35** J4
Woodnewton Nhants......**88** F5
Wood Norton Norfk.....**106** B6
Woodplumpton
Lancs...........................**121** G4
Woodrising Norfk............**92** B3
Wood's Corner E Susx ...**20** D2
Woodseaves Staffs...........**99** H7
Woodsetts Rothm..........**115** K5
Woodsford Dorset **14** E4
Wood's Green E Susx......**33** H6
Woodside Br For **42** F6
Woodside Fife...............**187** G5
Woodside Gt Lon............**45** G6
Woodside P & K.............**195** K8
Woodstock Oxon.............**57** H5
Woodston C Pete............**89** H4
Wood Street Norfk........**107** H7
Wood Street Village
Surrey............................**30** F2
Woodton Norfk................**93** G5
Woodtown Devon............**22** F6
Woodvale
Crematorium
Br & H **19** J4
Wood Walton Cambs......**89** J7

Woofferton Shrops..........**69** K2
Wookey Somset **26** D3
Wookey Hole Somset **26** D2
Wool Dorset.....................**14** F5
Woolacombe Devon.........**23** G3
Woolage Green Kent **35** H5
Woolaston Gloucs...........**54** E7
Woolaston Common
Gloucs...........................**54** E7
Woolavington
Somset **25** M3
Woolbeding W Susx **30** E6
Woolbrook Devon............**12** E5
Wooler Nthumb.............**168** E4
Woolfardisworthy
Devon............................**11** J3
Woolfardisworthy
Devon............................**22** E7
Woolfords S Lans...........**176** D6
Woolhampton
W Berk...........................**41** L6
Woolhope Herefs............**69** L7
Woolland Dorset **14** E2
Woolley BaNES................**39** H6
Woolley Cambs................**89** G8
Woolley Wakefd.............**123** L7
Woolley Edge
Services Wakefd **123** K7
Woolmere Green
Worcs **71** G2
Woolmer Green Herts **59** L4
Woolminstone
Somset **13** K2
Woolpit Suffk..................**77** L3
Woolstaston Shrops **83** J4
Woolsthorpe Lincs.........**102** D5
Woolsthorpe-by-
Colsterworth
Lincs...........................**102** F7
Woolston C Sotn **16** E1
Woolston Shrops..............**97** L7
Woolston Somset.............**25** H4
Woolston Somset.............**26** F5
Woolston Warrtn............**112** F4
Woolstone Gloucs............**55** L3
Woolstone M Keyn...........**74** C6
Woolstone Oxon **40** F3
Woolston Green
Devon..............................**7** H3
Woolton Lpool................**112** B4
Woolton Hill Hants.........**41** H7
Woolverstone Suffk........**78** E6
Woolverton Somset.........**27** H2
Woolwich Gt Lon............**45** H4
Woonton Herefs..............**69** G4
Woore Shrops...................**99** G4
Wootten Green Suffk......**92** F8
Wootton Bed...................**74** E5
Wootton Kent..................**35** G5
Wootton N Linc.............**126** D7
Wootton Nhants..............**73** L3
Wootton Oxon.................**57** H4
Wootton Oxon.................**57** J7
Wootton Staffs..............**100** C4
Wootton Bassett
Wilts.............................**40** B4
Wootton Bridge IoW.......**17** G4
Wootton Courtenay
Somset **24** E3
Wootton Fitzpaine
Dorset **13** J4
Wootton Rivers Wilts......**40** D7
Wootton St
Lawrence Hants **29** L2
Wootton Wawen
Warwks..........................**71** L2
Worcester
Crematorium
Worcs **70** F4
Worcester Park
Gt Lon...........................**44** E6
Wordsley Dudley **84** F6
Worfield Shrops...............**84** D4
Workington Cumb.........**136** D2
Worksop Notts...............**115** L5

Worlaby N Linc 126 C7
Worlds End Hants........29 M8
Worlds End W Susx 19 J2
Worle N Som 38 A7
Worleston Ches E........98 F2
Worlingham Suffk........93 J5
Worlington Devon 11 H3
Worlington Suffk........91 G8
Worlingworth Suffk........78 F2
Wormbridge Herefs........54 B2
Wormegay Norfk........90 F2
Wormelow Tump
Herefs........54 C3
Wormhill Derbys........114 C6
Wormingford Essex........61 M2
Worminghall Bucks........57 M6
Wormington Gloucs........71 J7
Wormit Fife........186 F3
Wormleighton
Warwks........72 F4
Wormley Herts........60 B6
Wormley Surrey........30 F4
Wormshill Kent........34 B3
Wormsley Herefs........69 H5
Worplesdon Surrey........30 F2
Worrall Sheff........114 F3
Worsbrough Barns........115 G2
Worsbrough Bridge
Barns........115 G2
Worsbrough Dale
Barns........115 G2
Worsley Salfd........113 H2
Worstead Norfk........107 G7
Worsthorne Lancs........122 C4
Worston Devon 6 E5
Worston Lancs........122 B3
Worth Kent........35 J4
Wortham Suffk........92 C7
Worthen Shrops........83 G3
Worthenbury
Wrexhm........98 B4
Worthing Norfk........106 B8
Worthing W Susx........18 F5
Worthing
Crematorium
W Susx........18 F4
Worthington Leics........101 H7
Worth Matravers
Dorset........15 H6
Wortley Barns........114 F2
Wortley Leeds........123 K4
Worton N York........131 H2
Worton Wilts........39 L8
Wortwell Norfk........92 F6
Wotton-under-Edge
Gloucs........39 H2
Wotton Underwood
Bucks........58 B5
Woughton on the
Green M Keyn........74 C6
Wouldham Kent........46 B7
Wrabness Essex........62 E2
Wrafton Devon........23 H4
Wragby Lincs........117 J6
Wragby Wakefd........124 C6
Wrangaton Devon 7 G4
Wrangle Lincs........104 C3
Wrangway Somset 25 H7
Wrantage Somset 25 L6
Wrawby N Linc........126 C8
Wraxall N Som........38 C6
Wraxall Somset 26 E4
Wray Lancs........130 B6
Wraysbury W & M........43 G5
Wrayton Lancs........130 C5
Wrea Green Lancs........120 E4
Wreay Cumb........148 D5
Wrecclesham Surrey........30 D3
Wrekenton Gatesd........151 G3
Wrelton N York........134 B3
Wrenbury Ches E........98 E3
Wreningham Norfk........92 E4
Wrentham Suffk........93 K6
Wrentnall Shrops........83 H3
Wressle E R Yk........125 G4
Wressle N Linc........126 B8

Wrestlingworth
C Beds........75 J5
Wretton Norfk........91 G4
Wrexham Wrexhm........97 M3
Wribbenhall Worcs........84 E7
Wrinehill Staffs........99 H3
Wrington N Som........38 C7
Writhlington BaNES........27 G1
Writtle Essex........61 G6
Wrockwardine
Wrekin........84 B2
Wroot N Linc........116 B2
Wrose C Brad........123 H3
Wrotham Kent........33 G2
Wroughton Swindn........40 C4
Wroxall IoW........17 G6
Wroxall Warwks........72 B1
Wroxeter Shrops........83 L2
Wroxham Norfk........107 G8
Wroxham Barns
Norfk........107 G7
Wroxton Oxon........72 E6
Wyaston Derbys........100 D4
Wyberton East Lincs 104 B4
Wyboston Bed........75 H3
Wybunbury Ches E........99 G3
Wychbold Worcs........71 G2
Wychnor Staffs........85 L1
Wyck Rissington
Gloucs........56 D4
Wycliffe Dur........140 E4
Wycoller Lancs........122 D3
Wycomb Leics........102 C7
Wycombe Marsh
Bucks........42 E3
Wyddial Herts........60 B2
Wye Kent........34 E5
Wyke C Brad........123 H5
Wyke Dorset 27 H6
Wyke Champflower
Somset........26 F4
Wykeham N York........134 E3
Wyken Covtry........86 D7
Wyken Shrops........84 D4
Wyke Regis Dorset........14 C6
Wykey Shrops........98 B7
Wylam Nthumb........150 E3
Wylde Green Birm........85 K5
Wylye Wilts........28 A4
Wymeswold Leics........101 L7
Wymington Bed........74 D2
Wymondham Leics 102 D8
Wymondham Norfk........92 D3
Wynford Eagle
Dorset 14 B3
Wyre Forest
Crematorium
Worcs........84 E8
Wyre Piddle Worcs........71 G5
Wysall Notts........101 L6
Wythall Worcs........85 J7
Wytham Oxon 57 J6
Wythenshawe Manch ..113 J4
Wyton Cambs........89 K8
Wyton E R Yk........126 F4
Wyverstone Suffk........78 C2
Wyverstone Street
Suffk........78 B2

Y

Yaddlethorpe N Linc....116 E1
Yafforth N York........141 H7
Yalberton Torbay........7 K4
Yalding Kent........33 J3
Yanwath Cumb........138 D2
Yanworth Gloucs........56 B5
Yapham E R Yk........125 J1
Yapton W Susx........18 D5
Yarborough N Som........38 B8
Yarburgh Lincs........118 E3
Yarcombe Devon........13 G2
Yard Devon........24 B6
Yardley Birm........85 K6

Yardley
Crematorium
Birm........85 K6
Yardley Gobion
Nhants........73 L5
Yardley Hastings
Nhants........74 C3
Yardley Wood Birm 85 K7
Yarkhill Herefs........69 L6
Yarley Somset........26 D3
Yarlington Somset........26 F5
Yarm S on T........141 K5
Yarmouth IoW........16 D4
Yarnbrook Wilts........27 K1
Yarnfield Staffs........99 K6
Yarnscombe Devon........23 J6
Yarnton Oxon........57 J5
Yarpole Herefs........69 J2
Yarrow Border........166 E4
Yarrow Feus Border 166 E4
Yarrowford Border......166 F4
Yarwell Nhants........88 F4
Yate S Glos........39 G4
Yateley Hants........42 D7
Yatesbury Wilts........40 B6
Yattendon W Berk........41 K5
Yatton Herefs........69 H2
Yatton N Som........38 B7
Yatton Keynell Wilts......39 K5
Yaverland IoW........17 H5
Yaxham Norfk........92 B2
Yaxley Cambs........89 H5
Yaxley Suffk........92 D8
Yazor Herefs........69 H5
Yeading Gt Lon........43 J4
Yeadon Leeds........123 J3
Yealand Conyers Lancs ..129 K5
Yealand Redmayne
Lancs........129 K4
Yealmpton Devon 6 E5
Yearsley N York........133 J5
Yeaton Shrops........98 B8
Yeaveley Derbys........100 D4
Yeavering Nthumb......168 D4
Yedingham N York......134 D4
Yelford Oxon........57 G6
Yell Shet........235 d3
Yelling Cambs........75 J3
Yelvertoft Nhants........87 H7
Yelverton Devon 6 D3
Yelverton Norfk........93 G3
Yenston Somset........27 G7
Yeoford Devon 11 H5
Yeolmbridge Cnwll 9 J7
Yeovil Somset........26 D7
Yeovil Crematorium
Somset........26 D7
Yeovil Marsh Somset......26 D7
Yeovilton Somset........26 D6
Yesnaby Ork........234 b5
Yetminster Dorset........14 B1
Yettington Devon........12 D5
Yetts o'Muckhart
Clacks........185 L6
Yew Tree Sandw........85 H4
Y Felinheli Gwynd......109 G7
Y Ferwig Cerdgn........65 G5
Y Ffor Gwynd........95 G5
Y Gyffylliog Denbgs......97 G2
Yielden Bed........74 E2
Yieldshields S Lans......176 B7
Yiewsley Gt Lon........43 H4
Y Maerdy Conwy........96 F4
Ynysboeth Rhondd........37 G2
Ynysddu Caerph........37 J2
Ynyshir Rhondd........36 F3
Ynystawe Swans........51 K5
Ynysybwl Rhondd........37 G2
Yockleton Shrops........83 H2
Yokefleet E R Yk........125 J5
Yoker C Glas........174 F5
York C York........124 F1
York City
Crematorium
C York........124 F2
Yorkletts Kent........34 E3

Yorkley Gloucs........54 F6
York Minster C York......124 F1
Yorkshire Dales
National Park 131 G4
York Town Surrey........42 E7
Youlgreave Derbys......114 E8
Youlthorpe E R Yk......134 B7
Youlton N York........133 G6
Yoxall Staffs........100 C8
Yoxford Suffk........79 H2
Y Rhiw Gwynd........94 D6
Ysbyty Ifan Conwy........96 C3
Ysbyty Ystwyth
Cerdgn........67 G1
Ysceifiog Flints........111 G7
Ystalyfera Neath........52 B6
Ystrad Rhondd........36 F2
Ystrad Aeron Cerdgn 66 C4
Ystradfellte Powys........52 E5
Ystradgynlais Powys....52 C6
Ystrad Meurig
Cerdgn........66 F2
Ystrad Mynach
Caerph........37 H2
Ystradowen V Glam......36 F5
Ythanbank Abers........217 G7
Ythanwells Abers........216 C6
Ythsie Abers........217 G7

Z

Zeal Monachorum
Devon........11 G4
Zeals Wilts........27 H5
Zelah Cnwll 4 C5
Zennor Cnwll 2 E4
Zouch Notts........101 J7
ZSL London Zoo
Gt Lon........44 F4
ZSL Whipsnade Zoo
C Beds........59 G4

Ireland

Map pages north

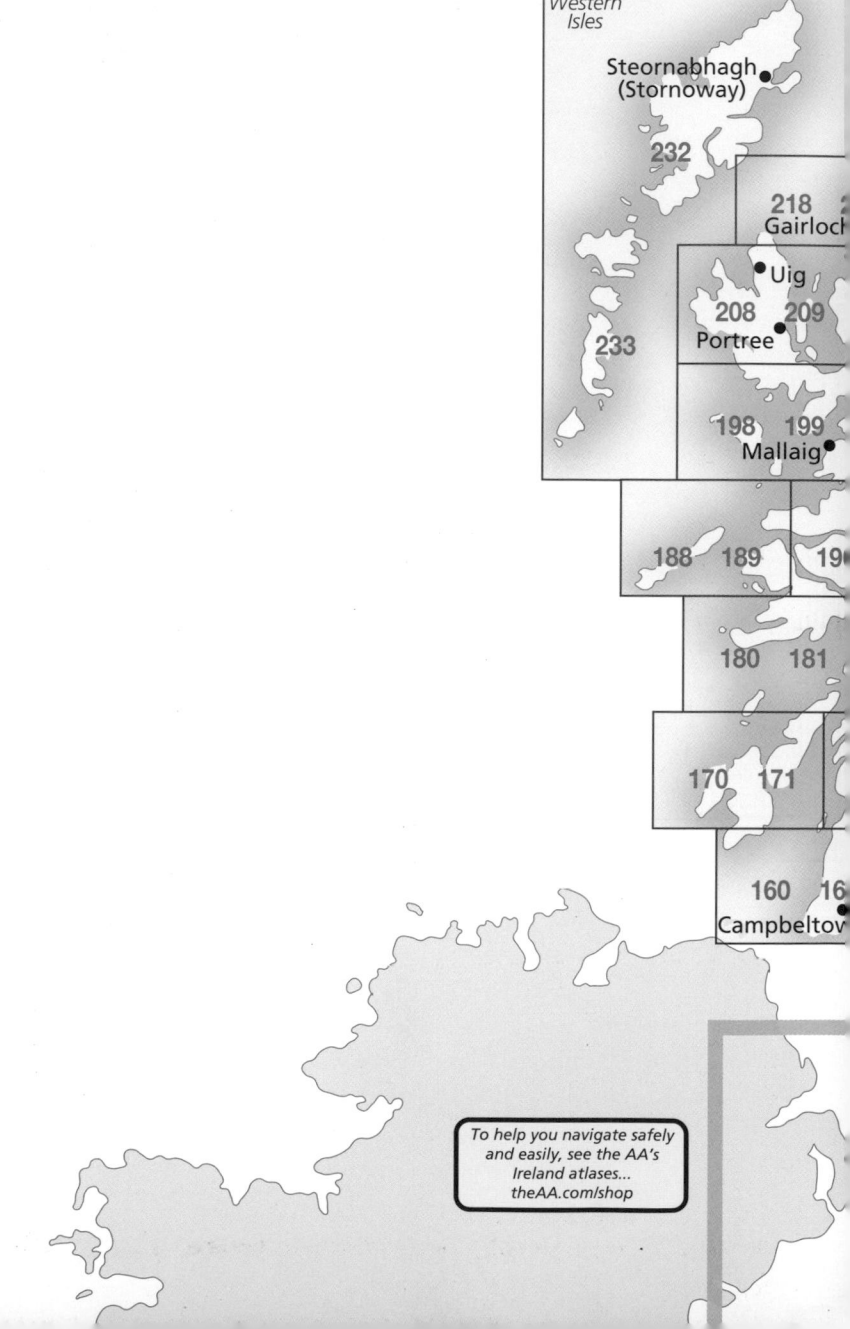

Western Isles

Steornabhagh•
(Stornoway)

232

218
Gairloch

•Uig
208 209
Portree•

233

198 199
Mallaig•

188 189 19

180 181

170 171

160 16
Campbeltov

To help you navigate safely
and easily, see the AA's
Ireland atlases...
theAA.com/shop